The PRENTICE HALL *Reader*

The PRENTICE HALL *Reader*

SEVENTH EDITION

GEORGE MILLER

University of Delaware

PEARSON

Prentice
Hall

Upper Saddle River, New Jersey 07458

Library of Congress

The Prentice Hall reader / [compiled by] George Miller. — 7th ed.
    p. cm.
  ISBN 0-13-182801-0 (Student book)
  ISBN 0-13-182802-9 (Annotated instructor's ed.)
  1.College readers. 2. English language—Rhetoric—Problems, exercises, etc.
  I. Miller, George.
PE1417.P74 2003
808'.0427—dc21   2003048219

Editor-in-Chief: Leah Jewell
Senior Acquisitions Editor: Corey Good
Assistant Editor: Karen Schultz
Editorial Assistant: Steve Kyritz
Executive Managing Editor: Ann Marie McCarthy
Production Liaison: Fran Russello
Project Manager: Terry Routley/Carlisle Communications
Prepress and Manufacturing Buyer: Mary Ann Gloriande
Art Director: Jayne Conte
Cover Designer: Bruce Kenselaar
Cover Art: Connie Hayes/SIS, Inc.
Director, Image Resource Center: Melinda Lee Reo
Manager, Rights & Permissions: Zina Arabia
Interior Image Specialist: Beth Boyd-Brenzel
Cover Image Specialist: Karen Sanatar
Image Permission Coordinator: Nancy Seise
Photo Researcher: Rachel Lucas
Marketing Manager: Brandy Dawson

This book was set in 10/12.5 Janson by Carlisle Communications, Ltd. and was
printed and bound by Courier Companies, Inc.. The cover was printed by Coral
Graphics.

Pages 610-615 constitute an extension of the copyright page.

Pearson Education Ltd.
Pearson Education Singapore
    Pte. Ltd.
Pearson Education Canada Ltd.
Pearson Education—Japan
Pearson Education Australia
    PTY. Limited

Pearson Education North Asia Ltd.
Pearson Educación de Mexico, S.A.
    de C.V.
Pearson Education Malaysia, Pte. Ltd.
Pearson Education, Upper Saddle River,
    New Jersey

PEARSON
Prentice
Hall

College 0-13-182801-0 (student text)
0-13-182802-9 (annotated instructor's edition)
10 9 8 7 6 5 4 3 2 1

High School 0-13-184662-0
10 9 8 7 6 5 4 3 2 1

For Valerie and Eric, their book

CONTENTS

THEMATIC CONTENTS   xvii

PREFACE   xxvii

HOW TO READ AN ESSAY   1
How Does Reading Help You Write? 1
How Does Writing Help You Read? 2
Active Rather than Passive Reading 3
Prereading 4
Reading 4
Rereading 5
A Sample Reading: **LEWIS THOMAS** / *On Cloning a Human
  Being* 7
Some Things to Remember When Reading 14

HOW TO WRITE AN ESSAY   16
A Writer's Subject 16
A Writer's Purpose 17
A Writer's Audience 17
Some Things to Remember 18
A Writer's Information 18
A Writer's Thesis 23
Revising an Essay 26
Is an Error-Free Paper an "A" Paper? 28
A Student Writer's Revision Process 29
Sample Student Essay: **TINA BURTON** / *The Watermelon
  Wooer* 31
Some Things to Remember When Revising 38

ONE

_____

GATHERING AND USING EXAMPLES   **39**

Where Can You Find Details and Examples?   40
How Do I Gather Details and Examples from My Experiences?   42
How Do I Gather Information from Outside Sources?   43
How Many Examples Are Enough?   44
Sample Student Essay: **FRANK SMITE** / *Looking for Love*   45
Some Things to Remember   47
Visualizing Examples   47
Example as a Literary Strategy: **BRET LOTT** / *Night*   48
Gathering and Using Examples in Writing for Your Other
  Courses   50
Visit the *Prentice Hall Reader*'s Website   51

ANNA QUINDLEN / *The Name Is Mine*   52
"I was given it at birth, and I have never changed it, although I married."

BOB GREENE / *Cut*   57
*"In traveling around the country, I have found that an inordinately large
proportion of successful men share that same memory—the memory of being cut
from a sports team as a boy."*

EDWIDGE DANTICAT / *Westbury Court*   65
*"Even now, I question what I remember about the children. Did they really die?
Or did their mother simply move away with them after the fire?"*

BRIAN DOYLE / *Being Brians*   71
*"There are 215 Brian Doyles in the United States, according to a World Wide
Web site called 'Switchboard,' which shows telephone numbers and addresses in
America."*

LESLIE HEYWOOD / *One of the Girls*   78
*"Female athletes fight the same unrealistic images that everyone fights, and
researchers are only beginning to understand the relationship between those
images and the 'female athlete triad'—eating disorders and exercise compulsion,
amenorrhea—that had me training until my bones fractured, my tendons ripped,
and I stuck my fingers down my throat."*
Prewriting and Rewriting Suggestions for Example   85

TWO

_____

NARRATION   **87**

What Do You Include in a Narrative?   88
How Do You Structure a Narrative?   89

How Are Narratives Told? 90

What Do You Write About If Nothing Ever Happened to You? 91

Sample Student Essay: **HOPE ZUCKER** / *The Ruby Slippers* 92

Some Things to Remember 96

Visualizing Narration 96

Narration as a Literary Strategy: **PEGGY MCNALLY** / *Waiting* 96

Using Narration in Your Writing for Other Courses 99

Visit the *Prentice Hall Reader's* Website 100

LANGSTON HUGHES / *Salvation* **101**

"*I was saved from sin when I was going on thirteen.*"

MAYA ANGELOU / *Sister Monroe* **106**

"*Each time they pried Sister Monroe loose from the preacher he took another deep breath and kept on preaching, and Sister Monroe grabbed him in another place, and more firmly.*"

RICK REILLY / *The Biggest Play of His Life* **111**

"*I want to let all of you guys know something about me.*"

JUDITH ORTIZ COFER / *Marina* **116**

"*I looked at my mother and she smiled at me; we now had a new place to begin our search for the meaning of the word woman.*"

EVANS D. HOPKINS / *Lockdown* **125**

"*I have endured lockdowns in buildings with little or no heat; lockdowns during which the authorities cut off the plumbing completely, so contraband couldn't be flushed away; and lockdowns where we weren't allowed to shower for more than a month.*"

Prewriting and Rewriting Suggestions for Narration 133

THREE

DESCRIPTION — 135

How Do You Describe an Object or a Place? 138

How Do You Describe a Person? 138

How Do You Organize a Description? 139

Does Description Mean Lots of Adjectives and Adverbs? 140

Sample Student Essay: **NADINE RESNICK** / *Natalie* 140

Some Things to Remember 143

Visualizing Description 143

Description as a Literary Strategy: **DUANE BIGEAGLE** / *Traveling to Town* 144

Using Description in Your Writing for Other Courses 147

Visit the *Prentice Hall Reader*'s Website   148

ERIC LIU / *Po-Po*   150
"For more than two decades, my mother's mother, Po-Po lived in a cinder-block apartment on the edge of New York's Chinatown."

N. SCOTT MOMADAY / *The Way to Rainy Mountain*   156
"I returned to Rainy Mountain in July. My grandmother had died in the spring, and I wanted to be at her grave."

WILLIAM LEAST HEAT MOON / *Nameless, Tennessee*   164
" 'You think Nameless is a funny name,' Miss Ginny said, 'I see it plain in your eyes. Well, you take yourself up north a piece to Difficult or Defeated or Shake Rag. Now them are silly names.' "

TERRY TEMPEST WILLIAMS / *The Village Watchman*   172
" 'Breech,' my mother told me of my brother's birth. 'Alan was born feet first. As a result, his brain was denied oxygen. He is special.' "

SCOTT RUSSELL SANDERS / *The Inheritance of Tools*   180
"At just about the hour when my father died, soon after dawn one February morning when ice coated the windows like cataracts, I banged my thumb with a hammer."

Prewriting and Rewriting Suggestions for Description   189

FOUR

DIVISION AND CLASSIFICATION   191

How Do You Choose a Subject?   194
How Do You Divide or Classify a Subject?   194
How Do You Structure a Division or Classification Essay?   196
Sample Student Essay: **EVAN JAMES** / *Riding the Rails: The American Hobo*   197
Some Things to Remember   199
Visualizing Division and Classification   199
Division and Classification as a Literary Strategy: **ELIZABETH BARRETT BROWNING** / *How Do I Love Thee?*   201
Using Division and Classification in Writing for Your Other Courses   202
Visit the *Prentice Hall Reader*'s Website   203

DAVID BODANIS / *What's in Your Toothpaste?*   204
"So it's chalk, water, paint, seaweed, antifreeze, paraffin oil, detergent, peppermint, formaldehyde, and fluoride. . . —that's the usual mixture raised to the mouth on the toothbrush for a fresh morning's clean."

BARBARA EHRENREICH / *In Defense of Talk Shows*   209

"As anyone who actually watches them knows, the talk shows are one of the most excruciatingly moralistic forums the culture has to offer."

FRANK GANNON / *English 99: Literacy among the Ruins*   **214**
"English 99 wasn't like most of the other courses at the college. It didn't 'count' as a course for the bachelor's degree."

JUDITH ORTIZ COFER / *The Myth of the Latin Woman: I Just Met a Girl Named Maria*   **223**
"Every time I give a reading, I hope the stories I tell, the dreams and fears I examine in my work, can achieve some universal truth that will get my audience past the particulars of my skin color, my accent, or my clothes."

BERNARD R. BERELSON / *The Value of Children: A Taxonomical Essay*   **231**
"Why do people want children? It is a simple question to ask, perhaps an impossible one to answer."

PICO IYER / *Why We Travel*   **240**
"Yet for me the first great joy of traveling is simply the luxury of leaving all my beliefs and certainties at home, and seeing everything I thought I knew in a different light, and from a crooked angle."

Prewriting and Rewriting Suggestions for Division and Classification   250

FIVE

COMPARISON AND CONTRAST   253

How Do You Choose a Subject?   256
Do You Always Find Both Similarities and Differences?   257
How Do You Use Analogy, Metaphor, and Simile?   258
How Do You Structure a Comparison and Contrast?   259
Sample Student Essay: **ALICIA GRAY** / *Subject vs. Keyword Searches*   261
Some Things to Remember   266
Visualizing Comparison and Contrast   266
Comparison and Contrast as a Literary Strategy: **MARTIN ESPADA** / *Coca-Cola and Coco Frio*   267
Using Comparison and Contrast in Writing for Your Other Courses   269
Visit the *Prentice Hall Reader*'s Website   270

ESMERALDA SANTIAGO / *Guavas*   **271**
"I had my last guava the day we left Puerto Rico. It was large and juicy, almost red in the center, and so fragrant that I didn't want to eat it because I would lose the smell."

WILLIAM ZINSSER / *The Transaction: Two Writing Processes*   *275*

> *"A school in Connecticut once held 'a day devoted to the arts,' and I was asked if I would come and talk about writing as a vocation. When I arrived I found that a second speaker had been invited—Dr. Brock . . . a surgeon who had recently begun to write."*

MARY PIPHER / *Academic Selves*   *279*

> *" 'When I started junior high I figured out that I'd have more friends if I focused on sports. Smart girls were nerds.' "*

ROBERT J. SAMUELSON / *Fun Ethic vs. Work Ethic?*   *284*

> *"In 1880, 58 percent of men 75 or older worked; the figure today is 8 percent. The factory workweek averaged about 60 hours, spread over six days."*

DANZY SENNA / *The Color of Love*   *289*

> *"We had this much in common: We were both women, and we were both writers. But we were as different as two people can be and still exist in the same family."*

MEGHAN DAUM / *Virtual Love*   *296*

> *"It was the courtship ritual that had seduced us. E-mail had become an electronic epistle, a yearned-for rule book. It allowed us to do what was necessary to experience love."*

Prewriting and Rewriting Suggestions for Comparison and Contrast   307

SIX

PROCESS   308

How Do You Choose a Subject to Write About?   310

How Do You Structure a Process Paper?   310

Sample Student Essay: **JULIE ANNE HALBFISH** / *How to Play Dreidel*   312

Some Things to Remember   314

Visualizing Process   315

Process as a Literary Strategy: **JANICE MIRIKITANI** / *Recipe 317*

Using Process in Writing for Your Other Courses   318

Visit the *Prentice Hall Reader*'s Website   319

LARS EIGHNER / *My Daily Dives in the Dumpster*   *320*

> *"I began scavenging by pulling pizzas out of the Dumpster behind a pizza delivery shop."*

NORA EPHRON / *Revision and Life: Take It from the Top— Again*   *327*

> *"I have been asked to write something for a textbook that is meant to teach college students something about writing and revision."*

DIANE COLE / *Don't Just Stand There*   333
"*Speaking up may not magically change a biased attitude, but it can change a person's behavior by putting a strong message across.*"

DAVID BROOKS / *The Culture of Martyrdom*   341
"*Suicide bombing is the crack cocaine of warfare. It doesn't just inflict death and terror on its victims, it intoxicates the people who sponsor it.*"

CHARLIE DROZDYK / *Into the Loop: How to Get the Job You Want after Graduation*   348
"*Finding a job by interviewing with firms that show up on your campus is like getting a job through the want ads—it's a passive take-what's-being-thrown-in-front-of-you approach.*"

LYNNE SHARON SCHWARTZ / *The Page Turner*   358
"*In the waiting hush, the page turner lowers her body onto a chair to the left and slightly behind the pianist's seat, the fabric of her slacks adjusting around her recalcitrant hips, the hem rising a trifle to reveal more of her boots.*"

Prewriting and Rewriting Suggestions for Process   365

SEVEN

CAUSE AND EFFECT   367

Why Do You Write a Cause and Effect Analysis?   369
How Do You Choose a Subject?   370
How Do You Isolate and Evaluate Causes and Effects?   370
How Do You Structure a Cause and Effect Analysis?   371
Sample Student Essay: **CATHY FERGUSON / *TV Aggression and Children*   373**
Some Things to Remember   376
Visualizing Cause and Effect   376
Cause and Effect as a Literary Strategy: **MARGE PIERCY / *Barbie Doll*   378**
Using Cause and Effect in Writing for Your Other Courses   379
Visit the *Prentice Hall Reader*'s Website   380

E. M. FORSTER / *My Wood*   381
"*What is the effect of property upon the character?*"

JOAN JACOBS BRUMBERG / *The Origins of Anorexia Nervosa*   387
"*By returning to its origins, we can see anorexia nervosa for what it is: a dysfunction in the bourgeois family system.*"

BRENT STAPLES / *Black Men and Public Space*   393
"*My first victim was a woman—white, well dressed, probably in her early twenties.*"

VERONICA CHAMBERS / *Dreadlocked*   **399**

"Hairdressers despaired like cowardly lion tamers at the thought of training my kinky hair. 'This is some hard hair,' they would say. I knew that I was not beautiful and I blamed it on my hair."

FOX BUTTERFIELD / *Why They Excel*   **405**

"When the Asian parents were asked why they think their children do well, they most often said 'hard work.' By contrast, American parents said 'talent.'"

MALCOLM GLADWELL / *The Trouble with Fries*   **412**

"Can fast food be fixed?"

Prewriting and Rewriting Suggestions for Cause and Effect   423

EIGHT

DEFINITION   425

How Much Do You Include in a Definition?   427
How Do You Structure a Definition?   428
Sample Student Essay: **SHERRY HECK** / *Infallible*   **429**
Some Things to Remember   432
Visualizing Definition   432
Definition as a Literary Strategy: **ALICE JONES** / *The Foot*   **434**
Using Definition in Writing for Your Other Courses   435
Visit the *Prentice Hall Reader*'s Website   436

BOB GREENE / *Adults Only*   **437**

" 'Adult content' on a movie or television show should be read as a warning against becoming the kind of adult who welcomes such things into his or her life."

JUDY BRADY / *I Want a Wife*   **441**

"I belong to that classification of people known as wives. I am A Wife."

ROBIN D. G. KELLEY / *The People in Me*   **446**

" 'So what are you?' I don't know how many times people have asked me that. 'Are you Puerto Rican? Dominican? Indian or something? You must be mixed.' "

AMY TAN / *Mother Tongue*   **451**

"Language is the tool of my trade. And I use them all—all the Englishes I grew up with."

JOHN HOLLANDER / *Mess*   **459**

"Mess is a state of mind."

MARGARET ATWOOD / *The Female Body*   **465**

"I agree it's a hot topic. But only one? Look around, there's a wide range."

Prewriting and Rewriting Suggestions for Definition   472

NINE

ARGUMENT AND PERSUASION   **472**

How Do You Analyze Your Audience? 475
What Does It Take to Persuade Your Reader? 476
How Do You Make Sure That Your Argument Is Logical? 478
How Do You Structure an Argument? 479
Sample Student Essay: **BETH JAFFE** / *Lowering the Cost of a College Education* 481
Some Things to Remember 484
Visualizing Argument and Persuasion 484
Argument and Persuasion as a Literary Strategy: **WILFRED OWEN** / **Dulce et Decorum Est** 486
Using Argument and Persuasion in Writing for Your Other Courses 487
Visit the *Prentice Hall Reader*'s Website 489

MARTIN LUTHER KING JR. / *I Have a Dream*   *490*
"With this faith we will be able to work together, to pray together, to struggle together, to go to jail together, to stand up for freedom together, knowing that we will be free one day."

JONATHAN RAUCH / *The Marrying Kind*   *497*
"Couples are simply more willing to live together without tying the knot. Whether this is a bad thing is a contentious question, but it is almost certainly not a good thing."

LINDA LEE / *The Case Against College*   *502*
"Eventually I asked myself, 'Is he getting $1,000 a week's worth of education?' Heck no. That's when I began wondering why everyone needs to go to college."

DAVID GELERNTER / *What Do Murderers Deserve?*   *506*
"We execute murderers in order to make a communal proclamation: that murder is intolerable. A deliberate murder embodies evil so terrible that it defiles the community."

THE NEW YORKER / *Help for Sex Offenders*   *512*
"If castration helps, why not let them have what they want?"

PETER SINGER / *The Singer Solution to World Poverty*   *515*
"The formula is simple: whatever money you're spending on luxuries, not necessities, should be given away."

RICHARD RODRIGUEZ / *None of This Is Fair*   *525*
" 'It's all very simple this year. You're a Chicano. And I am a Jew. That's the only real difference between us.' "

Prewriting and Rewriting Suggestions for Argument and Persuasion 531

TEN

REVISING   533

Analyzing Your Own Writing   534
Keeping a Revision Log   535
Using Peer Readers   536
Using Your School's Writing Center or a Writing Tutor   538
Using an OWL   539
Conferencing with Your Instructor   539
Proofreading Your Paper   540
Visualizing Revision   542
Revisers at Work   543
Visit the *Prentice Hall Reader*'s Website   543

REVISION CASE STUDY:
GORDON GRICE / *Caught in the Widow's Web*   544
                      Journal Entries: The Black Widow   550
                      A Conversation with Gordon Grice   555

APPENDIX

FINDING, USING, AND DOCUMENTING SOURCES   558

Finding Sources   558
Web Searching Tips   565
Using Sources   571
Documenting Your Sources   575
Electronic Sources   583
Annotated Sample Student Research Paper (MLA Documentation
  Style):   **AMY RUBENS** / *Ecotourism: Friend or Foe?*   584

GLOSSARY   600

CREDITS   610

INDEX   616

THEMATIC CONTENTS

AUTOBIOGRAPHY AND BIOGRAPHY

BRET LOTT / *Night*   48

ANNA QUINDLEN / *The Name Is Mine*   52

BOB GREENE / *Cut*   57

EDWIDGE DANTICAT / *Westbury Court*   65

BRIAN DOYLE / *On Being Brians*   71

LANGSTON HUGHES / *Salvation*   101

MAYA ANGELOU / *Sister Monroe*   106

RICK REILLY / *The Biggest Play of His Life*   111

JUDITH ORTIZ COFER / *Marina*   116

EVANS HOPKINS / *Lockdown*   125

DUANE BIGEAGLE / *Traveling to Town*   144

ERIC LIU / *Po-Po*   150

N. SCOTT MOMADAY / *The Way to Rainy Mountain*   156

WILLIAM LEAST HEAT MOON / *Nameless, Tennessee*   164

TERRY TEMPEST WILLIAMS / *The Village Watchman*   172

SCOTT RUSSELL SANDERS / *The Inheritance of Tools*   180

ELIZABETH BARRETT BROWNING / *How Do I Love Thee?*   201

FRANK GANNON / *English 99*   214

JUDITH ORTIZ COFER / *The Myth of the Latin Woman*   223

ESMERALDA SANTIAGO / *Guavas*   271

DANZY SENNA / *The Color of Love*   289

MEGHAN DAUM / *Virtual Love*   296

LARS EIGHNER / *My Daily Dives in the Dumpster*   320

NORA EPHRON / *Revision and Life*   327

E. M. FORSTER / *My Wood*   381

BRENT STAPLES / *Black Men and Public Space*   393

VERONICA CHAMBERS / *Dreadlocked*   399

ROBIN D. G. KELLEY / *The People in Me*   446

AMY TAN / *Mother Tongue*   461

RICHARD RODRIGUEZ / *None of This Is Fair*   525

CHILDREN AND FAMILY

BRET LOTT / *Night*   48

ANNA QUINDLEN / *The Name Is Mine*   52

EDWIDGE DANTICAT / *Westbury Court*   65

JUDITH ORTIZ COFER / *Marina*   116

ERIC LIU / *Po-Po*   150

N. SCOTT MOMADAY / *The Way to Rainy Mountain*   156

TERRY TEMPEST WILLIAMS / *The Village Watchman*   172

SCOTT RUSSELL SANDERS / *The Inheritance of Tools*   180

BERNARD BERELSON / *The Value of Children*   231

DANZY SENNA / *The Color of Love*   289

JOAN JACOBS BRUMBERG / *The Origins of Anorexia Nervosa*   387

FOX BUTTERFIELD / *Why They Excel*   405

JUDY BRADY / *I Want a Wife*   441

ROBIN D. G. KELLEY / *The People in Me*   446

AMY TAN / *Mother Tongue*   451

VIOLENCE AND PUNISHMENT

EVANS HOPKINS / *Lockdown*   125

DAVID BROOKS / *The Culture of Martyrdom*   341

BOB GREENE / *Adults Only*   437

WILFRED OWEN / Dulce et Decorum Est   488

DAVID GELERNTER / *What Do Murderers Deserve?*   506

THE NEW YORKER / *Help for Sex Offenders*   512

MEDIA AND COMPUTERS

BARBARA EHRENREICH / *In Defense of Talk Shows*   209

MEGHAN DAUM / *Virtual Love*   296

DAVID BROOKS / *The Culture of Martyrdom*   341

MARGARET ATWOOD / *The Female Body*   465

STEREOTYPES, PREJUDICE, AND THE STRUGGLE FOR EQUALITY

LESLIE HEYWOOD / *One of the Girls*   78

RICK REILLY / *The Biggest Play of His Life*   111

EVANS HOPKINS / *Lockdown*   125

TERRY TEMPEST WILLIAMS / *The Village Watchman*   172

JUDITH ORTIZ COFER / *The Myth of the Latin Woman*   223

JANICE MIRIKITANI / *Recipe*   317

DIANE COLE / *Don't Just Stand There*   333

MARGE PIERCY / *Barbie Doll*   377

BRENT STAPLES / *Black Men and Public Space*   393

VERONICA CHAMBERS / *Dreadlocked*   399

JUDY BRADY / *I Want a Wife*   441

ROBIN D. G. KELLEY / *The People in Me*   446

AMY TAN / *Mother Tongue*   451

MARGARET ATWOOD / *The Female Body*   465

MARTIN LUTHER KING, JR. / *I Have a Dream*   490

JONATHAN RAUCH / *The Marrying Kind*   497

RICHARD RODRIGUEZ / *None of This Is Fair*   525

WOMEN'S ROLES, WOMEN'S RIGHTS

ANNA QUINDLEN / *The Name Is Mine*   52

LESLIE HEYWOOD / *One of the Girls*   78

JUDITH ORTIZ COFER / *Marina*   116

JUDITH ORTIZ COFER / *The Myth of the Latin Woman*   223

MARY PIPHER / *Academic Selves*   279

DANZY SENNA / *The Color of Love*   289

JANICE MIRIKITANI / *Recipe*   317

JOAN JACOBS BRUMBERG / *The Origins of Anorexia Nervosa*   387

VERONICA CHAMBERS / *Dreadlocked*   399

JUDY BRADY / *I Want a Wife*   441

AMY TAN / *Mother Tongue*   451

MARGARET ATWOOD / *The Female Body*   465

GROWING OLDER

ANNA QUINDLEN / *The Name Is Mine*   52

BOB GREENE / *Cut*   57

LANGSTON HUGHES / *Salvation*   101

JUDITH ORTIZ COFER / *Marina*   116

ERIC LIU / *Po-Po*   150

N. SCOTT MOMADAY / *The Way to Rainy Mountain*   156

TERRY TEMPEST WILLIAMS / *The Village Watchman*   172

SCOTT RUSSELL SANDERS / *The Inheritance of Tools*   180

ESMERALDA SANTIAGO / *Guavas*   271

NORA EPHRON / *Revision and Life*   327

AMY TAN / *Mother Tongue*   451

HUMOR AND SATIRE

LANGSTON HUGHES / *Salvation*   101

MAYA ANGELOU / *Sister Monroe*   106

DAVID BODANIS / *What's in Your Toothpaste?*   204

FRANK GANNON / *English 99*   214

WILLIAM ZINSSER / *The Transaction*   275

JANICE MIRIKITANI / *Recipe*   317

MARGE PIERCY / *Barbie Doll*   377

JUDY BRADY / *I Want a Wife*   441

MARGARET ATWOOD / *The Female Body*   465

MEN AND WOMEN

ANNA QUINDLEN / *The Name Is Mine*   52

JUDITH ORTIZ COFER / *Marina*   116

ELIZABETH BARRETT BROWNING / *How Do I Love Thee?*   201

JUDITH ORTIZ COFER / *The Myth of the Latin Woman*   223

MEGHAN DAUM / *Virtual Love*   296

JUDY BRADY / *I Want a Wife*   441

MARGARET ATWOOD / *The Female Body*   465

RACE, CLASS, AND CULTURE

EDWIDGE DANTICAT / *Westbury Court*   65

LANGSTON HUGHES / *Salvation*   101

MAYA ANGELOU / *Sister Monroe*   106

JUDITH ORTIZ COFER / *Marina*   116

EVANS HOPKINS / *Lockdown*   125

N. SCOTT MOMADAY / *The Way to Rainy Mountain*   156

WILLIAM LEAST HEAT MOON / *Nameless, Tennessee*   164

BARBARA EHRENREICH / *In Defense of Talk Shows*   209

FRANK GANNON / *English 99*   214

JUDITH ORTIZ COFER / *The Myth of the Latin Woman*   223

BERNARD BERELSON / *The Value of Children*   231

DANZY SENNA / *The Color of Love*   289

JANICE MIRIKITANI / *Recipe*   317

LARS EIGHNER / *My Daily Dives in the Dumpster*   320

DAVID BROOKS / *The Culture of Martyrdom*   341

BRENT STAPLES / *Black Men and Public Space*   393

VERONICA CHAMBERS / *Dreadlocked*   399

FOX BUTTERFIELD / *Why They Excel*   405

ROBIN D. G. KELLEY / *The People in Me*   446

AMY TAN / *Mother Tongue*   451

MARTIN LUTHER KING, JR. / *I Have a Dream*   490

RICHARD RODRIGUEZ / *None of This Is Fair*   525

TRAVEL AND NATURE

DUANE BIGEAGLE / *Traveling to Town*   144

N. SCOTT MOMADAY / *The Way to Rainy Mountain*   156

WILLIAM LEAST HEAT MOON / *Nameless, Tennessee*   164

PICO IYER / *Why We Travel*   240

GORDON GRICE / *Caught in the Widow's Web*   544

PSYCHOLOGY AND BEHAVIOR

ANNA QUINDLEN / *The Name Is Mine*   52

BOB GREENE / *Cut*   57

LESLIE HEYWOOD / *One of the Girls*   78

PEGGY MCNALLY / *Waiting*   96

EVANS HOPKINS / *Lockdown*   125

TERRY TEMPEST WILLIAMS / *The Village Watchman*   172

BARBARA EHRENREICH / *In Defense of Talk Shows*   209

FRANK GANNON / *English 99*   214

JUDITH ORTIZ COFER / *The Myth of the Latin Woman* 223

BERNARD BERELSON / *The Value of Children* 231

PICO IYER / *Why We Travel* 240

ESMERALDA SANTIAGO / *Guavas* 271

MARY PIPHER / *Academic Selves* 279

ROBERT J. SAMUELSON / *Fun Ethic vs. Work Ethic?* 284

DANZY SENNA / *The Color of Love* 289

MEGHAN DAUM / *Virtual Love* 296

JANICE MIRIKITANI / *Recipe* 317

LARS EIGHNER / *My Daily Dives in the Dumpster* 320

NORA EPHRON / *Revision and Life* 327

DIANE COLE / *Don't Just Stand There* 333

DAVID BROOKS / *The Culture of Martyrdom* 341

E. M. FORSTER / *My Wood* 381

JOAN JACOBS BRUMBERG / *The Origins of Anorexia Nervosa* 387

BRENT STAPLES / *Black Men and Public Space* 393

VERONICA CHAMBERS / *Dreadlocked* 399

FOX BUTTERFIELD / *Why They Excel* 405

MALCOLM GLADWELL / *The Trouble with Fries* 412

MARGARET ATWOOD / *The Female Body* 465

JONATHAN RAUCH / *The Marrying Kind* 497

DAVID GELERNTER / *What Do Murderers Deserve?* 506

THE NEW YORKER / *Help for Sex Offenders* 512

PETER SINGER / *The Singer Solution* 515

READING, WRITING, AND LANGUAGE

ANNA QUINDLEN / *The Name Is Mine* 52

BRIAN DOYLE / *On Being Brians* 71

FRANK GANNON / *English 99* 214

WILLIAM ZINSSER / *The Transaction*   275

MEGHAN DAUM / *Virtual Love*   296

NORA EPHRON / *Revision and Life*   327

DIANE COLE / *Don't Just Stand There*   333

AMY TAN / *Mother Tongue*   451

JOHN HOLLANDER / *Mess*   459

MARGARET ATWOOD / *The Female Body*   465

SCHOOL AND COLLEGE

BOB GREENE / *Cut*   57

LESLIE HEYWOOD / *One of the Girls*   78

RICK REILLY / *The Biggest Play of His Life*   111

FRANK GANNON / *English 99*   214

MARY PIPHER / *Academic Selves*   279

CHARLIE DROZDYK / *Into the Loop*   348

FOX BUTTERFIELD / *Why They Excel*   405

LINDA LEE / *The Case Against College*   502

RICHARD RODRIGUEZ / *None of This Is Fair*   525

SELF-DISCOVERY

ANNA QUINDLEN / *The Name Is Mine*   52

BOB GREENE / *Cut*   57

LANGSTON HUGHES / *Salvation*   101

N. SCOTT MOMADAY / *The Way to Rainy Mountain*   156

WILLIAM LEAST HEAT MOON / *Nameless, Tennessee*   164

TERRY TEMPEST WILLIAMS / *The Village Watchman*   172

SCOTT RUSSELL SANDERS / *The Inheritance of Tools*   180

ELIZABETH BARRETT BROWNING / *How Do I Love Thee?*   201

FRANK GANNON / *English 99*   214

JUDITH ORTIZ COFER / *The Myth of the Latin Woman*   223

PICO IYER / *Why We Travel*   240

ESMERALDA SANTIAGO / *Guavas*   271

DANZY SENNA / *The Color of Love*   289

MEGHAN DAUM / *Virtual Love*   296

JANICE MIRIKITANI / *Recipe*   317

NORA EPHRON / *Revision and Life*   327

E. M. FORSTER / *My Wood*   381

BRENT STAPLES / *Black Men and Public Space*   393

VERONICA CHAMBERS / *Dreadlocked*   399

AMY TAN / *Mother Tongue*   451

JOHN HOLLANDER / *Mess*   459

RICHARD RODRIGUEZ / *None of This Is Fair*   525

PREFACE

The Prentice Hall Reader is predicated on two premises: that reading plays a vital role in learning how to write and that writing and reading can best be organized around the traditional division of discourse into a number of structural patterns. Such a division is not the only way that the forms of writing can be classified, but it does have several advantages.

First, practice in these structural patterns encourages students to organize knowledge and to see the ways in which information can be conveyed. How else does the mind know except by classifying, comparing, defining, or seeking cause and effect relationships? Second, the most common use of these patterns occurs in writing done in academic courses. There students are asked to narrate a chain of events, to describe an artistic style, to classify plant forms, to compare two political systems, to tell how a laboratory experiment was performed, to analyze why famine occurs in Africa, to define a philosophical concept, or to argue for or against building a space station. Learning how to structure papers using these patterns is an exercise that has immediate application in students' other academic work. Finally, because the readings use these patterns as structural devices, they offer an excellent way in which to integrate reading into a writing course. Students can see the patterns at work and learn how to use them to become more effective writers and better, more efficient readers.

WHAT IS NEW IN THE SEVENTH EDITION

The seventh edition of *The Prentice Hall Reader* features 54 essays, 15 of which are new, and another 11 papers written by student writers. Also new to this edition are 9 poems or short, short stories that show the organizational strategies at work. As in the previous editions, the readings are chosen on the basis of several criteria: how well they demonstrate a particular pattern of organization, appeal to a freshman audience, and promote interesting and appropriate discussion and writing activities.

The seventh edition of *The Prentice Hall Reader* includes a number of new features:

- *Literary Examples of Each Organizational Strategy.* A poem or short, short story has been added to each of the nine chapters. These creative examples show how the strategies can be used to structure not just essays, but poetry and fiction as well. Each selection has discussion questions and writing suggestions.

- *New Prewriting and Rewriting Suggestions.* Each of the 9 chapters ends with a list of prewriting and rewriting suggestions for that particular strategy. The suggestions offer students a convenient checklist of appropriate activities.

- *Writing Links.* Each essay has a "Writing Link" that focuses students' attention on how the writer uses punctuation, word choice, sentence structure, typographical devices, and paragraph skills to create an effective essay. The links will help build bridges between the content of the essays and the writing skills they reveal.

- *New Chapter Introductions.* Each chapter introduction has been rewritten to emphasize the visual display of information.

The seventh edition retains and improves upon some of the popular student features from earlier editions:

- *Visualizing.* Sections in each chapter show how the writing strategy is embodied in visual forms. A panel cartoon is a narrative, a technical drawing details a process, advertisements (even for products that do not exist!) show persuasion at work.

- *Writing in Other Disciplines.* Each chapter provides examples of how the traditional patterns of organization are used in writing for other college courses.

- *Prereading Questions.* These questions help connect the reading to students' experience and focus their reading attention.

- *Writers on Writing.* Writers share their observations on the process of finding a subject, composing, and revising.
- *Links to the Website.* The Prentice Hall Reader has a massive site at http://www.prenhall.com/miller. Additional materials for discussion, background information and reading suggestions, additional writing suggestions, and a group of Web links are available for every reading in every chapter. Each chapter also has Web-based writing tasks, asking students to visit a site or a series of sites, gather information, and respond to a writing prompt. Students can use the *Reader* as they learn how to navigate the Web to find sources of information for their papers.
- *Tips on Web Searching.* Students who find that their Web searches yield too many matches can get help in defining searches more narrowly.
- *Writing Suggestions.* Between the writing suggestions offered in the *Reader* itself and the additional topics found at the Website, the *Reader* has nearly 500 writing suggestions.

OTHER DISTINCTIVE FEATURES OF THIS TEXT

PROSE IN REVISION

As every writing instructor knows, getting students to revise is never easy. Having finished a paper, most students do not want to see it again, let alone revise it. Furthermore, for many students revising means making word substitutions and correcting grammatical and mechanical errors—changes that instructors regard as proofreading, not revising. To help make the need for revision more vivid and to show how writers revise, the *Prentice Hall Reader* includes three features:

1. Chapter 10: Revising. A complete chapter with a lengthy introduction offers specific advice on how to revise. A case study of Gordon Grice's essay on the black widow spider documents the evolution of the essay from notebook entries to its original publication in a small literary journal.

2. The introduction to each chapter of readings includes a first draft of a student essay, a comment on the draft's strengths and weaknesses, and a final, revised draft. These essays,

realistic examples of student writing, model the student revision process.

3. A list of specific prewriting and rewriting activities can be found at the end of each chapter of readings.

SELECTIONS

The seventh edition of *The Prentice Hall Reader* offers instructors flexibility in choosing readings. No chapter has fewer than five selections and most have six or more. The readings are scaled in terms of length and sophistication. The selections in each chapter begin with a student essay and the selections from professional writers are arranged so that they increase in length and in difficulty and sophistication.

WRITING SUGGESTIONS

Each reading is followed by four writing suggestions: the first is a journal writing suggestion; the second calls for a paragraph-length response; the third, an essay; and the fourth, an essay involving research. Each of the suggestions is related to the content of the reading and each calls for a response in the particular pattern or mode being studied. The material in the Annotated Instructor's Edition includes a fifth writing suggestion for each reading. Even more writing suggestions can be found at the *Prentice Hall Reader* Website at http://www.prenhall.com/miller.

INTRODUCTIONS

The introduction to each chapter offers clear and succinct advice to the student on how to write that particular type of paragraph or essay. The introductions anticipate questions, provide answers, and end with a checklist, titled "Some Things to Remember," to remind students of the major concerns they should have when writing.

HOW TO READ AN ESSAY

The first introductory section offers advice on how to read an essay, following prereading, reading, and rereading models. A sample analysis of an essay by Lewis Thomas shows how to use this reading model to prepare an essay for class.

HOW TO WRITE AN ESSAY

The section, "How to Write an Essay," offers an overview of every stage of the writing process, starting with advice on how to define a subject, purpose, and audience and an explanation of a variety of prewriting techniques. The section also shows students how to write a thesis statement, how to decide where to place that statement in an essay, and how to approach the problems of revising an essay. Finally it contains a student essay as well as two drafts of the student's two opening paragraphs.

ANNOTATED INSTRUCTOR'S EDITION

An annotated edition of *The Prentice Hall Reader* is available to instructors. Each of the selections in the text is annotated with

- A Teaching Strategy that suggests ways in which to teach the reading and to keep attention focused on how the selection works as a piece of writing
- A suggested link to other writing and organizational strategies found in the reading
- Appropriate background information that explains allusions or historical contexts
- Specific class and collaborative learning activities that can be used with the reading
- A critical reading activity
- Possible responses to all of the discussion questions included within the text
- Tips on "related readings" that suggest how to pair essays in the reader
- An additional writing suggestion

INSTRUCTOR'S QUIZ BOOKLET

A separate *Instructor's Quiz Booklet* for *The Prentice Hall Reader* is available from your Prentice Hall representative. The booklet contains two quizzes for each selection in the reader—one on content and the other on vocabulary. Each quiz has five multiple-choice questions. The quizzes are intended to be administered and graded quickly. They provide the instructor with a brief and efficient means of testing the student's ability to extract significant ideas from the readings and of demonstrating his or her understanding of certain vocabulary words as they are used in the essays. Keys to both content and vocabulary quizzes are included at the back of the *Quiz Booklet.*

TEACHING WRITING WITH "THE PRENTICE HALL READER"

A separate manual on planning the writing and the reading in a composition course is available from your Prentice Hall representative. Primarily addressed to the new graduate teaching assistant or the adjunct instructor, the manual includes sections on teaching the writing process, including how to use prewriting activities, to conference, to design and implement collaborative learning activities, and to grade. In addition, it provides advice on how to plan a class discussion of a reading and how to avoid pointless discussions. An appendix contains an index to all of the activities and questions in *The Prentice Hall Reader* that involve grammatical, mechanical, sentence- or paragraph-level subjects, three additional sample syllabi, and a variety of sample course materials including self-assessment sheets, peer editing worksheets, and directions for small group activities.

"THE PRENTICE HALL READER" WEBSITE

The *Reader* has an extensive Website that includes additional resources for both the student and the instructor for every essay in the *Reader.* The Website is divided into sections on Related Readings (print or on-line documents that are related to the topic under discussion or to the author), Background Information, Web Resources (with hot-linked sites so that the students can immediately access these sites), and Additional Writing Suggestions. Each chapter also has writing tasks that involve examining Websites and documents. The Website adds a new dimension to the *Reader* and allows instructors to integrate the World Wide Web into their freshman English courses. Additional student essays are also available there and you can submit the best of your students' work for inclusion as well!

George Miller
University of Delaware

ACKNOWLEDGMENTS

Although writing is a solitary activity, no one can write without the assistance of others. This text owes much to many people: To the staff at Prentice Hall who have continued to play a large role in helping to develop this reader, especially Phil Miller, former president, Humanities and Social Science; Leah Jewell, editor-in-chief; Corey Good, acquisitions editor; Karen Schultz assistant editor; Brandy Dawson, marketing manager; Fran Russello, production liaison; my production team at Carlisle Communications, Terry Routley, senior project editor; Mark Gallaher, development editor; and Mary Dalton-Hoffman, permissions specialist.

To my reviewers, who wrote extensive critiques of the manuscript and made many helpful suggestions: Barbara J. Grossman, Essex County College; Elaine M. Ferguson, McMurry University; Elizabeth Jean Milewicz, Jacksonville State University; Megan O'Neill, Stetson University; Michael Hricik, Westmoreland County Community College; Deanna Mascle, Morehead State University; Allison Smith, Louisiana Technical University; Robert Dornsite, Creighton University; Mildred Melendez, Sinclair Community College; Heidi E. Ajrami, Victoria College; Durr Walker, Copiah-Lincoln Community College; Allan Grant, Southwestern Community College; Ann T. Roberts, Texas State Technical College.

To the writing program staff at the University of Delaware, especially John Jebb. To my former students—both graduate and undergraduate—who tested materials, offered suggestions, and contributed essays to the introductions. To the University of Delaware Library and its staff, especially Pat Arnott.

To my wife Vicki, who makes everything possible. And finally to my children, Lisa, Jon, Craig, Valerie, Eric, Evan, Adam, Nathan, and Alicia and Eric Gray, who have learned over the years to live with a father who writes.

HOW TO READ
AN ESSAY

When your grade in most writing courses is determined by the papers that you write, rather than by examinations based on the essays that you read in the course, you might wonder why any instructor would assign "readings" in a writing course. How do these two seemingly very different activities fit together?

HOW DOES READING HELP YOU WRITE?

You read in a writing course for three purposes: First, the essays are a source of information: you learn by reading, and what you learn can then, in turn, be used in your writing. Any paper that involves research, for example, requires selective, critical reading on your part as you search for and evaluate sources. Second, readings offer a perspective on a particular subject, one with which you might agree or disagree. In this sense readings can serve as catalysts to spark writing. Many of the writing suggestions in this text grow out of the readings, asking you to explore some aspect of the subject more fully, to reply to a writer's position, or to expand on or refine that position. Finally, readings offer models to a writer; they show you how another writer dealt with a particular subject or a particular writing problem, and they demonstrate writing strategies. Other writing suggestions in this text ask you to employ the same strategy used in a reading with a different subject in an essay of your own.

The first two purposes—readings as a source of information or as a stimulus to writing—are fairly obvious, but the third purpose might seem confusing. Exactly how are you, as a student writer, to use an essay written by a professional writer as an example or model? Are you to suppose to sound like Margaret Atwood or Bob Greene or Maya Angelou? Are you to imitate their styles or the structures that they use in their essays?

To model, in the sense that the word is being used here, does not mean to produce an imitation. You are not expected to use the same organizational structure or to imitate someone else's style, tone, or approach. Rather, what you can learn from these writers is how to handle information; how to adapt writing to a particular audience; how to structure the body of an essay; how to begin, make transitions, and end; how to construct effective paragraphs and achieve sentence variety. In short, the readings represent an album of performances, examples that you can use to study writing techniques.

Models or examples are important to you as a writer because you learn to write effectively in the same way that you learn to do any other activity. You study the rules or advice on how it is done; you practice, especially under the watchful eye of an instructor or a coach; and you study how others have mastered similar problems and techniques. A young musician learns how to read music and play an instrument, practices daily, studies with a teacher, and listens to and watches how other musicians play. A baseball player learns the proper offensive and defensive techniques, practices daily, is supervised by a coach, and listens to the advice and watches the performance of other players. As a writer in a writing class, you do the same thing: follow the advice offered by your instructor and textbooks, practice by writing and revising, listen to the advice and suggestions of your fellow students, and study the work of other writers.

HOW DOES WRITING HELP YOU READ?

Reading and writing actually benefit each other: being a good reader will help you become a more effective writer, and being a good writer will help you become a more effective reader. As a writer, you learn how to plan an essay, how to use examples to support a thesis, how to structure an argument, how to make an effective transition from one point to another. You learn how to write beginnings, middles, and ends, and most especially you learn how essays can be organized. For example, through reading you learn that comparison and contrast essays can be organized in either the subject-by-subject or the point-by-point pattern, that narratives are structured chronologically, and that cause and effect analyses are linear and sequential. When you read other essays, you look for structure and pattern, realizing that such devices are not only creative tools you use in writing but also analytical ones that can be used in reading. By revealing to you an underlying organizational pattern, such devices help you understand what the essay says. To become an efficient reader, however, you need to exercise the same care and attention that you do when you write. You do that by becoming an active rather than a passive reader.

ACTIVE RATHER THAN PASSIVE READING

Every reader first reads a piece of writing for plot or subject matter. On that level, the reader wants to know what happens, what is the subject, whether it is new or interesting. Generally that first reading is done quickly, even, in a sense, superficially. The reader is a spectator waiting passively to be entertained or informed. Then, if it is important for the reader to use that piece of writing in some way, to understand it in detail and in depth, the next stage of active reading begins. On this level, the reader asks questions, seeks answers, looks for organizational structures, and concentrates on themes and images or on the thesis and the quality of evidence presented. Careful reading requires this active participation of the reader. Writing and reading are, after all, social acts, and as such they involve an implied contract between writer and audience. A writer's job is to communicate clearly and effectively; a reader's job is to read attentively and critically.

Because as a reader you need to become an active participant in this process of communication, you should always read any piece of writing you are using in a course or on your job more than once. Rereading an essay or a textbook involves the same types of critical activities that you use when rereading a poem, a novel, or a play and demands your attention and your active involvement as a reader. You must examine how the author embodies meaning or purpose in prose. You must seek answers to a variety of questions: How does the author structure the essay? How does the author select, organize, and present information? To whom is the author writing? How does that audience influence the essay?

You can increase your effectiveness as an active and critical reader by following the same three-stage model that you use as a writer: divide your time into prereading, reading, and rereading activities.

PREREADING

Before you begin reading an essay in this text, look first at the biographical headnote that describes the author and her or his work and that identifies where and when the essay was originally published, including any special conditions or circumstances that surrounded or influenced its publication. The headnote ends with two "Before Reading" questions that encourage you to connect aspects of the reading to your experiences and to anticipate the writer's thought. A careful reading of this material can help prepare you to read the essay.

Look next at the text of the essay itself. What does the title tell you about the subject or the tone? A serious, dignified title such as "The Value of Children: A Taxonomical Essay" (p. 231) sets up a very different set of expectations than a playful title such as "The Trouble with Fries" (p. 412). Page through the essay—are there any obvious subdivisions in the text (extra spaces, sequence markers, subheadings) that signal an organizational pattern? Does the paragraphing suggest a particular structure? You might also read the first sentence in every paragraph to get a general sense of what the essay is about and where the author is going.

Finally, look at the series of questions that follow each selection. These questions always ask about subject and purpose, structure and audience, and vocabulary and style. Read through them so that you know what to look for when you read the essay. Before you begin to read, make sure that you have a pen or pencil, some paper on which to take notes, and a dictionary in which to check the meanings of unfamiliar words.

READING

When you begin to read a selection in this book, you already have an important piece of information about its structure. Each selection was chosen to demonstrate a particular type of writing (narration, description, exposition, and argumentation) and a particular pattern of organization (chronological, spatial, division and classification, comparison and contrast, process, cause and effect, definition, induction or deduction). As you read, think about how the author organized the essay. On a separate sheet of paper, construct a brief outline. That will help you focus your attention on how the whole essay is put together.

Remember that an essay will typically express a particular idea or assertion **(thesis)** about a **subject** to an **audience** for a particular reason **(purpose).** Probably one reading of an essay will be enough for you to answer questions about **subject,** but you may have to reread the essay several times to identify the author's **thesis** and **purpose.** Keep these three elements separate and clear in your own mind. It will help to answer each of the following questions as you read and reread:

1. **Subject:** What is this essay about?
2. **Thesis:** What particular point is the author trying to make about this subject?
3. **Audience:** To whom is the author writing? Where did the essay first appear? How does its intended audience help shape the essay and influence its language and style?
4. **Purpose:** Why is the author writing this? Is the intention to entertain? To inform? To persuade?

Effective writing contains specific, relevant details and examples. Look carefully at the writer's choice of examples. Remember that the author made a conscious decision to include each of these details. Ideally, each is appropriate to the subject and each contributes to the thesis and purpose.

REREADING

Rereading, like rewriting, is not always a discrete stage in a linear process. Just as you might pause after writing several sentences and then go back and make some immediate changes, so as a reader, you might stop at the end of a paragraph and then go back and reread what you have just read. Depending on the difficulty of the essay, it might take several rereadings for you to be able to answer the questions posed about the writer's thesis and purpose. Even if you feel certain about your understanding of the essay, a final rereading is important.

In that rereading, focus on the essay as an example of a writer's craft. Look carefully at the paragraphing. How effective is the introduction to the essay? The conclusion? Have you ever used a similar strategy to begin or end an essay? How do both reflect the writer's purpose? Audience? Pay attention to the writer's sentence structures. How do these sentences differ from the ones that you typically write? Does the author employ a variety of sentence types and lengths? Is there anything unusual about the author's word choices? Do you use a similar range of vocabulary when you write? Remember that the writer of essays is just as conscious of craft as the poet, the novelist, or the playwright.

A SAMPLE READING

Before you begin reading in the seventh edition of *The Prentice Hall Reader*, you can see how to use these techniques of prereading, reading, and rereading in the following essay, which has been annotated over the course of several readings. Following the essay are the reader's prereading, reading, and rereading notes.

ON CLONING A HUMAN BEING

Lewis Thomas

Lewis Thomas (1913–1993) was born in Flushing, New York, and received his M.D. from Harvard University. He served on the medical faculty at Johns Hopkins, Tulane, Cornell, and Yale before assuming the position of chancellor of the Memorial Sloan-Kettering Cancer Center in New York. Thomas published widely in his research specialty, pathology, the study of diseases and their causes.

In 1971 he began contributing a 1,200-word monthly column, focusing on current topics related to medicine and biological science, to the New England Journal of Medicine. *Titled "Notes of a Biology Watcher," the column proved highly popular with professionals who subscribed to the journal as well as nonspecialists. Several collections of these essays have been published, including* The Lives of a Cell: Notes of a Biology Watcher *(1974),* The Medusa and the Snail *(1979),* Late Night Thoughts on Listening to Mahler's Ninth Symphony *(1983), and* Fragile Species *(1992).*

In "On Cloning a Human Being," originally published in the New England Journal of Medicine, *Thomas sets out to analyze the effect that an experiment to clone a human being would have on the rest of the world.*

BEFORE READING

Connecting: What do you know about cloning, both in fact and from science fiction? Do you find cloning a positive technological development or a frightening one?

Anticipating: What seems to be Thomas's attitude toward cloning? As a scientist, does he express the opinion you expect?

It is now theoretically possible to recreate an identical creature from any animal or plant, from the DNA contained in the nucleus of any somatic cell. A single plant root-tip cell can be teased and seduced into conceiving a perfect copy of the whole plant; a frog's intestinal epithelial cell possesses the complete instructions needed for a new, same frog. If the technology were further

1

Definition of cloning

advanced, you could do this with a human being, and there are now startled predictions all over the place that this will in fact be done, someday, in order to provide a version of immortality for carefully selected, especially valuable people.

2   The cloning of humans is on most of the lists of things to worry about from Science, along with behavior control, genetic engineering, <u>transplanted heads</u>, <u>computer poetry</u>, and the <u>unrestrained growth of plastic flowers</u>.

Joking here.

3   Cloning is the most dismaying of prospects, mandating as it does the elimination of sex with only a metaphoric elimination of death as compensation. It is almost no comfort to know that one's cloned, identical surrogate lives on, especially when the living will very likely involve edging one's real, now aging self off to the side, sooner or later. It is hard to imagine anything like filial affection or respect for a single, unmated nucleus; harder still to think of one's new, self-generated self as anything but an absolute, desolate orphan. Not to mention the complex interpersonal relationship involved in raising one's self from infancy, teaching the language, enforcing discipline, instilling good manners, and the like. How would you feel if you became an incorrigible juvenile delinquent by proxy, at the age of fifty-five?

Two versions of the same person living at once—the original and the clone. Wild idea.

proxy: person acting for another person

4   The public questions are obvious. Who is to be selected, and on what qualifications? How to handle the risks of misused technology, such as self-determined cloning by the rich and powerful but socially objectionable, or the cloning by governments of dumb, docile masses for the world's work? What will be the effect on all the uncloned rest of us of human sameness? After all, we've accustomed ourselves through hundreds of millennia to the continual exhilaration of uniqueness; each of us is totally different, in a fundamental sense, from all the other four billion. Selfness is an essential fact of life. The thought of human

4-paragraph introduction sets up negatives about cloning

nonselfness, precise sameness, is terrifying, when you think about it.

Well, don't think about it, because it isn't a probable possibility, not even as a long shot for the distant future, in my opinion. I agree that you might clone some people who would look amazingly like their parental cell donors, but the odds are that they'd be almost as different as you or me, and certainly more different than any of today's identical twins.

The time required for the experiment is only one of the problems, but a formidable one. Suppose you wanted to clone a <u>prominent, spectacularly successful diplomat, to look after the Middle East problems of the distant future</u>. You'd have to catch him and persuade him, probably not very hard to do, and extirpate a cell. But then you'd have to wait for him to grow up through embryonic life and then for at least forty years more, and you'd have to be sure all observers remained patient and unmeddlesome through his unpromising, ambiguous childhood and adolescence.

Moreover, you'd have to be sure of recreating his environment, perhaps down to the last detail. "Environment" is a word which really means people, so you'd have to do a lot more cloning than just the diplomat himself.

This is a very important part of the cloning problem, largely overlooked in our excitement about the cloned individual himself. You don't have to agree all the way with B. F. Skinner to acknowledge that the environment does make a difference, and when you examine what we really mean by the word "environment" it comes down to other human beings. We use euphemisms and jargon for this, like "social forces," "cultural influences," even Skinner's "verbal community," but what is meant is the dense crowd of nearby people who talk to, listen to, smile or frown at, give to, withhold from, nudge, push, caress, or flail out at the individual. No matter what the ⟨genome⟩ says, these people have a lot to do with shaping a char-

5 Thesis: Cloning human beings is not really possible.

6 Reason 1: Time involved

"valuable person"

7 Reason 2: Environment would have to be created

8
To be the same, the clone would have to have the same environment

genome: genetic organism

acter. Indeed, if all you had was the genome, and no people around, you'd grow a sort of vertebrate plant, nothing more.

9

So, to start with, you will undoubtedly need to clone the <u>parents.</u> No question about this. This means the diplomat is out, even in theory, since you couldn't have gotten cells from both his parents at the time when he was himself just recognizable as an early social treasure. You'd have to limit the list of clones to people already certified as sufficiently valuable for the effort, with both parents still alive. The parents would need cloning and, for consistency, <u>their parents</u> as well. I suppose you'd also need the usual informed-consent forms, filled out and signed, not easy to get if I know parents, even harder for grandparents.

Casual chain: clone parents, grandparents, family, people outside the family who came in contact with the individual, the whole world.

10

But this is only the beginning. It is the whole family that really influences the way a person turns out, not just the parents, according to current psychiatric thinking. Clone the family.

11

Then what? The way each member of the family develops has already been determined by the environment set around him, and this environment is more people, <u>people outside the family,</u> schoolmates, acquaintances, lovers, enemies, carpool partners, even, in special circumstances, peculiar <u>strangers across</u> the aisle on the subway. Find them, and clone them.

Isn't this an exaggeration?

12

But there is no end to the protocol. Each of <u>the outer contacts has his own surrounding family,</u> and his and their outer contacts. Clone them all.

13

To do the thing properly, with any hope of ending up with a genuine duplicate of a <u>single person,</u> you really have no choice. You <u>must</u> clone the world, no less.

He's really joking here

14

We are not ready for an experiment of this size, nor, I should think, are we willing. <u>For one thing, it would mean replacing today's world by an entirely identical world to follow immediately, and this means no new, natural, spontaneous, random, chancy children. No children at all, except for the manufactured doubles of those now on the scene. Plus all those identical adults, including all of to-</u>

day's politicians, all seen double. It is too much to contemplate.

Moreover, when the whole experiment is fi-   15
nally finished, fifty years or so from now, how could you get a responsible scientific reading on the outcome? Somewhere in there would be the original clonee, probably lost and overworked, now well into middle age, but everyone around him would be precise duplicates of today's everyone. It would be today's same world, filled to   With the world
overflowing with duplicates of today's people and   cloned, every-
their same, duplicated problems, probably all   thing would be
resentful at having had to go through our whole   the same,
thing all over, sore enough at the clone to make   leading to dis-
endless trouble for him, if they found him.   satisfaction

And obviously, if the whole thing were done   16
precisely right, they would still be casting about for ways to solve the problem of universal dissatisfaction, and sooner or later they'd surely begin to look around at each other, wondering who should be cloned for his special value to society, to get us out of all this. And so it would go, in regular cycles, perhaps forever.

I once lived through a period when I wondered   17
what Hell could be like, and I stretched my imagination to try to think of a perpetual sort of damnation. I have to confess, I never thought of anything like this.

I have an alternative suggestion, if you're look-   18
ing for a way out. Set cloning aside, and don't try it. Instead, go in the other direction. Look for   The author's
ways to get mutations more quickly, new variety,   real purpose
different songs. Fiddle around, if you must fiddle,   comes out
but never with ways to keep things the same, no   here; ties
matter who, not even yourself. Heaven, some-   to paragraph
where ahead, has got to be a change.   4.

PREREADING NOTES

The headnote indicates that the author, Lewis Thomas, was a physician and medical researcher and that most of his essays— including this one—were written for the New England Journal of

<u>Medicine</u>. These facts and the title "On Cloning a Human Being" initially suggest that this will be a pretty serious, probably dry essay and that it may be full of a lot of technical information. However, scanning the essay by looking at the first sentence in each paragraph shows the tone to be fairly informal: paragraph 5, for example, begins, "Well, don't think about it. . . ." It is also clear from a quick scan of the essay that it is really on <u>not</u> cloning a human being. Thomas is focusing on the problems involved in cloning human beings and seems to say that it will never happen.

READING NOTES

Outline:

par. 1 Introduction to cloning and predictions that "especially valuable people" will be cloned

pars. 2–4 Worries about cloning

par. 5 Thomas says cloning "isn't a probable possibility"

par. 6 Reason 1: Too much time involved in any experiment with human cloning

pars. 7–15 Reason 2: Since individuals are shaped by their environments, to clone a person would require cloning his or her parents, grandparents, the whole family, "the world, no less." People are not ready to replace today's world with "an entirely identical world to follow immediately," so everyone would hate the original clonee for causing all the trouble.

par. 16 The cloning cycle would have to start again to duplicate someone who could "solve the problem of universal dissatisfaction" with the original cloning experiment.

par. 17 To Thomas, this would be worse than Hell.

par. 18 Instead of cloning, it would be better to experiment with "ways to get mutations more quickly, new variety, different songs."

After an initial reading, it is clear that Thomas's subject is cloning and predictions that "valuable people" will be cloned experimentally in the future. He states his thesis explicitly in paragraph 5: cloning "isn't a probable possibility, not even as a long shot for the distant future. . . ." Even though the essay was written for the <u>New England Journal of Medicine,</u> it would seem that Thomas intended to reach a general educated audience; for example, he includes very little specialized terminology and doesn't assume any particular medical or scientific expertise. His purpose seems to be basically to inform, to explain to his audience why cloning of human beings isn't likely to happen in the future.

But in explaining why human beings aren't likely to be cloned, Thomas gives reasons that seem exaggerated. Could it really be necessary to clone the whole world, as he says? Why would he want to suggest that the effects of cloning a single human being would be so drastic?

REREADING NOTES

Rereading the essay reveals that Thomas is deliberately pushing the idea of cloning a human being to the point of absurdity. His tone is humorous from the beginning: in paragraph 2, for example, he lists as some of our worries about science—"transplanted heads, computer poetry, and the unrestrained growth of plastic flowers." When he describes the effects of an experiment in cloning an important diplomat and what would really be required to clone a human being (pars. 10–13), he builds each paragraph up to its logical—and increasingly absurd—conclusion: "Clone the family." "Find them, and clone them." "Clone them all." "You must clone the world, no less." In paragraph 14 he pushes the absurdity one step further, imagining a world where there are no longer unique children who grow up to be unique adults but only identical doubles of those who already exist—"including all of today's politicians. . . . It is too much to contemplate." The next two paragraphs continue in this vein, ending with the most absurd idea of all: that another cloning would have to take place of the person who could get everyone out of this mess. "And so it would go," Thomas says, "in regular cycles, perhaps forever."

Thomas is saying that it is absurd to imagine that an exact replica of another human being could ever be cloned; given the fact that the clone would necessarily grow up under different influences, the two might look alike, but "they'd be almost as different as you and me, and certainly more different than any of today's identical twins" (par. 5). Moreover, an even more substantial point emerges on rereading: there can be no benefit from cloning human beings to begin with. "Precise sameness," Thomas says, "is terrifying" (par. 4), an idea that he returns to in his conclusion, where he suggests that it is better for humans to experiment with "mutations," "variety," and "change" than with clones.

Thomas's purpose, therefore, seems to be more than simply informing readers about the impossibility of creating a human clone; at the core, he is arguing for a view of human nature that recognizes the value of "variety" over some standard of "perfection," and his method is to do so in an entertainingly humorous way.

Each of the essays in the seventh edition of *The Prentice Hall Reader* will repay you for the time and effort you put into reading it carefully and critically. Each essay shows an artful craftsperson at work, solving the problems inherent in communicating experiences, feelings, ideas, and opinions to an audience. Each writer is someone from whom you, as a reader and as a thinker, can learn. So when your instructor assigns a selection from the text, remember that as a reader you must assume an active role. Don't assume that reading an essay once—to see what it is "about"—will mean that you are prepared to write about it or that you have learned all that you can learn from the essay. Ask questions, seek answers to those questions, analyze, and reread.

SOME THINGS TO REMEMBER WHEN READING

1. Read the headnote to the selection. How does this information help you understand the writer and the context in which the selection was written?
2. Look at the questions that precede and follow each reading. They will help focus your attention on the important aspects of the selection. After you read, write out answers to each question.
3. Read through the selection first to see what happens and to satisfy your curiosity.
4. Reread the selection several times, taking notes or underlining as you go.

5. Write or locate in the essay a thesis statement. Remember that the thesis is the particular point that the writer is trying to make about the subject.

6. Define a purpose for the essay. Why is the writer writing? Does the author make that purpose explicit?

7. Imagine the audience for such an essay. Who is the likely reader? What does that reader already know about the subject? Is the reader likely to have any preconceptions or prejudices about the subject?

8. Isolate a structure in the selection. How is it put together? Into how many parts can it be divided? How do those parts work together? Outline the essay.

9. Be sure that you understand every sentence. How does the writer vary the sentence structures?

10. Look up every word that you cannot define with some degree of certainty. Remember that you might misinterpret what the author is saying if you simply skip over the unfamiliar words.

11. Reread the essay one final time, reassembling its parts into the artful whole that it was intended to be.

HOW TO WRITE AN ESSAY

Watching a performance, whether it is athletic or artistic, our attention is focused on the achievement displayed in that moment. In concentrating on the performance, however, we might forget about the extensive practice that lies behind that achievement. Writing is no different. Typically, writers rely on perspiration, not inspiration. An effective final product depends on careful preliminary work.

A WRITER'S SUBJECT

The first step in writing is to determine a subject, what a piece of writing is about. The majority of writing tasks that you face either in school or on the job require you to write in response to a specific assignment. Your instructor, for example, might ask you to use the specific writing suggestions that follow each reading in this book. Before you begin work on any writing assignment, take time to study what is being asked. What limits have already been placed on the assignment? What are the key words (for example, *compare, analyze, define*) used in the assignment?

Once you have a subject, the next step is to restrict, focus, or narrow that subject into a workable topic. Although the words *subject* and *topic* are sometimes used interchangeably, think of *subject* as the broader, more general word. You move from a subject to a *topic* by limiting or restricting what you will include or cover. The shift from subject to topic is a gradual one that is not marked by a clearly definable line. Just remember that a topic is a more restricted version of a larger subject.

A Writer's Purpose

A writer writes to fulfill three fundamental purposes: *to entertain, to inform,* and *to persuade.* Obviously, those purposes are not necessarily separate: an interesting, maybe even humorous, essay that documents the health hazards caused by smoking can, at the same time, attempt to persuade the reader to give up smoking. In this case the main purpose is still persuasion; entertainment and information play subordinate roles in catching the reader's interest and in providing appropriate evidence for the argument being advanced.

These three purposes are generally associated with the traditional division of writing into four forms—narration, description, exposition (including classification, comparison and contrast, process, cause and effect, and definition), and argumentation. *Narrative* or *descriptive essays* typically tell a story or describe a person, object, or place in order to entertain a reader and re-create the experience. *Expository essays* primarily provide information for a reader. *Argumentative* or *persuasive essays* seek to move a reader, to gain support, to advocate a particular type of action.

A Writer's Audience

Audience is a key factor in every writing situation. Writing is, after all, a form of communication and as such implies an audience. In many writing situations, your audience is a controlling factor that affects both the content of your paper and the style in which it is written. An effective writer learns to adjust to an audience and to write for that audience, for a writer, like a performer, needs and wants an audience.

Writers adjust their style and tone on a spectrum ranging from informal to formal. Articles that appear in popular, wide-circulation magazines often are written in the first person, use contractions, favor popular and colloquial words, and contain relatively short sentences and paragraphs. Articles in more scholarly journals exhibit a formal style that involves an objective and serious tone, a more advanced vocabulary, and longer and more complicated sentence and paragraph constructions. In the informal style, the writer injects his or her personality into the prose; in the formal style, the writer remains detached and impersonal. A writer adopts whatever style seems appropriate for a particular audience or context. An effective writer does not have just one style or voice but many.

Some Things to Remember

Before you begin to prewrite, you need to think about your subject, purpose, and audience. Remind yourself of their importance in your writing process by completing the following sentences:

1. My general subject is _____ .
2. My more specific topic is _____ .
3. My purpose is to _____ .
4. My intended audience is _____ .

A Writer's Information

What makes writing entertaining, informative, or persuasive is information—specific, relevant detail. If you try to write without gathering information, you end up skimming the surface of your subject, even if you "know" something about it.

How you go about gathering information on your topic depends on your subject and your purpose for writing. Some topics, such as those involving a personal experience, require a memory search; other assignments, such as describing a particular place, require careful observation. Essays that convey information or argue particular positions often require gathering information through research. Some possible strategies for gathering information and ideas about your topic are listed here. Before you start this step in your prewriting, remember three things.

First, remember that *different tactics work for different topics and for different writers.* You might find that freewriting is great for some assignments but not for others. As a writer, explore your options. Don't rule out any strategy until you have tried it. Second, remember that *prewriting activities sometimes produce information and sometimes just produce questions that you will then need to answer.* In other words, prewriting often involves learning what you don't know, what you need to find out. Learning to ask the right questions is just as important as knowing the right answers. Third, remember that *these prewriting activities are an excellent way in which to find a focus, to narrow a subject, or to suggest a working plan for your essay.* As you begin to explore a subject or topic, the possibilities spread out before you. Try not to be wedded to a particular topic or thesis until you have explored a subject through prewriting activities.

LISTING DETAILS FROM PERSONAL EXPERIENCE OR OBSERVATION

Even your most unforgettable experience has probably been forgotten in part. If you are going to re-create it for a reader, you will have to do some active searching among your memories. By focusing your attention, you can slowly recall more details. Ask yourself a series of questions about the chronology of the experience. For example, start with a particular detail and then try to stimulate your memory: What happened just before? Just after? Who was there? Where did the experience take place? Why did it happen? When did it happen? How did it happen?

Sense impressions, like factual details, fade from memory. In the height of the summer, it is not easy to recall a crisp fall day. Furthermore, sensory details are not always noticed, let alone recorded. How many times have you passed by a particular location without really seeing it?

Descriptions, like every other form of writing, demand specific information, and the easiest way to gather that detail is to observe. Before you try to describe a person, place, or object, take some time to list specific details on a piece of paper. At first record everything you notice. Do not worry about having too much, for you can always edit later. At this stage it is better to have too much than to have too little.

The next step is to decide what to include in your description and what to exclude. As a general principle, an effective written description does not try to record everything. The selection of detail should be governed by your purpose in the description. Ask yourself what you are trying to show or reveal. For what reason? What is particularly important about this person, place, or object? A description is not the verbal equivalent of a photograph or a tape recording.

FREEWRITING

Putting words down on a page or a computer screen can be very intimidating. Your editing instincts immediately want to take over—are the words spelled correctly? Are the sentences complete? Do they contain any mechanical or grammatical errors? Not only must you express your ideas in words, but suddenly those words must be the correct words.

When you translate thoughts into written words and edit those words at the same time, writing can seem impossible. Instead of allowing ideas to take shape in words or allowing the writing to stimulate your thinking, you become fearful of committing anything to paper.

Writing, however, can stimulate thought. Every writer has experienced times when an idea became clear because it was written down. If those editing instincts can be turned off, you can use writing as a way of generating ideas about a paper.

Freewriting is an effective way to deal with this dilemma. Write without stopping for a fixed period of time—a period as short as ten minutes or as long as an hour. Do not stop; do not edit; do not worry about mistakes. If you find yourself stuck for something to write, repeat the last word or phrase you wrote until a new thought comes to mind. You are looking for a focus point—an idea or a subject for a paper. You are trying to externalize your thinking into writing. What emerges is a free association of ideas. Some are relevant; some are worthless. After you have ideas on paper, you can then decide what is worth saving, developing, or simply throwing away.

You can also do freewriting on a computer. One technique many writers find effective is to use the contrast control to darken the screen until it is completely black. Then as you write you won't be distracted by errors and typos or be tempted to stop and read what you have already written. Freewriting in this way provides an opportunity to free-associate almost as you might when you are speaking.

JOURNALS

A daily journal can be an effective seedbed of ideas for writing projects. Such a journal should not be a daily log of your activities (got up, went to class, had lunch) but rather a place where you record ideas, observations, memories, and feelings. Set aside a specific notebook or a pad of paper in which to keep your journal. Try to write for at least ten minutes every day. Over a period of time—such as a semester—

you will be surprised how many ideas for papers or projects you will accumulate. When you are working on a paper, you might want to confine part of your daily journal entries to that particular subject.

BRAINSTORMING AND MAPPING

Brainstorming is oral freewriting among a group of people jointly trying to solve a problem by spontaneously contributing ideas. Whatever comes to mind, no matter how obvious or unusual, gets said. The hope is that out of the jumble of ideas that surface, some possible solutions to the problem will be found.

Although brainstorming is by definition a group activity, it can also be done by the individual writer. In the center of a blank sheet of paper, write down a key word or phrase referring to your subject. Then in the space around your subject, quickly jot down any ideas that come to mind. Do not write in sentences—just key words and phrases. Because you are not filling consecutive lines with words and because you have space in which the ideas can be arranged, this form of brainstorming often suggests structural relationships. You can increase the usefulness of such an idea generator by adding graphic devices such as circles, arrows, or connecting lines to indicate the possible relationships among ideas. These devices can be added to your brainstorming sheet later, and they become a map to the points you might want to cover in your essay.

FORMAL QUESTIONING

One particularly effective way to gather information on any topic is to ask yourself questions about it. This allows you to explore the subject from a variety of angles. After all, the secret to finding answers always lies in knowing the right questions to ask. A good place to start is with the list of questions presented here. Remember, though, that not every question is appropriate for every topic.

Illustration
1. What examples of _____ can be found?
2. In what ways are these things examples of _____?
3. What details about _____ seem the most important?

Comparison and Contrast

1. To what is _____ similar? List the points of similarity.
2. From what is _____ different? List the points of difference.
3. Which points of similarity or difference seem most important?
4. What does the comparison or contrast tell the reader about _____?

Division and Classification

1. Into how many parts can _____ be divided?
2. How many parts is _____ composed of?
3. What other category of things is _____ most like?
4. How does _____ work?
5. What are _____'s component parts?

Process

1. How many steps or stages are involved in _____?
2. In what order do those steps or stages occur?

Cause and Effect

1. What precedes _____?
2. Is that a cause of _____?
3. What follows _____?
4. Is that an effect of _____?
5. How many causes of _____ can you find?
6. How many effects of _____ can you find?
7. Why does _____ happen?

Definition

1. How is _____ defined in a dictionary?
2. Does everyone agree about the meaning of _____?
3. Does _____ have any connotations? What are they?
4. Has the meaning of _____ changed over time?
5. What words are synonymous with _____?

Argument and Persuasion

1. How do your readers feel about _____?
2. How do you feel about _____?
3. What are the arguments in favor of _____? List those arguments in order of strength.
4. What are the arguments against _____? List those arguments in order of strength.

INTERVIEWING

Typically you gather information for college papers by locating printed or electronic sources—books, articles, reports, e-texts. Depending on your topic, however, printed or electronic sources are not always available. In that case, people often represent a great source of information for a writer. Obviously you should choose someone who has special credentials or knowledge about the subject.

Interviewing requires some special skills and tact. When you first contact someone to request an interview, always explain who you are, what you want to know, and how you will use the information. Remember that specific questions will produce more useful information than general ones. Take notes that you can expand later, or use a tape recorder. Keep attention focused on the information that you need, and do not be afraid to ask questions to keep your informant on the subject. If you plan to use direct quotations, make sure that the wording is accurate. If possible, check the quotations with your source one final time.

A WRITER'S THESIS

For informative and argumentative essays, the information-gathering stage of the writing process is the time in which to sharpen your topic and to define first a tentative or working thesis for your paper and then a final thesis. Even narrative and descriptive essays may be strengthened by the development of a thesis at this stage.

Thesis is derived from a Greek word that means "placing" or "position" or "proposition." When you formulate a thesis, you are defining your position on the subject. A thesis lets your reader know exactly where you stand. Because it represents your "final" position, a thesis is typically something that you develop and refine as you move through the prewriting stage, testing out ideas and gathering information. Don't try to start with a final thesis; begin with a tentative thesis (also called a *hypothesis*, from the Greek for "supposition"). Allow your final position to emerge based on what you have discovered in the prewriting stage.

Before you write a thesis statement, you need to consider the factors that will control or influence the form your thesis will take. For example, a thesis is a reflection of your purpose in writing. If your purpose is to persuade your audience to do or to believe something, your thesis will urge the reader to accept that position. If your purpose is to convey information to your reader, your thesis will forecast your main points and indicate how your paper will be organized.

Your thesis will also be shaped by the scope and length of your paper. Your topic and your thesis must be manageable within the space you have available; otherwise, you end up skimming the surface. A short paper requires a more precise focus than a longer one. As a result, when you move from subject to topic to thesis, make sure that each step is more specific and has an increasingly sharper focus. To check that focusing process, ask yourself the following questions:

- What is my general subject?
- What is my specific topic within that general subject area?
- What is my position on that specific topic?

WRITING A THESIS STATEMENT

When you have answered the questions about your purpose, when you have sharpened your general subject into a topic, when you have defined your position toward that topic, you are ready to write a thesis statement. The process is simple. You write a thesis statement by linking together your topic and your position on that topic.

Subject:	Violence on television
Topic:	The impact that viewing televised violence has on young children
Thesis:	Televised violence makes young children numb to violence in the real world, distorts their perceptions of how people behave, and teaches them how to be violent.

An effective thesis, like any position statement, has a number of characteristics.

1. A thesis should clearly signal the purpose of the paper.
2. A thesis should state or take a definite position. It tells the reader what will be covered in the paper.
3. A thesis should express that definite position in precise, familiar terms. Avoid vague, abstract, or complicated technical terms.
4. A thesis should offer a position that can be explored or expanded within the scope of the paper. Remember that in moving from a general subject to a thesis, you have narrowed and sharpened your focus.

PLACING A THESIS IN YOUR PAPER

Once you have written a thesis for your paper or essay, you must make two final decisions. First, you have to decide whether to include that explicit statement in your paper or just allow your paper's structure and content to imply the thesis. Second, if you decide to include a thesis statement, you must determine where to place it in your paper. For example, should it appear in the first paragraph or at some point later in the paper?

If you look carefully at examples of professional writing, you will discover that neither question has a single answer. Writers make these decisions based on the type of paper they are writing. As a student, however, you can follow several guidelines. Most pieces of writing done in college—either papers or essay examinations—should have explicit thesis statements. Typically, those statements should be placed early in the paper (although the thesis for a narrative or descriptive essay may typically come at the end). The thesis will not always be in the first paragraph, as your introduction might be designed to attract a reader's attention. Nevertheless, placing a thesis statement early in your paper will guarantee that the reader knows exactly what to expect.

Every argumentative or persuasive paper should have an explicitly stated thesis. Where you place that thesis depends on whether the paper is structured deductively or inductively. A deductive argument begins with a general truth and then moves to a specific application of that truth, so such an arrangement requires that the thesis be stated early. Conversely, an inductive argument moves in the opposite direction, starting with specific evidence and then moving to a conclusion, an arrangement that requires that the thesis be withheld until near the end of the paper.

Similarly, whenever your strategy in a paper is to build to a conclusion, a realization, or a discovery, you can withhold an explicit statement of your thesis until late in the paper. An early statement would spoil the suspense.

REVISING AN ESSAY

The idea of revising a paper may not sound appealing in the least. By the time you have finished the paper, the last thing you want to do is revise it. Nevertheless, revising is a crucial step in the writing process, one you cannot afford to skip.

The word *revision* literally means "to see again." You do not revise a paper just by proofreading it for mechanical and grammatical errors, which is an expected final step in the writing process. Instead, a revision takes place after a draft of a whole paper or part of it has been completed, after a period of time has elapsed and you have had a chance to get some advice or criticism on what you wrote, after you can see what you wrote, not what you *think* you wrote. Revision should also involve an active, careful scrutiny on your part of every aspect of your paper—your subject, thesis, purpose, audience, paragraph structures, sentence constructions, and word choice.

BEGINNING A REVISION

Revision should start not with the smallest unit—the choice of a particular word—but with the largest—the choice of subject, thesis, purpose, audience, and organization. A revision in its broadest sense involves a complete rethinking of a paper from idea through execution. Once you have finished a paper, think first about these five groups of questions—if possible, write out answers to each:

1. What is my *subject?* Is it too large? Too small? Is it interesting? Is it fresh or informative?
2. What is my *thesis?* Do I have a precise position on my subject? Have I stated that thesis in a single sentence? Do I see the difference between having a subject and having a thesis?
3. What is my *purpose?* Why did I write *this* paper? Have I expressed my purpose in my thesis statement? Is everything in the paper related to that purpose?

4. Whom do I imagine as my *audience?* Who will read this? What do these people already know about the subject? Have I written the paper with that audience in mind?
5. How is my paper *structured?* Have I followed the advice on structure given in the chapter introductions to this text? Is the organization of my paper clear and inevitable? Can it be outlined easily? Have I provided enough examples and details?

USING THE ADVICE OF OTHERS

Another great help in revising is to find an editor or a critic. If your writing instructor has the time to look at your draft or if your college or university has a writing center or a writing tutor program, you can get the advice of an experienced, trained reader. If your paper or part of it is discussed in class, listen to your classmates' comments as a way of gauging how successful your writing has been. If your writing class uses peer editing, you can study the responses of your editors for possible areas for revision.

Peer evaluation works best when readers start with a series of specific directions—questions to answer or things to look for. If you are interested in trying peer evaluation, you and a classmate could start with an editing checksheet adapted from the "Some Things to Remember" section at the end of each introductory chapter in this book. Whenever you are responding to someone else's writing, remember that your comments are always more valuable if they are specific and suggest ways in which changes could be made.

It is often difficult to accept criticism, but if you want to improve your writing skills, you need someone to say, "Why not do this?" After all, you expect that an athletic coach or a music or dance teacher will offer criticism. Your writing instructor plays the same role, and the advice and criticism he or she offers is meant to make your writing more effective; it is not intended as a personal criticism of you or your abilities.

JUDGING LENGTH

After you have finished a draft of a paper, look carefully at how your response measures up to your instructor's guidelines about the length of the paper. Such guidelines are important in that they give you some idea of the amount of space that you will need to develop and illustrate your thesis sufficiently. If your papers are consistently short, you have probably not included enough examples or illustrating details.

Writing the suggested number of words does not, of course, guarantee a good essay, but writing only half of the suggested number because you fail to develop and illustrate your thesis can result in a lower grade.

Similarly, if your papers consistently exceed your instructor's guidelines, you have probably not sufficiently narrowed your subjects or you may have included too many details and examples. Of the material available to support, develop, and illustrate a thesis, some is more significant and relevant than the rest. Never try to include everything—select the best, the most appropriate, the most convincing.

CHECKING PARAGRAPHS

The qualities of a good paragraph—things like unity, coherence, organization, and completeness—have been stressed in every writing course you have taken. When you revise your paper, look carefully at each paragraph to see if it exhibits those qualities. How often have you paragraphed? If you have only one or two paragraphs in a several-page essay, you have not clearly indicated the structure of your essay to your reader or your essay does not have a clear, logical organization. At the opposite extreme, if you have many short paragraphs, you are overparagraphing, probably shifting ideas too quickly and failing to develop each one adequately. A good paragraph is meaty; a good essay is not a string of undeveloped ideas or bare generalizations.

IS AN ERROR-FREE PAPER AN "A" PAPER?

Although good, effective writing is mechanically and grammatically correct, you cannot reverse the equation. It is perfectly possible to write a paper that has no "errors" but is still a poor paper. An effective paper fulfills the requirements of the assignment, has something interesting or meaningful to say, and provides specific evidence and examples rather than vague generalizations. Effective writing is a combination of many factors: appropriate content, focused purpose, clear organization, and fluent expression.

Although perfect grammar and mechanics do not make a perfect paper, such things are important. Minor errors are like static in your writing. Too many of them distract your reader and focus the reader's attention not on your message but on your apparent carelessness. Minor errors can undermine your reader's confidence in you as a qualified authority. If you make errors in spelling or punctuation, for example, your reader might assume that you made similar errors in reporting information. So while revision is not just proofreading, proofreading should be a part of the revision process.

When you draft using a computer, always print out a hard-copy version of your paper for proofreading. Most writers find that they miss more errors when they proofread only on screen. Also keep in mind that while your word processor's spell-check function will catch many spelling errors, it won't identify mistakes that occur because two words sound alike but are spelled differently (*its* and *it's*, for example) or typos that result in a correctly spelled word (such as *the* for *they*). You need to proofread carefully yourself for mistakes like these.

A STUDENT WRITER'S REVISION PROCESS

The writing and rewriting process as outlined in this section can be seen in the evolution of Tina Burton's essay "The Watermelon Wooer." Tina's essay was written in response to a totally open assignment: she was asked to write an essay using examples, due in three weeks. The openness of the assignment proved initially frustrating to Tina. When she first began work on an essay, she started with a completely different topic. That weekend, however, she went home to visit her parents. Her grandfather had died a few months before, and the family was sorting through some photographs and reminiscing about him. Suddenly, Tina had the idea she wanted: she would write about her grandfather and her ambivalent feelings toward him. Once she had defined this specific topic, she also determined her purpose (to inform about her grandfather and her mixed feelings, as well as to entertain through a vivid description of this unusual old man) and her audience (her instructor and classmates).

Tina's first written work on the assignment came when she made a list of about thirty things that she remembered about him. "The list had to be cut," Tina said, "so I marked off things that were too bawdy or too unbelievable. I wanted to portray him as sympathetic," she added, "but I was really afraid that the whole piece would come off as too sentimental or drippy."

At the next class meeting, the instructor set aside some time for prewriting activities. The teacher recommended that the students try either a freewriting or a brainstorming exercise. Tina did the brainstorming that appears next.

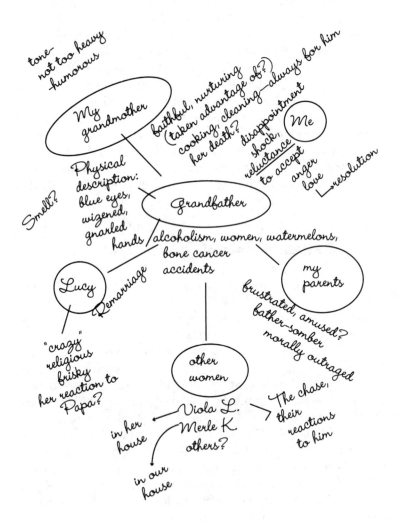

tone—
not too heavy
—humorous

My grandmother

faithful, nurturing
(taken advantage of?)
cooking, cleaning—always for him
her death?

disappointment
shock,
reluctance
to accept

Me

anger
love

resolution

Smell?

Physical
description:
blue eyes,
wizened,
gnarled
hands

Grandfather

alcoholism, women, watermelons,
bone cancer
accidents

my
parents

frustrated, amused?
father—somber
morally outraged

Lucy

Remarriage

"crazy"
religious
frisky
her reaction to
Papa?

other
women

Viola L.
Merle K.
others?

The chase,
their
reactions
to him

in her
house

in our
house

From here, Tina wrote a complete draft in one sitting. She had the most difficulty with the beginning of the essay. "I kept trying to describe him, but I found that I was including too much," she commented. The breakthrough came through the advice of two other students in the class. The first page of the first draft of Tina's essay follows. The handwritten comments were provided by Kathrine Varnes.

EARLIER DRAFT

THE WATERMELON WOOER

When someone you love dearly behaves in

a manner that offends you, do you stop loving

that person? Do you lose all respect for that

person because you cannot forget the act (that
repulsive [?]

you judged as repulsive?) On the contrary, you
Eventually,?   *

might (eventually) fondly recall the once offensive   *I have a
personal
behavior. (Perhaps,) in time, you might even   dislike for
this 3-word
transition
understand why you found the behavior
so?

loathesome. Maybe, you will reach a point in

time when you will be unable to think of your
someway
loved one without thinking of the once   to
condense?
questionable behavior. Such is the case with my

grandfather.

Before I tell the story of how my

grandfather behaved in ways that I could neither

understand nor tolerate, I must first (give some

introduce?
background information on) him. A wizened little

man with dancing blue eyes and hands gnarled

from years of carpentry work, "Papa" was a

notorious womanizer and an alcoholic. Born and

raised in Halifax County, Virginia, he spent most

of his life building houses, distilling and selling

corn liquor, and chasing women. After he and my

grandmother had been married for thirty years or

so, he decided to <u>curtail some of his wild behavior</u>

both of these things? or respect by curtailing?

<u>and treat her with more respect.</u> Actually, he

remained faithful to her only after he discovered

that she was ill and probably wouldn't be around

to feed and nurture him for much longer. ~~So, as you~~

didn't
~~can see~~, <u>m</u>y grandfather (does not) have a <u>spotless</u>,

reputation
or even a remotely commendable (record of

personal achievements.)

Use alternative diction to soften tone?

REVISED DRAFT

"Kathrine wanted me to condense and to find a way in which to jump right into the essay," Tina noted. "She also said, 'You're trying to tell too much. Let the story tell itself. Try to think of one thing that might capture something essential or important about him.' " In a second peer edit, Tina sought the advice of Stephen Palley, another classmate. Stephen offered these comments on this first page of the second draft.

THE WATERMELON WOOER

my grandfather never really (settled down)   characterize an
Let me tell you a story about my   essential part
   of his eccentricity

grandfather—~~and, I guess, me too. I don't pretend~~   Intro?

~~to know whether my story will shock, offend,~~

~~amuse, or bore.~~ I only know that I feel the need to

   it
tell ~~the story~~.

   For a time he
   ~~Before I tell the story of how my~~

~~grandfather~~ behaved in ways that I could   but eventually

neither understand nor tolerate, I must first

(*I see him now*)   *Let me introduce*
introduce him. A wizened little man with ~~dancing~~

~~blue eyes~~ and hands ~~gnarled from years of~~

~~carpentry work~~, "Papa" was a notorious   smell?

womanizer and an alcoholic. Born and raised in   It's funny
   but when
Halifax County, Virginia, he spent most of his life   I think of my
   grandfather
building houses, distilling and selling corn liquor,   I think 1st
   of the way
and chasing women. After he and my grandmother   he smelled

had been married for thirty years or so, he decided

to show her some respect by curtailing his wild

behavior. Actually, he remained faithful to her only   Miller
   ponies,
after he discovered that she was ill and probably   fertilizer

wouldn't be around to feed and nurture him for

much longer. Papa didn't have a spotless reputation.

"Stephen offered me quite a few helpful suggestions," Tina recalled, "but he also suggested something that I just didn't quite feel comfortable with." As you can see in the revised draft, Tina had queried Stephen about possibly including her memories of odor. In a conversation Stephen urged Tina to substitute memories of smells for memories of sight. In the end, though, Tina observed, "I just couldn't do what Stephen suggested."

FINAL DRAFT

Before the three weeks were over, Tina actually wrote five separate drafts of her essay. "Everything here is true," she said, "but I worried so much about what I included, because I didn't want to embarrass anyone in my family. Throughout the process," she added, "I was also worried about my tone. I wanted it to be funny; I wanted my readers to like my grandfather and his watermelon adventures."

Reproduced here is Tina's final draft of her essay. Note that she concludes with a thesis that summarizes her main point.

THE WATERMELON WOOER

Tina M. Burton

I see him now, sprawled on our couch, clutching a frayed afghan, one brown toenail escaping his sock. His darting eyes are betraying his withered body.

Born and raised in backwoods Virginia, my grandfather spent most of his life building houses, distilling and selling corn liquor, and chasing women. After he and my grandmother had been married for thirty years or so, he decided to show her some respect by curtailing his wild behavior. Actually, he remained faithful to her only after he discovered that she was ill and probably wouldn't be around to feed and nurture him much longer. Papa didn't have a spotless reputation.

Because he'd been on the wagon for several years and hadn't had any affairs for the last ten years, my family thought that Papa would continue to behave in a "respectable" manner even after my grandmother died. I guess we were hoping for some sort of miracle. After my grandmother died in 1983, Papa became a rogue again: he insisted on reveling in wild abandon. When my father found out that Papa was drinking heavily again and crashing his car into mailboxes, houses, and other large obstacles, he asked Papa to move into our house. The fact that three of Papa's female neighbors had complained to the police about Papa's exposing himself probably had something to do with my father's decision.

The year that Papa lived with us rivaled the agony of Hell.

I was always Papa's favorite grandchild, his "gal," and I worshipped him from the time that I was old enough to spend summers with him on his farm. Until I saw him every day, witnessed for myself his sometimes lewd behavior and his odd personality quirks, I never really believed the stories about him that I had heard from my mother and father. Every morning, he baited my mother with comments like "the gravy's too thick," "my room's too cold," "your kids are too loud," and "the phone rings too often." Against my mother's wishes, he smoked in the house. In mixed company, he gleefully explained how to have sex in an inner tube in the ocean without getting caught and gave detailed physical descriptions of the women he'd had sex with. It surprised me how much my opinion of Papa changed in one year.

During this one year, Papa did many things that I thought were embarrassing and inexcusable. I came face-to-face with the "dark" side of his personality. One week after moving into my parents' home, Papa began to sneak the orange juice from the refrigerator and doctor it with Smirnoff's vodka. I knew he'd been pickling his brain with alcohol for years and that this was part of the disease, but he'd said that he'd gone dry. Besides, he was violating my father's most important rule: no alcohol in the house. I didn't know that his drinking was only the first of a long line of incredible acts.

The behaviors that ultimately endeared Papa to me, that made me forgive him his shortcomings, are also those which I recall with a great deal of sadness. These are the memories of him that I treasure, the stories that I will tell to my grandchildren when they are old enough to deal with graphic material. A year ago, I never would have believed that I could fondly remember, much less write about, these episodes.

For about a year, Papa engaged in what I refer to as the "watermelon affairs." Perhaps because he had lived on a vegetable farm for the majority of his life Papa had a special affinity for a wide variety of fruits and vegetables. Especially dear to him were watermelons. So, he assumed that other elderly people, particularly women, shared his proclivity for produce. One week after he moved into my parent's house, he embarked upon his mission—to woo with watermelons as many women as he could.

A shrewd man, possessed of a generous supply of common sense and watermelons, Papa decided to seduce a woman who lived very close to him. This woman happened to be my maternal grandmother who also lived in our house. Unaware of his lascivious intentions and bent on helping him assuage his grief over the loss of his wife. Grandmother Merle prepared special meals for Papa and spent long hours conversing with him about farming, grandchildren, and life in the "Old South." Merle assumed that the watermelons Papa brought to her were nothing more than a token of his appreciation for her kindness. When Papa grabbed a part of Merle that she preferred to remain untouched, these conversations came to an abrupt halt. Of course, we were mortified by his inappropriate behavior, but I suspect that my parents secretly were amused. While Papa's indiscretion with Merle was upsetting, at least no one other than members of my immediate family knew about the incident. His next romantic adventure earned him immediate notoriety in the neighborhood. One afternoon, huge watermelon in hand, he trotted over to visit Viola Lampson, a decrepit and cranky elderly woman with whom my family had been friendly for twenty years. Twenty minutes after Papa entered her house, the police came. Poor Viola was in a state of disrepair because my grandfather had been chasing her around her kitchen table demanding kisses. Fortunately, the policeman who arrived at the scene of the crime was quite understanding and polite; he advised my father to keep a careful watch on Papa at all times. My somber father was very embarrassed. Finally, we were all beginning to see the relationship between watermelons and women. He'd disappear with a watermelon and return with the police.

I was mortified by Papa's lecherous desire for other women. After all, wasn't he supposed to be grieving over the death of my grandmother, his wife of fifty years? I resigned myself to the fact that I never would love him or respect him in the manner that I once had. For a while, I avoided his company and refused to answer his frequent questions about why I was avoiding him. I didn't think about why he was behaving the way he was; I simply cast judgement on his behavior and shut myself off from him. Not until Papa remarried did I even try to understand his needs or his behavior.

Approximately one year after his wife died, Papa remarried. Finally, he found a woman who not only loved watermelon but also loved him and his frisky behavior. Lucy, often referred to as "crazy Lucy" by her neighbors who had heard her speak of miracle healings and visions of Christ, wed Papa and took him into her already jam-packed home. Amazingly, she convinced him to stop drinking and to refrain from molesting other women. She could not, however, convince Papa to "get the religion" as she called it. My family was nonplussed both by Papa's decision to remarry at age 77 and to stop drinking after all these years. We all were annoyed by the fact that Lucy convinced him to do in several months what we had been trying to get him to do for many years.

Not until I learned that Papa was dying of bone cancer did I try to understand why he needed to remarry and why I found that fact unbearable. Until this time, I harbored the feeling that Papa somehow was degrading the memory of my grandmother by remarrying. His attempted seductions of women disturbed me, but his decision to marry Lucy saddened me. Only after I spent many afternoons with Papa and Lucy did I realize that they truly loved each other. More importantly, I realized that Papa, devastated by his wife's death, was afraid to be alone in his old age. Perhaps sensing his illness, even though he knew nothing of its development at this time, he wanted to recapture some of his stamina, some of his youth. He really wasn't searching for someone to replace my grandmother: he simply wanted to have a companion to comfort him, to distract him from his grief.

Fortunately, I accepted Papa's actions and resolved my conflict with him before he died. Once again, I was his "gal" in spirit, and I even came to love and respect Lucy. Now, I find that I cannot conjure images of Papa without thinking of watermelons and his romantic escapades. The acts that once troubled me eventually allowed me to glimpse the frail side of my grandfather, to see him as a human being possessed of fears and flaws rather than a cardboard ideal.

SOME THINGS TO REMEMBER WHEN REVISING

1. Put your paper aside for a period of time before you attempt to revise it.
2. Seek the advice of your instructor or a writing center tutor or the help of classmates.
3. Reconsider your choice of topic. Were you able to treat it adequately in the space you had available?
4. State your thesis in a sentence as a way of checking your content. Is everything in the paper relevant to that thesis?
5. Check to make sure that you have given enough examples to clarify your topic, to support your argument, or to make your thesis clear. Relevant specifics convince and interest a reader.
6. Look through the advice given in each of the introductions to this text. Have you organized your paper carefully? Is its structure clear?
7. Define your audience. To whom are you writing? What assumptions have you made about your audience? What changes are necessary to make your paper clear and interesting to that audience?
8. Check the guidelines your instructor provided. Have you done what was asked? Is your paper too short or too long?
9. Examine each sentence to make sure that it is complete and grammatically correct. Try for a variety of sentence structures and lengths.
10. Look carefully at each paragraph. Does it obey the rules for effective paragraph construction? Do your paragraphs clearly indicate the structure of your essay?
11. Check your word choice. Have you avoided slang, jargon, and clichés? Have you used specific words? Have you used appropriate words for your intended audience?
12. Proofread one final time.

GATHERING AND USING EXAMPLES

Settling into your seat, you look at the midterm essay question that your professor has just handed out in your Introduction to Sociology course:

> Part II. Essay (25%). Identify the advantages or disadvantages of a "voucher" or "choice" system in providing education from public funds. Be sure to provide specific examples drawn from the assigned readings.

The success of your answer depends upon gathering and organizing appropriate examples from the course readings. A good answer will have specifics, not just generalizations and personal opinions. That realization about effective, successful writing applies to all types of writing: Effective writing in any form depends on details and examples. Relevant details and examples make writing interesting, informative, and persuasive. If you try to write without having gathered these essential specifics, you are forced to skim the surface of your subject, relying on generalizations, incomplete and sometimes inaccurate details, and unsubstantiated opinions. Without specifics, even a paper with a strong, clearly stated thesis becomes superficial. For example, how convinced would you be by the following argument?

> In their quest for big-time football programs, American universities have lost sight of their educational responsibilities. Eager for the revenues and alumni support that come with winning teams, universities exploit their football players. They do not care if the players get an education. They care only that they remain academically eligible to play for four seasons. At many schools only a small percentage of these athletes graduate. Throughout their

college careers, they are encouraged to take easy courses and to put athletics first. It does not matter how they perform in the classroom as long as they distinguish themselves every Saturday afternoon. This exploitation should not be allowed to continue. Universities have a responsibility to educate their students, not to use them to gain publicity and to raise money.

Even if you agree with the writer's thesis, the paragraph does not go beyond the obvious. The writer generalizes, and probably distorts as a result. What the reader gets is an opinion unsupported by any evidence. For example, you might reasonably ask questions about the statement "At many schools only a small percentage of these athletes graduate."

How many schools?
How small a percentage?
How does this percentage compare with that of nonathletes? After
all, not everyone who starts college ends up graduating.

To persuade your reader—even just to interest your reader—you need specific information, details and examples that illustrate the points you are trying to make.

WHERE CAN YOU FIND DETAILS AND EXAMPLES?

You gather details and examples either from your own experiences and observations or from research. Your sources vary, depending on what you are writing about. For example, *Life* magazine once asked writer Malcolm Cowley for an essay on what it was like to turn eighty. Cowley was already eighty years old, so he had a wealth of firsthand experiences from which to draw. Since nearly all of Cowley's readers were younger than eighty, he decided to show his readers what it was like to be old by providing a simple list of the occasions on which his body reminds him that he is old:

—when it becomes an achievement to do thoughtfully, step by step,
what he once did instinctively
—when his bones ache
—when there are more and more little bottles in the medicine
cabinet, with instructions for taking four times a day
—when he fumbles and drops his toothbrush (butterfingers)
—when his face has bumps and wrinkles, so that he cuts himself
while shaving (blood on the towel)
—when year by year his feet seem farther from his hands
—when he can't stand on one leg and has trouble pulling on his pants

—when he hesitates on the landing before walking down a flight of
  stairs
—when he spends more time looking for things misplaced than he
  spends using them after he (or more often his wife) has found them
—when he falls asleep in the afternoon
—when it becomes harder to bear in mind two things at once
—when a pretty girl passes him in the street and he doesn't turn his
  head

Much of what you might be writing about, however, lies outside
of your own experiences and observations. David Guterson, for example, set out to write a magazine article for *Harper's* about the Mall
of America in Minneapolis. He chose to begin his essay with a series
of facts:

> Last April, on a visit to the new Mall of America near Minneapolis, I
> carried with me the public-relations press kit provided for the benefit
> of reporters. It included an assortment of "fun facts" about the mall:
> 140,000 hot dogs sold each week, 10,000 permanent jobs, 44
> escalators and 17 elevators, 12,750 parking places, 13,300 short tons
> of steel, $1 million in cash disbursed weekly from 8 automatic-teller
> machines. Opened in the summer of 1992, the mall was built on the
> 78-acre site of the former Metropolitan Stadium, a five-minute drive
> from the Minneapolis–St. Paul International Airport. With 4.2
> million square feet of floor space—including twenty-two times the
> retail footage of the average American shopping center—the Mall of
> America was "the largest fully enclosed combination retail and family
> entertainment center in the United States."

The accumulation of facts—taken from the press kit—becomes
a way of catching the reader's attention. In a nation impressed by size,
what better way to "capture" the country's largest mall than by heap-
ing up facts and statistics.

As the examples in this chapter show, writers sometimes draw
exclusively on their personal experiences, as do both Anna Quindlen
in "The Name Is Mine" and Edwidge Danticat in "Westbury Court."
At other times, though, writers mix examples drawn from their personal experiences with information gathered from outside sources.
Leslie Heywood in "One of the Girls" draws upon her own experiences as a Division I track and cross country runner, but then adds the
examples of the athletic achievements of Gertrude Ederle and
Kathrine Switzer. Heywood also reflects on the impact that Title IX
has had on women's athletics and on the dangers that young women
athletes still face—from themselves and from society. Brian Doyle in
"Being Brians" used the information provided in letters from the 215

other Brian Doyles that he located in the United States. Remember that regardless of where you find them, specific, relevant details and examples are very important in everything you write. They add life and interest to your writing, and they support or illustrate the points you are trying to make.

How Do I Gather Details and Examples from My Experiences?

Even when you are narrating an experience that happened to you or describing something that you saw, you will have to spend some time remembering the event, sorting out the details of the experience, and deciding which examples best support the point that you are trying to make. The best place to start in your memory and observation search is with the advice offered in "How to Write an Essay" (pp. 00–00) and by considering the resources available to you. Exploring a personal experience, as the following diagram suggests, can involve a number of different activities:

Probing memory

Looking for photographs

FROM PERSONAL EXPERIENCE   **Revisiting places**

Reexperiencing sense impressions

Talking with people who were also there

Looking for material evidence (scrapbooks, letters, journals)

Many of the essays in this and later chapters begin with the writer's memories, experiences, and observations. Anna Quindlen, for example, draws only on a series of experiences in her married life to write "The Name Is Mine." Edwidge Danticat recalls an experience that occurred nearly twenty years earlier, one which she has never forgotten. Similarly, Bob Greene's "Cut" begins with his own experience. Even when writers add information from sources outside of their personal experiences—as Leslie Heywood in "One of the Girls" and Brian Doyle in "Being Brians"—observation and personal experience might still play a significant role in shaping the essay.

How Do I Gather Information
from Outside Sources?

When you think about researching a subject, you might only think of going to a library to look up your topic in the on-line catalog or a database or logging on to the World Wide Web to search for appropriate sites. As varied as these search methods are, you can also find information in many other ways, as the following diagram suggests:

Locating books

Visiting a library   **Using databases**

Finding other media resources

FROM RESEARCH   **Interviewing knowledgeable people**

Searching the Web

**Gathering documentation provided
by other knowledgeable sources**

The experiences of other people can also be excellent sources of information. Bob Greene, for example, recounts the experiences of four men who were also cut from athletic teams when they were young. Brian Doyle's "Being Brians" depends upon information offered by the "other" Brian Doyles to whom he wrote. That gathered information is mixed with or tempered by details from Doyle's own life. Leslie Heywood has written extensively about women athletes and modern culture; she has spent years not only directly experiencing what it is to be a competitive athlete and a woman, but also studying, researching, and publishing in these areas. Her essay reflects a complex mix of sources.

When you use information gathered from outside sources—whether those sources are written texts, electronic media, or interviews—it is important that you document those sources. Though it is true that articles in newspapers and magazines do not provide the type of documentation that you find in a paper written for a college course, recognize that you are a student and not a reporter. Be sure to ask your instructor how you are to document quotations and paraphrases—is it all right just to mention the sources in the text, or do you need to provide formal parenthetical documentation? Additional advice and a sample paper can be found in the Appendix, "Finding,

Using, and Documenting Sources," pp. 000–000. Be sure to read that material before you hand in a paper that uses outside sources.

HOW MANY EXAMPLES ARE ENOUGH?

It would make every writer's job much easier if there were a single, simple answer to the question of how many examples to use. Instead, the answer is "enough to interest or convince your reader." Sometimes one fully developed example might be enough. Advertisements for organizations such as Save the Children and the Christian Children's Fund often tell the story of a specific child in need of food and shelter. The single example, accompanied by a photograph, is enough to persuade many people to sponsor a child.

Readers aren't going to respond to a statement like "Millions of people are starving throughout the world." Not only is the statement too general, most of us would throw up our hands in frustration. What can I do about millions? On the other hand, I can help one child on a monthly basis. Anna Quindlen in "The Name Is Mine" focuses on a single example drawn from her own experience—using that example as a way to make her point about the significance and the consequences of keeping your own name.

Save One Child

These are the children who best matched your search criteria. Would you like to refine your <u>search</u>.

Sponsorships

Name:	Basavaraju
Age:	9
Country:	India
	☐ Sponsor Basavaraju

Name:	Aldrin
Age:	6
Country:	Honduras
	☐ Sponsor Aldrin

Name:	Gervin
Age:	12
Country:	Honduras
	☐ Sponsor Gervin

[Sponsor] [Refine Your Search]

At other times you might need to use many details and examples. These need to be appropriate, accurate, and convincing. If you are actively involved in a national political party on your college campus, your chances of persuading your classmates to vote for members of your party for Congress will probably depend upon providing them specific examples of what your candidate stands for and how she or he has voted in the past. Responsible voters are not swayed by vague general statements such as "I support public prayer, or environmental responsibility, or a strong national defense."

On the other hand, when you write from personal experience, your readers might not demand the same level of detail and accuracy in your examples. In "Cut," Bob Greene writes about how being cut from the junior high school basketball team changed his life. To support his thesis and extend it beyond his own personal experience, Greene includes the stories of four other men who had similar experiences. But why give five examples of the same experience? Why not three or seven? There is nothing magical about the number five—Greene might have used five because he had that much column space in the magazine—but the five give authority to Greene's assertion, or at least they create the illusion of authority. To prove the validity of Greene's thesis would require a proper statistical sample. Only then could it be said with some certainty that the experience of being cut makes men superachievers later in life. In most writing situations, however, thoroughness is not needed. If the details and examples are well chosen and relevant, the reader is likely to accept your assertions.

SAMPLE STUDENT ESSAY

Frank Smite, recently divorced and recently returned to college, chose to work on an essay about the difficulties that older single or newly single people have in meeting people they can date. "Young college kids have it easy," Frank complained. "You are constantly surrounded by eligible people your own age. Try meeting someone when you're thirty-five, slightly balding, just divorced, and working all day." His first draft of the opening of his essay appears here:

MY SEARCH FOR LOVE

My wife and I separated and then quickly divorced a year ago. I figured that I would be able to forget some of the pain by returning to dating. At first, I was excited about the prospect of meeting new people. It made me feel young again. Besides, this time I'd be able to avoid the problems that led to my divorce. While I'm not exactly a male movie star—I'm thirty-five, a little overweight, kind of thin on the top, and have one daughter who I desperately miss seeing every day—I figured that romance was just around the corner.

It wasn't until I started to look for people to ask out that I realized how far away that corner was. Frankly, in my immediate world, there seemed to be no one who was roughly my age and unmarried. That's when I began to look at the various ways that people in my situation can meet people. I attended several meetings of the local Parents Without Partners group, but that didn't seem promising; I joined a computerized dating service; and, believe it or not, I started reading the "personals" in the newspaper.

When Frank came to revise his essay, he had his instructor's comments and the reactions of several classmates. Everyone agreed that he had an excellent subject and some good detail, but several readers were a little troubled by Frank's overuse of "I." One reader asked Frank if he could make his essay focus a little less on his own immediate experience and a little more on what anyone in his position might do. His instructor suggested that with the right type of revision, Frank might be able to publish his essay in the local newspaper—after all, she noted, many people are in the same situation. His instructor also suggested that Frank might eliminate the reference to his daughter and how much he misses her. Although those feelings are important, that is not where Frank wanted to center the essay. Frank liked the idea of sharing his experiences with a wider audience. His revised introduction—complete with a new title—follows.

LOOKING FOR LOVE

Ask any single or divorced adult about the problems of meeting "prospective partners" and you are likely to get a litany of complaints and horrifying experiences. No longer can people rely on introductions from well-meaning friends. After all, most of those friends are also looking for love. Matchmaking has become big business—even, in fact, a franchised business.

Today the search for love takes many forms, from bar hopping, to organizations such as Parents Without Partners, to computerized and videotaped "search services," to singles groups organized around a shared concern (for example, those who are concerned about the environment or who love books). A little more desperate (and risky and certainly tacky) is the newspaper classified. Titled "Getting Personal" in my local newspaper, advertisements typically read like this one running today: "Single white female, pretty, petite blond, 40's ISO [in search of] WM [white male] for a perfect relationship (it does exist!)."

SOME THINGS TO REMEMBER

1. Use details and examples—effective writing depends on them.
2. For some subjects you can find the illustrations you need from your own experiences and observations. You will, however, probably need to work at remembering and gathering those specifics.
3. For some subjects you will need to do some type of research—interviewing people, looking up material in your school's library, using the Internet and the World Wide Web to locate relevant documents and sites. Remember as well that you are always connecting your observations with knowledge that you have acquired in other courses and other experiences.
4. Choose examples that are relevant and accurate. Quality is more important than quantity. Make sure your examples support your argument or illustrate the points you are trying to make. If you use an outside authority—an interview, a printed text, an electronic source—make sure that the source is knowledgeable and accurate. Remember also to document those sources.
5. The number of details and examples you need necessarily varies. Sometimes one will do; sometimes you will need many. If you want your readers to do or to believe something, you will need to supply some evidence to gain their support or confidence.

VISUALIZING EXAMPLES

If you represent a land trust and you are trying to solicit donations from individuals, how do you make the value of your project vivid? Do you use a simple statistic? "We have 23,000 acres of conserved land under our permanent care." It's hard to imagine that much land

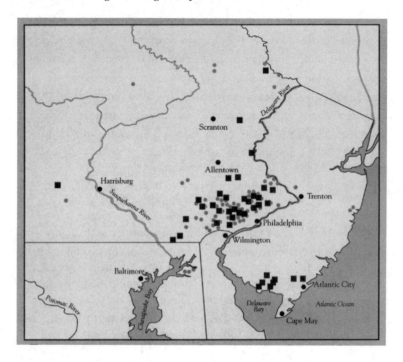

and a photograph or two will hardly do the subject justice. Moreover, how do you convey a sense of those 23,000 acres, especially if they are located in heavily populated areas. After all, 23,000 acres in parts of the West, Midwest, or Southwest is different from 23,000 acres in the area around Philadelphia, Pennsylvania. Notice the strategy used here. By locating those areas held in trust on a map, the Natural Lands Trust makes the significance of those holdings much more vivid to the potential contributor. Here the individual pieces are represented by squares and circles; the aggregate, depicting all of the specific areas, is much more impressive and persuasive.

EXAMPLE AS A LITERARY STRATEGY

We could find examples in any literary work, but Bret Lott's very short story "Night" uses a single example to capture a continuing painful reality. A father wakes up to hear what he thinks is his child breathing. It seems at first like an ordinary experience, but we quickly discover what that single example reveals.

NIGHT

Bret Lott

He woke up. He thought he could hear their child's breathing in the next room, the near-silent, smooth sound of air in and out. He touched his wife. The room was too dark to let him see her, but he felt her movement, the shift of blanket and sheet.

"Listen," he whispered.

"Yesterday," she mumbled. "Why not yesterday," and she moved back into sleep.

He listened harder, though he could hear his wife's breath, thick and heavy next to him, there was beneath this the thin frost of his child's breathing.

The hardwood floor was cold beneath his feet. He held out a hand in front of him, and when he touched the doorjamb, he paused, listened again, heard the life of his child.

His fingertips led him along the hall and to the next room. Then he was in the doorway of a room as dark, as hollow as his own. He cut on the light.

The room, of course, was empty. They had left the bed just as their child had made it, the spread merely thrown over bunched and wrinkled sheets, the pillow crooked at the head. The small blue desk was littered with colored pencils and scraps of construction paper, a bottle of white glue.

He turned off the light and listened. He heard nothing, then backed out of the room and moved down the hall, back to his room, his hands at his sides, his fingertips helpless.

This happened each night, like a dream, but not.

DISCUSSION QUESTIONS

1. What does this experience reveal to the reader? Is the single example sufficient to capture the emotion that the father feels? Would more examples, more experiences, be necessary?

2. Who narrates the experience? How does that point of view contribute to the story? What would the story be like if it were told by the father?

3. At what point in the story do you realize what is happening? Why might the author not reveal what has happened earlier?
4. Which of the descriptive details in the story seem most effective? Why?
5. What effect does the final sentence have?

WRITING SUGGESTIONS

Lott does not tell us how the parents felt; he allows the single example to reveal the loss that the father feels. It is simple and sparse, but extremely effective. Think about an emotion or feeling that you have had and then try to capture and convey that emotion or feeling in a single example. You might think about the following as possible starting points for your essay:

a. A life-changing event—something that has forever changed your life or your expectations
b. A loss—of a person, a pet, a personal possession
c. A discovery or a realization—a moment of insight into life, your identity, your future

Gathering and Using Examples in Writing for Your Other Courses

Almost all the writing you do in college will require you to gather and use details and examples to support your ideas and to demonstrate that you have mastered the materials covered in the course. Here are some samples of the kinds of writing assignments you might complete that would require the use of examples.

- **American History.** For an assignment asking that you explore some aspect of slave life prior to the Civil War, you might draw on examples from slave narratives to support the thesis that despite the practice of slave owners separating slave families by selling individual members to sometimes far-distant owners, many families were surprisingly successful at maintaining close bonds extending among several generations.
- **Film Studies.** For an assignment asking you to explore an important theme running through the work of a film director of your choice, you might explore the theme of entrapment in

the films of Alfred Hitchcock by looking in depth at four or five of his films.

- **Business Management.** For a paper on effective management styles, you might draw on examples you find in your reading, as well as from your own work experience, to illustrate some specific leadership qualities of strong managers.

- **Psychology.** For an essay exam question about how the different roles we play in our lives create problems of adjustment and psychological coherence, you might present real or hypothetical examples of particular individuals and their life roles to explain how such contradictions can be handled.

- **Environmental Science.** For an assignment asking you to explore the problems presented when a unique natural environment is threatened, you might, in choosing to write about the Florida Everglades, present a variety of examples of changes that have occurred in the plant and animal life of that ecosystem due to the effects of agricultural irrigation runoff.

VISIT THE PRENTICE HALL READER'S WEBSITE

When you have finished reading an essay, check out the additional material available at the *Reader*'s Website at www.prenhall.com/miller. For each reading, you will find a list of related readings connected with the topic or the author; additional background information; a group of relevant "hot-linked" Web resources (just click on the site you want to visit); and still more writing suggestions.

GATHERING AND USING EXAMPLES

Ever tried reading an on-line newspaper? Most of the major newspapers have extensive Websites that include searchable archives. Visit four major newspapers and sample what's available. Then using the Web as your information resource, write a review of what you found. Your starting points can be found at www. prenhall. com/miller.

THE NAME IS MINE

Anna Quindlen

Born in 1953, Anna Quindlen attended Barnard College in New York City. She enjoyed a successful career at The New York Times, *where she wrote three different weekly columns, including her syndicated column, "Public and Private," for which she won the 1992 Pulitzer Prize for commentary. Since leaving the* Times, *she has published several successful novels, the most recent of which is* Blessings *(2002).*

This essay first appeared in "Life in the 30's," a weekly column that Quindlen wrote for the Times *from 1986 to 1988. Based on her own experiences as a mother, a wife, and a journalist, the column attracted millions of readers and was syndicated in some sixty other newspapers. She ended the column because of its personal nature: "It wasn't just that I was in the spotlight; it was like I was in the spotlight naked. . . . I became public property."*

On Writing: *Quindlen writes on a laptop computer and observes, "I listen to all those authors who say they write longhand in diaries they buy in London, and I say, 'Get a life.' " A perfectionist who "wants every sentence to be the best it can be," Quindlen notes, "I don't want anything to be loose or sloppy."*

BEFORE READING

Connecting: Can you remember times when your "identity" was defined not by yourself but by your association with someone else, when you were the child *of*, the sibling *of*, the spouse *of*, the parent *of*, the employee *of*? How did these occasions make you feel?

Anticipating: Every decision we make has consequences—some of which we are immediately aware of and some of which only emerge later. What are the consequences of Quindlen's decision not to take her husband's name?

1   I am on the telephone to the emergency room of the local hospital. My elder son is getting stitches in his palm, and I have called to make myself feel better, because I am at home, waiting, and my husband is there, holding him. I am 34 years old, and I am crying like a child,

making a slippery mess of my face. "Mrs. Krovatin?" says the nurse, and for the first time in my life I answer "Yes."

This is a story about a name. The name is mine. I was given it 2 at birth, and I have never changed it, although I married. I could come up with lots of reasons why. It was a political decision, a simple statement that I was somebody and not an adjunct of anybody, especially a husband. As a friend of mine told her horrified mother, "He didn't adopt me, he married me."

It was a professional and a personal decision, too. I grew up 3 with an ugly dog of a name, one I came to love because I thought it was weird and unlovable. Amid the Debbies and Kathys of my childhood, I had a first name only my grandmothers had and a last name that began with a strange letter. "Sorry, the letters, I, O, Q, U, V, X, Y and Z are not available," the catalogues said about monogrammed key rings and cocktail napkins. Seeing my name in black on white at the top of a good story, suddenly it wasn't an ugly dog anymore.

But neither of these are honest reasons, because they assume 4 rational consideration, and it so happens that when it came to changing my name, there was no consideration, rational or otherwise. It was mine. It belonged to me. I don't even share a checking account with my husband. Damned if I was going to be hidden beneath the umbrella of his identity.

It seemed like a simple decision. But nowadays I think the only 5 simple decisions are whether to have grilled cheese or tuna fish for lunch. Last week, my older child wanted an explanation of why he, his dad and his brother have one name, and I have another.

My answer was long, philosophical and rambling—that is to 6 say, unsatisfactory. What's in a name? I could have said disingenuously. But I was talking to a person who had just spent three torturous, exhilarating years learning names for things, and I wanted to communicate to him that mine meant something quite special to me, had seemed as form-fitting as my skin, and as painful to remove. Personal identity and independence, however, were not what he was looking for; he just wanted to make sure I was one of them. And I am—and then again, I am not. When I made this decision, I was part of a couple. Now, there are two me's, the me who is the individual and the me who is part of a family of four, a family of four in which, in a small way, I am left out.

A wise friend who finds herself in the same fix says she never 7 wants to change her name, only to have a slightly different identity as a family member, an identity for pediatricians' offices and parent-teacher conferences. She also says that the entire situation reminds her of the women's movement as a whole. We did these things as individuals, made these decisions about ourselves and what we wanted to be and do. And they were good decisions, the right decisions. But we based them on individual choice, not on group dynamics. We thought in terms of our sense of ourselves, not our relationships with others.

8   Some people found alternative solutions: hyphenated names, merged names, matriarchal names for the girls and patriarchal ones for the boys, one name at work and another at home. I did not like those choices; I thought they were middle grounds, and I didn't live much in the middle ground at the time. I was once slightly disdainful of women who went all the way and changed their names. But I now know too many smart, independent, terrific women who have the same last names as their husbands to be disdainful anymore. (Besides, if I made this decision as part of a feminist world view, it seems dishonest to turn around and trash other women for deciding as they did.)

9   I made my choice. I haven't changed my mind. I've just changed my life. Sometimes I feel like one of those worms I used to hear about in biology, the ones that, chopped in half, walked off in different directions. My name works fine for one half, not quite as well for the other. I would never give it up. Except for that one morning when I talked to the nurse at the hospital, I always answer the question "Mrs. Krovatin?" with "No, this is Mr. Krovatin's wife." It's just that I understand the down side now.

10   When I decided not to disappear beneath my husband's umbrella, it did not occur to me that I would be the only one left outside. It did not occur to me that I would ever care—not enough to change, just enough to think about the things we do on our own and what they mean when we aren't on our own anymore.

QUESTIONS ON SUBJECT AND PURPOSE

1. Why did Quindlen not change her last name when she married?
2. How does she feel about her decision now?
3. Since Quindlen does not plan to change her name, what purpose might she have in writing the essay?

QUESTIONS ON STRATEGY AND AUDIENCE

1. The essay could begin at the second paragraph. Why might Quindlen have chosen to begin the essay with the telephone call experience?

2. In paragraph 9, Quindlen returns to the incident at the hospital. How does this device help hold the essay together?
3. The essay appeared in a column headed "Life in the 30's." How might that affect the nature of the audience who might read the essay?

QUESTIONS ON VOCABULARY AND STYLE

1. At the beginning of paragraphs 2 and 9, Quindlen uses three very short simple sentences in a row. Why?
2. Twice in the essay (paragraphs 4 and 10), Quindlen refers to coming under her husband's "umbrella." What is the effect of such an image?
3. Be able to define the following words: *disingenuously* (paragraph 6) and *disdainful* (8).

WRITING SUGGESTIONS

1. **For Your Journal.** Do you have any desire to change your name? If so, why? If not, why not? In your journal, explore what changing or not changing your name might mean. Would "you" be any different?
2. **For a Paragraph.** In a paragraph, explore the meaning that you find in your last name. How does that name define you?
3. **For an Essay.** In paragraph 6, Quindlen remarks, "There are two me's, the me who is the individual and the me who is part of a family of four." Everyone experiences such moments of awareness. Think about those times when you have been "two," and in an essay, explore the dilemma posed by being an individual and, at the same time, a part of a larger whole.
4. **For Research.** How widespread and recent is the phenomenon of women not taking their husbands' names? Research the phenomenon through the various databases that your library has. A crucial problem will be identifying the subject headings and keywords to use in your search. If you have problems, ask a reference librarian for some guidance. Remember as well that people make excellent sources of information. Then, using that research, write an essay for one of the following audiences:
   a. An article intended for a male audience

      b. An article intended for an audience of unmarried women who might be considering such a decision

      c. A traditional research paper for a college course

 WEBSITE LINK

What percentage of women in the United States choose not to take their husband's name? What socioeconomic factors influence that decision? Find out at www.prenhall.com/miller.

 WRITING LINK: DICTION

Quindlen uses a number of words and phrases that are colloquial and perhaps too informal. Make a list of these. Why might she mix levels of diction in the essay? How does word choice contribute to the voice that she projects in the essay? What does that suggest about your own writing?

CUT

Bob Greene

Bob Greene was born in Columbus, Ohio, in 1947 and received a B.J. from Northwestern University in 1969. A columnist and essayist, Greene's most recent books are Duty: A Father, His Son, and the Man Who Won the War *(2000) and* Once Upon a Town: The Miracle of the North Platte Canteen *(2002).*
On Writing: *Greene is, in many ways, a reporter of everyday events. He rarely tries to be profound but concentrates instead on "human interest" stories, the experiences that we all share. "Beyond entertaining or informing [my readers]," he has said, "the only responsibility I feel is . . . to make sure that they get to the last period of the last sentence of the last paragraph of the story . . . I feel I have a responsibility to make the story interesting enough for them to read all the way through." In this essay from* Esquire, *a magazine aimed at a male audience, Greene relates the stories of five successful men who shared the experience of being "cut from the team." Does being cut, Greene wonders, make you a superachiever later in life?*

BEFORE READING

Connecting: Was there ever a time when you realized that you were not going to be allowed to participate in something that you wanted very much? Did someone tell you, "You're not good enough," or did you realize it yourself?

Anticipating: Writers recount personal experiences for some reason, and that reason is never just "here is what happened to me"; instead, writers focus on the significance of the experience. What significance does Greene see in these narratives?

I remember vividly the last time I cried. I was twelve years old, in the   1
seventh grade, and I had tried out for the junior high school basketball team. I walked into the gymnasium; there was a piece of paper tacked to the bulletin board.

It was a cut list. The seventh-grade coach had put it up on the   2
board. The boys whose names were on the list were still on the team; they were welcome to keep coming to practices. The boys whose

names were not on the list had been cut; their presence was no longer desired. My name was not on the list.

3   I had not known the cut was coming that day. I stood and stared at the list. The coach had not composed it with a great deal of subtlety; the names of the very best athletes were at the top of the sheet of paper, and the other members of the squad were listed in what appeared to be a descending order of talent. I kept looking at the bottom of the list, hoping against hope that my name would miraculously appear there if I looked hard enough.

4   I held myself together as I walked out of the gym and out of the school, but when I got home I began to sob. I couldn't stop. For the first time in my life, I had been told officially that I wasn't good enough. Athletics meant everything to boys that age; if you were on the team, even a substitute, it put you in the desirable group. If you weren't on the team, you might as well not be alive.

5   I had tried desperately in practice, but the coach never seemed to notice. It didn't matter how hard I was willing to work; he didn't want me there. I knew that when I went to school the next morning I would have to face the boys who had not been cut—the boys whose names were on the list, who were still on the team, who had been judged worthy while I had been judged unworthy.

6   All these years later, I remember it as if I were still standing right there in the gym. And a curious thing has happened: in traveling around the country, I have found that an inordinately large proportion of successful men share that same memory—the memory of being cut from a sports team as a boy.

7   I don't know how the mind works in matters like this; I don't know what went on in my head following that day when I was cut. But I know that my ambition has been enormous ever since then; I know that for all of my life since that day, I have done more work than I had to be doing, taken more assignments than I had to be taking, put in more hours than I had to be spending. I don't know if all of that came from a determination never to allow myself to be cut again—never to allow someone to tell me that I'm not good enough again—but I know it's there. And apparently it's there in a lot of other men, too.

8   Bob Graham, thirty-six, is a partner with the Jenner & Block law firm in Chicago. "When I was sixteen, baseball was my whole life," he said. "I had gone to a relatively small high school, and I had been on the team. But then my family moved, and I was going to a much bigger high school. All during the winter months I told everyone that I was a ballplayer. When spring came, of course I went out for the team.

"The cut list went up. I did not make the team. Reading that 9
cut list is one of the clearest things I have in my memory. I wanted not
to believe it, but there it was.

"I went home and told my father about it. He suggested that 10
maybe I should talk to the coach. So I did. I pleaded to be put
back on the team. He said there was nothing he could do; he said he
didn't have enough room.

"I know for a fact that it altered my perception of myself. My 11
view of myself was knocked down; my self-esteem was lowered. I felt
so embarrassed; my whole life up to that point had revolved around
sports, and particularly around playing baseball. That was the group
I wanted to be in—the guys on the baseball team. And I was told that
I wasn't good enough to be one of them.

"I know now that it changed me. I found out, even though I 12
couldn't articulate it at the time, that there would be times in my life
when certain people would be in a position to say 'You're not good
enough' to me. I did not want that to happen ever again.

"It seems obvious to me now that being cut was what started 13
me in determining that my success would always be based on my own
abilities, and not on someone else's perceptions. Since then I've always been something of an overachiever; when I came to the law firm
I was very aggressive in trying to run my own cases right away, to be
the lead lawyer in the cases with which I was involved. I made partner at thirty-one; I never wanted to be left behind.

"Looking back, maybe it shouldn't have been that important. It 14
was only baseball. You pass that by. Here I am. That coach is probably still there, still a high school baseball coach, still cutting boys off
the baseball team every year. I wonder how many hundreds of boys
he's cut in his life?"

Maurice McGrath is senior vice-president of Genstar Mortgage Cor- 15
poration, a mortgage banking firm in Glendale, California. "I'm
forty-seven years old, and I was fourteen when it happened to me, and
I still feel something when I think about it," he said.

"I was in the eighth grade. I went to St. Philip's School in 16
Pasadena. I went out for the baseball team, and one day at practice the
coach came over to me. He was an Occidental College student who
had been hired as the eighth-grade coach.

"He said, 'You're no good.' Those were his words. I asked him 17
why he was saying that. He said, 'You can't hit the ball. I don't want
you here.' I didn't know what to do, so I went over and sat off to the
side, watching the others practice. The coach said I should leave the
practice field. He said that I wasn't on the team, and that I didn't belong there anymore.

18   "I was outwardly stoic about it. I didn't want anyone to see how I felt. I didn't want to show that it hurt. But oh, did it hurt. All my friends played baseball after school every day. My best friend was the pitcher on the team. After I got whittled down by the coach, I would hear the other boys talking in class about what they were going to do at practice after school. I knew that I'd just have to go home.

19   "I guess you make your mind up never to allow yourself to be hurt like that again. In some way I must have been saying to myself, 'I'll play the game better.' Not the sports game, but anything I tried. I must have been saying, 'If I have to, I'll sit on the bench, but I'll be part of the team.'

20   "I try to make my own kids believe that, too. I try to tell them that they should show that they're a little bit better than the rest. I tell them to think of themselves as better. Who cares what anyone else thinks? You know, I can almost hear that coach saying the words. 'You're no good.' "

21   Author Malcolm MacPherson *(The Blood of His Servants)*, forty, lives in New York. "It happened to me in the ninth grade, at the Yalesville School in Yalesville, Connecticut," he said. "Both of my parents had just been killed in a car crash, and as you can imagine, it was a very difficult time in my life. I went out for the baseball team, and I did pretty well in practice.

22   "But in the first game I clutched. I was playing second base; the batter hit a pop-up, and I moved back to catch it. I can see it now. I felt dizzy as I looked up at the ball. It was like I was moving in slow motion, but the ball was going at regular speed. I couldn't get out of the way of my own feet. The ball dropped to the ground. I didn't catch it.

23   "The next day at practice, the coach read off the lineup. I wasn't on it. I was off the squad.

24   "I remember what I did: I walked. It was a cold spring afternoon, and the ground was wet, and I just walked. I was living with an aunt and uncle, and I didn't want to go home. I just wanted to walk forever.

25   "It drove my opinion of myself right into a tunnel. Right into a cave. And when I came out of the cave, something inside of me wanted to make sure in one manner or another that I would never again be told I wasn't good enough.

26   "I will confess that my ambition, to this day, is out of control. It's like a fire. I think the fire would have pretty much stayed in control if I hadn't been cut from that team. But that got it going. You don't slice ambition two ways; it's either there or it isn't. Those of us

who went through something like that always know that we have to
catch the ball. We'd rather die than have the ball fall at our feet.

"Once that fire is started in us, it never gets extinguished, un-   27
til we die or have heart attacks or something. Sometimes I wonder
about the home-run hitters; the guys who never even had to worry
about being cut. They may have gotten the applause and the attention back then, but I wonder if they ever got the fire. I doubt it. I think
maybe you have to get kicked in the teeth to get the fire started.

"You can tell the effect of something like that by examining the   28
trail you've left in your life, and tracing it backward. It's almost like
being a junkie with a need for success. You get attention and applause
and you like it, but you never quite trust it. Because you know that
back then you were good enough if only they would have given you a
chance. You don't trust what you achieve, because you're afraid that
someone will take it away from you. You know that it can happen; it
already did.

"So you try to show people how good you are. Maybe you don't
go out and become Dan Rather; maybe you just end up owning the   29
Pontiac dealership in your town. But it's your dealership, and you're
the top man, and every day you're showing people that you're good
enough."

Dan Rather, fifty-two, is anchor of the CBS *Evening News.* "When   30
I was thirteen, I had rheumatic fever," he said. "I became extremely
skinny and extremely weak, but I still went out for the seventh-
grade baseball team at Alexander Hamilton Junior High School in
Houston.

"The school was small enough that there was no cut as such;   31
you were supposed to figure out that you weren't good enough, and
quit. Game after game I sat at the end of the bench, hoping that
maybe this was the time I would get in. The coach never even looked
at me; I might as well have been invisible.

"I told my mother about it. Her advice was not to quit. So I   32
went to practice every day, and I tried to do well so that the coach
would be impressed. He never even knew I was there. At home in my
room I would fantasize that there was a big game, and the three guys
in front of me would all get hurt, and the coach would turn to me and
put me in, and I would make the winning hit. But then there'd be another game, and the late innings would come, and if we were way
ahead I'd keep hoping that this was the game when the coach would
put me in. He never did.

"When you're that age, you're looking for someone to tell you   33
you're okay. Your sense of self-esteem is just being formed. And what

that experience that baseball season did was make me think that perhaps I wasn't okay.

34   "In the last game of the season something terrible happened. It was the last of the ninth inning, there were two outs, and there were two strikes on the batter. And the coach turned to me and told me to go out to right field.

35   "It was a totally humiliating thing for him to do. For him to put me in for one pitch, the last pitch of the season, in front of all the other boys on the team . . . I stood out there for that one pitch, and I just wanted to sink into the ground and disappear. Looking back on it, it was an extremely unkind thing for him to have done. That was nearly forty years ago, and I don't know why the memory should be so vivid now; I've never known if the coach was purposely making fun of me—and if he was, why a grown man would do that to a thirteen-year-old boy.

36   "I'm not a psychologist. I don't know if a man can point to one event in his life and say that that's the thing that made him the way he is. But when you're that age, and you're searching for your own identity, and all you want is to be told that you're all right . . . I wish I understood it better, but I know the feeling is still there."

QUESTIONS ON SUBJECT AND PURPOSE

1. Greene's "cuts" all refer to not making an athletic team. What other kinds of "cuts" can you experience?

2. It is always risky to speculate on an author's purpose, but why would Greene write about this? Why reveal to everyone something that hurt so much?

3. How might Greene have gone about gathering examples of other men's similar experiences? Why would they be willing to contribute? Would everyone who has been cut be so candid?

4. What can be said in the coaches' defense? Should everyone who tries out be automatically guaranteed a place on the team?

QUESTIONS ON STRATEGY AND AUDIENCE

1. Greene structures his essay in an unusual way. How can the essay be divided? Why give a series of examples of other men who were "cut"?

2. How many examples are enough? What if Greene had used two examples? Eight examples? How would either extreme have influenced your reaction as a reader?

3. Greene does not provide a final concluding paragraph. Why?
4. Are you skeptical after you have finished the essay? Does everyone react to being cut in the same way? What would it take to convince you that these reactions are typical?

QUESTIONS ON VOCABULARY AND STYLE

1. How would you characterize the tone of Greene's essay? How is it achieved? Through language? Sentence structure? Paragraphing?
2. Why does Greene allow each man to tell his own story? Why not just summarize their experiences? Each story is enclosed in quotation marks. Do you think that these were the exact words of each man? Why?
3. What do *inordinately* (paragraph 6) and *stoic* (18) mean?

WRITING SUGGESTIONS

1. **For Your Journal.** Greene attributes enormous significance to a single experience; he feels that it literally changed his entire life. Try to remember some occasions when a disappointment seemed to change your life by changing your expectations for yourself. In your journal, list some possible instances, and then explore one.
2. **For a Paragraph.** As children, we imagine ourselves doing or being anything we want. As we grow older, however, we discover that our choices become increasingly limited; in fact, each choice we make seems to cut off whole paths of alternative choices. We cannot be or do everything that we once thought we could. Choose a time in your life when you realized that a particular expectation or dream would never come true. In a paragraph, narrate that experience. Be sure to make the significance of your realization clear to your reader.
3. **For an Essay.** Describe an experience similar to the one that Greene narrates. It might have happened in an academic course during your school years, in a school or community activity, in athletics, or on the job: we can be "cut," "released," or "fired" from almost anything. Remember to make your narrative vivid through the use of detail and to make the significance of your narrative clear to the reader.
4. **For Research.** Check the validity of Greene's argument. Is there any evidence from research studies about the

psychological effects of such vivid rejections? Using print and on-line sources (if they are available), see what you can find. A reference librarian can help you start your search for information. Use that research in an essay about the positive or negative effects of such experiences. Remember to document all sources. You might write your paper in one of the following forms (each has a slightly different audience):

a. A conventional research paper for a college course

b. An article for a popular magazine (for example, *Esquire, Working Woman, Parents'*)

c. A feature article for your school's newspaper

WEBSITE LINK

Greene's essay originally appeared in *Esquire*, not *Sports Illustrated* or *Sporting News*. Want to see why?—compare the magazines (Hint: You can do it electronically).

WRITING LINK: TRANSITIONS

Greene uses *ands* and *buts* to connect many sentences in his essay. We use both words in oral speech much more than in writing. Why might Greene use them in the essay? How do they contribute to the essay? What cautions might there be in linking sentences together in this way?

WESTBURY COURT

Edwidge Danticat

Edwidge Danticat (1969–) was born in Port-au-Prince, Haiti. At the age of twelve she came to New York City to join her parents who had emigrated some years earlier. She earned a degree in French literature from Barnard College and an M.F.A. from Brown University. At twenty-six she was a finalist for a National Book Award for her collection of short stories Krik? Krak! *Her other books include* Breath, Eyes, Memory *(1994),* The Farming of Bones *(1998), and* Behind the Mountains *(2002).*

On Writing: *Danticat's native languages were Haitian Creole and French. She comments, "My writing in English is a consequence of my migration, in the same way that immigrant children speaking to each other in English is a consequence of their migration." She continues, "When I first started writing, I wasn't thinking about publishing it. I was working at writing. . . . Writing in any language is difficult. . . . I like to walk and think things out. . . . I prefer silence when writing. That was hard to come by when growing up with three [brothers]."*

BEFORE READING

Connecting: Danticat writes of a tragic experience that occurred when she was fourteen and living in Brooklyn. Do you have a particular sad or joyful experience that you connect with a place that you lived?

Anticipating: The core experience about which Danticat writes in the essay occurred almost twenty years ago. Why does she remember it now? What significance does it still have for her?

When I was fourteen years old, we lived in a six-story brick build-   1
ing in a cul-de-sac off of Flatbush Avenue, in Brooklyn, called Westbury Court. Beneath the building ran a subway station through which
rattled the D, M, and Q trains every fifteen minutes or so. Though
there was graffiti on most of the walls of Westbury Court, and hills of
trash piled up outside, and though the elevator wasn't always there
when we opened the door to step inside and the heat and hot water
weren't always on, I never dreamed of leaving Westbury Court until
the year of the fire.

2   I was watching television one afternoon when the fire began. I loved television then, especially the afternoon soap operas, my favorite of which was *General Hospital.* I would bolt out of my last high school class every day, pick up my youngest brother, Karl, from day care, and watch *General Hospital* with him on my lap while doing my homework during the commercials. My other two brothers, André and Kelly, would later join us in the apartment, but they preferred to watch cartoons in the back bedroom.

3   One afternoon while *General Hospital* and afternoon cartoons were on, a fire started in apartment 6E, across the hall. There in that apartment lived our new neighbors, an African-American mother and her two boys. We didn't know the name of the mother, or the names and ages of her boys, but I venture to guess that they were around five and ten years old.

4   I didn't know a fire had started until two masked, burly firemen came knocking on our door. My brothers and I rushed out into the hallway filled with smoke and were quickly escorted down to the first floor by some other firemen already on our floor. While we ran by, the door to apartment 6E had already been knocked over by the fire squad and inside was filled with bright flames and murky smoke.

5   All of the tenants of the building who were home at that time were crowded on the sidewalk outside. My brothers and I, it seemed, were the last to be evacuated. Clutching my brothers' hands, I wondered if I had remembered to lock our apartment door. Was there anything valuable we could have taken?

6   An ambulance screeched to a stop in front of the building, and the two firemen who had knocked on our door came out carrying the pliant and lifeless bodies of the two children from across the hall. Their mother jumped out of the crowd and ran toward them, screaming, "My babies—not my babies," as the children were lowered into the back of the ambulance and transferred into the arms of the emergency medical personnel. The fire was started by the two boys, after their mother had stepped out to pick up some groceries at the supermarket down the street. They had been playing with matches.

7   (Later my mother would tell us, "See, this is what happens to children who play with matches. Sometimes it is too late to say, 'I shouldn't have.' " My brother Kelly, who has fascinated with fire and liked to hold up a match to the middle of his palm until the light fizzled out, gave up this party trick after the fire.)

8   We were quiet that afternoon when both our parents came home. We were the closest to the fire in the building, and the most religious of our parents' friends saw it as a miracle that we had escaped safe and sound. When my mother asked how come I, the old-

est one, hadn't heard the children scream or hadn't smelled the smoke coming from across the hall, I confessed that I had been watching *General Hospital* and was too consumed in the intricate plot.

(After the fire, my mother had us stay with a family on the sec- 9 ond floor for a few months, after school. I felt better not having to be wholly responsible for myself and my brothers, in case something like that fire should ever happen again.)

The apartment across the hall stayed empty for a long time, 10 and whenever I walked past it, a piece of its inner skeleton would squeak, and occasionally burnt wood that might have been hanging by a fragile singed thread would crash down and cause a domino effect of further ruptures, unleashed like those children's last cries, which I had not heard because I had been so wrapped up in the made-up drama of a world where, even though the adults' lives were often in turmoil, the children came home to the welcoming arms of waiting mommies and nannies who served them freshly baked cookies on porcelain plates and helped them to remove their mud-soaked boots, if it was raining, lest they soil the lily-white carpets. But should their boots accidentally sully the carpet, or should their bright yellow raincoats inadvertently drip on the sparkling linoleum, there would be a remedy for that as well. And if their house should ever catch fire, a smart dog or a good neighbor would rescue them just in time, and the fire trucks would come right quick because some attentive neighbor would call them.

Through the trail of voices that came up to comfort us, I heard 11 that the children's mother would be prosecuted for negligence and child abandonment. I couldn't help but wonder, would our parents have suffered the same fate had it been my brothers and me who were killed in the fire?

When they began to repair the apartment across the hall, I 12 would occasionally sneak out to watch the workmen. They were shelling the inside of the apartment and replacing everything from the bedroom closets to the kitchen floors. I never saw the mother of the dead boys again and never heard anything of her fate.

A year later, after the apartment was well polished and painted, 13 two blind Haitian brothers and their sister moved in. They were all musicians and were part of a group called les Frères Parent, the Parent Brothers. Once my parents allowed my brothers and me to come home from school to our apartment, I would always listen carefully for our new tenants, so I'd be the first to know if anything went awry.

What I heard coming from the apartment soon after they 14 moved in was music, "engagé" music, which the brothers were composing to protest against the dictatorship in Haiti, from which they had fled. The Parent Brothers and their sister, Lydie, did nothing but rehearse a cappella most days when they were not receiving religious and political leaders from Haiti and from the Haitian community in New York.

15   The same year after the fire, a cabdriver who lived down the hall in 6J was killed on a night shift in Manhattan; a good friend of my father's, a man who gave great Sunday afternoon parties in 6F, died of cirrhosis of the liver. One day while my brothers and I were at school and my parents were at work, someone came into our apartment through our fire escape and stole my father's expensive camera. That same year a Nigerian immigrant was shot and killed in front of the building across the street. To appease us, my mother said, "Nothing like that ever happens out of the blue. He was in a fight with someone." It was too troublesome for her to acknowledge that people could die randomly, senselessly, at Westbury Court or anywhere else.

16   Every day on my way back from school, I hurried past the flowers and candles piled in front of the spot where the Nigerian, whose name I didn't know, had been murdered. Still I never thought I was living in a violent place. It was an elevated castle above a clattering train tunnel, a blind alley where children from our building and the building across the street had erected a common basketball court for hot summer afternoon games, an urban yellow brick road where hopscotch squares dotted the sidewalk next to burned-out, abandoned cars. It was home.

17   My family and I moved out of Westbury Court three years after the fire. Every once in a while, though, the place came up in conversation, linked to either a joyous or a painful memory. One of the girls who had scalded her legs while boiling a pot of water for her bath during one of those no-heat days got married last year. After the burglar had broken into the house and taken my father's camera, my father—an amateur photography buff—never took another picture.

18   My family and I often reminisce about the Parent Brothers when we see them in Haitian newspapers or on television; we brag that we knew them when, before one of the brothers became a senator in Haiti and the sister, Lydie, became mayor of one of the better-off Haitian suburbs, Pétion-Ville. We never talk about the lost children.

19   Even now, I question what I remember about the children. Did they really die? Or did their mother simply move away with them after the fire? Maybe they were not even boys at all. Maybe they were two girls. Or one boy and one girl. Or maybe I am struggling to phase them out of my memory altogether. Not just them, but the fear that their destiny could have so easily been mine and my brothers'.

A few months ago, I asked my mother, "Do you remember the   20
children and the fire at Westbury Court?"

Without missing a flutter of my breath, my mother replied,   21
"Oh those children, those poor children, their poor mother. Sometimes it is too late to say, 'I shouldn't have.' "

QUESTIONS ON SUBJECT AND PURPOSE

1. How long ago did the fire take place? What details in the
   story allow you to arrive at an approximate answer?
2. How many examples of life at Westbury Court does Danticat
   include?
3. Why might the essay be titled "Westbury Court"? What does
   that suggest about the essay? How appropriate would a title
   such as "Sometimes It Is Too Late" have been?

QUESTIONS ON STRATEGY AND AUDIENCE

1. In paragraphs 7 and 21, Danticat repeats her mother's
   observation: "Sometimes it is too late to say, 'I shouldn't
   have.' " Why?
2. Danticat encloses paragraphs 7 and 9 within parentheses. Why?
3. What is it about the essay and the experiences that it relates
   that might appeal to a reader?

QUESTIONS ON VOCABULARY AND STYLE

1. What is the effect of the typical televised depiction of children
   returning home in paragraph 10?
2. In paragraph 16, Danticat describes Westbury Court as an
   "elevated castle," "a blind alley," "an urban yellow brick road."
   What are these figures of speech called?
3. Be prepared to define the following words: *pliant* (paragraph
   6), *sully* (10), *appease* (15).

WRITING SUGGESTIONS

1. **For Your Journal.** Everyone has had scary experiences, but
   sometimes an experience will forever change the way we think
   or act. In your journal brainstorm about some past
   experiences that altered your later life. Jot down both a short

account of what happened and a sentence or two about the significance of that single experience.

2. **For a Paragraph.** Expand your journal entry into a paragraph. Concentrate on a single event, focusing especially on its significance.

3. **For an Essay.** "Sometimes it is too late to say, 'I shouldn't have.' " Use the mother's observation for the basis of an essay in which you explore an example or series of related examples or experiences that taught you the truth (or the falseness) of such a claim.

4. **For Research.** When children suddenly and unexpectedly die, schools (elementary, secondary, colleges, and universities) often have grief counselors available for their peers. What do we know about the impact that the sudden death of a friend or a classmate might have on a peer? Research the topic—or an aspect of the topic—and present your findings in a longer essay. If you recall a similar experience from your life, you might use that as a departure point for your paper.

 WEBSITE LINK

Unsure how to start the research paper suggested above? Check out some of the starting places offered at the Website.

 WRITING LINK: COMMA USAGE

Select one or more of Danticat's paragraphs and see if you can explain why she uses each comma. A grammar book will help you remember the rules of comma use. Good choices are paragraphs 1–3, or 7–8, or 12–14. Remember that we use commas (and other marks of punctuation) to help our readers see the structures of our sentences.

BEING BRIANS

Brian Doyle

Brian Doyle is the editor of Portland Magazine *at the University of Port-land and the author of three essay collections:* Two Voices *(1996; with his father,* Jim Doyle), Credo *(1999), and* Saints Passionate & Peculiar *(2002). Doyle's essays have been frequently included in* Best American Essays *and* Best Spiritual Writing.

On Writing: *Doyle commented about the essay: "Being Brians may be especially useful for young writers as an example of a stray idea pursued to effect; the essay form, perhaps more than any other, lends itself to the diligent and open-minded chasing of ideas wherever they may lead. In this case they led to peculiar humor and finally to poignancy; as so much of life does; which is why writing essays is so emotionally nutritious; and when they work, when they sing, when they have pop and verve and life and zest and muscle, they maybe advance the universe of the heart two inches. Which is pretty cool. And a prayer."*

BEFORE READING

Connecting: Have you ever met someone who has the same first and last name as you? What was your reaction? Was it ever a source of confusion (misdirected mail, telephone calls)?

Anticipating: In his first sentence Doyle notes that there are 215 Brian Doyles in the United States. How does Doyle select and organize those examples?

There are 215 Brian Doyles in the United States, according to a   1
World Wide Web site called "Switchboard," which shows telephone
numbers and addresses in America.

We live in forty states; more of us live in New York than in any   2
other state. Several of us live on streets named for women (Laura, Ce-
celia, Nicole, Jean, Joyce). A startling number of us live on streets and
in towns named for flora (Apple, Ash, Bay, Berry, Chestnut, Hickory,
Maple, Oak, Palm, Poinsettia, Sandalwood, and Teak) or fauna (Bee,
Bobolink, Buck, Buffalo, Bull, Fox, Gibbon, Hawk, Wildcat).

Some of us live on streets named in the peculiarly American   3
fashion for a bucolic natural place that doesn't exist, a pastoral Eden of

the imagination, the sort of name that has become de rigueur for housing developments: Bellarbor, Greenridge, Cresthaven, Cricklewood, Knollwood, Pleasant Hill, Shady Nook, Skyridge, Spring Winds.

4   And there are Brian Doyles in uncategorizable but somehow essentially American places (Vacation Lane, Enchanted Flame Street, Freedom Road, Sugar Land) and in some places that seem to me especially American in their terse utility: Main Street, Rural Route, United States Highway, Old Route, New Road.

5   One of us is paralyzed from the chest down; one of us is eighteen and "likes to party"; one of us played second base very well indeed for the New York Yankees in the 1978 World Series; several of us have had problems with alcohol and drugs; one of us is nearly finished with his doctorate in theology; one of us is a nine-year-old girl; one of us works for Promise Keepers; one was married while we were working on this essay; one welcomed a new baby; one died.

6   The rest of us soldier on being Brian Doyle.

7   "Tell me a little bit about yourself," I wrote us recently:
How did you get your name? What do you do for work? What are your favorite pursuits? Hobbies? Avocations? Have any of us named our sons Brian? What Irish county were your forebearers from? Where were you born? Where did you go to college? What's your wife's name?

8   Brian the doctoral student in theology at the Catholic University of America:
I ride my bike and search for new microbrews. No children. We still have family in County Kerry. They live on a dairy farm and moved out of the thatched-roof cottage about fifteen years ago, but it still stands on the property.

9   Brian the New England field representative for Promise Keepers, "a Christian ministry dedicated to uniting men in vital relationships so that they might be godly influences in their world":
My wife and I are committed to honoring Jesus Christ in our lives, marriage, and in all that we do. He is Central to our daily living.

10   Brian of Waltham, Mass., in a handwritten note:
I am a union ironworker in Boston and have been iron working for twenty-three years. I am pretty much a free spirit.

11   Brian the undergraduate at the University of Kansas:
Hiked 700 miles of the Pacific Crest Trail. Biked from Newport, Ore., to San Francisco down Highway 101. I don't know much about my name, but now you got me curious.

12   Brian of Leicester, Mass.:
I am forty-nine years old and was injured in the military back in 1969. I was wounded three times in Vietnam and got to walk off the plane, but within two months I was involved in a motor-vehicle accident while home on leave and I became paralyzed from the chest down. I have worked

as a police dispatcher for my local highway department. I am currently retired as I decided a few years ago that it was time to enjoy life right now. My wife Shirley is legally blind with a degenerative eye disease. So let's go for the gusto and enjoy while we can. Hope to hear back from you.

I write back to Brain of Leicester and tell him that I am grateful for his courteous note. I think about him in his wheelchair and his wife who cannot see and the days and months he must have spent on his back after his car crash thinking about the irony of surviving warfare only to be savagely injured on a highway, and by then it is time to put my sons and daughter to bed, which I do with the sharp flavor of gratitude in my mouth. 13

Brian of Livonia, Mich.: 14
I have four daughters—Nicole, Meghan, Adrienne, and Stèphanie. Sons? What are sons?

Brian of Livonia adds a genealogical note about our surname, which is an English translation of the Gaelic word *"dubhghaill,"* or "dark stranger," a word often used in early times to denote a Dane. Doyle is now the twelfth most common name in Ireland. Brian of Livonia also points out that the name "Brian" hails from the last Irish high king, or *ard righ*, Brian Boru, slain in 1014 in the battle of Clontarf. 15

Brian Doyle in Poughkeepsie, N.Y.: 16
I know of a few other Brian Doyles—a plumbing-supply salesperson, a local restaurateur, and an IBM public-relations official—but have met none of them. I have been asked several times if I played second base for the New York Yankees in 1978. Of course, I confess that I am this same person who nearly won the 1978 World Series MVP Award—but later confess to this lie.

Brian of Naples, Fla.: 17
Recently divorced, though very much in love again with a wonderful woman. Early life at home was very confusing, and I took refuge in hiding in mind and mood alterers, i.e., alcohol and drugs. I have not indulged in such behavior in over seven years. I was in the air-conditioning field for fifteen years, but as I became more aware it just didn't feel right.

Next morning I count up the number of letters that have come back stamped UNDELIVERABLE or NO LONGER AT THIS ADDRESS or that have the new resident's angry, scrawled HE DOESN'T LIVE HERE ANYMORE!!!! on them in large, annoyed block letters: forty-three. Where are those Brian Doyles? The Lost Brian Doyles, addresses gone bad, addresses rotten, addresses thrown out on the compost heap, moldering. 18

Denise Doyle, of Saltillo, Pa., in a handwritten letter: 19
We thought your letter was very neat! Brian is self-employed in the carpenter field: building, remodeling, etc. He loves to fish and hunt. We have

a daughter, Brianne, named after her daddy, age nine. Brian is a laid back sort of guy and has a lot of care for other people.

20   Calm, compassionate, caring—it's a Brian Doyle thing.

21   Brian in Houston, Tex.: Likes cold beer.

22   Brian in Braintree, Mass.: Named for Brian Boru. Parents: Francis and Frances, both Irish natives. Brian was the goalkeeper on the University of Lowell's 1979 national championship hockey team, had a cup of coffee with the National Hockey League's Phoenix Coyotes, and once played in a high school hockey game in which both goalies were named Brian Doyle.

23   Brian of Valley Cottage, N.Y.: Father called him Boru as a boy. Appalachian Trail nut:

I've hiked the trail from Maine to Georgia, and I guess you could say that I'm a woodsman, eastern style.

24   Remembers with affection his cousin Brian Doyle, who died a few years ago in Pittston, Pa., where his father's people, fleeing *An Gorta Mor,* the horrendous Irish Famine of 1845–1851, landed in America to work the coal mines.

25   Not unlike some of my father's ancestors, who fled Wicklow and Cork from what my grandmother called "the Horror" and became bartenders, bricklayers, cigar dealers, steelworkers, die cutters, freight clerks, and bookkeepers in the 10th, 18th, 20th, and 34th wards of Pittsburgh, this line eventually producing my grandfather, James Aloysius Doyle, who with Sophia Holthaus produced another James Aloysius Doyle, my father, who with Ethel Clancey produced another James Aloysius Doyle, my brother, nicknamed Seamus, who died as a baby, my mother discovering him seemingly asleep in his stroller on a bright April morning in New York in 1946, which discovery plunged my parents into a great blackness, but eventually they recovered, as much as possible, and they made a daughter and four more sons, one of whom is named for Brian Boru, high king of Ireland until his last day at Clontarf.

26   Obituary notice in the *Morning Oregonian,* Thursday, May 22:

Brian Doyle, died May 16, age 42. Veteran, United States Army; spent last 15 years of life working as mail handler for United States Postal Service. Accomplished figure skater, competed for U.S. Olympic teams in 1976 and 1980. Gifts in his memory are to be sent to the St. Vincent de Paul Society, a Catholic organization that collects food and clothes for the poor.

27   What Brian died of the article does not say. Nor, for all the facts, does it say who he was. It doesn't say who or how he loved. It doesn't report the color of his eyes. It doesn't show the shape of his ambition, the tenor of his mind, the color of his sadness, the bark of his laugh.

It doesn't say with what grace or grace-lessness he bore his name, how he was carved by it, how his character and personality and the bounce in his step were shaped and molded by its ten letters, how he learned, slowly and painstakingly, to write as a child and so saw himself on paper, how he learned to pick the quick song of "Brian" out of the soup of sound swirling around him as an infant, how he sat in the first row at school because his surname began early in the alphabet, how other schoolchildren tried to edit and mangle and nick his name—Brian the Lion, Lying Brian, Oily Doyle, Lace Doyley—how he was fascinated as a small boy sitting at his grandmother's knee and watching her sew a lace doily, the word "doily" squirming in his mouth, his tongue tumbling over "Doyle" and "doily" for days afterward. Probably as a boy he added up the letters and admired the symmetry of his first and last names, as I did. Probably he spent a few moments, once, late on a rainy summer afternoon, bored, writing "Mrs. Brian Doyle" to see what it looked like, to hold the dangerous idea of a wife on paper for a moment, as I did. Probably he saw and heard his name misspelled, as we all did on applications and reports and certificates and letters and phone calls: Brain Doyel, Brian Dooley, Bryan Doyle, Brien Doyle, Brian Dalkey, even Brian Dahlia once, the woman at the other end of the scratchy phone doing her best to spell what she so dimly heard, to make real the faraway sound of a name.

QUESTIONS ON SUBJECT AND PURPOSE

1. How many Brian Doyles can you find in the essay? Count them.
2. To what extent is Brian Doyle, the author, the subject of the essay?
3. What purpose might the essay have? Is it simply a catalogue of some of the Brian Doyles in the United States?

QUESTIONS ON STRATEGY AND AUDIENCE

1. How did Doyle gather his information?
2. The last example in the essay is the obituary of a Brian Doyle. Why might Doyle choose to end with this example?
3. Only a few of Doyle's readers will be named "Brian Doyle." What assumptions must Doyle make about his readers and their potential interest in the essay?

QUESTIONS ON VOCABULARY AND STYLE

1. What does the title "Being Brians" suggest? When the essay was reprinted in *Harper's Magazine*, the title was changed to "The Lives of Brians." Which title do you like better? Why?
2. In paragraph 6, Doyle writes, "the rest of us soldier on being Brian Doyle." What do you call the expression "soldier on"? What does it mean?
3. Be prepared to define the following words: *flora* (paragraph 2), *fauna* (2), *bucolic* (3), *de rigueur* (3), *terse* (4).

WRITING SUGGESTIONS

1. **For Your Journal.** In your journal reflect on what your name means to you. Were you named for someone? What does your name suggest about you? Do you like your name? Why or why not?
2. **For a Paragraph.** Explore your own experiences with your name—in the past or the present. Focus on a single example. Do people mispronounce or misspell your name? Were you ever teased about it? Did it seem "too old" for you as a child, or "too young" for you now? Or is it perfect for you?
3. **For an Essay.** Use the paragraph writing as a starting point in an essay exploring your name. Where did it come from? Who chose it? Why? What does it mean? Look up your name in a dictionary of names. Run your name through a Web search engine. What do you find? Ask your parent(s). Use your own past experiences as a resource. What experiences have you had with it? Would you change it if you could? Why? Did you have a nickname? Where did it come from? Does it seem more like the "real" you?
4. **For Research.** How are children named in other cultures? Select either one culture or perhaps two quite different cultures and research how names are selected for children. How much variety is there? Are names always drawn from ancestors? Are names seen as symbolic? Are names always conventional? In your research you might want to do a number of interviews in addition to locating printed or on-line sources. Always be sure to document your sources carefully.

WEBSITE LINK

How many people in the United States share your name? You can start by doing a search on a Web directory such as "Switchboard." Visit the *Prentice Hall Reader* Website for some places to begin.

WRITING LINK: INTRODUCING QUOTATIONS

Much of the information in Doyle's essay comes from information provided by the other Brian Doyles in the United States. How does Doyle introduce these quotations? What consistent pattern does he use? What does this suggest about how to integrate quotations into your own essay?

ONE OF THE GIRLS
Leslie Heywood

Leslie Heywood (1964–), a former Division I track and cross country runner and currently a competitive powerlifter, is an associate professor of English and Cultural Studies at the State University of New York, Binghamton. She has an M.F.A. in poetry from the University of Arizona and a Ph.D. in English and Critical Theory from the University of California, Irvine. Her books include Bodymakers: A Cultural Anatomy of Women's Body Building *(1998) and* Pretty Good for a Girl: A Memoir *(1998), from which this selection is taken.*

The Preamble to Title IX of the Education Amendments of 1972 reads: "No person in the United States shall, on the basis of sex, be excluded from participation in, be denied the benefits of, or be subject to discrimination under any educational programs or activity receiving financial assistance." Among the many areas of gender inequality that Title IX has addressed are the opportunities for young women to participate in scholastic sports.

On Writing: *Asked about her writing habits, Heywood replied: "Some of my very best writing ideas come during a long run. Titles, an elusive piece of an argument, even a compelling voice often emerge in the cadence of my steps on a trail through the woods where there is nothing but quiet, deer, and wild turkeys. Something about physical movement, a steady heartbeat, the endorphin buzz, seems to catalyze my thinking."*

BEFORE READING

Connecting: The title of the book from which this essay is taken is *Pretty Good for a Girl.* Have you ever heard that phrase used in conversation? In what context might that expression be used? What does it seem to imply?

Anticipating: For Heywood, has it been enough just to provide equal opportunities for young women to participate in sports? Is anything more necessary?

1   When Gertrude Ederle swam the English Channel in 1926, two hours faster than any of the men who had preceded her, people began to think that women might not be so weak. Imagine her there, her hair cropped short like a flapper, looking into the water and say-

ing *I will.* Imagine the pull of the water that day, the fierceness of the currents, her fearlessness as she greased up. For her, unlike the world that followed her swim, it wasn't a question of whether she could but how fast she would do it. Not wavering a bit, she coats herself from head to foot and heads out. As her face touches water and she takes her first stroke, what she feels is how a wolf feels setting in for an all-day run: she feels right. Her hand passes high above the water with precision and she feels the currents, rolling her over the way they would rough up a boat. Her heart opens with joy, it will be a fight, her muscles pulling the water for hours while exhaustion sets in and she keeps moving. Nothing can stop her, not the manta rays whose tentacles leave a blistering kiss around her throat, not the weather so bad there is an advisory for boats. Twelve hours in, nervous to see the waver in her stroke, the way her arms dip and weave, the way she floats in the seconds in between, her companions pace the deck, lean over the water, cupping their hands in a shout. Gertrude, they say, you should stop. But they're speaking another language, live different lives in which a body doesn't ask itself to dig itself in, to rally, to find an energy that simply doesn't exist, to explode from that gray space of silence and dread into a muscle that is supple, feeling blood beginning to tingle again, ready to bear itself on, to the limit, to the limit, to feel what *is.* No, she says, I have to go.

Forty-one years later, Kathrine Switzer knew she could go the 26.2 miles it took to run the Boston Marathon, knew the feel of the hills and the wind on her skin, knew where she had to dig to scale that inevitable wall, rising at mile 18, when her muscles start to sag and her back is tight far beyond the pounding of her heart stabbing like scabby birch bark. From training runs, she knew the breathing it takes to soar over that wall, the way she had to close her mind to the creeping exhaustion contracting her back, the ache that spreads and spreads like shooting stars of blood rushing through a limb too long compressed, iron spikes between the shoulders. She knew she was up to it. Every day she rose in the morning longing for that ache and the strength that would break in lemon waves, electric. Many times her feet kept moving, still in stride, the air sharp through her lungs past startled pines and leafless maples, through snow and ice, then rain and glittering sleeves of summer green. And every time she scaled that wall and ran beyond those pressing hands along her spine, she opened up. Legs firm and sure, lungs silver-tanked, her strides taking the ground like a monster breathing. *I can do this. Here I am. Watch me run.* And Switzer wants to run like this in an official race, to see it, feel it measured. One for the girls, for the books.

3   But in 1967, women are not allowed to run. Still she needs to do it. She covers her body and her tracks. She enters the Boston Marathon, K. Switzer, number 261, and goes to the starting line thickened by sweats. A hooded head. No face. The gun goes off and she takes off with the pack, her training partners around her. They start at a decent pace, and breathing, settle in. The hood gathering her face and the top of her head makes her hot. Hothead. Sweat. Two miles in, she pushes it back, her chin-length hair falling free. She looks at her training partner and smiles. Her arms pump, her legs are steady.

4   But rushing at her from the corner is the race director, mid-sixties heavy in a long dark coat, stabbing his arms toward the number on her chest. *No girls allowed.* Her partner steps between them, and she pulls away, still running. They leave the race director behind. But then comes another, hips spread wide, rushing at her in heavy boots. Look at his lips curling back from his teeth, *a woman will not compete in this race, not ever, not if it is up to me.* His coat flies up as he grabs at her, his eyes narrowed to a slit. Her partner rushes between them again as Kathrine turns and slips away. For 24.2 more miles. Her heart beats even heavier, adrenaline strong. *I will do this.* And this time there is no wall rising at mile 18. This time, the four hours and twenty minutes it takes her to finish are a lime-long breeze. Pain in her ankles, ball joints of her hips, steel clamps on her neck, she breathes easy. Heart steadier than ever. When the newspapers mob the race director and ask him to speak, he says that he is "hurt to think that an American girl would go where she is not wanted. If that girl were my daughter I would spank her." So they turn to Switzer. Ask her why she runs. Because running makes her "strong, all there." It is another five years, 1972, before women are allowed to run, pound out the long roads laid by the still-grown trees. Stronger than strong. All there. They come. They run.

5   This is where I begin. Title IX of the Education Act of 1972, that law that made gender discrimination illegal, made athletes of millions of girls like me. No more female incompetence and physical weakness, *you throw like a girl, no girls allowed, why don't you just go home.* Not now, excuse me. Stepping out.

6   So now she is everywhere around us, staring back at you from the television screen, from women's magazines: a fierce babe with biceps, straight shoulders, a proud look, claiming the planet for her own. Gabby Reece. Lisa Leslie. Rebecca Lobo. Mia Hamm. She's given to us in blacks and in whites: you can see the stark beauty of her body like straight-line cords. She's no one you would mess with. She's someone you might like to become. She's beautiful. She's strong.

She's proud. She's doing it for herself: you project on her all the strength you've never felt, all the invulnerability you've never mustered, all the desire for self-sufficiency and completion you've never owned. She has it. You want it. Look closer.

Are you the one she's looking at when she asks if you'll let her play sports? Are you the one who'll prepare her to win? Are you the one who follows, looks, watches her step out and stride? If she lets you touch her, is it because she wants to be touched? What if she turned from her chiseled silhouette, poised, and looked you in the face? What if she could speak? What if she could tell you a story you haven't heard, not yet, what if the image of perfection took on some blood and began to tell you? Would you listen? Would you follow her voice like a glistening chime? Would her story take you over, overcome where you need her to stay—way up there pedestaled, just out of reach, an image of hope and a goal that you can become—sometime soon, next month or next week? But who is she? How does she live? What does she think about, what does she eat? Who touches her, who does she touch? Her muscles, her body, her pillars of strength—what's inside her? Is her life like yours, like your best friend's? Look closer. 7

There are some great Nike ads out there that are a gateway to my vanished world, where I used to win races and everyone knew. In the black-and-white images, dreams, possibilities beckon to girls, welcome them into the world. Sports can give us that place, but a lot of work needs to be done before we've finished that race. Female athletes fight the same unrealistic images everyone fights, and researchers are only beginning to understand the relationship between those images and the "female athlete triad"—eating disorders and exercise compulsion, amenorrhea—that had me training until my bones fractured, my tendons ripped, and I stuck my fingers down my throat or simply didn't eat to stay lean. Nobody's been quite loud enough in saying that the female athlete triad is almost surely connected to all the old negative ideas about girls—girls trying to prove beyond a shadow of a doubt that they are not what those ideas say they are: weak, mild, meek, meant to serve others instead of achieving for themselves. The ideas that made the race directors chase Kathrine Switzer away. 8

Are those ideas really gone? Let's face it—many of the images of female athletes out there are more about having a great butt or a great set of pecs than they are about winning races and feeling confident. If we really want a society where, as one of the young girls in the Nike ads says, "I can be anything I want to be," each of us will have to do everything we can to make this dream more than words 9 sliding easily out of the mouth. We need to make sure Title IX is enforced so that as many girls as possible have the opportunity to play sports. We need to make sure girls are treated as athletes, not just pretty girls. We need to continue the research that's been started on all the different aspects of girls' and women's lives, which shows sports' potential to give us a sense of competence and power—like that feeling deep in my lungs as, running by, I dared the very cacti not to see me.

10   Because national attention has turned to female athletes, because we are no longer disparaged or scorned, or seen as exceptions to the woman-as-weakness rule, I know some things now I didn't know then. I belonged to the first wave of women in sports after Title IX, part of the gathering wave that ballooned the stats from 300,000 girls in interscholastic athletics to the 2.25 million who play today. Is it really safe now? Can we begin to try out some of the new ideas about competing, ideas I was struggling with competing against Sheila in the gym? Can we smile at each other without being fake? Can we find ways to get out there, still swallowing the world, still roaring like Tarzan swinging mightily on his vines, and not have to knock everyone else off the vines just so it looks like we're the one who soars best? Can we move toward what, in her new book, *Embracing Victory*, Mariah Burton Nelson names "the Champion" model of competition, which "respects all contestants, including the self"?

11   The old competitive model—what I did—led many of us from an earlier generation to the female athlete triad, and we missed out on the true benefits of sports. Can we revise people's ideas about girls enough so that my ghost will give up having to prove herself, and the other girls running in her place won't have to erase whole worlds inside themselves just so someone will notice them, just so they can stand out and win?

12   In spite of everything that happened I continued in sport. I knew instinctively what research is proving now: sports, if not played in the way I did, where everyone around you had to be stomped out with boots to their face because there was only one winner and it had to be you—if played a little differently than this, sports help with depression. They help with what the books call self-esteem: feeling the sun on your warm face, walking across the field like a giant, feeling that just for a moment, the world belongs to you.

13   Running and lifting are as much a part of my life as is the quiet in-and-out of my steady chest. I write this book with hopes that other girls will have some support I didn't have and won't make the same mistakes. So here's to many, many more women's hockey teams and

Picabo Streets—and to the women and men who'll work hard to make it possible for every young girl to burn bright as the sun without paying the price of self-destruction. And then when there are girls all around who are stronger and with better biceps than me, well, I just might be able to deal with it.

QUESTIONS ON SUBJECT AND PURPOSE

1. For Heywood, what benefits do sports hold for women?
2. Did Heywood herself only experience benefits from competing in sports? Were there any drawbacks or problems?
3. This essay forms the final chapter or epilogue to Heywood's memoir. What final thoughts does she want to leave with her reader?

QUESTIONS ON STRATEGY AND AUDIENCE

1. Why might Heywood have titled the essay "One of the Girls"?
2. Paragraph 7 is composed entirely of rhetorical questions—questions that provoke thought rather than require response. Specifically, to whom are those questions addressed? Define that "you."
3. As the headnote explains, this essay appeared in her memoir, not a magazine. What assumptions might Heywood have made about a book-reading audience rather than a magazine-reading audience?

QUESTIONS ON VOCABULARY AND STYLE

1. When Heywood writes of the "blistering kiss" (paragraph 1) of the manta ray or the "ache that spreads . . . like shooting stars of blood" (2), what type of language is she using?
2. In narrating Ederle's swim and Switzer's run, Heywood shifts to the present tense (for example, "she takes her first stroke" or "she takes off with the pack") rather than the past tense ("took"), even though the events occurred in the past. Why tell the story in this way?
3. Be prepared to define the following words: *flapper* (1), *supple* (1), *glistening* (7), *amenorrhea* (8), *disparaged* (10).

WRITING SUGGESTIONS

1. **For Your Journal.** How do you view women athletes? Are your images only positive? Do you stereotype women athletes? In your journal explore that idea—with reference to yourself (if you are a woman athlete) or to others.

2. **For a Paragraph.** How does our society seem to view women athletes? Look for advertisements, for example, that depict women athletes. Are they depicted in the same way as male athletes are? For a paragraph writing, pick a particular advertisement and explore the image that is projected.

3. **For an Essay.** Extend your analysis of the depiction of women athletes in our culture into an essay. If you are using advertisements, make sure that you gather them from a range of magazines. You might also use other visual examples—film, television, photographs, or drawings illustrating articles.

4. **For Research.** How did Title IX influence the women's athletic program at your school? Visit the Athletic Department and your school's library and archives and research the development of women's athletics since 1972. Then using that research—with specific facts and appropriate quotations—write an essay in which you trace that impact. Be sure to document your sources. You might want to submit your final paper to your school's newspaper for possible publication.

 WEBSITE LINK

What impact has Title IX of the Educational Amendments had on the education (not just sports participation) of young women in the United States? It's pretty amazing—see for yourself.

 WRITING LINK: SENTENCE FRAGMENTS

What is the difference between a sentence fragment and a sentence? How many fragments can you find in Heywood's essay? Are they intentional or unintentional? Why might she use them if she knows that they are fragments? What is the danger in using fragments in your writing?

PREWRITING SUGGESTIONS FOR GATHERING AND USING EXAMPLES

1. Don't try to rush the example gathering stage of your prewriting. Good writing depends upon good examples—quality is more important than quantity. Before sitting down to write, try to spend a day just jotting down examples.

2. Depending on your topic, examples can come from personal experience, from interviews with sources, or from information gathered in printed or on-line sources. Think about where you might find the best examples and remember that finding examples often requires research on your part.

3. Remember that the examples you select are chosen for a reason: to support a point or a thesis that you are making. On a separate sheet of paper, jot down each example and then next to it explain in a sentence how the example supports the larger point you are trying to make.

4. Think about possible ways in which the examples in your essay can be ordered or organized. If you are narrating an event, do you use a chronological order or a flashback? If you are using examples to support an argument, do you start with your strongest example or end with it? Make an organizational strategy for your essay.

5. Plan an opening strategy for your essay—maybe you will start with a vivid example or maybe with a statement of your thesis. Your opening paragraph is really important since that is where you will either catch your readers or lose them.

REWRITING SUGGESTIONS FOR GATHERING AND USING EXAMPLES

1. If you are writing about yourself, it is especially important to keep your readers interested. They need to feel how significant this experience was. Do not just tell them; show them. One way to do this is to dramatize the experience, to tell it as if it were happening at that moment. Did you?

2. Arrange your examples in a variety of ways—you can cut and paste to get different arrangements. Which order seems to work best? Consider your alternatives. Don't just assume that your essay can be assembled in only one way.

3. How effective is your conclusion? Do you just stop? Do you just repeat in slightly altered words what you said in your introduction? Brainstorm another different way in which to end.

4. If you interviewed people in your research or if you used information from printed or on-line sources, make sure that you punctuated your quotations properly and that you documented those sources (check the Appendix for guidelines on both).

5. Find someone to read your essay—a friend, roommate, classmate, or tutor in a writing center. Ask your reader for some constructive criticism, and listen to what you hear.

NARRATION

Once upon a time . . .
Did you hear the one about?
What did you two do last night?
Well, officer, it was like this . . .
What happened at the Battle of Gettysburg?

What follows each of those lines is a story or a narrative. All stories, whether they are personal experiences, jokes, novels, histories, films, or television serials, have the same essential ingredients: a series of events arranged in a chosen order and told by a narrator for some particular purpose.

On the simplest level, all stories are made up of three elements:

beginning (the initiating action)	
middle	**PLOT**
end (the concluding action)	

As these terms suggest, stories are told in time—the fundamental arrangement of those events is chronological. But stories do not always begin at the beginning. The time order of events can be rearranged by using flashbacks. Stories can begin with the last event in the chronological sequence or with any event that falls into the middle.

Stories also involve tellers, or narrators, who relate the story. The narrators of stories almost always either tell the story themselves ("I"—a first-person point of view) or tell the story as an observer (a third-person point of view).

First person ("I was saved from sin when I was going on thirteen.")	**POINT**
Third person ("One of the captains of the high school football team had something big he wanted to tell the other players.")	**OF** **VIEW**

Finally, stories have a purpose, a reason for being told, and that purpose controls the narrative and its selection of detail. As you start to write your narrative, always ask yourself what point you are trying to make. Force yourself to finish the following statement:

I am telling this story because _____.   **PURPOSE**

Any type of writing can use narration; it is not something found only in personal experience essays or in fiction. Narration can also be used as examples to support a thesis, as Bob Greene does in "Cut" (Chapter 1) where he provides five personal narratives to support his assertion that being cut from an athletic team can make a person a superachiever later in life. Narration can also be found mixed with description in William Least Heat Moon's "Nameless, Tennessee" (Chapter 3) or underlying a persuasive argument in Richard Rodriguez's "None of This Is Fair" (Chapter 9). In fact, you can find examples of narration in readings throughout this text.

What Do You Include in a Narrative?

> Just tell me what happened!
> Get to the punch line!

No one, probably not even your mother, wants to hear everything you did today. Readers, like listeners, want you to be selective, for some things are more important or interesting than others. Historians have to select out of a mass of data what they will include and emphasize; they have to choose a place to begin and a place to end. Even in relating personal experiences, you must condense and select. Generally, you need to pare away, to cut out the unnecessary and the uninteresting. What you include depends, of course, on what happened and, more important, on the purpose or meaning that you are trying to convey.

Maya Angelou's story of "Sister Monroe" actually blends two experiences, widely separated in time, into a single story. The story opens on a Sunday morning in church, but Sister Monroe's comic performance does not occur on that morning. Once the initial story is underway, Angelou shifts to an earlier point in time, on a morning when Sister Monroe seized Reverend Taylor ("once she [Sister Monroe] hadn't been to church for a few months . . . she got the spirit and started shouting"). Angelou focuses our attention on the significant action—she doesn't relate every event that occurred.

HOW DO YOU STRUCTURE A NARRATIVE?

Time structures all narratives, although events need not always be arranged in chronological order. A narrative can begin at one point in time and then "flash back" to an earlier action or event. Langston Hughes's "Salvation" begins with a narrator looking back at an experience that occurred when he was thirteen, although the story itself is told in the order in which it happened. The most typical inversion is to begin at the end of the narrative and then to move backward in time to explain how that end was reached. More complex narratives may shift several times back and forth between incidents in the past or between the past and the present. Two cautions are obvious: first, do not switch time too frequently, especially in short papers; second, make sure that any switches you make are clearly marked for your readers.

Remember as well that you control where your narrative begins and ends. For example, Evans Hopkins begins "Lockdown" with a predawn visit from two prison guards in armored vests and riot helmets; he does not begin with an account of the events that led to the lockdown or with the events that led to his imprisonment. Those details Hopkins fills in later, for they are not as dramatic or central to the points that he is trying to make. In a similar way, you might want to build your narrative to a climactic moment of insight that concludes the story. A formal, summary conclusion tacked on to a narrative essay sometimes actually obscures the significance of the experience.

Writers frequently change or modify an actual personal experience in order to tell the story more effectively, heighten the tension, or make their purpose clearer. In her essay "On Keeping a Notebook," essayist and novelist Joan Didion remarks:

> I tell what some would call lies. "That's simply not true," the members of my family frequently tell me when they come up against my memory of a shared event. "The party was *not* for you, the spider was *not* a black widow, *it wasn't that way at all.*" Very likely they are right, for not only have I always had trouble distinguishing between what happened and what merely might have happened, but I remain unconvinced that the distinction, for my purposes, matters.

"*It's plotted out. I just have to write it.*"

Keep your plots simple. Do not approach your construction of plot like this writer. © *The New Yorker Collection 1996 Charles Barsotti from cartoonbank.com. All Rights Reserved.*

Whenever you recall an experience, even if it happened last week, you do not necessarily remember it exactly as it occurred. The value of a personal narrative does not rest on relating the original experience with absolute accuracy. It does not matter, for example, whether the scene with Sister Monroe in the Christian Methodist Episcopal Church occurred exactly as Maya Angelou describes it years later. What does matter is that it could have happened as she describes it and that it is faithful to Angelou's purpose.

HOW ARE NARRATIVES TOLD?

Two things are especially important in relating your narrative. First, you need to choose a point of view from which to tell the story. Personal experience narratives, such as those by Hughes, Angelou, and Hopkins, are generally told in the first person: the narrator is an actor in the story. Historical narratives and narratives used as illustrations in a larger piece of writing are generally told in the third person. The historian or the reporter, for example, stands outside the narrative and provides an objective view of the actions described. Rick Reilly describes the coming out experience of high school football player Corey Johnson as a narrator outside of the story—this is what happened to this person, Reilly is saying. In "Marina" Judith Ortiz Cofer mixes first-person and third-person narration. The essay begins with a first-person account of how she and her mother went for a walk after an argument. They encounter a distinguished older gentleman with a little girl, and that meeting leads to the "story within the story," the tale of Marina and Kiki, which Cofer narrates in the third person. Once that story is finished, Cofer returns to the first person as she and her mother ponder the significance of the tale. Point of view can vary in one other way. The narrator can reveal only his or her own thoughts (using what is known as the limited point of view), or the narrator can reveal what anyone else in the narrative thinks or feels (using the omniscient, or all-knowing, point of view).

Second, you need to decide whether you are going to "show" or "tell" or mix the two. You "show" in a narrative by dramatizing a scene and creating dialogue. Hughes re-creates his experience for the reader by showing what happened and by recording some of the conversation that took place the night he was "saved from sin." Telling, by contrast, is summarizing what happened. For example, the story of Marina and Kiki in Cofer's "Marina" is told to the reader by the narrator. Marina and Kiki never talk; the story within the story contains no dialogue. Showing makes a narrative more vivid, for it allows the reader to experience the scene directly. Telling allows you to include a greater number of events and details. Either way, selectivity is necessary. Even when the experience being narrated took place over a short period of time—such as Hughes's experiences one evening at church—a writer cannot dramatize everything that happened. When an experience lasts four-and-a-half months, as does the lockdown Hopkins describes, a writer could never summarize events on a day-to-day basis. Each writer selects the moments that best give shape and significance to the experience.

WHAT DO YOU WRITE ABOUT IF NOTHING EVER HAPPENED TO YOU?

It is easy to assume that the only things worth writing about are once-in-a-lifetime experiences—a heroic or death-defying act, a personal tragedy, an Olympic medal-winning performance. It is likely that few readers have been in a lockdown in a prison, and probably not many have heard a tale like that of Marina and Kiki; but a good personal narrative does not need to be based on an extraordinary experience. In fact, ordinary experiences, because they are about things familiar to every reader, are often the best sources for personal narratives. There is nothing extraordinary, for example, about the events Langston Hughes relates in "Salvation," even though Hughes's experience was a turning point in his life. Bob Greene in "Cut" (Chapter 1) narrates the kind of story—about being "cut" from a team—that is all too familiar to most readers; in one way or another, probably everyone has experienced a similar rejection and subsequent disappointment.

The secret to writing an effective personal narrative is twofold. First, you must tell your story artfully, following the advice outlined in this chapter's introduction. Simply relating what happened is not enough, however, for you must do a second, equally important thing: you must reveal a purpose in your tale. Purposes can be many. You might offer insight into human behavior or motivation; you might mark a significant moment in your life; you might reveal an awareness of what it is to be young and to have dreams; you might reflect on the precariousness of life and inevitability of change and decay; you might even use your experience to argue, as Evans Hopkins does, for a change in social attitudes. However you use your narrative, what is important is that your story have a point, a reason for being, and that you make that reason clear to your reader.

SAMPLE STUDENT ESSAY

Hope Zucker decided to write about a powerful childhood memory—a pair of red shoes that became her "ruby slippers" and the key to the Land of Oz.

EARLIER DRAFT

MY NEW SHOES

When you are four years old anything longer than five minutes feels like eternity, so when the clerk told me and my mom that it would take three to four weeks for my new shoes to arrive, I was almost in tears. Since seeing *The Wizard of Oz,* I had thought of little else other than owning a pair of ruby slippers. My dreams were full of spinning houses, little munchkins, flying monkeys, and talking lions. All I wanted was to be Dorothy, and the shoe store had made a promise to find me a pair of red mary-janes which would hopefully take me to Munchkin Land and Oz.

For the next three weeks I made all the preparations I could think of in order to become Dorothy. It did not matter how convincing Judy Garland was because I knew in my heart that I was the true Dorothy. I sang "Somewhere Over the Rainbow" day and night, and I played dress up with an old light blue checked dress of my mother's. I even went as far as to carry my dog in a basket, but that did not work out too well. I had my mom braid my long brown hair, and after I insisted, she tied a light blue ribbon around each braid. I skipped wherever I went, and I even went as far as coloring part of our driveway with chalk to create my very own yellow brick road.

The only thing missing to my new persona was my ruby slippers. After my mother explained to me that three weeks really was not that far off in the future, I decided to help the store in their search for my red mary-janes. For a month I called the store everyday when I got home from preschool. Mr. Rogers and Big Bird could wait because there was nothing in the whole wide world that was more important than my red patent leather shoes. By the end of the month, the nice little old ladies at the store knew me by name and thought that I was the cutest child. Lucky for them, they did not have to put up with me.

Finally, after what seemed like years, the lady on the other side of the phone said that yes, my shiny red shoes had arrived. Now I had only to plead with my mother to get her to make a special trip into the city. After a few days of delay and a great deal of futile temper tantrums, my mom took me to the store. I could hardly contain my excitement. During the ride, I practiced the one and only line that only the real Dorothy could say, "There's no place like home." And of course, I clicked my beat up boondockers three times each time I recited my part. It was all practice for the real thing.

As we pulled into the parking lot, all the little old ladies inside the store waved to me as if they had been expecting me for days. I finally got to see my shoes, and they were as perfect as I knew they'd be. I was practically jumping out of my seat when she began to remove the stiff tissue paper surrounding my shoes, so rather than wait for her to fit my little feet into my slippers, I grabbed them from her and did it myself. They were the prettiest pair of shoes any girl could have!

For the next few weeks I was Dorothy and I'd stop everyone I'd see in order to prove it by tapping my heels together and saying, "There's no place like home." But soon my feet grew too big for my ruby slippers, and as I graduated into the next larger size, I no longer wanted to be Dorothy. As I grew up, so did my dreams. Cinderella, now she was someone to be! Yet, once again that phase, like the phases I am going through now, passed fairly quickly.

Hope made enough copies of her essay so that the whole class could read and then discuss it. After reading her essay to the class, Hope asked her classmates for their reactions. Several students suggested that she tighten her narrative, eliminating details that were not essential to the story. Most of their suggestions were centered in paragraphs 4 and 5. "Why mention Mr. Rogers and Big Bird?" someone asked. "I didn't want you to have to wait several days to pick them up, and I didn't want to be reminded of your temper," commented another. When Hope came to revise her draft, she used this advice. She also eliminated a number of clichés and made a significant change in the ending of the paper. Notice how much more effective the final version is as the result of these minor revisions.

REVISED DRAFT

THE RUBY SLIPPERS

To a four-year old, anything longer than five minutes feels like eternity, so when the clerk told me and my mom that it would take three to four weeks for my new shoes to arrive, I was almost in tears. Since seeing <u>The Wizard of Oz,</u> I had thought of little else other than owning a pair of ruby slippers. My dreams were full of spinning houses, little munchkins, flying monkeys, and talking lions. All I wanted was to be Dorothy, and the shoe store had made a promise to find me a pair of red mary-janes which would hopefully take me to Munchkin Land and Oz.

For the next three weeks I made all the preparations I could think of in order to become Dorothy. It did not matter how convincing Judy Garland was because I knew in my heart that I was the true Dorothy. I sang "Somewhere Over the Rainbow" day and night, and I played dress up with an old light blue checked dress of my mother's. I even went as far as to carry my dog in a basket. My mom braided my long brown hair, and after I insisted, she tied a light blue ribbon around each braid. I skipped everywhere I went and colored part of our driveway with chalk to create my very own yellow brick road.

The only thing missing was my ruby slippers. After my mother explained that three weeks really was not that far off, I decided to help the store in their search for my red mary-janes. For a month I called the store everyday when I got home from preschool. By the end of the month, the ladies at the store knew me by name.

Finally, the woman on the other end of the phone said that yes, my shiny red shoes had arrived. I could hardly contain my excitement. During the ride, I practiced the one line that only the real Dorothy could say, "There's no place like home." And of course, I clicked my beat up loafers three times each time I recited that line. It was all practice for the real thing.

As we pulled into the parking lot, all the ladies inside the store waved to me as if they had been expecting me. I finally got to see my shoes, and they were as perfect as I had imagined. I was practically jumping out of my seat when she began to remove the stiff tissue paper surrounding my shoes, so rather than wait for her to fit my little feet into my slippers, I grabbed them from her and did it myself. They were the prettiest pair of shoes any girl could have!

For the next few weeks I was Dorothy and I'd stop everyone I'd see in order to prove it by tapping my heels together and saying, "There's no place like home." But soon my feet grew too big for my ruby slippers, and as I graduated into the next larger size, I no longer wanted to be Dorothy. As I grew up, so did my dreams.

SOME THINGS TO REMEMBER

1. Decide first why you are telling the reader *this* story. You must have a purpose clearly in mind.
2. Choose an illustration, event, or experience that can be covered adequately within the space limitations you face. Do not try to narrate the history of your life in an essay!
3. Decide on which point of view you will use. Do you want to be a part of the narrative or an objective observer? Which is more appropriate for your purpose?
4. Keeping your purpose in mind, select the details or events that seem the most important or the most revealing.
5. Arrange those details in an order—either a strict chronological one or one that employs a flashback. Remember to keep your verb tenses consistent and to signal any switches in time.
6. Remember the differences between showing and telling. Which method will be better for your narrative?

VISUALIZING NARRATION

Narratives do not always involve or even require words. Visual sequences can also tell stories—remember that the earliest films were silent! Comic or cartoon strips, comic books, and graphic novels all involve narration. Here cartoonist Roz Chast has fun with a story "template" (a pattern). Think how many stories can ultimately be reduced to the pattern—"once upon a time," "suddenly," "luckily," and "happily ever after." Notice how the panel exhibits the characteristics of a narrative—a series of events arranged in a chronological order told (shown) by a narrator (artist) for some particular purpose (to entertain). See page 97.

NARRATION AS A LITERARY STRATEGY

All stories—whether they are personal essays, imaginative fictions, journalistic reports, or histories—contain the same essential ingredients: a series of events arranged in an order structured through time recounted by a "narrator" for some particular purpose. Narratives can range from hundreds, even thousands, of pages to only a single paragraph. Peggy McNally's short story "Waiting" is an example of what is called "micro fiction," a genre that is limited to a maximum of 250 words. See page 98.

WAITING

Peggy McNally

Five days a week the lowest-paid substitute teacher in the district drives her father's used Mercury to Hough and 79th, where she eases it, mud flaps and all, down the ramp into the garage of Patrick Henry Junior High, a school where she'll teach back-to-back classes without so much as a coffee break and all of this depressing her until she remembers her date last night, and hopes it might lead to bigger things, maybe love, so she quickens her pace towards the main office to pick up her class lists with the names of students she'll never know as well as she has come to know the specials in the cafeteria, where she hopes the coffee will be perking and someone will have brought in those donuts she has come to love so much, loves more than the idea of teaching seventh-graders the meaning of a poem, because after all she's a sub who'll finish her day, head south to her father's house, and at dinner, he'll ask her how her job is going, and she'll say okay, and he'll remind her that it might lead to a full-position with benefits but she knows what teaching in that school is like, and her date from last night calls to ask if she's busy and she says yes because she's promised her father she'd wash his car and promises to her father are sacred since her mother died, besides it is the least she can do now that he lets her drive his car five days a week towards the big lake, to the NE corner of Hough and 79th and you know the rest.

DISCUSSION QUESTIONS

1. McNally composes her story as a single sentence. Why might she have chosen to do this? How does the story's form (as a single sentence) relate to what is occurring in the story?

2. The story contains a number of details, yet the woman is never named. Why is she nameless?

3. Who narrates the story? Why might this point of view be used? What would happen if the point of view were changed?

4. Stories have beginnings, middles, and ends. Is there an end to McNally's story? What shape does the story seem to take and why? How is that shape appropriate to what happens in the story?

5. What central impression does the story leave in your mind?

WRITING SUGGESTIONS

Often we find ourselves locked into repetitive patterns, small daily or weekly cycles that define us. Think about a pattern that you see in your own life. In a short personal essay, narrate that cycle for your readers. You don't need to use McNally's story as a structural model; you can narrate the story from the first person, and you can include dialogue if you wish. Remember, though, to have a purpose for your narrative. What does the pattern reveal about you? As a possible starting point, you might consider the following:

a. A bad (or good) habit or behavior

b. Situations in which you know how you will always react

c. An endless quarrel or disagreement

Using Narration in Writing for Your Other Courses

Various kinds of college writing assignments will require you to use narration, at least in part. Most of these will involve third-person narration rather than first-person experiential writing—although you may occasionally be asked to write about your own experiences as a means of exploring particular issues raised in a course. Here are some examples of assignments that would include narration.

- **Chemistry.** In a lab report discussing the results of an experimental procedure, in one section you would objectively recount the method used in conducting the procedure.

- **History/American Studies.** For an oral history project, you might be asked to interview a senior family member or another older person to relate that person's experiences during an important period of history.

- **Education.** For an assignment asking you to observe and report on child development during the first-grade, you might write up a final case study tracing the progress of the particular child you observed over the first three months of school.

- **Engineering.** In completing a project studying the viability of replacing a less expensive lubricant for the one currently used in particular manufacturing process, you might be assigned an interim report tracing your progress in testing and evaluating other lubricants.

- **Literature.** In studying a short story, you might be asked to write a creative response, retelling the story from the perspective of a character different from the original narrator.
- **Communications.** For an essay exam question, you might be asked to trace the development of the American broadcast industry.

VISIT THE PRENTICE HALL READER'S WEBSITE

When you have finished reading an essay, check out the additional material available at the *Reader*'s Website at www.prenhall. com/ miller. For each reading, you will find a list of related readings connected with the topic or the author; additional background information; a group of relevant "hot-linked" Web resources (just click on the site you want to visit); and still more writing suggestions.

NARRATING

Have you ever visited the National Air and Space Museum in Washington, D.C.? Did you know that it is increasingly possible to "see" museum exhibits on-line? Visit one of the on-line exhibitions now available at the National Air and Space. The site is hot-linked at the *Reader*'s Website and is just a click away. Once you have seen the exhibit, practice your narration skills with the paragraph-writing assignment.

SALVATION

Langston Hughes

Born in Joplin, Missouri, Langston Hughes (1902–1967) was an important figure in the Harlem Renaissance. He is best known for his jazz- and blues-inspired poetry, though he was also a talented prose writer and playwright. Among his writings are Simple Speaks His Mind *(1950), the first of four volumes of some of his best-loved stories; and* Ask Your Mama: 12 Moods for Jazz *(1961), one of his later, angry collections of poetry, fueled by emotions surrounding the civil rights movements.*

The Big Sea: An Autobiography *(1940), published when Hughes was thirty-eight years old, is a memoir of his early years, consisting of a series of short narratives focusing on events and people. After the death of his grandmother, Hughes was raised by Auntie Reed, one of his grandmother's friends. Uncle Reed, Auntie's husband, was, as Hughes notes in* The Big Sea, *"a sinner and never went to church as long as he lived . . . but both of them were very good and kind. . . . And no doubt from them I learned to like both Christians and sinners equally well."*

On Writing: *Hughes once noted that, to him, the prime function of creative writing is "to affirm life, to yeah-say the excitement of living in relation to the vast rhythms of the universe of which we are a part, to untie the riddles of the gutter in order to closer tie the knot between man and God."*

BEFORE READING

Connecting: Was there a time in your teenage years when you were disappointed by someone or something?

Anticipating: No narrative recounts every minute of an experience. Writers must leave out far more than they include. What events connected with this experience does Hughes leave out of his narrative? Why?

I was saved from sin when I was going on thirteen. But not really   1
saved. It happened like this. There was a big revival at my Auntie Reed's church. Every night for weeks there had been much preaching, singing, praying, and shouting, and some very hardened sinners had been brought to Christ, and the membership of the church had grown by leaps and bounds. Then just before the revival ended, they

held a special meeting for children, "to bring the young lambs to the fold." My aunt spoke of it for days ahead. That night I was escorted to the front row and placed on the mourners' bench with all the other young sinners, who had not yet been brought to Jesus.

2   My aunt told me that when you were saved you saw a light, and something happened to you inside! And Jesus came into your life! And God was with you from then on! She said you could see and hear and feel Jesus in your soul. I believed her. I had heard a great many old people say the same thing and it seemed to me they ought to know. So I sat there calmly in the hot, crowded church, waiting for Jesus to come to me.

3   The preacher preached a wonderful rhythmical sermon, all moans and shouts and lonely cries and dire pictures of hell, and then he sang a song about the ninety and nine safe in the fold, but one little lamb was left out in the cold. Then he said: "Won't you come? Won't you come to Jesus? Young lambs, won't you come?" And he held out his arms to all us young sinners there on the mourners' bench. And the little girls cried. And some of them jumped up and went to Jesus right away. But most of us just sat there.

4   A great many old people came and knelt around us and prayed, old women with jet-black faces and braided hair, old men with work-gnarled hands. And the church sang a song about the lower lights are burning, some poor sinners to be saved. And the whole building rocked with prayer and song.

5   Still I kept waiting to *see* Jesus.

6   Finally all the young people had gone to the altar and were saved, but one boy and me. He was a rounder's son named Westley. Westley and I were surrounded by sisters and deacons praying. It was very hot in the church, and getting late now. Finally Westley said to me in a whisper: "God damn! I'm tired o' sitting here. Let's get up and be saved." So he got up and was saved.

7   Then I was left all alone on the mourner's bench. My aunt came and knelt at my knees and cried, while prayers and song swirled all around me in the little church. The whole congregation prayed for me alone, in a mighty wail of moans and voices. And I kept waiting serenely for Jesus, waiting, waiting—but he didn't come. I wanted to see him, but nothing happened to me. Nothing! I wanted something to happen to me, but nothing happened.

8   I heard the songs and the minister saying: "Why don't you come? My dear child, why don't you come to Jesus? Jesus is waiting for you. He wants you. Why don't you come? Sister Reed, what is this child's name?"

9   "Langston," my aunt sobbed.

"Langston, why don't you come? Why don't you come and be   10
saved? Oh, Lamb of God! Why don't you come?"

Now it was really getting late. I began to be ashamed of myself,   11
holding everything up so long. I began to wonder what God thought
about Westley, who certainly hadn't seen Jesus either, but who was
now sitting proudly on the platform, swinging his knickerbockered
legs and grinning down at me, surrounded by deacons and old women
on their knees praying. God had not struck Westley dead for taking
his name in vain or for lying in the temple. So I decided that maybe
to save further trouble, I'd better lie, too, and say that Jesus had come,
and get up and be saved.

So I got up.   12

Suddenly the whole room broke into a sea of shouting, as they   13
saw me rise. Waves of rejoicing swept the place. Women leaped in the
air. My aunt threw her arms around me. The minister took me by the
hand and led me to the platform.

When things quieted down, in a hushed silence, punctuated by   14
a few ecstatic "Amens," all the new young lambs were blessed in the
name of God. Then joyous singing filled the room.

That night, for the last time in my life but one—for I was a big   15
boy twelve years old—I cried. I cried, in bed alone, and couldn't stop.
I buried my head under the quilts, but my aunt heard me. She woke
up and told my uncle I was crying because the Holy Ghost had come
into my life, and because I had seen Jesus. But I was really crying because I couldn't bear to tell her that I had lied, that I had deceived
everybody in the church, that I hadn't seen Jesus, and that now I
didn't believe there was a Jesus any more, since he didn't come to help
me.

QUESTIONS ON SUBJECT AND PURPOSE

1. Who narrates the story? From what point in time is it told?
2. What does the narrator expect to happen when he is to be
   saved? What does happen?
3. Why does the narrator cry at the end of the story?
4. What was Hughes's attitude toward his experience when it
   first happened? At the time he originally wrote this selection?
   How does the opening sentence reflect that change in
   attitude?

QUESTIONS ON STRATEGY AND AUDIENCE

1. Why did Hughes not tell the story in the present tense? How would doing so change the story?
2. How much dialogue is used in the narration? Why does Hughes not use more?
3. Why does Hughes blend telling with showing in the story?
4. How much time is represented by the events in the story? Where does Hughes compress the time in his narrative? Why does he do so?

QUESTIONS ON VOCABULARY AND STYLE

1. What is the effect of the short paragraphs (5, 9, and 12)? How does Hughes use paragraphing to help shape his story?
2. How much description does Hughes include in his narrative? What types of details does he single out?
3. What is the effect of the exclamation marks used in paragraph 2?
4. Try to identify or explain the following phrases: *the ninety and nine safe in the fold* (paragraph 3), *the lower lights are burning* (4), *a rounder's son* (6), *knickerbockered legs* (11).

WRITING SUGGESTIONS

1. **For Your Journal.** What can you remember from your early teenage years? In your journal, first make a list of significant moments—both high and low points—and then re-create one moment in prose.
2. **For a Paragraph.** We have all been disappointed by someone or something in our life. Single out a particular moment from your past. After spending some time remembering what happened and how you felt, narrate that experience for a general reader in a paragraph. Remember that your paragraph must reveal what the experience meant to you. Try using some dialogue.
3. **For an Essay.** Have you ever experienced anything that changed your life? It does not need to be a dramatic change—

perhaps just a conviction that you will *never* do that again or that you will *always* be sure to do that again. In an essay, narrate for a reader that experience. Remember that your narrative should illustrate or prove the experience's significance to you.

4. **For Research.** Does Hughes seem to be serious about his experience—did he "lose" his faith as a result of what happened? Find other examples of Hughes's writing (check your college's library catalog for books by Hughes and perhaps also some of the on-line databases). Then, in an essay, analyze the significance (or insignificance) of this event in Hughes's writing. Be sure to formulate an explicit thesis about the importance of the event in Hughes's work. Be sure to document any direct quotations or information taken from other sources.

 WEBSITE LINK

Did you think that the episode that Hughes narrates in the essay actually happened? Did you think it really did become a memory that Hughes never forgot? Check out the biographical background for the essay at the Website.

 WRITING LINK: ADJECTIVES AND ADVERBS

First, be sure you can identify adjectives and adverbs. Then go through Hughes's narrative and make a list of all of the adjectives and adverbs that you can find. Are there as many as you expected? Sometimes we assume that vividness in writing comes from using many adjectives and adverbs. Is that true here? What parts of speech make Hughes's narrative vivid? What does that suggest about writing narration and description?

SISTER MONROE

Maya Angelou

Maya Angelou was born Marguerita Johnson in St. Louis, Missouri, in 1928. A talented performing artist as well as a poet and autobiographer, Angelou has used much of her writing to explore the American black female identity. Her most significant writings have been her six volumes of autobiography (1970–2002).

The following selection is from the first of Angelou's memoirs, I Know Why the Caged Bird Sings *(1970), a work that describes her early years in Stamps, Arkansas. One critic called that work a "revealing portrait of the customs and harsh circumstances of black life in the segregated South." Here in a brilliantly comic moment, Angelou recalls how Sister Monroe "got the spirit" one Sunday morning at church.*

On Writing: *In an interview about her goals as a writer, Angelou observed: "When I'm writing, I am trying to find out who I am, who we are, what we're capable of, how we feel, how we lose and stand up. . . . But I'm also trying for the language. I'm trying to see how it can really sound. I really love language. I love it for what it does for us, how it allows us to explain the pain and the glory, the nuances and delicacies of our existence. And then it allows us to laugh. . . . We need language."*

BEFORE READING

Connecting: As a spectator, when do you find a physical mishap, such as a fight or fall, comic? What is necessary for us to laugh at "slapstick comedy" and not be concerned about the welfare of the people involved?

Anticipating: How does Angelou create humor in this narrative? What makes it funny?

1   In the Christian Methodist Episcopal Church the children's section was on the right, cater-cornered from the pew that held those ominous women called the Mothers of the Church. In the young people's section the benches were placed close together, and when a child's legs no longer comfortably fitted in the narrow space, it was an indication to the elders that that person could now move into the intermediate area (center church). Bailey and I were allowed to sit with the

other children only when there were informal meetings, church socials or the like. But on the Sundays when Reverend Thomas preached, it was ordained that we occupy the first row, called the mourners' bench. I thought we were placed in front because Momma was proud of us, but Bailey assured me that she just wanted to keep her grandchildren under her thumb and eye.

Reverend Thomas took his text from Deuteronomy. And I was   2 stretched between loathing his voice and wanting to listen to the sermon. Deuteronomy was my favorite book in the Bible. The laws were so absolute, so clearly set down, that I knew if a person truly wanted to avoid hell and brimstone, and being roasted forever in the devil's fire, all she had to do was memorize Deuteronomy and follow its teaching, word for word. I also liked the way the word rolled off the tongue.

Bailey and I sat alone on the front bench, the wooden slats   3 pressing hard on our behinds and the backs of our thighs. I would have wriggled just a bit, but each time I looked over at Momma, she seemed to threaten, "Move and I'll tear you up," so, obedient to the unvoiced command, I sat still. The church ladies were warming up behind me with a few hallelujahs and praise the Lords and Amens, and the preacher hadn't really moved into the meat of the sermon.

It was going to be a hot service.   4

On my way into church, I saw Sister Monroe, her open-faced   5 gold crown glinting when she opened her mouth to return a neighborly greeting. She lived in the country and couldn't get to church every Sunday, so she made up for her absences by shouting so hard when she did make it that she shook the whole church. As soon as she took her seat, all the ushers would move to her side of the church because it took three women and sometimes a man or two to hold her.

Once she hadn't been to church for a few months (she had   6 taken off to have a child), she got the spirit and started shouting, throwing her arms around and jerking her body, so that the ushers went over to hold her down, but she tore herself away from them and ran up to the pulpit. She stood in front of the altar, shaking like a freshly caught trout. She screamed at Reverend Taylor. "Preach it. I say, preach it." Naturally he kept on preaching as if she wasn't standing there telling him what to do. Then she screamed an extremely fierce "I said, preach it" and stepped up on the altar. The Reverend kept on throwing out phrases like home-run balls and Sister Monroe made a quick break and grasped for him. For just a second, everything and everyone in the church except Reverend Taylor and Sister Monroe hung loose like stockings on a washline. Then she caught the minister by the sleeve of his jacket and his coattail, then she rocked him from side to side.

7   I have to say this for our minister, he never stopped giving us the lesson. The usher board made its way to the pulpit, going up both aisles with a little more haste than is customarily seen in church. Truth to tell, they fairly ran to the minister's aid. Then two of the deacons, in their shiny Sunday suits, joined the ladies in white on the pulpit, and each time they pried Sister Monroe loose from the preacher he took another deep breath and kept on preaching, and Sister Monroe grabbed him in another place, and more firmly. Reverend Taylor was helping his rescuers as much as possible by jumping around when he got a chance. His voice at one point got so low it sounded like a roll of thunder, then Sister Monroe's "Preach it" cut through the roar, and we all wondered (I did, in any case) if it would ever end. Would they go on forever, or get tired out at last like a game of blindman's bluff that lasted too long, with nobody caring who was "it"?

8   I'll never know what might have happened, because magically the pandemonium spread. The spirit infused Deacon Jackson and Sister Willson, the chairman of the usher board, at the same time. Deacon Jackson, a tall, thin, quiet man, who was also a part-time Sunday school teacher, gave a scream like a falling tree, leaned back on thin air and punched Reverend Taylor on the arm. It must have hurt as much as it caught the Reverend unawares. There was a moment's break in the rolling sounds and Reverend Taylor jerked around surprised, and hauled off and punched Deacon Jackson. In the same second Sister Willson caught his tie, looped it over her fist a few times, and pressed down on him. There wasn't time to laugh or cry before all three of them were down on the floor behind the altar. Their legs spiked out like kindling wood.

9   Sister Monroe, who had been the cause of all the excitement, walked off the dais, cool and spent, and raised her flinty voice in the hymn, "I came to Jesus, as I was, worried, wounded, and sad, I found in Him a resting place and He has made me glad."

10   The minister took advantage of already being on the floor and asked in a choky little voice if the church would kneel with him to offer a prayer of thanksgiving. He said we had been visited with a mighty spirit, and let the whole church say Amen.

11   On the next Sunday, he took his text from the eighteenth chapter of the Gospel according to St. Luke, and talked quietly but seriously about the Pharisees, who prayed in the streets so that the public would be impressed with their religious devotion. I doubt that anyone got the message—certainly not those to whom it was directed. The deacon board, however, did appropriate funds for him to buy a new suit. The other was a total loss.

QUESTIONS ON SUBJECT AND PURPOSE

1. Who is the narrator? How old does she seem to be? How do you know?
2. Why does Sister Monroe behave as she does?
3. How does the section on the narrator and Bailey act as a preface to the story of Sister Monroe? Is it relevant, for example, that the narrator's favorite book of the Bible is Deuteronomy?

QUESTIONS ON STRATEGY AND AUDIENCE

1. Part of the art of narration is knowing what events to select. Look carefully at Angelou's story of Sister Monroe (paragraphs 5–9). What events does she choose to include in her narrative?
2. How is Sister Monroe described? Make a list of all of the physical particulars we are given about her. How, other than direct description, is Sister Monroe revealed to the reader?
3. What shift occurs between paragraphs 5 and 6? Did you notice it the first time you read the selection?

QUESTIONS ON VOCABULARY AND STYLE

1. Other than a few words uttered by Sister Monroe, Angelou uses no other dialogue in the selection. How, then, is the story told? What advantage does this method have?
2. Writing humor is never easy. Having a funny situation is essential, but in addition, the story must be told in the right way. (Remember how people can ruin a good joke?) How does Angelou's language and style contribute to the humor in the selection?
3. How effective are the following images:
   a. "She stood in front of the altar, shaking like a freshly caught trout" (paragraph 6).
   b. "The Reverend kept on throwing out phrases like home-run balls" (6).
   c. "Everyone in the church . . . hung loose like stockings on a washline" (6).
   d. "Their legs spiked out like kindling wood" (8).

WRITING SUGGESTIONS

1. **For Your Journal.** Observe people for a day. In your journal, make a list of the funny or comic moments that you notice. Select one of those moments and first describe the situation you witnessed, then analyze why it seemed funny to you.

2. **For a Paragraph.** Everyone has experienced a funny, embarrassing moment—maybe it happened to you or maybe you just witnessed it. In a paragraph, narrate that incident for your reader. Remember to keep the narrative focused.

3. **For an Essay.** Select a "first" from your experience—your first day in junior high school, your first date, your first time driving a car, your first day on a job or at college. Re-create that first for your reader. Remember to shape your narrative, and select only important contributing details. Focus your narrative around a significant aspect of that first experience, whether it was funny or serious.

4. **For Research.** What is an autobiography? Is it always a factual account of events in the writer's life? Is it ever "made up" or fictional? Is it ever propagandistic? What purposes do autobiographies have? Select an autobiography written by someone who interests you—check your college's library catalog for possibilities. Then analyze that work as an autobiography. Do not summarize. Instead, formulate a thesis about what you see as the writer's sense of purpose in the book. Support your argument with evidence from the text, and be sure to document your quotations.

 WEBSITE LINK

The Web has a number of sites with extensive information about Maya Angelou, including interviews, and even audio and video clips that you can hear and watch on your computer's screen. Visit the *Reader*'s Website for the links.

 WRITING LINK: FIGURATIVE LANGUAGE

First, be sure you can identify figurative language, especially simile and metaphor (see the Glossary, p. 604). Then go through Angelou's narrative and make a list of all the similes and metaphors you can find. What effect do these devices have on Angelou's narrative? Why does she use them? Have you tried creating similes and metaphors in your own narrative writing? What cautions should you be aware of when you use these devices?

THE BIGGEST PLAY OF HIS LIFE

Rick Reilly

Rick Reilly (1958–) is a senior writer for Sports Illustrated. *Author of the weekly "Life of Reilly" column, Reilly has been voted National Sportswriter of the Year seven times. His recent books include the novel* Slo-Mo: My Untrue Story *(1999) and* The Life of Reilly: The Best of "Sports Illustrated's" *Rick Reilly (2000).*

On Writing: *At the Sports Illustrated "Your Turn" site, Reilly posted the following on-line query from a novice writer: "I'm a freshman in high school, and I try to use some of your techniques in my writing. However, my journalism teacher says I'm too sarcastic and mean-spirited. I say I'm witty and honest. She says I use too many analogies. I say analogies are like balloons [sic] fun to throw around, and nobody ever has enough of them. Do you have any suggestions on how to tone down one's style for high school writing?" Reilly responded, "(a) I'd learn to spell. (b) Analogies are wonderful, if they work. If they don't, they sit there on the page and scream at you. (c) Every once in awhile, you need to be like Sears—find your softer side. You need more than one gear to get through the race. My gut feeling is you should probably listen to your teacher."*

BEFORE READING

Connecting: Do you remember a time when you confessed something to someone? Maybe a fear? A medical condition? An accident? A misdemeanor?

Anticipating: What does the title of the essay suggest to you? As you read, think about the title as a clue to the story that Reilly is narrating.

One of the captains of the high school football team had something big he wanted to tell the other players. "I was so anxious," remembers middle linebacker Corey Johnson, a senior at Masconomet High in Topsfield, Massachusetts, "I thought I was going to vomit."

He took a hard gulp. "I want to let all of you guys know something about me." He tried not to let his voice quake. "I'm coming out as an openly gay student here."

His teammates' eyes and mouths went wide as soup plates. "I hope this won't change anything," Corey quickly went on. "I didn't

come on to you last year in the locker room, and I won't this year. I
didn't touch you last year in the locker room, and I won't this year."

4   Awkward silence.

5   "Besides, who says you guys are good enough anyway?"

6   And you know what happened? They laughed! But that's not
the best part. The best part is what happened next. Nothing.

7   Corey's teammates had no problem with his sexual orientation.
His coach had no problem with it. His mom and dad and his sister
had no problem with it. His teachers, his counselor—nobody—had a
problem with it.

8   O.K., somebody scrawled FOOTBALL FAG on a door at school.
True, one cementhead parent asked coach Jim Pugh to have the team
take a new vote on the captaincy, but Pugh told him to stuff it. And,
yeah, one week the opposing team's captain kept hollering, "Get the
fag!" but his coach finally benched him (and Masconomet fricasseed
that team 25–0).

9   No opponent refused to play against Corey. No opposing
coach said, "Boys, the Lord wants you to go out and crush that hea-
then!" Nobody held up a sign at a Masconomet game that read
WHICH SIDE ARE YOU ON, COREY? Nope. Corey Johnson, guard-
linebacker, wrestler, lacrosse player, just went out and played his senior football season, same as ever. Masconomet did well (7–4 for the
season, 25–8 with Corey, a two-way starter for three years). Now
Corey is getting on with his life, hopeful as ever. He'll graduate with
his class next month, think about playing small-college football, and
become a gay activist, a journey that began on Sunday at the Millennium March on Washington for Equality.

10   Can't wait for Corey to be on a gay parade float when some
beer-bellied yahoo hollers, "Hey, girls! Shoe sale next corner!" The
football captain might turn the poor schmo into a smudge mark.

11   Corey can take the hits now, but hiding the truth about himself
was so depressing in his sophomore and junior years that he let his
grades drop, skipped practice, and even skipped school. When an
adult friend started ripping homosexuals at a Super Bowl party in January 1998, Corey couldn't decide whether to punch him or cry. He
knew he had to do something.

12   First, he told a guidance counselor he was gay and then a few
teachers. They all supported him. A year later he told his parents.
Fine. Then his best friend, Sean. Uh-oh. Big problem. Sean started
crying. Corey asked him what was wrong. "I'm sorry you couldn't
share this with me before," Sean said. They're still best friends.

13   Since coming out, Corey says, he has heard from "hundreds"
on the Internet, including athletes who wish they had the guts to

come out, too. "But," says Corey, "they always say, 'At my school? No way. It'd be impossible.' "

At Masconomet, a public school with an enrollment of thirteen   14
hundred, Corey is the football captain who had even more moral courage than physical. He's admired by his teammates. In fact, nothing much changed between them, except on bus rides home after wins, when the whole team sang *YMCA* together. Well, it isn't *Hunker Down, You Hairy Bulldogs*, but it works.

Maybe we're actually getting somewhere in the U.S. A young   15
man who leads young men comes out as gay, and it makes such a ruckus you can still hear the crickets chirp. In fact, last month the Boston Gay, Lesbian, and Straight Education Network handed its Visionary Award not just to Corey, but also to his teammates. Can you imagine that? A high school football team getting an award for *tolerance?*

When I was growing up, my best friend was a hilarious kid I'll   16
call Danny. Along about high school, he stopped coming around. Then, in college, he showed up in the Gay Club photo in the yearbook. After that, Danny didn't take my calls.

It's lousy feeling. I guess I'm not the kind of person he could've   17
shared that with.

QUESTIONS ON SUBJECT AND PURPOSE

1. To what extent does Reilly seem surprised about the outcome of Johnson's experience?
2. Where did Reilly get his information about this story? Do you think he was present when Johnson came out to his teammates? During the season? At the award banquet? On what do you base your opinion?
3. What purpose might Reilly have had in writing the essay?

QUESTIONS ON STRATEGY AND AUDIENCE

1. From what point of view is the story told? Who is telling the story?
2. What shift occurs in the final two paragraphs of the essay?
3. The essay originally appeared in *Sports Illustrated*. What assumptions could you make about Reilly's sense of his audience?

QUESTIONS ON VOCABULARY AND STYLE

1. In paragraph 3, Reilly writes, "his teammates' eyes and mouths went wide as soup plates." What is that figure of speech called? How does it contribute to the description? What if Reilly just wrote "his teammates' eyes and mouths went wide"?

2. Can you find instances in the essay in which Reilly's word choice and tone provide clear clues to how he feels about Johnson's experience?

3. Be prepared to define the following words: *fricasseed* (paragraph 8) and *yahoo* (10).

WRITING SUGGESTIONS

1. **For Your Journal.** Brainstorm about a time when you feared telling someone something. Perhaps it was your parents, teachers, classmates, or friends. Maybe you did something of which you knew people wouldn't approve. Maybe it involved sharing a fear or a medical, mental, or physical problem. Maybe it was an addiction or self-destructive behavior. Try to remember that moment when you shared your problem.

2. **For a Paragraph.** Expand your journal writing into a paragraph that re-creates that moment. Try to include a little dialogue to make the moment more vivid. As an alternative, you might write about something that you would like to reveal to someone.

3. **For an Essay.** Use your journal and paragraph writing as a starting point for an essay. Narrate your experience of acknowledging or making public something you kept hidden. As an alternative, you might use the experience of someone you know—perhaps a sibling or a friend—and choose to tell that story as a third-person narrator. Reilly's essay could be a model for a narration like this.

4. **For Research.** What type of advice do counselors, psychologists, and psychiatrists offer to people who are reluctant to acknowledge something to other people. Perhaps it might be an eating disorder, an emotional or physical problem, a paralyzing fear, or a self-destructive impulse. Research the types of advice that might be given. Rather than trying to offer advice that would fit any situation, you might want to narrow down the topic first. Remember that you can

interview counselors or doctors at your school, as well as consult on-line or printed sources. Be sure to document anything that you have taken from a source.

WEBSITE LINK

If you enjoyed Reilly's style and like reading about sports, check out the *Sports Illustrated* Website where you can find an archive of Reilly's past columns. Some on-line databases available through your library might allow you to read these columns. Check the *Reader*'s Website for address suggestions.

WRITING LINK: SENTENCE FRAGMENTS

How many sentence fragments can you find in Reilly's essay? List them and then rewrite each in order to make it a complete sentence. What do you need to add in each case? Why might Reilly have used fragments in these places rather than complete sentences?

MARINA

Judith Ortiz Cofer

Judith Ortiz Cofer was born in Puerto Rico in 1952. Her family settled in Patterson, New Jersey, in 1954, but frequently returned to the Island. She is currently a professor of English and creative writing at the University of Georgia. Her most recent book is Woman in Front of the Sun: On Becoming a Writer *(2000). "Marina" is taken from Cofer's collection of her essays* Silent Dancing: A Partial Remembrance of a Puerto Rican Childhood *(1990).*

On Writing: *Cofer observes, "Much of my writing begins as a meditation on past events. But memory for me is the 'jumping off' point; I am not, in my poetry and fiction writing, a slave to memory. I like to believe that the poem or story contains the 'truth' of art rather than the factual, historical truth that the journalist, sociologist, scientist—most of the rest of the world—must adhere to."*

BEFORE READING

Connecting: How would you define the word *woman?* What does that word mean to you?

Anticipating: What does the story of Marina have to do with Cofer and her mother? Or is Cofer merely setting the scene in which the story of Marina is told?

1   Again it happened between my mother and me. Since her return to Puerto Rico after my father's death ten years before, she had gone totally "native," regressing into the comfortable traditions of her extended family and questioning all of my decisions. Each year we spoke more formally to each other, and each June, at the end of my teaching year, she would invite me to visit her on the Island—so I could see for myself how much I was missing out on.

2   These yearly pilgrimages to my mother's town where I had been born also, but which I had left at an early age, were for me symbolic of the clash of cultures and generations that she and I represent. But I looked forward to arriving at this lovely place, my mother's lifetime dream of home, now endangered by encroaching "progress."

Located on the west coast, our pueblo is a place of contrasts: 3
the original town remains as a tiny core of ancient houses circling the
church, which sits on a hill, the very same where the woodcutter
claimed to have been saved from a charging bull by a lovely dark Lady
who appeared floating over a treetop. There my mother lives, at the
foot of this hill; but surrounding this postcard scene there are shopping malls, a Burger King, a cinema. And where the sugar cane fields
once extended like a green sea as far as the eye could see: condomini-
ums, cement blocks in rows, all the same shape and color. My mother
tries not to see this part of her world. The church bells drown the
noise of traffic, and when she sits on her back porch and looks up at
the old church built by the hands of generations of men whose last
names she would not recognize, she feels safe—under the shelter of
the past.

During the twenty years she spent in "exile" in the U.S. often 4
alone with two children, waiting for my father, she dedicated her time
and energy to creating a "reasonable facsimile" of a Puerto Rican
home, which for my brother and me meant that we led a dual existence: speaking Spanish at home with her, acting out our parts in her
traditional play, while also daily pretending assimilation in the classroom, where in the early sixties, there was no such thing as bilingual
education. But, to be fair, we were not the only Puerto Rican children
leading a double life, and I have always been grateful to have kept my
Spanish. My trouble with Mother comes when she and I try to define
and translate key words for both of us, words such as "woman" and
"mother." I have a daughter too, as well as a demanding profession as a
teacher and writer. My mother got married as a teenager and led a life
of isolation and total devotion to her duties as mother. As a Penelope-
like wife, she was always waiting, waiting, waiting, for the return of
her sailor, for the return to her native land.

In the meantime, I grew up in the social flux of the sixties in 5
New Jersey, and although I was kept on a steady diet of fantasies
about life in the tropics, I liberated myself from her plans for me,
got a scholarship to college, married a man who supported my need
to work, to create, to travel and to experience life as an individual.
My mother rejoices at my successes, but is often anxious at how
much time I have to spend away from home, although I keep as-
suring her that my husband is as good a parent as I am, and a much
better cook. Her concern about my familial duties is sometimes a
source of friction in our relationship, the basis for most of our arguments. But, in spite of our differences, I miss her, and as June approaches, I yearn to be with her in her tiny house filled with her
vibrant presence. So I pack up and go to meet my loving adversary

in her corner of the rapidly disappearing "paradise" that she waited so long to go home to.

6   It was after a heated argument one afternoon that I sought reconciliation with my mother by asking her to go with me for a walk down the main street of the pueblo. I planned to request stories about the town and its old people, something that we both enjoy for different reasons: she likes recalling the old days, and I have an insatiable curiosity about the history and the people of the Island which have become prominent features in my work.

7   We had been walking around the church when we saw a distinguished looking old man strolling hand-in-hand with a little girl. My mother touched my arm and pointed to them. I admired the pair as the old man, svelte and graceful as a ballet dancer, lifted the tiny figure dressed up in pink lace onto a stool at an outdoor cafe.

8   "Who is he?" I asked my mother, trying not to stare as we pretended to examine the menu taped on the window.

9   "You have heard his story at your grandmother's house."

10   She took my elbow and led me to a table at the far end of the cafe. "I will tell it to you again, but first I will give you a hint about who he is: he has not always been the man he is today."

11   Though her "hint" was no help, I suddenly recalled the story I had heard many years earlier as told by my grandmother, who had started the tale with similar words, "People are not always what they seem to be, that is something we have all heard, but have you heard about the one who ended up being what he was but did not appear to be?" Or something like that. Mamá could turn any story—it did not have to be as strange and fascinating as this one—into an event. I told my guess to my mother.

12   "Yes," she nodded, "he came home to retire. You know he has lived in Nueva York since before you were born. Do you remember the story?"

13   As we continued our walk, my mother recounted for me her mother's dramatic tale of a famous incident that had shaken the town in Mamá's youth. I had heard it once as a child, sitting enthralled at my grandmother's knee.

14   In the days when Mamá was a young girl, our pueblo had not yet been touched by progress. The cult of the Black Virgin had grown strong as pilgrims traveled from all over the island to visit the shrine, and the Church preached chastity and modesty as the prime virtues for the town's daughters. Adolescent girls were not allowed to go anywhere without their mothers or *dueñas*—except to a certain river that no man was allowed to approach.

15   Río Rojo, the river that ran its course around the sacred mountain where the Virgin had appeared, was reserved for the maidens of

the pueblo. It was nothing but a stream, really, but crystalline, and it was bordered by thick woods where the most fragrant flowers and herbs could be found. This was a female place, a pastoral setting where no true *macho* would want to be caught swimming or fishing. Nature had decorated the spot like a boudoir—royal poin- 16 cianas extended their low branches for the girls to hang their clothes, and the mossy grass grew like a plush green carpet all the way down to the smooth stepping-stones where they could sun themselves like *favoritas* in a virginal harem.

As a "grown" girl of fifteen, Mamá had led her sisters and other 17 girls of the pueblo to bathe there on hot summer afternoons. It was a place of secret talk and rowdy play, of freedom from mothers and chaperones, a place where they could talk about boys, and where they could luxuriate in their bodies. At the río, the young women felt free to hypothesize about the secret connection between their two concerns: their changing bodies and boys.

Sex was the forbidden topic in their lives, yet these were the 18 same girls who would be given to strangers in marriage before they were scarcely out of childhood. In a sense, they were betrayed by their own protective parents who could bring themselves to explain neither the delights, nor the consequences of sex to their beloved daughters. The prevailing practice was to get them safely married as soon after puberty as possible—because nature would take its course one way or another. Scandal was to be avoided at all costs.

At the río, the group of girls Mamá grew up with would squeal 19 and splash away their last few precious days as children. They would also wash each other's hair while sitting like brown nyads upon the smooth rocks in the shallow water. They had the freedom to bathe nude, but some of them could not break through a lifetime of training in modesty and would keep their chemises and bloomers on. One of the shyest girls was Marina. She was everyone's pet.

Marina was a lovely young girl with her *café-con-leche* skin and 20 green eyes. Her body was willowy and her thick black Indian hair hung down to her waist. Her voice was so soft that you had to come very close to hear what she was saying during the rare times when she did speak. Everyone treated Marina with special consideration, since she had already known much tragedy by the time she reached adolescence. It was due to the traumatic circumstances of her birth, as well as her difficult life with a reclusive mother, all the girls believed, that Marina was so withdrawn and melancholy as she ended her fifteenth year. She was surely destined for convent life, they all whispered when Marina left their company, as she often did, to go sit by herself on the bank, and to watch them with her large, wet, melancholy eyes.

21   Marina had fine hands and all the girls liked for her to braid their hair at the end of the day. They argued over the privilege of sitting between her legs while Marina ran her long fingers through their hair like a cellist playing a soothing melody. It caused much jealousy that last summer before Mamá's betrothal (which meant it was the last summer she could play at the río with her friends) when Marina chose to keep company only with Kiki, the mayor's fourteen year old daughter who had finally won permission from her strict parents to bathe with the pueblo's girls at the river.

22   Kiki would be a pale fish among the golden tadpoles in the water. She came from a Spanish family who believed in keeping the bloodlines pure, and she had spent all of her childhood in the cool shade of mansions and convent schools. She had come to the pueblo to prepare for her debut into society, her *quinceañera*, a fifteenth birthday party where she would be dressed like a princess and displayed before the Island's eligible bachelors as a potential bride.

23   Lonely for the company of girls her age, and tired of the modulated tones of afternoons on the verandah with her refined mother, Kiki had pressured her father to give her a final holiday with the other girls, whom she would see going by the mansion, singing and laughing on their way to the río. Her father began to see the wisdom of her idea when she mentioned how democratic it would seem to the girls' parents for the mayor's daughter to join them at the river. Finally, he agreed. The mother took to her bed with a sick headache when she thought of her lovely daughter removing her clothes in front of the uncouth spawn of her husband's constituents: rough farmers and their sun-darkened wives.

24   Kiki removed all her clothes with glee as soon as the group arrived at the river. She ran to the water tossing lace, satin, and silk over her head. She behaved like a bird whose cage door had been opened for the first time. The girls giggled at the sight of the freckles on her shoulders, her little pink nipples, like rosebuds, her golden hair. But since she was the mayor's daughter, they dared not get too close. They acted more like her attendants than her friends. Kiki would have ended up alone again if it had not been for Marina.

25   Marina was awestruck by the exuberant Kiki; and Kiki was drawn to the quiet girl who watched the others at play with such yearning. Soon the two girls were inseparable. Marina would take Kiki's wet hair, like molten gold, into her brown hands and weave it into two perfect plaits which she would pin to the girl's head like a crown. It was fascinating to watch how the two came together wordlessly, like partners in a *pas de deux*.

It was an idyllic time, until one afternoon Marina and Kiki did   26
not return to the river from an excursion into the woods where they
had ostensibly gone to gather flowers. Mamá and her friends searched
for them until nearly dark, but did not find them. The mayor went in
person to notify Marina's mother of the situation. What he found was
a woman who had fallen permanently into silence: secluded in a secret place of shadows where she wished to remain.

It was the events of one night long ago that had made her aban-   27
don the world.

Marina's mother had lost her young husband and delivered her   28
child prematurely on the same night. The news that her man had
been drowned in a fishing accident had brought on an agonizing labor. She had had a son, a tiny little boy, perfect in his parts, but sickly.
The new mother, weakened in body and mind by so much pain, had
decided that she preferred a daughter for company. Hysterically, she
had begged the anxious midwife to keep her secret. And as soon as she
was able to walk to church, she had the child dressed in a flowing
gown of lace and had her christened Marina. Living the life a recluse,
to which she was entitled as a widow, and attended by her loyal nurse,
and later, by her quiet obedient Marina, the woman had slipped easily out of reality.

By the time Marina was old enough to discover the difference   29
between her body and the bodies of her girlfriends, her mother had
forgotten all about having borne a son. In fact, the poor soul would
have been horrified to discover a man under her roof. And so Marina
kept up appearances, waiting out her body's dictates year by year. The
summer that Kiki joined the bathers at the río, Marina had made up
her mind to run away from home. She had been in torment until the
blonde girl had appeared like an angel, bringing Marina the balm of
her presence and the soothing touch of her hands.

The mayor found the woman sitting calmly in a rocking chair.   30
She looked like a wax figure dressed in widow's weeds. Only her elegant hands moved as she crocheted a collar for a little girl's dress. And
although she smiled deferentially at the men speaking loudly in her
parlor, she remained silent. Silence was the place she had inhabited
for years, and no one could draw her out now.

Furious, the mayor threatened to have her arrested. Finally it   31
was the old nurse who confessed the whole sad tale—to the horror of
the mayor and his men. She handed him an envelope with *Papá y
Mamá* written on its face in Kiki's hand. In a last show of control, the
mayor took the sealed letter home to read in the privacy of the family mansion where his wife was waiting, still under the impression that
the two girls had been kidnapped for political reasons.

32   Kiki's letter explained briefly that she and *Marino* had eloped. They had fallen in love and nothing and no one could change their minds about getting married. She had sold her pearl necklace—the family heirloom given to her by her parents to wear at her quinceañera, and they were using the money for passage on the next steamship out of San Juan to New York.

33   The mayor did not finish his term in office. He and his wife, now a recluse, exiled themselves to Spain.

34   "And Marina and Kiki?" I had asked Mamá, eager for more details about Kiki and Marino. "What happened to them?"

35   "What happens to *any* married couple?" Mamá had replied, putting an end to her story. "They had several children, they worked, they got old . . . " She chuckled gently at my naiveté.

36   On our way back through town from our walk, Mother and I again saw Marino with his pretty granddaughter. This time he was lifting her to smell a white rose that grew from a vine entangled on a tree branch. The child brought the flower carefully to her nose and smelled it. Then the old man placed the child gently back on the ground and they continued their promenade, stopping to examine anything that caught the child's eye.

37   "Do you think he made a good husband?" I asked my mother.

38   "He would know what it takes to make a woman happy," she said as she turned to face me, and winked in camaraderie.

39   As I watched the gentle old man and the little girl, I imagined Marina sitting alone on the banks of a river, his heart breaking with pain and wild yearnings, listening to the girls asking questions he could have answered; remaining silent; learning patience, until love would give him the right to reclaim his original body and destiny. Yet he would never forget the lessons she learned at the río—or how to handle fragile things. I looked at my mother and she smiled at me; we now had a new place to begin our search for the meaning of the word *woman*.

QUESTIONS ON SUBJECT AND PURPOSE

1. In what way is the essay about "the clash of cultures and generations" (paragraph 2)?
2. Why does Marina not reveal his identity before?
3. Why might Cofer want to retell the story of Marina?

QUESTIONS ON STRATEGY AND AUDIENCE

1. How many narratives are there in the essay?
2. What is the effect of the riddles—"He has not always been the man he is today" (paragraph 10) and "Have you heard about

the one who ended up being what he was but did not appear to be?" (11)?

3. Although it really does not matter one way or another, as you read the story of Marina and Kiki, did you think it might have actually happened?

QUESTIONS ON VOCABULARY AND STYLE

1. How is the story of Marina narrated?
2. What is the effect of the mother's reply to Cofer's question "What happened to them?" (paragraph 34)?
3. Be prepared to define the following words: *encroaching* (paragraph 2), *insatiable* (6), *svelte* (7), *boudoir* (16), *traumatic* (20), *uncouth* (23), *ostensibly* (26).

WRITING SUGGESTIONS

1. **For Your Journal.** Make a list of the characteristics that you associate with the word *woman* or the word *man*.
2. **For a Paragraph.** Use the list of characteristics that you made for your journal to write a paragraph in which you narrate an event or an action that demonstrates or reveals someone as being either a man or a woman.
3. **For an Essay.** "Clashes of cultures and generations" are inevitable. Choose a time in which you were aware that your behavior or values were in conflict with those of your parents or grandparents. Narrate the event, but at the same time explore why you did what you did and how it made you feel. Were you right, or do you now see that they were right and you were wrong?
4. **For Research.** To what extent does Cofer explore similar themes in her other work? Find other examples of her writing (see the headnote and check the catalog and databases available at your library). Another good source of information is interviews that Cofer has granted. A number of these have appeared in print, and the full text of some is available through electronic databases. Once you have gathered your information, write an essay analyzing her writing to isolate her central concerns. Be sure to formulate a thesis about the themes that occur in her writing; do not just summarize what you have read. Be sure to document your sources.

WEBSITE LINK

Several extensive interviews with Cofer are available from on-line databases and others can be found in print sources in your school's library. Check out the possibilities at the Website.

WRITING LINK: COLONS

What is the mark of punctuation called the colon? How do you use that mark in your writing? Cofer uses the colon a number of times in her essay (see paragraphs 3, 6, 10, 17, and 26). Study how she uses them. Can you write a rule or two for the use of the colon working just from Cofer's essay?

LOCKDOWN

Evans D. Hopkins

A former inmate at Nottoway Correctional Center in Virginia and writer for the Black Panther Party, Evans Hopkins was paroled in 1997 after serving sixteen years for armed robbery. He has published essays in the Washington Post, Nerve, *and* The New Yorker, *where this essay first appeared.*

BEFORE READING

Connecting: What associations do you have with the words *prison* and *prisoner?*

Anticipating: Before you start to read, write down in a sentence or two how you feel about people sentenced to prison. For example, how should they be treated while they are in jail? Then read the essay.

I know something serious has happened when I wake up well before dawn to discover two guards wearing armored vests and riot helmets taking a head count. I'd gone to bed early this August evening, so that I might write in the early morning, as is my custom, before the prison clamor begins. So when I wake up I have no idea what was going down while I slept. But it's apparent that the prison is on "full lockdown status." At the minimum, we will be locked in our cells twenty-four hours a day for the next several days.

While lockdowns at Nottoway Correctional Center in Virginia are never announced in advance, I'm not altogether surprised by this one. The buzz among the eleven-hundred-man prison population was that a lockdown was imminent. The experienced prisoner knows to be prepared for a few weeks of complete isolation.

But I'm hardly prepared for the news I receive later in the day from a local TV station: two corrections officers and two nurses were taken hostage by three prisoners, following what authorities are calling "a terribly botched escape attempt" that included a fourth man. The incident was ended around 5:30 A.M. by a Department of Corrections strike-force team, with the hostages unharmed. However, according to authorities, eight of the rescuers, including the warden, were slightly wounded when a shotgun was discharged accidentally.

4   Oh, God, I think. Forget a few weeks. No telling how long we'll be on lock *now*. I try to take heart by telling myself, "It's nothing you haven't seen before, might as well take the opportunity to get the old typewriter pumpin', maybe even finish your book."

5   The idea that most people have of prison life consists of images from worst-case-scenario movies, or from news footage of local jails. Visitors to prison often comment on how surprised they are to see men moving around, without apparent restraint, having believed that prisoners are kept in their cells most of the time. In modern prisons, however, there is usually lots of orderly movement, as inmates go about the activities of normal life: working, eating, education, recreation, etc.

6   In a well-run institution, long lockdowns—where all inmate movement stops—are aberrations. Yet major institutions lock down regularly, for short periods, so that the prison can be searched for weapons and other contraband. Lockdowns are also called for emergencies, as this one has been at Nottoway, or, in fact, for any reason deemed necessary for security.

7   By the second week of the lockdown, one of our hot meals has been replaced with a bag lunch—four slices of bread, two slices of either cheese or a luncheon meat, and a small piece of plain cake or, more rarely, fruit. Since counsellors or administrative personnel must do most of the cooking, the lockdown menu usually consists of meals that require minimal culinary skills. Today we have chili-mac (an ungodly concoction of macaroni and ground beef), along with three tablespoons of anemic mixed vegetables and a piece of plain cake—all served on a disposable aluminum tray the size of a hard-cover book.

8   We have not yet been allowed out to shower, so I lay newspaper on the concrete floor and bathe at the sink. There is a hot water tap, in contrast to the cells at the now demolished State Penitentiary, in Richmond, where I served the first several years of my life sentence for armed robbery, and where I went through many very long lockdowns.

9   I have endured lockdowns in buildings with little or no heat; lockdowns during which authorities cut off the plumbing completely, so contraband couldn't be flushed away; and lockdowns where we weren't allowed out to shower for more than a month. I have been in prison since 1981, and my attitude has had to be "I can do time on the moon," if that is what's called for. So I'm not about to let this lockdown faze me. (Besides, I am in what is known as the "honor building," where conditions are marginally better.)

10   Around one o'clock in the morning, the three guards of the "shower squad" finally get around to our building. They have full riot

gear on, and a Rottweiler in tow. One by one, we are handcuffed and escorted to the shower stalls at the center of the dayroom area. As I walk past the huge dog, I turn my head to keep an eye on it. The beast suddenly lunges against the handler's leash and barks at me with such ferocity that I actually feel the force of air on my face. I walk to the shower with feigned insouciance, but my heart is pumping furiously. I can forget sleeping for a while.

Back in the cell, I contemplate what's happening to this place. 11 Information about the hostage incident has been trickling in. While the show of force seems absurd to those of us here in the honor building, I have heard reports of assaults on guards in the cell houses of the main compound, where the treatment of the inmates is said to have been more severe. On the night of the original incident, some men in a section of one building refused to return to their cells, and in at least one section there was open rebellion—destruction and burning.

Today a memorandum from the warden is passed out, and the 12 warden himself appears on a video broadcast on the prison's TV system. He announces that there will be no visitation until some time in October—about two months from now.

Other restrictions are to be imposed, he says, including imme- 13 diate implementation of a new Department of Corrections guideline, stripping all prisoners of most personal property: televisions with screens larger than five and a half inches; any tape player other than a Walkman; nearly all personal clothing (jeans, nongray sweatsuits, colored underwear, etc.); and—most devastating for me—*all type-writers*.

I find this news disquieting, to say the least, and I decide to lie 14 down, to try to get some sleep. This is difficult, as men are yelling back and forth from their cells, upset about this latest development. Many of them have done ten or fifteen years, like me, obeying all the rules and saving the meagre pay from prison jobs to buy a few personal items—items that we must now surrender.

I awaken in the night, sweating and feverish in the humid sum- 15 mer air. Sitting on the edge of my bed while considering my plight, I look at photographs of my family. My eyes rest on the school portrait of my son, taken shortly before he died from heart disease ten years ago, at age twelve. Sorrow overwhelms me, and I find myself giving in to grief, then to great, mournful sobs.

The tears stop as suddenly as they began. It has been years since 16 I've wept so, and I realize that the grief has been only a trigger—that I am, by and large, really feeling sorry for myself. This is no good, if I'm to survive with my mind and spirit intact. I can't afford to succumb to self-pity.

17   This new day begins shortly after 8 A.M., when three guards come to my cell door. One of them says, "We're here to escort you to Personal Property. You have to pack up everything in your cell, and they will sort out what you have to send out, and what you can keep, over there."

18   He looks through the long, narrow vertical slot in the steel door and—seeing all the books, magazines, journal notebooks, and piles of papers I have stacked around the cell—shakes his head in disbelief. "Looks like you're gonna need a lot of boxes," he says. I have the accumulated papers, magazines, and books of a practicing freelance writer. The only problem is that my "office" is about as big as your average bathroom—complete with toilet and sink, but with a steel cot where your bathtub would be.

19   Now the new rules say twelve books, twelve magazines, twelve audiotapes. Period. And "a reasonable number of personal and legal papers." I wonder how much of all this stuff they will say is reasonable, when sometimes even I question the sanity of holding on to so much. But who knows *when* I'll be able to get to any files, manuscripts, books, and notes that I send home? I finish packing after three hours, ending up with twelve full boxes. I sit and smoke a cigarette while waiting for the guards to return, and contemplate the stacked boxes filling the eight feet between the cot and the door. *Where are all the books, plays, and film scripts I dreamed of producing?*

20   As I walk to the property building, on the far side of the compound, the sun is bright, the sky is cloudless, and the air of the Virginia countryside is refreshing. I look away from the fortress-gray concrete buildings of the prison, and out through the twin perimeter fences and the gleaming rolls of razor wire, to note that the leaves of a distant maple have gone to orange. I realize that the season has changed since I was last out of the building.

21   I am accompanied by three guards. Two push a cart laden with my boxes, grumbling; the third, an older man I know, walks beside me, making small talk.

22   "Man, things are really changing here," this guard says. Lowering his voice so that the other two cannot hear him, he tells me that he considered transferring to work at another institution, but that the entire system is now going through similar changes.

23   Back in my cell, I don't have the energy to unpack the four boxes I've returned with. I am glad to have at least salvaged the part of the manuscripts I've worked on over the years.

24   I lie upon the bed like a mummy, feet crossed at the ankle and hands folded over my chest, and try to meditate. However, with my tape player gone (along with my television), I have no music to drown

out the sounds coming from the cell house. A wave of defeat settles over me.

I think of what I've often told people who ask about my 25 crime—that I got life for a robbery in which no one was hurt. I'll have to rephrase that from now on. If robbery can be said to be theft by force, I can't help but feel like I've just been robbed. And I've most certainly been *hurt*. Maybe that's the whole idea, I think—to injure us, eye for an eye.

Perhaps I should acknowledge that the lockdown—and, in- 26 deed, all these years—have damaged me more than I want to believe. But self-pity is anathema to the prisoner, and self-doubt is deadly to the writer.

I get up quickly, pull out a yellow pad and ballpoint from one 27 of the boxes, and stuff spongy plugs in my ears to block out the noise. I know that if I don't go back to work immediately—on *something*— the loss of my typewriter may throw up a block that I'll never over-come.

Just before Christmas, the lockdown officially ends. The four 28 and a half months have taken their toll on everyone. There have been reports of two or three suicides. Some inmates have become unhinged, and can be seen shuffling around, on Thorazine or some-thing.

Things are far from being back to "normal operations." There 29 is now the strictest control of *all* movement; attack dogs are every-where and officers escort you wherever you go. The gym is closed, and recreation and visitation privileges have been drastically cur-tailed. At least the educational programs, which were once touted as among the best in the state's prison system, are to resume again in the new year.

On Christmas Eve, the first baked "real chicken on the bone" 30 since summer is served. But the cafeteria-style serving line has been replaced with a wall of concrete blocks. Now the prisoner gets a stan-dard tray served through a small slot at the end of the wall.

As I hasten to finish my food in the allotted fifteen minutes, I 31 look at the men from another building in the serving line. There is a drab sameness to the men, all dressed in the required ill-fitting uni-form of denim jeans, blue work shirts, and prison jackets.

I spot a friend of more than fifteen years, whom I haven't 32 seen in months. I can only wave and call out a greeting, for as we are seated separately, "mingling" with men from another building is nearly impossible in the chow hall. "I'm a grandfather now," he shouts to me, beaming. "I've got some pictures to show you, when we get a chance." Then he remembers the strict segregation by building now, and his smile fades. He knows that I may never get a chance to see them.

33   I notice a large number of new faces among the men in line. Most of them are black. Many are quite young, with a few appearing to be still in their teens.

34   Such young men are a primary reason for the new lockdown policies, which are calculated largely to contain the "eighty-five-per-centers"—those now entering Virginia's growing prison system, who must serve eighty-five per cent of their sentences, under new, no-parole laws.

35   Virginia, like most states and the federal government, has passed punitive sentencing laws in recent years. This has led to an unprecedented United States prison/jail population of more than a million six hundred thousand—about three times what it was when I entered prison, sixteen years ago. In the resulting expansion of the nation's prison systems, authorities have tended to dispense with much of the rehabilitative programming once prevalent in America's penal institutions.

36   When I was sent to the State Penitentiary, in 1981, I was twenty-six—the quintessential angry young black male. However, there was a very different attitude toward rehabilitation at that time, particularly as regards education. I was able to take college courses for a number of years on a Pell grant. Vocational training was available, and literacy (or at least enrollment in school) was encouraged and increased one's chances for making parole.

37   In the late seventies, there was a growing recognition that rehabilitation programs paid off in lower rates of recidivism. But things began to change a few years later. First, the highly publicized violence of the crack epidemic encouraged mandatory minimum sentencing. The throw-away-the-key fever really took off in 1988, when George Bush's Presidential campaign hit the Willie Horton hot button, and sparked the tough-on-crime political climate that continues to this day. The transformation was nearly complete when President Clinton endorsed the concept of "three strikes you're out" in his 1994 State of the Union address. And when Congress outlawed Pell grants for prisoners later that year the message became clear: We really don't give a damn if you change or not.

38   Although the men are glad, after more than four months, to be out of their cells, there is little holiday spirit; it's just another day. Several watch whatever banality is on the dayroom TV screen. Most sit on the stainless-steel tables and listlessly play cards to kill time, while others wait for a place at the table. Some wait to use one of two telephones, while others, standing around in bathrobes or towels, wait for a shower stall to become available.

Most of the men in this section of the building are in their for-   39
ties or fifties, with a few elderly. It strikes me that for most of them
prison has become a life of waiting: waiting in line to eat, for a phone
call, the mail, or a visit. Or just waiting for tomorrow—for parole and
freedom. For the older ones, with no hope of release, I suppose that
they wait for the deliverance of death.

As I record the day in my notebook, I find myself thinking   40
about my aunt's grandnephew—her adopted son. He was rumored to
have been dealing drugs, and he was shot dead in the doorway of her
home on Thanksgiving Day, just over a month ago; my father, who is
seventy-five, was called to comfort her. With violence affecting so
many lives, one can understand the desire—driven by fear—to lock
away young male offenders. But considering their impoverished,
danger-filled lives, I wonder whether the threat of being locked up for
decades can really deter them from crime.

I understand the philosophy behind the increased use of long   41
sentences and harsh incarceration. The idea is to make prison a sec-
ular hell on earth—a place where the young potential felon will fear
to go, where the ex-con will fear to return. But an underlying theme
is that "these people" are irredeemable "predators" (i.e., "animals"),
who are without worth. Why, then, provide them with the opportunity to rehabilitate—or give them any hope?

Still, what really bothers me is knowing that many thousands   42
of the young men entering prison now may *never* get the "last
chance to change," which I was able to put to good use—in an era
that, I'm afraid, is now in the past. And more disturbing, to my
mind, are the long "no hope" sentences given to so many young
men now—they can be given even to people as young as thirteen
and fourteen. Although I personally remain eligible for parole—
and in all likelihood will be released eventually—I can't help thinking of all the young lives that are now being thrown away. I know
that if I had been born in another time I might very well have suffered the same fate.

QUESTIONS ON SUBJECT AND PURPOSE

1. How long does the lockdown last? How many specific days
   during that period does Hopkins write about?
2. At what point in the essay does Hopkins move away from his
   narrative account of the lockdown? What does Hopkins then
   do in the essay?
3. What objectives might Hopkins have in writing his essay?

QUESTIONS ON STRATEGY AND AUDIENCE

1. At times, Hopkins seems to talk to himself—even using quotation marks around his words, as in paragraph 4. Why? What is the effect of this strategy?
2. Hopkins uses white space to separate sections of the essay. How many divisions are there?
3. Who might Hopkins imagine as his readers? To whom is he writing? How do you know?

QUESTIONS ON VOCABULARY AND STYLE

1. When the Rottweiler lunges at him, Hopkins writes, "I walk to the shower with feigned insouciance" (paragraph 10). What is the effect of his word choice?
2. Hopkins chooses to quote a few remarks that the guards make when he is asked to pack up his possessions (paragraphs 17, 18, and 22). Why?
3. Be prepared to define the following words: *clamor* (paragraph 1), *aberrations* (6), *insouciance* (10), *anathema* (26), *punitive* (35), *quintessential* (36), *recidivism* (37), *banality* (38).

WRITING SUGGESTIONS

1. **For Your Journal.** Spend some time thinking about instances in which a personal experience that you had might be used to argue for a change in society's attitudes. For example, were you ever discriminated against for any reason? Were you ever needlessly embarrassed or ridiculed for something? Make a list of some possible experiences.
2. **For a Paragraph.** Look at the list of personal experiences that you made for your journal. Select one of those experiences and in a paragraph narrate what happened and then reflect on the significance of that experience. Try to make your reader see the injustice that was done.
3. **For an Essay.** If you have written the paragraph in Suggestion 2, treat that as a draft for a longer, fuller narrative. Write an essay in which you narrate a personal experience for a specific purpose. If you are having trouble finding a suitable experience from your own life, you might want to narrate the experience of someone else.

4. **For Research.** What evidence is there to support or to refute the idea that prison can be a place for rehabilitation, can offer a "last chance to change"? Research the problem using your library's resources. Some on-line or CD-ROM databases would also be good places to start. You might want to talk to a reference librarian for search strategy suggestions. Use your findings to argue for or against providing educational or vocational opportunities to people in prison.

 WEBSITE LINK

Some additional essays by Hopkins can be found in on-line e-journals and in the *Washington Post*'s newspaper archives. The links can be found at the Website, as can a number of sources about prisons. Background information for an argument on the need for or the opposition to educational programs in prisons is also available.

 WRITING LINK: DASHES

What is the mark of punctuation called the dash? How do you use that mark in your writing? How does a dash differ from parentheses or a comma? When might you use one and not the others? Hopkins uses dashes throughout his essay. Could you write a rule for the use of the dash using Hopkins's sentences as examples?

PREWRITING SUGGESTIONS FOR NARRATION

1. Several days before your essay is due, set aside some time to brainstorm about your paper. If you are writing about a personal experience, you will discover that, with time, you will slowly remember more and more details. Do you need to do some research for your essay? Interview someone? Do the gathering and the note-taking before you start to write.

2. Complete the following sentence: "I am narrating this story so that my reader will see . . . ." As you gather information and plan your draft, use your thesis statement to decide what details to include and what to exclude.

3. Look carefully at your choice of point of view. Personal narratives are nearly always told from the first person ("I"); historical narratives and journalistic stories are generally told in the third person ("they," "she," "he"). How are you planning to narrate your essay?

4. Remember that your narrative must have a beginning, a middle, and an end; but stories don't have to be told in strict chronological order. You can use flashbacks. Be sure to structure your account so that it has the shape necessary for a story.

5. Look again at the narratives in this chapter. Think about how each story is organized. Do you see any strategies that might work in your essay?

REWRITING SUGGESTIONS FOR NARRATION

1. Look again at your title. An informative, even catchy, title is a tremendous asset to an essay. If yours seems a little boring, brainstorm some other possibilities.

2. A successful narrative has a shape and a purpose. You do not need to include everything that happened, just those events relevant to the experience and its significance. Look again at the narratives in this chapter. Notice what they include, but also what they exclude. Does your narrative show the same economy?

3. Did you use any dialogue? Sparing use will probably make your narrative more vivid—it will show rather than tell. Dialogue, though, can slow a story down, so look at how the writers in this chapter integrate dialogue into their essays.

4. Remember to catch your reader's attention in the first paragraph. Look closely at your introduction. Ask a friend to read just that paragraph. Does your friend want to continue reading?

5. Look at your conclusion. How did you end? Did you lead up to a climactic moment, or did you just end with a flat conclusion ("And so you can see why this experience was important to me")? Compare how the writers in this chapter end their narratives. You might be able to use a similar strategy.

DESCRIPTION

The birth of a baby
A week at the beach
A wedding
A senior prom

How do we memorialize such occasions? With photographs—color snapshots, digital pictures, picture postcards, professionally-taken portraits. We are surrounded by images. The advertisements in our magazines contain few words; even novels today are increasingly a mixture of words and images (graphic novels). "A picture is worth a thousand words" the cliché goes—and not surprisingly the claim itself was the invention of an American advertising executive.

We cannot deny the power of the visual. Look, for example, at the photograph by John McCarthy of a sod house probably taken in the 1880s in North Dakota. If we wanted to know what a settler's life was like on the Northern Great Plains, if we wanted to see the physical reality of that life, what better way than to study a group of photographs?

At the same time, though, words can do something that photographs never can. Photographs are static—a visual, but unchanging, moment captured in time. What were the people in the photograph thinking? What were they feeling? What impression did the landscape leave on their minds and lives? What was it like to go to bed and wake each morning in a sod house? How cold did it get in winter? How wet and damp in the spring? Descriptions in words never attempt to capture a photographic reality. Instead, images are filtered through the mind of the writer—the writer evokes our feelings, our memories. The writer of description records what she or he saw as

Nebraska State Historical Society Photograph

important in the image. For example, three of the writers in this chapter write about people important in their lives. Would their descriptions have been more effective—or even unnecessary—if they had included a photograph of the person about whom they were writing? Of course not. In each case, what is important about the person is not that static, external appearance but rather what the person being described meant to the writer.

Like narration, description is an everyday activity. You describe to a friend what cooked snails really taste like, how your favorite perfume smells, how your body feels when you have a fever, how a local band sounded last night. Description re-creates sense impressions, ideas, and feelings by translating them into words.

That translation is not always easy. For one thing, when you have a firsthand experience, all of your senses are working at the same time: you see, taste, smell, feel, hear; you experience feelings and have thoughts about the experience. When you convey that experience to a reader or a listener, you can only record one sense impression at a time. Furthermore, sometimes it is difficult to find an adequate translation for a particular sense impression—how do you describe the smell of musk perfume or the taste of freshly squeezed orange juice? But the translation of sense impressions into words offers two distinct advantages. First, ideally it isolates the most important aspects of the experience, ruling out anything else that might distract your reader's attention. Second, it makes those experiences more permanent. Sensory impressions decay in seconds, but written descriptions survive indefinitely.

Consider Darcy Frey's description of Russell Thomas, a star basketball player at a Brooklyn, New York, high school, as he practices on a playground in August:

> At this hour Russell usually has the court to himself; most of the other players won't come out until after dark, when the thick humid air begins to stir with night breezes and the court lights come on. But this evening is turning out to be a fine one—cool and foggy. The low, slanting sun sheds a feeble pink light over the silvery Atlantic a block away, and milky sheets of fog roll off the ocean and drift in tatters along the project walkways. The air smells of sewage and saltwater. At the far end of the court, where someone has torn a hole in the chicken wire fence, other players climb through and begin warming up.

Traditionally, descriptions are divided into two categories: objective and subjective. In objective description, you record details without making any personal evaluation or reaction. For example, Roger Angell offers this purely objective description of a baseball, recording weight, dimensions, colors, and material:

> It weighs just five ounces and measures between 2.86 and 2.94 inches in diameter. It is made of a composition-cork nucleus encased in two thin layers of rubber, one black and one red, surrounded by 121 yards of tightly wrapped blue-gray wool yarn, 45 yards of white wool yarn, 53 more yards of blue-gray wool yarn, 150 yards of fine cotton yarn, 53 more yards of blue-gray wool yarn, 150 yards of fine cotton yarn, a coat of rubber cement, and a cowhide (formerly horsehide) exterior, which is held together with 216 slightly raised red cotton stitches.

Few descriptions outside of science writing, however, are completely objective. Instead of trying to include every detail, writers choose details carefully. That process of selection is determined by the writer's purpose and by the impression that the writer wants to create. For example, when Eric Liu visits his grandmother, he washes his hands in the bathroom before eating. As he looks around, his eye is drawn to a strange assortment of details: "a frayed toothbrush in a plastic Star Trek mug I'd given her in 1979, stiff washrags and aged pantyhose hanging from a clothesline, medicine bottles and hair dye cluttered on the sinktop." Liu captures a loneliness and a sadness through those details. Not everyone looking at the room would have "seen" what Liu did.

In subjective description, you are free to interpret details for your reader; your choice of words and images can be suggestive, emotional, and value-loaded. Subjective description frequently makes use of figurative language—similes and metaphors that forge connections in the reader's mind. When Gordon Grice in "Caught in the Widow's

Web" (another descriptive essay found in the Case Study in Chapter 10) sees the debris that litters the ground under the spider's web, he sees "the husks of consumed insects, their antennae stiff as gargoyle horns." When Scott Russell Sanders looks at his smashed thumbnail, he sees "a crescent moon" that "month by month . . . rose across the pink sky of my thumbnail."

Descriptions serve a variety of purposes, but in every case it is important to make that purpose clear to your reader. Sometimes description is done solely to record the facts, as in Angell's description of the baseball, or to evoke an atmosphere, as in Frey's description of an August evening at a basketball court in Brooklyn. More often description is used as support for other purposes. Gordon Grice, in describing the black widow, is not trying just to describe a spider accurately. He uses description to emphasize the evil or malevolence that he sees embodied in the "flower of natural evil." The spider is more than just a physical thing; it becomes a symbol.

How Do You Describe an Object or a Place?

The first task in writing a description is to decide what you want to describe. As in every other writing task, making a good choice means that the act of writing will be easier and probably more successful. Before you begin, keep two things in mind. First, there is rarely any point in describing a common object or place—something every reader has seen—unless you do it in a fresh and perceptive way. Roger Angell describes a baseball, but he does so by dissecting it, giving a series of facts about its composition. Probably most of Frey's readers had at least seen pictures of a project playground, but after reading his description, what they are left with is a sense of vividness—this passage evokes or re-creates in our minds a mental picture of that evening.

Second, remember that your description must create a focused impression. To do so, you need to select details that contribute to your purpose. This will give you a way of deciding which details out of the many available are relevant. Details in a description must be carefully chosen and arranged; otherwise, your reader will be overwhelmed or bored by the accumulation of detail.

How Do You Describe a Person?

Before you begin to describe a person, remember an experience that everyone has had. You have read a novel and then seen a film or a made-for-television version, and the two experiences did not mesh. The characters, you are convinced, just did not look like the actors and actresses: "She was thinner and blond" or "He was all wrong—not big enough, not rugged enough." Any time you read a narrative that contains a character—either real or fictional—you form a mental picture of the person, and that picture is generally not based on any physical description that the author has provided. In fact, in many narratives, authors provide only minimal description of the people involved. For example, if you look closely at the Thurmond Watts family in William Least Heat Moon's "Nameless, Tennessee," you will find almost no physical description of the people. Thurmond, we are told, is "tall" and "thin"—those are the only adjectives used to describe him. The rest of the family—his wife, Miss Ginny; his sister-in-law, Marilyn; and his daughter, Hilda—are not physically described at all. Nevertheless, we get a vivid sense of all four as people.

Fictional characters or real people are created or revealed primarily through ways other than direct physical description. What a person does or says, for example, also reveals personality. The reader "sees" Alan in Terry Tempest Williams's "The Village Watchman" in part through what he does (for example, his behavior at the bowling alley) and through what he says. The Wattses, in Least Heat Moon's description, are revealed by how they react, what they say, how their speech sounds, what they consider to be important. These are the key factors in re-creating Least Heat Moon's experience for the reader.

In fact, descriptions of people should not try to be verbal portraits recording physical attributes in photographic detail. Words finally are never as efficient in doing that as photographs. If the objective in describing a person is not photographic accuracy, what then is it? Go back to the advice offered earlier in this introduction: decide first what impression you want to create in your reader. Why are you describing this person? What is it about this person that is worth describing? In all likelihood the answer will be something other than physical attributes. Once you know what that something is, you can then choose the details that best reveal or display the person.

HOW DO YOU ORGANIZE A DESCRIPTION?

You have found a subject; you have studied it—either firsthand or in memory; you have decided on a reason for describing this particular subject; you have selected details that contribute to that reason or purpose. Now you need to organize your paragraph or essay. Descriptions, like narratives, have principles of order, although the principles vary depending on what sensory impressions are involved. When the primary descriptive emphasis is on seeing, the most obvious organization is spatial—moving from front to back, side to side, outside to inside, top to bottom, general to specific. The description moves as a camera would. Roger Angell's description of a baseball moves outward from the cork nucleus through the layers of rubber, wool yarn, and rubber cement to the cowhide exterior.

Other sensory experiences might be arranged in order of importance, from the most obvious to the least—the loudest noise at the concert, the most pervasive odor in the restaurant—or even in chronological order. Eric Liu's description of his visit to his grandmother is structured chronologically—from his arrival at her apartment building to their farewell embrace.

DOES DESCRIPTION MEAN LOTS OF ADJECTIVES AND ADVERBS?

You can create an image without providing a mountain of adjectives and adverbs—just as you imagine what a character looks like without being told. When Terry Tempest Williams describes Alan's behavior at the bowling alley, the scene and Alan come alive for the reader: "When it was Alan's turn, it was an event. Nothing subtle. His style was Herculean. Big man. Big ball. Big roll. Big bang. Whether it was a strike or a gutter ball, he clapped his hands, spun around on the floor, clapped his thighs, and cried, 'Goddamn! Did you see that one? Send me another ball, sweet Jesus!'" One of the greatest dangers in writing a description lies in trying to describe too much, trying to qualify every noun with at least one adjective and every verb with an adverb. Precise, vivid nouns and verbs will do most of the work for you.

SAMPLE STUDENT ESSAY

Nadine Resnick chose to describe her favorite childhood toy, a stuffed doll she had named Natalie.

PRETTY IN PINK

Standing in the middle of the aisle, staring up at the world as most children in nursery school do, something pink caught my eye. Just like Rapunzel in her high tower, there was a girl inside a cardboard and plastic prison atop a high shelf that smiled down at me. I pointed to the doll and brought her home with me that same day. Somehow I knew that she was special.

She was named Natalie. I do not know why, but the name just seemed perfect, like the rest of her. Natalie was less than twelve inches tall and wore a pink outfit. Her hands and grimacing face were made of plastic while the rest of her body was stuffed with love. She had brown eyes and brown hair, just like me, which peeked through her burgundy and pink-flowered bonnet. Perhaps the most unusual feature about her was that my mom had tattooed my name on her large bottom so that if Natalie ever strayed from me at nursery school or at the supermarket, she would be able to find me.

There was some kind of magic about Natalie's face. I think it was her grin from ear to ear. Even if I had played with her until she was so dirty that most of her facial features were hidden, Natalie's never-ending smile usually shown through. When I neglected her for days to play with some new toy and then later returned, her friendly smirk was still there. When I was left home alone for a few hours, her smile assured me that I need not be afraid. Natalie's bright smile also cheered me up when I was sick or had a bad day. And she always had enough hugs for me.

As I was growing up, Natalie and her beaming face could usually be found somewhere in my room—on my bed, in her carriage, hiding under a pile of junk, and later piled in my closet with the rest of my other dolls and stuffed animals. When I got older, I foolishly decided that I no longer needed such childish toys. So I put Natalie and the rest of my stuffed animals in a large black plastic bag in a dark corner of the basement. I now realize that the basement really is not an honorable place for someone who has meant so much to me. But, I will bet that she is still smiling anyway.

Nadine had a chance to read her essay to a small group of class-mates during a collaborative editing session. Everyone liked the essay and most of their suggested changes were fairly minor. For example, several people objected to her choice of the words *grimaced* and *smirk*, feeling that such words were not appropriate choices for a lovable doll. Another student, however, suggested a revision in the final para-graph. "It seems like you put her farther and farther away from you as you got older. Why don't you emphasize that distancing by having it occur in stages?" he commented. When Nadine rewrote her essay, she made a number of minor changes in the first three paragraphs and then followed her classmate's idea in the fourth paragraph.

NATALIE

Standing in the store's aisle, staring up at the world as most pre-school children do, something pink caught my eye. Just like Rapunzel in her high tower, a girl trapped inside a cardboard and plastic prison atop a high shelf smiled down at me. I pointed to the doll and brought her home with me that same day. Somehow I knew that she was special.

She was named Natalie. I do not know why, but the name just seemed perfect, like the rest of her. Natalie was less than twelve inches tall and wore a pink outfit. Her hands and smiling face were made of plastic while the rest of her body was plumply stuffed. Just like me, she had brown eyes and brown hair which peeked through her burgundy and pink-flowered bonnet. Perhaps her most unusual feature was my name tattooed on her bottom so that if Natalie ever strayed from me at nursery school or at the supermarket, she would be able to find me.

Natalie's face had a certain glow, some kind of magic. I think it was her grin from ear to ear. After I had played with her, no matter how dirty her face was, Natalie's never-ending smile still beamed through. When I neglected her for days to play with some new toy and then later returned, her friendly grin was still there. Years later, when I was old enough to be left home alone for a few hours, her smile assured me that I need not be afraid. Natalie's bright smile also cheered me up when I was sick or had a bad day. And she always had enough hugs for me.

As I was growing up, Natalie and her beaming face could usually be found somewhere in my room. However, she seemed to move further away from me as I got older. Natalie no longer slept with me; she slept in her own carriage. Then she rested on a high shelf across my room. Later she made her way into my closet with the rest of the dolls and stuffed animals that I had outgrown. Eventually, I decided that I no longer needed such childish toys, so I put Natalie and my other stuffed animals in a large black plastic bag in a dark cellar corner. Even though I abandoned her, I am sure that Natalie is still smiling at me today.

SOME THINGS TO REMEMBER

1. Choose your subject carefully, making sure that you have a specific reason or purpose in mind for whatever you describe.
2. Study or observe your subject—try to see it or experience it in a fresh way. Gather details; make a list; use all your senses.
3. Use your purpose as a way of deciding which details ought to be included and which excluded.
4. Choose a pattern of organization to focus your reader's attention.
5. Use precise, vivid nouns and verbs, as well as adjectives and adverbs, to create your descriptions.

VISUALIZING DESCRIPTION

Remember the cliché: "A picture is worth a thousand words"? Frankly, some things can't be adequately described in words alone. Imagine how difficult it would be to assemble a complex object if its set of instructions included only words and no pictures. Words might be crucial to creating an impression, focusing a reader's attention, or conveying precise information, but they are not adequate for every task. Consider the illustrator's anatomical sketch of the human back on page 107. It accompanies an article on "Low-Back Pain" aimed at a general audience. Here the illustrator reveals the complex muscle structures that surround the spine. Can you imagine trying to describe with only words the muscles found in the human back? See page 145.

DESCRIPTION AS A LITERARY STRATEGY

Description is often intertwined with narration as it is in "Traveling to Town," a poem by Duane BigEagle that recalls a regular experience that occurred during his childhood near the Osage Reservation in Oklahoma. As he explains in a note to the poem, "Monkey Ward" was the name many people used to refer to catalog merchandiser Montgomery Ward—once a competitor of Sears. As you read the poem, think about how sparse, but effective, the use of description is here. See page 146.

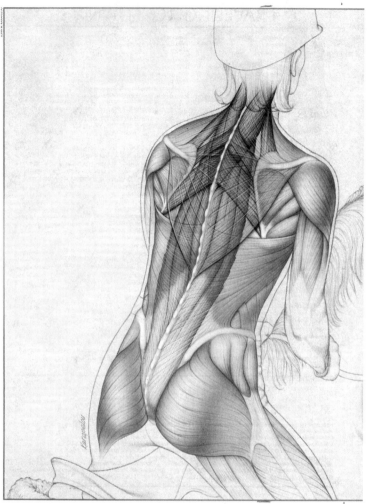

LOWER BACK consists of numerous structures, any of which may be responsible for pain. The most obvious are the powerful muscles that surround the spine. Other potential sources of pain include the strong ligaments that connect vertebrae; the disks that lie between vertebrae, providing cushioning; the facet joints, which help to ensure smooth alignment and stability of the spine; the vertebral bones themselves; blood vessels; and the nerves that emerge from the spine.

TRAVELING TO TOWN

Duane BigEagle

When I was very young,
we always went to town
in the flatbed wagon.
We'd leave as soon as the day's first heat
had stopped the mare's breath
from forming a cloud
in the air.
Kids sprawled in the back
among the dusty bushels
of corn and beans.
As we rode down main street,
the town revealed itself
backwards
for my sister and me to see.
We loved the brick and sandstone buildings
and the farmer's market
with its sawdust floor.
Best of all
was Monkey Ward
with its large wood paneled center room
and little wires
with paper messages
that flew back and forth
like trained birds.
We finally got to Safeway
where Grandma did the shopping
and Grandpa sat outside
on the brick steps in the sunlight
watching all the grandkids.
From a shady coolness
on the other side of the street
the ice cream store
would call to us
with its banging screen door.
Grandpa always had money for ice cream
and we'd ride home down main street
licking ice cream
watching the town reveal itself
backwards again
in afternoon sun.

DISCUSSION QUESTIONS

1. Probably few readers have ridden to town in a horse-drawn wagon. Despite the lack of similar experiences, can you visualize the scene that BigEagle is describing? Why or why not?
2. The trip presumably takes an entire day. Out of the whole experience, what does BigEagle describe? Why these things?
3. Description doesn't always mean surrounding nouns with clusters of adjectives and verbs with adverbs. Focus on a detail or two in the poem that adds to the description. What does BigEagle do to make the detail seem vivid? What does that suggest about writing effective descriptions?
4. What is the overall impression that BigEagle seems to be trying to convey to his readers? How do the individual details contribute to that impression?
5. How is the description organized in the poem?

WRITING SUGGESTIONS

Describe an experience out of your childhood or adolescence. Notice that description often works best when it is sparsely done. Some possible places to start could include the following prompts:

a. An experience you had with your grandparents or parents
b. A place that you (or you and your family) regularly visited
c. A trip—a ride, for example, in a car, train, bus, subway, or airplane

Using Description in Your Writing for Other Courses

Description can be involved in a number of different college writing assignments. Most such descriptive writing will be objective, focusing on exact details rather than on your personal responses, but you might occasionally be asked to evaluate something you describe more aesthetically. Here are some examples of writing assignments that would involve description.

- **Art History.** An assignment asking for a detailed analysis of a painting would necessarily include a detailed description of its pictorial elements, both objectively and with an eye toward the aesthetic qualities of the work.

- **Geology.** On an exam you might be required to identify a variety of different mineral samples by describing their specific physical characteristics.
- **Anthropology.** For an anthropological field study, you might be asked for a closely observed description of the physical appearance and social interactions of the members of a clearly defined social group.
- **Anatomy.** Following your class's examination of a laboratory specimen, you might be asked to write a brief paper describing its specific anatomical structures in detail.
- **American Studies.** In a unit on American architecture, you might choose to write a paper focusing on a particular architectural style—the main features of which you would describe fully—to suggest what that style reflects about American values at a particular period in history.
- **Theater/Dramatic Literature.** On an essay exam, you might be asked to describe the physical theaters in which plays were presented at the times of the playwrights Sophocles, Shakespeare, and Ibsen.

VISIT THE PRENTICE HALL READER'S WEBSITE

When you have finished reading an essay, check out the additional material available at the *Reader*'s Website at www.prenhall. com/miller. For each reading, you will find a list of related readings connected with the topic or the author; additional background information; a group of relevant "hot-linked" Web resources (just click your computer's mouse and automatically visit the sites listed); and still more writing suggestions.

DESCRIPTION

The Library of Congress in Washington, D.C., has 60 spectacular on-line exhibitions covering a broad range of topics, time frames, and geographical regions in the United States—see a fabulous collection of old baseball cards, watch Edison's films made during the Spanish American War in 1898, view over 900 photographs of the Northern Great Plains during the first decades of the twentieth century. For an overview of the exhibits and for a writing topic that invites you to describe what you saw on your virtual experience, go to the *Reader*'s Website.

PO-PO

Eric Liu

Eric Liu (1968–   ) graduated from Yale and in 1991 founded The
Next Progressive, *a quarterly journal of Democratic Party politics and culture. In 1993, he joined President Clinton's speech-writing staff as its
youngest and only Asian American member. A contributor to MSNBC,
Slate,* The Washington Post, *and* USA Weekend, *Liu also edited* Next:
Young American Writers on the New Generation *(1994). This essay is
taken from* The Accidental Asian: Notes of a Native Speaker *(1998).*

On Writing: *In* The Accidental Asian, *Liu considers issues of personal
identity—both as an Asian American and simply as an American. He longs, he
says, to be grounded in a historical tradition and wonders if he should focus on
"Asian American history: the trials of people before my time, whose estrange-
ment from the mainstream years ago made possible my entry into the mainstream today." Liu goes on: "And I think here in this narrative is a source of
belonging. But then I wonder: Should I stop with Asian American stories?
Should I even begin there?" Then he explains that as a speechwriter for President Clinton his specialty was to compose memorial speeches for victims of
tragedies such as plane crashes and for military personnel killed in battle. He
discovered that his speech to honor the fiftieth anniversary of World War II's D-
Day, delivered at the American cemetary in Normandy, allowed him to participate in "a nation's memory" and "something I, too, could claim."*

BEFORE READING

Connecting: What memories or associations come immediately to
mind when you think about one of your parents or grandparents?

Anticipating: Liu is writing about his memories of his maternal
grandmother. Out of the many memories that he has, why might he
choose to recount his memory of a visit to her apartment? How do
the included details affect our sense of Po-Po?

1   For more than two decades, my mother's mother, Po-Po, lived in a
cinder-block one-bedroom apartment on the edge of New York's
Chinatown. She was twenty floors up, so if you looked straight out
from the main room, which faced north, one block appeared to melt
into the next, all the way to the spire of the Empire State off in the

distance. This was a saving grace, the view, since her own block down below was not much to look at. Her building, one of those inter-changeable towers of 1970s public housing, was on the lower east side of the Lower East Side, at the corner of South and Clinton. It was, as the realtors say, only minutes from the Brooklyn Bridge and South Street Seaport, although those landmarks, for all she cared, might as well have been in Nebraska. They weren't part of the world Po-Po in-habited, which was the world that I visited every few months during the last years of her life.

My visits followed a certain pattern. I'd get to her apartment   2
around noon, and when I knocked on the door I could hear her scur-rying with excitement. When she opened the door, I'd be struck, al-ways as if for the first time, by how tiny she was: four feet nine and shrinking. She wore loose, baggy clothes, nylons, and ill-fitting old glasses that covered her soft, wrinkled face. It was a face I recognized from my own second-grade class photo. *Eh, Po-Po, ni hao maaa?* She offered a giggle as I bent to embrace her. With an impish smile, she proclaimed my American name in her Yoda-like voice: *Areek.* She got a kick out of that. As she shuffled to the kitchen, where Li Tai Tai, her caregiver, was preparing lunch, I would head to the bathroom, trained to wash my hands upon entering Po-Po's home.

In the small bath were the accessories of her everyday life: a   3
frayed toothbrush in a plastic Star Trek mug I'd given her in 1979, stiff washrags and aged pantyhose hanging from a clothesline, med-icine bottles and hair dye cluttered on the sinktop. I often paused for a moment there, looking for my reflection in the filmy, clouded mirror, taking a deep breath or two. Then I would walk back into the main room. The place was neat but basically grimy. Some of the furniture—the lumpy couch, the coffee table with old magazines and congealed candies, the lawn chair where she read her Chinese news-paper through a magnifying glass—had been there as long as I could remember. The windowsill was crammed with plants and flowers. The only thing on the thickly painted white wall was a calendar. *Your house looks so nice*, I'd say in a tender tone of Mandarin that I used only with her. On a tray beside me, also surveying the scene, was a faded black-and-white portrait of Po-Po as a beautiful young woman dressed in Chinese costume. *Lai chi ba*, Po-Po would say, inviting me to eat.

Invariably, there was a banquet's worth of food awaiting me on   4
the small kitchen table: *hongshao* stewed beef, a broiled fish with scal-lions and ginger, a leafy green called *jielan*, a soup with chicken and winter melon and radishes, tofu with ground pork, stir-fried shrimp still in their salty shells. Po-Po ate sparingly, and Li Tai Tai, in her

mannerly Chinese way, adamantly refused to dine with us, so it was up to me to attack this meal. I gorged myself, loosening my belt within the half hour and sitting back dazed and short of breath by the end. No matter how much I put down, Po-Po would express disappointment at my meager appetite.

5   As I ate she chattered excitedly, pouring forth a torrent of opinions about politics in China, Hong Kong pop singers, the latest developments in Taiwan. After a while, she'd move into stories about people I'd never met, distant relations, half brothers killed by the Communists, my grandfather, who had died when I was a toddler. Then she'd talk about her friends who lived down the "F" train in Flushing or on the other side of Chinatown and who were dying one by one, and she'd tell me about seeing Jesus after she'd had a cancer operation in 1988, and how this blond Jesus had materialized and said to her in Chinese, *You are a good person, too good to die now. Nobody knows how good you are. Nobody appreciates you as much as I do.* I would sit quietly then, not sure whether to smile. But just as she approached the brink she would take a sip of 7UP and swerve back to something in the news, perhaps something about her heroine, the Burmese dissident Aung San Suu Kyi. She was an incredible talker, Po-Po, using her hands and her eyes like a performer. She built up a tidal momentum, relentless, imaginative, spiteful, like a child.

6   I generally didn't have much to say in response to Po-Po's commentary, save the occasional Chinese-inflected *Oh?* and *Wah!* I took in the lilt of her Sichuan accent and relied on context to figure out what she was saying. In fact, it wasn't till I brought my girlfriend to meet Po-Po that I realized just how vague my comprehension was. *What did she say?* Carroll would ask. *Um, something about, something, I think, about the president of Taiwan.* Of course, I'm not sure Po-Po even cared whether I understood. If I interjected, she'd cut me off with a hasty *bushide—no, it's not that*—a habit I found endearing in small doses but that my mother, over a lifetime, had found maddening.

7   If there was a lull, I might ask Po-Po about her health, which would prompt her to spring up from her chair and, bracing herself on the counter, kick her leg up in the air. *I do this ten times every morning at five,* she would proudly say in Chinese. *Then this,* she'd add, and she would stretch her arms out like little wings, making circles with her fingertips. *And last week I had a headache, so I rubbed each eye like this thirty-six times.* Pretty soon I was out of my chair, too, laughing, rubbing, kicking, as Po-Po schooled me in her system of exercises and home remedies. We did this every visit, like a ritual.

8   Time moved so slowly when I was at Po-Po's. After lunch, we might sit on the couch next to each other or go to her room so she

could tell me things that she didn't want Li Tai Tai to hear. We would rest there, digesting, our conversation turning more mellow. I might pull out of my bag a small keepsake for her, a picture of Carroll and me, or a souvenir from a recent vacation. She would show me a bundle of poems she had written in classical Chinese, scribbled on the backs of the small cardboard rectangles that come with travel packs of Kleenex. She would recount how she'd been inspired to write this poem or that one. Then she would open a spiral notebook that she kept, stuffed with news clippings and filled with idioms and sentences she had copied out of the Chinese newspaper's daily English lesson: *Let's get a move on. I don't like the looks of this.* At my urging, she'd read the sentences aloud, tentatively. I would praise her warmly, she would chuckle, and then she might show me something else, a photo album, a book about *qigong.*

One day she revealed to me her own way of prayer, demon-   9
strating how she sat on the side of her bed at night and clasped her hands, bowing as if before Buddha, repeating in fragile English, *God bless me? God bless me? God bless me?* Another time she urgently recited to me a short story that had moved her to tears, but I understood hardly a word of it. On another visit she fell asleep beside me, her glasses still on, her chin tucked into itself. And so the hours would pass, until it was time for me to go—until, that is, I had decided it was time to go, for she would have wanted me to stay forever—and I would hold her close and stroke her knotted back and tell her that I loved her and that I would miss her, and Po-Po, too modest to declare her heart so openly, would nod and press a little red envelope of money into my hand and say to me quietly in Chinese, *How I wish I had wings so I could come see you where you live.*

QUESTIONS ON SUBJECT AND PURPOSE

1. Liu recounts a typical visit to his grandmother's New York City apartment. How often does he visit her?
2. Why might Liu have written about his grandmother?
3. Why would a reader be interested in reading about someone else's grandmother?

QUESTIONS ON STRATEGY AND AUDIENCE

1. How does Liu structure his essay?
2. How would you describe the feelings that Liu has about Po-Po? What evidence from the essay could you cite to support your answer?

3. Why might Liu have chosen to end his account of a typical visit with the incidents related in paragraph 9?

QUESTIONS ON VOCABULARY AND STYLE

1. What is the effect of the final sentence of the essay?
2. Liu italicizes scraps of dialogue in the essay—for example, Po-Po's remarks and questions. What is the effect of including these little scraps of conversation?
3. Be prepared to define the following words: *scurrying* (paragraph 2), *scallions* (4), *tofu* (4), *adamantly* (4), *dissident* (5).

WRITING SUGGESTIONS

1. **For Your Journal.** How would you describe your parents' attitude toward their parents? How would you describe your attitude toward your grandparents? In your journal, explore both subjects. (If you are an older student, you could explore your and your children's attitudes toward your parents.)
2. **For a Paragraph.** In a paragraph, write a description of someone who is significantly older than you are—preferably a grandparent or someone at least a generation older. As a prewriting exercise, try to make a visit to your subject or to at least talk with the person on the telephone. Observe, listen, take notes. Try to capture your person in a paragraph.
3. **For an Essay.** Extend your paragraph into an essay. Do not just describe the person photographically. Use descriptive details—for example, about the person's behavior, environment, language, or values—to reveal character. Consider using some dialogue.
4. **For Research.** America is a society that worships youth and shuns old age. Old people are often not figures to be respected or honored but burdens to be cared for by hired professionals. In many other societies, however, the elderly are treated very differently. Research a society that honors its old. Do not just report on how the elderly are seen or treated in this society. Formulate a thesis that explains why this society behaves in this way. You will first need to identify those societies—a reference librarian can help you start a search through a source such as the Library of Congress Subject Headings (see the Appendix: "Finding, Using, and Documenting Sources").

WEBSITE LINK

In an interview, "Asian Integration," Liu talks about race and identity in America. The text is available from an on-line bookstore. The interview is instantly accessible through the *Reader*'s Website.

 WRITING LINK: COMMAS

Select one or more of Liu's paragraphs and study how he uses commas in each sentence. See if you can find an explanation in a grammar book for why each comma is used. Look at your own writing. Do you use commas in the same way? Remember that commas—and all marks of punctuation—help your reader to see the structure of the sentence.

THE WAY TO RAINY MOUNTAIN

N. Scott Momaday

Navarre Scott Momaday was born in Lawton, Oklahoma, in 1934. He earned a B.A. from the University of New Mexico and a Ph.D. in English from Stanford University. Professor of English, artist, editor, poet, and novelist, Momaday is above all a storyteller committed to preserving and interpreting the rich oral history of the Kiowa Indians. His work includes a book of Kiowa folktales, The Journey of Tai-me *(1967), which he revised as* The Way to Rainy Mountain *(1969), and the Pulitzer Prize-winning novel,* House Made of Dawn *(1968). His most recent book is* The Man Made of Words *(1997), a collection of essays, stories, and "passages."*

This essay originally appeared in the magazine The Reporter *in 1967, but Momaday revised it and used it as the introduction to* The Way to Rainy Mountain.

On Writing: *Momaday commented: "There's a lot of frustration in writing. I heard an interview with a writer not long ago in which the interviewer said, tell me, is writing difficult? And the writer said, oh, no . . . no, of course not. He said, 'All you do is sit down at a typewriter, you put a page in it, and then you look at it until beads of blood appear on your forehead. That's all there is to it.' There are days like that."*

BEFORE READING

Connecting: In what way does one of your relatives, perhaps a grandparent or a great-grandparent, connect you to a part of your family's past?

Anticipating: How and why does Momaday interlink descriptions of the landscape with descriptions of his grandmother?

1   A single knoll rises out of the plain in Oklahoma, north and west of the Wichita Range. For my people, the Kiowas, it is an old landmark, and they gave it the name Rainy Mountain. The hardest weather in the world is there. Winter brings blizzards, hot tornadic winds arise in the spring, and in summer the prairie is an anvil's edge. The grass turns brittle and brown, and it cracks beneath your feet. There are green belts along the rivers and creeks, linear groves of hickory and pecan, willow and witch hazel. At a distance in July or August the

steaming foliage seems almost to writhe in fire. Great green and yellow grasshoppers are everywhere in the tall grass, popping up like corn to sting the flesh, and tortoises crawl about on the red earth, going nowhere in the plenty of time. Loneliness is an aspect of the land. All things in the plain are isolate; there is no confusion of objects in the eye, but one hill or one tree or one man. To look upon that landscape in the early morning, with the sun at your back, is to lose the sense of proportion. Your imagination comes to life, and this, you think, is where Creation was begun.

I returned to Rainy Mountain in July. My grandmother had   2 died in the spring, and I wanted to be at her grave. She had lived to be very old and at last infirm. Her only living daughter was with her when she died, and I was told that in death her face was that of a child.

I like to think of her as a child. When she was born, the Kiowas   3 were living the last great moment of their history. For more than a hundred years they had controlled the open range from the Smoky Hill River to the Red, from the headwaters of the Canadian to the fork of the Arkansas and Cimarron. In alliance with the Comanches, they had ruled the whole of the southern Plains. War was their sacred business, and they were among the finest horsemen the world has ever known. But warfare for the Kiowas was preeminently a matter of disposition rather than of survival, and they never understood the grim, unrelenting advance of the U.S. Cavalry. When at last, divided and ill-provisioned, they were driven onto the Staked Plains in the cold rains of autumn, they fell into panic. In Palo Duro Canyon they abandoned their crucial stores to pillage and had nothing then but their lives. In order to save themselves, they surrendered to the soldiers at Fort Sill and were imprisoned in the old stone corral that now stands as a military museum. My grandmother was spared the humiliation of those high gray walls by eight or ten years, but she must have known from birth the affliction of defeat, the dark brooding of old warriors.

Her name was Aho, and she belonged to the last culture to   4 evolve in North America. Her forebears came down from the high country in western Montana nearly three centuries ago. They were a mountain people, a mysterious tribe of hunters whose language has never been positively classified in any major group. In the late seventeenth century they began a long migration to the south and east. It was a journey toward the dawn, and it led to a golden age. Along the way the Kiowas were befriended by the Crows, who gave them the culture and religion of the Plains. They acquired horses, and their ancient nomadic spirit was suddenly free of the ground. They acquired Tai-me, the sacred Sun Dance doll, from that moment the object and symbol of their worship, and so shared in the divinity of the sun. Not least, they acquired the sense of destiny, therefore courage and pride. When they entered upon the southern Plains they had been transformed. No longer were they slaves to the simple necessity of survival; they were a lordly and dangerous society of fighters and thieves, hunters and priests of the sun. According to their origin myth, they entered the world through a hollow log. From one point of view, their migration was the fruit of an old prophecy, for indeed they emerged from a sunless world.

5   Although my grandmother lived out her long life in the shadow of Rainy Mountain, the immense landscape of the continental interior lay like memory in her blood. She could tell of the Crows, whom she had never seen, and of the Black Hills, where she had never been. I wanted to see in reality what she had seen more perfectly in the mind's eye, and traveled fifteen hundred miles to begin my pilgrimage.

6   Yellowstone, it seemed to me, was the top of the world, a region of deep lakes and dark timber, canyons and waterfalls. But, beautiful as it is, one might have the sense of confinement there. The skyline in all directions is close at hand, the high wall of the woods and deep cleavages of shade. There is a perfect freedom in the mountains, but it belongs to the eagle and the elk, the badger and the bear. The Kiowas reckoned their stature by the distance they could see, and they were bent and blind in the wilderness.

7   Descending eastward, the highland meadows are a stairway to the plain. In July the inland slope of the Rockies is luxuriant with flax and buckwheat, stonecrop and larkspur. The earth unfolds and the limit of the land recedes. Clusters of trees, and animals grazing far in the distance, cause the vision to reach away and wonder to build upon the mind. The sun follows a longer course in the day, and the sky is immense beyond all comparison. The great billowing clouds that sail upon it are shadows that move upon the grain like water, dividing light. Farther down, in the land of the Crows and Blackfeet, the plain is yellow. Sweet clover takes hold of the hills and bends upon itself to cover and seal the soil. There the Kiowas paused on their way; they had come to the place where they must change their lives. The sun is at home on the plains. Precisely there does it have the certain character of a god. When the Kiowas came to the land of the Crows, they could see the dark lees of the hills at dawn across the Bighorn River, the profusion of light on the grain shelves, the oldest deity ranging after the solstices. Not yet would they veer southward to the caldron of the land that lay below; they must wean their blood from the northern winter and hold the mountains a while longer in their view. They bore Tai-me in procession to the east.

A dark mist lay over the Black Hills, and the land was like iron. 8
At the top of a ridge I caught sight of Devil's Tower up-thrust against
the gray sky as if in the birth of time the core of the earth had broken
through its crust and the motion of the world was begun. There are
things in nature that engender an awful quiet in the heart of man;
Devil's Tower is one of them. Two centuries ago, because they could
not do otherwise, the Kiowas made a legend at the base of the rock.
My grandmother said:

> Eight children were there at play, seven sisters and their brother.
> Suddenly the boy was struck dumb; he trembled and began to run
> upon his hands and feet. His fingers became claws, and his body was
> covered with fur. Directly there was a bear where the boy had been.
> The sisters were terrified; they ran, and the bear after them. They
> came to the stump of a great tree, and the tree spoke to them. It bade
> them climb upon it, and as they did so it began to rise into the air.
> The bear came to kill them, but they were just beyond its reach. It
> reared against the tree and scored the bark all around with its claws.
> The seven sisters were borne into the sky, and they became the stars
> of the Big Dipper.

From that moment, and so long as the legend lives, the Kiowas have
kinsmen in the night sky. Whatever they were in the mountains, they
could be no more. However tenuous their well-being, however much
they had suffered and would suffer again, they had found a way out of
the wilderness.

My grandmother had a reverence for the sun, a holy regard that 9
now is all but gone out of mankind. There was a wariness in her, and
an ancient awe. She was a Christian in her later years, but she had
come a long way about, and she never forgot her birthright. As a child
she had been to the Sun Dances; she had taken part in those annual
rites, and by them she had learned the restoration of her people in the
presence of Tai-me. She was about seven when the last Kiowa Sun
Dance was held in 1887 on the Washita River above Rainy Mountain
Creek. The buffalo were gone. In order to consummate the ancient
sacrifice—to impale the head of a buffalo bull upon the medicine
tree—a delegation of old men journeyed into Texas, there to beg and
barter for an animal from the Goodnight herd. She was ten when the
Kiowas came together for the last time as a living Sun Dance culture.
They could find no buffalo; they had to hang an old hide from the sacred tree. Before the dance could begin, a company of soldiers rode
out from Fort Sill under orders to disperse the tribe. Forbidden without cause the essential act of their faith, having seen the wild herds
slaughtered and left to rot upon the ground, the Kiowas backed away
forever from the medicine tree. That was July 20, 1890, at the great

bend of the Washita. My grandmother was there. Without bitterness, and for as long as she lived, she bore a vision of deicide.

10   Now that I can have her only in memory, I see my grandmother in the several postures that were peculiar to her: standing at the wood stove on a winter morning and turning meat in a great iron skillet; sitting at the south window, bent above her beadwork, and afterwards, when her vision failed, looking down for a long time into the fold of her hands; going out upon a cane, very slowly as she did when the weight of age came upon her; praying. I remember her most often at prayer. She made long, rambling prayers out of suffering and hope, having seen many things. I was never sure that I had the right to hear, so exclusive were they of all mere custom and company. The last time I saw her she prayed standing by the side of her bed at night, naked to the waist, the light of a kerosene lamp moving upon her dark skin. Her long, black hair, always drawn and braided in the day, lay upon her shoulders and against her breasts like a shawl. I do not speak Kiowa, and I never understood her prayers, but there was something inherently sad in the sound, some merest hesitation upon the syllables of sorrow. She began in a high and descending pitch, exhausting her breath to silence; then again and again—and always the same intensity of effort, of something that is, and is not, like urgency in the human voice. Transported so in the dancing light among the shadows of her room, she seemed beyond the reach of time. But that was illusion; I think I knew then that I should not see her again.

11   Houses are like sentinels in the plain, old keepers of the weather watch. There, in a very little while, wood takes on the appearance of great age. All colors wear soon away in the wind and rain, and then the wood is burned gray and the grain appears and the nails turn red with rust. The windowpanes are black and opaque; you imagine there is nothing within, and indeed there are many ghosts, bones given up to the land. They stand here and there against the sky, and you approach them for a longer time than you expect. They belong in the distance; it is their domain.

12   Once there was a lot of sound in my grandmother's house, a lot of coming and going, feasting and talk. The summers there were full of excitement and reunion. The Kiowas are a summer people; they abide the cold and keep to themselves, but when the season turns and the land becomes warm and vital they cannot hold still; an old love of going returns upon them. The aged visitors who came to my grandmother's house when I was a child were made of lean and leather, and they bore themselves upright. They wore great black hats and bright ample shirts that shook in the wind. They rubbed fat upon their hair and wound their braids with strips of colored cloth. Some of them

painted their faces and carried the scars of old and cherished enmities. They were an old council of warlords, come to remind and be reminded of who they were. Their wives and daughters served them well. The women might indulge themselves; gossip was at once the mark and compensation of their servitude. They made loud and elaborate talk among themselves, full of jest and gesture, fright and false alarm. They went abroad in fringed and flowered shawls, bright beadwork and German silver. They were at home in the kitchen, and they prepared meals that were banquets.

There were frequent prayer meetings, and great nocturnal   13
feasts. When I was a child I played with my cousins outside, where the lamplight fell upon the ground and the singing of the old people rose up around us and carried away into the darkness. There were a lot of good things to eat, a lot of laughter and surprise. And afterwards, when the quiet returned, I lay down with my grandmother and could hear the frogs away by the river and feel the motion of the air.

Now there is a funeral silence in the rooms, the endless wake of   14
some final word. The walls have closed in upon my grandmother's house. When I returned to it in mourning, I saw for the first time in my life how small it was. It was late at night, and there was a white moon, nearly full. I sat for a long time on the stone steps by the kitchen door. From there I could see out across the land; I could see the long row of trees by the creek, the low light upon the rolling plains, and the stars of the Big Dipper. Once I looked at the moon and caught sight of a strange thing. A cricket had perched upon the handrail, only a few inches away from me. My line of vision was such that the creature filled the moon like a fossil. It had gone there, I thought, to live and die, for there, of all places, was its small definition made whole and eternal. A warm wind rose up and purled like the longing within me.

The next morning I awoke at dawn and went out on the dirt   15
road to Rainy Mountain. It was already hot, and the grasshoppers began to fill the air. Still, it was early in the morning, and the birds sang out of the shadows. The long yellow grass on the mountain shone in the bright light, and a scissortail hied above the land. There, where it ought to be, at the end of a long and legendary way, was my grandmother's grave. Here and there on the dark stones were ancestral names. Looking back once, I saw the mountain and came away.

QUESTIONS ON SUBJECT AND PURPOSE

  1. What event triggers Momaday's essay?
  2. How many "journeys" are involved in Momaday's story?

3. Why might Momaday have titled the essay "The Way to Rainy Mountain"? Why not, for example, refer more specifically to the event that has brought him back?

QUESTIONS ON STRATEGY AND AUDIENCE

1. Why might Momaday retell the legend of the "seven sisters" (paragraph 8)? How does that fit into his essay?
2. How much descriptive detail does Momaday give of his grandmother? Go through the essay, and isolate each physical detail the reader is given.
3. What expectations might Momaday have of his audience? How might those expectations affect the essay?

QUESTIONS ON VOCABULARY AND STYLE

1. Identify the figure of speech used in each of these descriptions:
   a. "in summer the prairie is an anvil's edge" (paragraph 1)
   b. "the highland meadows are a stairway to the plain" (7)
   c. "the land was like iron" (8)
   d. "houses are like sentinels in the plain" (11)
2. Between the essay's first appearance in a magazine and its inclusion in a book of essays two years later, Momaday added two new paragraphs, now 6 and 7. What do these paragraphs add to the essay?
3. Be prepared to define the following words: *knoll* (paragraph 1), *writhe* (1), *pillage* (3), *nomadic* (4), *luxuriant* (7), *lees* (7), *solstices* (7), *veer* (7), *tenuous* (8), *deicide* (9), *enmities* (12), *purled* (14), *hied* (15).

WRITING SUGGESTIONS

1. **For Your Journal.** What memories do you have of a grandparent or a great-grandparent? When you think of that person, what comes to mind? In your journal, make a list of those memories—sights, sounds, smells, associations of any sort.
2. **For a Paragraph.** In a substantial paragraph, analyze the effects that Momaday achieved by adding paragraphs 6 and 7 to the essay.
3. **For an Essay.** Momaday once told an interviewer, "I believe that the Indian has an understanding of the physical world and

of the earth as a spiritual entity that is his, very much his own. The non-Indian can benefit a good deal by having that perception revealed to him." What do such perceptions reveal to the non-Indian?

4. **For Research.** What part have geography and other aspects of the natural world played in determining who you are? If you had to undertake a "pilgrimage" to a place or a geographical location or to retrack a migration, where would you go? What were the stages on the journey? Research part of your own family history, and write a research paper in which you trace out that journey for a reader. You might want to start by talking with your relatives. Then use research—in the library, in archives, in electronic databases, in atlases, in talks with people—to fill out the story for your reader. Be sure to acknowledge all of your sources.

 WEBSITE LINK

Among the Web resources for information about Momaday is a long, detailed interview with him that includes extensive audio clips—the link is at www.prenhall.com/miller.

 WRITING LINK: SENTENCE VARIETY

Teachers often urge students to explore a variety of sentence types, not to rely, for example, on writing strings of simple sentences. Look at paragraph 10 in Momaday's essay. The long first sentence, a complex series of parallel clauses introduced by a colon and separated by semicolons, ends with a single participle, *praying*. That seven-line sentence is followed by a simple sentence that grows out of that participle. The remainder of the paragraph shows other patterns at work—long compound sentences held together with coordinating conjunctions and complex sentences containing dependent clauses. How do the sentences' structures reflect their meaning? What does Momaday gain by varying his sentence structures? What does this suggest about your own writing?

NAMELESS, TENNESSEE

William Least Heat Moon

William Least Heat Moon was born William Trogdon in Missouri in 1939 and earned a Ph.D. in English from the University of Missouri in 1973. Trogdon's father created his pen name in memory of their Sioux forefather. His books include Blue Highways: A Journey into America *(1982),* PrairyErth *(1991), and* River-Horse: A Voyage Across America *(1999), an account of his five-thousand mile journey across America's waterways from New York harbor to the Pacific Ocean. The following essay is from* Blue Highways, *an account of Least Heat Moon's 14,000-mile journey through American backroads in a converted van called* Ghost Dancing. *Its title refers to the blue ink used by map publisher Rand McNally to indicate smaller, or secondary, roads.*

On Writing: *Asked about his writing, Least Heat Moon observed: "Woody Allen once said the hardest thing in writing is going from nothing to something. And I think he's right. I struggle so much getting that first draft down. My writing draws so much upon every bit that I am, that I feel drained when I finish a book, and it's years before I'm ready to write again."*

BEFORE READING

Connecting: If you could get in an automobile and drive off, and time, money, and responsibilities posed no obstacles, where would you go?

Anticipating: "Nameless, Tennessee" does more than just faithfully record everything Least Heat Moon saw while visiting the Wattses. The narrative has a central focus that controls the selection of detail. What is that focus?

1   Nameless, Tennessee, was a town of maybe ninety people if you pushed it, a dozen houses along the road, a couple of barns, same number of churches, a general merchandise store selling Fire Chief gasoline, and a community center with a lighted volleyball court. Behind the center was an open-roof, rusting metal privy with PAINT ME on the door, in the hollow of a nearby oak lay a full pint of Jack Daniel's Black Label. From the houses, the odor of coal smoke.

2   Next to a red tobacco barn stood the general merchandise with a poster of Senator Albert Gore, Jr., smiling from the window. I knocked. The door opened partway. A tall, thin man said, "Closed up. For good," and started to shut the door.

"Don't want to buy anything. Just a question for Mr. Thur-   3
mond Watts."

The man peered through the slight opening. He looked me   4
over. "What question would that be?"

"If this is Nameless, Tennessee, could he tell me how it got   5
that name?"

The man turned back into the store and called out, "Miss   6
Ginny! Somebody here wants to know how Nameless come to be
Nameless."

Miss Ginny edged to the door and looked me and my truck   7
over. Clearly, she didn't approve. She said, "You know as well as I
do, Thurmond. Don't keep him on the stoop in the damp to tell
him." Miss Ginny, I found out, was Mrs. Virginia Watts, Thurmond's wife.

I stepped in and they both began telling the story, adding a de-   8
tail here, the other correcting a fact there, both smiling at the fool-
ishness of it all. It seems the hilltop settlement went for years without
a name. Then one day the Post Office Department told the people if
they wanted mail up on the mountain they would have to give the
place a name you could properly address a letter to. The community
met; there were only a handful, but they commenced debating. Some
wanted patriotic names, some names from nature, one man recommended in all seriousness his own name. They couldn't agree, and
they ran out of names to argue about. Finally, a fellow tired of the talk;
he didn't like the mail he received anyway. "Forget the durn Post Office," he said. "This here's a nameless place if I ever seen one, so leave
it be." And that's just what they did.

Watts pointed out the window. "We used to have signs on the   9
road, but the Halloween boys keep tearin' them down."

"You think Nameless is a funny name," Miss Ginny said. "I see   10
it plain in your eyes. Well, you take yourself up north a piece to Difficult or Defeated or Shake Rag. Now them are silly names."

The old store, lighted only by three fifty-watt bulbs, smelled of   11
coal oil and baking bread. In the middle of the rectangular room,
where the oak floor sagged a little, stood an iron stove. To the right
was a wooden table with an unfinished game of checkers and a stool
made from an apple-tree stump. On shelves around the walls sat
earthen jugs with corncob stoppers, a few canned goods, and some of
the two thousand old clocks and clockworks Thurmond Watts
owned. Only one was ticking, the others he just looked at. I asked how
long he'd been in the store.

"Thirty-five years, but we closed the first day of the year. We're   12
hopin' to sell it to a churchly couple. Upright people. No athians."

"Did you build this store?"   13

14   "I built this one, but it's the third general store on the ground. I fear it'll be the last. I take no pleasure in that. Once you could come in here for a gallon of paint, a pickle, a pair of shoes, and a can of corn."

15   "Or horehound candy," Miss Ginny said. "Or corsets and salves. We had cough syrups and all that for the body. In season, we'd buy and sell blackberries and walnuts and chestnuts, before the blight got them. And outside, Thurmond milled corn and sharpened plows. Even shoed a horse sometimes."

16   "We could fix up a horse or a man or a baby," Watts said.

17   "Thurmond, tell him we had a doctor on the ridge in them days."

18   "We had a doctor on the ridge in them days. As good as any doctor alivin'. He'd cut a crooked toenail or deliver a woman. Dead these last years."

19   "I got some bad ham meat one day," Miss Ginny said, "and took to vomitin'. All day, all night. Hangin' on the drop edge of yonder. I said to Thurmond, 'Thurmond, unless you want shut of me, call the doctor.'"

20   "I studied on it," Watts said.

21   "You never did. You got him right now. He come over and put three drops of iodeen in half a glass of well water. I drank it down and the vomitin' stopped with the last swallow. Would you think iodeen could do that?"

22   "He put Miss Ginny on one teaspoon of spirits of ammonia in well water for her nerves. Ain't nothin' works better for her to this day."

23   "Calms me like the hand of the Lord."

24   Hilda, the Wattses' daughter, came out of the backroom. "I remember him," she said. "I was just a baby. Y'all were talkin' to him, and he lifted me up on the counter and gave me a stick of Juicy Fruit and a piece of cheese."

25   "Knew the old medicines," Watts said. "Only drugstore he needed was a good kitchen cabinet. None of them anteebeeotics that hit you worsen your ailment. Forgotten lore now, the old medicines, because they ain't profit in iodeen."

26   Miss Ginny started back to the side room where she and her sister Marilyn were taking apart a duck-down mattress to make bolsters. She stopped at the window for another look at Ghost Dancing. "How do you sleep in that thing? Ain't you all cramped and cold?"

27   "How does the clam sleep in his shell?" Watts said in my defense.

28   "Thurmond, get the boy a piece of buttermilk pie afore he goes on."

29   "Hilda, get some buttermilk pie." He looked at me. "You like good music?" I said I did. He cranked up an old Edison phonograph,

the kind with the big morning-glory blossom for a speaker, and put on a wax cylinder. "This will be 'My Mother's Prayer,'" he said. While I ate buttermilk pie, Watts served as disc jockey of 30 Nameless, Tennessee. "Here's 'Mountain Rose.'" It was one of those moments that you know at the time will stay with you to the grave: the sweet pie, the gaunt man playing the old music, the coals in the stove glowing orange, the scent of kerosene and hot bread. "Here's 'Evening Rhapsody.'" The music was so heavily romantic we both laughed. I thought: It is for this I have come.

Feathered over and giggling, Miss Ginny stepped from the side 31 room. She knew she was a sight. "Thurmond, give him some lunch. Still looks hungry."

Hilda pulled food off the woodstove in the backroom: home- 32 butchered and canned whole-hog sausage, home-canned June apples, turnip greens, cole slaw, potatoes, stuffing, hot cornbread. All delicious.

Watts and Hilda sat and talked while I ate. "Wish you would 33 join me."

"We've ate," Watts said. "Cain't beat a woodstove for flavorful 34 cookin'."

He told me he was raised in a one-hundred-fifty-year-old cabin 35 still standing in one of the hollows. "How many's left," he said, "that grew up in a log cabin? I ain't the last surely, but I must be climbin' on the list."

Hilda cleared the table. "You Watts ladies know how to cook." 36

"She's in nursin' school at Tennessee Tech. I went over for one 37 of them football games last year there at Coevul." To say *Cookeville*, you let the word collapse in upon itself so that it comes out "Coevul."

"Do you like football?" I asked. 38

"Don't know. I was so high up in that stadium, I never opened 39 my eyes."

Watts went to the back and returned with a fat spiral notebook 40 that he set on the table. His expression had changed. "Miss Ginny's *Deathbook.*"

The thing startled me. Was it something I was supposed to 41 sign? He opened it but said nothing. There were scads of names written in a tidy hand over pages incised to crinkliness by a ball-point. Chronologically, the names had piled up: Wives, grandparents, a stillborn infant, relatives, friends close and distant. Names, names. After each, the date of the unknown finally known and transcribed. The last entry bore yesterday's date.

"She's wrote out twenty years' worth. Ever day she listens to the 42 hospital report on the radio and puts the names in. Folks come by to check a date. Or they just turn through the books. Read them like a scrapbook."

43   Hilda said, "Like Saint Peter at the gates inscribin' the names."

44   Watts took my arm. "Come along." He led me to the fruit cellar under the store. As we went down, he said, "Always take a newborn baby upstairs afore you take him downstairs, otherwise you'll incline him downwards."

45   The cellar was dry and full of cobwebs and jar after jar of home-canned food, the bottles organized as a shopkeeper would: sausage, pumpkin, sweet pickles, tomatoes, corn relish, blackberries, peppers, squash, jellies. He held a hand out toward the dusty bottles. "Our tomorrows."

46   Upstairs again, he said, "Hope to sell the store to the right folk. I see now, though, it'll be somebody offen the ridge. I've studied on it, and maybe it's the end of our place." He stirred the coals. "This store could give a comfortable livin', but not likely get you rich. But just gettin' by is dice rollin' to people nowadays. I never did see my day guaranteed."

47   When it was time to go, Watts said, "If you find anyone along your ways wants a good store—on the road to Cordell Hull Lake—tell them about us."

48   I said I would. Miss Ginny and Hilda and Marilyn came out to say goodbye. It was cold and drizzling again. "Weather to give a man the weary dismals," Watts grumbled. "Where you headed from here?"

49   "I don't know."

50   "Cain't get lost then."

51   Miss Ginny looked again at my rig. It had worried her from the first as it had my mother. "I hope you don't get yourself kilt in that durn thing gallivantin' around the country."

52   "Come back when the hills dry off," Watts said. "We'll go lookin' for some of them round rocks all sparkly inside."

53   I thought a moment. "Geodes?"

54   "Them's the ones. The country's properly full of them."

QUESTIONS ON SUBJECT AND PURPOSE

1. At one point in the narrative (paragraph 30), Least Heat Moon remarks, "I thought: It is for this I have come." What does he seem to be suggesting? What is the "this" that he finds in Nameless?

2. Why do "Miss Ginny's *Deathbook*" (paragraph 40) and the "fruit cellar" (44) seem appropriate details?

3. What might have attracted Least Heat Moon to this place and these people? What does he want you to sense? Is there anything in his description and narrative that suggests how he feels about Nameless?

QUESTIONS ON STRATEGY AND AUDIENCE

1. After you have read the selection, describe each member of the Watts family. Describe the exterior and interior of their store. Then carefully go through the selection and see how many specific descriptive details the author uses. List them.
2. What devices other than direct description does Least Heat Moon use to create the sense of place and personality? Make a list, and be prepared to tell how those devices work.
3. How is the narrative arranged? Is the order just spatial and chronological?
4. This selection is taken from *Blue Highways: A Journey into America*, a bestseller for nearly a year. Why would a travel narrative full of stories such as this be so appealing to an American audience?

QUESTIONS ON VOCABULARY AND STYLE

1. Least Heat Moon attempts to reproduce the pronunciation of some words—for example, *athians* (paragraph 12), *iodeen* (21), and *anteebeeotics* (25). Make a list of all such phonetic spellings. Why does Least Heat Moon do this? Do you think he captures all of the Wattses' accent or just some part of it? Is the device effective?
2. Examine how Least Heat Moon uses dialogue in his description. How are the Wattses revealed by what they say? How much of what was actually said during the visit is recorded? Can you find specific points in the story where Least Heat Moon obviously omits dialogue?
3. Try to define or explain the following words and phrases: *horehound candy* (paragraph 15), *bolsters* (26), *buttermilk pie* (28), *incised to crinkliness by a ballpoint* (41), *weary dismals* (48), *gallivantin' around* (51).

WRITING SUGGESTIONS

1. **For Your Journal.** Have you ever encountered or experienced a person, a place, or an event that seemed cut off from the modern world? In your journal, try to recall a few such experiences.

2. **For a Paragraph.** Virtually every campus has a building or a location that has acquired a strange or vivid name (for example, the cafeteria in the Student Center known as "The Scrounge"). In a paragraph, describe such a place to a friend who has never seen it. Remember to keep a central focus— you want to convey an atmosphere more than a verbal photograph.

3. **For an Essay.** Look for an unusual business in your town or city (a barber shop, a food co-op, a delicatessen or diner, a secondhand clothing store, a specialized boutique). In an essay, describe the place. Your essay will need to have a focus—a central impression or thesis—that will govern your selection of details. It will probably work best if you also include some descriptions of people and dialogue.

4. **For Research.** Least Heat Moon is fascinated by unusual names and often drives considerable distances to visit towns with names such as Dime Box, Hungry Horse, Liberty Bond, Ninety-Six, and Tuba City. Choose an unusual place name (town, river, subdivision, topographical feature) from your home state and research the origin of the name. A reference librarian can show you how to locate source materials. If possible, contact your local historical society or public library for help or interview some knowledgeable local residents. Using your research, write an essay about how that name was chosen. Remember to document your sources.

 WEBSITE LINK

Want to read an excerpt from Least Heat Moon's new book, *River-Horse*, an account of a 5,000-mile water voyage across America in a small boat named *Nikawa?* Is there really a Nameless, Tennessee? Visit the *Reader'*s Website.

WRITING LINK: WRITING DIALOGUE

Writing dialogue is never easy, but there are times when dialogue is extremely effective. Select a group of paragraphs from the essay and rewrite them using no dialogue. You could simply have your narrator indirectly report what was said. What is lost when the dialogue is removed? What does this suggest about the effectiveness of dialogue? Study the dialogue that Least Heat Moon uses. What can you learn by watching him at work?

THE VILLAGE WATCHMAN

Terry Tempest Williams

Terry Tempest Williams (1955–   ), a fifth-generation Mormon, grew up within sight of Great Salt Lake. Williams has written and edited a number of books including the recent The New Genesis: A Mormon Reader on Land and Community *(1999) and* Leap *(2000).*

"The Village Watchman" first appeared in Between Friends *(1994), a collection of essays; it was reprinted in her collection of essays titled* An Unspoken Hunger *(1994).*

On Writing: *A writer deeply concerned about environmental issues, Williams has observed that she writes "through my biases of gender, geography, and culture, that I am a woman whose ideas have been shaped by the Colorado Plateau and the Great Basin, that these ideas are then sorted out through the prism of my culture—and my culture is Mormon. Those tenets of family and community that I see at the heart of that culture are then articulated through story."*

BEFORE READING

Connecting: In her essay, Williams writes of our attitude toward people who are "mentally disabled or challenged": "We see them for who they are not, rather than for who they are." What does that sentence mean to you?

Anticipating: Williams is writing about her memories of her uncle. Out of the many that she has, why might she select the ones that she does? How does each included detail or incident affect our sense of Alan?

1   Stories carved in cedar rise from the deep woods of Sitka. These totem poles are foreign to me, this vertical lineage of clans: Eagle, Raven, Wolf, and Salmon. The Tlingit craftsmen create a genealogy of the earth, a reminder of mentors, a reminder that we come into this world in need of proper instruction. I sit on the soft floor of this Alaskan forest and feel the presence of Other. The totem before me is called "Wolf Pole" by locals. The Village Watchman sits on top of Wolf's head with his knees drawn to his chest, his hands holding them tight against his body. He wears a red and black striped hat. His eyes are direct, deep set, painted blue.

The expression on his face reminds me of a man I loved, a man   2
who was born into this world feet first. "Breech," my mother told me
of her brother's birth. "Alan was born feet first. As a result, his brain
was denied oxygen. He is special." As a child, I was impressed by this
information. I remember thinking that fish live underwater. Maybe
Alan had gills, maybe he didn't need a face-first gulp of air like the
rest of us. The amniotic sea he had floated in for nine months delivered him with a fluid memory. He knew something. Other.

There is a story of a boy who was kidnapped from his village by   3
the Salmon People. He was taken from his family to learn the ways of
water. When he returned many years later to his home, he was recognized by his own as a holy man privy to the mysteries of the unseen
world. Twenty years after my uncle's death, I wonder if Alan could
have been that boy.

But our culture tells a different story, more alien. My culture   4
calls people of sole births retarded, handicapped, mentally disabled or
challenged. We see them for who they are not, rather than for who
they are.

My grandmother, Lettie Romney Dixon, wrote in her journal,   5
"It wasn't until Alan was 16 months old that a busy doctor cruelly
broke the news to us. Others may have suspected our son's limitations
but to those of us who loved him so unquestionably, lightning struck
without warning. I hugged my sorrow to myself. I felt abandoned and
lost. I wouldn't accept the verdict. Then we started the trips to a mul-
titude of doctors. Most of them were kind and explained that our
child was like a car without brakes, like an electric wire without insu-
lation. They gave us no hope for a normal life."

Normal. Latin: *normalis; norma*, a rule: conforming with or con-   6
stituting an accepted standard, model, or pattern, especially corresponding to the median or average of a large group in type,
appearance, achievement, function, or development.

Alan was not normal. He was unique; one and only; single; sole;   7
unusual; extraordinary; rare. His emotions were not measured, his
curiosity not bridled. In a sense, he was wild like a mustang in the
desert, and like most wild horses, he was eventually rounded up.

He was unpredictable. He created his own rules and they   8
changed from moment to moment. Alan was 12 years old, hyperac-
tive, mischievous, easily frustrated, and unable to learn in traditional
ways. The situation was intensified by his seizures. Suddenly, without
warning, he would stiffen like a rake, fall forward, and crash to the
ground, hitting his head. My grandparents could not keep him home
any longer. They needed professional guidance and help. In 1957,
they reluctantly placed their youngest child in an institution for

handicapped children called the American Fork Training School. My grandmother's heart broke for the second time.

9   Once again, from her journal: "Many a night my pillow is wet from tears of sorrow and senseless dreamings of 'if things had only been different,' or wondering if he is tucked in snug and warm, if he is well and happy, if the wind still bothers him. . . ."

10   The wind may have continued to bother Alan: certainly the conditions he was living under were less than ideal, but there was much about his private life his family never knew. What we did know was that Alan had an enormous capacity for adaptation. We had no choice but to follow him.

11   I followed him for years.

12   Alan was ten years my senior. In my mind, he was mythic. Everything I was taught not to do, Alan did. We were taught to be polite, to not express displeasure or anger in public. Alan was sheer, physical expression. Whatever was on his mind he vocalized and usually punctuated with colorful speech. We would go bowling as a family on Sundays. Each of us would take our turn, hold the black ball to our chest, take a few steps, swing our arm back, forward, glide, and release. The ball would roll down the alley, hit a few pins; we would wait for the ball to return, and then take our second run. Little emotion was shown. When it was Alan's turn, it was an event. Nothing subtle. His style was Herculean. Big man. Big ball. Big roll. Big bang. Whether it was a strike or a gutter ball, he clapped his hands, spun around on the floor, slapped his thighs, and cried, "Goddamn! Did you see that one? Send me another ball, sweet Jesus!" And the ball was always returned.

13   I could count on my uncle for a straight answer. He taught me that one of the remarkable aspects of being human was to hold opposing views in our mind at once.

14   "How are you doing?" I would ask.

15   "Ask me how I am feeling?" he answered.

16   "Okay, how are you feeling?"

17   "Today? Right now?"

18   "Yes."

19   "I am very happy and very sad."

20   "How can you be both at the same time?" I asked in all seriousness, a girl of nine or ten.

21   "Because both require each other's company. They live in the same house. Didn't you know?"

22   We would laugh and then go on to another topic. Talking to my uncle was always like entering a maze of riddles. Ask a question. Answer with a question and see where it leads you.

My younger brother Steve and I spent a lot of time with Alan.   23
He offered us shelter from the conventionality of a Mormon family.
At our home during Christmas, he would direct us in his own nativ-
ity plays. "More—" he would say to us, making wide gestures with his
hands. "Give me more of yourself." He was not like anyone we knew.
In a culture where we were taught to be seen and not heard. Alan was
our mirror.

We could be different, too. His unquestioning belief in us as   24
children, as human beings, was in startling contrast to the way we saw
the public react to him. It hurt us. We could never tell if it hurt him.

Each week, Steve and I would accompany our grandparents   25
south to visit Alan. It was an hour's drive to the school from Salt Lake
City, mostly through farmlands. We would enter the grounds, pull
into the parking lot to a playground filled with huge papier-mâché
storybook figures (a 20-foot pied piper, a pumpkin carriage with Cinderella inside, the old woman who lived in a shoe), and nine times out
of ten, Alan would be standing outside his dormitory waiting for us.
We would get out of the car and he would run toward us and throw
his powerful arms around us. His hugs cracked my back and at times
I had to fight for my breath. My grandfather would calm him down
by simply saying, "We're here, son. You can relax now."

Alan was a formidable man, now in his early twenties, stocky   26
and strong. His head was large, with a protruding forehead that bore
many scars, a line-by-line history of seizures. He always had on someone else's clothes—a tweed jacket too small, brown pants too big, a
striped golf shirt that didn't match. He showed us that appearances
didn't matter, personality did. If you didn't know him, he could look
frightening. It was an unspoken rule in our family that the character
of others was gauged by how they treated Alan. The only consistent
thing about his attire was that he always wore a silver football helmet
from Olympus High School, where my grandfather was coach. It was
a loving, practical solution to protect Alan when he fell.

"Part of the team," my grandfather would say as he slapped Alan   27
affectionately on the back, "You're a Titan, son, and I love you."

The windows to the dormitory were dark, reflecting Mount   28
Timpanogos to the east. It was hard to see inside, but I knew what the
interior held. It looked like an abandoned gymnasium without bleach-
ers, filled with hospital beds. The stained white walls and yellow-
waxed floors offered no warmth. The stench was nauseating: sweat
and urine trapped in the oppression of stale air. I recall the dirty sheets,
the lack of privacy, and the almond-eyed children who never rose from
their beds. And then I would turn around and face Alan's cheerfulness,
the open and loving manner in which he would introduce me to his

friends, the pride he exhibited as he showed me around his home. I kept thinking, "Doesn't he see how bad this is, how poorly they are being treated?" His words would return to me: "I am very happy and very sad."

29   For my brother and me, Alan was guide, elder. He was fearless. But neither one of us will ever be able to escape the image of Alan kissing his parents good-bye after an afternoon with family and slowly walking back to his dormitory. Before we drove away, he would turn toward us, take off his silver helmet, and wave. The look on his face haunts me still.

30   Alan liked to talk about God. Perhaps it was in these private conversations that our real friendship was forged.

31   "I know Him," he would say when all the adults were gone.

32   "You do?" I asked.

33   "I talk to Him every day."

34   "How?"

35   "I talk to Him in my prayers. I listen and then I hear His voice."

36   "What does He tell you?"

37   "He tells me to be patient. He tells me to be kind. He tells me that He loves me."

38   In Mormon culture, children are baptized as members of the Church of Jesus Christ of Latter-day Saints when they turn 8 years old. Alan had never been baptized because my grandparents believed it should be his choice, not something simply taken for granted. When he turned 22, he expressed a sincere desire to join the church. A date was set immediately.

39   The entire Dixon clan convened in the Lehi chapel, a few miles north of the group home where Alan was then living. We were there to support and witness his conversion. As we walked toward the meetinghouse where this sacred rite was to be performed, Alan had a violent seizure. My grandfather and uncle Don, Alan's elder brother, dropped down with him, holding his head and body as every muscle thrashed on the pavement like a school of netted fish brought on deck. I didn't want to look, but to walk away would have been worse. We stayed with him, all of us.

40   "Talk to God,—" I heard myself saying under my breath. "I love you, Alan."

41   "Can you hear me, darling?" It was my grandmother, holding her son's hand.

42   By now, many of us were gathered on our knees around him, our trembling hands on his rigid body.

43   Alan opened his eyes. "I want to be baptized," he said. The men helped him to his feet. The gash on his left temple was deep. Blood

dripped down the side of his face. My mother had her arm around my grandmother's waist. Shaken, we all followed him inside.

Alan's father and brother stopped the bleeding and bandaged the pressure wound, then helped him change into the designated white garments for baptism. He entered the room with great dignity and sat on the front pew with a dozen or more 8-year-old children seated on either side. Row after row of family sat behind him. 44

"Alan Romney Dixon." His name was called by the presiding bishop. Alan rose from the pew and met his brother Don, also dressed in white, who took his hand and led him down the blue-tiled stairs into the baptismal font filled with water. They faced the congregation. Don raised his right arm to the square in the gesture of a holy oath as Alan placed his hands on his brother's left forearm. The sacred prayer was offered in the name of the Father, the Son, and the Holy Ghost, after which my uncle put his right hand behind Alan's shoulder and gently lowered him into the water for a baptism by complete immersion. 45

Alan emerged from the holy waters like an angel. 46

Six years later, I found myself sitting with my uncle at a hospital where he was being treated for a severe ear infection. I was 18. He was 28. 47

"Alan," I asked, "what is it really like to live inside your body?" 48

He crossed his legs and placed both hands on the arms of the chair. His brown eyes were piercing. 49

"I can't tell you what it's like except to say I feel pain for not being seen as the person I am." 50

A few days later, Alan died—alone, unique, one and only, single—in American Fork, Utah. 51

The Village Watchman sits on top of his totem with Wolf and Salmon. It is beginning to rain in the forest. I find it curious that this spot in southeast Alaska has brought me back into relation with my uncle, this man who came into the world feet first. He reminds me of what it means to live and love with a broken heart; how nothing is sacred, how everything is sacred. He was a weather vane, at once a storm and a clearing. 52

Shortly after his death, Alan appeared to me in a dream. We were standing in my grandmother's kitchen. He was leaning against the white stove with his arms folded. 53

"Look at me now, Terry," he said, smiling. "I'm normal—perfectly normal." And then he laughed. We both laughed. 54

He handed me his silver football helmet, which was resting on the counter, kissed me, and opened the back door. 55

"Do you recognize who I am?" 56

On this day in Sitka, I remember. 57

QUESTIONS ON SUBJECT AND PURPOSE

1. What associations do you have with the word *normal?* Does Williams's definition (paragraph 6) challenge those associations?
2. In two places (paragraphs 5 and 9), Williams quotes from her grandmother's journal. What is the effect of these quotations?
3. Why would a reader be interested in a tribute to her uncle? Do you find the story moving?

QUESTIONS ON STRATEGY AND AUDIENCE

1. Why does Williams begin and end with the references to the totem poles in Alaska?
2. At several places, Williams reproduces—or rather re-creates—conversations she had with Alan (for example, paragraphs 14–21, 31–37, and 48–50). Why? What is the effect of these sections?
3. What expectations might Williams have about her audience and their reaction to Alan?

QUESTIONS ON VOCABULARY AND STYLE

1. At a number of points in the essay, Williams quotes Alan. What do these quotations add to her description?
2. What is the effect of Alan's question, "Do you recognize who I am?"
3. Be prepared to define the following words: *privy* (paragraph 3) and *convened* (39).

WRITING SUGGESTIONS

1. **For Your Journal.** Select a vivid memory that involves a family member or a close friend who touched your life. In your journal, describe for yourself what you remember. Do not worry about trying to be too focused. Concentrate on recovering memories.
2. **For a Paragraph.** In a paragraph, try to "capture" that person. Remember that your description needs a central focus or purpose. Why are you writing about this person? What is important for the reader to know about this person? Select

details to reveal the person to your reader rather than simply telling the reader what to think.

3. **For an Essay.** In writing about Alan, Williams achieves two purposes: she memorializes her uncle, and she comments on society's perceptions of persons who are "mentally disabled or challenged." Try for a similar effect in an essay about someone who has touched your life. Remember that your essay needs to have a duel purpose or thesis.

4. **For Research.** Explore our society's reactions to people who are, to use Williams's words, "retarded, handicapped, mentally disabled or challenged." How does society see such people? How are they treated or portrayed? This is a large subject, so you will need to find a way to focus your research and writing. You could concentrate on changes in reaction over time (early twentieth century versus late in the century), portrayals (or their lack) in the popular media, family attitudes versus outsiders' attitudes, or reactions to a specific disability (such as Down's syndrome). Textbooks might be one place to start. You will need to establish a list of possible subject headings and keywords before you start searching library resources, on-line databases, and the World Wide Web. Remember to document your sources, including any information that you obtain through interviews.

 WEBSITE LINK

A listing of sites dealing with specific genetic or birth conditions and additional writing suggestions can be found at the Website.

 WRITING LINK: TOPIC SENTENCES

Select some of the longer paragraphs in Williams's essay. Look carefully at the first sentence in the paragraph. How does that sentence serve to control the details that are included in what follows? Even though many of Williams's paragraphs are narrative in nature, she still forecasts their structure through those first sentences. What does this suggest about your own paragraphs in your essays?

THE INHERITANCE OF TOOLS

Scott Russell Sanders

Born in Memphis, Tennessee, in 1945, Scott Russell Sanders received a Ph.D. from Cambridge University. Currently a professor of English at Indiana University, Sanders is a novelist, an essayist, and a science fiction writer. He has contributed fiction and essays to many journals and magazines and has published numerous books, including the recent collection of essays The Force of Spirit *(2000).*

Sanders writes often about his childhood and his efforts to "ground" himself. In another of his collections of essays, Secrets of the Universe *(1991), Sanders describes growing up with an alcoholic father, noting that he "wants to drag into the light what eats at me—the fear, the guilt, the shame—so that my own children may be spared."*

On Writing: *Commenting on the development of his writing style from academic prose to creative writing and essays, Sanders observed: "I flouted the rules I learned about writing in school. I played with sound, strung images together line after line, flung out metaphors by the handful. Sin of sins, I even mixed metaphors, the way any fertile field will sprout dozens of species of grass and flower and fern. I let my feelings and opinions show. . . . I drew shamelessly on my own life. I swore off jargon and muddle and much. I wrote in the active voice."*

BEFORE READING

Connecting: Can you think of something that you learned how to do from a family member or friend?

Anticipating: In what ways is "The Inheritance of Tools" an appropriate title for the essay? What is the essay about?

1   At just about the hour when my father died, soon after dawn one February morning when ice coated the windows like cataracts, I banged my thumb with a hammer. Naturally I swore at the hammer, the reckless thing, and in the moment of swearing I thought of what my father would say: "If you'd try hitting the nail it would go in a whole lot faster. Don't you know your thumb's not as hard as that hammer?" We both were doing carpentry that day, but far apart. He was building cupboards at my brother's place in Oklahoma; I was at

home in Indiana putting up a wall in the basement to make a bedroom for my daughter. By the time my mother called with news of his death—the long distance wires whittling her voice until it seemed too thin to bear the weight of what she had to say—my thumb was swollen. A week or so later a white scar in the shape of a crescent moon began to show above the cuticle, and month by month it rose across the pink sky of my thumbnail. It took the better part of a year for the scar to disappear, and every time I noticed it I thought of my father.

The hammer had belonged to him, and to his father before him. 2 The three of us have used it to build houses and barns and chicken coops, to upholster chairs and crack walnuts, to make doll furniture and book shelves and jewelry boxes. The head is scratched and pock-marked, like an old plowshare that has been working rocky fields, and it gives off the sort of dull sheen you see on fast creek water in the shade. It is a finishing hammer, about the weight of a bread loaf, too light, really, for framing walls, too heavy for cabinetwork, with a curved claw for pulling nails, a rounded head for pounding, a fluted neck for looks, and a hickory handle for strength.

The present handle is my third one, bought from a lumberyard 3 in Tennessee down the road from where my brother and I were help-ing my father build his retirement house. I broke the previous one by trying to pull sixteen-penny nails out of floor joists—a foolish thing to do with a finishing hammer, as my father pointed out. "You ever hear of a crowbar?" he said. No telling how many handles he and my grandfather had gone through before me. My grandfather used to cut down hickory trees on his farm, saw them into slabs, cure the planks in his hayloft, and carve handles with a drawknife. The grain in hick-ory is crooked and knotty, and therefore rough, hard to split, like the grain in the two men who owned this hammer before me.

After proposing marriage to a neighbor girl, my grandfather 4 used this hammer to build a house for his bride on a stretch of river bottom in northern Mississippi. The lumber for the place, like the hickory for the handle, was cut on his own land. By the day of the wedding he had not quite finished the house, and so right after the ceremony he took his wife home and put her to work. My grand-mother had worn her Sunday dress for the wedding, with a fringe of lace tacked on around the hem in honor of the occasion. She removed this lace and folded it away before going out to help my grandfather nail siding on the house. "There she was in her good dress," he told me some fifty-odd years after that wedding day, "hold-ing up them long pieces of clapboard while I hammered, and to-gether we got the place covered up before dark." As the family grew to four, six, eight, and eventually thirteen, my grandfather used this hammer to enlarge his house room by room, like a chambered nautilus expanding his shell.

5   By and by the hammer was passed along to my father. One day he was up on the roof of our pony barn nailing shingles with it, when I stepped out the kitchen door to call him for supper. Before I could yell, something about the sight of him straddling the spine of that roof and swinging the hammer caught my eye and made me hold my tongue. I was five or six years old, and the world's commonplaces were still news to me. He would pull a nail from the pouch at his waist, bring the hammer down, and a moment later the *thunk* of the blow would reach my ears. And that is what had stopped me in my tracks and stilled my tongue, that momentary gap between seeing and hearing the blow. Instead of yelling from the kitchen door, I ran to the barn and climbed two rungs up the ladder—as far as I was allowed to go—and spoke quietly to my father. On our walk to the house he explained that sound takes time to make its way through air. Suddenly the world seemed larger, the air more dense, if sound could be held back like any ordinary traveler.

6   By the time I started using this hammer, at about the age when I discovered the speed of sound, it already contained houses and mysteries for me. The smooth handle was one my grandfather had made. In those days I needed both hands to swing it. My father would start a nail in a scrap of wood, and I would pound away until I bent it over.

7   "Looks like you got ahold of some of those rubber nails," he would tell me. "Here, let me see if I can find you some stiff ones." And he would rummage in a drawer until he came up with a fistful of more cooperative nails. "Look at the head," he would tell me. "Don't look at your hands, don't look at the hammer. Just look at the head of that nail and pretty soon you'll learn to hit it square."

8   Pretty soon I did learn. While he worked in the garage cutting dovetail joints for a drawer or skinning a deer or tuning an engine, I would hammer nails. I made innocent blocks of wood look like porcupines. He did not talk much in the midst of his tools, but he kept up a nearly ceaseless humming, slipping in and out of a dozen tunes in an afternoon, often running back over the same stretch of melody again and again, as if searching for a way out. When the humming did cease, I knew he was faced with a task requiring great delicacy or concentration, and I took care not to distract him.

9   He kept scraps of wood in a cardboard box—the ends of two-by-fours, slabs of shelving and plywood, odd pieces of molding—and everything in it was fair game. I nailed scraps together to fashion what I called boats or houses, but the results usually bore only faint resem-

blance to the visions I carried in my head. I would hold up these constructions to show my father, and he would turn them over in his
hands admiringly, speculating about what they might be. My cobbled-
together guitars might have been alien spaceships, my barns might
have been models of Aztec temples, each wooden contraption might
have been anything but what I had set out to make.

Now and again I would feel the need to have a chunk of wood   10
shaped or shortened before I riddled it with nails, and I would clamp
it in a vise and scrape at it with a handsaw. My father would let me lacerate the board until my arm gave out, and then he would wrap his
hand around mine and help me finish the cut, showing me how to use
my thumb to guide the blade, how to pull back on the saw to keep it
from binding, how to let my shoulder do the work.

"Don't force it," he would say, "just drag it easy and give the   11
teeth a chance to bite."

As the saw teeth bit down, the wood released its smell, each kind   12
with its own fragrance, oak or walnut or cherry or pine—usually pine
because it was the softest, easiest for a child to work. No matter how
weathered and gray the board, no matter how warped and cracked,
inside there was this smell waiting, as of something freshly baked. I
gathered every smidgen of sawdust and stored it away in coffee cans,
which I kept in a drawer of the workbench. When I did not feel like
hammering nails I would dump my sawdust on the concrete floor of
the garage and landscape it into highways and farms and towns, running miniature cars and trucks along miniature roads. Looming as
huge as a colossus, my father worked over and around me, now and
again bending down to inspect my work, careful not to trample my
creations. It was a landscape that smelled dizzyingly of wood. Even
after a bath my skin would carry the smell, and so would my father's
hair, when he lifted me for a bedtime hug.

I tell these things not only from memory but also from recent ob-   13
servation, because my own son now turns blocks of wood into nailed
porcupines, dumps cans full of sawdust at my feet and sculpts highways
on the floor. He learns how to swing a hammer from the elbow instead
of the wrist, how to lay his thumb beside the blade to guide a saw, how
to tap a chisel with a wooden mallet, how to mark a hole with an awl
before starting a drill bit. My daughter did the same before him, and
even now, on the brink of teenage aloofness, she will occasionally drag
out my box of wood scraps and carpenter something. So I have seen my
apprenticeship to wood and tools reenacted in each of my children, as
my father saw his own apprenticeship renewed in me.

The saw I use belonged to him, as did my level and both of my   14
squares, and all four tools had belonged to his father. The blade of the

saw is the bluish color of gun barrels, and the maple handle, dark from the sweat of hands, is inscribed with curving leaf designs. The level is a shaft of walnut two feet long, edged with brass and pierced by three round windows in which air bubbles float in oil-filled tubes of glass. The middle window serves for testing if a surface is horizontal, the others for testing if a surface is plumb or vertical. My grandfather used to carry this level on the gun-rack behind the seat in his pickup, and when I rode with him I would turn around to watch the bubbles dance. The larger of the two squares is called a framing square, a flat steel elbow, so beat up and tarnished you can barely make out the rows of numbers that show how to figure the cuts on rafters. The smaller one is called a try square, for marking right angles, with a blued steel blade for the shank and a brass-faced block of cherry for the head.

15   I was taught early on that a saw is not to be used apart from a square: "If you're going to cut a piece of wood," my father insisted, "you owe it to the tree to cut it straight."

16   Long before studying geometry, I learned there is a mystical virtue in right angles. There is an unspoken morality in seeking the level and the plumb. A house will stand, a table will bear weight, the sides of a box will hold together only if the joints are square and the members upright. When the bubble is lined up between two marks etched in the glass tube of a level, you have aligned yourself with the forces that hold the universe together. When you miter the corners of a picture frame, each angle must be exactly forty-five degrees, as they are in the perfect triangles of Pythagoras, not a degree more or less. Otherwise the frame will hang crookedly, as if ashamed of itself and of its maker. No matter if the joints you are cutting do not show. Even if you are butting two pieces of wood together inside a cabinet, where not one except a wrecking crew will ever see them, you must take pains to insure that the ends are square and the studs are plumb.

17   I took pains over the wall I was building on the day my father died. Not long after that wall was finished—paneled with tongue-and-groove boards of yellow pine, the nail holes filled with putty and the wood all stained and sealed—I came close to wrecking it one afternoon when my daughter ran howling up the stairs to announce that her gerbils had escaped from their cage and were hiding in my brand new wall. She could hear them scratching and squeaking behind her bed. Impossible! I said. How on earth could they get inside my drum-tight wall? Through the heating vent, she answered. I went downstairs, pressed my ear to the honey-colored wood, and heard the *scritch scritch* of tiny feet.

"What can we do?" my daughter wailed. "They'll starve to   18
death, they'll die of thirst, they'll suffocate."

"Hold on," I shouted, "I'll think of something."   19

While I thought and she fretted, the radio on her bedside table   20
delivered us the headlines. Several thousand people had died in a city
in India from a poisonous cloud that had leaked overnight from a
chemical plant. A nuclear-powered submarine had been launched.
Rioting continued in South Africa. An airplane had been hijacked in
the Mediterranean. Authorities calculated that several thousand
homeless people slept on the streets within sight of the Washington
Monument. I felt my usual helplessness in face of all these calamities.
But here was my daughter weeping because her gerbils were holed up
in a wall. This calamity I could handle.

"Don't worry," I told her. "We'll set food and water by the heat-   21
ing vent and lure them out. And if that doesn't do the trick, I'll tear
the wall apart until we find them."

She stopped crying and gazed as me. "You'd really tear it apart?   22
Just for my gerbils? The *wall?*" Astonishment slowed her down only
for a second, however, before she ran to the workbench and began
tugging at drawers, saying, "Let's see, what'll we need? Crowbar.
Hammer. Chisels. I hope we don't have to use them—but just in case."

We didn't need the wrecking tools. I never had to assault my   23
handsome wall, because the gerbils eventually came out to nibble at
a dish of popcorn. But for several hours I studied the tongue-and-
groove skin I had nailed up on the day of my father's death, considering where to begin prying. There were no gaps in that wall, no
crooked joints.

I had botched a great many pieces of wood before I mastered the   24
right angle with a saw, botched even more before I learned to miter a
joint. The knowledge of these things resides in my hands and eyes and
the webwork of muscles, not in the tools. There are machines for
sale—powered miter boxes and radial-arm saws, for instance—that
will enable any casual soul to cut proper angles in boards. The skill is
invested in the gadget instead of the person who uses it, and this is
what distinguishes a machine from a tool. If I had to earn my keep by
making furniture or building houses, I suppose I would buy powered
saws and pneumatic nailers; the need for speed would drive me to it.
But since I carpenter only for my own pleasure or to help neighbors
or to remake the house around the ears of my family, I stick with hand
tools. Most of the ones I own were given to me by my father, who also
taught me how to wield them. The tools in my work-bench are a double inheritance, for each hammer and level and saw is wrapped in a
cloud of knowing.

25   All of these tools are a pleasure to look at and to hold. Merchants would never paste NEW NEW NEW! signs on them in stores. Their designs are old because they work, because they serve their purpose well. Like folksongs and aphorisms and the grainy bits of language, these tools have been pared down to essentials. I look at my claw hammer, the distillation of a hundred generations of carpenters, and consider that it holds up well beside those other classics— Greek vases, Gregorian chants, *Don Quixote*, barbed fish hooks, candles, spoons. Knowledge of hammering stretches back to the earliest humans who squatted beside fires chipping flints. Anthropologists have a lovely name for those unworked rocks that served as the earliest hammers. *Dawn stones*, they are called. Their only qualification for the work, aside from hardness, is that they fit the hand. Our ancestors used them for grinding corn, tapping awls, smashing bones. From dawn stones to this claw hammer is a great leap in time, but no great distance in design or imagination.

26   On that iced-over February morning when I smashed my thumb with the hammer, I was down in the basement framing the wall that my daughter's gerbils would later hide in. I was thinking of my father, as I always did whenever I built anything, thinking how he would have gone about the work, hearing in memory what he would have said about the wisdom of hitting the nail instead of my thumb. I had the studs and plates nailed together all square and trim, and was lifting the wall into place when the phone rang upstairs. My wife answered, and in a moment she came to the basement door and called down softly to me. The stillness in her voice made me drop the framed wall and hurry upstairs. She told me my father was dead. Then I heard the details over the phone from my mother. Building a set of cupboards for my brother in Oklahoma, he had knocked off work early the previous afternoon because of cramps in his stomach. Early this morning, on his way into the kitchen of my brother's trailer, maybe going for a glass of water, so early that no one else was awake, he slumped down on the linoleum and his heart quit.

27   For several hours I paced around inside my house, upstairs and down, in and out of every room, looking for the right door to open and knowing there was no such door. My wife and children followed me and wrapped me in arms and backed away again, circling and staring as if I were on fire. Where was the door, the door, the door? I kept wondering. My smashed thumb turned purple and throbbed, making me furious. I wanted to cut it off and rush outside and scrape away the snow and hack a hole in the frozen earth and bury the shameful thing.

28   I went down into the basement, opened a drawer in my workbench, and stared at the ranks of chisels and knives. Oiled and sharp,

as my father would have kept them, they gleamed at me like teeth. I took up a clasp knife, pried out the longest blade and tested the edge on the hair of my forearm. A tuft came away cleanly, and I saw my father testing the sharpness of tools on his own skin, the blades of axes and knives and gouges and hoes, saw the red hair shaved off in patches from his arms and the backs of his hands. "That will cut bear," he would say. He never cut a bear with his blades, now my blades, but he cut deer, dirt, wood. I closed the knife and put it away. Then I took up the hammer and went back to work on my daughter's wall, snugging the bottom plate against a chalk line on the floor, shimming the top plate against the joists overhead, plumbing the studs with my level, making sure before I drove the first nail that every line was square and true.

QUESTIONS ON SUBJECT AND PURPOSE

1. What is the subject of Sanders's essay? Is it tools? His father's death?
2. Is Sanders's father or grandfather (or his children) ever described in the story? How are they revealed to the reader?
3. What "door" (paragraph 27) is Sanders searching for?
4. What exactly has Sanders inherited from his father?

QUESTIONS ON STRATEGY AND AUDIENCE

1. How does Sanders use time to structure his essay? Is the story told in chronological order?
2. What is the function of each of the following episodes or events in the essay?
   A. The sore thumb
   B. "A mystical virtue in right angles" (paragraph 16)
   C. The wall he was building
3. What expectations does Sanders seem to have about his audience?

QUESTIONS ON VOCABULARY AND STYLE

1. How much dialogue does Sanders use in the story? What does the dialogue contribute?
2. Throughout the essay, Sanders makes use of many effective similes and metaphors. Make a list of six such devices. What

does each contribute to the essay? How fresh and arresting are these images?

3. Be able to define each of the following words or phrases: *plowshare* (paragraph 2), *sixteen-penny nails* (3), *chambered nautilus* (4), *rummage* (7), *lacerate* (10), *smidgen* (12), *plumb* (14), *miter* (24), *aphorisms* (25), *shimming* (28).

WRITING SUGGESTIONS

1. **For Your Journal.** The word *inheritance* may suggest money or property that is bequeathed to a descendent. But you can "inherit" many things that are far less tangible. In your journal, explore what you might have inherited from someone in your family—perhaps a talent, an interest, an ability, or an obsession.

2. **For a Paragraph.** Study the childhood scenes or episodes that Sanders includes in his essay—for example, calling his father to supper (paragraph 5), hammering nails (6–9), landscaping with sawdust (12). Notice how Sanders re-creates sensory experiences. Then in a paragraph, re-create a similar experience from your childhood. Remember to evoke sensory impressions for your reader—sight, sound, smell, touch.

3. **For an Essay.** Think about a skill, talent, or habit that you have learned from or share with a family member. In addition to the ability or trait, what else have you "inherited"? How does it affect your life? In an essay, describe the inheritance and its effect on you.

4. **For Research.** The passing on of traditional crafts or skills is an important part of cultural tradition. Choose a society that interests you, and find a particular craft that is preserved from one generation to another. It might also be something that has been preserved in your family's religious or ethnic heritage. In a research paper, document the nature of the craft and the methods by which the culture ensures its transmission. What is important about this craft? What does it represent to that society? Why bother to preserve it?

   WEBSITE LINK

Another view of Sanders's relationship with his father can be found in his essay "Under the Influence," which can be read on-line. The hotlink is available at the Website.

WRITING LINK: DASHES

Sanders often uses dashes to insert material into his sentences and to add material to the ends of sentences. Make a list of each use, and on the basis of that sample, write some "rules" for the use of the dash in writing. What other punctuation alternatives would Sanders have had in each case? Could he have used commas? Parentheses? What would have been the difference?

PREWRITING SUGGESTIONS FOR DESCRIPTION

1. Start your description by making a list of details that reveal how you feel or how you want your reader to feel about the place, person, or subject. What is the emotion, the impression, the understanding that you want to convey to your readers?

2. Using the details you have gathered, write a purpose statement for your descriptive essay. Use that purpose statement as a way of testing each detail that you plan to include. Do all of your details contribute to your purpose?

3. If possible, reexperience the place, person, or subject of your essay. Go and visit. Take notes. Listen. Look. Jot down details.

4. Plan a structure for your essay. Consider writing out the steps in that structure on index cards. Play with various organizational arrangements of the cards. Does your description move spatially, from most obvious to least obvious? Does time underlie the structure of your description?

5. Plan an opening for your essay. Try to think of at least three possible ways in which to begin. Write out the possibilities on separate cards or sheets. Ask some friends to read just the opening paragraph(s) and then to vote for their favorite.

REWRITING SUGGESTIONS FOR DESCRIPTION

1. Check to make sure that you have used vivid nouns and verbs to carry most of the descriptive burden. How many adjectives and adverbs have you used?

2. Have you been too heavy-handed in emphasizing the significance or importance that you see in the object of your description? Remember, you are trying to reveal significance; you are not lecturing your reader on the "meaning" of your description.

3. Go through your essay and underline every descriptive detail. Are there too many? Are you trying to make the reader experience too much? Compare your descriptive technique with those of other writers in this chapter.

4. Find readers for your draft—a roommate, a classmate, a writing center tutor. Ask your readers for honest advice. What did they like about the essay? Did it hold their attention? Did it create in them the impression you wanted to create? If not, why not? Ask for their suggestions and then carefully weigh each as you revise.

5. Look carefully at the title you have selected. Remember "Essay #2" is not a title. Titles catch your readers' attention; titles help attract your audience. Brainstorm a number of possibilities before settling on a final one.

DIVISION AND CLASSIFICATION

Division and classification are closely related methods of analysis, but you can remember the difference by asking yourself whether you are analyzing a single thing or analyzing two or more things. Division occurs when a single subject is subdivided into its parts. To cut a pizza into slices, to list the ingredients in a can of soup or a box of cereal,

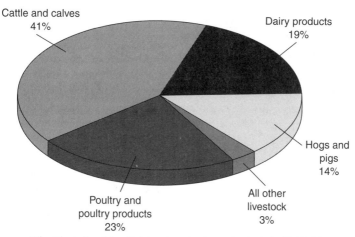

Cattle and calves
41%

Dairy products
19%

Hogs and pigs
14%

All other livestock
3%

Poultry and poultry products
23%

The ideal visual for division is a pie chart. A whole is divided into parts. Here for example is a U.S. Department of Agriculture chart on the value of livestock and poultry sold in the United States. *U.S. Department of Agriculture, National Agricultural Statistics Services.*

or to create a pie chart is to perform a division. The key is that you begin with a single thing.

We can also divide a subject in writing. In the following excerpt from a "chemistry primer" for people interested in cooking, Harold McGee uses division twice—first to subdivide the atom into its smaller constituent particles and second to subdivide the "space" within the atom into two areas (nucleus and shell):

> An atom is the smallest particle into which an element can be subdivided without losing its characteristic properties. The atom too is divisible into smaller particles, electrons, protons, and neutrons, but these are the building blocks of all atoms, no matter of what element. The different properties of the elements are due to the varying combinations of subatomic particles contained in their atoms. The Periodic Table arranges the elements in order of the number of protons contained in one atom of each element. That number is called the atomic number.
>
> The atom is divided into two regions: the nucleus, or center in which the protons and neutrons are located, and a surrounding "orbit," or more accurately a "cloud" or "shell," in which the electrons move continuously. Both protons and neutrons weigh about 2000 times as much as electrons, so practically all of an atom's mass is concentrated in the nucleus.

Similarly, David Bodanis in an essay in this chapter uses division to structure a discussion of toothpaste; he analyzes its composition, offering some surprising insights into the "ingredients" we brush with every morning. Barbara Ehrenreich in "In Defense of Talk Shows" also uses division when she analyzes the distinctive features that a number of different television talk shows exhibit. She treats the shows—hosted by people such as Montel Williams, Sally Jessy Raphael, and Geraldo Rivera—as a single subject that can then be divided or analyzed into its component parts. Ehrenreich does not classify television talk shows; rather, she analyzes the common characteristics that such shows share. Frank Gannon divides students in his English 99 class into three groups.

Division, then, is used to show the components of a larger subject; it helps the reader understand a complex whole by considering it in smaller units.

Classification, instead of starting with a single subject and then subdividing it into smaller units, begins with two or more items that are then grouped or classified into categories. Newspapers, for example, contain "classified" sections in which advertisements for the same type of goods or services are grouped or classified together. A classification must have at least two categories.

- A — GENERAL WORKS
- B — PHILOSOPHY, PSYCHOLOGY, RELIGION
- C — AUXILIARY SCIENCES OF HISTORY
- D — HISTORY (GENERAL) AND HISTORY OF EUROPE
- E — HISTORY: AMERICA
- F — HISTORY: AMERICA
- G — GEOGRAPHY, ANTHROPOLOGY, RECREATION
- H — SOCIAL SCIENCES
- J — POLITICAL SCIENCE
- K — LAW
- L — EDUCATION
- M — MUSIC AND BOOKS ON MUSIC
- N — FINE ARTS
- P — LANGUAGE AND LITERATURE
- Q — SCIENCE
- R — MEDICINE
- S — AGRICULTURE
- T — TECHNOLOGY
- U — MILITARY SCIENCE
- V — NAVAL SCIENCE
- Z — BIBLIOGRAPHY, LIBRARY SCIENCE, INFORMATION RESOURCES (GENERAL)

In the Library of Congress Classification System, books are first organized by "main classes" or by what we might call "subjects." Each class is assigned a letter of the alphabet. By knowing the Library of Congress's system, you can browse the sections knowing that books on these general headings will be grouped together.

Depending on how many items you start with and how different they are, you can end up with quite a few categories. Consider the books in your school's library—they have to be arranged or classified in some way so that they can be easily found. Many schools use the Library of Congress Classification System, which organizes books by their subject matter. The sciences, especially the biological sciences, make extensive use of classification. You probably remember, in at least rough form, the taxonomic classification you learned in high school biology. It begins by setting up five kingdoms (animals, plants, monera, fungi, and protista) and then moves downward to increasingly narrower categories (phylum or division, class, order, family, genus, species).

Most classifications outside of the sciences are not as precisely and hierarchically defined. For example, E. B. White uses classification to discuss the three different groups of people who make up New York City:

There are roughly three New Yorks. There is, first, the New York of the man or woman who was born here, who takes the city for granted and accepts its size and its turbulence as natural and inevitable. Second, there is the New York of the commuter—the city that is devoured by locusts each day and spat out each night. Third, there is the New York of the person who was born somewhere else and came to New York in quest of something. Of these three trembling cities the greatest is the last—the city of final destination, the city that is a goal.

In this chapter, Bernard R. Berelson's classification of the reasons people want children is precisely and logically ordered—something we would expect in an essay that is titled "The Value of Children: A Taxonomical Essay" and that uses headings to display its organizational pattern clearly. More informally, in "Why We Travel" Pico Iyer classifies the reasons why people are fascinated by travel.

HOW DO YOU CHOOSE A SUBJECT?

In choosing your subject for either division or classification, be sure to avoid the obvious approach to the obvious topic. Every teacher has read at some point a classification essay placing teachers into three groups based solely on the grade level at which they teach: elementary school teachers teach in elementary school, middle school teachers teach in middle school, and high school teachers teach in high school. Although the classification is complete and accurate, such a subject and approach are likely to lead you into writing that is boring and simply not worth your time or your reader's. No subject is inherently bad, but if you choose to write about something common, you need to find an interesting angle from which to approach it. Before you begin to write, answer two questions: first, what is your purpose? and second, will your reader learn something or be entertained by what you plan to write?

HOW DO YOU DIVIDE OR CLASSIFY A SUBJECT?

Since both division and classification involve separation into parts—either dividing a whole into pieces or sorting many things into related groups or categories—you have to find ways in which to divide or group. Those ways can be objective and formal, such as the classification schemes used by biologists or by Bernard Berelson, or subjective and informal, like Pico Iyer's in "Why We Travel." Either way, several things are particularly important.

First, you subdivide or categorize for a reason or a purpose, and your division or classification should be made with that end in mind.

Bernard R. Berelson in "The Value of Children: A Taxonomical Essay" places people's reasons for wanting children into six categories: biological, cultural, political, economic, familial, and personal. His purpose is to explain the various factors that motivate people to want children, and these six categories represent the spectrum of reasons why adults want children. Berelson does not include, for example, a category labeled "accidental," for such a heading would be irrelevant to his stated purpose.

Second, your division or classification must be complete—you cannot omit pieces or leave items unclassified. How complete your classification needs to be depends on your purpose. Iyer's reasons for "Why We Travel" probably do not represent all the possible reasons for traveling, but Iyer is not attempting to list everything. He is focusing on what he regards as the most significant reasons. Berelson, by contrast, sets out to be exhaustive, to isolate all of the reasons people at any time or in any place have wanted children. As a result, he has to include some categories that are essentially irrelevant for most Americans. For example, probably few Americans ever want children for political reasons, that is, because their government encourages them or forbids them to have children. But in some societies at certain times political reasons have been important. Therefore, Berelson must include that category as well.

Third, the categories or subdivisions you establish need to be parallel in form. In mathematical terms, the categories should share a lowest common denominator. A simple and fairly effective test for parallelism is to see whether your categories are all phrased in similar grammatical terms. Berelson, for example, defines his categories (the reasons for wanting children) in exactly parallel form:

+Biological
+Cultural
+Political
+Economic
+Familial
+Personal
    Personal power
    Personal competence
    Personal status
    Personal extension
    Personal experience
    Personal pleasure

For this reason, you should not establish a catch-all category that you label something like "Other." When Berelson is finished with his classification scheme, no reasons for wanting children are left unaccounted for; everything fits into one of the six subdivisions. Finally, your categories or subdivisions should be mutually exclusive; that is, items should belong in only one category.

HOW DO YOU STRUCTURE A DIVISION OR CLASSIFICATION ESSAY?

The body of a division or classification essay will have as many parts as you have subdivisions or categories. Each subdivision or category will probably be treated in a single paragraph or in a group of related paragraphs. Gannon, for example, uses a very symmetrical form in his essay: he cites three different types of students in his English 99 class and he treats each in a parallel way. Not every essay will be so evenly and perfectly divided. Judith Ortiz Cofer's essay "The Myth of the Latin Woman" uses narrative examples to establish and explore the common stereotypes of the "Latin woman" that she has encountered. Though the essay has a clear, chronological structure, Cofer analyzes the myth in sections of varying length.

Once you have decided how many subdivisions or categories you will have and how long each one will be, you have to decide in what order to arrange those parts or categories. Sometimes you must devise your own order. Iyer, for example, could have arranged his reasons in any order. Nothing in the material itself determines the sequence. However, not all divisions or classifications have the same flexibility in their arrangement. Some invite, imply, or even demand a particular order. For example, if you were classifying films using the ratings established by the motion picture industry, you would essentially have to follow the G, PG, PG-13, R, and NC-17 sequence; you could begin at either end, but it would not make sense to begin with one of the middle categories.

Having an order underlying your division or classification can be a great help for both you and your reader. It allows you to know where to place each section, dictating the order you will follow. It gives your reader a clear sense of direction. Berelson, for example, in "The Value of Children: A Taxonomical Essay," arranges the reasons that people have children in an order that "starts with chemistry and proceeds to spirit." That is, he deals first with the biological reasons for wanting children and moves finally to the most spiritual of reasons, love.

SAMPLE STUDENT ESSAY

Evan James had chosen to write his term paper for his introductory American studies course on the hobo in America. He had read widely in the library about the phenomenon, so he had plenty of information, but he was having trouble getting started and getting organized. He took his draft to the Writing Center.

EARLIER DRAFT

HOBOS

Among the many social problems that the United States faced at the turn of this past century was that of the "hobo." My interest in hobos came about because of the book The Ways of the Hobo that we read. The term hobo, the dictionary says, was probably derived from the greeting "Ho! Beau!" commonly used by vagrants to greet each other, although other possibilities have been suggested as well. The number of hobos in the United States at the turn of the century was large because of soldiers returning from the Civil War and because increasing mechanization had reduced the number of jobs in factories and businesses. In fact, the unemployment rate in the late 1800s ran as high as 40% of the workforce. We think that unemployment rates of 6% are unacceptable today!

Actually hobos were careful about how they referred to themselves. Today, for example, we might use the words hobo, tramp, and bum interchangeably. I was surprised to learn that among the hobos themselves, the distinctions were clear. A hobo was a migrant worker, a tramp was a migrant nonworker, and a bum was a nonmigrant nonworker.

When the tutor asked about the problems Evan saw in his essay, Evan listed a couple: he thought the introduction was flat and boring and the essay didn't move smoothly from sentence to sentence ("I think I just jump around from idea to idea"). The tutor and Evan collaborated on a list of the qualities that make a good introduction. They also discussed how writers can group information and make transitions. In the process of revising, Evan found a stronger, more interesting way to begin, and he reparagraphed and developed his opening paragraphs to reflect an analysis both by division and by cause and effect.

R E V I S E D   D R A F T

RIDING THE RAILS: THE AMERICAN HOBO

Although homelessness and vagrancy might seem to be a distinctively modern phenomenon, the problem is probably less acute today (in terms of percentage of our total population) than it was at the turn of the twentieth century. At that time, a series of factors combined to create a large migratory population comprised almost exclusively of young males.

The Civil War was an uprooting experience for thousands of young men. Many left home in their teenage years, had acquired no job skills during their military service, and had grown accustomed to the nomadic life of the soldier—always on the move, living off the land, sleeping in the open. As the armies disbanded, many young men chose not to return home but to continue wandering the countryside.

Even if these former soldiers had wanted to work, few jobs were available to absorb the thousands of men who were mustered out. Increasingly, mechanization in the last decades of the 1800s brought the loss of jobs. In a world before unemployment benefits and social welfare, unemployment encouraged migration. The problem worsened in the 1870s when the country spiraled into a depression. Businesses failed, construction sagged, and the unemployment rate soared to an estimated 40%. Men, looking for work, took to the road.

Such men were called by a variety of names. One was <u>hobo</u>. The origin of that word is unknown. It has been suggested that <u>hobo</u> might be a shortened form of the Latin phrase <u>homo bonus</u> ("good man") or derived from the greeting "Ho! Beau!" commonly used among vagrants (dictionaries favor this suggestion). Other possibilities include a shortened form of the phrase "homeward bound" or "hoe boy," a term used in the eighteenth century for migrant farm workers.

Strictly speaking, not everyone who took to the road should be called a hobo. "Real" hobos were quick to insist on a series of distinctions. The words hobo, tramp, and bum were not interchangeable. By definition within the hobo community, the term hobo referred to a migrant worker, tramp to a migrant nonworker, and bum to a nonmigrant nonworker.

Obviously, the motives of the men traveling the road varied widely. Some were in search of work—migrant agricultural workers were an accepted fact by the turn of the century. Others were fleeing from the law, from family responsibilities, from themselves. Many were alcoholics; some were mentally impaired. All, though, were responding to a version of the American myth—the hope that a better future lay somewhere (geographically) ahead and that, meanwhile, the open road was the place to be.

SOME THINGS TO REMEMBER

1. In choosing a subject for division or classification, ask yourself, first, what is my purpose? and second, will my reader learn something or be entertained by my paper?
2. Remember that your subdivision or classification should reflect your purpose—that is, the number of categories or parts is related to what you are trying to do.
3. Make sure that your division or classification is complete. Do not omit any pieces or items. Everything should be accounted for.
4. Take care that the parts or categories are phrased in parallel form.
5. Avoid a category labeled something such as "Other" or "Miscellaneous."
6. Remember to make your categories or subdivisions mutually exclusive.
7. Once you have established your subdivisions, check to see whether there is an order implied or demanded by your subject.
8. As you move from one subdivision to another, provide markers for the reader so that the parts are clearly labeled.

VISUALIZING DIVISION AND CLASSIFICATION

Did you ever think about how many trees it took to provide your Sunday newspaper? J. B. Handelsman's cartoon is a reminder of the

© *The New Yorker Collection 1998 by J. B. Handelsman from cartoonbank.com. All Rights Reserved.*

relationship between a newspaper and the trees it takes to produce it. The cartoon visually depends on division. The tree about to be harvested for newsprint is playfully subdivided into the newspaper's sections. Division occurs when a single subject (a tree, a Sunday newspaper) is subdivided into its parts. At least one section of a newspaper—the classifieds—shows, as its name suggests, classification at work. Advertisements for the same types of goods (real estate, houses, pets) or services or employment opportunities are grouped or classified together. Consider the number of these small advertisements in your Sunday newspaper. The only way that you can find what you are looking for is if the advertisements are grouped together (or classified) under headings. Without such a classification scheme, the Sunday reader would be faced with hundreds of small advertisements arranged in a random order.

DIVISION AND CLASSIFICATION AS A LITERARY STRATEGY

Victorian poet Elizabeth Barrett wrote a series of sonnets to poet Robert Browning during their courtship. She did not show him the sonnets until some months after they were married. She thought that the sonnets were too private to ever be published, but her husband disagreed. In Sonnet 43 in the series, Barrett "counted" the ways in which she loved Browning. Notice how she "divides" her love for him:

HOW DO I LOVE THEE

Elizabeth Barrett

How do I love thee? Let me count the ways.
I love thee to the depth and breadth and height
My soul can reach, when feeling out of sight
For the ends of Being and ideal Grace.
I love thee to the level of everyday's
Most quiet need, by sun and candle-light.
I love thee freely, as men strive for Right;
I love thee purely, as they turn from Praise.
I love thee with the passion put to use
In my old griefs, and with my childhood's faith.
I love thee with a love I seemed to lose
With my lost saints,—I love thee with the breath,
Smiles, tears, of all my life!—and, if God choose,
I shall but love thee better after death.

DISCUSSION QUESTIONS

1. Barrett has one love, but it is a love that she sees as showing itself in many different ways. Using the punctuation of the poem as a clue, how many ways are "counted" in the poem?

2. Is there a sense of progression or movement in the ways in which Barrett loves? Is the division organized in any particular sequence? Could the ways be organized in different order?

3. What stylistic device(s) does Barrett use to help her reader "count" the ways?

4. How does Barrett vary the pattern in the final two lines of the poem?

5. How does Barrett bring the poem to an end? Judging simply from what is being said, how do we know that the poem is now finished?

WRITING SUGGESTIONS

The American greeting card industry flourishes because most of us have difficulty putting our feelings into words. It is much easier to buy a card with the appropriate preprinted sentiment. In a paragraph express your thanks, gratitude, love, affection, devotion, whatever, to someone important to you. Do so using division as an organizational pattern. Possible starting points might include the following:

a. A note of thanks to the person or persons responsible for helping you through school

b. A note to a child (maybe your own child, your sibling, your niece or nephew)

c. A note to someone who is a model for you (such as a coach, a grandparent, a former teacher, a close friend)

Using Division and Classification in Writing for Your Other Courses

Many kinds of college writing assignments will call for analysis—dividing a theory, event, cultural movement, historical period, literary style, or other broad subject into its component elements and examining how each contributes to the whole. Others will require classifying subjects—artistic works, kinds of behavior, individual thinkers and writers, natural phenomena, biological organisms—into established categories based on 5 characteristic they share with others in that category—historical periods, groupings established by expert opinion or specific theories, artistic movements, and the like. Here are some examples of writing assignments that would require division (analysis) or classification.

- **Economics.** For an independent research paper in a contemporary economics course, you might be asked to read the work of a contemporary economist and analyze the theories presented in terms of labor, markets, and the distribution of wealth.
- **Art History or Introduction to Music.** For an exam, you might be asked to look at or listen to a number of works, classify each according to the period during which it was probably created, and write a paragraph or two explaining your reasoning in each case.
- **Sociology or Psychology.** As part of a case study of a particular group of your choice, you might be asked to classify the behaviors you observe according to the kinds of patterns you've learned about in the course.
- **Communications.** For a writing assignment asking you to examine bias in the media, you might observe and read a number of news reports focusing on the same subject or issue and then write a paper classifying each according to the level of bias it seemed to exhibit—for example, highly biased, somewhat biased, essentially neutral—based on criteria you establish prior to your research.
- **Physics.** On an exam, you might be asked to judge the conductivity of various solids based on an analysis of their atomic structure.

VISIT THE PRENTICE HALL READER'S WEBSITE

When you have finished reading an essay, check out the additional material available at the *Reader*'s Website at www.prenhall. com/miller. For each reading, you will find a list of related readings connected with the topic or the author; additional background information; a group of relevant "hot-linked" Web resources (just click your computer's mouse and automatically visit the sites listed); and still more writing suggestions.

DIVIDING AND CLASSIFYING

Visit the "Electronic" Newsstand and browse through 900 different magazines organized into 25 categories. Then write a paragraph based on your "surfing" experience. Want to see additional examples of classification and division schemes? Visit the *Reader*'s Website.

WHAT'S IN YOUR TOOTHPASTE

David Bodanis

Raised in Chicago, David Bodanis earned a degree in mathematics from the University of Chicago and did postgraduate work in theoretical biology and population genetics. He traveled to London and then to Paris, where he began his journalism career as a copyboy at the International Herald Tribune. *Bodanis has a special talent for explaining complex concepts in simple, yet entertaining, language. His most recent book is* E = Mc^2: A Biography of the World's Most Famous Equation *(2000).*

This essay is excerpted from The Secret House *(1986). One reviewer noted: "The book explores the gee-whiz science that sits unnoticed under every homeowner's nose." If you are appalled to discover what is in your toothpaste, you ought to read Bodanis's account of some mass-produced ice cream that contains "leftover cattle parts that no one else wants."*

BEFORE READING

Connecting: Most of us are well aware of the toxic nature of some common products, but there are many others that we assume are safe and maybe even good for us. Think about the things that you use, eat, or drink every day. Which ones have you never worried about?

Anticipating: Is Bodanis being fair and objective in his essay? How can you judge?

1   Into the bathroom goes our male resident, and after the most pressing need is satisfied it's time to brush the teeth. The tube of toothpaste is squeezed, its pinched metal seams are splayed, pressure waves are generated inside, and the paste begins to flow. But what's in this toothpaste, so carefully being extruded out?

2   Water mostly, 30 to 45 percent in most brands: ordinary, everyday simple tap water. It's there because people like to have a big gob of toothpaste to spread on the brush, and water is the cheapest stuff there is when it comes to making big gobs. Dripping a bit from the tap onto your brush would cost virtually nothing; whipped in with the rest of the toothpaste the manufacturers can sell it at a neat and accountant-pleasing $2 per pound equivalent. Toothpaste manufacture is a very lucrative occupation.

Second to water in quantity is chalk: exactly the same material 3
that schoolteachers use to write on blackboards. It is collected from
the crushed remains of long-dead ocean creatures. In the Cretaceous
seas chalk particles served as part of the wickedly sharp outer skeleton that these creatures had to wrap around themselves to keep from
getting chomped by all the slightly larger other ocean creatures they
met. Their massed graves are our present chalk deposits.

The individual chalk particles—the size of the smallest mud 4
particles in your garden—have kept their toughness over the aeons,
and now on the toothbrush they'll need it. The enamel outer coating
of the tooth they'll have to face is the hardest substance in the body—
tougher than skull, or bone, or nail. Only the chalk particles in toothpaste can successfully grind into the teeth during brushing, ripping
off the surface layers like an abrading wheel grinding down a boulder
in a quarry.

The craters, slashes, and channels that the chalk tears into the 5
teeth will also remove a certain amount of build-up yellow in the carnage, and it is for that polishing function that it's there. A certain
amount of unduly enlarged extra-abrasive chalk fragments tear such
cavernous pits into the teeth that future decay bacteria will be able to
bunker down there and thrive; the quality control people find it almost impossible to screen out these errant super-chalk pieces, and
government regulations allow them to stay in.

In case even the gouging doesn't get all the yellow off, another 6
substance is worked into the toothpaste cream. This is titanium diox-
ide. It comes in tiny spheres, and it's the stuff bobbing around in white
wall paint to make it come out white. Splashed around onto your
teeth during the brushing it coats much of the yellow that remains.
Being water soluble it leaks off in the next few hours and is swallowed,
but at least for the quick glance up in the mirror after finishing it will
make the user think his teeth are truly white. Some manufacturers
add optical whitening dyes—the stuff more commonly found in
washing machine bleach—to make extra sure that that glance in the
mirror shows reassuring white.

These ingredients alone would not make a very attractive con- 7
coction. They would stick in the tube like a sloppy white plastic lump,
hard to squeeze out as well as revolting to the touch. Few consumers
would savor rubbing in a mixture of water, ground-up blackboard
chalk, and the whitener from latex paint first thing in the morning.
To get around that finicky distaste the manufacturers have mixed in a
host of other goodies.

To keep the glop from drying out, a mixture including glycerine 8
glycol—related to the most common car antifreeze ingredient—is

whipped in with the chalk and water, and to give *that* concoction a bit of substance (all we really have so far is wet colored chalk) a large helping is added of gummy molecules from the seaweed *Chondrus Crispus*. This seaweed ooze spreads in among the chalk, paint, and antifreeze, then stretches itself in all directions to hold the whole mass together. A bit of paraffin oil (the fuel that flickers in camping lamps) is pumped in with it to help the moss ooze keep the whole substance smooth.

9   With the glycol, ooze, and paraffin we're almost there. Only two major chemicals are left to make the refreshing, cleansing substance we know as toothpaste. The ingredients so far are fine for cleaning, but they wouldn't make much of the satisfying foam we have come to expect in the morning brushing.

10   To remedy that every toothpaste on the market has a big dollop of detergent added too. You've seen the suds detergent will make in a washing machine. The same substance added here will duplicate that inside the mouth. It's not particularly necessary, but it sells.

11   The only problem is that by itself this ingredient tastes, well, too like detergent. It's horribly bitter and harsh. The chalk put in toothpaste is pretty foul-tasting too for that matter. It's to get around that gustatory discomfort that the manufacturers put in the ingredient they tout perhaps the most of all. This is the flavoring, and it has to be strong. Double rectified peppermint oil is used—a flavorer so powerful that chemists know better than to sniff it in the raw state in the laboratory. Menthol crystals and saccharin or other sugar simulators are added to complete the camouflage operation.

12   Is that it? Chalk, water, paint, seaweed, antifreeze, paraffin oil, detergent, and peppermint? Not quite. A mix like that would be irresistible to the hundreds of thousands of individual bacteria lying on the surface of even an immaculately cleaned bathroom sink. They would get in, float in the water bubbles, ingest the ooze and paraffin, maybe even spray out enzymes to break down the chalk. The result would be an uninviting mess. The way manufacturers avoid that final obstacle is by putting something in to kill the bacteria. Something good and strong is needed, something that will zap any accidentally intrudant bacteria into oblivion. And that something is formaldehyde—the disinfectant used in anatomy labs.

13   So it's chalk, water, paint, seaweed, antifreeze, paraffin oil, detergent, peppermint, formaldehyde, and fluoride (which can go some way towards preserving children's teeth)—that's the usual mixture raised to the mouth on the toothbrush for a fresh morning's clean. If it sounds too unfortunate, take heart. Studies show that thorough brushing with just plain water will often do as good a job.

QUESTIONS ON SUBJECT AND PURPOSE

1. Bodanis explains to the reader what toothpaste is composed of. Is his description objective? Could it appear, for example, in an encyclopedia?
2. After reading the essay, you might feel that Bodanis avoids certain crucial issues about the composition of toothpaste. Does he raise for you any questions that he does not answer?
3. What might Bodanis's purpose be? Is he arguing for something? Is he attacking something?

QUESTIONS ON STRATEGY AND AUDIENCE

1. How does Bodanis seem to arrange or order his division?
2. Bodanis gives the most space (three paragraphs) to chalk. Why? What is his focus in the section?
3. What could Bodanis expect about his audience?

QUESTIONS ON VOCABULARY AND STYLE

1. How would you characterize the tone of the essay?
2. Bodanis links most of the ingredients to their use in another product. Find these links, and be prepared to comment on the effect that these linkages have on the reader.
3. Be prepared to define the following words: *splayed* (paragraph 1), *extruded* (1), *lucrative* (2), *aeons* (4), *abrading* (4), *carnage* (5), *errant* (5), *finicky* (7), *dollop* (10), *gustatory* (11), *tout* (11), *intrudant* (12).

WRITING SUGGESTIONS

1. **For Your Journal.** Over a period of several days, keep a list of every product that you use or consume—everything from a lip balm to cosmetics to after-shave or cologne to mouthwash to chewing gum. When you really think about it, which ones would you like to know more about?
2. **For a Paragraph.** Select a common food or beverage, and subdivide it into its constituent parts. Use the contents label on the package as a place to start. You could use either the list of ingredients or the nutrition information. Present your division in a paragraph. Do not just describe what you find; rather, develop an attitude or thesis toward those findings.

Bodanis, for example, certainly expresses (or implies) how he feels about what he finds in toothpaste.

3. **For an Essay.** Americans exhibit widely differing attitudes toward the food they eat, in large part because they have the greatest choice of any people in the world. In an essay, classify the American eater. You can approach your subject from a serious or a comic point of view. Do not just describe types; your essay should either state or imply your feelings or judgments about your findings. Try to establish four to six categories.

4. **For Research.** Americans have become increasingly concerned about the additives that are put into food. Research the nature of food additives. How many are there? In general, what do they do? Develop a classification scheme to explain the largest groups or subdivisions. Be sure to adopt a stand or thesis about the use of such additives; also be sure to document your sources.

  WEBSITE LINK

Shocked to find out what's in your tube of toothpaste? That's nothing compared to the ingredients in a jar of baby food! Read a description from Bodanis's *The Secret Family* at the *Reader*'s Website.

  WRITING LINK: SUMMARY SENTENCES

Bodanis uses a summary sentence at times to repeat or reinforce the points that he has made so far—examples occur in paragraphs 7, 8, 9, 12, and 13. Why might he keep doing this? What is the effect of such summary or repetition? When might you use such a strategy in your own writing?

IN DEFENSE OF TALK SHOWS

Barbara Ehrenreich

Born in Butte, Montana, in 1941, Barbara Ehrenreich earned her Ph.D. in biology at Rockefeller University. After a period of university teaching, Ehrenreich turned to writing full time. A prolific writer, Ehrenreich's most recent book is Nickel and Dimed: On (Not) Getting By in America *(2001).*

On Writing: *Ehrenreich writes regularly for* The Progressive *and a wide range of other magazines, including* Time, *where "In Defense of Talk Shows" first appeared. Commenting on writing essays for magazines, she observed: "I don't see myself as writing polemics where I'm just trying to beat something into people's heads. An essay is like a little story, a short story, and I will obsess about what is the real point, what are the real connections, a long time before I ever put finger to keyboard."*

BEFORE READING

Connecting. Do you ever watch talk shows such as the ones that Ehrenreich mentions? What attracts you to them?

Anticipating. To what extent is the essay a "defense" of talk shows?

U p until now, the targets of Bill *(The Book of Virtues)* Bennett's cru-   1
sades have at least been plausible sources of evil. But the latest victim of his wrath—TV talk shows of the Sally Jessy Raphael variety—are in a whole different category from drugs and gangsta rap. As anyone who actually watches them knows, the talk shows are one of the most excruciatingly moralistic forums the culture has to offer. Disturbing and sometimes disgusting, yes, but their very business is to preach the middle-class virtues of responsibility, reason and self-control.

Take the case of Susan, recently featured on *Montel Williams* as   2
an example of a woman being stalked by her ex-boyfriend. Turns out Susan is also stalking the boyfriend and—here's the sexual frisson—has slept with him only days ago. In fact Susan is neck deep in trouble without any help from the boyfriend: She's serving a yearlong stretch of home incarceration for assaulting another woman, and home is the tiny trailer she shares with her nine-year-old daughter.

3   But no one is applauding this life spun out of control. Montel scolds Susan roundly for neglecting her daughter and failing to confront her role in the mutual stalking. A therapist lectures her about this unhealthy "obsessive kind of love." The studio audience jeers at her every evasion. By the end Susan has lost her cocky charm and dissolved into tears of shame.

4   The plot is always the same. People with problems—"husband says she looks like a cow," "pressured to lose her virginity or else," "mate wants more sex than I do"—are introduced to rational methods of problem solving. People with moral failings—"boy crazy," "dresses like a tramp," "a hundred sex partners"—are introduced to external standards of morality. The preaching—delivered alternately by the studio audience, the host and the ever present guest therapist—is relentless. "This is wrong to do this," Sally Jessy tells a cheating husband. "Feel bad?" Geraldo asks the girl who stole her best friend's boyfriend. "Any sense of remorse?" The expectation is that the sinner, so hectored, will see her way to reform. And indeed, a Sally Jessy update found "boy crazy," who'd been a guest only weeks ago, now dressed in schoolgirlish plaid and claiming her "attitude {had} changed"—thanks to the rough-and-ready therapy dispensed on the show.

5   All right, the subjects are often lurid and even bizarre. But there's no part of the entertainment spectacle, from *Hard Copy* to *Jade*, that doesn't trade in the lurid and bizarre. At least in the talk shows, the moral is always loud and clear: Respect yourself, listen to others, stop beating on your wife. In fact it's hard to see how *The Bill Bennett Show*, if there were to be such a thing, could deliver a more pointed sermon. Or would he prefer to see the feckless Susan, for example, tarred and feathered by the studio audience instead of being merely booed and shamed?

6   There is something morally repulsive about the talks, but it's not anything Bennett or his co-crusader Senator Joseph Lieberman has seen fit to mention. Watch for a few hours, and you get the claustrophobic sense of lives that have never seen the light of some external judgment, of people who have never before been listened to, and certainly never taken seriously if they were. "What kind of people would let themselves be humiliated like this?" is often asked, sniffily, by the shows' detractors. And the answer, for the most part, is people who are so needy—of social support, of education, of material resources and self-esteem—that they mistake being the center of attention for being actually loved and respected.

7   What the talks are about, in large part, is poverty and the distortions it visits on the human spirit. You'll never find investment

bankers bickering on *Rolonda*, or the host of *Gabrielle* recommending therapy to sobbing professors. With few exceptions the guests are drawn from trailer parks and tenements, from bleak streets and narrow, crowded rooms. Listen long enough, and you hear references to unpaid bills, to welfare, to twelve-hour workdays and double shifts. And this is the real shame of the talks: that they take lives bent out of shape by poverty and hold them up as entertaining exhibits. An announcement appearing between segments of *Montel* says it all: The show is looking for "pregnant women who sell their bodies to make ends meet."

This is class exploitation, pure and simple. What next—"home-   8
less people so hungry they eat their own scabs"? Or would the next step be to pay people outright to submit to public humiliation? For $50 would you confess to adultery in your wife's presence? For $500 would you reveal your thirteen-year-old's girlish secrets on *Ricki Lake*? If you were poor enough, you might.

It is easy enough for those who can afford spacious homes and   9
private therapy to sneer at their financial inferiors and label their pathetic moments of stardom vulgar. But if I had a talk show, it would feature a whole different cast of characters and category of crimes than you'll ever find on the talks: "CEOs who rake in millions while their employees get downsized" would be an obvious theme, along with "Senators who voted for welfare and Medicaid cuts"—and, if he'll agree to appear, "well-fed Republicans who dithered about talk shows while trailer-park residents slipped into madness and despair."

QUESTIONS ON SUBJECT AND PURPOSE

1. Write a thesis statement—or find one—for the essay.
2. According to Ehrenreich, why would people agree to appear on these talk shows?
3. What makes such shows "morally repulsive" (paragraph 6)?

QUESTIONS ON STRATEGY AND AUDIENCE

1. How does Ehrenreich divide or analyze the distinctive common features of the talk shows?
2. Why are such shows popular?
3. What expectations does Ehrenreich seem to have about her audience?

QUESTIONS ON VOCABULARY AND STYLE

1. In paragraphs 4 and 5, Ehrenreich uses an extended metaphor to explain the pattern that the shows follow. What is that metaphor? (Check the Glossary for a definition of *metaphor.*)
2. How would you characterize the tone of the rhetorical questions that Ehrenreich asks in paragraph 8? (Check the Glossary for a definition of *tone.*)
3. Be prepared to define the following words: *excruciatingly* (paragraph 1), *frisson* (2), *hectored* (4), *lurid* (5), *feckless* (5), *dithered* (9).

WRITING SUGGESTIONS

1. **For Your Journal.** All forms of media—compact discs, software programs, magazines, books, television or radio shows, even Websites—try to mimic whatever has been successful. For example, if one television show about "friends" or a new primetime game show is popular, expect next season to see several other imitators. Select one medium, and make notes in your journal about the similarities that you see among the items that belong in that category.
2. **For a Paragraph.** Expand your observations from your journal into a paragraph. Try for the same type of analysis or division that Ehrenreich achieves. Focus your paragraph around a single shared element.
3. **For an Essay.** Expand your paragraph analysis or division into a full essay. You are analyzing the elements that a series of similar media products share—for example, the common elements of television cooking shows or of magazines intended for teenage girls. Remember that the choice of medium is yours—software programs, magazines, advertisements, Websites. You will probably want to analyze three or four shared elements. How do these shared elements work together? To what purpose or goal do all of these things contribute?
4. **For Research.** Test your analysis by checking research done on the subject. Using the resources of your library, and perhaps of on-line databases and the World Wide Web, see what other writers have said. Remember that information will appear in communication journals, marketing and business journals, trade papers for that particular medium, and

scholarly and general journals and magazines. A keyword search might be a good place to begin. If you are having trouble gathering information, ask a reference librarian.

WEBSITE LINK

Did you know that most of the television talk shows have their own Websites, complete with additional photographs, backstage "live" minicams, and other special features? Find out where to go.

WRITING LINK: TONE AND DICTION

Assuming a spectrum from formal to informal, where would you place Ehrenreich's essay on that scale? Identify those features in her prose (such as word choice and sentence structure) that support your opinion. Under what circumstances do you want your writing to be formal? When can it be informal?

ENGLISH 99: LITERACY AMONG THE RUINS

Frank Gannon

Frank Gannon (1952–   ) has published essays in magazines such as The New Yorker, GQ, Atlantic Monthly, *and* National Review. *The author of several books, Gannon's* Midlife Irish: Discovering My Family and Myself *will appear in 2003.*

"English 99" first appeared in Harper's *Magazine in an issue with the theme "New Hope for American Education."*

On Writing: *Gannon observes, "I'm a humorist. I'm not a very talented writer, but I do what I can. . . . I write every day except Sunday. I use a word processor now. I used to think that the first typewriter I used when I first started to make money was 'magic,' but I got over that. I always write in the same room, but I know that if it burned down, I would get another one. And then that would be 'magic'."*

BEFORE READING

Connecting: Think about the classes in which you are enrolled now. Are there certain "types" or categories of students in those classes? If you had to classify those students, what categories would you use?

Anticipating. Where does the focus of the essay lie? Is it about the students who were enrolled in English 99? Is it about Gannon's experience as a teacher? Is it about both?

1   Recently, a small college asked me to teach. I was told that I'd be teaching writing. This sounded pretty good to me. It might be interesting, and I might find some kid who was very talented. Then I would bring him along, nurture the talent, and, at the end of the movie, when he was winning the Nobel Prize for Literature, he would say, "I want to thank Frank Gannon, who first taught me how to write." Then they'd show me, a really old guy in a hospital bed watching him accept the Nobel Prize on television. He'd say some little dumb thing that the kid used to say when he was first learning how to be great from me. Something from the time when he was rebellious and I was crusty-but-lovable . . . Then they would play "triumphant" music.

I bought a herringbone jacket. I couldn't find one with those 2
leather elbow patches. I tried at Men's Wearhouse. The sales guy told
me they didn't make them anymore, but the guy looked like the ser-
geant in *Gomer Pyle* and probably didn't travel in academic circles, so
I doubt that he knew.

But the coat was very tweedy. I put it on and looked at myself in 3
the mirror. I used Robin Williams in *Good Will Hunting* as my goal
and I was very close.

I thought I would be teaching some kind of nonfiction creative- 4
writing thing at the college. I was told that not enough students were
interested. The little college was hard up for money, and small
classes, such as my proposed "English 393: Nonfiction Writing,"
were not very profitable.

Instead, I wound up teaching a class called English 99, a prof- 5
itable course. English 99 wasn't like most of the other courses at the
college. It didn't "count" as a course for the bachelor's degree. It was
held in a college classroom, but taking it didn't give you any credits
toward a degree. English 99 was a pass/fail course for students who,
according to the college, were going to be "overly challenged" by the
introductory English course, English 101. English 101 at the college
was not the intellectual equivalent of boot camp, but many of the students at the college weren't ready for that kind of hurdle. The class
met for one hour three times a week. After a student passed English
99, he or she would be theoretically prepared to take the first college
English course.

The administration at the college didn't like to draw attention 6
to English 99 because the course didn't "work." Most of those who
took English 99 never seemed to get anywhere close to graduating,
and a lot of them, discouraged by the rigor of English 99, wouldn't
ever take another college course for the rest of their lives.

The truth of the matter was that English 99 was there so that 7
the college could get some money from these kids before they flunked
out or quit. The college was shockingly expensive. Its main appeal
was that it almost never rejected anyone who applied.

This whole thing was pretty cloudy from a moral perspective, 8
but that wasn't a big factor for me, a person of cloudy morality. Compared with, say, the Sopranos, I was still semi-moral, sort of. At least
I told myself that.

For me the troublesome moral implications were settled by two 9
deciding factors: A) I could always say, in the immortal words of
Joseph Goebbels: "Hey, I just work here." B) Dental.

I liked the life of a professor. I spent much of my days reading 10
the books I never got around to when I was a student, and it was

pleasant putting on my professor costume and walking around on the campus.

11   A student would see me and say, "Dr. Gannon." I would wave in a low-key, academic way. I wasn't really a "doctor" or anything; I was just a magazine writer. But the students didn't know that. They assumed that I, like all the other professors, had a Ph.D.

12   I was a pseudo-professor. "Dr. Gannon." That sounded strange but good. I'd always wave. I thought of getting a pipe.

13   Of course, I was an impostor. But so was the class I taught. I was posing as a professor and English 99 was posing as a college course.

14   There were three definite types of students in the class: Bored-looking girls, jocks, and, this year, a new category: Bosnian refugees. A wealthy alumnus of the college had established a grant for the victims of the war in Bosnia. The young Bosnians at the college were there because of the grant. It enabled them to enroll in the college, take courses, and, hopefully, start a new life in America.

15   Many of these Bosnian young people had been college students in their native country before the war had shattered their lives. Now that they were in America it was no longer important that they were Serbs or Croats or Christians or Muslims. They were now Bosnian people beginning over in America.

16   A lot of the Bosnian kids were extremely bright. Some of them had been pre-med and pre-law students before the tragic war, but because most of these kids were just learning English, they were natural candidates for English 99.

17   So the situation was set. Two huge vehicles, the "Horror-of-the-World Truck" and the "Stupidity-of-the-World Truck," were about to run into each other. I was there to watch. If this had involved insurance, the police and the insurance company would have interrogated me. As it was, I just watched.

18   (I have disguised the identities of both the college and the students for reasons that will, I think, become obvious to the reader.)

19   There was no "seating chart" in English 99, so anyone could sit anywhere in the room, but, for some reason, the classes always segregated themselves. The groups all sat together, which, I thought, underlined their status as specific groups. The English 99 classroom was large, and there was enough room to establish a sort of buffer zone of empty desks around each group.

20   Again, the three groups were:
1. The Bored-Looking Girls
2. The Jocks
3. The Refugees

After the first day of class, no one ever changed desks, so the   21
sense of three distinct groups was emphasized. This was, of course, a
writing-exercise class, so the content of the writing was not as important as the form. The idea was to get the students good enough at
writing English that they could have a chance in English 101.

The first day, I tried to explain writing English to the class. I   22
told them that writing was more like playing golf or the piano than it
was like other courses. Writing wasn't really a subject to be studied.
That is, writing English prose was more a skill than a body of acquired knowledge, like, say, history, or psychology, or biology. It was
an activity more than something that can be studied. You don't *learn*
it, you learn how to *do* it.

I used a lot of metaphors to get across this general idea. It was   23
like juggling. Like riding a bicycle. Keep doing it and one day you
wake up and you can do it. If you don't quit, you will get it. It is like
golf. It is like tennis. It is like the hula hoop. It is like jumping rope.
Like riding a bicycle.

It was very difficult to come up with something they had all   24
done. The three groups—the bored-looking girls, the jocks, and the
refugees—were like three separate countries. They were all trying to
get to the same general place. But they were starting from places a
million miles apart.

The writing of the three groups was very, very distinct, very   25
particular. The writing of the bored-looking girls could never be mistaken for the writing of the jocks or the writing of the refugees. Except for the fact that they were written in English, the writings of the
three groups were DRASTICALLY different.

Because we were just concerned with writing in general, I found   26
it best to let the students write about anything they wanted. Despite
that fact, however, the students wrote in-class essay after in-class essay on the same subjects.

The bored-looking girls always wrote about three topics. Topic   27
one can be called "LIFE IS HARD":

> It is very hard to have a relationship with a guy because it is hard to
> meet a guy that you like. When you meet them they never turn out
> to be the way you want them to be. Like this guy I went out with last
> summer. I thought he was sweet but I found out that he lied all the
> time. Right to my face. Incredible.

Topic two was "I CAN'T DO ANYTHING":

> I always say I'm going to do something and then I never do it. Like
> this morning. I said that I was going to math class but I went to the

Jiffy Mart and I bought a slushy and I drank it in the car with my girlfriend Mandy and it was hard to go to math class because it's so boring. I didn't go so I didn't get my makeup test. So now I'm behind. I hate that. I have to apply myself.

Topic three was "I AM TIRED":

Today my roommate woke me up and I looked at the alarm clock and I was like I am so late! I just threw some clothes on and I didn't even put on much makeup and then I was like I'm so late anyway and I just went back to sleep. I have to stop doing this. It is very stressful because today's young person has drugs and peer pressure and yet is expected to go to college.

28   The jocks also had three subjects. One was "I HAVE FUN":

Last week my friends and I drove down to the beach and got a room. In the daytime we just hung out at the pool and at night we would go out and get some beer and go to places. We got there around nine and it was pretty empty. But by ten there were a lot of girls and we all met girls. It was just kick back and have some fun. And we had a good time. In the morning we got a bite to eat and then just hung out by the pool and caught some rays and drank a couple of beers. One afternoon we went to this mall they have near there. I bought some shoes. It was great. But then we had to go back to college again.

The jocks' topic two was "I NEED FREEDOM":

Why is it that the drinking age is twenty-one? That is so stupid because a person knows what he's doing and why should he have to wait until somebody says it's all right. And it just makes you want to drink more and if you can be in the army when you are eighteen then it doesn't make sense. You can get killed for the same country you can't drink in. It doesn't do any good and everyone knows it's stupid. In Europe I hear it isn't like that. Why can't it be like that in America? Don't get me wrong. You should drink sensibly. Like when we drink we always have a designated driver.

Three was "WHAT I CAN DO GOOD":

I started playing baseball when I was eight with T-ball. When I was twelve our team had won the region. I was the pitcher for that game and I have always had a good arm. When I was in high school we were second in the state and I won every game I pitched except one that I got hurt in. One year we won our division and it was awesome. I was like about the best player on that team. When I got to college I was nervous because I didn't have confidence about playing on this level but my dad said just relax and do the best you can and the first day I hit the ball real good so now I feel better about everything and I'm really looking forward to this year.

The refugees had only one theme, "LIFE": 29

> When I was ten the war came in and people lost lives. We only have water on some days. People saw shooting and war came closer. I was in a building and a bomb went off and my friend was killed. I had to leave country without family. It changes everything. But war kept getting closer until we must leave. I walked by people dead in street. Cetnik and anti-Serb leave because nothing is left.

***

> In Sarajevo soldiers say that they will bring a dream of making things fair. People I live with call Melmed in Bijeljina. Relatives all killed. U.N. has blue helmets take care of small problems. Milosevic and Karadzic do not do what they said. Can't help. Now I live in America and go to college here. I am trying to learn English. Difficult. First night was in Brooklyn. Very scary at night.

Sometimes the refugees write things that, if written by one of 30 the other groups, would get me to write "nice detail" in the margin. Many times the only thing I could ever think of to write was "good." Sometimes I would look at the word after I wrote it and cross it out because it seemed like a stupid thing to write. So I would just circle things and correct sentences.

> Adnan lived next door has hand blown in war.

I corrected it.

> Adnan, who lived next door, had his hand blown off in the war.

Then I crossed out my corrected sentence. Sometimes after 31 reading a few refugee papers I felt that instead of teaching English I was unlearning English.

Our class was at eight-thirty in the morning. Sometimes I 32 would get there a few minutes late. There would be students waiting outside the room. I unlocked the door to let the students in. Then I said, "I need coffee." I'd excuse myself and go downstairs to get coffee. When I got back, I saw a student paper on my desk:

> Some people so hungry they eat tree. They put tree in boil water to make soft tree. Since began rationing green corn is best thing. But army and air force have nice meals. Here everything good.

Some of the Refugee Group's papers were narrative in nature. 33

> My sister had friend. She said that soldiers took her off the street and hurt and then let her go. Then she cries never would come out of room. People say forget. That is hard for her. She stay in room.

I remember circling the verb and writing, "agreement?" 34

35   At the end of every semester I would have to give grades to the students. The only two grades were "Pass" and "Fail." I passed and failed a lot of bored-looking girls and a lot of jocks. Mostly they passed. You could take English 99 more than once, and a lot of students took it two and even three times. I never failed a refugee. I knew that English 101 would be hard for many of them, but I thought that I might be teaching English 99 again, and I still wouldn't be able to "correct" anything.

36   After a few weeks of English 99, I desperately wanted it to end. It had a bad effect on me. I started to dread Mondays, Wednesdays, and Fridays. The dean's secretary called me one day. It was right after class, and I was thinking about an essay I had just read. The essay was about Sarajevo, about hiding.

37   I had just finished reading an essay about how guys can be so thoughtless that it's not even funny. Before that I had read an essay about people who wear designer clothes and how they are so snotty. Before that I read what happens when a bomb goes off in the middle of the night in your apartment building.

38   The dean wanted to see me. I was very happy to go.

39   The dean, a polite balding man in his late forties, told me, in a pleasant voice, that the college was trying to "get leaner." He was sorry, and this had nothing to do with my work, but he was going to have to cut me loose. I said that I appreciated everything the college had done for me. He said that I was "on the top of our list" if they ever hired more professors. We shook hands.

40   I was going to walk back up to my office. I remembered what I was doing when I left. I still had a lot more essays to read, but I went outside and walked home trying not to think in sentences.

QUESTIONS ON SUBJECT AND PURPOSE

1. What is English 99?
2. How much of the essay is devoted to talking about Gannon's experience with the three types of students? What does the rest of the essay focus on?
3. What purpose might Gannon have had in the essay? Is this a condemnation of pre-Freshman English writing courses? Of students? Is the essay comic? Exaggerated?

QUESTIONS ON STRATEGY AND AUDIENCE

1. What is the effect of the opening paragraph in the essay? What does it suggest about the essay that follows? How does it become a lens through which we read the essay?

2. Why might Gannon quote some examples from the students' writing? Do you think these are actual examples? Why or why not?
3. Who might Gannon be imagining as his reader?

QUESTIONS ON VOCABULARY AND STYLE

1. Why might Gannon choose to capitalize the topics about which the students write?
2. How would you characterize the tone of Gannon's essay? Is he serious? Detached? Prejudiced? How is that tone achieved?
3. Be prepared to define the following words: *nurture* (paragraph 1) and *rigor* (6).

WRITING SUGGESTIONS

1. **For Your Journal.** Think about the other subjects that you are studying this semester. How might division or classification be used to present some idea central to the subject matter of those courses? In your journal make a list of possible subjects or ideas.
2. **For a Paragraph.** Using your journal as a starting point, select one idea or concept and in a paragraph using either division or classification, present that idea to a general reader.
3. **For an Essay.** For an essay, consider two alternative topics. First, expand your paragraph writing into an essay. Remember that you are writing to a general audience and make sure that you avoid highly technical language or unfamiliar terms. Or, second, use the research paper topic as a departure point. In an essay, explore the types of learning that you have experienced during your years in school. What is the range of teaching methods and objectives that you have encountered? What seems to be the rationale for each? This second alternative could provide the basis for a comic essay in the style of Gannon.
4. **For Research.** Increasingly, researchers have realized that people learn in many different ways—that there are "multiple intelligences." Thomas Armstrong identifies eight: linguistic, logical/mathematical, spatial, kinesthetic, musical, interpersonal, intrapersonal, and naturalist. Research the concept of multiple intelligences—the Website will suggest

some places to start. Then, in a research essay, show how some or all of those intelligences have come into play during your own education.

WEBSITE LINK

To find available resources on learning about Thomas Armstong's concept of "multiple intelligences," check out the Website.

WRITING LINK: PARAGRAPHING

Look carefully at how and why Gannon develops paragraphs in the essay. In places, his paragraphs are quite long; in others, quite short. What seems to be the strategy behind that paragraphing? Working just from the essay, try to write a series of suggestions for when writers might begin a new paragraph. What does Gannon's paragraphing suggest about your own writing?

THE MYTH OF THE LATIN WOMAN: I JUST MET A GIRL NAMED MARIA

Judith Ortiz Cofer

Judith Ortiz Cofer's "Marina" is one of the readings in Chapter 2, and biographical information about her can be found in that headnote.

On Writing: *Cofer comments about living in and writing about two cultures: "The very term 'bilingual' tells you I have two worlds. At least now, they're very strictly separated, but when I was growing up it was a constant shift back and forth. I think my brain developed a sense of my world and my reality as being composed of two halves. But I'm not divided in them. I accept them, and I think they have basically been the difference that has allowed me to write things that are not like anybody else's."*

BEFORE READING

Connecting. Have you ever been treated as a stereotype? Have people ever expected certain things of you (good or bad) because of how you were classified in their eyes?

Anticipating. What expectations would you have of a "Latin woman"? Or a "Latin man"? Do those expectations coincide with those about which Cofer writes?

On a bus trip to London from Oxford University where I was earning some graduate credits one summer, a young man, obviously fresh from a pub, spotted me and as if struck by inspiration went down on his knees in the aisle. With both hands over his heart he broke into an Irish tenor's rendition of "Maria" from *West Side Story*. My politely amused fellow passengers gave his lovely voice the round of gentle applause it deserved. Though I was not quite as amused, I managed my version of an English smile: no show of teeth, no extreme contortions of the facial muscles—I was at this time of my life practicing reserve and cool. Oh, that British control, how I coveted it. But "Maria" had followed me to London, reminding me of a prime fact of my life: you can leave the island, master the English language, and travel as far as you can, but if you are a Latina, especially one like me

1

who so obviously belongs to Rita Moreno's gene pool, the island travels with you.

2   This is sometimes a very good thing—it may win you that extra minute of someone's attention. But with some people, the same things can make *you* an island—not a tropical paradise but an Alcatraz, a place nobody wants to visit. As a Puerto Rican girl living in the United States and wanting like most children to "belong," I resented the stereotype that my Hispanic appearance called forth from many people I met.

3   Growing up in a large urban center in New Jersey during the 1960s, I suffered from what I think of as "cultural schizophrenia." Our life was designed by my parents as a microcosm of their *casas* on the island. We spoke in Spanish, ate Puerto Rican food bought at the *bodega*, and practiced strict Catholicism at a church that allotted us a one-hour slot each week for mass, performed in Spanish by a Chinese priest trained as a missionary for Latin America.

4   As a girl I was kept under strict surveillance by my parents, since my virtue and modesty were, by their cultural equation, the same as their honor. As a teenager I was lectured constantly on how to behave as a proper *señorita*. But it was a conflicting message I received, since the Puerto Rican mothers also encouraged their daughters to look and act like women and to dress in clothes our Anglo friends and their mothers found too "mature" and flashy. The difference was, and is, cultural; yet I often felt humiliated when I appeared at an American friend's party wearing a dress more suitable to a semi-formal than to a playroom birthday celebration. At Puerto Rican festivities, neither the music nor the colors we wore could be too loud.

5   I remember Career Day in our high school, when teachers told us to come dressed as if for a job interview. It quickly became obvious that to the Puerto Rican girls "dressing up" meant wearing their mother's ornate jewelry and clothing, more appropriate (by mainstream standards) for the company Christmas party than as daily office attire. That morning I had agonized in front of my closet, trying to figure out what a "career girl" would wear. I knew how to dress for school (at the Catholic school I attended, we all wore uniforms), I knew how to dress for Sunday mass, and I knew what dresses to wear for parties at my relatives' homes. Though I do not recall the precise details of my Career Day outfit, it must have been a composite of these choices. But I remember a comment my friend (an Italian American) made in later years that coalesced my impressions of that day. She said that at the business school she was attending, the Puerto Rican girls always stood out for wearing "everything at once." She meant, of course, too much jewelry, too many accessories. On that

day at school we were simply made the negative models by the nuns, who were themselves not credible fashion experts to any of us. But it was painfully obvious to me that to the others, in their tailored skirts and silk blouses, we must have seemed "hopeless" and "vulgar." Though I now know that most adolescents feel out of step much of the time, I also know that for the Puerto Rican girls of my generation that sense was intensified. The way our teachers and classmates looked at us that day in school was just a taste of the cultural clash that awaited us in the real world, where prospective employers and men on the street would often misinterpret our tight skirts and jingling bracelets as a "come-on."

Mixed cultural signals have perpetuated certain stereotypes— 6 for example, that of the Hispanic woman as the "hot tamale" or sexual firebrand. It is a one-dimensional view that the media have found easy to promote. In their special vocabulary, advertisers have designated "sizzling" and "smoldering" as the adjectives of choice for describing not only the foods but also the women of Latin America. From conversations in my house I recall hearing about the harassment that Puerto Rican women endured in factories where the "bossmen" talked to them as if sexual innuendo was all they understood, and worse, often gave them the choice of submitting to their advances or being fired.

It is custom, however, not chromosomes, that leads us to choose 7 scarlet over pale pink. As young girls, it was our mothers who influenced our decisions about clothes and colors—mothers who had grown up on a tropical island where the natural environment was a riot of primary colors, where showing your skin was one way to keep cool as well as to look sexy. Most important of all, on the island, women perhaps felt freer to dress and move more provocatively since, in most cases, they were protected by the traditions, mores, and laws of a Spanish/Catholic system of morality and machismo whose main rule was: *You may look at my sister, but if you touch her I will kill you.* The extended family and church structure could provide a young woman with a circle of safety in her small pueblo on the island; if a man "wronged" a girl, everyone would close in to save her family honor.

My mother has told me about dressing in her best party clothes 8 on Saturday nights and going to the town's plaza to promenade with her girlfriends in front of the boys they liked. The males were thus given an opportunity to admire the women and to express their admiration in the form of *piropos:* erotically charged street poems they composed on the spot. (I have myself been subjected to a few *piropos* while visiting the island, and they can be outrageous, although custom dictates that they must never cross into obscenity.) This ritual, as

I understand it, also entails a show of studied indifference on the woman's part; if she is "decent," she must not acknowledge the man's impassioned words. So I do understand how things can be lost in translation. When a Puerto Rican girl dressed in her idea of what is attractive meets a man from the mainstream culture who has been trained to react to certain types of clothing as a sexual signal, a clash is likely to take place. I remember the boy who took me to my first formal dance leaning over to plant a sloppy, over-eager kiss painfully on my mouth; when I didn't respond with sufficient passion, he remarked resentfully: "I thought you Latin girls were supposed to mature early," as if I were expected to *ripen* like a fruit or vegetable, not just grow into womanhood like other girls.

9   It is surprising to my professional friends that even today some people, including those who should know better, still put others "in their place." It happened to me most recently during a stay at a classy metropolitan hotel favored by young professional couples for weddings. Late one evening after the theater, as I walked toward my room with a colleague (a woman with whom I was coordinating an arts program), a middle-aged man in a tuxedo, with a young girl in satin and lace on his arm, stepped directly into our path. With his champagne glass extended toward me, he exclaimed "Evita!"

10   Our way blocked, my companion and I listened as the man half-recited, half-bellowed "Don't Cry for Me, Argentina." When he finished, the young girl said: "How about a round of applause for my daddy?" We complied, hoping this would bring the silly spectacle to a close. I was becoming aware that our little group was attracting the attention of the other guests. "Daddy" must have perceived this too, and he once more barred the way as we tried to walk past him. He began to shout-sing a ditty to the tune of "La Bamba"—except the lyrics were about a girl named Maria whose exploits rhymed with her name and gonorrhea. The girl kept saying "Oh, Daddy" and looking at me with pleading eyes. She wanted me to laugh along with the others. My companion and I stood silently waiting for the man to end his offensive song. When he finished, I looked not at him but at his daughter. I advised her calmly never to ask her father what he had done in the army. Then I walked between them and to my room. My friend complimented me on my cool handling of the situation, but I confessed that I had really wanted to push the jerk into the swimming pool. This same man—probably a corporate executive, well-educated, even worldly by most standards—would not have been likely to regale an Anglo woman with a dirty song in public. He might have checked his impulse by assuming that she could be somebody's wife or mother, or at least *somebody* who might take offense. But, to him,

I was just an Evita or a Maria: merely a character in his cartoon-populated universe.

Another facet of the myth of the Latin woman in the United 11
States is the menial, the domestic—Maria the housemaid or counter-girl. It's true that work as domestics, as waitresses, and in factories is all that's available to women with little English and few skills. But the myth of the Hispanic menial—the funny maid, mispronouncing words and cooking up a spicy storm in a shiny California kitchen—has been perpetuated by the media in the same way that "Mammy" from *Gone with the Wind* became America's idea of the black woman for generations. Since I do not wear my diplomas around my neck for all to see, I have on occasion been sent to that "kitchen" where some think I obviously belong.

One incident has stayed with me, though I recognize it as a mi- 12
nor offense. My first public poetry reading took place in Miami, at a restaurant where a luncheon was being held before the event. I was nervous and excited as I walked in with notebook in hand. An older woman motioned me to her table, and thinking (foolish me) that she wanted me to autograph a copy of my newly published slender volume of verse, I went over. She ordered a cup of coffee from me, assuming I was the waitress. (Easy enough to mistake my poems for menus, I suppose.) I know it wasn't an intentional act of cruelty. Yet of all the good things that happened later, I remember that scene most clearly, because it reminded me of what I had to overcome before anyone would take me seriously. In retrospect I understand that my anger gave my reading fire. In fact, I have almost always taken any doubt in my abilities as a challenge, the result most often being the satisfaction of winning a convert, of seeing the cold, appraising eyes warm to my words, the body language change, the smile that indicates I have opened some avenue for communication. So that day as I read, I looked directly at that woman. Her lowered eyes told me she was embarrassed at her faux pas, and when I willed her to look up at me, she graciously allowed me to punish her with my full attention. We shook hands at the end of the reading and I never saw her again. She has probably forgotten the entire incident, but maybe not.

Yet I am one of the lucky ones. There are thousands of Latinas 13
without the privilege of an education or the entrees into society that I have. For them life is a constant struggle against the misconceptions perpetuated by the myth of the Latina. My goal is to try to replace the old stereotypes with a much more interesting set of realities. Every time I give a reading, I hope the stories I tell, the dreams and fears I examine in my work, can achieve some universal truth that will get my audience past the particulars of my skin color, my accent, or my clothes.

14   I once wrote a poem in which I called all Latinas "God's brown daughters." This poem is really a prayer of sorts, offered upward, but also, through the human-to-human channel of art, outward. It is a prayer for communication and for respect. In it, Latin women pray "in Spanish to an Anglo God / with a Jewish heritage," and they are "fervently hoping / that if not omnipotent, / at least He be bilingual."

QUESTIONS ON SUBJECT AND PURPOSE

1. What exactly is a stereotype? Where does the word *stereotype* come from?
2. What are the stereotypes or "myths" of the Latin woman that Cofer has experienced?
3. What is Cofer's announced goal in writing?

QUESTIONS ON STRATEGY AND AUDIENCE

1. At what point in time does the essay begin? Why does Cofer start with this example?
2. How does Cofer use time or chronology as a structural device in her essay?
3. Who does Cofer imagine as her reader? How can you tell?

QUESTIONS ON VOCABULARY AND STYLE

1. What does Cofer mean when she writes, "It is custom, however, not chromosomes, that leads us to choose scarlet over pale pink"?
2. What does *machismo* (paragraph 7) mean?
3. Be prepared to define the following words: *coveted* (paragraph 1), *microcosm* (3), *coalesced* (5), *innuendo* (6), *mores* (7), *regale* (10), *menial* (11), *faux pas* (12).

WRITING SUGGESTIONS

1. **For Your Journal.** Probably most people have in one way or another been stereotyped by someone else. Stereotyping is not reserved only for individuals from particular races or cultures. Think about the wide range of other stereotypes that exists in our culture, based on gender, age, physical appearance, hair or clothing styles, language dialects, or geography. In your journal, make a list of such stereotypes, focusing on either

those that have been applied to you or those that you have consciously or unconsciously applied to others.

2. **For a Paragraph.** Using your journal writing as a prewriting exercise, take one of the stereotypes and in a paragraph develop one aspect of that stereotype and how it is evidenced by others or by yourself.

3. **For an Essay.** Expand your paragraph into an essay. Remember now that you are fully exploring a stereotype that you yourself have encountered or that you apply to others. Stereotypes are everywhere—they are not encountered solely by people from different cultures, races, or religions. For example, has anyone ever considered you a "dumb blonde" or a "nerd" or a "jock"? What aspects of personality do people expect when they see you as a stereotype (or do you expect when you see someone else as a stereotype)? Classify these reactions.

4. **For Research.** Think about the stereotypes that Americans commonly hold about people from another culture. Cultural differences sometimes produce a great deal of misunderstanding. Select a culture (or some aspect of that culture) that seems to be widely misunderstood by most Americans. Research the cultural differences, and present your findings in an essay. One excellent source of information would be interviews with students from other countries and cultures. Where do they see those misunderstandings occurring most frequently? Your library, on-line databases, and the World Wide Web can also be good sources of information when you are able to narrow your search with appropriate specific subjects and keywords. Be sure to document all of your sources and to ask permission of any interviewees.

 WEBSITE LINK

A range of on-line and print interviews with Cofer can be found at the Website.

WRITING LINK: PARENTHESES

Cofer uses a number of parentheses in her writing. What are the rules that govern the use of parentheses? How do they differ from a pair of commas or a pair of dashes? Look closely at how Cofer uses parentheses. Can you construct some rules or suggestions for their use based on her sentences? Under what set of circumstances might you enclose material within parentheses in your own writing?

THE VALUE OF CHILDREN:
A TAXONOMICAL ESSAY

Bernard R. Berelson

Bernard R. Berelson (1912–1979) was born in Spokane, Washington, and received a Ph.D. from the University of Chicago. He divided his time between the academic world and the world of international development assistance. In 1962, he joined the Population Council, eventually serving as its president until his retirement in 1974. Berelson published extensively on population policy and the prospects for fertility declines in developing countries.

Berelson's concern with population policy is obvious in this essay reprinted from the Annual Report *of the Population Council. Using a clear scheme of classification, Berelson analyzes the reasons why people want children.*

BEFORE READING

Connecting: The phrase "the value of children" might seem a little unusual. What, for example, was your "value" to your parents? If you have children, in what sense do they have "value" to you?

Anticipating. Despite the many reasons for having or wanting children, people in many societies today consciously choose to limit the number of children that they have. How might Berelson explain this phenomenon?

Why do people want children? It is a simple question to ask, perhaps an impossible one to answer. 1

Throughout most of human history, the question never seemed to need a reply. These years, however, the question has a new tone. It is being asked in a nonrhetorical way because of three revolutions in thought and behavior that characterize the latter decades of the twentieth century: the vital revolution in which lower death rates have given rise to the population problem and raise new issues about human fertility; the sexual revolution from reproduction; and the women's revolution, in which childbearing and -rearing no longer are being accepted as the only or even the primary roles of half the human race. Accordingly, for about the first time, the question of 2 why people want children now can be asked, so to speak, with a straight face.

3   "Why" questions of this kind, with simple surfaces but profound depths, are not answered or settled; they are ventilated, explicated, clarified. Anything as complex as the motives for having children can be classified in various ways, and any such taxonomy has an arbitrary character to it. This one starts with chemistry and proceeds to spirit.

THE BIOLOGICAL

4   Do people innately want children for some built-in reason of physiology? Is there anything to maternal instinct, or parental instinct? Or is biology satisfied with the sex instinct as the way to assure continuity?

5   In psychoanalytic thought there is talk of the "child-wish," the "instinctual drive of physiological cause," "the innate femaleness of the girl direct(ing) her development toward motherhood," and the wanting of children as "the essence of her self-realization," indicating normality. From the experimental literature, there is some evidence that man, like other animals, is innately attracted to the quality of "babyishness."

6   If the young and adults of several species are compared for differences in bodily and facial features, it will be seen readily that the nature of the difference is apparently the same almost throughout the phylogenetic scale. Limbs are shorter and much heavier in proportion to the torso in babies than in adults. Also, the head is proportionately much larger in relation to the body than is the case with adults. On the face itself, the forehead is more prominent and bulbous; the eyes large and perhaps located as far down as below the middle of the face, because of the large forehead. In addition, the cheeks may be round and protruding. In many species there is also a greater degree of overall fatness in contrast to normal adult bodies. . . . In man, as in other animals, social prescriptions and customs are not the sole or even primary factors that guarantee the rearing and protection of babies. This seems to indicate that the biologically rooted releaser of babyishness may have promoted infant care in primitive man before societies ever were formed, just as it appears to do in many animal species. Thus this releaser may have a high survival value for the species of man.*

*Eckhard H. Hess, "Ethology and Developmental Psychology," in Paul H. Musser, ed., *Carmichael's Manual of Child Psychology*, Vol. 1 (New York: Wiley, 1970), pp. 20–21.

In the human species the question of social and personal moti-   7
vation distinctively arises, but that does not necessarily mean that the
biology is completely obliterated. In animals the instinct to reproduce
appears to be all; in humans is it something?

THE CULTURAL

Whatever the biological answer, people do not want all the children   8
they physically can have—no society, hardly any woman. Everywhere
social traditions and social pressures enforce a certain conformity to
the approved childbearing pattern, whether large numbers of children in Africa or small numbers in Eastern Europe. People want children because that is "the thing to do"—culturally sanctioned and
institutionally supported, hence about as natural as any social behavior can be.

Such social expectations, expressed by everyone toward every-   9
one, are extremely strong in influencing behavior even on such an important element in life as childbearing and on whether the outcome
is two children or six. In most human societies, the thing to do gets
done, for social rewards and punishments are among the most powerful. Whether they produce lots of children or few and whether the
matter is fully conscious or not, the cultural norms are all the more
effective if, as often, they are rationalized as the will of God or the
hand of fate.

THE POLITICAL

The cultural shades off into political considerations: reproduction for   10
the purposes of a higher authority. In a way, the human responsibility to perpetuate the species is the grandest such expression—the human family pitted politically against fauna and flora—and there
always might be people who partly rationalize their own childbearing
as a contribution to that lofty end. Beneath that, however, there are
political units for whom collective childbearing is or has been explicitly encouraged as a demographic duty—countries concerned with
national glory or competitive political position; governments concerned with the supply of workers and soldiers; churches concerned
with propagation of the faith or their relative strength; ethnic minorities concerned with their political power; linguistic communities
competing for position; clans and tribes concerned over their relative
status within a larger setting. In ancient Rome, according to the Oxford English Dictionary, the proletariat—from the root *proles*, for

progeny—were "the lowest class of the community, regarded as contributing nothing to the state but offspring": and a proletaire was
"one who served the state not with his property but only with his offspring." The world has changed since then, but not all the way.

THE ECONOMIC

11   As the "new home economics" is reminding us in its current attention
to the microeconomics of fertility, children are economically valuable. Not that that would come as a surprise to the poor peasant who
consciously acts on the premise, but it is clear that some people want
children or not for economic reasons.

12   Start with the obvious case of economic returns from children
that appears to be characteristic of the rural poor. To some extent,
that accounts for their generally higher fertility than that of their urban and wealthier counterparts: labor in the fields; hunting, fishing,
animal care; help in the home and with the younger children; dowry
and "bride-wealth"; support in later life (the individualized system of
social security).

13   The economics of the case carries through on the negative side
as well. It is not publicly comfortable to think of children as another
consumer durable, but sometimes that is precisely the way parents do
think of them, before conception: another child or a trip to Europe;
a birth deferred in favor of a new car, the nth child requiring more expenditure on education or housing. But observe the special characteristics of children viewed as consumer durables: they come only in
whole units; they are not rentable or returnable or exchangeable or
available on trial; they cannot be evaluated quickly; they do not come
in several competing brands or products; their quality cannot be
pretested before delivery; they usually are not available for appraisal
in large numbers in one's personal experience; they themselves participate actively in the household's decisions. And in the broad view,
both societies and families tend to choose standard of living over
number of children when the opportunity presents itself.

THE FAMILIAL

14   In some societies people want children for what might be called familial reasons: to extend the family line or the family name; to propitiate the ancestors; to enable the proper functioning of religious
rituals involving the family (e.g., the Hindu son needed to light the
father's funeral pyre, the Jewish son needed to say Kaddish for the

dead father). Such reasons may seem thin in the modern, secularized society but they have been and are powerful indeed in other places.

In addition, one class of family reasons shares a border with the following category, namely, having children in order to maintain or improve a marriage: to hold the husband or occupy the wife; to repair or rejuvenate their marriage; to increase the number of children on the assumption that family happiness lies that way. The point is underlined by its converse: in some societies the failure to bear children (or males) is a threat to the marriage and a ready cause for divorce. 15

Beyond all that is the profound significance of children to the very institution of the family itself. To many people, husband and wife alone do not seem a proper family—they need children to enrich the circle, to validate its family character, to gather the redemptive influence of offspring. Children need the family, but the family seems also to need children, as the social institution uniquely available, at least in principle, for security, comfort, assurance, and direction in a changing, often hostile, world. To most people, such a home base, in the literal sense, needs more than one person for sustenance and in generational extension. 16

THE PERSONAL

Up to here the reasons for wanting children primarily refer to instrumental benefits. Now we come to a variety of reasons for wanting children that are supposed to bring direct personal benefits. 17

Personal Power. As noted, having children sometimes gives one parent power over the other. More than that, it gives the parents power over the child(ren)—in many cases, perhaps most, about as much effective power as they ever will have the opportunity of exercising on an individual basis. They are looked up to by the child(ren), literally and figuratively, and rarely does that happen otherwise. Beyond that, having children is involved in a wider circle of power: 18

> In most simple societies the lines of kinship are the lines of political power, social prestige and economic aggrandizement. The more children a man has, the more successful marriage alliances he can arrange, increasing his own power and influence by linking himself to men of greater power or to men who will be his supporters. . . . In primitive and peasant societies, the man with few children is the man of minor influence and the childless man is virtually a social nonentity.* 19

---

*Burton Benedict, "Population Regulation in Primitive Societies," in Anthony Ellison, *Population Control* (London: Penguin, 1970), pp. 176–77.

20   *Personal Competence.* Becoming a parent demonstrates competence in an essential human role. Men and women who are closed off from other demonstrations of competence, through lack of talent or educational opportunity or social status, still have this central one. For males, parenthood is thought to show virility, potency, *machismo.* For females it demonstrates fecundity, itself so critical to an acceptable life in many societies.

21   *Personal Status.* Everywhere parenthood confers status. It is an accomplishment open to all, or virtually all, and realized by the overwhelming majority of adult humankind. Indeed, achieving parenthood surely must be one of the two most significant events in one's life—that and being born in the first place. In many societies, then and only then is one considered a real man or a real woman.

22   Childbearing is one of the few ways in which the poor can compete with the rich. Life cannot make the poor man prosperous in material goods and services but it easily can make him rich with children. He cannot have as much of anything else worth having, except sex, which itself typically means children in such societies. Even so, the poor still are deprived by the arithmetic; they have only two or three times as many children as the rich whereas the rich have at least forty times the income of the poor.

23   *Personal Extension.* Beyond the family line, wanting children is a way to reach for personal immortality—for most people, the only way available. It is a way to extend oneself indefinitely into the future. And short of that, there is simply the physical and psychological extension of oneself in the children, here and now—a kind of narcissism: there they are and they are mine (or like me).

24   *Look in thy glass and tell the face thou viewest,*
       Now is the time that face should form another;
       But if thou live, remember'd not to be,
       Die single, and thine image dies with thee.

       —Shakespeare's Sonnets, III

25   *Personal Experience.* Among all the activities of life, parenthood is a unique experience. It is a part of life, or personal growth, that simply cannot be experienced in any other way and hence is literally an indispensable element of the full life. The experience has many profound facets: the deep curiosity as to how the child will turn out; the renewal of self in the second chance; the reliving of one's own childhood; the redemptive opportunity; the challenge to shape another human being; the sheer creativity and self-realization involved. For a large proportion of the world's women, there was and probably still is nothing else for the grown female to do with her time and energy, as

society defines her role. And for many women, it might be the most emotional and spiritual experience they ever have and perhaps the most gratifying as well.

Personal Pleasure. Last, but one hopes not least, in the list of   26
reasons for wanting children is the altruistic pleasure of having them, caring for them, watching them grow, shaping them, being with them, enjoying them. This reason comes last on the list but it is typically the first one mentioned in the casual inquiry: "because I like children." Even this reason has its dark side, as with parents who live through their children, often to the latter's distaste and disadvantage. But that should not obscure a fundamental reason for wanting children: love.

There are, in short, many reasons for wanting children. Taken   27
together, they must be among the most compelling motivations in human behavior: culturally imposed, institutionally reinforced, psychologically welcome.

QUESTIONS ON SUBJECT AND PURPOSE

1. What is "the value of children"? How many different values does Berelson cite?
2. Berelson gives positive, negative, and neutral reasons for wanting children. Is the overall effect of the essay positive, negative, or neutral?
3. Which of Berelson's reasons seem most relevant in American society today? Which seem least relevant?

QUESTIONS ON STRATEGY AND AUDIENCE

1. How does Berelson organize his classification? Can you find an explicit statement of organization?
2. Could the classification have been organized in a different way? Would that have changed the essay in any way?
3. How effective is Berelson's introduction? His conclusion? Suggest other ways in which the essay could have begun or ended.

QUESTIONS ON VOCABULARY AND STYLE

1. Berelson asks a number of rhetorical questions (see the Glossary). Why does he ask them? Does he answer them? Does he "ventilate," "explicate," and "clarify" them (paragraph 3)?

2. Describe the tone of Berelson's essay—what does he sound like? Be prepared to support your statement with some specific illustrations from the text.

3. Be able to define the following words: *taxonomy* (paragraph 3), *physiology* (4), *phylogenetic* (6), *bulbous* (6), *sanctioned* (8), *fauna and flora* (10), *demographic* (10), *consumer durable* (13), *propitiate* (14), *sustenance* (16), *aggrandizement* (19), *nonentity* (19), *machismo* (20), *fecundity* (20), *narcissism* (23).

WRITING SUGGESTIONS

1. **For Your Journal.** In your journal, explore the reasons why you do or do not want to have children. Would you choose to limit the number of children that you have? Why or why not?

2. **For a Paragraph.** Using your journal writing as a starting point, in a paragraph classify the reasons for your decision. Focus on two or three reasons at most, and be sure to have some logical order to your arrangement.

3. **For an Essay.** Few issues are so charged in American society today as abortion. In an essay, classify the reasons why people are either pro-choice or pro-life. Despite your personal feelings on the topic, try in your essay to be as objective as possible. Do not write an argument for or against abortion or a piece of propaganda.

4. **For Research.** Studies have shown that as countries become increasingly industrialized, their population growth approaches zero. For example, India's fertility rate has declined from six infants per female reproductive lifetime to four. In China, the rate is now 2.3 (zero growth is 2.1). In a research paper, explore how increasingly industrialized societies—such as India, China, Costa Rica, or Sri Lanka—have changed their views of the "value" of children. Be sure to document your sources wherever appropriate.

WEBSITE LINK

Is the world still facing a population explosion? Have birth rates stabilized? Declined? What type of population growth will the world see in the next millennium? For variety of Web resources, visit www.prenhall.com/miller.

WRITING LINK: TYPOGRAPHICAL DEVICES

Berelson uses several different typographical devices to signal the structure of his essay (extra white space separating subdivisions, centered headings, indented italic headings). Such devices are common in magazines and newspapers. What do such devices do? Are they helpful to you as a reader? In what ways? Under what sets of circumstances might it be appropriate for you to use typographical devices in your own writing?

WHY WE TRAVEL
Pico Iyer

*Pico Iyer (1957–   ), as he writes in this essay, "was born, as the son of In-
dian parents, in England, moved to America at seven." One of the country's
foremost travel writers, Iyer is the author of a number of books, the most recent of which is* The Global Soul: Jet Lag, Shopping Malls, and the
Search for Home *(2000). "Why We Travel" first appeared in* Salon Travel.
On Writing: *Iyer comments: "Writing should be an act of communication more than of mere self-expression—a telling of a story rather than
a flourishing of skills. . . . Writing . . . should, ideally, be as spontaneous and
urgent as a letter to a lover, or a message to a friend who has just lost a parent. And because of the ways a writer is obliged to tap in private the selves
that even those closest to him never see, writing is, in the end, that oddest of
anomalies: an intimate letter to a stranger."*

BEFORE READING

Connecting. Do you like to travel? What is it about travel that either excites us or sometimes frightens us?

Anticipating. As you read, think about the reasons that Iyer offers
for why we travel. Which reason seems most familiar or understandable to you? Can you think of any reasons that Iyer does not include?

1   We travel, initially, to lose ourselves; and we travel, next, to find
ourselves. We travel to open our hearts and eyes and learn more about
the world than our newspapers will accommodate. We travel to bring
what little we can, in our ignorance and knowledge, to those parts of
the globe whose riches are differently dispersed. And we travel, in
essence, to become young fools again—to slow time down and get
taken in, and fall in love once more. The beauty of this whole process
was best described, perhaps, before people even took to frequent flying, by George Santayana in his lapidary essay "The Philosophy of
Travel." We "need sometimes," the Harvard philosopher wrote, "to
escape into open solitudes, into aimlessness, into the moral holiday of
running some pure hazard, in order to sharpen the edge of life, to
taste hardship, and to be compelled to work desperately for a moment
at no matter what."

I like that stress on work, since never more than on the road are   2
we shown how proportional our blessings are to the difficulty that
precedes them; and I like the stress on a holiday that's "moral" since
we fall into our ethical habits as easily as into our beds at night. Few
of us ever forget the connection between "travel" and "travail," and I
know that I travel in large part in search of hardship—both my own,
which I want to feel, and others', which I need to see. Travel in that
sense guides us toward a better balance of wisdom and compassion—
of seeing the world clearly, and yet feeling it truly. For seeing without feeling can obviously be uncaring; while feeling without seeing
can be blind.

Yet for me the first great joy of traveling is simply the luxury of   3
leaving all my beliefs and certainties at home, and seeing everything
I thought I knew in a different light, and from a crooked angle. In that
regard, even a Kentucky Fried Chicken outlet (in Beijing) or a
scratchy revival showing of *Wild Orchids* (on the Champs-Elysées)
can be both novelty and revelation: In China, after all, people will pay
a whole week's wages to eat with Colonel Sanders, and in Paris,
Mickey Rourke is regarded as the greatest actor since Jerry Lewis.

If a Mongolian restaurant seems exotic to us in Evanston, Illi-   4
nois, it only follows that a McDonald's would seem equally exotic in
Ulan Bator—or, at least, equally far from everything expected.
Though it's fashionable nowadays to draw a distinction between the
"tourist" and the "traveler," perhaps the real distinction lies between
those who leave their assumptions at home and those who don't:
Among those who don't, a tourist is just someone who complains,
"Nothing here is the way it is at home," while a traveler is one who
grumbles, "Everything here is the same as it is in Cairo—or Cuzco or
Kathmandu." It's all very much the same.

But for the rest of us, the sovereign freedom of traveling comes   5
from the fact that it whirls you around and turns you upside down, and
stands everything you took for granted on its head. If a diploma can
famously be a passport (to a journey through hard realism), a passport
can be a diploma (for a crash course in cultural relativism). And the
first lesson we learn on the road, whether we like it or not, is how provisional and provincial are the things we imagine to be universal.
When you go to North Korea, for example, you really do feel as if
you've landed on a different planet—and the North Koreans doubt-
less feel that they're being visited by an extra-terrestrial too (or else
they simply assume that you, as they do, receive orders every morning
from the Central Committee on what clothes to wear and what route
to use when walking to work, and you, as they do, have loudspeakers
in your bedroom broadcasting propaganda every morning at dawn,

and you, as they do, have your radios fixed so as to receive only a single channel).

6   We travel, then, in part just to shake up our complacencies by seeing all the moral and political urgencies, the life-and-death dilemmas, that we seldom have to face at home. And we travel to fill in the gaps left by tomorrow's headlines: When you drive down the streets of Port-au-Prince, for example, where there is almost no paving and women relieve themselves next to mountains of trash, your notions of the Internet and a "one world order" grow usefully revised. Travel is the best way we have of rescuing the humanity of places, and saving them from abstraction and ideology.

7   And in the process, we also get saved from abstraction ourselves, and come to see how much we can bring to the places we visit, and how much we can become a kind of carrier pigeon—an anti-Federal Express, if you like—in transporting back and forth what every culture needs. I find that I always take Michael Jordan posters to Kyoto and bring woven ikebana baskets back to California; I invariably travel to Cuba with a suitcase piled high with bottles of Tylenol and bars of soap and come back with one piled high with salsa tapes, and hopes, and letters to long-lost brothers.

8   But more significantly, we carry values and beliefs and news to the places we go, and in many parts of the world, we become walking video screens and living newspapers, the only channels that can take people out of the censored limits of their homelands. In closed or impoverished places, like Pagan or Lhasa or Havana, we are the eyes and ears of the people we meet, their only contact with the world outside and, very often, the closest, quite literally, they will ever come to Michael Jackson or Bill Clinton. Not the least of the challenges of travel, therefore, is learning how to import—and export—dreams with tenderness.

9   By now all of us have heard (too often) the old Proust line about how the real voyage of discovery consists not in seeing new places but in seeing with new eyes. Yet one of the subtler beauties of travel is that it enables you to bring new eyes to the people you encounter. Thus even as holidays help you appreciate your own home more—not least by seeing it through a distant admirer's eyes—they help you bring newly appreciative—distant—eyes to the places you visit. You can teach them what they have to celebrate as much as you celebrate what they have to teach. This, I think, is how tourism, which so obviously destroys cultures, can also resuscitate or revive them, how it has created new "traditional" dances in Bali, and caused craftsmen in India to pay new attention to their works. If the first thing we can bring the Cubans is a real and balanced sense of what contemporary America is like, the second—and perhaps more important—thing we can bring

them is a fresh and renewed sense of how special are the warmth and beauty of their country, for those who can compare it with other places around the globe.

Thus travel spins us round in two ways at once: It shows us the sights and values and issues that we might ordinarily ignore; but it also, and more deeply, shows us all the parts of ourselves that might otherwise grow rusty. For in traveling to a truly foreign place, we inevitably travel to moods and states of mind and hidden inward passages that we'd otherwise seldom have cause to visit.

On the most basic level, when I'm in Thailand, though a teetotaler who usually goes to bed at 9:00 P.M., I stay up till dawn in the local bars; and in Tibet, though not a real Buddhist, I spend days on end in temples, listening to the chants of sutras. I go to Iceland to visit the lunar spaces within me, and, in the uncanny quietude and emptiness of that vast and treeless world, to tap parts of myself generally obscured by chatter and routine.

We travel, then, in search of both self and anonymity—and, of course, in finding the one we apprehend the other. Abroad, we are wonderfully free of caste and job and standing; we are, as Hazlitt puts it, just the "gentlemen in the parlour," and people cannot put a name or tag to us. And precisely because we are clarified in this way, and freed of inessential labels, we have the opportunity to come into contact with more essential parts of ourselves (which may begin to explain why we may feel most alive when far from home).

Abroad is the place where we stay up late, follow impulse, and find ourselves as wide open as when we are in love. We live without a past or future, for a moment at least, and are ourselves up for grabs and open to interpretation. We even may become mysterious—to others, at first, and sometimes to ourselves—and, as no less a dignitary than Oliver Cromwell once noted, "A man never goes so far as when he doesn't know where he is going."

There are, of course, great dangers to this, as to every kind of freedom, but the great promise of it is that, traveling, we are born again, and able to return at moments to a younger and a more open kind of self. Traveling is a way to reverse time, to a small extent, and make a day last a year—or at least forty-five hours—and traveling is an easy way of surrounding ourselves, as in childhood, with what we cannot understand. Language facilitates this cracking open, for when we go to France, we often migrate to French and the more childlike self, simple and polite, that speaking a foreign language educes. Even when I'm not speaking pidgin English in Hanoi, I'm simplified in a positive way, and concerned not with expressing myself but simply with making sense.

15   So travel, for many of us, is a quest for not just the unknown but the unknowing; I, at least, travel in search of an innocent eye that can return me to a more innocent self. I tend to believe more abroad than I do at home (which, though treacherous again, can at least help me to extend my vision), and I tend to be more easily excited abroad, and even kinder. And since no one I meet can "place" me—no one can fix me in my résumé—I can remake myself for better, as well as, of course, for worse (if travel is notoriously a cradle for false identities, it can also, at its best, be a crucible for truer ones). In this way, travel can be a kind of monasticism on the move: On the road, we often live more simply (even when staying in a luxury hotel), with no more possessions than we can carry, and surrendering ourselves to chance.

16   And that is why many of us travel in search not of answers but of better questions. I, like many people, tend to ask questions of the places I visit, and relish most the ones that ask the most searching questions back of me. In Paraguay, for example, where one car in every two is stolen, and two-thirds of the goods on sale are smuggled, I have to rethink my every Californian assumption. And in Thailand, where many young women give up their bodies in order to protect their families—to become better Buddhists—I have to question my own too-ready judgments.

17   "The ideal travel book," Christopher Isherwood once said, "should be perhaps a little like a crime story in which you're in search of something." And it's the best kind of something, I would add, if it's one that you can never quite find.

18   I remember, in fact, after my first trips to Southeast Asia, more than a decade ago, how I would come back to my apartment in New York and lie in my bed, kept up by something more than jet lag, playing back in my memory, over and over, all that I had experienced, and paging wistfully through my photographs and reading and rereading my diaries, as if to extract some mystery from them. Anyone witnessing this strange scene would have drawn the right conclusion: I was in love.

19   For if every true love affair can feel like a journey to a foreign country, where you can't quite speak the language and you don't know where you're going and you're pulled ever deeper into the inviting darkness, every trip to a foreign country can be a love affair, where you're left puzzling over who you are and whom you've fallen in love with. All the great travel books are love stories, by some reckoning— from the *Odyssey* and the *Aeneid* to the *Divine Comedy* and the New Testament—and all good trips are, like love, about being carried out of yourself and deposited in the midst of terror and wonder.

And what this metaphor also brings home to us is that all travel   20
is a two-way transaction, as we too easily forget, and if warfare is one
model of the meeting of nations, romance is another. For what we all
too often ignore when we go abroad is that we are objects of scrutiny
as much as the people we scrutinize, and we are being consumed by
the cultures we consume, as much on the road as when we are at
home. At the very least, we are objects of speculation (and even desire) who can seem as exotic to the people around us as they do to us.

We are the comic props in Japanese home movies, the oddities   21
in Malian anecdotes, and the fall guys in Chinese jokes; we are the
moving postcards or bizarre *objects trouvés* that villagers in Peru will
later tell their friends about. If travel is about the meeting of realities,
it is no less about the mating of illusions: You give me my dreamed-
of vision of Tibet, and I'll give you your wished-for California. And
in truth, many of us, even (or especially) the ones who are fleeing
America abroad, will get taken, willy-nilly, as symbols of the American Dream.

That, in fact, is perhaps the most central and most wrenching   22
of the questions travel proposes to us: how to respond to the dream
that people tender to you? Do you encourage their notions of a Land
of Milk and Honey across the horizon, even if it is the same land
you've abandoned? Or do you try to dampen their enthusiasm for a
place that exists only in the mind? To quicken their dreams may, after all, be to matchmake them with an illusion; yet to dash them may
be to strip them of the one possession that sustains them in adversity.

That whole complex interaction—not unlike the dilemmas we   23
face with those we love (how do we balance truthfulness and tact?)—
is partly the reason why so many of the great travel writers, by nature,
are enthusiasts: not just Pierre Loti, who famously, infamously, fell in
love wherever he alighted (an archetypal sailor leaving offspring in
the form of *Madame Butterfly* myths), but also Henry Miller, D. H.
Lawrence, and Graham Greene, all of whom bore out the hidden
truth that we are optimists abroad as readily as pessimists at home.
None of them was by any means blind to the deficiencies of the places
around them, but all, having chosen to go there, chose to find something to admire.

All, in that sense, believed in "being moved" as one of the points   24
of taking trips, and "being transported" by private as well as public
means; all saw that "ecstasy" ("ex-stasis") tells us that our highest moments come when we're not stationary, and that epiphany can follow
movement as much as it precipitates it. I remember once asking the
great travel writer Norman Lewis if he'd ever be interested in writing

on apartheid South Africa. He looked at me, astonished. "To write well about a thing," he said, "I've got to like it!"

25   At the same time, as all this is intrinsic to travel, from Ovid to O'Rourke, travel itself is changing as the world does, and with it, the mandate of the travel writer. It's not enough to go to the ends of the earth these days (not least because the ends of the earth are often coming to you); and where a writer like Jan Morris could, a few years ago, achieve something miraculous simply by voyaging to all the great cities of the globe, now anyone with a Visa card can do that. So where Morris, in effect, was chronicling the last days of the empire, a younger travel writer is in a better position to chart the first days of a new empire, postnational, global, mobile, and yet as diligent as the Raj in transporting its props and its values around the world.

26   In the mid-nineteenth century, the British famously sent the Bible and Shakespeare and cricket round the world; now a more international kind of empire is sending Madonna and the Simpsons and Brad Pitt. And the way in which each culture takes in this common pool of references tells you as much about them as their indigenous products might. Madonna in an Islamic country, after all, sounds radically different from Madonna in a Confucian one, and neither begins to mean the same as Madonna on East 14th Street. When you go to a McDonald's outlet in Kyoto, you will find Teriyaki McBurgers and Bacon Potato Pies. The place mats offer maps of the great temples of the city, and the posters all around broadcast the wonders of San Francisco. And—most crucial of all—the young people eating their Big Macs, with baseball caps worn backward and tight 501 jeans, are still utterly and inalienably Japanese in the way they move, they nod, they sip their oolong teas—and never to be mistaken for the patrons of a McDonald's outlet in Rio, Morocco, or Managua. These days a whole new realm of exotica arises out of the way one culture colors and appropriates the products of another.

27   The other factor complicating and exciting all of this is people, who are, more and more, themselves as many-tongued and mongrel as cities like Sydney or Toronto or Hong Kong. I am in many ways an increasingly typical specimen, if only because I was born, as the son of Indian parents, in England, moved to America at seven, and cannot really call myself an Indian, an American, or an Englishman. I was, in short, a traveler at birth, for whom even a visit to the candy store was a trip through a foreign world where no one I saw quite matched my parents' inheritance, or my own. And though some of this is involuntary and tragic—the number of refugees in the world, which came to just 2.5 million in 1970, is now at least 27.4 million— it does involve, for some of us, the chance to be transnational in a hap-

pier sense, able to adapt anywhere, used to being outsiders every-where, and forced to fashion our own rigorous sense of home. (And if nowhere is quite home, we can be optimists everywhere.)

Besides, even those who don't move around the world find the 28 world moving more and more around them. Walk just six blocks in Queens or Berkeley, and you're traveling through several cultures in as many minutes; get into a cab outside the White House, and you're often in a piece of Addis Ababa. And technology too compounds this (sometimes deceptive) sense of availability, so that many people feel they can travel around the world without leaving the room—through cyber-space or CD-ROMs, videos and virtual travel. There are many challenges in this, of course, in what it says about essential notions of family and community and loyalty, and in the worry that air-conditioned, purely synthetic versions of places may replace the real thing—not to mention the fact that the world seems increasingly in flux, a moving target quicker than our notions of it. But there is, for the traveler at least, the sense that learning about home and learning about a foreign world can be one and the same thing.

All of us feel this from the cradle, and know, in some sense, that 29 all the significant movement we ever take is internal. We travel when we see a movie, strike up a new friendship, get held up. Novels are often journeys as much as travel books are fictions; and though this has been true since at least as long ago as Sir John Mandeville's colorful fourteenth-century accounts of a Far East he'd never visited, it's an even more shadowy distinction now, as genre distinctions join other borders in collapsing.

In Mary Morris's *House Arrest*, a thinly disguised account of 30 Castro's Cuba, the novelist reiterates, on the copyright page, "All dialogue is invented. Isabella, her family, the inhabitants, and even *laisla* itself are creations of the author's imagination." On page 172, however, we read, "*La isla*, of course, does exist. Don't let anyone fool you about that. It just feels as if it doesn't. But it does." No wonder the travel-writer narrator—a fictional construct (or not)?—confesses to devoting her travel magazine column to places that never existed. "Erewhon," after all, the undiscovered land in Samuel Butler's great travel novel, is just "nowhere" rearranged.

Travel, then, is a voyage into that famously subjective zone, the 31 imagination, and what the traveler brings back is—and has to be—an ineffable compound of himself and the place, what's really there and what's only in him. Thus Bruce Chatwin's books seem to dance around the distinction between fact and fancy. V. S. Naipaul's recent book *A Way in the World* was published as a nonfictional "series" in England and a "novel" in the United States. And when some of the stories in Paul Theroux's half-invented memoir, *My Other Life*, were published in *The New Yorker*, they were slyly categorized as "Fact and Fiction."

32   And since travel is, in a sense, about the conspiracy of perception and imagination, the two great travel writers, for me, to whom I constantly return are Emerson and Thoreau (the one who famously advised that "traveling is a fool's paradise," and the other who "traveled a good deal in Concord"). Both of them insist on the fact that reality is our creation, and that we invent the places we see as much as we do the books that we read. What we find outside ourselves has to be inside ourselves for us to find it. Or, as Sir Thomas Browne sagely put it, "We carry within us the wonders we seek without us. There is Africa and her prodigies in us."

33   So, if more and more of us have to carry our sense of home inside us, we also—Emerson and Thoreau remind us—have to carry with us our sense of destination. The most valuable Pacifics we explore will always be the vast expanses within us, and the most important Northwest Crossings the thresholds we cross in the heart. The virtue of finding a gilded pavilion in Kyoto is that it allows you to take back a more lasting, private Golden Temple to your office in Rockefeller Center.

34   And even as the world seems to grow more exhausted, our travels do not, and some of the finest travel books in recent years have been those that undertake a parallel journey, matching the physical steps of a pilgrimage with the metaphysical steps of a questioning (as in Peter Matthiessen's great *The Snow Leopard*), or chronicling a trip to the farthest reaches of human strangeness (as in Oliver Sacks's *Island of the Colorblind*, which features a journey not just to a remote atoll in the Pacific but to a realm where people actually see light differently). The most distant shores, we are constantly reminded, lie within the person asleep at our side.

35   So travel, at heart, is just a quick way of keeping our minds mobile and awake. As Santayana, the heir to Emerson and Thoreau with whom I began, wrote, "There is wisdom in turning as often as possible from the familiar to the unfamiliar; it keeps the mind nimble; it kills prejudice, and it fosters humor." Romantic poets inaugurated an era of travel because they were the great apostles of open eyes. Buddhist monks are often vagabonds, in part because they believe in wakefulness. And if travel is like love, it is, in the end, mostly because it's a heightened state of awareness, in which we are mindful, receptive, undimmed by familiarity and ready to be transformed. That is why the best trips, like the best love affairs, never really end.

QUESTIONS ON SUBJECT AND PURPOSE

1. What is the distinction between a "tourist" and a "traveler"?
2. Iyer likens travel to falling in love. Why does he think that this analogy is appropriate?
3. Would it make a difference if Iyer had titled his essay "Why I Travel"? Would changing the pronoun have changed the essay?

QUESTIONS ON STRATEGY AND AUDIENCE

1. What strategy does Iyer use in his opening paragraph? Does it catch your attention?
2. Toward the end of the essay, Iyer cites Emerson and Thoreau as two travel writers to whom he constantly returns. In what way does he see these two nontravelers as illuminating?
3. What expectations does Iyer seem to have about his audience? What evidence from the essay can you cite to support your answer?

QUESTIONS ON VOCABULARY AND STYLE

1. What figure of speech is Iyer using when he writes, "we travel . . . to lose ourselves; and we travel . . . to find ourselves" (paragraph 1). What effect does it create?
2. In paragraph 21, Iyer refers to "bizarre *objets trouvés.*" What does that expression mean?
3. Be prepared to define the following words: *lapidary* (paragraph 1), *travail* (2), *provisional* (5), *provincial* (5), *complacencies* (6), *resuscitate* (9), *uncanny* (11), *educes* (14), *willy-nilly* (21), *epiphany* (24), *indigenous* (26), *ineffable* (31).

WRITING SUGGESTIONS

1. **For Your Journal.** Have you traveled? Do you plan to? Have you considered a semester abroad? Or an exchange program? Do you want to travel after college? Have you considered joining the Peace Corps? In your journal, brainstorm about why travel is important to you. If it is not, speculate on why it is not.
2. **For a Paragraph.** Expand your journal writing into a paragraph. Focus on the primary reason you want or do not want to travel.

3. **For an Essay.** In an essay organized around a classification scheme, offer reasons to students why they should, or should not, consider traveling, going on a semester abroad, or participating in an exchange program. You might imagine that your essay will appear in your school's newspaper. Whichever side you take, remember to respect the opinions of those who disagree with you—you are trying to point out reasons for doing or not doing something; you are not insulting or making fun of people who feel differently.

4. **For Research.** Are Iyer's assertions about the reasons why we travel and the benefits that we derive from travel borne out in research? Using a variety of sources, test out the validity of Iyer's reasons. What evidence is there that travel does the things that he claims?

WEBSITE LINK

Have you ever considered becoming a "virtual" traveler if you do not have the time or money to do the real thing? Check out some possibilities and visit the countries that Iyer mentions in his essay.

WRITING LINK: PARALLELISM

Iyer frequently uses parallelism—within sentences, within paragraphs. Go through the essay and see how many instances of parallel structure you can find. What is the effect of this frequent use of parallelism. What does this suggest about parallelism in your own writing?

PREWRITING SUGGESTIONS FOR DIVISION AND CLASSIFICATION

1. Make a list of possible subjects for division or classification. Brainstorm for each possible topic; concentrate on just getting some ideas down. Is your topic going to require observation? Interviewing people? Doing some sort of research? Plan how you are going to gather and develop each idea.

2. Remember that the number of parts or the number of categories in your essay has to be manageable. You cannot subdivide into a dozen pieces or a dozen categories and keep your paper a reasonable length. As a rough rule, in a two- to four-page essay, you probably should have not more than six parts or categories. If you have more, see if they can be grouped under some larger headings.

3. Your parts or categories need to be phrased in parallel form. Be sure you know what parallelism means. Make a list of the parts and categories. Have you written them so that they all are in the same grammatical form?

4. Remember that your paper needs an organizational principle. Once you have selected a subject, jot down what you see as the divisions or the categories in which the subject will be treated. Put each division or category on a separate index card. Try moving around the order of the cards. Do you see alternate arrangements?

5. Ask yourself what purpose you want your essay to have. Write down that purpose statement. Test out your purpose statement on peer readers. Ask them if they would find an essay with this topic and purpose potentially interesting.

REWRITING SUGGESTIONS FOR DIVISION AND CLASSIFICATION

1. Once you have a draft, write out a one- or two-sentence summary of your essay. Ask two peers to read that summary statement. Insist that they be honest. Do they find your subject and approach potentially interesting? Why or why not? Remember that there are no bad subjects, just bad approaches to subjects. Do you need to reconsider how you approached your subject?

2. Look again at how you organized the body of your essay. Why did you begin and end where you did? Did you move from largest to smallest? Most important to least important? What principle of order does the body of your essay reveal?

3. Have you accounted for everything in your division or classification? Make sure that there are not things that you have omitted. Avoid a final part or category that you label

"other" or "miscellaneous." Rethink your groupings if that has occurred, and try to eliminate that final catch-all group.

4. Do you have adequate links or transitions as you move from one division or category to another? Underline those links to make sure that they are there and that they are effective.

5. Look again at your introduction. Have you tried to catch your readers' interest? Or have you written a standard thesis introduction? First impressions are very important in catching and holding readers.

COMPARISON AND CONTRAST

Whenever you decide between two alternatives, you engage in comparison and contrast. Which DVD player is the best value or has the most attractive set of features? Which professor's section of Introductory Sociology should you register for in the spring semester? In both cases, you make the decision by comparing alternatives on a series of relevant points and then deciding which has the greatest advantages.

In comparison and contrast, subjects are set in opposition in order to reveal their similarities and differences. Comparison involves finding similarities between two or more things, people, or ideas; contrast involves finding differences. Comparison and contrast writing tasks can involve, then, three activities: emphasizing similarities, emphasizing differences, or emphasizing both. Visually, comparison and contrast can be seen through a Venn diagram: the two or more subjects share some, but not all, things.

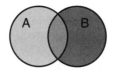

In a cartoon originally published in the *Utne Reader*, the Tour de France (the famous bicycle race) is compared with a Tour de America (which does not exist). By changing the background and the bikers' eyes, the artist creates a vivid contrast.

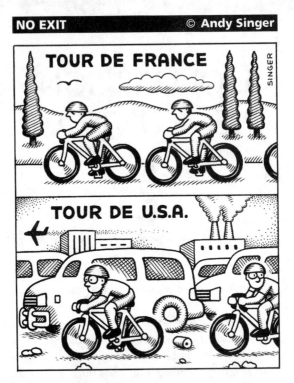

NO EXIT   © **Andy Singer**

Biking is a popular recreation in the United States, but not always a safe sport in America's urbanized areas. *Andy Singer*

   Comparison and contrast often involves visual displays of the
similarities and differences—things such as lists, tables, and charts—
but it also occurs using just words. John Fischer uses comparison in
this paragraph to emphasize the similarities between Ukrainians and
Texans:

> The Ukrainians are the Texans of Russia. They believe they can
> fight, drink, ride, sing, and make love better than anybody else in the
> world, and if pressed will admit it. Their country, too, was a
> borderland—that's what Ukraine means—and like Texas it was
> originally settled by outlaws, horse thieves, land-hungry farmers, and
> people who hadn't made a go of it somewhere else. Some of these
> hard cases banded together, long ago, to raise hell and livestock.
> They called themselves Cossacks, and they would have felt right at
> home in any Western movie. Even today the Ukrainians cherish a

wistful tradition of horsemanship, although most of them would feel as uncomfortable in a saddle as any Dallas banker. They still like to wear knee-high boots and big, furry hats, made of gray or Persian lamb, which are the local equivalent of the Stetson.

Fischer emphasizes only similarities. He tries to help his readers understand a foreign country by likening it to a place far more familiar to most Americans. Fischer concentrates on four similarities, which could be outlined:

Ukrainians and Texans

1. Believe that they are good at fighting, drinking, singing, making love
2. Are descended from people willing to take risks
3. Cherish a tradition of horsemanship
4. Wear high boots and big hats

Henry Petroski, in his essay "The Gleaming Silver Bird and the Rusty Iron Horse," contrasts air travel and train travel, emphasizing their differences.

The airplane lets us fly and forget. We are as gods, even in coach class, attended by young, smiling stewards and stewardesses who bring us food, drink, and entertainment. From the window of the airplane we marvel at the cities far beneath us, at the great land formations and waterways, and at the clouds. Political boundaries are forgotten, and the world is one. Everything is possible.

Nothing is forgotten on the train, however. The right of way is strewn with the detritus of technology, and technology's disruptiveness is everywhere apparent. Outside the once-clean picture window of the train, which has probably slowed down to pass over a deteriorating roadbed under repair, one sees not heaven in the clouds but the graveyards of people and machines. One cannot help but notice how technology has changed the land and the lives of those who live beside the rails. The factory abandoned is a blight not easily removed; the neglected homes of myriad factory (and railroad?) workers are not easily restored.

Petroski treats his two subjects in two separate paragraphs, emphasizing their differences. A simple outline of the paragraph would look like this:

Airplanes

1. We are as gods, passing over the earth—we see only the "big" picture, the world at a distance.
2. The view is an optimistic one—differences are eliminated.

Trains

1. We see out the dirty train windows all of the decay and deterioration that borders railroad tracks. We see the grimy details, not the "big" picture.
2. The view is a pessimistic one—we are constantly reminded of the "cost" of technology.

Like every writing task, comparison and contrast is done to achieve a particular purpose. In practical situations, you use it to help make a decision. You compare DVD players or professors in order to make an intelligent choice. In academic situations, comparison and contrast allows you to analyze two or more subjects carefully and thoroughly on the basis of a series of shared similarities or differences.

HOW DO YOU CHOOSE A SUBJECT?

Many times, especially on examinations in other academic courses, the subject for comparison and contrast is already chosen for you. On an economics examination you are asked, "What are the main differences between the public and private sectors?" In political science you are to "compare the political platforms of the Republican and Democratic parties in the last presidential election." At other times, however, you must choose the subject for comparison and contrast yourself.

The choice of subject is crucial. It is best to limit your paragraph or essay to subjects that have obvious similarities or differences. Esmeralda Santiago compares her experiences with guavas as a child and later in life; William Zinsser compares his writing process to Dr. Brock's; Mary Pipher contrasts the educational experiences and encouragements given to adolescent girls and boys; Robert J. Samuelson explores differences in our attitudes toward work over the past century; Danzy Senna compares and contrasts herself with her grandmother; Meghan Daum is shocked to find that her "virtual love" Pete is much better than the "real" Pete.

Two other cautions are also important. First, be sure that you have a reason for making the comparison or contrast and that it will reveal something new or important to give your comparison or contrast an interesting thesis. Meghan Daum begins a "virtual," that is, an electronic, on-line relationship with an admirer named Pete. The romance flourishes until she meets the "real" Pete. Although the two have an electronic but "old-fashioned kind of courtship," although neither had lied or pretended to be someone else, although the two "real" people are the same as the two "virtual" people, the romance instantly dies when they meet each other in person. Daum uses comparison and contrast to make a point not just about this one relationship, but about our needs and our frustrations in trying to establish lasting relationships in contemporary society. She comments, "our need to worship somehow fuses with our need to be worshipped."

Second, limit your comparison and contrast to important points; do not try to cover everything. Mary Pipher, for example, focuses on how our educational system treats adolescent girls differently than adolescent boys. She does not write about parental expectations or other educational influences.

Do You Always Find Both Similarities and Differences?

You can compare and contrast only if there is some basic similarity between the two subjects: John Fischer compares two groups of people—Ukrainians and Texans; Henry Petroski compares two modes of transportation—the airplane and the railroad. There is no point in comparing two totally unrelated subjects; for example, the mind could be compared to a computer since both process information, but there would be no reason to compare a computer to an airplane. Remember, too, that some similarities will be obvious and hence not worth writing about. It would be pointless for William Zinsser to observe that both he and Dr. Brock write on word processors, use dictionaries, or work best in a quiet study. This does not mean that similarities are not important or should not be mentioned. Danzy Senna sees a number of similarities between herself and her grandmother—both are writers, both are strong-willed and outspoken. At the same time, she is also struck by the differences in their backgrounds and their expectations.

Once you have chosen your subject, make a list of the possible points of comparison and contrast. Be sure that those points are shared. Zinsser, for example, organizes his comparison and contrast around six questions. To each of the six, Zinsser gives first Dr. Brock's response and then his own. The contrast depends on the two responses to each of the six questions. If Brock had answered one group of three and Zinsser a different group of three, the contrast would not have worked.

HOW DO YOU USE ANALOGY, METAPHOR, AND SIMILE?

Writing a comparison often involves constructing an analogy, an extended comparison in which something complex or unfamiliar is likened to something simple or familiar. The reason for making the analogy is to help your reader more easily understand or visualize the more complex or unfamiliar subject. For example, if you are trying to explain how the hard disk on your computer is organized, you might use the analogy of a file cabinet. The hard disk, you write, is the file cabinet, which is partitioned off into directories (the file drawers), each of which contains subdirectories (the hanging folders), which in turn contain the individual files (the manila folders in which documents are stored). Think of the icons on your computer screen to display this relationship metaphorically.

Analogies are also used to provide a new way of seeing something. J. Anthony Lukas, for example, explains his attraction to the game of pinball by an analogy:

> Pinball is a metaphor for life, pitting man's skill, nerve, persistence, and luck against the perverse machinery of human existence. The playfield is rich with rewards: targets that bring huge scores, bright lights, chiming bells, free balls, and extra games. But is it replete with perils, too: culs-de-sac, traps, gutters, and gobble holes down which the ball may disappear forever.

Lukas's analogy does not seek to explain the unfamiliar. Probably every reader has seen a pinball game. Rather, the analogy invites the reader to see the game in a fresh way. The suggested similarity might help the reader understand why arcade games such as pinball have a particular significance or attraction.

Two common forms of analogy in writing are metaphor and simile. A metaphor directly identifies one thing with another. When Henry Petroski contrasts air travel and train travel (see p. 255), he uses metaphors—the airplane is a "silver bird" and the train is an "iron horse."

A simile, as its name suggests, is also a comparison based on a point or points of similarity. A simile differs from a metaphor by using the word *like* or *as* to link the two things being compared. In this sense, a simile suggests, rather than directly establishes, the comparison. On the February morning when his father died, Scott Russell Sanders saw that the ice "coated the windows like cataracts." Seventeenth-century poet Robert Herrick found a witty similarity: "Fain would I kiss my Julia's dainty leg,/Which is as white and hairless as an egg."

Be careful when you create analogies, similes, and metaphors. Do not try to be too clever, or your point will seem forced. But do not avoid such devices altogether. Used sparingly, these compressed comparisons can be evocative and effective.

How Do You Structure a Comparison and Contrast?

Comparison and contrast is not only an intellectual process but also a structural pattern that can be used to organize paragraphs and essays. In comparing and contrasting two subjects, three organizational models are available.

Subject-by-Subject (all of subject A and then all of subject B)

A.
  1.
  2.
  3.
B.
  1.
  2.
  3.

Esmeralda Santiago basically uses a subject-by-subject structure in her essay, treating the experience of eating ripe guavas in paragraphs 2 through 4 and unripe guavas in paragraphs 5 through 7. The subject-by-subject pattern for comparison and contrast works in paragraph units. If your comparison paper is fairly short, you could treat all of subject A in a paragraph or group of paragraphs and then all of subject B in a paragraph or group of paragraphs. If your paper is fairly long and the comparisons are fairly complicated, you might want to use either the point-by-point or mixed pattern.

Point-by-Point (point 1 in A, then point 1 in B)

A1/B1
A2/B2
A3/B3

William Zinsser's comparison of his writing process with that of Dr. Brock uses a point-by-point pattern of contrast. The two authors take turns responding to a series of six questions asked by students. The essay then follows a pattern that can be described as A1B1, A2B2, A3B3, A4B4, A5B5, A6B6. In replying to the fourth question, for example, about whether or not feeling "depressed or unhappy" will affect their writing, Brock and Zinsser reply:

> "Probably it will," Dr. Brock replied. "Go fishing. Take a walk."
> "Probably it won't," I said. "If your job is to write every day, you learn to do it like any other job."

The point-by-point, or alternating, pattern emphasizes the individual points of comparison or contrast rather than the subject as a whole. In college writing, this pattern most frequently devotes a sentence, a group of sentences, or a paragraph to each point, alternating between subject A and subject B. If you use the alternating pattern, you must decide how to order your points—for instance, by beginning or by ending with the strongest or most significant.

Mixed Sequence (includes both subject-by-subject and point-by-point)

A.
  1.
  2.

B.
  1.
  2.

A3/B3
etc.

In longer pieces of writing, writers typically mix the subject-by-subject and point-by-point patterns. Such an arrangement provides variety and can make the points of comparison and contrast much more vivid for the reader. Robert J. Samuelson begins his essay with a subject-by-subject pattern. Paragraphs 1 and 2 discuss working conditions in the 1880s, while paragraph 3 focuses on contemporary working conditions. Separating the two subjects—work then and work today—forces the reader to make the comparisons mentally. By paragraph 4, Samuelson highlights a contrast by using the point-by-point structure:

The lowest-paid 10 percent of workers in 1890 worked about two hours more a day than the richest 10 percent (11 hours versus 9 hours). A century later the best-paid 10 percent labored an hour more a day than the poorest-paid 10 percent (8.5 hours versus 7.5 hours).

Much of the examination writing that you do in college probably should be organized either as subject-by-subject or point-by-point since these are the clearest structures for short responses. Many of the essays that you encounter in magazines and newspapers will use a mixed pattern in order to achieve flexibility and variety.

SAMPLE STUDENT ESSAY

As part of the library research paper unit in Freshman English, Alicia Gray's class had been talking about searching their school's on-line library catalog for relevant books. The instructor had mentioned a number of times that card catalogs could be searched for both subjects and keywords since the software program allowed for both. To give the students practice in both kinds of searches, Meghan, their instructor, gave them a worksheet to do for homework. On the way out of class, Alicia stopped and remarked to her instructor, "I always just do a key-word search," she said, "and it always seems like I find plenty of material." She added, "Since we have the capability to do a keyword search, isn't doing a subject search just unnecessary and even old-fashioned?" "Do the worksheet," Meghan replied. "Maybe," she added, "you could compare and contrast the two methods for your essay which is due next week." A week later, Alicia brought to class the following rough draft of her essay comparing keyword and subject searches.

EARLIER DRAFT

SUBJECT VS. KEYWORD SEARCHES

When it is time to start gathering information for your research paper in Freshman English, you will need to consult our Library's on-line catalog. The card catalog is a listing of the books that our library holds. Those books are catalogued, or listed, by author, title, subject, and keyword. Since normally we start by looking for books about our intended topic—rather than for specific titles by specific authors—we must start with either subject searches or keyword searches. What exactly is the difference between these two types of searches and how do you know when to use each?

When librarians refer to a "subject" search, they mean something quite specific and different from a "keyword." The term subject in library catalogs refers to a large listing of subject headings that are used by the Library of Congress to catalog a book. In fact, if you want to do a subject search in a library catalog, you don't start with the catalog itself. Instead you go to a multivolume series of books entitled the <u>Library of Congress Subject Headings</u>. Those books list alphabetically the various headings under which the Library of Congress files books. That listing is complete with cross-references, that is, with references to broader terms and to narrower, more specific terms. When catalogers at the Library of Congress look at new books, they do not just randomly assign a heading or a group of headings to the book, nor do they take the heading from a word in the book's title. Instead, they choose a heading or headings from the published list.

The principle behind the subject headings is to group related books under one heading. So instead of filing books about "the death penalty," "capital punishment," "death by lethal injection" under three separate subject headings, the Library of Congress uses a single subject heading ("capital punishment") and then provides cross-references from any other synonymous terms. The subject heading can also be followed by a whole series of other headings (for example, "capital punishment—history"). These other, more specific headings are very important because the Library of Congress always tries to assign the most specific subject heading to a book that it can. You never want to look under a large general heading if a more specific one is used. And how do you know if a more specific heading exists? You need to check the printed collection of headings currently in use. Subject headings impose a control on the vocabulary words used for headings.

In contrast, keyword searches look for words that are present somewhere in the book's record—typically in its title or subtitle, its author, its publisher. A keyword search retrieves information only when that word or group of words that you have entered appear in a record. That means there is no attempt at controlling the vocabulary. A book that had the phrase "the death penalty" somewhere in the title could be retrieved only if you typed in the keywords "death" and "penalty." A book on the same subject that used "capital punishment" would never appear—and keyword searches do not suggest related synonyms to you. Moreover, the presence of the key words would not necessarily mean that the book would be about the "death penalty" in the sense of "capital punishment." The words could appear in the title of novel or a collection of poems; they could refer to vastly different and unrelated circumstances—"the death penalty in ancient Rome." And, if you don't indicate the relationship (for example, immediately next to each other) that the two (or more) terms are to have, you'll end up retrieving a mountain of records that have the terms "death" and "penalty" somewhere in the record (for example, "The Penalty of Life: The Death of John Sayce").

Keyword searches have an advantage in that they can be used to find the very specific words for which you might be looking. Maybe those words haven't yet been added to the subject headings. Since subject headings depend on printed lists, subject headings are slow to react to new fields of study or new technologies.

Alicia shared the opening paragraphs of her rough draft with a classmate during in-class peer editing. The instructor had asked the students to concentrate on the organizational pattern used in the body of the essay and on the introduction. After reading Alicia's paper, her partner Sara LaBarca offered some advice on revising the draft. "You have lots of information," she said, "but your main pattern of development is subject-by-subject except for the fifth paragraph where you switch to point-by-point. Maybe you should try doing more with the point-to-point, otherwise by the time your readers come to the second half of your essay they might forget the contrasts you established in the first half." "I also think you need a strong introduction," she added. "You have a good thesis statement, but, well, frankly, I found the opening paragraph a little boring." Alicia tried to take Sara's advice and revised the opening of her essay and reorganized the body.

MINIMIZING THE GUESSWORK IN A LIBRARY SEARCH

The Cecil County Community College Library has twenty books dealing with the death penalty, but unless you pay attention to the next couple of pages, you will never find most of them. Why? Because no single search strategy will lead you to all twenty books.

Looking for book sources is more complicated than you might think. A successful search will require two different types of searches—a subject and a keyword search. They are very different kinds of searches with different rules and results. But to maximize your sources for a quality research paper, you will need to know how to do both.

In both subject and keyword searches, you are looking for single words or phrases that will lead you to the books you need. Those subject or keyword terms come from two different places. The term subject in library catalogs refers to a large alphabetized listing of subject headings that are assigned by the Library of Congress when cataloging a book. You find an appropriate heading not by guessing as you stand at a computer terminal, but by looking in a multivolume series of books entitled Library of Congress Subject Headings. When catalogers at the Library of Congress look at new books, they do not just randomly assign a heading or a group of headings to the book, nor do they necessarily take the heading from a word in the book's title. Instead, they choose a heading or headings from the published list. A keyword, on the other hand, is a significant word, generally a noun, that is typically in a book's title or subtitle. Unlike a subject search where the categories are "controlled" (that is, someone has predetermined what subject headings will be used), a keyword search is, in one sense, guesswork. You think of an important word or phrase that might describe the topic about which you want information and you try that. Just like any time you guess, though, there are risks. A keyword search retrieves information only when that word or group of words that you have entered appears in a record.

"If I have the choice of having to look things up in a set of books or of just guessing, I'll guess," you might reply. But before

you reject subject searches, consider the problem of synonyms—
that is, words or phrases that mean roughly the same thing. A
controlled subject search groups related books under one heading.
So instead of filing books about "the death penalty," "capital
punishment," and "death by lethal injection" under three separate
subject headings, the Library of Congress uses a single subject
heading ("capital punishment") and then provides cross references
from any other synonymous terms. In contrast, you can only
retrieve a book in a keyword search if it has those specific words
somewhere in its record. A book that had the phrase "the death
penalty" somewhere in the title could be retrieved only if you
typed in the keywords "death" and "penalty." A book on the same
subject that used "capital punishment" would never appear, and
keyword searches do not suggest related synonyms to you.
Moreover, the presence of the key words would not necessarily
mean that the book would be about the "death penalty" in the
sense of "capital punishment." The words could appear in the title
of a novel or a collection of poems; they could refer to vastly
different and unrelated circumstances—"the death penalty in
ancient Rome." And, if you don't indicate the relationship (for
example, immediately next to each other) that the two (or more)
terms are to have, you'll end up retrieving a mountain of records
that have the terms "death" and "penalty" somewhere in the
record (for example, "The Penalty of Life: The Death of John
Sayce").

Keyword searches have some distinct advantages, however.
Since subject searches are controlled, the Library of Congress tries
to find existing appropriate terms under which to file books—even
if they end up having to use more general terms. Although new
subject headings are regularly added to the lists, emerging fields
and technologies are rarely represented adequately in the subject
headings. On the other hand, since keywords do not depend on
any pre-existing published categories and since no one has tried to
classify those keywords into categories, keywords can be the best
way to look for books on new and emerging subjects. In that sense,
a keyword can be far more precise (if you guess the right one!)
than a subject heading.

SOME THINGS TO REMEMBER

1. Limit your comparison and contrast to subjects that can be adequately developed in a paragraph or an essay.
2. Make sure that the subjects you are comparing and contrasting have some basic similarities. Make a list of similarities and differences before you begin to write.
3. Decide why the comparison or contrast is important. What does it reveal? Remember to make the reason clear to the reader.
4. Decide what points of comparison or contrast are the most important or the most revealing. In general, omit any points of comparison that would be obvious to anybody.
5. Decide which of the three patterns of comparison and contrast best fits your purpose: subject-by-subject, point-by-point, or mixed.
6. Remember to make clear to your reader when you are switching from one subject to another or from one point of comparison to another.

VISUALIZING COMPARISON AND CONTRAST

This advertisement uses comparison and contrast to make a point about racial stereotyping. The same man appears in both photographs. In one, however, his skin color is darkened—that is the only difference between the two photographs. The advertisement asks you to make a quick judgment by comparing and contrasting the two photographs and answering the question, "Which man looks guilty?" Although comparison and contrast is an important way by which we know things (What is this similar to? How is this different from that?), the advertisement also suggests that we can react uncritically on the basis of a simple comparison.

Which man looks guilty? If you picked the man on the right, you're wrong. Wrong for judging people based on the color of their skin. Because if you look closely, you'll see they're the same man. Unfortunately, racial stereotyping like this happens every day. On America's highways, police stop drivers based on their skin color rather than for the way they are driving. For example, in Florida 80% of those stopped and searched were black and Hispanic, while they constituted only 5% of all drivers. These humiliating and illegal searches are violations of the Constitution and must be fought. Help us defend your rights. Support the ACLU. www.aclu.org **american civil liberties union**

COMPARISON AND CONTRAST AS A LITERARY STRATEGY

Poet Martin Espada uses comparison and contrast to structure his poem "Coca-Cola and Coco Frio." As you read the poem, notice the points of comparison and contrast that Espada develops and think about what the comparison and contrast is intended to reveal. See page 268.

COCA-COLA AND COCO FRIO
Martin Espada

On his first visit to Puerto Rico,
island of family folklore,
the fat boy wandered
from table to table
with his mouth open.
At every table, some great-aunt
would steer him with cool-spotted hands
to a glass of Coca-Cola.
One even sang to him, in all the English
she could remember, a Coca-Cola jingle
from the forties. He drank obediently, though
he was bored with this portion, familiar
from soda fountains in Brooklyn.

Then, at a roadside stand off the beach, the fat boy
opened his mouth to coco frio, a coconut
chilled, then scalped by a machete
so that a straw could inhale the clear milk.
The boy tilted the green shell overhead
and drooled coconut milk down his chin;
suddenly, Puerto Rico was not Coca-Cola
or Brooklyn, and neither was he.

For years afterwards, the boy marveled at an island
where the people drank Coca-Cola
and sang jingles from World War II
in a language they did not speak,
while so many coconuts in the trees
sagged heavy with milk, swollen
and unsuckled.

DISCUSSION QUESTIONS

1. How does Espada organize his comparison and contrast in the poem? In what ways are the two drinks similar? In what ways are they different?
2. What is it about the two drinks that catches Espada's attention? Why might he have written the poem? What is he trying to reveal?

3. What does the boy discover? How does the comparison and contrast lead to that discovery?
4. What image is developed in the final two lines of the poem? What is that image called? How is it also an example of comparison and contrast?
5. What is the significance of the word "unsuckled" in the final line? Who should consume the nourishment that the coconuts supply? Why?

WRITING SUGGESTIONS

Espada uses something from American popular culture to comment on the "island of [his] family folklore." Think about conflicts that you have experienced between how something is done in your culture in contrast to how it is done in another. The conflicts, for example, could result from differences in culture, in age, in religion, in values, in expectations, or in social or economic backgrounds. As a departure point, you might consider the following possible conflicts:

a. Between you and your parents
b. Between you and your grandparents
c. Between you and your siblings

Using Comparison and Contrast in Writing for Your Other Courses

Writing assignments and essay test questions that require comparison and contrast are common throughout the college curriculum. Instructors will often ask that you consider two subjects in depth, pointing out similarities and differences between them in order to demonstrate your familiarity with both subjects as well as to show how well you can apply the analytical concepts and skills being taught in the course. Here are some examples of writing assignments that would require comparison and contrast.

- **Literature.** For a five- to six-page paper, you might be asked to compare two works by the same author, one written early and one from later in his or her career, in order to analyze the development of the writer's style and the central themes explored in the works. Similarly, you might be asked to look at two works by different authors with similar themes in order to discuss similarities and differences in the development of these themes.

- **Life Sciences.** An exam question might ask that you compare and contrast two theories of evolutionary change—for example, natural selection and punctuated equilibrium.
- **Political Science.** For a research assignment to evaluate the role government plays in a particular aspect of a nation's economy, you might compare the United States' policies toward industrial planning with those of another major world power, such as Japan.
- **Theater History.** On an essay exam, you might be asked to compare the physical structure of the theaters where ancient Greek plays were performed with the kinds of theaters Shakespeare's plays were originally performed in two thousand years later.
- **Business Management.** For a research paper, you might be asked to compare how two different companies responded to a public relations challenge—for example, an outbreak of salmonella poisoning at a fast-food chain or accusations that a restaurant chain discriminated against minority customers—and then to explain which response you find the more effective and the more ethical.

VISIT THE PRENTICE HALL READER'S WEBSITE

When you have finished reading an essay, check out the additional material available at the *Reader*'s Website at www.prenhall. com/miller. For each reading, you will find a list of related readings connected with the topic or the author; additional background information; a group of relevant "hot-linked" Web resources (just click your computer's mouse and automatically visit the sites listed); and still more writing suggestions.

COMPARING AND CONTRASTING

Most of us are familiar with the "supermarket tabloids," those newspapers with the sensational headlines and photographs sold in the check-out lanes of supermarkets. Are they an accurate source of information? How do they compare with a regular newspaper? Visit the *National Enquirer* on-line and compare it with a newspaper such as *The Christian Science Monitor.* Comparison is easy with hot-links at the *Reader*'s Website.

GUAVAS

Esmeralda Santiago

Esmeralda Santiago (1948–) was born in San Juan, Puerto Rico, and came to the United States at the age of thirteen. A Harvard graduate with an M.F.A. from Sarah Lawrence, Santiago is a founder of CantoMedia, a film and media production company. This essay appeared as the Prologue to When I Was Puerto Rican *(1993), an autobiographical memoir that Santiago continued in her recent* Almost a Woman *(1998), which was adapted for a 2002* Masterpiece Theatre *production.*

On Writing: *Santiago observes, "Writing memoir involves chipping away at things in small increments, like a sculptor does to a piece of marble, until the image inside emerges. The process of writing my memoirs involved solitary and painful self-examination."*

BEFORE READING

Connecting: Do you remember a particular food that you associate with childhood? Something that was special to you? Something that you particularly enjoyed?

Anticipating: Why does Santiago no longer eat guavas?

There are guavas at the Shop & Save. I pick one the size of a tennis 1
ball and finger the prickly stem end. It feels familiarly bumpy and firm. The guava is not quite ripe; the skin is still a dark green. I smell it and imagine a pale pink center, the seeds tightly embedded in the flesh.

A ripe guava is yellow, although some varieties have a pink 2
tinge. The skin is thick, firm, and sweet. Its heart is bright pink and almost solid with seeds. The most delicious part of the guava surrounds the tiny seeds. If you don't know how to eat a guava, the seeds end up in the crevices between your teeth.

When you bite into a ripe guava, your teeth must grip the 3
bumpy surface and sink into the thick edible skin without hitting the center. It takes experience to do this, as it's quite tricky to determine how far beyond the skin the seeds begin.

4   Some years, when the rains have been plentiful and the nights cool, you can bite into a guava and not find many seeds. The guava bushes grow close to the ground, their branches laden with green then yellow fruit that seem to ripen overnight. These guavas are large and juicy, almost seedless, their roundness enticing you to have one more, just one more, because next year the rains may not come.

5   As children, we didn't always wait for the fruit to ripen. We raided the bushes as soon as the guavas were large enough to bend the branch.

6   A green guava is sour and hard. You bite into it at its widest point, because it's easier to grasp with your teeth. You hear the skin, meat, and seeds crunching inside your head, while the inside of your mouth explodes in little spurts of sour.

7   You grimace, your eyes water, and your cheeks disappear as your lips purse into a tight O. But you have another and then another, enjoying the crunchy sounds, the acid taste, the gritty texture of the unripe center. At night, your mother makes you drink castor oil, which she says tastes better than a green guava. That's when you know for sure that you're a child and she has stopped being one.

8   I had my last guava the day we left Puerto Rico. It was large and juicy, almost red in the center, and so fragrant that I didn't want to eat it because I would lose the smell. All the way to the airport I scratched at it with my teeth, making little dents in the skin, chewing small pieces with my front teeth, so that I could feel the texture against my tongue, the tiny pink pellets of sweet.

9   Today, I stand before a stack of dark green guavas, each perfectly round and hard, each $1.59. The one in my hand is tempting. It smells faintly of late summer afternoons and hopscotch under the mango tree. But this is autumn in New York, and I'm no longer a child.

10   The guava joins its sisters under the harsh fluorescent lights of the exotic fruit display. I push my cart away, toward the apples and pears of my adulthood, their nearly seedless ripeness predictable and bittersweet.

QUESTIONS ON SUBJECT AND PURPOSE

1. Where is Santiago at the start of the essay? What triggers her memory?

2. Santiago never buys the guava. Why not?

3. The essay appears at the start of Santiago's book *When I Was Puerto Rican* with the heading "Prologue: How to Eat a Guava." Can you think of other appropriate or suggestive titles for the essay?

QUESTIONS ON STRATEGY AND AUDIENCE

1. How does Santiago structure her comparison and contrast? Is it subject-by-subject or point-by-point or a mix of the two? What other structure underlies the essay?
2. Santiago's essay is taken from a memoir. What is a memoir? What do you expect in one?
3. What assumption about audience must the writer of a memoir make?

QUESTIONS ON VOCABULARY AND STYLE

1. In paragraph 7, how does Santiago suggest what happens to your mouth when you bite into a sour guava?
2. At the end of the essay, Santiago writes of apples and pears as being "bittersweet." What is "bittersweet"? In what ways might the apples and pears be "bittersweet"?
3. Be prepared to define the following word: *grimace* (paragraph 7).

WRITING SUGGESTIONS

1. **For Your Journal.** Sense impressions—sights, sounds, smells, touches—are a powerful stimulus to memory. Think back to your childhood. Do you associate a particular sense experience with that time? The perfume your mother wore? The sound of your father whistling? The texture or taste of your favorite cookie? Pick a period from your childhood and make a list of the sense impressions that you remember.
2. **For a Paragraph.** Using your journal as a prewriting exercise, select one of the remembered experiences and re-create it in a paragraph. Try to capture that sensual memory in words as Santiago does.
3. **For an Essay.** Santiago's essay contrasts, in part, a childhood experience with an adult experience—a "once I grew up I stopped doing . . . " theme. In an essay, make a similar comparison and contrast. Perhaps there was a climactic moment when you suddenly realized things had changed, that you had changed.

4. **For Research.** Santiago's memoir is about growing up and making the transition from the innocence of childhood to the experience of adulthood, but it is also about the problems of cultural identity—am I Puerto Rican or American? Research the problem of how people who immigrate to the United States (or to any other country) confront these issues. What does it mean to be a part of two cultures? Is it always problematic? Have you faced this problem? Do you know someone—a friend or classmate—who has? How can this contrast be made vivid to students for whom this is not an issue?

 WEBSITE LINK

The Web offers a wide variety of resources. Visit Santiago's own Website, read an interview with her, check out reviews of her work— all at the *Reader*'s Website. You can also find out everything about guavas.

 WRITING LINK: COMMAS

Go through Santiago's essay and underline each use of the comma. Then explain why a comma was used there. You might check a grammar handbook for help if you need it. How many different examples of comma use can you find in the essay?

THE TRANSACTION: TWO WRITING PROCESSES

William Zinsser

William Zinsser (1922–) has been an editor, critic, editorial writer, college teacher, and writing consultant. He is the author of many books including On Writing Well: An Informal Guide to Writing Nonfiction *(sixth edition, 1998), a textbook classic of which* The New York Times *wrote: "It belongs on any shelf of serious reference works for writers."*

On Writing: *As someone who earns his living as a writer, Zinsser sees writing as hard work. "The only way to learn to write," he has observed, "is to force yourself to produce a certain number of words on a regular basis." In an interview, he once remarked: "I don't think writing is an art. I think sometimes it's raised to an art, but basically it's a craft, like cabinet making or carpentry."*

BEFORE READING

Connecting: If you had to describe your writing process to a group of younger students, what would you say?

Anticipating: Why should writing seem so easy to Brock and so difficult to Zinsser? If he finds it so difficult, why does Zinsser continue to write?

A school in Connecticut once held "a day devoted to the arts," and   1
I was asked if I would come and talk about writing as a vocation. When I arrived I found that a second speaker had been invited—Dr. Brock (as I'll call him), a surgeon who had recently begun to write and had sold some stories to magazines. He was going to talk about writing as an avocation. That made us a panel, and we sat down to face a crowd of students and teachers and parents, all eager to learn the secrets of our glamorous work.

Dr. Brock was dressed in a bright red jacket, looking vaguely   2
bohemian, as authors are supposed to look, and the first question went to him. What was it like to be a writer?

He said it was tremendous fun. Coming home from an arduous   3
day at the hospital, he would go straight to his yellow pad and write

his tensions away. The words just flowed. It was easy. I then said that writing wasn't easy and wasn't fun. It was hard and lonely, and the words seldom just flowed.

4   Next Dr. Brock was asked if it was important to rewrite. Absolutely not, he said. "Let it all hang out," he told us and whatever form the sentences take will reflect the writer at his most natural. I then said that rewriting is the essence of writing. I pointed out that professional writers rewrite their sentences repeatedly over and over and then rewrite what they have rewritten.

5   "What do you do on days when it isn't going well?" Dr. Brock was asked. He said he just stopped writing and put the work aside for a day when it would go better. I then said that the professional writer must establish a daily schedule and stick to it. I said that writing is a craft, not an art, and that the man who runs away from his craft because he lacks inspiration is fooling himself. He is also going broke.

6   "What if you're feeling depressed or unhappy?" a student asked. "Won't that affect your writing?"

7   Probably it will, Dr. Brock replied. Go fishing. Take a walk. Probably it won't, I said. If your job is to write every day, you learn to do it like any other job.

8   A student asked if we found it useful to circulate in the literary world. Dr. Brock said he was greatly enjoying his new life as a man of letters, and he told several stories of being taken to lunch by his publisher and his agent at Manhattan restaurants where writers and editors gather. I said that professional writers are solitary drudges who seldom see other writers.

9   "Do you put symbolism in your writing?" a student asked me.

10   "Not if I can help it," I replied. I have an unbroken record of missing the deeper meaning in any story, play or movie, and as for dance and mime, I have never had any idea of what is being conveyed.

11   "I *love* symbols!" Dr. Brock exclaimed, and he described with gusto the joys of weaving them through his work.

12   So the morning went, and it was a revelation to all of us. At the end Dr. Brock told me he was enormously interested in my answers—it had never occurred to him that writing could be hard. I told him I was just as interested in *his* answers—it had never occurred to me that writing could be easy. Maybe I should take up surgery on the side.

13   As for the students, anyone might think we left them bewildered. But in fact we probably gave them a broader glimpse of the writing process than if only one of us had talked. For there isn't any "right" way to do such personal work. There are all kinds of writers and all kinds of methods, and any method that helps you to say what you want to say is the right method for you. . . .

QUESTIONS ON SUBJECT AND PURPOSE

1. Zinsser uses contrast to make a point about how people write. What is that point?
2. How effective is the beginning? Would the effect have been lost if Zinsser had opened with a statement similar to his final sentence?
3. What process do you use when you write? Does it help in any way to know what other people do? Why? Why not?

QUESTIONS ON STRATEGY AND AUDIENCE

1. Which method of development does Zinsser use for his example? How many points of contrast does he make?
2. Would it have made any difference if he had used another pattern of development? Why?
3. How effective are the short paragraphs? Should they be longer?

QUESTIONS ON VOCABULARY AND STYLE

1. What makes Zinsser's story humorous? Try to isolate several aspects of humor.
2. Zinsser uses a number of parallel structures in his narrative. Make a list of them, and be prepared to show how they contribute to the narrative's effectiveness.
3. Be able to explain or define the following: *avocation* (paragraph 1), *bohemian* (2), *arduous* (3), *mime* (10), *gusto* (11), *drone* (12).

WRITING SUGGESTIONS

1. **For Your Journal.** How do you feel about writing? How do you feel about having other people read your writing? Is writing a source of great anxiety? Of pleasure? In your journal, explore those feelings.
2. **For a Paragraph.** Using the details provided by Zinsser, rewrite the narrative using a subject-by-subject pattern. Choose either writer, and put together his advice in a single paragraph. Be sure to formulate a topic sentence that will control the paragraph.
3. **For an Essay.** Let's be honest—writing instructors and textbooks offer one view of the writing process, but the

practice of most writers can differ sharply. Prewriting and revising get squeezed out when a paper is due and only one night is available. In an essay, compare and contrast your typical behavior as a writer with the process outlined in this text. Do not be afraid to be truthful.

4. **For Research.** Compare the creative processes of two or more artists. You can choose painters, musicians, dancers, writers, actors—anyone involved in the creative arts. Check your library's catalog and the various periodical indexes and electronic databases for books and articles about the creative work of each person. Try to find interviews or statements in which the artists talk about how they work. If you are having trouble finding information, ask a reference librarian to help you. Be sure to document your sources.

 WEBSITE LINK

Interested in some on-line help for your writing? A list of sites is available at www.prenhall.com/miller.

 WRITING LINK: SENTENCE VARIETY

Rewrite paragraph 12 in the essay, casting it into simple sentences, each of which is followed by a period. What is the difference between your new paragraph and the one that Zinsser originally wrote? How does the punctuation of the original help reflect and emphasize Zinsser's meaning?

ACADEMIC SELVES

Mary Pipher

Mary Pipher earned her B.A. in cultural anthropology from the University of California at Berkeley and a Ph.D. in psychology from the University of Nebraska. A clinical psychologist in private practice, she is the author of Reviving Ophelia: Saving the Selves of Adolescent Girls *(1994), which was on* The New York Times *best-seller list for 149 weeks, and* Another Country: Navigating the Emotional Terrain of Our Elders *(1999). This selection is taken from* Reviving Ophelia.

BEFORE READING

Connecting: In the years that you were in middle or high school, did you ever feel as if boys and girls were treated differently?

Anticipating: As you read Pipher's essay, try to decide which of the three patterns for comparison and contrast (point-by-point, subject-by-subject, or mixed) she uses.

Schools have always treated girls and boys differently. What is new   1
in the nineties is that we have much more documentation of this phenomenon. Public awareness of the discrimination is increasing. This is due in part to the American Association of University Women (AAUW), which released a study in 1992 entitled "How Schools Shortchange Girls."

In classes, boys are twice as likely to be seen as role models, five   2
times as likely to receive teachers' attention and twelve times as likely to speak up in class. In textbooks, one-seventh of all illustrations of children are of girls. Teachers chose many more classroom activities that appeal to boys than to girls. Girls are exposed to almost three times as many boy-centered stories as girl-centered stories. Boys tend to be portrayed as clever, brave, creative, and resourceful, while girls are depicted as kind, dependent and docile. Girls read six times as many biographies of males as of females. Even in animal stories, the animals are twice as likely to be males. (I know of one teacher who, when she reads to her classes, routinely changes the sex of the characters in the stories so that girls will have stronger role models.)

3   Analysis of classroom videos shows that boys receive more classroom attention and detailed instruction than girls. They are called on more often than girls and are asked more abstract, open-ended and complex questions. Boys are more likely to be praised for academics and intellectual work, while girls are more likely to be praised for their clothing, behaving properly and obeying rules. Boys are likely to be criticized for their behavior, while girls are criticized for intellectual inadequacy. The message to boys tends to be: "You're smart, if you would just settle down and get to work." The message to girls is often: "Perhaps you're just not good at this. You've followed the rules and haven't succeeded."

4   Because with boys failure is attributed to external factors and success is attributed to ability, they keep their confidence, even with failure. With girls it's just the opposite. Because their success is attributed to good luck or hard work and failure to lack of ability, with every failure, girls' confidence is eroded. All this works in subtle ways to stop girls from wanting to be astronauts and brain surgeons. Girls can't say why they ditch their dreams, they just "mysteriously" lose interest.

5   Some girls do well in math and continue to like it, but many who were once good at math complain that they are stupid in math. Girl after girl tells me, "I'm not good in math." My observations suggest that girls have trouble with math because math requires exactly the qualities that many junior-high girls lack—confidence, trust in one's own judgment and the ability to tolerate frustration without becoming overwhelmed. Anxiety interferes with problem solving in math. A vicious circle develops—girls get anxious, which interferes with problem solving, and so they fail and are even more anxious and prone to self-doubt the next time around.

6   When boys have trouble with a math problem, they are more likely to think the problem is hard but stay with it. When girls have trouble, they think they are stupid and tend to give up. This difference in attribution speaks to girls' precipitous decline in math. Girls need to be encouraged to persevere in the face of difficulty, to calm down and believe in themselves. They need permission to take their time and to make many mistakes before solving the problem. They need to learn relaxation skills to deal with the math anxiety so many experience.

7   The AAUW study found that as children go through school, boys do better and feel better about themselves and girls' self-esteem, opinions of their sex and scores on standardized achievement tests all decline. Girls are more likely than boys to say that they are not smart

enough for their dream careers. They emerge from adolescence with a diminished sense of their worth as individuals.

Gifted girls seem to suffer particularly with adolescence. Lois 8 Murphy found that they lose IQ points as they become feminized. In the 1920s Psychologist Louis Terman studied gifted children in California. Among the children, the seven best writers were girls and all the best artists were girls, but by adulthood all the eminent artists and writers were men.

Junior high is when girls begin to fade academically. Partly this 9 comes from the very structure of the schools, which tend to be large and impersonal. Girls, who tend to do better in relationship-based, cooperative learning situations, get lost academically in these settings. Partly it comes from a shift girls make at this time from a focus on achievement to a focus on affiliation. In junior high girls feel enormous pressure to be popular. They learn that good grades can even interfere with popularity. Lori learned to keep quiet about grades. She said, "Either way I lose. If I make a good grade, they are mad. If I make a bad grade, they spread it around that even I can screw up." Another girl said, "When I started junior high I figured out that I'd have more friends if I focused on sports. Smart girls were nerds." Another, who almost flunked seventh grade, told me, "All I care about is my friends. Grades don't matter to me."

I saw a seventh-grader who was failing everything. I asked her 10 why and she said, "My friends and I decided that making good grades wasn't cool." Her story has a happy ending, not because of my work, but because the next year, in eighth grade, she and her friends had another meeting and decided that it was now "cool" to make good grades. My client's academic situation improved enormously.

This tendency for girls to hide their academic accomplishments 11 is an old one. Once on a date I was particularly untrue to myself. Denny and I went to the A&W Root Beer Drive-In on Highway 81, and he asked me what I would like. Even though I was famished I ordered only a small Coke. (Nice girls didn't eat too much.) Then he asked about my six-week grades. I had made As, but I said I had two Cs and was worried my parents would be mad. I can still remember his look of visible relief.

QUESTIONS ON SUBJECT AND PURPOSE

1. According to Pipher why do young girls "fade academically"?
2. Although Pipher cites a study done by the American Association of University Women (paragraph 1), she does not

quote from the study or specifically document the "facts" that she provides. Does that affect your reading experience of the essay? Do you, for example, doubt anything that she says?

3. What purpose might Pipher have in her essay? Notice the title and subtitle of the book from which this is taken in the introductory information.

QUESTIONS ON STRATEGY AND AUDIENCE

1. In paragraphs 9 and 10, Pipher introduces examples of young girls reacting to peer pressure. How do these examples work in the essay?

2. In the final paragraph, Pipher relates a personal experience. What is the effect of telling that story about her own life?

3. To whom is Pipher writing? Would the imagined or intended audience be adolescent girls? Someone else?

QUESTIONS ON VOCABULARY AND STYLE

1. What effect does Pipher gain by quoting—rather than summarizing—the remarks of the girls in paragraphs 9 and 10?

2. Reread paragraph 11. Does it seem unusual that Pipher is able to recall such detailed information from her own past? Does it really matter whether or not each detail is accurate and truthful?

3. Be prepared to define the following words: *docile* (paragraph 2), *precipitous* (6), *persevere* (6).

WRITING SUGGESTIONS

1. **For Your Journal.** Pipher is writing about the educational and peer experiences that adolescent girls have. Do similar discrimination and pressure extend into the college years? Think about male and female students at your school. Do they behave differently in class? Do males talk more? Do professors call on males more often? Is peer pressure a factor in academic success or failure? For several days, just listen and watch what is going on in your classes and elsewhere on campus. Take notes in your journal.

2. **For a Paragraph.** Use your journal to provide the examples for a paragraph in which you explore gender differences in your college's classrooms.

3. **For an Essay.** Expand your paragraph writing into an essay. What differences do you see between male and female students, in the classroom, in the laboratory, in their expectations, in their assumptions?

4. **For Research.** Your essay dealt with your own experience and observation and the experiences and observations of fellow students. Does the body of scholarly research see any difference between how men and women are treated in college classrooms? Is there any perceived difference in peer pressure? In expectations? Is it suddenly acceptable to be a "brilliant" student in college if you are a woman? In an essay that includes research in printed or on-line sources, compare and contrast the educational experience for men and women in college. Be sure to document your sources.

 WEBSITE LINK

A number of interviews with Pipher are available on-line. A good place to start is with the listing at the Website.

 WRITING LINK: PARALLELISM

Throughout the essay, Pipher makes extensive use of parallelism—in words, in sentences, and in groups of sentences. Review the concept of parallelism, and then see how many examples you can find in the essay. What effect does Pipher gain by using these types of structures?

FUN ETHIC VS. WORK ETHIC?

Robert J. Samuelson

Robert J. Samuelson is a graduate of Harvard and an award-winning news-paper and magazine writer. He writes a biweekly column on socioeconomic is-sues for Newsweek, *as well as columns for a number of newspapers including* The Washington Post, The Los Angeles Times, *and* The Boston Globe. *"Fun Ethic vs. Work Ethic?" originally appeared in* Newsweek.

On Writing: *In the Acknowledgments to his 1995 book* The Good Life and Its Discontents, *Samuelson reflects on the process of writing and revision. He had earlier abandoned the project because, he says, "I could never quite master the tone and organization that would satisfy my infor-mal rule: never write a book you wouldn't want to read." Picking up the project again several years later, he "wrote and rewrote," revising in part based on the suggestions of other readers who "helped me see better exactly what I was trying to say" and "how to be more precise and concise." "It's not easy to be honest in criticizing without being discouraging," he goes on to say, but the readers of his drafts "all managed that feat."*

BEFORE READING

Connecting: Once you have graduated from college, what expecta-tions do you have about a job? What should the job do for *you*?

Anticipating: As you read, think about the major changes that we have seen in the world of work since the 1880s.

1   The transformation of labor since the creation of Labor Day a cen-tury ago tells, in many ways, the story of modern America. Paid labor was then all-consuming, generally backbreaking, done mainly by men, often dangerous and, of course, endless—that is, most men worked until they couldn't. In 1880, 58 percent of men 75 or older worked; the figure today is 8 percent. The factory workweek averaged about 60 hours, spread over six days. Sunday was a day of rest and prayer, but not really recreation.

2   Economic historian Stuart Bruchey has written: "By present standards the age of America's first Industrial Revolution must be re-garded as callous in its relative indifference to the welfare and safety of workers. The unemployed worker was cast adrift. As a rule, there

was no such thing as public relief, and private charity was either insufficient or offered only on demeaning terms. The risks of injury or death on the job were grievously high." From 1880 to 1900 about 35,000 workers died and 500,000 were injured annually in work accidents, he reports. This was in a work force between one ninth of today's (in 1880) and one fifth (in 1900).

It was the oppressive and precarious nature of employment that   3
led the Knights of Labor to agitate in the early 1880s for an annual celebration that would honor the dignity of ordinary workers—a campaign that culminated with Congress's designating a national holiday in 1894. Since then, work has slowly become less demanding of our time and bodies. In 1998 there were 5,100 on-the-job deaths, a seventh of accidents outside the workplace. Although dangerous and degrading jobs remain, most of us trudge to offices, where the greatest threat is getting stuck in an elevator or, more seriously, developing a repetitive-stress injury. In factories, automation has reduced risks dramatically. Machines perform operations that once mangled hands and arms.

Similarly, a gradual explosion of leisure has completely changed   4
how Americans think about their daily lives. It is no longer a simple rotation of work, sleep, eat. We now cram our days with TV, restaurants, shopping, soccer, PTA meetings and health clubs. Curiously, the poor may have benefited more from this than the wealthy, according to economist Dora Costa of the Massachusetts Institute of Technology. By her estimates, the lowest-paid 10 percent of workers in 1890 worked about two hours more a day than the richest 10 percent (11 hours versus 9 hours). A century later the best-paid 10 percent labored an hour more a day than the poorest-paid 10 percent (8.5 hours versus 7.5 hours).

Just what caused this reversal isn't clear. Perhaps the highest-   5
paid workers and managers are also the most committed, passionate and besieged. Or they may feel pressured to stay longer to protect their positions. Whatever the explanation, work's burdens (if not benefits) have become more evenly distributed. And for everyone— including, now, the half of the work force who are women— expectations have broadened.

Jobs should not just improve our incomes, we think. Like candy   6
and cars, they should also enhance psychic well-being. They should be gratifying and stimulating. Every Labor Day produces a pile of reports on the state of working America. Perhaps the most interesting this year comes from Karlyn Bowman of the American Enterprise Institute, who has assembled public-opinion data on recent worker attitudes. Pollsters reflect public tastes and therefore ask questions like

whether we feel our jobs have "importance to society," allow us "to influence decisions made at work" or provide agreeable friends. A century ago, had polling existed, questions would have been cruder: "Do you expect to die on the job?" Or "Do you make enough to feed your family?" In 1888 a typical family spent 45 percent of its budget on food; the comparable figure today is about 14 percent.

7   In many respects, the polls show remarkable stability. For example, 45 percent of workers report being "very satisfied" and 44 percent "moderately satisfied" with their jobs, according to the National Opinion Research Center at the University of Chicago. In 1972 the results were similar (49 percent and 37 percent, respectively). When Americans detest their jobs, they tend to quit. But there are hints of change. One survey asks "whether work is the important thing—and the purpose of leisure time is to recharge people's batteries so they can do a better job or . . . leisure is the important thing—and the purpose of work is to make it [leisure] possible." In 1975, 48 percent of respondents rated work as "the important thing" versus 36 percent for leisure. By 2000 the numbers had reversed—43 percent chose leisure and 34 percent work.

8   "It's the movement from the work ethic to the fun ethic," says Thomas Riehle of Ipsos-Reid, a survey firm. But, as Riehle notes, the work ethic is not collapsing so much as the boundaries between work and leisure are blurring—a combination that often produces stress and confusion. According to a new Ipsos-Reid poll, about 43 percent of workers say they bring work home or are "on call"; similarly, 30 percent admit using the Internet or e-mail at work for play or personal matters. Companies are now routinely expected to help workers balance family and job demands. There is some success. One poll in Bowman's collection finds that 47 percent of workers rated their companies as "very accommodating" and 33 percent as "somewhat accommodating" in reconciling job and family pressures.

9   The late economist Herbert Stein once attributed America's progress to the fact that "100 million people got up every morning to do the best they could for themselves and their children." The figure today would be about 140 million, but the appraisal was equally true a century ago, when workers numbered 28 million. What has changed is that work has become less manual and more mental, less regimented and more collaborative, and—as an activity—less economic and more social. To Stein, freedom was the key. It allowed people to strive to earn the most for themselves and be the most productive for society. Although this remains true, we have amended freedom to include some fun.

QUESTIONS ON SUBJECT AND PURPOSE

1. What was it like to be a worker in 1880?
2. What are the "work ethic" and the "fun ethic"?
3. What does Samuelson's purpose seem to be?

QUESTIONS ON STRATEGY AND AUDIENCE

1. Why might Samuelson begin with statistics about work in 1880? How effective is paragraph 1 as an introduction to the essay?
2. How important are the statistics that Samuelson cites in his essay? What would it be like if these facts were omitted?
3. The essay originally appeared in *Newsweek* magazine. Who reads *Newsweek*? What could Samuelson expect of his audience?

QUESTIONS ON VOCABULARY AND STYLE

1. In paragraph 7, Samuelson quotes the phrase, "to recharge people's batteries." What would you call this expression?
2. How would you characterize the tone of the essay? Do you get any sense of Samuelson's personality? Why or why not? How does the tone work with the essay's purpose?
3. Be prepared to define the following words: *callous* (paragraph 2), *demeaning* (2), *precarious* (3), *culminated* (3).

WRITING SUGGESTIONS

1. **For Your Journal.** What are your expectations about your first job after college? What is it going to be like? Will it be demanding? Fulfilling? Will work be a priority in your life? Will work give you the means to enjoy your leisure? In your journal, jot down a list of those expectations. If possible, talk with a parent or grandparent. Ask them to review your list. What is their reaction to your expectations?
2. **For a Paragraph.** Using the information gathered from your parents' or grandparents' reaction (or anyone who is at least a generation older than you), write a paragraph in which you compare and contrast the attitudes and expectations of the two generations toward work.

3. **For an Essay.** Expand your paragraph writing into an essay. You will want to interview a number of adults who are at least a generation older than you and a number of your peers. Do the two groups share any expectations and attitudes? Do they disagree on certain things? What does the comparison and contrast reveal about the two generations? Does it explain any conflicts or disagreements?

4. **For Research.** The average American worker gets two weeks of paid vacation each year. In contrast workers in many other countries get four weeks of vacation. Some analysts have argued that American workers prefer higher salaries to longer vacations. Research the problem. How do American attitudes toward vacation differ from the attitudes in other industrialized societies? Why?

 WEBSITE LINK

For some suggestions about places to start researching labor statistics and attitudes toward work, check the *Reader's* Website.

 WRITING LINK: INTEGRATING QUOTATIONS

Look carefully at how Samuelson integrates quotations from other sources into his essay. Where do those quotations tend to come in his sentences? How does he introduce and punctuate them? What can you learn from Samuelson about using quotations in your own papers?

THE COLOR OF LOVE

Danzy Senna

*Danzy Senna (1970–   ) is a graduate of Stanford University with an
M.F.A. from the University of California, Irvine. She is currently teaching at
the College of the Holy Cross in Worcester, Massachusetts. The daughter of a
White mother and a Black father, Senna is particularly interested in multira-
cial identity in the United States, which she explores in her first novel,* Cauc-
asia *(1998). "The Color of Love" first appeared in* O, The Oprah *Magazine.*

On Writing: *In an interview, Senna commented: "I'm not interested in memoir, or purely autobiographical writing. I'm more interested in
what might have happened than what really did."*

BEFORE READING

Connecting: "The Color of Love" focuses on the conflict between
Senna and her grandmother. Are there some fundamental ways in
which you and a grandparent are opposites?

Anticipating: Is the conflict between Senna and her grandmother
ever resolved in the essay? Why or why not?

W e had this much in common: We were both women, and we were   1
both writers. But we were as different as two people can be and still
exist in the same family. She was ancient—as white and dusty as
chalk—and spent her days seated in a velvet armchair, passing judgments on the world below. She still believed in noble bloodlines; my
blood had been mixed at conception. I believed there was no such
thing as nobility or class or lineage, only systems designed to keep
some people up in the big house and others outside, in the cold.

   She was my grandmother. She was Irish but from that country's   2
Protestant elite, which meant she seemed more British than anything.
She was an actress, a writer of plays and novels and still unmarried in
her thirties when she came to America to visit. One night while in
Boston, she went to a dinner party, where she was seated next to a
young lawyer with blood as blue as the ocean. Her pearl earring fell
in his oyster soup—or so the story goes—and they fell in love. My
grandmother married that lawyer and left her native Ireland for New
England.

3   How she came to have black grandchildren is a story of opposites. It was 1968 in Boston when her daughter—my mother—a small,
blonde Wasp poet, married my father, a tall and handsome black intellectual, in an act that was as rebellious as it was hopeful. The products of that unlikely union—my older sister, my younger brother and
I—grew up in urban chaos, in a home filled with artists and political
activists. The old lady across the river in Cambridge seemed to me an
endangered species. Her walls were covered with portraits of my ancestors, the pale and dead men who had conquered Africa and built
Boston long before my time. When I visited, their eyes followed me
from room to room with what I imagined to be an expression of scorn.
Among the portraits sat my grandmother, a bird who had flown in to
remind us all that there had indeed been a time when lineage and caste
meant something. To me, young and dark and full of energy, she was
the missing link between the living and the dead.

4   But her blood flowed through me, whether I liked it or not. I
grew up to be a writer, just like her. And as I struggled to tell my own
stories—about race and class and post–civil rights America—I wondered who my grandmother had been before, in Dublin, when she was
friend and confidante to literary giants such as William Butler Yeats
and Samuel Beckett. Once, while snooping in her bedroom, I discovered her novels, the ones that had been published in Ireland when she
was my age. I stared at her photograph on the jacket and wondered
about the young woman who wore a mischievous smile. Had she ever
worried about becoming so powerful that no man would want her?
Did she now feel that she had sacrificed her career and wild Irish-
woman dreams to become a wife and mother and proper Bostonian?

5   I longed to know her—to love her. But the differences between
us were real and alive, and they threatened to squelch our fragile connection. She was an alcoholic. In the evening, after a few glasses of
gin, she could turn vicious. Though she held antiquated racist views,
my grandmother would still have preferred to see my mother married
and was saddened when my parents split in the seventies. She believed
that a woman without a man was pitiable. The first question she always asked me when she saw me: "Do you have a man?" The second
question: "What is he?" That was her way of finding out his race and
background. She looked visibly pleased if he was a Wasp, neutral if he
was Jewish and disappointed if he was black.

6   My mother ignored her hurtful comments but felt them just the
same. She spent her visits to my grandmother's house slamming
dishes in the kitchen, hissing her anger just out of hearing range, then
raving, on the drive home, about what awful thing her mother had
said this time. Like my mother, I knew the rule: I was not to disre-

spect elders. She was old and gray and would soon be gone. But I had inherited my grandmother's short temper. When I got angry, even as a child, I felt as if blood were rushing around in my head, red waves battering the shore. Words spilled from my mouth—cutting, vicious words that I regretted.

One autumn day in Cambridge, at my grandmother's place, I lost my temper. I was home from college for the holidays, staying in her guest room. I woke from a nap to the sound of her enraged voice shouting at what I could only imagine was the television.   7

"Idiot! You damn fool!" she bellowed. "You stupid, stupid woman!" It has to be *Jeopardy!*, I thought. She must be yelling at those tiny contestants on the screen. She knows the answers to those questions better than they do. But when the shouting went on for a beat too long, I went to the top of the stairs and looked down into the living room. She was speaking to a real person: her cleaning lady, a Greek woman named Mary, who was on her hands and knees, nervously gathering the shards of a broken vase. My grandmother stood over her, hands on hips, cursing.   8

"You fool," my grandmother repeated. "How in bloody hell could you have done something so stupid?"   9

"Grandma." I didn't shout her name but said it loudly enough that she, though hard of hearing, glanced up.   10

"Oh, darling!" she piped, suddenly cheerful. "Would you like a cup of tea? You must be dreadfully tired."   11

Mary was on her feet again. She smiled nervously at me, then rushed into the kitchen with the pieces of the broken vase.   12

I told myself to be a good girl, to be polite. But something snapped. I marched down the stairs, and even she noticed something on my face that made her sit in her velvet chair.   13

"Don't you ever talk to her that way," I shouted. "Where do you think you are? Slavery was abolished long ago."   14

I stood over her, tall and long-limbed, daring her to speak. My grandmother shook her head. "It's about race, isn't it?"   15

"Race?" I said, baffled. "Mary's white. This is about respect—treating other human beings with respect."   16

She wasn't hearing me. All she saw was color. "The tragedy about you," she said soberly, "is that you are mixed." I felt those waves in my head: "Your tragedy is that you're old and ignorant," I spat. "You don't know the first thing about me."   17

She cried into her hands. She seemed diminished, a little old woman. She looked up only to say, "You are a cruel girl."   18

I left her apartment trembling yet feeling exhilarated by what I had done. But my elation soon turned to shame. I had taken on an old   19 lady. And for what? Her intolerance was, at her age, deeply entrenched. My rebuttals couldn't change her.

20   Yet that fight marked the beginning of our relationship. I've since decided that when you cease to express anger toward those who have hurt you, you are essentially giving up on them. They are dead to you. But when you express anger, it is a sign that they still matter, that they are worth the fight.

21   After that argument, my grandmother and I began a conversation. She seemed to see me clearly for the first time, or perhaps she, a "cruel girl" herself, had simply met her match. And I no longer felt she was a relic. She was a living, breathing human being who deserved to be spoken to as an equal.

22   I began visiting her more. I would drive to Cambridge and sit with her, eating mixed nuts and sipping ginger ale, regaling her with tales of my latest love drama or writing project. In her presence, I was proudly black and young and political, and she was who she was: subtly racist, terribly elitist and awfully funny. She still said things that angered me: She bemoaned my mother's marriage to my father, she said that I should marry not for love but for money, and she told me that I needn't identify as black, since I didn't look it. I snapped back at her. But she, with senility creeping in, didn't seem to hear me; each time I came, she said the same things.

23   Last summer I went into hiding to work on my second novel at a writers' retreat in New Hampshire. The place was a kind of paradise for creative souls, a hideaway where every writer had his or her own cabin in the woods with no phone or television—no distractions to speak of. But I was miserable. I could not write. Even the flies outside my window seemed to whisper, "Go out and play. Forget the novel. Leave it till tomorrow."

24   I woke one morning at four, the light outside my window still blue. I felt panic and sadness, though I didn't know why I got up, dressed and went outside for a walk through the forest. But the panic persisted, and I began to cry. I assumed that my writer's block had seized me suddenly.

25   That night I ate dinner in the main house and received a call on the pay phone from my mother. She told me my grandmother had fallen and broken her leg. But that wasn't all; she had subsequently suffered a heart attack. Her other organs were failing. I had to hurry if I wanted to say good-bye.

26   I drove to Boston that night, not believing that we could be losing her. She would make it. I was certain. Sure, she was ninety-two, frail, unable to walk steadily. But she was lucid, and her tongue was as sharp as ever. Somehow I had imagined her as indestructible, made immortal by power and cruelty and wit.

The woman I found in the hospital bed was barely recognizable. My grandmother had always been fussy about her appearance. She never showed her face without makeup. Even in the day, when it was just she and the cleaning lady, she dressed as if she were ready for a cocktail party. At night she usually had cocktail parties; doddering old men hovered around her, sipping Scotch and bantering about theater and politics.

My grandmother's face had swollen to twice its normal size, and tubes came out of her nose. She had struggled so hard to pull them out that the nurses had tied her wrists to the bed rails. Her hair was gray and thin. Her body was withered and bruised, barely covered by the green hospital gown.

Her hazel eyes were all that was still recognizable, but the expression in them was different from any I had ever seen on her—terror. She was terrified to die. She tried to rise when she saw me, and her eyes pleaded with me to help her, to save her, to get her out of this mess. I stood over her, and I felt only one thing: overwhelming love. Not a trace of anger. That dark gray rage I'd felt toward her was gone as I stroked her forehead and told her she would be okay, even knowing she would not.

For two days, my mother, her sisters and I stood beside my grandmother, singing Irish ballads and reading passages to her from the works of her favorite novelist, James Joyce. For the first time, she could not talk. At one point, she gestured wildly for pen and paper. I brought her the pen and the paper and held them up for her, but she was too weak for even that. What came out was only a faint, incomprehensible line.

In death we are each reduced to our essence: the spirit we are when we are born. The trappings we hold on to our whole lives—our race, our money, our sex, our age, our politics—become irrelevant. My grandmother became a child in that hospital bed, a spirit about to embark on an unknown journey, terrified and alone, no matter how many of us were crowded around her. In the final hours, even her skin seemed to lose its wrinkles and take on a waxy glow. Then, finally, the machines around us went silent as she left us behind to squabble in the purgatory of the flesh.

QUESTIONS ON SUBJECT AND PURPOSE

1. In what sense is this a comparison and contrast essay? What is being compared and contrasted?
2. Why might Senna have titled the essay "The Color of Love"? Does love have a color?

3. Does the essay transcend the personal? That is, do you as a reader feel that Senna's experience is relevant to you?

QUESTIONS ON STRATEGY AND AUDIENCE

1. What shift occurs in the essay in paragraphs 7–19?
2. What is the significance of the scene that occurs in paragraphs 7–19?
3. In what way is the writing of the essay similar to the fight between Senna and her grandmother?

QUESTIONS ON VOCABULARY AND STYLE

1. What is your sense of the narrator? Do you find her sympathetic?
2. What is the effect of the use of dialogue in paragraphs 7–19?
3. Be prepared to define the following words: *antiquated* (paragraph 5), *shards* (8), *elation* (19), *regaling* (22), *lucid* (26), *doddering* (27).

WRITING SUGGESTIONS

1. **For Your Journal.** What generational conflicts have you experienced within your own family? Are there conflicts between you and your grandparents, between your parents and your grandparents, between you and your parents? Jot down some ideas and possible scenes in your journal. Try to think not only about an issue on which the two disagree, but also about a possible scene where that disagreement is clearly revealed.
2. **For a Paragraph.** Using your journal as a departure point, create for the reader that conflict in a paragraph. Try not just to tell the reader; try also to show how the two sides revealed their differences.
3. **For an Essay.** Expand your paragraph into an essay. Remember that the conflicts are likely to be rooted in a set of values or a particular expectation. Even if you feel that one side is completely wrong, it is at least possible to understand why the person feels the way that he or she does. Remember that your experience is probably not unique—that is, that most of your readers have experienced similar things. Like

Senna, try to include at least one dramatized scene with some dialogue.

4. **For Research.** Select one or more significant differences or conflicts between generations. Look for a charged issue—such things as race relations, attitudes toward sex or money, views of gender roles, or work ethics. What are the significant factors or experiences that fuel those conflicts? What can you learn from research and interviews? What explains the differences between the two generations and their attitudes toward this subject?

WEBSITE LINK

Read an interview with Senna, check out reviews of her book, and locate additional information—all on the Web.

WRITING LINK: PUNCTUATION

Choose one of the paragraphs in the essay (good choices would include paragraphs 1, 3, 4, 5, 6, 29), and look closely at how Senna punctuates her sentences. Using a grammar book, try to find the reason why each mark is appropriate in its particular content. When do you use a colon, a semicolon, a dash? What are the most common uses of the comma? What does the variety of Senna's punctuation suggest about your own writing? Do you use a variety of punctuation marks?

Virtual Love

Meghan Daum

Meghan Daum graduated from Vassar College and earned an M.F.A. at Columbia University. Her essays and articles have appeared in The New Yorker, The New York Times Book Review, GQ, Vogue *and* Self, *among others, and have been collected in* My Misspent Youth *(2001). "Virtual Love" first appeared in* The New Yorker.

On Writing: *Asked about her writing, Daum commented: "The subjects that I find most fascinating concern ideas or events that have not only affected me personally but seem to resonate with the culture at large. Though I am often called a 'confessional' writer, I am less interested in 'confessing' than in using specific experiences as a tool for looking at more general or abstract phenomena in the world. The key to writing about yourself without falling into solipsism is to explore issues that transcend the merely personal and shed a new light on the experiences that many of us share. It also helps to have a sense of humor and respect for the absurdity of life by not taking yourself too seriously."*

BEFORE READING

Connecting: Do you think that it is possible to "fall in love" with someone that you have never met face-to-face?

Anticipating: What is it about this "virtual" relationship that attracts Daum?

1   It was last November; fall was drifting away into an intolerable chill. I was at the end of my twenty-sixth year, and was living in New York City, trying to support myself as a writer, and taking part in the kind of urban life that might be construed as glamorous were it to appear in a memoir in the distant future. At the time, however, my days felt more like a grind than like an adventure: hours of work strung between the motions of waking up, getting the mail, watching TV with my roommates, and going to bed. One morning, I logged on to my America Online account to find a message under the heading "is this the real meghan daum?" It came from someone with the screen name PFSlider. The body of the message consisted of five sentences, written entirely in lower-case letters, of perfectly turned flattery: something about PFSlider's admiration of some newspaper and magazine

articles I had published over the last year and a half, something about
his resulting infatuation with me, and something about his being a
sportswriter in California.

I was engaged for the thirty seconds that it took me to read the 2
message and fashion a reply. Though it felt strange to be in the position of confirming that I was indeed "the real meghan daum," I managed to say, "Yes, it's me. Thank you for writing." I clicked the "Send
Now" icon, shot my words into the void, and forgot about PFSlider
until the next day, when I received another message, this one headed
"eureka."

"wow, it is you," he wrote, still in lower case. He chronicled the 3
various conditions under which he'd read my few-and-far-between
articles—a boardwalk in Laguna Beach, the spring-training press-
room for a baseball team that he covered for a Los Angeles newspaper. He confessed to having a crush on me. He referred to me as
"princess daum." He said he wanted to have lunch with me during
one of his two annual trips to New York.

The letter was outrageous and endearingly pathetic, possibly 4
the practical joke of a friend trying to rouse me out of a temporary
writer's block. But the kindness pouring forth from my computer
screen was bizarrely exhilarating, and I logged off and thought about
it for a few hours before writing back to express how flattered and
"touched"—this was probably the first time I had ever used that word
in earnest—I was by his message.

I am not what most people would call a computer person. I have 5
no interest in chat rooms, newsgroups, or most Websites. I derive a
palpable thrill from sticking a letter in the United States mail. But I
have a constant low-grade fear of the telephone, and I often call people with the intention of getting their answering machines. There is
something about the live voice that I have come to find unnervingly
organic, as volatile as live television. E-mail provides a useful antidote
for my particular communication anxieties. Though I generally send
and receive only a few messages a week, I take comfort in their silence
and their boundaries.

PFSlider and I tossed a few innocuous, smart-assed notes back 6
and forth over the week following his first message. Let's say his name
was Pete. He was twenty-nine, and single. I revealed very little about
myself, relying instead on the ironic commentary and forced witti-
cisms that are the conceit of so many E-mail messages. But I quickly
developed an oblique affection for PFSlider. I was excited when there
was a message from him, mildly depressed when there wasn't. After a
few weeks, he gave me his phone number. I did not give him mine,
but he looked it up and called me one Friday night. I was home. I

picked up the phone. His voice was jarring, yet not unpleasant. He held up more than his end of the conversation for an hour, and when he asked permission to call me again I granted it, as though we were of an earlier era.

7   Pete—I could never wrap my mind around his name, privately thinking of him as PFSlider, "E-mail guy," or even "baseball boy"— began phoning me two or three times a week. He asked if he could meet me, and I said that that would be O.K. Christmas was a few weeks away, and he told me that he would be coming back East to see his family. From there, he would take a short flight to New York and have lunch with me.

8   "It is my off-season mission to meet you," he said.

9   "There will probably be a snowstorm," I said.

10   "I'll take a team of sled dogs," he answered.

11   We talked about our work and our families, about baseball and Bill Clinton and Howard Stern and sex, about his hatred for Los Angeles and how much he wanted a new job. Sometimes we'd find each other logged on simultaneously and type back and forth for hours.

12   I had previously considered cyber-communication an oxymoron, a fast road to the breakdown of humanity. But, curiously, the Internet—at least in the limited form in which I was using it—felt anything but dehumanizing. My interaction with PFSlider seemed more authentic than much of what I experienced in the daylight realm of living beings. I was certainly putting more energy into the relationship than I had put into many others. I also was giving Pete attention that was by definition undivided, and relishing the safety of the distance between us by opting to be truthful instead of doling out the white lies that have become the staple of real life. The outside world—the place where I walked around avoiding people I didn't want to deal with, peppering my casual conversations with half-truths, and applying my motto "Let the machine take it" to almost any scenario—was sliding into the periphery of my mind.

13   For me, the time on-line with Pete was far superior to the phone. There were no background noises, no interruptions from "call waiting," no long-distance charges. Through typos and misspellings, he flirted maniacally. "I have an absurd crush on you," he said. "If I like you in person, you must promise to marry me." I was coy and conceited, telling him to get a life, baiting him into complimenting me further, teasing him in a way I would never have dared to do in person, or even on the phone. I would stay up until 3 A.M. typing with him, smiling at the screen, getting so giddy that when I quit I couldn't fall asleep. I was having difficulty recalling what I used to do at night. It was as if he and I lived together in our own quiet space—a space

made all the more intimate because of our conscious decision to block everyone else out. My phone was tied up for hours at a time. No one in the real world could reach me, and I didn't really care.

Since my last serious relationship, I'd had the requisite number 14 of false starts and five-night stands, dates that I wasn't sure were dates, and emphatically casual affairs that buckled under their own inertia. With PFSlider, on the other hand, I may not have known my suitor, but, for the first time in my life, I knew the deal: I was a desired person, the object of a blind man's gaze. He called not only when he said he would call but unexpectedly, just to say hello. He was protected by the shield of the Internet; his guard was not merely down but nonexistent. He let his phone bill grow to towering proportions. He told me that he thought about me all the time, though we both knew that the "me" in his mind consisted largely of himself. He talked about me to his friends, and admitted it. He arranged his holiday schedule around our impending date. He managed to charm me with sports analogies. He didn't hesitate. He was unblinking and unapologetic, all nerviness and balls to the wall.

And so PFSlider became my everyday life. All the tangible stuff 15 fell away. My body did not exist. I had no skin, no hair, no bones. All desire had converted itself into a cerebral current that reached nothing but my frontal lobe. There was no outdoors, no social life, no weather. There was only the computer screen and the phone, my chair, and maybe a glass of water. Most mornings, I would wake up to find a message from PFSlider, composed in Pacific time while I slept in the wee hours. "I had a date last night," he wrote. "And I am not ashamed to say it was doomed from the start because I couldn't stop thinking about you."

I fired back a message slapping his hand. "We must be careful 16 where we tread," I said. This was true but not sincere. I wanted it, all of it. I wanted unfettered affection, soul-mating, true romance. In the weeks that had elapsed since I picked up "is this the real meghan daum?" the real me had undergone some kind of meltdown—a systemic rejection of all the savvy and independence I had worn for years, like a grownup Girl Scout badge.

Pete knew nothing of my scattered, juvenile self, and I did my 17 best to keep it that way. Even though I was heading into my late twenties, I was still a child, ignorant of dance steps and health insurance, a prisoner of credit-card debt and student loans and the nagging feeling that I didn't want anyone to find me until I had pulled myself into some semblance of an adult. The fact that Pete had literally seemed to discover me, as if by turning over a rock, lent us an aura of fate which I actually took half-seriously. Though skepticism seemed like the obvious choice in this strange situation, I discarded it precisely because it was the obvious choice, because I wanted a more interesting narrative than cynicism would ever allow. I was a true believer in the urban dream: the dream of years of struggle, of getting a break, of making it. Like most of my friends, I wanted someone to love me, but I wasn't supposed to need it. To admit to loneliness was to smack the face of progress, to betray the times in which we lived. But PFSlider derailed me. He gave me all of what I'd never even realized I wanted.

18   My addiction to PFSlider's messages indicated a monstrous narcissism, but it also revealed a subtler desire, which I didn't fully understand at that time. My need to experience an old-fashioned kind of courtship was stronger than I had ever imagined. And the fact that technology was providing an avenue for such archaic discourse was a paradox that both fascinated and repelled me. Our relationship had an epistolary quality that put our communication closer to the eighteenth century than to the impending millennium. Thanks to the computer, I was involved in a well-defined courtship, a neat little space in which he and I were both safe to express the panic and the fascination of our mutual affection. Our interaction was refreshingly orderly, noble in its vigor, dignified despite its shamelessness. It was far removed from the randomness of real-life relationships. We had an intimacy that seemed custom-made for our strange, lonely times. It seemed custom-made for me.

19   The day of our date, a week before Christmas, was frigid and sunny. Pete was sitting at the bar of the restaurant when I arrived. We shook hands. For a split second, he leaned toward me with his chin, as if to kiss me. He was shorter than I had pictured, though he was not short. He struck me as clean-cut. He had very nice hands. He wore a very nice shirt. We were seated at a very nice table. I scanned the restaurant for people I knew, saw none, and couldn't decide how I felt about that.

20   He talked, and I heard nothing he said. I stared at his profile and tried to figure out whether I liked him. He seemed to be saying nothing in particular, but he went on forever. Later, we went to the Museum of Natural History and watched a science film about storm chasers. We walked around looking for the dinosaurs, and he talked so much that I wanted to cry. Outside, walking along Central Park West at dusk, through the leaves, past the yellow cabs and the splendid lights of Manhattan at Christmas, he grabbed my hand to kiss me and I didn't let him. I felt as if my brain had been stuffed with cotton. Then, for some reason, I invited him back to my apartment. I gave him a few beers and finally let him kiss me on the lumpy futon in my bedroom. The radiator clanked. The phone rang and the machine

picked up. A car alarm blared outside. A key turned in the door as one
of my roommates came home. I had no sensation at all—only a clear
conviction that I wanted Pete out of my apartment. I wanted to hand
him his coat, close the door behind him, and fight the ensuing emptiness by turning on the computer and taking comfort in PFSlider.

When Pete finally did leave, I berated myself from every angle: 21
for not kissing him on Central Part West, for letting him kiss me at
all, for not liking him, for wanting to like him more than I had wanted
anything in such a long time. I was horrified by the realization that I
had invested so heavily in a made-up character—a character in whose
creation I'd had a greater hand than even Pete himself. How could I,
a person so self-congratulatingly reasonable, have been sucked into a
scenario that was more akin to a television talk show than to the relatively full and sophisticated life I was so convinced I led? How could
I have received a fan letter and allowed it to go this far?

The next day, a huge bouquet of FTD flowers arrived from him.   22
No one had ever sent me flowers before. I forgave him. As human beings with actual flesh and hand gestures and Gap clothing, Pete and
I were utterly incompatible, but I decided to pretend otherwise. He
returned home and we fell back into the computer and the phone, and
I continued to keep the real world safely away from the desk that held
them. Instead of blaming him for my disappointment, I blamed the
earth itself, the invasion of roommates and ringing phones into the
immaculate communication that PFSlider and I had created.

When I pictured him in the weeks that followed, I saw the im-   23
age of a plane lifting off over an overcast city. PFSlider was other-
worldly, more a concept than a person. His romance lay in the notion
of flight, the physics of gravity defiance. So when he offered to send
me a plane ticket to spend the weekend with him in Los Angeles I
took it as an extension of our blissful remoteness, a three-dimensional
E-mail message lasting an entire weekend.

The temperature of the runway at J.F.K. was seven degrees   24
Fahrenheit. Our DC-10 sat for three hours waiting for deicing. Finally, it took off over the frozen city, and the ground below shrank
into a drawing of itself. Phone calls were made, laptop computers
were plopped onto tray tables. The recirculating air dried out my
contact lenses. I watched movies without the sound and told myself
that they were probably better that way. Something about the plastic
interior of the fuselage and the plastic forks and the din of the air and
the engines was soothing and strangely sexy.

Then we descended into LAX. We hit the tarmac, and the seat-   25
belt signs blinked off. I hadn't moved my body in eight hours, and now
I was walking through the tunnel to the gate, my clothes wrinkled, my

hair matted, my hands shaking. When I saw Pete in the terminal, his face seemed to me just as blank and easy to miss as it had the first time I'd met him. He kissed me chastely. On the way out to the parking lot, he told me that he was being seriously considered for a job in New York. He was flying back there next week. If he got the job, he'd be moving within the month. I looked at him in astonishment. Something silent and invisible seemed to fall on us. Outside, the wind was warm, and the Avis and Hertz buses ambled alongside the curb of Terminal 5. The palm trees shook, and the air seemed as heavy and palpable as Pete's hand, which held mine for a few seconds before dropping it to get his car keys out of his pocket. He stood before me, all flesh and preoccupation, and for this I could not forgive him.

26   Gone were the computer, the erotic darkness of the telephone, the clean, single dimension of Pete's voice at 1 A.M. It was nighttime, yet the combination of sight and sound was blinding. It scared me. It turned me off. We went to a restaurant and ate outside on the sidewalk. We strained for conversation, and I tried not to care that we had to. We drove to his apartment and stood under the ceiling light not really looking at each other. Something was happening that we needed to snap out of. Any moment now, I thought. Any moment and we'll be all right. These moments were crowded with elements, with carpet fibers and automobiles and the smells of everything that had a smell. It was all wrong. The physical world had invaded our space.

27   For three days, we crawled along the ground and tried to pull ourselves up. We talked about things that I can no longer remember. We read the Los Angeles *Times* over breakfast. We drove north past Santa Barbara to tour the wine country. I felt like an object that could not be lifted, something that secretly weighed more than the world itself. Everything and everyone around us seemed imbued with a California lightness. I stomped around the countryside, an idiot New Yorker in my clunky shoes and black leather jacket. Not until I studied myself in the bathroom mirror of a highway rest stop did I fully realize the preposterousness of my uniform. I was dressed for war. I was dressed for my regular life.

28   That night, in a tiny town called Solvang, we ate an expensive dinner. We checked into a Marriott and watched television. Pete talked at me and through me and past me. I tried to listen. I tried to talk. But I bored myself and irritated him. Our conversation was a needle that could not be threaded. Still, we played nice. We tried to care, and pretended to keep trying long after we had given up. In the car on the way home, he told me that I was cynical, and I didn't have the presence of mind to ask him just how many cynics he had met who would travel three thousand miles to see someone they barely knew.

Pete drove me to the airport at 7 A.M. so I could make my eight-   29
o'clock flight home. He kissed me goodbye—another chaste peck
that I recognized from countless dinner parties and dud dates. He
said that he'd call me in a few days when he got to New York for his
job interview, which we had discussed only in passing and with no reference to the fact that New York was where I happened to live. I returned home to frozen January. A few days later, he came to New
York, and we didn't see each other. He called me from the plane taking him back to Los Angeles to tell me, through the static, that he had
got the job. He was moving to my city.

PFSlider was dead. There would be no meeting him in distant   30
hotel lobbies during the baseball season. There would be no more
phone calls or E-mail messages. In a single moment, Pete had completed his journey out of our mating dance and officially stepped into
the regular world—the world that gnawed at me daily, the world that
fostered those five-night stands, the world where romance could not
be sustained, because so many of us simply did not know how to do
it. Instead, we were all chitchat and leather jackets, bold proclaimers
of all that we did not need. But what struck me most about this affair
was the unpredictable nature of our demise. Unlike most cyber-
romances, which seem to come fully equipped with the inevitable set
of misrepresentations and false expectations, PFSlider and I had
played it fairly straight. Neither of us had lied. We'd done the best we
could. Our affair had died from natural causes rather than virtual ones.

Within a two-week period after I returned from Los Angeles, at   31
least seven people confessed to me the vagaries of their own E-mail
affairs. This topic arose, unprompted, in the course of normal conversation. I heard most of these stories in the close confines of smoky
bars and crowded restaurants, and we all shook our heads in bewil-
derment as we told our tales, our eyes focussed on some point in the
distance. Four of these people had met their correspondents, by trav-
elling from New Haven to Baltimore, from New York to Montana,
from Texas to Virginia, and from New York to Johannesburg. These
were normal people, writers and lawyers and scientists. They were all
smart, attractive, and more than a little sheepish about admitting just
how deeply they had been sucked in. Mostly, it was the courtship ritual that had seduced us. E-mail had become an electronic epistle, a
yearned-for rule book. It allowed us to do what was necessary to experience love. The Internet was not responsible for our remote, frag-
mented lives. The problem was life itself.

The story of PFSlider still makes me sad, not so much because   32
we no longer have anything to do with each other but because it forces
me to see the limits and the perils of daily life with more clarity than

I used to. After I realized that our relationship would never transcend the screen and the phone—that, in fact, our face-to-face knowledge of each other had permanently contaminated the screen and the phone—I hit the pavement again, went through the motions of everyday life, said hello and goodbye to people in the regular way. If Pete and I had met at a party, we probably wouldn't have spoken to each other for more than ten minutes, and that would have made life easier but also less interesting. At the same time, it terrifies me to admit to a firsthand understanding of the way the heart and the ego are snarled and entwined like diseased trees that have folded in on each other. Our need to worship somehow fuses with our need to be worshipped. It upsets me still further to see how inaccessibility can make this entanglement so much more intoxicating. But I'm also thankful that I was forced to unpack the raw truth of my need and stare at it for a while. It was a dare I wouldn't have taken in three dimensions.

33   The last time I saw Pete, he was in New York, three thousand miles away from what had been his home, and a million miles away from PFSlider. In a final gesture of decency, in what I later realized was the most ordinary kind of closure, he took me out to dinner. As the few remaining traces of affection turned into embarrassed regret, we talked about nothing. He paid the bill. He drove me home in a rental car that felt as arbitrary and impersonal as what we now were to each other.

34   Pete had known how to get me where I lived until he came to where I lived: then he became as unmysterious as anyone next door. The world had proved to be too cluttered and too fast for us, too polluted to allow the thing we'd attempted through technology ever to grow in the earth. PFSlider and I had joined the angry and exhausted living. Even if we met on the street, we wouldn't recognize each other, our particular version of intimacy now obscured by the branches and bodies and falling debris that make up the physical world.

QUESTIONS ON SUBJECT AND PURPOSE

1. What is a "virtual" love?
2. In paragraph 18, Daum writes, "My need to experience an old-fashioned kind of courtship was stronger than I had ever imagined." How could an Internet romance be old-fashioned?
3. What is Daum saying or implying about "real" relationships in our society?

QUESTIONS ON STRATEGY AND AUDIENCE

1. What is the central contrast in Daum's essay?
2. The essay can be roughly divided into half. Where does the second half of the essay begin? What is the event that begins the second half?
3. Realistically, how large is Daum's audience? That is, to whom is she writing? How did you react to her essay?

QUESTIONS ON VOCABULARY AND STYLE

1. In paragraph 12, Daum writes: "I had previously considered cyber-communication an *oxymoron*." What is an "oxymoron"? What does she mean by that sentence?
2. Pete accuses Daum of being "cynical" (paragraph 28). What does that mean?
3. Be prepared to define the following words: *construed* (paragraph 1), *palpable* (5), *volatile* (5), *innocuous* (6), *conceit* (6), *periphery* (12), *unfettered* (16), *archaic* (18), *epistolary* (18), *berated* (21), *imbued* (27), *demise* (30), *vagaries* (31).

WRITING SUGGESTIONS

1. **For Your Journal.** Think about the times in your relationships—with a family member, a close friend, someone you were dating, someone to whom you might have been engaged or even married—when you suddenly realized something about the other person that really changed the way in which you "saw" that person. It could be a change for the better or for the worse. What you are looking for basically is a contrast—a before and an after. In your journal, first, make a list of possible subjects and, second, write two sentences for each about the before and after experience.
2. **For a Paragraph.** Using your journal as a prewriting exercise, explore one of these before and after situations in a paragraph.
3. **For an Essay.** Expand your paragraph writing into an essay. Look back at the guidelines for the assignment above. Remember that you are basically working on a contrast—what you had thought or assumed before and the reality that you discovered after.

4. **For Research.** The remarkable thing about Daum's "virtual" relationship was that it was honest—neither person pretended to be different from whom they were; neither "doled out white lies." Why do people often change their identities or their personalities in cyberspace? Research the problem. What you are exploring are the contrasts that occur between people's real life identities and personalities and the virtual identities and personalities that they assume. What do we know about these contrasts? Why do they occur? You might find that databases of articles are better sources for information than your school's on-line library catalog. Check with a reference librarian for search strategy suggestions. Be sure to document any direct quotations, paraphrases, or ideas that you take from your sources.

 WEBSITE LINK

Other essays by Daum are available on-line. Links are available at the *Reader*'s Website. Web search engines also turn up a wide variety of sources about on-line courtships.

 WRITING LINK: SENTENCE VARIETY

At several points in the essay, Daum intentionally repeats the same sentence structure—for example, the final three sentences in paragraph 3; the first three sentences in paragraph 5; the final nine sentences in paragraph 14. See if you can locate other examples. Specifically, what types of opening structures does Daum repeat and why? Usually teachers caution students about repeating the same types of sentences. Are they effective here? If so, why? What does this suggest about your own writing?

PREWRITING SUGGESTIONS FOR COMPARISON AND CONTRAST

1. Jot down ideas on possible subjects that might be compared or contrasted. Make lists, freewrite, brainstorm, whatever works best for you. At first just concentrate on generating ideas.
2. Once you have a working list, develop a series of points on which the two subjects might be compared or contrasted. Number those points in descending order of importance.
3. Explain in one sentence (a thesis) why you are making this comparison or contrast.
4. Remember that your points of comparison and contrast must be parallel in grammatical form. Look at your list of points and rewrite any that are not parallel.
5. Decide on whether the best organizational strategy will be point-by-point, subject-by-subject, or a mix of the two. Plan the organization of your paper by making an outline.

REWRITING SUGGESTIONS FOR COMPARISON AND CONTRAST

1. Look carefully at the points of comparison or contrast that you have developed. Are they truly significant or interesting? No one wants you to list every possible comparison or contrast. Concentrate on the key ones. Have you adequately developed each point? For example, are the body paragraphs in your draft more than two or three sentences long?
2. Evaluate your organizational strategy. Experiment with another order. Cut apart your paragraphs with scissors and move the blocks around.
3. Look again at your introduction. Ask some friends to read it. On the basis of your introduction, do they want to keep reading?
4. Honestly evaluate your conclusion. Did you just stop, or did you really write a conclusion? Does your final paragraph seem to emphasize the points that you are making in the essay? Does it reinforce your thesis?
5. Check your title. Every paper needs a real title—not something descriptive like "Essay #1." If necessary, force yourself to write at least three different titles before you choose one.

PROCESS

A recipe in a cookbook
A textbook discussion of how the body converts food into energy
    and fat
Directions on how to install a CD changer in your car
An on-line explanation of an earthquake

What do each of these have in common? Each is a process analysis—either a set of directions for how to do something (make lasagna or install a CD changer) or a description of how something happens or is done (food is converted or the earth "quakes"). These two different types of process writing have two different purposes.

The function of a set of directions is to allow the reader to duplicate the process. For example, *The Amy Vanderbilt Complete Book of Etiquette* offers the following step-by-step advice to the young executive woman about how to handle paying for a business lunch or dinner.

> No one likes a man who is known never to pick up a check. In today's world, people are going to feel the same about a woman who is known never to pick up a tab. The woman executive is going to have to learn how to pay gracefully when it's her turn.
>
> In order to save embarrassment all around, who will pay for the next business lunch should be decided without question in advance. If it's a woman's turn, she should make it very clear over the telephone or face to face when the appointment is made that she will be paying. She has only to say with a smile that it really is her turn. She should name the time and the place, call the restaurant, and make the reservation in her name.

At the end of lunch she should unobtrusively ask for the bill, add the waiter's tip to the total without an agonizing exercise in mathematics, and then use her credit card or sign her name and her company's address to the back of the check (if she has a charge account there). If she does this quietly, no one around them need be aware of her actions.

Several readings in this chapter similarly offer advice or instructions. Lars Eighner in "My Daily Dives in the Dumpster" describes both how to "dive" into dumpsters and what the process eventually taught him about life and human acquisitiveness. Diane Cole offers the reader suggestions on how to respond to distasteful and bigoted remarks. Charlie Drozdyk offers advice to soon-to-graduate college students on how to "get the job you want after graduation."

Not every example of process is a set of directions about how to do something. Process can also be used to tell the reader how something happens or is made. Harold McGee, for example, explains to his readers how chewing gum, the quintessential American product, is made. McGee's paragraph is not a recipe. Instead, its function is to provide a general view of the manufacturing process.

Today, chewing gum is made mostly of synthetic polymers, especially styrene-butadiene rubber and polyvinyl acetate, though 10 to 20% of some brands is still accounted for by chicle or jelutong, a latex from the Far East. The crude gum base is first filtered, dried, and then cooked in water until syrupy. Powdered sugar and corn syrup are mixed in, then flavorings and softeners—vegetable oil derivatives that make the gum easier to chew—and the material is cooked, kneaded to an even, smooth texture, cut, rolled thin, and cut again into strips, and packaged. The final product is about 60% sugar, 20% corn syrup, and 20% gum materials.

Nora Ephron in "Revision and Life" describes her own revision process; David Brooks describes the process through which martyrdom has become an end rather than a means in the Arab-Israeil conflict; Lynne Sharon Schwartz records the role of "The Page Turner" in a concert performance. None of these essays is meant to describe a process that we are to perform or imitate. Ephron describes her own process of revision as also a process of maturing or aging. Brooks attempts to explain a phenomena that many Americans do not understand. Schwartz describes the process of watching a concert from the viewpoint of an audience member who, in turn, focuses on the process followed by the pianist's page turner.

How Do You Choose a Subject to Write About?

Choosing a subject is not a problem if you have been given a specific assignment—to describe how a congressional bill becomes a law, how a chemistry experiment was performed, how to write an A paper for your English course. Often, however, you have to choose your own subject. Several considerations are crucial in making that decision.

First, choose a subject that can be adequately described or analyzed in the space you have available. When Nora Ephron in "Revision and Life" traces her revision process, she isolates three decades in her life—her 20s, 30s, and 40s. She alternates paragraphs dealing with her evolving attitudes toward revision with paragraphs establishing links between revision and life. At 20, she revised nothing; at 40, she is increasingly drawn to revision. Ephron does not try to identify every change that occurred during those three decades. Instead, she confines her analysis to the major periods.

Second, in a process analysis, as in any other writing assignment, identify the audience to whom you are writing. What does that audience already know about your subject? Are you writing to a general audience, an audience of your fellow classmates, or a specialized audience? You do not want to bore your reader with the obvious, nor do you want to lose your reader in a tangle of unfamiliar terms and concepts. Your choice of subject and certainly your approach to it should be determined by your audience. Charlie Drozdyk's essay on job-seeking strategies for young college students appeared in *Rolling Stone* magazine; to appeal to readers of this publication, he focused on interviewing people who held relatively "glamorous" positions in publishing, on Wall Street, in advertising, in fashion design, in interior design, and in television. David Brooks's essay appeared in *Atlantic Monthly*, a literary magazine aimed at older, sophisticated readers. Brooks writes to an American audience, an audience who is puzzled by the suicide bombings in the Middle East, but also probably more sympathetic to the Israelis than to the Palestinians. Identifying your audience—what they might be interested in, what they already know—will help in both selecting a subject and deciding how or what to write about it.

How Do You Structure a Process Paper?

If you have ever tried to assemble something from a set of directions, you know how important it is that each step or stage in the process be clearly defined and properly placed in the sequence. Because process

"Some assembly required." Most of us have come to fear those words. Directions—the most common form of process writing—must be clear and correctly ordered. The success of a set of directions is always easy to measure—did they work? *www.CartoonStock.com*

always involves a series of events or steps that must be done or must occur in proper order, the fundamental structure for a process paragraph or essay will be chronological.

Since proper order is essential, begin your planning by making a list of the various steps in the process. Once your list seems complete, arrange the items in the order in which they are performed or in which they occur. Check to make sure that nothing has been omitted or misplaced. If your process is a description of how to do or make something, you should check your arranged list by performing the process according to the directions you have assembled so far. This ordered list will serve as the outline for your process paper.

Converting your list or outline into a paragraph or an essay is the next step. Be sure that all of the phrases on your outline have been turned into complete sentences and that any technical terms have been carefully explained for your reader. You will also need some way of signaling to your reader each step or stage in the process. On your list, you probably numbered the steps, but in your paragraph or essay you generally cannot use such a device. More commonly, process papers employ various types of step or time markers to indicate order. Step markers like *first, second,* and *third* can be used at the beginning of sentences or paragraphs devoted to each individual stage. Time markers like *begin, next, in three minutes,* or *while this is being done* remind the reader of the proper chronological sequence.

SAMPLE STUDENT ESSAY

As part of her student-teaching assignment, Julie Anne Halbfish was asked by her cooperating teacher to write out a set of directions on how to play dreidel, a game associated with the Jewish holiday Hanukkah. Most of the students in the seventh-grade class in which Julie was student-teaching had never played the game.

EARLIER DRAFT

HOW TO PLAY DREIDEL

A dreidel is a small top with four sides. On each side is a Hebrew letter. The letters correspond to the first letters in each word of the Hebrew phrase "<u>Nes gadol haya sham</u>," which means "A great miracle happened there." That phrase refers to the military victory of the Maccabees over the Greeks and the story of the small jug of olive oil that burned for eight days. The corresponding Hebrew letters on the dreidel are called <u>nun</u> [נ], <u>gimel</u> [ג], <u>hay</u> [ה], and <u>shin</u> [ש].

Many people have heard the Hanukkah song "Dreidel," but most are unfamiliar with how to play the traditional children's game of the same name. The rules are actually quite simple.

To start the game, every player receives ten pieces of "money" (usually peanuts, candies, pennies, or anything else the players choose to play for) and a dreidel. Each player puts two pieces of money into the "pot" and then spins the dreidel. When the dreidel stops spinning, the letter that is on the side facing up determines how many pieces the player takes from or adds to the pot. If the dreidel lands on <u>nun</u>, the player takes nothing. If it lands on <u>gimel</u>, the player takes all of the pot. If the dreidel lands on <u>hay</u>, the player receives half of the pot. Finally, if the dreidel lands on shin, the player must put two additional pieces into the pot. After as many rounds of play as the players want, the game ends, and whoever has the most goodies is declared the winner. However, the reason so many people love this game is that everyone ends up with treats to enjoy, so nobody loses.

After Julie had finished a draft of her essay, she showed her paper to Adam Helenic, a fellow classmate. At first, Adam simply praised the draft—"It's good; it's clear; it's fine, Julie." But Julie would not settle for simple approval. When pushed, Adam made several suggestions. Since many students have heard the dreidel song, he urged her somehow to work at least part of the song into the essay—maybe as an attention-getting introduction. He also suggested that she reorder paragraphs 1 and 2 and that she tighten up her prose in a number of places. When Julie revised her set of directions, she tried to incorporate all of the changes that Adam had suggested. Interestingly, when Julie set out to check her "facts" about the song and the game, she used the World Wide Web. She found a computerized dreidel game that you might like to try (you can play at http://www.jcn18.com/spinner.htm).

Revised Draft

HOW TO PLAY DREIDEL

I have a little dreidel,
I made it out of clay.
And when it's dry and ready,
Oh, dreidel I shall play!
It has a lovely body,
With legs so short and thin.
And when it gets all tired,
It drops and then I win.

During Hanukkah, we often hear the "Dreidel" song, but most people have never actually played the traditional children's game to which the song refers. The game is quite simple, and since every player is sure to win something, dreidel is a popular Hanukkah game.

A dreidel is a small, four-sided top, traditionally made out of clay. On each side is a Hebrew letter. The letters correspond to the first letters in each word of the Hebrew phrase "<u>Nes gadol haya sham</u>," which means "A great miracle happened there." That phrase refers to the military victory of the Maccabees over the Greeks and the story of the small jug of olive oil that miraculously burned for eight days. The corresponding Hebrew letters on the dreidel are called <u>nun</u> [נ], <u>gimel</u> [ג], <u>hay</u> [ה], and <u>shin</u> [ש].

To start the game, every player receives ten pieces of "money" (usually peanuts, candies, pennies, or anything else the players choose to play for) and a dreidel. Each player puts two pieces of money into the "pot" and then spins the dreidel. When the dreidel is spinning, the players are encouraged to sing a Hanukkah song or to shout "<u>Gimel</u>!" When the dreidel stops spinning, the letter that is on the side facing up determines how many pieces the player takes from or adds to the pot. If the dreidel lands on <u>nun</u>, the player takes nothing. If it lands on <u>gimel</u>, the player takes all of the pot. If the dreidel lands on <u>hay</u>, the player receives half of the pot. Finally, if the dreidel lands on <u>shin</u>, the player must put two additional pieces into the pot.

After as many rounds of play as the players want, the game ends, and whoever has the most goodies is declared the winner. Whether you win or not, no one really loses since everyone ends up with treats to enjoy.

SOME THINGS TO REMEMBER

1. Choose a subject that can be analyzed and described within the space you have available.
2. Remember that process takes one of two forms, reflecting its purpose: either to tell the reader how to do something or to tell the reader how something happens. Make sure that you have a purpose clearly in mind before you start your paper.
3. Identify your audience and write to that audience. Ask yourself, "Will my audience be interested in what I am writing about?" and "How much does my audience know about this subject?"

4. Make a list of the steps or stages in the process.

5. Order or arrange a list, checking to make sure nothing is omitted or misplaced.

6. Convert the list into paragraphs using complete sentences. Remember to define any unfamiliar terms or concepts.

7. Use step or time markers to indicate the proper sequence in the process.

8. Check your process one final time to make sure that nothing has been omitted. If you are describing how to do something, use your paper as a guide to the process. If you are describing how something happens, ask a friend to read your process analysis to see whether it is clear.

VISUALIZING PROCESS

Any set of illustrated instructions is a perfect example of process at work: First, attach piece A to piece B with fastener C. As anyone who has ever assembled anything knows, illustrated, step-by-step instructions are vitally important. Mere words aren't enough; illustrations must accompany the text. Not every process narrative, however, tells us how to do something. Process can also be used to explain to us how something is done or how it works. This short, illustrated article on the Zamboni ice-resurfacing machine is an example of a visualized process. The illustrations that accompany the text allow us to understand how an ice-resurfacing machine works. See page 316.

PROCESS AS A LITERARY STRATEGY

Janice Mirikitani, a third-generation Japanese American, uses process in her poem "Recipe." As the title and its list of "ingredients" suggests, the poem might at first seem like a set of directions that you would find in a magazine—"how to create the illusion of having round eyes." As you read the poem, think first about how Mirikitani uses the elements of a process analysis to structure her poem. See page 317.

WORKING KNOWLEDGE

ICE-RESURFACING MACHINES

by Richard F. Zamboni
President, Frank J. Zamboni & Co.

I f you have ever been to a skating rink or watched figure skating or hockey on television, you have probably seen my name before. Chances are good it was on the front of the unusual-looking vehicle that periodically traveled around the rink, making the chipped, pockmarked ice surface as smooth as glass.

The first such ice-resurfacing machine was built in the 1940s by my father, Frank J. Zamboni, who with his brother and cousin owned and operated the Paramount Iceland skating rink in Paramount, Calif. That ungainly but effective invention, the result of seven years of trial-and-error development, went into regular use at the Paramount rink in 1949. A year later figure-skating legend and actress Sonja Henie (*above, left*) saw the machine in use and immediately ordered two of them for her touring skating show. Those two, the third and fourth machines built, were seen in arenas all over the U.S. and Europe, effectively announcing the arrival of mechanized ice resurfacing. Today, although it has one competitor in Canada and five in Europe, Frank J. Zamboni & Co.

EARLY ZAMBONIS, such as this one from 1950, were built around existing jeeps or Jeep chassis.

has become literally synonymous with ice resurfacing and is the largest producer by far of ice-resurfacing machines. Some 6,000 of our machines are in operation, at least two thirds of the world's total. The current line consists of seven models ranging from small, tractor-pulled units starting at about $7,000 to a state-of-the-art, battery-powered model that costs around $80,000.

ZAMBONI MACHINE has a large bin in front to collect ice shavings scraped by a blade in the conditioner, behind the rear tires. Tanks underneath the bin and in front of the driver store water for conditioning and cleaning the ice.

TANK FOR WASH WATER

VERTICAL SCREW CONVEYOR

TANK FOR FRESH WATER

WASH WATER SUCTION PUMP

WASH WATER HOSE

HORIZONTAL SCREW CONVEYOR

TOWEL

BLADE

ICE-MAKING WATER DISCHARGE

WASH WATER DISCHARGE

CONDITIONER at the rear of the machine has a blade that shaves a thin layer of ice as screw conveyors remove the shavings. Meanwhile jets of water clean the ice by flushing dirt and debris toward a vacuum hose (*orange*). This dirty water is filtered for reuse. Finally, a towel spreads the ice-making water, which sprays out of holes in a discharge pipe (*light blue*) at 82 degrees Celsius (180 degrees Fahrenheit).

RECIPE

Janice Mirikitani

Round Eyes
Ingredients: scissors, Scotch magic transparent tape.
eyeliner—water based, black.
Optional: false eyelashes.
Cleanse face thoroughly.
For best results, powder entire face, including eyelids.
(lighter shades suited to total effect desired)
With scissors, cut magic tape ¹⁄₁₆" wide, ¼"–½" long—depending on length of
eyelid.
Stick firmly onto mid-upper eyelid area
(looking down into handmirror facilitates finding adequate surface)
If using false eyelashes, affix first on lid, folding any excess lid over the base
of eyelash with glue.
Paint black eyeliner on tape and entire lid.
Do not cry.

DISCUSSION QUESTIONS

1. How do you think that Mirikitani feels about "round eyes"? Is she trying simply to describe how to create that illusion? Is her poem trying to be "helpful"?
2. How would you characterize the tone of the poem? What in the poem provides evidence for your viewpoint?
3. How does the process structure contribute to the poem's effect? For example, what initial expectation did you have about the poem? Did your expectations change as you read? Where?
4. Is there anything in the "steps" of the process that seems unusual?
5. What makes this a poem and not a helpful set of instructions?

WRITING SUGGESTIONS

As this poem suggests, process does not have to be used in a simple, expository way. Mirikitani uses it to make a comment about a social issue, about cultural pressure and values. Explore a similar issue using a process model—either a set of directions or a description of how something works. Some possibilities for topics might include:

a. Underage drinking or smoking
b. The desire to change your "looks" (for example, hair coloring, body piercing, hair straightening or curling, plastic surgery, purging)
c. The desire to conform to your peers (for example, behavior, dress, attitude)

Using Process in Writing for Your Other Courses

Writing that explains processes is common in the sciences, where you may often be asked to demonstrate your understanding of natural biological or physical processes by tracing them in detail. Although less common in the humanities, writing assignments requiring this pattern do turn up with some frequency in courses that deal with contemporary institutions and culture, courses that focus on any aspect of human development, and courses for which writing instructions might be part of the curriculum. Here are some examples of writing assignments that would require you to use the process pattern.

- **Life Sciences.** On an exam, you might be asked to trace the life cycle of a particular organism.
- **Communications.** For a research project on the telecommunications industry, you might write a paper recounting the stages involved in the development of a new television series.
- **Computer Science.** As part of a team developing an original software program, you might be asked to write a user's manual documenting how to use the program.
- **American Government.** On an essay exam, you might be asked to examine in detail the procedure by which a bill is introduced in Congress and ultimately enacted into law.
- **Physical Education.** As part of teacher training, you might be asked to write out instructions for a particular game or exercise.
- **Psychology.** For a short paper on learning disabilities, you might trace the cognitive process that results in the reversal of letters that troubles many dyslexic readers.

VISIT THE PRENTICE HALL READER'S WEBSITE

When you have finished reading an essay, check out the additional material available at the *Reader's* Website at www.prenhall.com/miller. For each reading, you will find a list of related readings connected with the topic or the author; additional background information; a group of relevant "hot-linked" Web resources (just click your computer's mouse and automatically visit the sites listed); and still more writing suggestions.

DESCRIBING A PROCESS

The World Wide Web is home to thousands of "how to . . ." process descriptions. Using a Web search engine, locate a subject of interest to you. Better yet, read the "help with searching" notes on your favorite search engine and learn how to improve your on-line searching techniques. Some possible sites to explore, along with paragraph writing assignments, can be found at the *Reader's* Website.

MY DAILY DIVES IN THE DUMPSTER

Lars Eighner

Born in 1948, Lars Eighner grew up in Houston, Texas. He attended the University of Texas at Austin but dropped out before graduation to do social work. In the mid-1980s, he lost his job as an attendant at a mental institution, which launched him on a three-year nightmare as a homeless person, with his dog, Lizbeth, as his companion. He later reworked these experiences as a book, Travels with Lizbeth *(1993), the final manuscript of which was written on a personal computer that Eighner found in a dumpster.*

On Writing: *Advice from Eighner's Website: "The best thing you can do for your writing is to learn to revise effectively. Sure, some natural geniuses may never have to revise a word, but the number of writers who consider themselves geniuses must outnumber the true geniuses by a factor of a thousand. And yes, some writers who practice revision for a long time eventually learn to avoid most mistakes so that their first drafts do not need much revision. But everyone else needs to* revise and revise and revise. *Putting a work through a spelling checker or a grammar checker is not revision. . . . Revision means changing words and phrases and sometimes changing whole sentences and paragraphs. Almost everyone's writing needs this kind of revision."*

BEFORE READING

Connecting: If you came across someone "diving" into a dumpster, what assumptions would you be likely to make about that person?

Anticipating: One would hope that few of Eighner's readers will ever have to dive into dumpsters to survive. What then can readers learn from his essay?

1   I began Dumpster diving about a year before I became homeless.

2   I prefer the term "scavenging" and use the word "scrounging" when I mean to be obscure. I have heard people, evidently meaning to be polite, use the word "foraging," but I prefer to reserve that word for gathering nuts and berries and such, which I do also, according to the season and opportunity.

3   I like the frankness of the word "scavenging." I live from the refuse of others. I am a scavenger. I think it a sound and honorable niche, although if I could I would naturally prefer to live the com-

fortable consumer life, perhaps—and only perhaps—as a slightly less wasteful consumer owing to what I have learned as a scavenger.

Except for jeans, all my clothes come from Dumpsters. Boom 4 boxes, candles, bedding, toilet paper, medicine, books, a typewriter, a virgin male love doll, change sometimes amounting to many dollars: All came from Dumpsters. And, yes, I eat from Dumpsters too.

There are a predictable series of stages that a person goes 5 through in learning to scavenge. At first the new scavenger is filled with disgust and self-loathing. He is ashamed of being seen and may lurk around trying to duck behind things, or he may try to dive at night. (In fact, this is unnecessary, since most people instinctively look away from scavengers.)

Every grain of rice seems to be a maggot. Everything seems to 6 stink. The scavenger can wipe the egg yolk off the found can, but he cannot erase the stigma of eating garbage from his mind.

This stage passes with experience. The scavenger finds a pair of 7 running shoes that fit and look and smell brand-new. He finds a pocket calculator in perfect working order. He finds pristine ice cream, still frozen, more than he can eat or keep. He begins to understand: People do throw away perfectly good stuff, a lot of perfectly good stuff.

At this stage he may become lost and never recover. All the 8 Dumpster divers I have known come to the point of trying to acquire everything they touch. Why not take it, they reason, it is all free. This is, of course, hopeless, and most divers come to realize that they must restrict themselves to items of relatively immediate utility.

The finding of objects is becoming something of an urban art. Even 9 respectable, employed people will sometimes find something tempting sticking out of a Dumpster or standing beside one. Quite a number of people, not all of them of the bohemian type, are willing to brag that they found this or that piece in the trash.

But eating from Dumpsters is the thing that separates the dilet- 10 tanti from the professionals. Eating safely involves three principles: using the senses and common sense to evaluate the condition of the found materials; knowing the Dumpsters of a given area and checking them regularly; and seeking always to answer the question, Why was this discarded?

Perhaps everyone who has a kitchen and a regular supply of 11 groceries has, at one time or another, eaten half a sandwich before discovering mold on the bread, or has gotten a mouthful of milk before realizing the milk had turned. Nothing of the sort is likely to happen to a Dumpster diver because he is constantly reminded that most food is discarded for a reason.

12   Yet perfectly good food can be found in Dumpsters. Canned goods, for example, turn up fairly often in the Dumpsters I frequent. All except the most phobic people would be willing to eat from a can even if it came from a Dumpster. I have few qualms about dry foods such as crackers, cookies, cereal, chips, and pasta if they are free of visible contaminates and still dry and crisp. Raw fruits and vegetables with intact skins seem perfectly safe to me, excluding, of course, the obviously rotten. Many are discarded for minor imperfections that can be pared away. Chocolate is often discarded only because it has become discolored as the cocoa butter de-emulsified.

13   I began scavenging by pulling pizzas out of the Dumpster behind a pizza delivery shop. In general, prepared food requires caution, but in this case I knew what time the shop closed and went to the Dumpster as soon as the last of the help left.

14   Because the workers at these places are usually inexperienced, pizzas are often made with the wrong topping, baked incorrectly, or refused on delivery for being cold. The products to be discarded are boxed up because inventory is kept by counting boxes: A boxed pizza can be written off; an unboxed pizza does not exist. So I had a steady supply of fresh, sometimes warm pizza.

15   The area I frequent is inhabited by many affluent college students. I am not here by chance; the Dumpsters are very rich. Students throw out many good things, including food, particularly at the end of the semester and before and after breaks. I find it advantageous to keep an eye on the academic calendar.

16   A typical discard is a half jar of peanut butter—though nonorganic peanut butter does not require refrigeration and is unlikely to spoil in any reasonable time. Occasionally I find a cheese with a spot of mold, which, of course, I just pare off, and because it is obvious why the cheese was discarded, I treat it with less suspicion than an apparently perfect cheese found in similar circumstances. One of my favorite finds is yogurt—often discarded, still sealed, when the expiration date has passed—because it will keep for several days, even in warm weather.

17   I avoid ethnic foods I am unfamiliar with. If I do not know what it is supposed to look or smell like when it is good, I cannot be certain I will be able to tell if it is bad.

18   No matter how careful I am I still get dysentery at least once a month, oftener in warm weather. I do not want to paint too romantic a picture. Dumpster diving has serious drawbacks as a way of life.

19   Though I have a proprietary feeling about my Dumpsters, I don't mind my direct competitors, other scavengers, as much as I hate the sodacan scroungers.

I have tried scrounging aluminum cans with an able-bodied companion, and afoot we could make no more than a few dollars a day. I can extract the necessities of life from the Dumpsters directly with far less effort than would be required to accumulate the equivalent value in aluminum. Can scroungers, then, are people who *must* have small amounts of cash—mostly drug addicts and winos.   20

I do not begrudge them the cans, but can scroungers tend to tear up the Dumpsters, littering the area and mixing the contents. There are precious few courtesies among scavengers, but it is a common practice to set aside surplus items: pairs of shoes, clothing, canned goods, and such. A true scavenger hates to see good stuff go to waste, and what he cannot use he leaves in good condition in plain sight. Can scroungers lay waste to everything in their path and will stir one of a pair of good shoes to the bottom of a Dumpster to be lost or ruined in the muck. They become so specialized that they can see only cans and earn my contempt by passing up change, canned goods, and readily hockable items.   21

Can scroungers will even go through individual garbage cans, something I have never seen a scavenger do. Going through individual garbage cans without spreading litter is almost impossible, and litter is likely to reduce the public's tolerance of scavenging. But my strongest reservation about going through individual garbage cans is that this seems to me a very personal kind of invasion, one to which I would object if I were a homeowner.   22

Though Dumpsters seem somehow less personal than garbage cans, they still contain bank statements, bills, correspondence, pill bottles, and other sensitive information. I avoid trying to draw conclusions about the people who dump in the Dumpsters I frequent. I think it would be unethical to do so, although I know many people will find the idea of scavenger ethics too funny for words.   23

Occasionally a find tells a story. I once found a small paper bag containing some unused condoms, several partial tubes of flavored sexual lubricant, a partially used compact of birth control pills, and the torn pieces of a picture of a young man. Clearly,the woman was through with him and planning to give up sex altogether.   24

Dumpster things are often sad—abandoned teddy bears, shredded wedding albums, despaired-of sales kits. I find diaries and journals. College students also discard their papers; I am horrified to discover the kind of paper that now merits an A in an undergraduate course.   25

Dumpster diving is outdoor work, often surprisingly pleasant. It is not entirely predictable; things of interest turn up every day, and some days there are finds of great value. I am always very pleased   26 when I can turn up exactly the thing I most wanted to find. Yet in spite of the element of chance, scavenging, more than most other pursuits, tends to yield returns in some proportion to the effort and intelligence brought to bear.

27   I think of scavenging as a modern form of self-reliance. After ten years of government service, where everything is geared to the lowest common denominator, I find work that rewards initiative and effort refreshing. Certainly I would be happy to have a sinecure again, but I am not heart-broken to be without one.

28   I find from the experience of scavenging two rather deep lessons. The first is to take what I can use and let the rest go. I have come to think that there is no value in the abstract. A thing I cannot use or make useful, perhaps by trading, has no value, however fine or rare it may be. (I mean useful in the broad sense—some art, for example, I would think valuable.)

29   The second lesson is the transience of material being. I do not suppose that ideas are immortal, but certainly they are longer-lived than material objects.

30   The things I find in Dumpsters, the love letters and rag dolls of so many lives, remind me of this lesson. Many times in my travels I have lost everything but the clothes on my back. Now I hardly pick up a thing without envisioning the time I will cast it away. This, I think, is a healthy state of mind. Almost everything I have now has already been cast out at least once, proving that what I own is valueless to someone.

31   I find that my desire to grab for the gaudy bauble has been largely sated. I think this is an attitude I share with the very wealthy— we both know there is plenty more where whatever we have came from. Between us are the rat-race millions who have confounded their selves with the objects they grasp and who nightly scavenge the cable channels looking for they know not what.

32   I am sorry for them.

QUESTIONS ON SUBJECT AND PURPOSE

1. Is the subject of Eighner's essay simply how to "dive" into a dumpster? What other points does he make?

2. A substantial part of the essay deals with scavenging for food. Why does Eighner devote so much space to this?

3. What larger or more general lesson or truth does Eighner see in his experiences? For example, for whom does Eighner say he feels sorry at the end of the essay?

QUESTIONS ON STRATEGY AND AUDIENCE

1. In what ways does the essay use process as a writing strategy?
2. What are the "predictable stages" that a scavenger goes through?
3. What assumptions does Eighner make about his audience?

QUESTIONS ON VOCABULARY AND STYLE

1. Why does Eighner prefer the term *scavenging* to a more ambiguous or better-sounding term?
2. In what way is Eighner's final sentence ironic? Why might he choose to make it a separate paragraph?
3. Be prepared to define the following words: *niche* (paragraph 3), *stigma* (6), *pristine* (7), *bohemian* (9), *dilettanti* (10), *phobic* (12), *qualms* (12), *de-emulsified* (12), *affluent* (15), *proprietary* (19), *sinecure* (27), *transience* (29), *gaudy* (31), *bauble* (31), *sated* (31).

WRITING SUGGESTIONS

1. **For Your Journal.** Suppose that suddenly you found yourself without a full-time job or financial support from your family. What would you do? Using an ordered sequence, plan out the steps that you would take in trying to deal with the situation.
2. **For a Paragraph.** In a world in which many Americans can find only low-paying jobs with no benefits, what advice could you offer to a young high school student today? In a paragraph organized according to a process structure, address that audience. Be sure to have a specific point or thesis to your paragraph. Try to avoid clichéd answers; just saying "go to college," for example, is not particularly good advice since many college students are not able to find well-paying, full-time jobs.
3. **For an Essay.** Where are you going in your life, and how do you plan to get there? What are your objectives, goals, or aspirations? Where do you hope to be in ten years? In twenty years? What are you doing now to try to achieve those goals? What should you be doing? In an essay, honestly examine your directions and your actions.
4. **For Research.** With corporate and business "downsizing," many Americans have suddenly found themselves out of work.

As advice for those trapped in such a situation, write a guide
to the resources available to the newly unemployed. Use a
process strategy as a way of providing step-by-step advice to
your audience. Contact local and state agencies to see what
help is available and how one goes about making an
application. Be sure to document your sources—including
interviews—wherever appropriate.

WEBSITE LINK

Eighner has a home page on the Web that includes a wide range of
information about his books, his other publications, and a bibliography of articles about him and his work. Check the Website.

WRITING LINK: COLON AND SEMICOLONS

Locate each instance in which Eighner uses a colon or a semicolon.
On the basis of these examples, write a series of rules that govern
colon and semicolon usage. How often do you use either mark in your
own writing? What does each mark do that cannot be done by another mark of punctuation?

REVISION AND LIFE: TAKE IT FROM THE TOP—AGAIN

Nora Ephron

Nora Ephron (1941–   ) graduated from Wellesley College and worked as a journalist and columnist for the New York Post, New York *magazine, and* Esquire. *She is also a successful screenplay writer and director whose credits include* Sleepless in Seattle *(1993),* You've Got Mail *(1998), and* Hanging Up *(2000). "Revision and Life," written in response to an invitation to participate in this textbook, was originally published in* The New York Times Book Review.

On Writing: *When asked about the autobiographical influences of her first novel, Ephron replied: "I've always written about my life. That's how I grew up. 'Take notes. Everything is copy.' All that stuff my mother [also a writer] said to us."*

BEFORE READING

Connecting: When it comes to writing, what does the word *revision* suggest to you?

Anticipating: When Ephron observes, "A gift for revision may be a developmental stage," what does she mean?

I have been asked to write something for a textbook that is meant to   1
teach college students something about writing and revision. I am happy to do this because I believe in revision. I have also been asked to save the early drafts of whatever I write, presumably to show these students the actual process of revision. This too I am happy to do. On the other hand, I suspect that there is just so much you can teach college students about revision; a gift for revision may be a developmental stage—like a 2-year-old's sudden ability to place one block on top of another—that comes along somewhat later, in one's mid-20s, say; most people may not be particularly good at it, or even interested in it, until then.

When I was in college, I revised nothing. I wrote out my papers   2
in longhand, typed them up and turned them in. It would never have crossed my mind that what I had produced was only a first draft and

that I had more work to do; the idea was to get to the end, and once you had got to the end you were finished. The same thinking, I might add, applied in life: I went pell-mell through my four years in college without a thought about whether I ought to do anything differently; the idea was to get to the end—to get out of school and become a journalist.

3   Which I became, in fairly short order. I learned as a journalist to revise on deadline. I learned to write an article a paragraph at a time—and I arrived at the kind of writing and revising I do, which is basically a kind of typing and retyping. I am a great believer in this technique for the simple reason that I type faster than the wind. What I generally do is to start an article and get as far as I can—sometimes no farther in than a sentence or two—before running out of steam, ripping the piece of paper from the typewriter and starting all over again. I type over and over until I have got the beginning of the piece to the point where I am happy with it. I then am ready to plunge into the body of the article itself. This plunge usually requires something known as a transition. I approach a transition by completely retyping the opening of the article leading up to it in the hope that the ferocious speed of my typing will somehow catapult me into the next section of the piece. This does not work—what in fact catapults me into the next section is a concrete thought about what the next section ought to be about—but until I have the thought the typing keeps me busy, and keeps me from feeling something known as blocked.

4   Typing and retyping as if you know where you're going is a version of what therapists tell you to do when they suggest that you try changing from the outside in—that if you can't master the total commitment to whatever change you want to make, you can at least do all the extraneous things connected with it, which make it that much easier to get there. I was 25 years old the first time a therapist suggested that I try changing from the outside in. In those days, I used to spend quite a lot of time lying awake at night wondering what I should have said earlier in the evening and revising my lines. I mention this not just because it's a way of illustrating that a gift for revision is practically instinctive, but also (once again) because it's possible that a genuine ability at it doesn't really come into play until one is older—or at least older than 25, when it seemed to me that all that was required in my life and my work was the chance to change a few lines.

5   In my 30's, I began to write essays, one a month for *Esquire* magazine, and I am not exaggerating when I say that in the course of writing a short essay—1,500 words, that's only six double-spaced typewritten pages—I often used 300 or 400 pieces of typing paper, so often did I type and retype and catapult and recatapult myself, some-

times on each retyping moving not even a sentence farther from the spot I had reached the last time through. At the same time, though, I was polishing what I had already written: as I struggled with the middle of the article, I kept putting the beginning through the typewriter; as I approached the ending, the middle got its turn. (This is a kind of polishing that the word processor all but eliminates, which is why I don't use one. Word processors make it possible for a writer to change the sentences that clearly need changing without having to retype the rest, but I believe that you can't always tell whether a sentence needs work until it rises up in revolt against your fingers as you retype it.) By the time I had produced what you might call a first draft—an entire article with a beginning, middle and end—the beginning was in more like 45th draft, the middle in 20th, and the end was almost newborn. For this reason, the beginnings of my essays are considerably better written than the ends, although I like to think no one ever notices this but me.

As I learned the essay form, writing became harder for me. I was   6
finding a personal style, a voice if you will, a way of writing that looked chatty and informal. That wasn't the hard part—the hard part was that having found a voice, I had to work hard month to month not to seem as if I were repeating myself. At this point in this essay it will not surprise you to learn that the same sort of thing was operating in my life. I don't mean that my life had become harder—but that it was becoming clear that I had many more choices than had occurred to me when I was marching through my 20's. I no longer lost sleep over what I should have said. Not that I didn't care—it was just that I had moved to a new plane of late-night anxiety: I now wondered what I should have done. Whole areas of possible revision opened before me. What should I have done instead? What could I have done? What if I hadn't done it the way I did? What if I had a chance to do it over? What if I had a chance to do it over as a different person? These were the sorts of questions that kept me awake and led me into fiction, which at the very least (the level at which I practice it) is a chance to rework the events of your life so that you give the illusion of being the intelligence at the center of it, simultaneously managing to slip in all the lines that occurred to you later. Fiction, I suppose, is the ultimate shot at revision.

Now I am in my 40's and I write screenplays. Screenplays—if   7
they are made into movies—are essentially collaborations, and movies are not a writer's medium, we all know this, and I don't want to dwell on the craft of screenwriting except insofar as it relates to revision. Because the moment you stop work on a script seems to be determined not by whether you think the draft is good but simply by

whether shooting is about to begin: if it is, you get to call your script a final draft; and if it's not, you can always write another revision. This might seem to be a hateful way to live, but the odd thing is that it's somehow comforting; as long as you're revising, the project isn't dead. And by the same token, neither are you.

8   It was, as it happens, while thinking about all this one recent sleepless night that I figured out how to write this particular essay. I say "recent" in order to give a sense of immediacy and energy to the preceding sentence, but the truth is that I am finishing this article four months after the sleepless night in question, and the letter asking me to write it, from George Miller of the University of Delaware, arrived almost two years ago, so for all I know Mr. Miller has managed to assemble his textbook on revision without me.

9   Oh, well. That's how it goes when you start thinking about revision. That's the danger of it, in fact. You can spend so much time thinking about how to switch things around that the main event has passed you by. But it doesn't matter. Because by the time you reach middle age, you want more than anything for things not to come to an end; and as long as you're still revising, they don't.

10   I'm sorry to end so morbidly—dancing as I am around the subject of death—but there are advantages to it. For one thing, I have managed to move fairly effortlessly and logically from the beginning of this piece through the middle and to the end. And for another, I am able to close with an exhortation, something I rarely manage, which is this: Revise now, before it's too late.

QUESTIONS ON SUBJECT AND PURPOSE

1. For Ephron, how are revision and life connected?
2. Why is fiction the "ultimate shot at revision" (paragraph 6)?
3. Is the essay about how to revise or about something else?

QUESTIONS ON STRATEGY AND AUDIENCE

1. How does Ephron structure her essay? What principle of order does she follow?
2. What might Ephron mean by her final sentence ("Revise now, before it's too late")?
3. It would have been a simple matter for Ephron to omit the references to this textbook (paragraphs 1 and 8). *The New York Times* audience, for example, would not be interested in knowing these details. Why might she have chosen to include these references in her essay?

QUESTIONS ON VOCABULARY AND STYLE

1. Have you ever heard the phrase "take it from the top—again"? In what context is it usually used? What might such a figure of speech be called?

2. Ephron refers to her strategy of retyping as a way of "catapulting" herself into the next section. Where does the verb *catapult* come from? What does it suggest?

3. Be prepared to define the following words: *pell-mell* (paragraph 2), *extraneous* (4), *exhortation* (10).

WRITING SUGGESTIONS

1. **For Your Journal.** What obstacles do you face when you try to revise something that you have written? Make a list of the ones that immediately come to mind. Add to your list as you finish each paragraph and essay during this course.

2. **For a Paragraph.** Formulate a thesis about Ephron's process of revision based on this essay. In a paragraph, assert your thesis and support it with appropriate evidence from the essay.

3. **For an Essay.** On the basis of your own experience as a writer and as a student in this course, argue for or against *requiring* revision in a college writing course. Should a student be forced to do it? Does revision always produce a better paper?

4. **For Research.** What role does revision play in the writing process of faculty and staff at your college or university? Interview a range of people—faculty (especially professors in disciplines other than English) and other professional staff members who write as a regular part of their job (for example, librarians, information officers, and admissions officers). Using notes from your interviews, write an essay about the revision practices of these writers. Your essay could be a feature article in the campus newspaper.

 WEBSITE LINK

Ephron is increasingly known as both a screenwriter and director. You can find detailed Web resources on all of her films, including stills, audio, and video clips. A list of places to start can be found at the Website.

WRITING LINK: PUNCTUATION

Information inserted into or added onto a sentence can be set off by commas, parentheses, or dashes. In paragraphs 5 and 6, Ephron uses all three marks. Study those paragraphs, and then offer an explanation for why Ephron chooses to punctuate each insertion or addition as she does.

DON'T JUST STAND THERE
Diane Cole

Diane Cole was born in Baltimore, Maryland, in 1952. Educated at Radcliffe College (B.A.) and Johns Hopkins University (M.A.), she is a freelance journalist well versed in psychological issues. Her most recent book, co-authored with Scott Wetzler, is Is It You or Is It Me?: How We Turn Our Emotions Inside Out and Blame Each Other *(1998). "Don't Just Stand There" originally appeared as part of a national campaign against bigotry in a special supplement to* The New York Times *titled "A World of Difference" (April 16, 1989), sponsored by the Anti-Defamation League of B'nai B'rith.*

On Writing: *In an article about her life as a writer, Cole wrote: "I've been scribbling things down for as long as I can remember. . . . And when [my fourth-grade teacher] encouraged me to keep on writing I thought: Maybe it's possible, maybe I can become a writer one day. And there was also the desire—maybe the need—to leave my mark, by writing something that would somehow be of use to others, whether it entertained, gave solace, provided practical information, or simply made another person smile."*

BEFORE READING

Connecting: Can you remember a time when you were told a joke that maligned your national or ethnic origin, race, religion, gender, sexual orientation, or age? How did you respond?

Anticipating: According to Cole and the experts that she cites, what are improper responses to such distasteful or bigoted remarks?

It was my office farewell party, and colleagues at the job I was about   1
to leave were wishing me well. My mood was one of ebullience tinged with regret, and it was in this spirit that I spoke to the office neighbor to whom I had waved hello every morning for the past two years. He smiled broadly as he launched into a long, rambling story, pausing only after he delivered the punch line. It was a very long pause because, although he laughed, I did not: This joke was unmistakably anti-Semitic.

I froze. Everyone in the office knew I was Jewish; what could he   2
have possibly meant? Shaken and hurt, not knowing what else to do,

I turned in stunned silence to the next well-wisher. Later, still angry, I wondered, what else should I—could I—have done?

3   Prejudice can make its presence felt in any setting, but hearing its nasty voice in this way can be particularly unnerving. We do not know what to do and often we feel another form of paralysis as well: We think, "Nothing I say or do will change this person's attitude, so why bother?"

4   But left unchecked, racial slurs and offensive ethnic jokes "can poison the atmosphere," says Michael McQuillan, adviser for racial/ethnic affairs for the Brooklyn borough president's office. "Hearing these remarks conditions us to accept them; and if we accept these, we can become accepting of other acts."

5   Speaking up may not magically change a biased attitude, but it can change a person's behavior by putting a strong message across. And the more messages there are, the more likely a person is to change that behavior, says Arnold Kahn, professor of psychology at James Madison University, Harrisonburg, Va., who makes this analogy: "You can't keep people from smoking in *their* house, but you can ask them not to smoke in *your* house."

6   At the same time, "Even if the other party ignores or discounts what you say, people always reflect on how others perceive them. Speaking up always counts," says LeNorman Strong, director of campus life at George Washington University, Washington, D.C.

7   Finally, learning to respond effectively also helps people feel better about themselves, asserts Cherie Brown, executive director of the National Coalition Building Institute, a Boston-based training organization. "We've found that, when people felt they could at least in this small way make a difference, that made them more eager to take on other activities on a larger scale," she says. Although there is no "cookbook approach" to confronting such remarks—every situation is different, experts stress—these are some effective strategies.

8   *When the "joke" turns on who you are—as a member of an ethnic or religious group, a person of color, a woman, a gay or lesbian, an elderly person, or someone with a physical handicap—shocked paralysis is often the first response. Then, wounded and vulnerable, on some level you want to strike back.*

9   Lashing out or responding in kind is seldom the most effective response, however. "That can give you momentary satisfaction, but you also feel as if you've lowered yourself to that other person's level," Mr. McQuillan explains. Such a response may further label you in the speaker's mind as thin-skinned, someone not to be taken seriously. Or it may up the ante, making the speaker, and then you, reach for new insults—or physical blows.

"If you don't laugh at the joke, or fight, or respond in kind to the   10
slur," says Mr. McQuillan, "that will take the person by surprise, and
that can give you more control over the situation." Therefore, in situations like the one in which I found myself—a private conversation
in which I knew the person making the remark—he suggests voicing
your anger calmly but pointedly: "I don't know if you realize what that
sounded like to me. If that's what you meant, it really hurt me."

State how *you* feel, rather than making an abstract statement   11
like, "Not everyone who hears that joke might find it funny." Coun-
sels Mr. Strong: "Personalize the sense of 'this is how I feel when you
say this.' That makes it very concrete"—and harder to dismiss.

Make sure you heard the words and their intent correctly by re-   12
peating or rephrasing the statement: "This is what I heard you say. Is
that what you meant?" It's important to give the other person the
benefit of the doubt because, in fact, he may *not* have realized that the
comment was offensive and, if you had not spoken up, would have had
no idea of its impact on you.

For instance, Professor Kahn relates that he used to include in   13
his exams multiple-choice questions that occasionally contained "incorrect funny answers." After one exam, a student came up to him in
private and said, "I don't think you intended this, but I found a number of those jokes offensive to me as a woman." She explained why.
"What she said made immediate sense to me," he says. "I apologized
at the next class, and I never did it again."

But what if the speaker dismisses your objection, saying, "Oh,   14
you're just being sensitive. Can't you take a joke?" In that case, you
might say, "I'm not so sure about that, let's talk about that a little
more." The key, Mr. Strong says, is to continue the dialogue, hear the
other person's concerns, and point out your own. "There are times
when you're just going to have to admit defeat and end it," he adds,
"but I have to feel that I did the best I could."

When the offending remark is made in the presence of others—   15
at a staff meeting, for example—it can be even more distressing than
an insult made privately.

"You have two options," says William Newlin, director of field   16
services for the Community Relations division of the New York City
Commission on Human Rights. "You can respond immediately at the
meeting, or you can delay your response until afterward in private.
But a response has to come."

Some remarks or actions may be so outrageous that they can-   17
not go unnoted at the moment, regardless of the speaker or the setting. But in general, psychologists say, shaming a person in public
may have the opposite effect of the one you want: The speaker will

deny his offense all the more strongly in order to save face. Further, few people enjoy being put on the spot, and if the remark really was not intended to be offensive, publicly embarrassing the person who made it may cause an unnecessary rift or further misunderstanding. Finally, most people just don't react as well or thoughtfully under a public spotlight as they would in private.

18 Keeping that in mind, an excellent alternative is to take the offender aside afterward: "Could we talk for a minute in private?" Then use the strategies suggested above for calmly stating how you feel, giving the speaker the benefit of the doubt, and proceeding from there.

19 At a large meeting or public talk, you might consider passing the speaker a note, says David Wertheimer, executive director of the New York City Gay and Lesbian Anti-Violence Project: You could write, "You may not realize it, but your remarks were offensive because . . ."

20 "Think of your role as that of an educator," suggests James M. Jones, Ph.D., executive director for public interest at the American Psychological Association. "You have to be controlled."

21 Regardless of the setting or situation, speaking up always raises the risk of rocking the boat. If the person who made the offending remark is your boss, there may be an even bigger risk to consider: How will this affect my job? Several things can help minimize the risk, however. First, know what other resources you may have at work, suggests Caryl Stern, director of the A World of Difference—New York City campaign: Does your personnel office handle discrimination complaints? Are other grievance procedures in place?

22 You won't necessarily need to use any of these procedures, Ms. Stern stresses. In fact, she advises, "It's usually better to try a one-on-one approach first." But simply knowing a formal system exists can make you feel secure enough to set up that meeting.

23 You can also raise the issue with other colleagues who heard the remark: Did they feel the same way you did? The more support you have, the less alone you will feel. Your point will also carry more validity and be more difficult to shrug off. Finally, give your boss credit—and the benefit of the doubt: "I know you've worked hard for the company's affirmative action programs, so I'm sure you didn't realize what those remarks sounded like to me as well as the others at the meeting last week. . . ."

24 If, even after this discussion, the problem persists, go back for another meeting, Ms. Stern advises. And if that, too, fails, you'll know what other options are available to you.

25 *It's a spirited dinner party, and everyone's having a good time, until one guest starts reciting a racist joke. Everyone at the table is white,*

including you. The others are still laughing, as you wonder what to say or do.

No one likes being seen as a party-pooper, but before deciding   26
that you'd prefer not to take on this role, you might remember that the person who told the offensive joke has already ruined your good time.

If it's a group that you feel comfortable in—a family gathering,   27
for instance—you will feel freer to speak up. Still, shaming the person by shouting "You're wrong!" or "That's not funny!" probably won't get your point across as effectively as other strategies. "If you interrupt people to condemn them, it just makes it harder," says Cherie Brown. She suggests trying instead to get at the resentments that lie beneath the joke by asking open-ended questions: "Grandpa, I know you always treat everyone with such respect. Why do people in our family talk that way about black people?" The key, Ms. Brown says, "is to listen to them first, so they will be more likely to listen to you."

If you don't know your fellow guests well, before speaking up   28
you could turn discreetly to your neighbors (or excuse yourself to help the host or hostess in the kitchen) to get a reading on how they felt, and whether or not you'll find support for speaking up. The less alone you feel, the more comfortable you'll be speaking up: "I know you probably didn't mean anything by that joke, Jim, but it really offended me. . . . " It's important to say that *you* were offended—not state how the group that is the butt of the joke would feel. "Otherwise," LeNorman Strong says, "you risk coming off as a goody two-shoes."

If you yourself are the host, you can exercise more control; you   29
are, after all, the one who sets the rules and the tone of behavior in your home. Once, when Professor Kahn's party guests began singing offensive, racist songs, for instance, he kicked them all out, saying, "You don't sing songs like that in my house!" And, he adds, "they never did again."

At school one day, a friend comes over and says, "Who do you think   30
you are, hanging out with Joe? If you can be friends with those people, I'm
through with you!"

Peer pressure can weigh heavily on kids. They feel vulnerable   31
and, because they are kids, they aren't as able to control the urge to fight. "But if you learn to handle these situations as kids, you'll be better able to handle them as an adult," William Newlin points out.

Begin by redefining to yourself what a friend is and examining   32
what friendship means, advises Amy Lee, a human relations specialist at Panel of Americans, an intergroup-relations training and educational organization. If that person from a different group fits your requirement for a friend, ask, "Why shouldn't I be friends with Joe?

We have a lot in common." Try to get more information about whatever stereotypes or resentments lie beneath your friend's statement. Ms. Lee suggests: "What makes you think they're so different from us? Where did you get that information?" She explains: "People are learning these stereotypes from somewhere, and they cannot be blamed for that. So examine where these ideas came from." Then talk about how your own experience rebuts them.

33   Kids, like adults, should also be aware of other resources to back them up: Does the school offer special programs for fighting prejudice? How supportive will the principal, the teachers, or other students be? If the school atmosphere is volatile, experts warn, make sure that taking a stand at that moment won't put you in physical danger. If that is the case, it's better to look for other alternatives.

34   These can include programs or organizations that bring kids from different backgrounds together. "When kids work together across race lines, that is how you break down the barriers and see that the stereotypes are not true," says Laurie Meadoff, president of CityKids Foundation, a nonprofit group whose programs attempt to do just that. Such programs can also provide what Cherie Brown calls a "safe place" to express the anger and pain that slurs and other offenses cause, whether the bigotry is directed against you or others.

35   In learning to speak up, everyone will develop a different style and a slightly different message to get across, experts agree. But it would be hard to do better than these two messages suggested by teenagers at CityKids: "Everyone on the face of the earth has the same intestines," said one. Another added, "Cross over the bridge. There's a lot of love on the streets."

QUESTIONS ON SUBJECT AND PURPOSE

1. According to Cole, why should we object to "racial slurs and offensive ethnic jokes"?

2. The body of Cole's essay (paragraphs 8–34) offers strategies to use when confronting offensive remarks or jokes. How does Cole divide or organize this part of her subject?

3. What purposes might Cole have had in writing the essay?

QUESTIONS ON STRATEGY AND AUDIENCE

1. Why does Cole begin the essay with a personal example (paragraphs 1 and 2)?

2. Cole quotes a number of authorities in her essay. Why? What do the quotations and the authorities contribute to the article?
3. Why might Cole include the final section—the advice to children about handling such situations among friends? What does this section suggest about her intended audience?

QUESTIONS ON VOCABULARY AND STYLE

1. Throughout the essay, Cole uses first- or second-person pronouns such as *I, you,* and *we.* Why? How would the essay differ if she used *one* or *he* or *she?*
2. At several points (in paragraph 23, for instance), Cole suggests a possible response to a situation, enclosing that remark within quotation marks. Why might she create these imagined sentences for her reader?
3. Be prepared to define the following words: *ebullience* (paragraph 1), *tinged* (1), *rift* (17), *volatile* (33).

WRITING SUGGESTIONS

1. **For Your Journal.** Would you honestly say that after reading Cole's essay you will respond as she suggests when you hear offensive remarks? Does it matter if they are directed at a group to which you belong or at another group? Start with a typical offensive remark that you have often heard, and plan a response to it. If you feel that you would still "just stand there," explain for yourself why you would choose not to react.
2. **For a Paragraph.** Studies from colleges and universities across the United States suggest that many students have cheated at some point during their college years. Typically, these students either plagiarized someone else's work in a paper or a laboratory report or copied answers on a quiz or an exam. Suppose that a friend asks to borrow your research paper or laboratory report, explaining that he or she wants to submit it as his or her own work, or that a friend tries to copy answers from your paper. How can you handle such a situation? In a process paragraph, explain a procedure for replying to that person.
3. **For an Essay.** Cole's essay describes a process—what to do when you encounter prejudice. Select another occasion when we might need advice on how to handle a similarly awkward situation, and write an essay offering advice on what to do.

4. **For Research.** Many colleges and universities have established policies for dealing with sexual harassment and discrimination. Research your own institution's position on these issues. See if, for example, a policy statement is available. You might also wish to interview members of the administration and faculty. Then, using your research, write an essay in which you explain to students how to handle a case of sexual harassment or discrimination.

 WEBSITE LINK

The Web has wonderful resources for dealing with discrimination—check out the sites maintained by the Anti-Defamation League of B'nai B'rith, the National Organization for Women, and the National Association for Colored People.

 WRITING LINK: SENTENCE VARIETY

Cole uses a variety of sentence structures in the essay. See if you can find examples of the following types of sentences: compound sentences linked with coordinating conjunctions; compound sentences linked with semicolons; sentences containing colons; short, simple sentences. What is the effect of the variety of sentences? Look at your own writing. Do you use a variety of sentence types?

THE CULTURE OF MARTYRDOM

David Brooks

David Brooks, a graduate of the University of Chicago, is a senior editor at
The Weekly Standard, *a contributing editor at* Newsweek, *a correspondent for* Atlantic Monthly, *and a political analyst for* The NewsHour
with Jim Lehrer. *His most recent book is* Bobos in Paradise: The New
Upper Class and How They Got There *(2000).* "The Culture of Martyrdom" *appeared in the* Atlantic Monthly *in the summer of 2002.*

On Writing: *In the Acknowledgments to* Bobos in Paradise,
*Brooks suggests the importance to professional writers of peer readers and editors. He thanks numerous readers of his manuscript for their "valuable advice" and, in particular, his editor, who "seemed to ponder every word" and
whose "comments improved it in ways great and small."*

BEFORE READING

Connecting: What does the word *martyr* mean to you?

Anticipating: Throughout the essay Brooks suggests that suicide
bombings are an "addiction." Why does he make this analogy? In his
mind, what justifies such a link?

Suicide bombing is the crack cocaine of warfare. It doesn't just inflict   1
death and terror on its victims; it intoxicates the people who sponsor it.
It unleashes the deepest and most addictive human passions—the thirst
for vengeance, the desire for religious purity, the longing for earthly
glory and eternal salvation. Suicide bombing isn't just a tactic in a
larger war; it overwhelms the political goals it is meant to serve. It
creates its own logic and transforms the culture of those who employ
it. This is what has happened in the Arab-Israeli dispute. Over the
past year suicide bombing has dramatically changed the nature of the
conflict.

   Before 1983 there were few suicide bombings. The Koran for-   2
bids the taking of one's own life, and this prohibition was still generally observed. But when the United States stationed Marines in
Beirut, the leaders of the Islamic resistance movement Hizbollah began to discuss turning to this ultimate terrorist weapon. Religious authorities in Iran gave it their blessing, and a wave of suicide bombings

began, starting with the attacks that killed about sixty U.S. embassy workers in April of 1983 and about 240 people in the Marine compound at the airport in October. The bombings proved so successful at driving the United States and, later, Israel out of Lebanon that most lingering religious concerns were set aside.

3   The tactic was introduced into Palestinian areas only gradually. In 1988 Fathi Shiqaqi, the founder of the Palestinian Islamic Jihad, wrote a set of guidelines (aimed at countering religious objections to the truck bombings of the 1980s) for the use of explosives in individual bombings; nevertheless, he characterized operations calling for martyrdom as "exceptional." But by the mid-1990s the group Hamas was using suicide bombers as a way of derailing the Oslo peace process. The assassination of the master Palestinian bomb maker Yahya Ayyash, presumably by Israeli agents, in January of 1996, set off a series of suicide bombings in retaliation. Suicide bombings nonetheless remained relatively unusual until two years ago, after the Palestinian leader Yasir Arafat walked out of the peace conference at Camp David—a conference at which Israel's Prime Minister, Ehud Barak, had offered to return to the Palestinians parts of Jerusalem and almost all of the West Bank.

4   At that point the psychology shifted. We will not see peace soon, many Palestinians concluded, but when it eventually comes, we will get everything we want. We will endure, we will fight, and we will suffer for that final victory. From then on the struggle (at least from the Palestinian point of view) was no longer about negotiation and compromise—about who would get which piece of land, which road or river. The red passions of the bombers obliterated the grays of the peace process. Suicide bombing became the tactic of choice, even in circumstances where a terrorist could have planted a bomb and then escaped without injury. Martyrdom became not just a means but an end.

5   Suicide bombing is a highly communitarian enterprise. According to Ariel Merari, the director of the Political Violence Research Center, at Tel Aviv University, and a leading expert on the phenomenon, in not one instance has a lone, crazed Palestinian gotten hold of a bomb and gone off to kill Israelis. Suicide bombings are initiated by tightly run organizations that recruit, indoctrinate, train, and reward the bombers. Those organizations do not seek depressed or mentally unstable people for their missions. From 1996 to 1999 the Pakistani journalist Nasra Hassan interviewed almost 250 people who were either recruiting and training bombers or preparing to go on a suicide mission themselves. "None of the suicide bombers—they ranged in age from eighteen to thirty-eight—conformed to the typi-

cal profile of the suicidal personality," Hassan wrote in *The New Yorker.* "None of them were uneducated, desperately poor, simple-minded, or depressed." The Palestinian bombers tend to be devout, but religious fanaticism does not explain their motivation. Nor does lack of opportunity, because they also tend to be well educated.

Often a bomber believes that a close friend or a member of his   6 family has been killed by Israeli troops, and this is part of his motivation. According to most experts, though, the crucial factor informing the behavior of suicide bombers is loyalty to the group. Suicide bombers go through indoctrination processes similar to the ones that were used by the leaders of the Jim Jones and Solar Temple cults. The bombers are organized into small cells and given countless hours of intense and intimate spiritual training. They are instructed in the details of *jihad*, reminded of the need for revenge, and reassured about the rewards they can expect in the afterlife. They are told that their families will be guaranteed a place with God, and that there are also considerable rewards for their families in this life, including cash bonuses of several thousand dollars donated by the government of Iraq, some individual Saudis, and various groups sympathetic to the cause. Finally, the bombers are told that paradise lies just on the other side of the detonator, that death will feel like nothing more than a pinch.

Members of such groups re-enact past operations. Recruits are   7 sometimes made to lie in empty graves, so that they can see how peaceful death will be; they are reminded that life will bring sickness, old age, and betrayal. "We were in a constant state of worship," one suicide bomber (who somehow managed to survive his mission) told Hassan. "We told each other that if the Israelis only knew how joyful we were they would whip us to death! Those were the happiest days of my life!"

The bombers are instructed to write or videotape final testi-   8 mony. (A typical note, from 1995: "I am going to take revenge upon the sons of the monkeys and the pigs, the Zionist infidels and the enemies of humanity. I am going to meet my holy brother Hisham Hamed and all the other martyrs and saints in paradise.") Once a bomber has completed his declaration, it would be humiliating for him to back out of the mission. He undergoes a last round of cleansing and prayer and is sent off with his bomb to the appointed pizzeria, coffee shop, disco, or bus.

For many Israelis and Westerners, the strangest aspect of the   9 phenomenon is the televised interview with a bomber's parents after a massacre. These people have just been told that their child has killed himself and others, and yet they seem happy, proud, and—should the opportunity present itself—ready to send another child off to the afterlife. There are two ways to look at this: One, the parents feel so wronged and humiliated by the Israelis that they would rather sacrifice their children than continue passively to endure. Two, the cult of suicide bombing has infected the broader culture to the point where large parts of society, including the bombers' parents, are addicted to the adrenaline rush of vengeance and murder. Both explanations may be true.

10   It is certainly the case that vast segments of Palestinian culture have been given over to the creation and nurturing of suicide bombers. Martyrdom has replaced Palestinian independence as the main focus of the Arab media. Suicide bombing is, after all, perfectly suited to the television age. The bombers' farewell videos provide compelling footage, as do the interviews with families. The bombings themselves produce graphic images of body parts and devastated buildings. Then there are the "weddings" between the martyrs and dark-eyed virgins in paradise (announcements that read like wedding invitations are printed in local newspapers so that friends and neighbors can join in the festivities), the marches and celebrations after each attack, and the displays of things bought with the cash rewards to the families. Woven together, these images make gripping packages that can be aired again and again.

11   Activities in support of the bombings are increasingly widespread. Last year the BBC shot a segment about so-called Paradise Camps—summer camps in which children as young as eight are trained in military drills and taught about suicide bombers. Rallies commonly feature children wearing bombers' belts. Fifth- and sixthgraders have studied poems that celebrate the bombers. At Al Najah University, in the West Bank, a student exhibition last September included a re-created scene of the Sbarro pizzeria in Jerusalem after the suicide bombing there last August: "blood" was splattered everywhere, and mock body parts hung from the ceiling as if blown through the air.

12   Thus suicide bombing has become phenomenally popular. According to polls, 70 to 80 percent of Palestinians now support it—making the act more popular than Hamas, the Palestinian Islamic Jihad, Fatah, or any of the other groups that sponsor it, and far more popular than the peace process ever was. In addition to satisfying visceral emotions, suicide bombing gives average Palestinians, not just PLO elites, a chance to play a glorified role in the fight against Israel.

13   Opponents of suicide bombings sometimes do raise their heads. Over the last couple of years educators have moderated the tone of textbooks to reduce and in many cases eliminate the rhetoric of holy

war. After the BBC report aired, Palestinian officials vowed to close the Paradise Camps. Nonetheless, Palestinian children grow up in a culture in which suicide bombers are rock stars, sports heroes, and religious idols rolled into one. Reporters who speak with Palestinians about the bombers notice the fire and pride in their eyes.

"I'd be very happy if my daughter killed Sharon," one mother told   14
a reporter from *The San Diego Union-Tribune* last November. "Even if she killed two or three Israelis, I would be happy." Last year I attended a dinner party in Amman at which six distinguished Jordanians—former cabinet ministers and supreme-court justices and a journalist—talked about the Tel Aviv disco bombing, which had occurred a few months earlier. They had some religious qualms about the suicide, but the moral aspect of killing teenage girls—future breeders of Israelis—was not even worth discussing. They spoke of the attack with a quiet sense of satisfaction.

It's hard to know how Israel, and the world, should respond to   15
the rash of suicide bombings and to their embrace by the Palestinian people. To take any action that could be viewed as a concession would be to provoke further attacks, as the U.S. and Israeli withdrawals from Lebanon in the 1980s demonstrated. On the other hand, the Israeli raids on the refugee camps give the suicide bombers a propaganda victory. After Yasir Arafat walked out of the Camp David meetings, he became a pariah to most governments, for killing the peace process. Now, amid Israeli retaliation for the bombings, the global community rises to condemn Israel's actions.

Somehow conditions must be established that would allow the   16
frenzy of suicide bombings to burn itself out. To begin with, the Palestinian and Israeli populations would have to be separated; contact between them inflames the passions that feed the attacks. That would mean shutting down the vast majority of Israeli settlements in the West Bank and Gaza and creating a buffer zone between the two populations. Palestinian life would then no longer be dominated by checkpoints and celebrations of martyrdom; it would be dominated by quotidian issues such as commerce, administration, and garbage collection.

The idea of a buffer zone, which is gaining momentum in Is-   17
rael, is not without problems. Where, exactly, would the buffer be? Terrorist groups could shoot missiles over it. But it's time to face the reality that the best resource the terrorists have is the culture of martyrdom. This culture is presently powerful, but it is potentially fragile. If it can be interrupted, if the passions can be made to recede, then the Palestinians and the Israelis might go back to hating each other in the normal way, and at a distance. As with many addictions, the solution is to go cold turkey.

QUESTIONS ON SUBJECT AND PURPOSE

1. What is a martyr?
2. What does the phrase "the culture of martyrdom" suggest to you?
3. What purpose or purposes might Brooks have in his essay?

QUESTIONS ON STRATEGY AND AUDIENCE

1. How effective is Brooks's introduction?
2. How does Brooks use process in his essay?
3. To whom is Brooks writing? What assumptions does he make about his audience? How can you tell?

QUESTIONS ON VOCABULARY AND STYLE

1. What does the expression "to go cold turkey" mean? From what context is it derived? What might we call such an expression?
2. How appropriate is Brooks's final sentence as a concluding statement for the essay?
3. Be prepared to define the following words: *obliterated* (paragraph 4), *infidels* (8), *visceral* (12), *pariah* (15), *quotidian* (16).

WRITING SUGGESTIONS

1. **For Your Journal.** In your journal, reflect on how you handle conflict—with parents, friends, authority figures, or people you perceive as "enemies." Be honest with yourself. Try to think of specific situations in which you were faced with a conflict. Make a list of several. What did you do in response to that conflict? What should you have done?
2. **For a Paragraph.** Conflict often provokes counterproductive reactions. Someone screams at us; we scream louder in response. Generally, we know how we ought to react, even if we rarely do so. Expand your journal writing into a paragraph. In the paragraph offer advice in a step-by-step process about how to handle a specific type of conflict. Possible situations might include a quarrel with your parents or with a sibling, a conflict with a teacher over a grade, resentment toward a friend who clearly takes advantage of you, or your response to someone who insults or demeans you.

3. **For an Essay.** "How to Negotiate Conflicts." Expand your paragraph into an essay offering advice to your contemporaries on how to handle a commonly encountered conflict. You might want to imagine that your essay will appear in your college or university newspaper. Remember that you can address serious conflicts such as sexual, racial, or ethnic discrimination, domestic abuse, or criminal and/or immoral behavior.

4. **For Research.** What proposals have been put forth for a settlement of the Arab-Israeli conflict? How have people suggested creating a peace? What are the key steps in such a process? Research the issue. Remember to treat both sides fairly—any resolution must be equally embraced by both sides.

 WEBSITE LINK

The Web offers a wide variety of sources for gathering information about the Arab-Israeli conflict and about suicide bombing. In addition, you can read interviews with Brooks and check out reviews of his most recent book.

 WRITING LINK: TOPIC SENTENCES

What is a topic sentence? Look carefully at Brooks's essay. Do his paragraphs always have topic sentences? Where are they placed in his paragraphs? How do they help you as a reader? What does Brooks's use of topic sentences suggest about your own writing?

INTO THE LOOP: HOW TO GET THE JOB YOU WANT AFTER GRADUATION

Charlie Drozdyk

Charlie Drozdyk has had a wide range of job experiences. He has worked for the Big Apple Circus and the Brooklyn Academy of Music. He has also been theater manager at the Criterion Center on Broadway, a researcher at CBS, a director of development for a film production company, a producer of videos, and a talent agent. He is the author of Hot Jobs Handbook *(1994) and* Jobs That Don't Suck *(1998). This essay originally appeared in* Rolling Stone *magazine.*

BEFORE READING

Connecting: At this point, what expectations do you have about your first job after college?

Anticipating: What seems like the most surprising piece of information or advice in the essay?

1   When Benjamin Braddock, Dustin Hoffman's bewildered twenty-something hero in *The Graduate*, finished college, he was hit with a mind-numbing barrage of good wishes from well-meaning friends. Who can forget that single depressing word of advice that sent Benjamin into catatonic shock—*plastics?* It was no wonder he wound up sleeping with his girlfriend's mother and hanging out all summer at the bottom of his parents' swimming pool.

2   In 1995, 1.38 million college graduates will find themselves in Benjamin's shoes. They might not share *all* of his summer adventures, but with the flip of a tassel, they will soon find themselves at the bottom of the employment pool. Whom are they going to listen to?

3   The truth is, Benjamin had it pretty good back in 1967. Not only were jobs being created as fast as the labor force would grow, but once a job seeker got a foot in the door at an IBM or a Grey Advertising, he or she could expect to stroll the halls for some 40 years while waiting for the gold watch. Unfortunately, the Fortune 500

companies that 20 years ago employed one in five of all Americans now employ fewer than one in 10. It's called corporate downsizing, and it's not over yet. In 1994 the largest U.S. companies dropped around 700,000 employees. But in spite of that, unemployment numbers are actually shrinking. The big guys may be busy handing out pink slips, but small employers are even busier signing up new hires. 4

But beware of *under*employment. Among the 30 fastest-growing occupations, 21 require no college degree. In fact, the 10 occupations that will pour the greatest number of jobs into the economy, in order, are salespeople (retail), registered nurses, cashiers, general office clerks, truck drivers, waiters/waitresses, nursing aides, janitors/cleaners, food-preparation workers and systems analysts. It is the service industry that will contribute the bulk—approximately two-thirds—of all new jobs. 5

So the question is, How can the class of 1995 put to use the $140 billion it spent on higher education last year? The graduates didn't spend five years—the average amount of time it now takes to get a B.A.—to land a job that doesn't require a college degree. Or did they? Well, the sad truth is that 25 percent of the class of 1995 will be working at jobs that don't require a college diploma. 6

They could always stay on campus. If you're planning on getting a master's degree, the odds of not using your education in a career will drop to 10 percent. For Ph.D.s the odds drop to a 4 percent chance. As you can see, the burger-flipping probability decreases with degrees earned. For those who are thinking about postponing the inevitable job thing, that's good news. 7

For anyone else eager to get on with a career, including Benjamin, if you're still looking, I've talked to plenty of people who have advice. And they're not talking plastics. 8

But before diving into how to get a job, there's one thing to keep in mind, and it's this: Bosses hate hiring people; in fact, they loathe and generally resent the entire process. Put yourself in a boss's shoes. The person they hired two years, or maybe just six months ago, has quit, and now they have to dig through the résumés on their desks and meet with a bunch of random strangers all over again. Or not. What they usually do is toss those résumés in the old circular file and call their friends and business associates, asking them if they know of anyone who's looking for a job. 9

This is exactly how Lauren Marino, a book editor at Hyperion (a trade-book publishing company owned by Disney), hired her assistant. She called the literary agencies she works with on a daily basis and asked her contacts if they knew anyone who was looking for a 10 job. "Not only do they know the business already," she says, "but if someone I know recommends them, then it's not going to be a complete waste of time meeting with them."

11   So how do you get to be the person who is recommended? Get in the loop. You will never even hear of most of the job openings out there if you're not in the loop. Once you get your first job, however, you're automatically in the loop. In many companies, workers are paid to talk to people at different companies all day. And it will instantly start to make sense how the average worker manages to change jobs 7.5 times between the ages of 18 and 30. As obnoxious as the word sounds, it's all about *networking*.

12   For recent graduates without the benefits of business contacts and associates, instant entry into the loop is through a connection. For a lot of people, the word *connection* is as loathsome as that other word. Friends will snivel, "Hey, man, he only got that job because he knows somebody." Absolutely. It's how the game works. So don't discount anyone as a connection—your neighbor, your parents' friends, your baby sitter from 10 years ago. Ask them if they know anyone— or know anyone who knows anyone—who works in the industry into which you want to get. Meet with as many people as you can for a five-minute informational interview, and then go in there and pick their brains: Are they hiring? Do they know anyone who is? (But let them think you're there to simply learn what they do. They know why you're really there.)

13   Don't worry that you'll be bugging them. As Bill Wright-Swadel, director of career services at Dartmouth College, says, "Most people who have an expertise love to talk about the things that they're knowledgeable about." Contacts aren't just about getting an interview, though. Once you've interviewed somewhere, find out if any alumni from your college work there—or any friend of a friend. Call that person, say you've just interviewed and ask him to make a call on your behalf. Basically, it's just someone giving testament that you're *one of them*. It's standard networking procedure—but something often ignored.

14   "People don't know how to network," says David McNulty, a recruiter for Smith Barney. "If you want to get hired by a Wall Street firm, you should find out who went to your school and who works in the firm and call them."

15   Melissa Statmore, human-resources manager at J. Walter Thompson advertising, agrees. "Use any connections you have," she says. "We love referrals. They're taken very seriously."

RECRUITING ROULETTE

Say, however, that you've got no connections. You've just crawled out   16
from under the rock of your undergraduate studies, your parents live
in Tibet, and you have no friends. There's always recruiting, right?
Yes and no. Finding a job by interviewing with firms that show up on
your campus is like getting a job through the want ads—it's a passive
take-what's-being-thrown-in-front-of-you-approach. And considering that employers will visit an average of 7.4 fewer campuses in 1995
than they did in 1994, it's also a somewhat dying approach.

If you're at one of the Ivy League schools, the University of Vir-   17
ginia, Stanford, Michigan or about a dozen select others, and if you
want to work for Smith Barney, you're lucky—the company will visit
your school. And if you want to work for J. Walter Thompson, and if
you're at Amherst, Yale, Colby or Bates, to name a random few, you're
also in luck. My senior year at school—not among the chosen few—I
remember seeing recruiters from a railroad, a pharmaceutical firm
and a company that had something to do with socks and underwear.

Even though it's March, and you haven't scored a job via re-   18
cruiting with some company you never really wanted to work for in
the first place, don't worry about it—you're probably better off. Remember Lauren Marino, the editor who was looking for an assistant?
When Marino was about to graduate, she interviewed on campus with
a printing company based in Tennessee and was offered a job. The
company then had to rescind the offer because of a hiring freeze, and
Marino was forced to continue searching. If the offer hadn't been re-
scinded, instead of loving her life as a book editor (at only 27) in New
York, she would be destined, as she puts it, to be "living in Kingsport,
Tenn., a member of the Junior League and would have 10 kids."

INTERN INTO THE LOOP

So don't fret that you blew off that recruiter. Truth is, if you're about   19
to graduate, it may not be you they're after. The new trend in recruiting is lassoing sophomores and juniors as interns, giving them a
summer or semester of experience and then hiring them as soon as
they're done with school. This gives the company a chance to see if
they fit in and saves time and money in training.

But just because you're about to graduate doesn't mean you   20
can't still intern. In fact, you probably should. In a survey by the College Placement Council, employers say that three out of 10 new hires
will be former interns. Christian Breheney is part of that 30 percent.
Right before she was about to graduate a semester early from Johns

Hopkins and armed with her Spanish major, she saw a flier on a bulletin board and ripped it off the wall. After she was offered the non-paying internship at *Late Night with David Letterman*, she put the flier back up.

21   Some of her friends thought that Breheney's decision to work for free was questionable. After all, she was about to be a college graduate. Her plan worked, though. After four months of commuting from New Jersey five days a week, working from 10 A.M. to 7 P.M., she got her break. A receptionist quit, and Breheney got the job. How? "If you're well liked and make a good impression, you can get hired right off of your internship," she says. Which is something that happens quite often, apparently, as she lists about a dozen full timers who started as interns.

22   Two years later and now the assistant to the head writer at the *Late Show with David Letterman*, Breheney has yet to send out a single résumé. It's just been a matter of "moving up that ladder," she says gleefully.

TEMP INTO THE LOOP

23   The cost-effective benefits in hiring interns—pretrained, proven commodities—are the same reason that temps (temporary employees who are hired to fill in when needed) are landing full-time jobs at the companies where they're assigned. Thirty-eight percent of all temporary workers are offered full-time employment while on an assignment.

24   Temping has become a recruiting technique in itself, not just a means of replacing somebody when he or she is out sick. It's becoming known as "temping to perm." As Jules Young, president of Friedman Personnel Agency, in West Hollywood, Calif., says: "Temping is like living with someone before you marry them. A lot of placement is based on chemistry between the people you're going to work with. That's why a temp is a good way to go—because it gives the employer a chance to check out whether the chemistry matches."

25   At many large companies like Nike or Paramount Pictures—as well as most of the faster-growing small companies (200 employees or fewer) that by the year 2000 will employ 85 percent of all Americans—a great way in, and a fairly common one, is through temping. The best way to go is to call the company you want to work for and ask which temp agency they use. Then call that agency, go in and pass its typing test and boom! You're in the door. Get familiar with some of the more popular computer programs (WordPerfect, Microsoft Word, Excel and Lotus 1-2-3)—the agencies are going to be looking for them.

THE PERSONNEL MYTH

We're practically programmed to do it. We make a list of the compa-   26
nies we want to work for, write a standard cover letter (changing the
name of the company and the person to whom we're sending it, of
course) and drop that and a résumé in the mailbox. A hundred letters
sent to 100 personnel departments. Probability alone suggests that at
least one or two interviews will come out of it, right? Not likely. You
know how many résumés Nike got in 1994? More than 23,000. It
hired 511 people. Smith Barney hired around 80 people last year
from a pool of applicants that numbered about 10,000. Do the math:
The odds aren't good.

When Lauren Marino decided to go into publishing, she sent   27
résumés to every publishing house in New York. You know how many
interviews she got? Zero. As she realizes now, "That was a huge waste
of my time. Personnel departments don't hire anybody. The only way
to get an editorial job in publishing is by knowing somebody or by
sending a letter directly to the editor."

Although it's not a rule to live by, most people don't use their   28
company's personnel departments for a job search. If you want to
work at a company, pinpoint which department you want to work in
and then find the person who can make a hiring decision. Approach
that person directly.

If you don't know anybody who knows anybody who knows   29
anybody who knows the person with whom you want to work—or
under—at a specific company, then you're going to have to be a little
resourceful. The first tactic is obvious. Cold-call them. Pick up the
phone and try to get the person on the line. Tell him truthfully how
you would really love to work for his company and would love to meet
with him for five minutes. Chances are you're not going to get past
this person's assistant, however.

This is exactly what happened to Michael Landau when he   30
called the national sales manager (he got her name from a friend) at
Nicole Miller, a New York fashion-design company. The first four
times he called, he got an assistant on the phone who was nice enough
but wouldn't put her boss on the phone. This is what assistants are for.

Figuring that the assistant probably left at around 6 P.M., Landau   31
called at 6:30, thinking the boss might still be there—and if so, would
pick up her own phone. She was, and she did. She was nice to him but
said there wasn't anything available. Standard stuff, but Landau was
persistent, and as luck would have it, the CEO of the company walked
into the sales manager's office. "Talk to this guy, he sounds good," the
sales manager said to her colleague. The exec repeated that the

company wasn't hiring but that it was, however, always interested in meeting good people.

32   At that moment, Landau decided to fly to New York, a trip he told them he just happened to be taking. Landau started out in sales and is now happily employed in the public-relations department at Nicole Miller.

SAY YES

33   This is the first thing you should know about interviewing: If someone asks you in an interview if you know a certain computer program (which you don't) or if you know how to drive a car (and you never have), just say yes. As Sheryl Vandermolen, a junior designer at Robert Metzger Interiors, says: "It's all about selling yourself and believing in yourself. Don't say you think you can, say you can—even if you don't know if you can."

RESEARCH

34   "Please do your research," says Cheryl Nickerson, director of employment for Nike. "Be able to ask intelligent questions about the company and what's going on in the industry. [As an employer] you're making a judgment about that person's curiosity, their willingness to learn and grow." And where do you find information about the company? Start by reading the firm's annual report. Not doing this is a "cardinal sin," says David McNulty of Smith Barney. Just call up the company and ask that a report be mailed to you. You don't even have to leave your couch.

GET PSYCHED

35   Employers want someone who's going to come in and kick ass. Interviews are about convincing the employer that you're that person. As Brian Johnson, co-owner of the Dogwater Cafe, a fast-growing restaurant chain in Florida, says, "When I'm interviewing, I'm looking for someone with a lot of energy who wants this job more than anything. I want them to basically beg me not to interview anybody else—that this is their job."

FOLLOW UP

36   When I was in Jules Young's office at the Friedman agency, a young woman who had just had an interview with someone at the William

Morris Agency called to report back that it had gone well. Without pausing, Young said, "Drop a note off to her in the morning thanking her and saying you really want the job. Drop it off in person to the reception desk."

"I don't think people [write thank-you notes] as much as they   37
think they should anymore," says Nike's Cheryl Nickerson. "If you're in the running, that special touch of following up to say thank you may be the edge that you need." Sometimes, however, a thank-you letter isn't enough to push you over that edge. You need to do more. You need to . . .

BE PERSISTENT

When Tracy Grandstaff interviewed for her first job, at MTV, she   38
was told that they would let her know quickly since they needed someone right away. "It took three months of me hounding this woman to get that job," she says. "I called her constantly. She couldn't make a decision." Finally, the woman told Grandstaff that it was between her and someone else and that she just couldn't decide. To which Grandstaff said, "Flat out: What do I have to say to you to give me the edge? What do you want to hear, and I'll say it. What do you want me to do? I'll do it." Apparently these questions were what the MTV executive wanted to hear. Grandstaff got the job.

BE NICE TO THE INTERVIEWER'S SECRETARY

A survey of executives at the country's largest companies found that   39
nearly two-thirds of the interviewers consider the opinion of their administrative assistants with regard to the interviewee who walks past them on their way in and out of their bosses' offices. So be smart and just say, "I just had some water, I'm fine, thank you," when they ask you if you would like anything to drink. Asking for a coffee, light, one sugar, isn't going to score you points.

There's no formula to any of this. Some applicants get really   40
lucky and land something quickly. Most, however, collect a few horror stories to tell. And that's the reality: At best, getting a job has always been an elusive and difficult task. So whatever you do, don't get sucked into that slacker pity party presently taking place on couches and in bars everywhere, the one that goes like this: "Man, there's no jobs available. The baby boomers took them all."

As Greg Drebin, vice president of programming at MTV, says,   41
"When people say, 'Well, now is a really hard time for the industry,' and all that . . . well, it's always a hard time. There's no such thing as

'Oh, it's hiring season; we've got all these jobs that just became available.' You know what? There's always jobs, and there's never jobs."

QUESTIONS ON SUBJECT AND PURPOSE

1. Drozdyk's opening example is drawn from a film, *The Graduate*, made in 1967. How effective is that example? Why might he use it?
2. Are there ever times in Drozdyk's essay when you disagree or feel uncomfortable with the advice that he is giving?
3. What assumptions does Drozdyk make about the reasons why people attend college? Do you agree with those assumptions?

QUESTIONS ON STRATEGY AND AUDIENCE

1. Why might Drozdyk title the essay "Into the Loop"?
2. Drozdyk quotes from a number of people throughout the essay. Why might he do so, and how effective is the strategy?
3. To whom is Drozdyk writing? How specifically can you define that audience?

QUESTIONS ON VOCABULARY AND STYLE

1. How would you characterize the tone of Drozdyk's essay? (See the Glossary for a definition of *tone*.)
2. Find examples of words or expressions that Drozdyk uses to connect with an audience of late teenagers and "twentysomethings."
3. Be prepared to define the following words and phrases: *barrage* (paragraph 1), *catatonic* (1), *snivel* (12), *rescind* (18), *proven commodities* (23), *cold-call* (29), *cardinal sin* (34).

WRITING SUGGESTIONS

1. **For Your Journal.** Jot down in your journal a list of possible internships or volunteer positions for which you might apply. Remember that such positions might not involve specific job skills but rather particular "people" skills that are transferable to many jobs. Visit your college's placement office for possible suggestions as well. Your major department might also be a source of information.

2. **For a Paragraph.** Using your list, the advice in Drozdyk's essay, and any advice that you can get from your college's placement office, write a paragraph in which you describe the process by which you (or anyone else) would apply for a specific internship or volunteer position.

3. **For an Essay.** Write an essay in which you offer advice on how an undergraduate at your college can locate and apply for internships and volunteer positions. With your instructor's approval, you might consider writing the essay for your school's student newspaper or as a brochure that could be handed out by the placement office.

4. **For Research.** In what ways is electronic communication changing the nature of a job search? For example, increasing numbers of individuals are mounting personal Web pages that advertise their talents and skills in ways somewhat similar to the old printed résumé. How are the new technologies influencing job search strategies? Research the problem and the future directions. Remember that source information will have to be current, so look for very recent books and articles. You might want to use the World Wide Web to find examples, as well, or interview people. In a researched essay, bring Drozdyk's advice up to date for the early 2000s.

WEBSITE LINK

Can the Web help you find a job? What Web resources are available for job seekers? If you post your résumé on the Web, will you find a job? The Website links you to some good advice.

WRITING LINK: INTEGRATING QUOTATIONS

Drozdyk uses a large number of quotations from interviewees. Look carefully at how he integrates these quotations into his essay. Try writing a set of guidelines for your classmates on how to integrate quotations into an essay.

THE PAGE TURNER

Lynne Sharon Schwartz

Lynne Sharon Schwartz (1939–   ) is the author of a number of books including novels, collections of essays, and a children's book. Some of her shorter work has been collected in A Lynne Sharon Schwartz Reader: Selected Prose and Poetry *(1992). Her most recent books are* Face to Face: A Reader in the World *(2000) and* In Solitary: Poems *(2002).*

On Writing: *In* Ruined by Reading *Schwartz writes about what she admires in other writers: "The good writer offers a new language, the silent language of the inner voice. . . . From Faulkner to Gertrude Stein to Virginia Woolf, the writers who claim our attention do so by voice and idiom, which are the audible manifestations of the mind. This is how it sounds inside, they declare. Listen, hear the shape within me. . . . [T]he only new thing under the sun is the sound of another voice."*

BEFORE READING

Connecting: If you have been to a piano concert—or seen one on television—have you ever noticed the page turner? Do you think that you, as a member of the audience, should notice a page turner?

Anticipating: What is it about the page turner that so captures Schwartz's attention?

1   The page turner appears from the wings and walks onstage, into the light, a few seconds after the pianist and the cellist, just as the welcoming applause begins to wane. By her precise timing the page turner acknowledges, not so much humbly as serenely, lucidly, that the applause is not meant for her: she has no intention of appropriating any part of the welcome. She is onstage merely to serve a purpose, a worthy purpose even if a bit absurd—a concession, amid the coming glories, to the limitations of matter and of spirit. Precision of timing, it goes without saying, is the most important attribute of a page turner. Also important is unobtrusiveness.

2   But strive though she may to be unobtrusive, to dim or diminish her radiance in ways known only to herself, the page turner cannot render herself invisible, and so her sudden appearance onstage is as exciting as the appearance of the musicians; it gives the audience an unantici-

pated stab of pleasure. The page turner is golden-tressed—yes, "tresses" is the word for the mass of hair rippling down her back, hair that emits light like a shower of fine sparkles diffusing into the glow of the stage lights. She is young and tall, younger and taller than either of the musicians, who are squarish, unprepossessing middle-aged men. She wears black, a suitable choice for one who should be unobtrusive. Yet the arresting manner in which her black clothes shelter her flesh, flesh that seems molded like clay and yields to the fabric with a certain playful, even droll resistance, defies unobtrusiveness. Her black long-sleeved knit shirt reaches just below her waist, and the fabric of her perfectly fitting black slacks stirs gently around her narrow hips and thighs. Beyond the hem of her slacks can be glimpsed her shiny, but not too conspicuously shiny, black boots with a thick two-inch heel. Her face is heart-shaped, like the illustrations of princesses in fairy tales. The skin of her face and neck and hands, the only visible skin, is pale, an off-white like heavy cream or the best butter. Her lips are painted magenta.

Of course she is not a princess or even a professional beauty   3
hired to enhance the decor but most likely, offstage, a music student, selected as a reward for achievement or for having demonstrated an ability to sit still and turn the pages at the proper moment. Or else she has volunteered for any number of practical reasons: to help pay for her studies, to gain experience of being onstage. Perhaps she should have been disqualified because of her appearance, which might distract from the music. But given the principles of fair play and equal opportunity, beauty can no more disqualify than plainness. For the moment, though, life offstage and whatever the page turner's place in it might be are far removed from the audience, transported as they are by the hair combed back from her high forehead and cascading in a loose, lacy mass that covers her back like a cloak.

In the waiting hush, the page turner lowers her body onto a   4
chair to the left and slightly behind the pianist's seat, the fabric of her slacks adjusting around her recalcitrant hips, the hem rising a trifle to reveal more of her boots. She folds her white hands patiently in her lap like lilies resting on the surface of a dark pond and fixes her eyes on the sheets of music on the rack, her body calm but alert for the moment when she must perform her task.

After the musicians' usual tics and fussing, the pianist's last-   5
minute swipes at face and hair, the cellist's slow and fastidious tuning of his instrument, his nervous flicking of his jacket away from his body as if to let his torso breathe, the music begins. The page turner, utterly still, waits. Very soon, she rises soundlessly and leans forward—and at this instant, with the right side of her upper body leaning over

the pianist, the audience inevitably imagines him, feels him, inhaling the fragrance of her breast and arm, of her cascading hair; they imagine she exudes a delicate scent, lightly alluring but not so alluring as to distract the pianist, not more alluring than the music he plays.

6   She stays poised briefly in that leaning position until with a swift movement, almost a surprise yet unsurprising, she reaches her hand over to the right-hand page. The upper corner of the page is already turned down, suggesting that the page turner has prepared the music in advance, has, in her patient, able manner (more like a lady in waiting, really, than an idle fairy-tale princess), folded down all the necessary corners so that she need not fumble when the moment arrives. At the pianist's barely perceptible nod, she propels the page in the blink of an eye through its small leftward arc and smooths it flat, then seats herself, her body drifting lightly yet firmly, purposefully, down to the chair. Once again the edge of her short shirt sinks into her waist and the folds of her slacks reassemble beguilingly over her hips; the hem of her slacks rises to reveal more of her shiny boots. With her back straight, her seated body making a slender black L shape, once again she waits with hands folded, and very soon rises, quite silently, to perform the same set of movements. Soon this becomes a ritual, expected and hypnotic, changeless and evocative.

7   The page turner listens attentively but appears, fittingly, unmoved by the music itself; her body is focused entirely on her task, which is a demanding one, not simply turning the pages at the proper moments but dimming her presence, suppressing everything of herself except her attentiveness. But as able as she proves to be at turning pages—never a split second late, never fumbling with the corners or making an excessive gesture—she cannot, in her helpless radiance, keep from absorbing all the visual energy in the concert hall. The performance taking place in the hall is a gift to the ear, and while all ears are fully occupied, satiated—the musicians being excellent, more than excellent, capable of seraphic sounds—the listeners' eyes are idle. The musicians are only moderately interesting to look at. The eyes crave occupation too. Offered a pleasure to match that of the ears, naturally the eyes accept the offering. They fix on the page turner—pale skin, black clothes, and gold tresses—*who surely knows she is being watched, who cannot deflect the gaze of the audience, only absorb it into the deep well of her stillness,* her own intent yet detached absorption in the music.

8   The very banality of her task lends her a dignity, adds a richness to her already rich presence, since it illustrates a crucial truth: banality is necessary in the making of splendid music, or splendid anything for that matter, much like the pianist's probable clipping of his fin-

gernails or the cellist's rosining of his bow, though such banalities are performed in private, which is just as well.

And then little by little, while the listeners' eyes yearn toward the page turner, it comes to appear that her purpose is not so banal after all, nor is she anything so common as a distraction. Instead it appears that she has an unusual and intimate connection with the music. She is not a physical expression of it, a living symbol; that would be too facile. More subtly, she might be an emanation of the music, a phantom conjured into being by the sounds, but her physical reality—her stylish clothes and shiny boots—contradicts this possibility, and besides, the audience has seen her enter minutes before the music began and can attest to her independent life. No, the connection must be this: though the pianist is clearly striking the keys and the cellist drawing the bow over the strings (with, incidentally, many unfortunate contortions of his face), it comes to seem, through the force of the audience's gaze, that the music is issuing from the page turner, effortlessly, or through some supernatural, indescribable effort, as she sits in her golden radiance and stillness. So that as the concert proceeds, the audience gazes ever more raptly at the page turner. By virtue of her beauty and their gaze, she has become an ineffable instrument—no longer a distraction but rather the very source of the music.

Though the concert is long, very long, the air in the hall remains charged with vitality, the seraphic sounds yielding an ecstasy for which the entranced listeners silently bless the page turner. But perhaps because the concert is long and the page turner is only human, not even a princess, she cannot maintain her aloof pose forever. Though not flagging in her task, without any lapse of efficiency, she begins to show her pleasure in the music as any ordinary person might: her eyelids tremble at a finely executed turn, her lips hint at a smile for a satisfying chord resolution. Her breathing is visible, her upper body rising and sinking with the undulations of the sounds swirling about her. She leans into the music, once or twice even swaying her body a bit. While undeniably pretty to watch, this relaxation of discipline is a sad portent. It suggests the concert has gone on almost long enough, that beauty cannot be endlessly sustained, and that we, too, cannot remain absorbed indefinitely in radiant stillness: we have our limits, even for ecstasy. Banality beckons us back to its leaden, relieving embrace. The ordinary, appreciative movements of the page turner are a signal that the concert will soon end. We feel an anticipatory nostalgia for the notes we are hearing, even for the notes we have not yet heard, have yet to hear, which will be the closing notes. The early notes of a concert lead us into a safe and luxuriant green meadow of sound, a kind of Eden of the ear, but there comes a point, the climax in the music's arc, when we grasp that the notes are curving back and leading us out of the meadow, back into silent and harsher weather.

11   And this impression of being led regrettably back to dailiness grows still stronger when now and then the pianist glances over at the page turner with a half-smile, a tacit acknowledgment related to some passage in the music, maybe to a little problem of page turning successfully overcome, a private performance within the public performance, which will remain forever unfathomed by the audience and for those instants makes us feel excluded. With their work almost over the performers can afford such small indulgences—a foretaste of the inevitable melancholy moment when audience and performers, alike excluded, will file out into their lives, stripped of this glory, relieved of its burden.

12   When the music ends, as it must, the page turner remains composed and still: unlike the musicians, she does not relax into triumphant relief. As they take their bows, they show intimate glimpses of themselves in the ardor of achievement, as well as a happy camaraderie—their arms around each other's shoulders—in which the page turner cannot share, just as she cannot share in the applause or show intimate glimpses of herself. She stands patiently beside her chair near the piano and then, with the same precise timing as at the start, leaves the stage a few seconds after the musicians, deftly gathering up the music from the rack to carry off with her, tidying up like a good lady in waiting.

13   The musicians reappear for more bows. The page turner does not reappear. Her service is completed. We understand her absence yet we miss her, as though an essential part of the lingering pleasure is being withheld, as though the essential instrument through which the music reached us has vanished along with the sounds themselves. We do not wish to think of what ordinary gestures she might now be performing off in the wings, putting the music away or lifting her hair off her neck with long staved-off weariness, released from the burden of being looked at. We cannot deny her her life, her future, yet we wish her to be only as she was onstage, in the beginning. We will forget how the musicians looked, but ever after when we revisit the music we will see the page turner—black clothes, golden hair, regal carriage—radiant and still, emitting the sounds that too briefly enraptured us.

QUESTIONS ON SUBJECT AND PURPOSE

1. In what way is this essay an example of a process narrative?
2. What does Schwartz leave out of her essay? That is, what doesn't she tell us about the concert?
3. How does the role of the page turner change in paragraph 9?

QUESTIONS ON STRATEGY AND AUDIENCE

1. Schwartz insists in paragraphs 1 and 2 that an important attribute of a page turner is that the person be "unobtrusive." What is ironic about that comment?
2. How is the essay told or narrated?
3. Does the essay describe only Schwartz's reaction? Does she ever imply that others saw and felt what she did?

QUESTIONS ON VOCABULARY AND STYLE

1. Schwartz uses a number of similes in her description of the page turner. Check the Glossary first to make sure you know what a simile is, and then locate the similes in the essay.
2. Would you say that Schwartz's essay is a vivid description? What makes an essay descriptive?
3. Be prepared to define the following words: *wane* (paragraph 1), *droll* (2), *recalcitrant* (4), *tics* (5), *fastidious* (5), *beguilingly* (6), *evocative* (6), *satiated* (7), *seraphic* (7), *banality* (8), *facile* (9), *emanation* (9), *raptly* (9), *ineffable* (9), *portent* (10), *camaraderie* (12).

WRITING SUGGESTIONS

1. **For Your Journal.** A live concert, regardless of the nature of the music it features—rock, ska, hip-hop, country, classical—is a performance, an experience that involves all the senses. Think about your experiences at a live concert. If possible, attend one at your school. Take notes, jot down your memories in your journal about what is happening or happened to you as a member of the audience during the entire performance.

2. **For a Paragraph.** Use your journal experiences as a basis for a paragraph. Remember that you are not "reviewing" the music. Schwartz, for example, never tells us what pieces the musicians played; she never comments on their specific execution of that music. Rather, she focuses on the visual perceptions and observations of an audience member—and by implication all audience members—during the performance. In your paragraph, focus on a single detail.

3. **For an Essay.** Expand your paragraph into an essay. You might want to follow your experience from beginning to end—that is, use a chronological pattern for your process narrative.

4. **For Research.** Tours by major recording artists today are generally complicated, elaborately staged, corporately sponsored affairs. Sometimes the tours even have names. Choose your favorite big-name artist or group and research the process by which they mount such elaborate productions. What is involved? How does the tour develop and what does it involve? What type of planning and strategy lies behind the production?

WEBSITE LINK

According to a story on the Web, an MIT inventor recently built an inexpensive automatic page turner, created at the request of musicians. How would that have changed Schwartz's essay!

WRITING LINK: ADJECTIVES

How does Schwartz use adjectives in her essay? Start with a definition of an adjective, and then pick one of Schwartz's paragraphs to analyze. Underline all of the adjectives in the paragraph. How many are there? We sometimes think that adjectives make writing and description vivid. Is that always true? What else can make your writing vivid?

PREWRITING SUGGESTIONS FOR PROCESS

1. Brainstorm some possible topics that lend themselves to a process narrative—how something is done, how to do something, the stages in which something occurred, or your plan for handling a situation. Do not commit too quickly to a particular topic—allow a couple of days for just thinking about possibilities. Jot down ideas; take notes.
2. Answer the question, "Why am I writing about this?" What purpose do you have in mind? Are you trying to inform your reader? Entertain your reader? Explore your own past or your motivations? Persuade your reader? Remember that an essay needs a purpose.
3. Think about the steps or stages in the process that you are describing. Remember that you probably need somewhere between three and six. If the process involves fewer than three, it might be too simple to justify an essay; if it has more than six, it might be too complicated. This is not an unbreakable rule; use it for guidance.
4. Are your steps or stages phrased in parallel form? Use a marker to underline the start of each new step or stage. Look at the underlined sentences. Are they parallel in grammatical form?
5. Consider how your steps or stages might be ordered. Is there an obvious place in which to start? To end? What about the middle of the process? If you do have options, experiment with some to see what you think might work best.

REWRITING SUGGESTIONS FOR PROCESS

1. Look carefully at the organizational strategy that you have used. Are the steps or stages in the process in a logical or chronological order? Could you construct a flowchart or a time line outlining those steps?
2. Have you clearly marked the steps or stages in the process in your essay? Have you used step ("first," "second") or time ("now," "then," "finally") markers to indicate the proper sequence for your reader?

3. Look again at your introduction and conclusion. Do you catch your reader's attention in your introduction? Do you have a clear thesis statement? Does your conclusion simply repeat what you said in your introduction? Or do you end on a thought-provoking note?

4. Never underestimate the power of a good title. Try to write at least four different titles for your paper. Ask some friends or classmates to evaluate each one.

5. Once you have a complete draft, find someone to read your essay and offer honest advice. Perhaps it might be a classmate? Maybe you could visit your school's Writing Center? Perhaps even your instructor might have the time to read your essay before you hand it in. Look for readers and then listen to what they say.

CAUSE AND EFFECT

I t is a rainy morning and you are late for class. Driving to campus in an automobile with faulty brakes, you have an accident. Considering the circumstances, the accident might be attributable to a variety of causes:

> You were driving too fast.
> The visibility was poor.
> The roads were slippery.
> The brakes did not work properly.

Visually, cause and effect can be displayed in diagrams, called "fishbone" diagrams, which are tools used to analyze and display possible causes. If we used a fishbone diagram to analyze your accident, it might look like this:

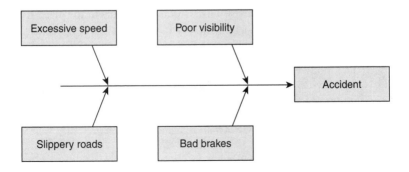

The diagram could also branch out further since the accident, in turn, could produce a series of consequences or effects:

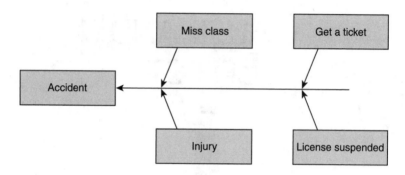

Susan Strasser, for example, uses a cause and effect strategy when she suggests that part of the popularity of fast-food restaurants lies in the appeal of "stylized, repetitive, stereotyped events." Notice how Strasser structures the following paragraph to show how this ritualization is one "cause" for such restaurants' popularity:

> People arrive at McDonald's—and to a lesser extent at the other chains—knowing what they will eat, what they will pay, what to say to the counter person and how she or he will respond, what the restaurant will look like—in short, knowing exactly what to expect and how to behave; children learn these expectations and behaviors early in life. For some, the ritual constitutes an attraction of these restaurants; they neither wish to cook nor to chat with a waitress as she intones and delivers the daily specials. The fast-food ritual requires no responsibility other than ordering (with as few words as possible) and paying; nobody has to set or clear the table, wash the dishes, or compliment the cook on her cuisine, the traditional responsibilities of husbands and children at the family dinner.*

Strasser turns her analysis of fast-food restaurants in the other direction—toward effects—when she discusses how "fast food eating" has affected mealtime rituals at home:

> Fast foods have changed eating habits far beyond the food itself; they have invaded the mealtime ritual even at home. The chief executive officer of Kraft, Inc., maintained that eating out accustomed people to "portion control" and therefore to accepting a processor's statement that a package of macaroni and cheese serves four.

---

*Susan Strasser, *Never Done: A History of American Housework* (New York: Random House, 1982), pp. 296–97.

"Generally speaking," one writer claimed in *Advertising Age*, "the homemaker no longer sets the table with dishes of food from which the family fills their plates—the individual plates are filled and placed before the family, no second helpings." Eating out even accustoms diners at the same table to eating different food, putting home meals of different prepared foods within the realm of possibility and altering the nature of parental discipline; freed from the "shut up— you'll eat what we're eating" rule, children experience the pleasures and also the isolation of individual free choice at earlier ages.*

Causes and effects can be either immediate or remote with reference to time. The lists regarding the hypothetical car accident suggest only immediate causes and effects, things that could be most directly linked in time to the accident. Another pair of lists of more remote causes and effects could be compiled—for example, your brakes were faulty because you did not have the money to fix them, or because of your accident, your insurance rates will go up.

Causes and effects can be either primary or secondary with reference to their significance or importance. If you had not been in a hurry and driving too fast, it might not have mattered that the visibility was poor, the roads were slippery, or your brakes were faulty. Similarly, if you or someone else had been injured, the other consequences would have seemed insignificant in comparison.

In some instances, causes and effects are linked in a causal chain: if you were driving too fast and tried to stop on slippery roads with inadequate brakes, each of those causes is interlinked in the inevitable accident. Likewise, the accident means that you will get a ticket, that ticket carries points against your license, your license could as a result be suspended, and either way your insurance rates will certainly climb.

WHY DO YOU WRITE A CAUSE AND EFFECT ANALYSIS?

Cause and effect analyses are intended to reveal the reasons why something happened or the consequences of a particular occurrence. E. M. Forster in "My Wood" examines the consequences of owning property. Joan Jacobs Brumberg in "The Origins of Anorexia Nervosa" examines some of the causes of anorexia nervosa, tracing the disease back to its origins in middle-class families in the nineteenth century. Brent Staples in "Black Men and Public Space" uses his own experiences as an urban night walker to explore the effects that he, as a black male, has on those who share the streets with him. Veronica Chambers in "Dreadlocked" explains both why she wears her hair in

dreadlocks and what those "dreads" suggest to people. Fox Butterfield in "Why They Excel" explores some of the reasons why Asian
and Asian American students do so well in academic studies. Finally,
Malcolm Gladwell in "The Trouble with Fries" tackles the question
of why, when we all know better, we consume so much fast food and
resist attempts to make it healthier for us.

Cause and effect analyses can also be used to persuade readers
to do or believe something. Fox Butterfield's analysis of the cultural
roots of Asian academic excellence is obviously meant to encourage
readers to reevaluate their own approach toward their children's education. Brent Staples's experiences as an urban night walker challenge all of us when we realize how quickly and easily we form
stereotypes—a young, large black man dressed casually on an urban
street must be dangerous, must be someone to avoid. Malcolm Gladwell, although he does not ask us to stop eating fast-food fries, does
force us to stop and think about our own behavior: why do we do this
even when we are fully aware that it is unhealthy?

How Do You Choose a Subject?

In picking a subject to analyze, first remember the limits of your assignment. The larger the subject, the more difficult it will be to do
justice to. Trying to analyze the causes of the Vietnam War or the effects of technology in five hundred words is an invitation to disaster.
Second, make sure that the relationships you see between causes and
effects are genuine. The fact that a particular event preceded another
does not necessarily mean that the first caused the second. In logic
this error is labeled *post hoc, ergo propter hoc* ("after this, therefore because of this"). If a black cat crossed the street several blocks before
your automobile accident, that does not mean that the cat was a cause
of the accident.

How Do You Isolate and Evaluate Causes and Effects?

Before you begin to write, take time to analyze and, if necessary, research your subject thoroughly. It is important that your analysis consider all of the major factors involved in the relationship. Relatively
few things are the result of a single cause, and rarely does a cause have
a single effect. Owning a piece of property—even if it is something

that cannot possibly be stolen—can have a number of effects on you, as E. M. Forster discovers. He becomes far more preoccupied by his property than he ever thought possible. Veronica Chambers discovers that her dreadlocks conjure up in people's minds a whole series of different identities. She is, in the eyes of others, simultaneously a "rebel child, Rasta mama, Nubian princess, drug dealer, unemployed artist, rock star, world-famous comedienne, and nature chick."

Depending on your subject, your analysis could be based on personal experience, thoughtful reflection and examination, or research. E. M. Forster's analysis of the effects of owning property is derived completely from studying his own reactions. Brent Staples draws on his own personal experiences and those of a fellow black journalist. Veronica Chambers's analysis of the effects of her dreadlocks is based on the reactions of those around her. Fox Butterfield relies on interviews and on statistical evidence gathered from library or database searches. Clearly Malcolm Gladwell has researched his essay on french fries, for he quotes from a number of print sources. Joan Jacobs Brumberg's essay is also built on extensive research, especially in sources in history, literature, medicine, and psychology. As these selections show, sometimes causes and effects are certain and unquestionable. At other times, the relationships are only probable or even speculative.

Once you have gathered a list of possible causes or effects, the next step is to evaluate each item. Any phenomenon can have many causes or many effects, so you will have to select the explanations that seem the most relevant or most convincing. Rarely should you list every cause or every effect you can find. Generally, you choose the causes or effects that are immediate and primary, although the choice is always determined by your purpose.

HOW DO YOU STRUCTURE A CAUSE AND EFFECT ANALYSIS?

By definition, causes precede effects, so a cause and effect analysis involves a linear or chronological order. Most commonly, you structure your analysis to reflect that sequence. If you are analyzing causes, typically you begin by identifying the subject that you are trying to explain and then move to analyze its causes. Malcolm Gladwell begins by narrating McDonald's founder Ray Kroc's role in the scientific development of the fast-food french fry. The perfection of the french fry has had, however, serious health consequences. Gladwell points to some possible solutions to the unhealthy french fry, but then explores why American consumers seem unwilling to demand that fast food become healthy food. Knowing the health risks, and having alternative answers at hand, why do we persist in eating unhealthy food?

If you are analyzing effects, typically you begin by identifying the subject that produced the effects and then move to enumerate or explain what those effects were. E. M. Forster begins by describing how he came to purchase his "wood" and then describes four distinct effects that ownership had on him.

A cause and effect analysis can also go in both directions. Veronica Chambers begins by remembering what it was like to have "bad" nappy hair and what that meant in the black community in the late 20th century. She explains the causes that led to her decision to wear her hair in dreadlocks. But Chambers also moves forward, looking then at the effects that her hairstyle had on others. "My hair," she writes, "says a lot of things."

Within these patterns, you face one other choice: If you are listing multiple causes or effects, how do you decide in what order to treat them? That arrangement depends on whether or not the reasons or consequences are linked in a chain. If they happen in a definite sequence, you would arrange them in an order to reflect that sequence—normally a chronological order (this happened, then this, and finally this). This linear arrangement is very similar to what you do in a process narrative except that your purpose is to answer the question *why* rather than *how*. In "Black Men and Public Space," Brent Staples follows a chronological pattern of development. He begins with his first experience as a night walker in Chicago and ends with his most recent experiences in Brooklyn. The essay includes a brief flashback as well, to his childhood days in Chester, Pennsylvania. As he is narrating his experiences, Staples explores the reasons why people react as they do when they encounter him at night on a city street. At the same time, Staples analyzes the impact or effects that their reactions have had on him.

But multiple causes and effects are not always linked. Brumberg's causes do not occur in any inevitable chronological order, nor do Forster's effects. If the causes or effects that you have isolated are not linked in a chain, you must find another way in which to order them. They could be arranged from immediate to remote, for example. When the degree of significance or importance varies, the most obvious structural choice would be to move from the primary to the secondary or from the secondary to the primary. Before you set any sequence, study your list of causes or effects to see whether any principle of order is evident—chronological, spatial, immediate to remote, primary to secondary. If you see a logical order, follow it.

For a cause and effect analysis, Cathy Ferguson chose to examine the effects that television's depiction of violence has on young children.

EARLIER DRAFT

TV AGGRESSION AND CHILDREN

Let's face it. Television producers are out to make money. Their main concern is with what sells. What does sell? Sensationalism. People like shocking stories. In the effort to sell, the limit of the outrageous on TV has been pushed far beyond what it was, say, ten years ago. Television aggression is one aspect of sensationalism that has been exploited to please a thrill-seeking audience. Television is not showing a greater number of aggressive scenes, but the scenes portray more violent and hostile acts. Psychologists, prompted by concerned parents, have been studying the effects of children viewing increased aggression, since the average program for kids contains twenty acts of violence per hour, while the overall average is only seven acts of violence per hour. Research reveals three outstanding consequences of viewing greater TV hostility. First of all, TV aggression numbs children to real-world violence. One experiment showed that even a brief exposure to a fairly violent show made kids indifferent to the same aggression in real life. Preschoolers are especially affected by TV violence because they are usually unable to distinguish between reality and fantasy. If they see a hostile act, they are liable to believe that it is reality and accept it as the norm.

This leads to the second effect of viewing TV aggression: a distorted perception of the world. Most TV shows do not present real-world consequences of violence; thus children are getting a false picture of their world. Some kids are led to believe that acts of hostility are normal, common, expected even, and may lead a fearfully restricted life. In general, however, most children learn not how to be afraid of violence but how to be violent, which is the third and most drastic effect of viewing television aggression. Almost all studies show that kids are more aggressive after they watch an aggressive show, like "Batman" or "Power Rangers," than after watching a pro-social show like "Barney and Friends" or a neutral show. So although sensationalism, especially violent sensationalism, is making money for TV producers, it is also creating a generation that is numb to real violence, has a distorted picture of the environment, and is itself more hostile. These effects are so palpable, it is now realized that the single best predictor of how aggressive an 18-year-old will be is how much aggressive television he watched when he was 8 years old.

After Cathy handed in her first draft, she had a conference with her instructor. The instructor commented on her effective use of examples. Because the essay contains specific evidence, the cause and effect analysis seems much more convincing.

Her instructor offered some specific advice about revisions in word choice, sentence structure, and paragraph division. He noted that the essay repeated the phrase "television aggression" or a related variant seven times. Since condensed forms can be confusing, he recommended that she indicate that what she was writing about was aggression, violence, or hostility depicted on television shows. Noting that her first draft begins with five very short sentences and a single-word sentence fragment, he urged her to combine the sentences to reduce the choppy effect. Finally, he recommended that she use paragraph divisions to separate the three effects that she discusses. That division would make it easier for her reader to see the structure of the paper.

Cathy's revision addressed each of the problems that had been discussed in conference. In addition, she made a number of minor changes to tighten the prose and make it clearer.

THE INFLUENCE OF TELEVISED VIOLENCE ON CHILDREN

Let's face it. Television producers are in business to make money. Their main concern is what sells, and nothing sells better than sensationalism. In an effort to gain a larger share of the audience, television producers now treat subject matter that would never have been acceptable ten years ago. The depiction of violence on television is one aspect of that sensationalism, exploited to please a thrill-seeking audience. The number of aggressive scenes shown on television has not increased, but those scenes now portray more violent and hostile acts. This is especially true on shows aimed at children.

Psychologists, prompted by concerned parents, have begun studying the effects on children of viewing this increased aggression. The average program for children contains twenty acts of violence per hour, compared to an overall average of seven acts of violence per hour. Research reveals three significant consequences of viewing violence on television.

First, aggressive acts on television numb children to real-world violence. One study showed that even a brief exposure to a fairly violent show made children indifferent to the same aggression in real life. Preschoolers are especially affected by television because they are usually unable to distinguish between reality and fantasy. If they see an aggressive act, they are likely to believe that it is real and so accept it as normal.

This potential confusion leads to the second effect of watching violence on television: a distorted perception of the world. Some children are led to believe that acts of hostility are normal, common, and even expected. As a result, these children may lead a restricted life, afraid of the violence that they imagine lurks everywhere.

In general, however, most children learn not to be afraid of violence but how to be violent—the third and most drastic effect of viewing aggression on television. Almost all studies show that children are more aggressive after they watch a show that includes violence than after watching a show that excludes it.

All three effects are so palpable that it is now realized the single best predictor of how aggressive an 18-year-old will be is how much violence he watched on television when he was 8 years old.

SOME THINGS TO REMEMBER

1. Choose a topic that can be analyzed thoroughly within the limits of the assignment.
2. Decide on a purpose: are you trying to explain or to persuade?
3. Determine an audience. For whom are you writing? What does your audience already know about your subject?
4. Analyze and research your subject. Remember to provide factual support wherever necessary. Not every cause and effect analysis can rely on unsupported opinion.
5. Be certain that the relationships you see between causes and effects are genuine.
6. Concentrate your efforts on immediate and primary causes or effects rather than on remote or secondary ones. Do not try to list every cause or every effect that you can.
7. Begin with the cause and then move to effects, or begin with an effect and then move to its causes.
8. Look for a principle of order to organize your list of causes or effects. It might be chronological or spatial, for example, or it might move from immediate to remote or from primary to secondary.
9. Remember that you are explaining why something happens or what will happen. You are not just describing how.

VISUALIZING CAUSE AND EFFECT

At the core of every murder mystery is the search for causes, or motives—a reason for committing the crime. George Booth's cartoon depends on our awareness of cause and effect. We know the effect of the falling potted begonia—Mr. Goodrich is dead. Mrs. Burlington Wells suggests a cause (which clearly rules out any possibility of her having a motive)—the plant "went off by accident." A likely story, we might reply!

*"This is Mrs. Burlington Wells. One of my begonias went
off by accident and killed Mr. Goodrich."*

"This is Mrs. Burlington Wells. One of my begonias went off by
accident and killed Mr. Goodrich." © *The New Yorker Collection 1998
by George Booth from cartoonbank.com. All Rights Reserved.*

CAUSE AND EFFECT AS A LITERARY STRATEGY

Marge Piercy's poem "Barbie Doll" uses a cause and effect structure
in order to comment on the physical ideals that society offers to
young women. As you read, think about what is the cause and what is
the effect and how those two elements are arranged in the poem. See
page 378.

BARBIE DOLL

Marge Piercg

This girlchild was born as usual
and presented dolls that did pee-pee
and miniature GE stoves and irons
and wee lipsticks the color of cherry candy.
Then in the magic of puberty, a classmate said:
You have a great big nose and fat legs.

She was healthy, tested intelligent,
possessed strong arms and back,
abundant sex drive and manual dexterity.
She went to and fro apologizing.
Everyone saw a fat nose on thick legs.

She was advised to play coy,
exhorted to come on hearty,
exercise, diet, smile and wheedle.
Her good nature wore out
like a fan belt.
So she cut off her nose and her legs
and offered them up.
In the casket displayed on satin she lay
with the undertaker's cosmetics painted on,
a turned-up putty nose,
dressed in a pink and white nightie.
Doesn't she look pretty? everyone said.
Consummation at last.
To every woman a happy ending.

DISCUSSION QUESTIONS

1. What happens to the "girlchild" in the story?
2. What is the cause and what is the effect in the poem?
3. What role does "Barbie" play in what happens?
4. In the final stanza what is the significance of details describing the woman's body?

5. What reaction might Piercy be trying to evoke in her readers? How is cause and effect being used in the poem?

WRITING SUGGESTIONS

It is difficult sometimes even to be aware of the pressures generated by popular culture yet alone to be able to deal with them. How are you influenced by what you see around you—by images in magazines, in advertisements, in films, in music, in television? To what extent are those images a problem? Do they ever make you do things you shouldn't, feel bad about yourself, or feel pressured to change or conform? Explore in an essay one aspect of the influence of popular culture on your life. Possible points of departure might include:

a. Your physical self—size, proportions, appearance
b. Your values or expectations in life—how do you measure success? happiness? fulfillment?
c. Your possessions

Using Cause and Effect in Writing for Your Other Courses

Writing to analyze causes and effects is common in many of the social sciences, in which research and study often involve an attempt to explain why people behave in certain ways or what the results of particular behaviors may be. Causal analysis is also common in the sciences, in which explaining the causes or effects of natural phenomena is a fundamental concern. Examples of assignments that would require analysis of causes or effects include the following.

- **Sociology or Communication.** For a research paper on the effects of racial or gender balance on group decision making, you might read about a number of jury decisions, considering closely the makeup of the juries in terms of race or gender, and write a paper explaining whether or not the makeup of each jury seemed to affect the eventual verdict.

- **Chemistry.** For an exam, you might be asked to trace the causal chain that leads to a specific chemical reaction.

- **History.** On an essay exam, you might be asked to explain the causes of the Great Depression (or another decisive period of history, such as the French Revolution or the collapse of the Soviet Union). Alternatively, you might be asked to discuss the effects of such a period.

- **Environmental Studies.** As part of an ongoing research assignment, you might be asked to draft an environmental impact statement, researching the short-term and long-term effects of a proposed development in your community.

- **Theater.** For a short interpretive paper, you might analyze one of Shakespeare's plays in terms of how its structure and characters were influenced by the physical conditions of English Renaissance theaters and the companies that acted the play.

- **Geology.** On an exam, you might be asked to explain the causes or effects (or both) of a phenomenon such as continental drift.

- **Education.** For a research paper on the effects of a controversial educational policy, you might research bilingual education to report on how successfully or unsuccessfully it seems to prepare students for English-language proficiency.

VISIT THE PRENTICE HALL READER'S WEBSITE

When you have finished reading an essay, check out the additional material available at the *Reader*'s Website at www.prenhall.com/miller. For each reading, you will find a list of related readings connected with the topic or the author; additional background information; a group of relevant "hot-linked" Web resources (just click your computer's mouse and automatically visit the sites listed); and still more writing suggestions.

TRACING CAUSES AND EFFECTS

What do you know about Alzheimer's disease? Visit the Alzheimer's Association Website and read about the causes and effects of the disease. Write a paragraph on this or another disease. A collection of links can be found at the *Reader*'s Website.

MY WOOD

E. M. Forster

Edward Morgan Forster (1879–1970) was born in London, England, and earned two undergraduate degrees and a master's degree from King's College, Cambridge University. He is best known as a novelist, but he also wrote short stories, literary criticism, biographies, histories, and essays. His novels, many of which have recently been made into popular films, include A Room with a View *(1908),* Howards End *(1910), and* A Passage to India *(1924). He published two collections of essays,* Abinger Harvest *(1936) and* Two Cheers for Democracy *(1951).*

On Writing: *Once, after having broken his right arm in a fall, Forster contemplated writing with his left hand: "The attempt to write with the left hand raises new hopes in the human heart. For how many years have our thoughts been transmitted by the nerves and muscles of the right hand. How much of their essence might not have been absorbed in the passage. Now when new organs are brought into play new thoughts or new parts of thoughts may find their way on to the page, how many old ones can be absent and fail to reach it. A physiological outcry may be raised at this. But at all events the thought that it may occur is new. . . . [T]he thoughts that have so long struggled for expression may at last find it."*

BEFORE READING

Connecting: What would you regard as the most important "thing" that you own? Why is it most important to you?

Anticipating: Forster observes that owning the wood made him feel "heavy." In what sense does it make him feel "heavy"?

A few years ago I wrote a book which dealt in part with the difficulties of the English in India. Feeling that they would have had no difficulties in India themselves, the Americans read the book freely. The more they read it the better it made them feel, and a cheque to the author was the result. I bought a wood with the cheque. It is not a large wood—it contains scarcely any trees, and it is intersected, blast it, by a public footpath. Still, it is the first property that I have owned, so it is right that other people should participate in my shame, and should ask themselves, in accents that will vary in horror, this   1 very important question: What is the effect of property upon the character? Don't let's touch economics; the effect of private ownership upon the community as a whole is another question—a more important question, perhaps, but another one. Let's keep to psychology. If you own things, what's their effect on you? What's the effect on me of my wood?

2   In the first place, it makes me feel heavy. Property does have this effect. Property produces men of weight, and it was a man of weight who failed to get into the Kingdom of Heaven. He was not wicked, that unfortunate millionaire in the parable, he was only stout; he stuck out in front, not to mention behind, and as he wedged himself this way and that in the crystalline entrance and bruised his well-fed flanks, he saw beneath him a comparatively slim camel passing through the eye of a needle and being woven into the robe of God. The Gospels all through couple stoutness and slowness. They point out what is perfectly obvious, yet seldom realized: that if you have a lot of things you cannot move about a lot, that furniture requires dusting, dusters require servants, servants require insurance stamps, and the whole tangle of them makes you think twice before you accept an invitation to dinner or go for a bathe in the Jordan. Sometimes the Gospels proceed further and say with Tolstoy that property is sinful; they approach the difficult ground of asceticism here, where I cannot follow them. But as to the immediate effects of property on people, they just show straightforward logic. It produces men of weight. Men of weight cannot, by definition, move like the lightning from the East unto the West, and the ascent of a fourteen-stone bishop into a pulpit is thus the exact antithesis of the coming of the Son of Man. My wood makes me feel heavy.

3   In the second place, it makes me feel it ought to be larger.

4   The other day I heard a twig snap in it. I was annoyed at first, for I thought that someone was blackberrying, and depreciating the value of the undergrowth. On coming nearer, I saw it was not a man who had trodden on the twig and snapped it, but a bird, and I felt pleased. My bird. The bird was not equally pleased. Ignoring the relation between us, it took fright as soon as it saw the shape of my face, and flew straight over the boundary hedge into a field, the property of Mrs. Henessy, where it sat down with a loud squawk. It had become Mrs. Henessy's bird. Something seemed grossly amiss here, something that would not have occurred had the wood been larger. I could not afford to buy Mrs. Henessy out, I dared not murder her, and limitations of this sort beset me on every side. Ahab did not want that vineyard—he only needed it to round off his property, preparatory to plotting a new curve—and all the land around my wood has become

necessary to me in order to round off the wood. A boundary protects. But—poor little thing—the boundary ought in its turn to be protected. Noises on the edge of it. Children throw stones. A little more, and then a little more, until we reach the sea. Happy Canute! Happier Alexander! And after all, why should even the world be the limit of possession? A rocket containing a Union Jack, will, it is hoped, be shortly fired at the moon. Mars. Sirius. Beyond which . . . But these immensities ended by saddening me. I could not suppose that my wood was the destined nucleus of universal dominion—it is so very small and contains no mineral wealth beyond the blackberries. Nor was I comforted when Mrs. Henessy's bird took alarm for the second time and flew clean away from us all, under the belief that it belonged to itself.

In the third place, property makes its owner feel that he ought   5 to do something to it. Yet he isn't sure what. A restlessness comes over him, a vague sense that he has a personality to express—the same sense which, without any vagueness, leads the artist to an act of creation. Sometimes I think I will cut down such trees as remain in the wood, at other times I want to fill up the gaps between them with new trees. But impulses are pretentious and empty. They are not honest movements towards money-making or beauty. They spring from a foolish desire to express myself and from an inability to enjoy what I have got. Creation, property, enjoyment form a sinister trinity in the human mind. Creation and enjoyment are both very, very good, yet they are often unattainable without a material basis, and at such moments property pushes itself in as a substitute, saying, "Accept me instead—I'm good enough for all three." It is not enough. It is, as Shakespeare said of lust, "the expense of spirit in a waste of shame": it is "Before, a joy proposed; behind, a dream." Yet we don't know how to shun it. It is forced on us by our economic system as the alternative to starvation. It is forced on us by an internal defect in the soul, by the feeling that in property may lie the germs of self-development and of exquisite or heroic deeds. Our life on earth is, and ought to be, material and carnal. But we have not learned to manage our materialism and carnality properly; they are still entangled with the desire for ownership, where (in the words of Dante) "Possession is one with loss."

And this brings us to our fourth and final point: the blackberries.   6

Blackberries are not plentiful in the meagre grove, but they are   7 easily seen from the public footpath which traverses it, and all too easily gathered. Foxgloves, too—people will pull up the foxgloves, and ladies of an educational tendency even grub for toadstools to show them on the Monday in class. Other ladies, less educated, roll down the bracken in the arms of their gentlemen friends. There is paper, there are tins. Pray, does my wood belong to me or doesn't it? And, if it does, should I not own it best by allowing no one else to walk there? There is a wood near Lyme Regis, also cursed by a public footpath, where the owner has not hesitated on this point. He has built high stone walls on each side of the path, and has spanned it by bridges, so that the public circulate like termites while he gorges on the black-berries unseen. He really does own his wood, this able chap. Dives in Hell did pretty well, but the gulf dividing him from Lazarus could be traversed by vision, and nothing traverses it here. And perhaps I shall come to this in time. I shall wall in and fence out until I really taste the sweets of property. Enormously stout, endlessly avaricious, pseudocreative, intensely selfish, I shall weave upon my forehead the quadruple crown of possession until those nasty Bolshies come and take it off again and thrust me aside into the outer darkness.

QUESTIONS ON SUBJECT AND PURPOSE

1. According to Forster, what are the consequences of owning property?
2. Is there any irony in buying property from the royalties earned from a book about England's problems in India?
3. What purpose or purposes might Forster have had in writing the essay?

QUESTIONS ON STRATEGY AND AUDIENCE

1. In what way is this a cause and effect essay?
2. Look at the conclusion of the essay. Why does Forster end in this way? Why not add a more conventional conclusion?
3. What expectations does Forster seem to have about his audience? How do you know?

QUESTIONS ON VOCABULARY AND STYLE

1. Characterize the tone of Forster's essay. Is it formal? Informal? How is that tone achieved?
2. Forster makes extensive use of allusion in the essay. Some of the names are easily recognizable; others are less so. Identify the following allusions (all but c are to biblical stories). How does each fit into the context of the essay?
    a. The wealthy man in the parable (paragraph 2)

    b. Ahab and the vineyard (4)

    c. Canute and Alexander (4)

    d. Dives and Lazarus (7)

3. Be able to define the following words: *asceticism* (paragraph 2), *stone* (2), *depreciating* (4), *pretentious* (5), *carnal* (5), *foxgloves* (7), *bracken* (7), *avaricious* (7), *Bolshies* (7).

WRITING SUGGESTIONS

1. For Your Journal. Commenting on the second effect of owning property, Forster observes: "it makes me feel it ought to be larger" (paragraph 3). To what extent does something you own make you want to own something more? Concentrate on the possession you value most highly. Does owning it ever make you want to own more? Explore the idea.

2. For a Paragraph. Select something you own that is important to you—a house, a car, a stereo system, a pet, something you use for recreation. In a paragraph, describe the consequences of owning it. How has it changed your life and behavior? Are there negative as well as positive consequences?

3. For an Essay. Extend your paragraph into an essay. Explore each of the consequences you described in a separate paragraph.

4. For Research. Property ownership has frequently been used throughout history as a precondition for full participation in the affairs of government (voting, for example). A number of states in this country applied such a restriction until the practice was declared unconstitutional. Using outside sources, write a research essay that explains and analyzes either the reasons for such practices or their negative consequence. Be sure to document your sources.

WEBSITE LINK

An "unofficial" Website devoted to E. M. Forster includes a wide range of links to related topics such as hypertext versions of some of Forster's novels and Merchant/Ivory Productions, the film company responsible for making, among others, the film versions of Forster's novels *Howards End* and *A Room with a View.*

WRITING LINK: WRITING CONCLUSIONS

Write a new ending for Forster's essay. Try one that follows the advice you have learned from writing the typical five-paragraph essay—that is, write a very conventional, English-class-sounding conclusion. What is the effect of adding this ending to the essay? What does this suggest about writing effective conclusions?

THE ORIGINS OF ANOREXIA NERVOSA

Joan Jacobs Brumberg

Born in 1944 in Mount Vernon, New York, Joan Jacobs Brumberg earned a Ph.D. in American history at the University of Virginia. She is the Stephen H. Weiss Presidential Fellow and Professor at Cornell University. She has written many articles and several books, including Fasting Girls: The Emergence of Anorexia Nervosa *(1988), which studies the disease from historical, social, and familial perspectives. Her most recent book is* The Body Project: An Intimate History of American Girls *(1997). The following selection is from* Fasting Girls *and was published in* Harper's *magazine.*

On Writing: *In her preface to* The Body Project, *Brumberg praised an editor for helping her achieve "accessibility" and "shed the girdle of academese that shapes so many historical accounts of the past."*

BEFORE READING

Connecting: What attitudes toward food and toward mealtime do the members of your family share? Do you have "family" meals? Are there any rituals connected with mealtime?

Anticipating: Brumberg defines a certain environment in which anorexia nervosa emerged. What are the essential conditions of that environment?

C ontrary to the popular assumption that anorexia nervosa is a pe-   1
culiarly modern disorder, the malady first emerged in the Victorian era—long before the pervasive cultural imperative for a thin female body. The first clinical descriptions of the disorder appeared in England and France almost simultaneously in 1873. They were written by two well-known physicians: Sir William Withey Gull and Charles Lasègue. Lasègue, more than any other nineteenth-century doctor, captured the rhythm of repeated offerings and refusals that signaled the breakdown of reciprocity between parents and their anorexic daughter. By returning to its origins, we can see anorexia nervosa for what it is: a dysfunction in the bourgeois family system.

2   Family meals assumed enormous importance in the bourgeois milieu, in the United States as well as in England and France. Middle-class parents prided themselves on providing ample food for their children. The abundance of food and the care in its preparation became expressions of social status. The ambience of the meal symbolized the values of the family. A popular domestic manual advised, "Simple, healthy food, exquisitely prepared, and served upon shining dishes and brilliant silverware . . . a gentle blessing, and cheerful conversation, embrace the sweetest communions and the happiest moments of life." Among the middle class it seems that eating correctly was emerging as a new morality, one that set its members apart from the working class.

3   At the same time, food was used to express love in the nineteenth-century bourgeois household. Offering attractive and abundant meals was the particular responsibility and pleasure of middle-class wives and mothers. In America the feeding of middle-class children, from infancy on, had become a maternal concern no longer deemed appropriate to delegate to wet nurses, domestics, or governesses. Family meals were expected to be a time of instructive and engaging conversation. Participation was expected on both a verbal and gustatory level. In this context, refusing to eat was an unabashedly antisocial act. Anorexic behavior was antithetical to the ideal of bourgeois eating. One advice book, *Common Sense for Maid, Wife, and Mother,* stated: "Heated discussion and quarrels, fretfulness and sullen taciturnity while eating, are as unwholesome as they are unchristian."

4   Why would a daughter affront her parents by refusing to eat? Lasègue's 1873 description of anorexia nervosa, along with other nineteenth-century medical reports, suggests that pressure to marry may have precipitated the illness.

5   Ambitious parents surely understood that by marrying well, at an appropriate moment, a daughter, even though she did not carry the family name, could help advance a family's social status—particularly in a burgeoning middle-class society. As a result, the issue of marriage loomed large in the life of a dutiful middle-class daughter. Although marriage did not generally occur until the girl's early twenties, it was an event for which she was continually prepared, and a desirable outcome for all depended on the ability of the parents and the child to work together—that is, to state clearly what each wanted or to read each other's heart and mind. In the context of marital expectations, a daughter's refusal to eat was a provocative rejection of both the family's social aspirations and their goodwill toward her. All of the parents' plans for her future (and their own) could be stymied by her peculiar and unpleasant alimentary nihilism.

Beyond the specific anxieties generated by marital pressure, the   6
Victorian family milieu in America and in Western Europe harbored
a mélange of other tensions and problems that provided the emotional preconditions for the emergence of anorexia nervosa. As love
replaced authority as the cement of family relations, it began to gen-
erate its own set of emotional disorders.

Possessiveness, for example, became an acute problem in Vic-   7
torian family life. Where love between parents and children was the
prevailing ethic, there was always the risk of excess. When love became suffocating or manipulative, individuation and separation from
the family could become extremely painful, if not impossible. In the
context of increased intimacy, adolescent privacy was especially problematic: For parents and their sexually maturing daughters, what constituted an appropriate degree of privacy? Middle-class girls, for
example, almost always had their own rooms or shared them with sisters, but they had greater difficulty establishing autonomous psychic
space. The well-known penchant of adolescent girls for novel-reading
was an expression of their need for imaginative freedom. Some parents, recognizing that their daughters needed channels for expressing
emotions, encouraged diary-keeping. But some of the same parents
who gave lovely marbled journals as gifts also monitored their content. Since emotional freedom was not an acknowledged prerogative
of the Victorian adolescent girl, it seems likely that she would have
expressed unhappiness in non-verbal forms of behavior. One such behavior was refusal of food.

When an adolescent daughter became sullen and chronically re-   8
fused to eat, her parents felt threatened and confused. The daughter
was perceived as willfully manipulating her appetite the way a younger
child might. Because parents did not want to encourage this behavior,
they often refused at first to indulge the favorite tastes or caprices of
their daughter. As emaciation became visible and the girl looked ill,
many violated the contemporary canon of prudent child-rearing and
put aside their moral objections to pampering the appetite. Eventually
they would beg their daughter to eat whatever she liked—and eat she
must, "as a sovereign proof of affection" for them. From the parents'
perspective, a return to eating was a confirmation of filial love.

The significance of food refusal as an emotional tactic within   9
the family depended on food's being plentiful, pleasing, and connected to love. Where food was eaten simply to assuage hunger,
where it had only minimal aesthetic and symbolic messages, or where
the girl had to provide her own nourishment, refusal of food was not
particularly noteworthy or defiant. In contrast, the anorexic girl was
surrounded by a provident, if not indulgent, family that was bound to
be distressed by her rejection of its largess.

10   Anorexia nervosa was an intense form of discourse that honored the emotional guidelines that governed the middle-class Victorian family. Refusing to eat was not as confrontational as yelling, having a tantrum, or throwing things; refusing to eat expressed emotional hostility without being flamboyant. And refusing to eat had the advantage of being ambiguous. If a girl repeatedly claimed lack of appetite she might indeed be ill and therefore entitled to special treatment and favors.

11   In her own way, the anorexic was respectful of what historian Peter Gay called "the great bourgeois compromise between the need for reserve and the capacity for emotion." The rejection of food, while an emotionally charged behavior, was also discreet, quiet, and ladylike. The unhappy adolescent who was in all other ways a dutiful daughter chose food refusal from within the symptom repertoire available to her. Precisely because she was not a lunatic, she selected a behavior that she knew would have some efficacy within her own family.

QUESTIONS ON SUBJECT AND PURPOSE

1. According to Brumberg, when did anorexia nervosa emerge as a definable disease? Why did it emerge in that particular time period?

2. On the basis of what Brumberg writes here, who is the most likely candidate for anorexia nervosa?

3. What purpose might Brumberg have in writing about anorexia nervosa?

QUESTIONS ON STRATEGY AND AUDIENCE

1. Why does Brumberg begin by referring to "the popular assumption that anorexia nervosa is a peculiarly modern disorder"?

2. To what extent does isolating the origins of anorexia nervosa help us understand the disorder in young people today?

3. Brumberg uses quite a few words that might be unfamiliar to many readers. What do her vocabulary choices imply about her sense of audience?

QUESTIONS ON VOCABULARY AND STYLE

1. In paragraphs 2 and 3, Brumberg quotes from two popular domestic manuals of the nineteenth century. What do the quotations contribute to her essay?
2. In paragraph 5, Brumberg uses the phrase "alimentary nihilism" with reference to anorexics. What does the phrase mean?
3. Be prepared to define the following words: *malady* (paragraph 1), *imperative* (1), *reciprocity* (1), *dysfunction* (1), *bourgeois* (1), *milieu* (2), *ambience* (2), *wet nurses* (3), *gustatory* (3), *unabashedly* (3), *antithetical* (3), *taciturnity* (3), *burgeoning* (5), *stymied* (5), *alimentary* (5), *nihilism* (5), *mélange* (6), *individuation* (7), *autonomous* (7), *penchant* (7), *prerogative* (7), *caprices* (8), *emaciation* (8), *assuage* (9), *largess* (9), *flamboyant* (10), *efficacy* (11).

WRITING SUGGESTIONS

1. **For Your Journal.** How would you characterize your mealtimes? Do you care about the circumstances in which you eat? Do you have to eat with someone else? Can you just grab something on the run? Explore your attitudes toward mealtime. Do not just accept what you are doing without thinking about it. What do you expect of meals? Why?
2. **For a Paragraph.** Define your "ideal" body. Then in a second paragraph speculate on the reasons why that body type or shape seems "ideal."
3. **For an Essay.** Cultural historians have observed that American society is "obesophobic" (excessively or irrationally fearful of fat and being fat). Certainly weight consciousness permeates American society and the weight-loss industries are multimillion dollar businesses. Why?
4. **For Research.** Anorexia nervosa is only one of a number of diseases that are common today but were previously unknown or undiagnosed. Other examples include Alzheimer's disease, osteoporosis, premenstrual syndrome, and chronic fatigue syndrome. Select a "new" disease or disorder, and research its history. When was it first defined? What might account for its emergence during the past decade or two? If you are using information from electronic sources, such as the World Wide Web, make sure that the information is authoritative. Be sure to document all of your sources, including electronic ones, wherever appropriate.

WEBSITE LINK

The Web has extensive resources for dealing with anorexia nervosa and other related eating disorders. A listing of key sites is available at the *Reader's* Website.

WRITING LINK: VOCABULARY

Brumberg uses quite a few words that are not part of most people's working vocabulary. Underline every unfamiliar word in the essay. Next to each unfamiliar word, write down what you guess it might mean. Check your guess against a dictionary definition.

BLACK MEN AND PUBLIC SPACE
Brent Staples

Born in Chester, Pennsylvania, Brent Staples graduated from Widener University in 1973 and earned a Ph.D. in psychology from the University of Chicago in 1982. He worked for the Chicago Sun-Times as a reporter before moving to The New York Times in 1985. In 1994 he published a memoir, Parallel Time: Growing Up in Black and White, *which tells the story of his childhood in Chester, a mixed-race, economically declining town. The book focuses on his younger brother, a drug dealer who died of gunshot wounds at age twenty-two.*
"Black Men and Public Space" was originally published in Ms. *magazine under the title "Just Walk on By: A Black Man Ponders His Power to Alter Public Space." In revised and edited form, it was reprinted in* Harper's *with the current title.*

On Writing: *In* Parallel Time, *Staples describes how, in his early twenties, he began to explore his voice as a writer: "I was carrying a journal with me everywhere. . . . I wrote on buses and on the Jackson Park el—though only at the stops to keep the writing legible. I traveled to distant neighborhoods, sat on the curbs, and sketched what I saw in words. Thursday meant free admission at the Art Institute. All day I attributed motives to people in paintings, especially people in Rembrandts. At closing time, I went to a nightclub in The Loop and spied on the patrons, copied their conversations, and speculated about their lives. The journal was more than 'a record of my inner transactions.' It was a collection of stolen souls from which I would one day construct a book."*

BEFORE READING

Connecting: What precautions do you take if you have to walk at night in public spaces?

Anticipating: Why does Staples whistle melodies from classical music when he walks at night? What effect does that particular "cowbell" have on people?

My first victim was a woman—white, well dressed, probably in her 1 early twenties. I came upon her late one evening on a deserted street in Hyde Park, a relatively affluent neighborhood in an otherwise mean, impoverished section of Chicago. As I swung onto the avenue behind her, there seemed to be a discreet, uninflammatory distance between us. Not so. She cast back a worried glance. To her, the youngish black man—a broad six feet two inches with a beard and billowing hair, both hands shoved into the pockets of a bulky military jacket—seemed menacingly close. After a few more quick glimpses, she picked up her pace and was soon running in earnest. Within seconds she disappeared into a cross street.

2   That was more than a decade ago. I was twenty-two years old, a graduate student newly arrived at the University of Chicago. It was in the echo of that terrified woman's footfalls that I first began to know the unwieldy inheritance I'd come into—the ability to alter public space in ugly ways. It was clear that she thought herself the quarry of a mugger, a rapist, or worse. Suffering a bout of insomnia, however, I was stalking sleep, not defenseless wayfarers. As a softy who is scarcely able to take a knife to a raw chicken—let alone hold one to a person's throat—I was surprised, embarrassed, and dismayed all at once. Her flight made me feel like an accomplice in tyranny. It also made it clear that I was indistinguishable from the muggers who occasionally seeped into the area from the surrounding ghetto. That first encounter, and those that followed, signified that a vast, unnerving gulf lay between nighttime pedestrians—particularly women— and me. And I soon gathered that being perceived as dangerous is a hazard in itself. I only needed to turn a corner into a dicey situation, or crowd some frightened, armed person in a foyer somewhere, or make an errant move after being pulled over by a policeman. Where fear and weapons meet—and they often do in urban America—there is always the possibility of death.

3   In that first year, my first away from my hometown, I was to become thoroughly familiar with the language of fear. At dark, shadowy intersections, I could cross in front of a car stopped at a traffic light and elicit the *thunk, thunk, thunk, thunk* of the driver—black, white, male, or female—hammering down the door locks. On less traveled streets after dark, I grew accustomed to but never comfortable with people crossing to the other side of the street rather than pass me. Then there were the standard unpleasantries with policemen, doormen, bouncers, cabdrivers, and others whose business it is to screen out troublesome individuals *before* there is any nastiness.

4   I moved to New York nearly two years ago and I have remained an avid night walker. In central Manhattan, the near-constant crowd cover minimizes tense one-on-one street encounters. Elsewhere—in SoHo, for example, where sidewalks are narrow and tightly spaced buildings shut out the sky—things can get very taut indeed.

After dark, on the warrenlike streets of Brooklyn where I live, I 5 often see women who fear the worst from me. They seem to have set their faces on neutral, and with their purse straps strung across their chests bandolier-style, they forge ahead as though bracing themselves against being tackled. I understand, of course, that the danger they perceive is not a hallucination. Women are particularly vulnerable to street violence, and young black males are drastically overrepresented among the perpetrators of that violence. Yet these truths are no solace against the kind of alienation that comes of being ever the suspect, a fearsome entity with whom pedestrians avoid making eye contact.

It is not altogether clear to me how I reached the ripe old age 6 of twenty-two without being conscious of the lethality nighttime pedestrians attributed to me. Perhaps it was because in Chester, Pennsylvania, the small, angry industrial town where I came of age in the 1960s, I was scarcely noticeable against a backdrop of gang warfare, street knifings, and murders. I grew up one of the good boys, had perhaps a half-dozen fistfights. In retrospect, my shyness of combat has clear sources.

As a boy, I saw countless tough guys locked away; I have since 7 buried several, too. They were babies, really—a teenage cousin, a brother of twenty-two, a childhood friend in his mid-twenties—all gone down in episodes of bravado played out in the streets. I came to doubt the virtues of intimidation early on. I chose, perhaps unconsciously, to remain a shadow—timid, but a survivor.

The fearsomeness mistakenly attributed to me in public places 8 often has a perilous flavor. The most frightening of these confusions occurred in the late 1970s and early 1980s, when I worked as a journalist in Chicago. One day, rushing into the office of a magazine I was writing for with a deadline story in hand, I was mistaken for a burglar. The office manager called security and, with an ad hoc posse, pursued me through the labyrinthine halls, nearly to my editor's door. I had no way of proving who I was. I could only move briskly toward the company of someone who knew me.

Another time I was on assignment for a local paper and killing 9 time before an interview. I entered a jewelry store on the city's affluent Near North Side. The proprietor excused herself and returned with an enormous red Doberman pinscher straining at the end of a leash. She stood, the dog extended toward me, silent to my questions, her eyes bulging nearly out of her head. I took a cursory look around, nodded, and bade her good night.

Relatively speaking, however, I never fared as badly as another black male journalist. He went to nearby Waukegan, Illinois, 10 a couple of summers ago to work on a story about a murderer who was born there. Mistaking the reporter for the killer, police officers hauled him from his car at gunpoint and but for his press credentials would probably have tried to book him. Such episodes are not uncommon. Black men trade tales like this all the time.

11   Over the years, I learned to smother the rage I felt at so often being taken for a criminal. Not to do so would surely have led to madness. I now take precautions to make myself less threatening. I move about with care, particularly late in the evening. I give a wide berth to nervous people on subway platforms during the wee hours, particularly when I have exchanged business clothes for jeans. If I happen to be entering a building behind some people who appear skittish, I may walk by, letting them clear the lobby before I return, so as not to seem to be following them. I have been calm and extremely congenial on those rare occasions when I've been pulled over by the police.

12   And on late-evening constitutionals I employ what has proved to be an excellent tension-reducing measure: I whistle melodies from Beethoven and Vivaldi and the more popular classical composers. Even steely New Yorkers hunching toward night-time destinations seem to relax, and occasionally they even join in the tune. Virtually everybody seems to sense that a mugger wouldn't be warbling bright, sunny selections from Vivaldi's *Four Seasons*. It is my equivalent of the cowbell that hikers wear when they know they are in bear country.

QUESTIONS ON SUBJECT AND PURPOSE

1. What does Staples mean by the phrase "public space"? In what way is he capable of altering it?
2. What types of evidence does Staples provide to illustrate his point—that black men can alter public space?
3. What purpose might Staples have had in writing the essay?

QUESTIONS ON STRATEGY AND AUDIENCE

1. In addition to cause and effect, what other structure is at work in the essay?
2. When the essay was first published, it was entitled "Just Walk on By." When it appeared in a slightly revised form, it was retitled, "Black Men and Public Space." What is the effect of the change in title?
3. The essay first appeared in *Ms.* magazine. What assumptions could Staples have had about his initial audience?

QUESTIONS ON VOCABULARY AND STYLE

1. What is the effect of Staples's opening sentence in the essay? Why does he write "my first victim"?
2. In paragraph 5, Staples writes the phrase "on the warrenlike streets of Brooklyn." What is a *warren?* To what does the term usually refer? Can you think of another word or phrase that Staples could have used instead that might be more vivid to most readers?
3. Be prepared to define the following words: *discreet* (paragraph 1), *dicey* (2), *errant* (2), *taut* (4), *warrenlike* (5), *bandolier* (5), *solace* (5), *entity* (5), *bravado* (7), *ad hoc* (8), *cursory* (9), *skittish* (11), *congenial* (11), *constitutionals* (12).

WRITING SUGGESTIONS

1. **For Your Journal.** Have you ever been frightened in a public space? Explore your memories or your recent experiences, and jot down a few such times. Try to capture a few details about each experience.
2. **For a Paragraph.** Select one of the experiences you entered in your journal for Suggestion 1, and narrate that experience in a paragraph. Why did you react as you did? Was your fear justified? You can also turn the topic around and describe a time when your presence frightened someone else while in a public space.
3. **For an Essay.** Regardless of our age or sex or color, we all provoke reactions from people who do not know us. Sometimes, in fact, we go out of our way to elicit a reaction—dressing in a certain way, driving a particular type of car, engaging in an unusual activity, wearing our hair in a peculiar style. Describe your image and behavior, and analyze how people react to you and why they react as they do.
4. **For Research.** Who mugs whom? Research the problem of assault or mugging either in the country as a whole or in your own community. What are your chances of being mugged? Who is likely to do it to you? Where is it most likely to happen? If you decide to focus on your own community or college campus, remember to interview the local police.

WEBSITE LINK

A Public Broadcasting Website offers video and audio clips of Staples; a list of his publications in *The New York Times* can be found at the newspaper's Website.

WRITING LINK: VERBS

Staples often uses vivid verbs in telling his story. Go through the essay and make a list of such verbs. What do they suggest about how to create an arresting story or description? Do you use verbs in the same way in your writing?

DREADLOCKED

Veronica Chambers

Veronica Chambers was born in Brooklyn, the daughter, she writes, of "two black Latinos from Panama." Educated at Simon's Rock College, she has worked as a journalist, editor, and photographer for magazines such as Sassy, Seventeen, Essence, The New York Times Magazine, Newsweek, *and, most recently,* Savoy. *She is the author of children's books and the novel* Mama's Girl *(1996). Her most recent book is* Having It All: Black Women and the Question of Success *(2003).*

On Writing: *In an interview aired on National Public Radio's* Anthem *series, Chambers said of her writing, "I go to poetry a lot. . . . I found, for example, in writing* Mama's Girl *that it was hard for me to read other people's memoirs. . . . So I read almost exclusively a lot of poetry . . . to keep myself with words, but not get myself mired in other stories."*

BEFORE READING

Connecting: What associations do you have with dreadlocks? Are those associations stereotypes?

Anticipating: What do Chambers's dreadlocks mean or symbolize to her?

I have two relationships with the outside world: One is with my hair, 1 and the other is with the rest of me. Sure, I have concerns and points of pride with my body. I like the curve of my butt but dislike my powerhouse thighs. My breasts, once considered too small, have been proclaimed perfect so often that not only am I starting to believe the hype, but also am booking my next vacation to a topless resort in Greece. But my hair. Oh, my hair.

I have reddish brown dreadlocks that fall just below shoulder 2 length. Eventually, they will cover my aforementioned breasts, at which time I will give serious thought to nude modeling at my local art school. I like my hair—a lot. But over the last eight years my dreadlocks have conferred upon me the following roles: rebel child, Rasta mama, Nubian princess, drug dealer, unemployed artist, rock star, world-famous comedienne, and nature chick. None of which is true. It has occurred to me more than once that my hair is a whole lot more interesting than I am.

3   Because I am a black woman, I have always had a complicated relationship with my hair. Here's a quick primer on the politics of hair and beauty aesthetics in the black community vis-à-vis race and class in the late 20th century: "Good" hair is straight and, preferably, long. Think Naomi Campbell. Diana Ross. For that matter, think RuPaul. "Bad" hair is thick and coarse, aka "nappy," and, often, short. Think Buckwheat in *The Little Rascals*. Not the more recent version, but the old one in which Buckwheat looked like Don King's grandson.

4   Understand that these are stereotypes: broad and imprecise. Some will say that the idea of "good" hair and "bad" hair is outdated. And it is less prevalent than in the '70s when I was growing up. Sometimes I see little girls with their hair in braids and Senegalese twists sporting cute little T-shirts that say HAPPY TO BE NAPPY and I get teary-eyed. I was born between the black power Afros of the '60s and the blue contact lenses and weaves of the '80s; in my childhood, no one seemed happy to be nappy at all.

5   I knew from the age of 4 that I had "bad" hair because my relatives and family friends discussed it as they might discuss a rare blood disease. "Something must be done," they would chick sadly. "I think I know someone," an aunt would murmur, referring to a hair-dresser as if she were a medical specialist. Some of my earliest memories are of Brooklyn apartments where women did hair for extra money. These makeshift beauty parlors were lively and loud, the air thick with the smell of lye from harsh relaxer, the smell of hair burning as the hot straightening comb did its job.

6   When did I first begin to desire hair that bounced? Was it because black Barbie wasn't, and still isn't, happy to be nappy? Was it Brenda, the redhead, my best friend in second grade? Every time she flicked her hair to the side, she seemed beyond sophistication. My hair bounced the first day back from the hairdresser's, but not much longer. "Don't sweat out that perm," my mother would call. But I found it impossible to sit still. Hairdressers despaired like cowardly lion tamers at the thought of training my kinky hair. "This is some hard hair," they would say. I knew that I was not beautiful and I blamed it on my hair.

7   The night I began to twist my hair into dreads, I was 19 and a junior in college. It was New Year's Eve and the boy I longed for had not called. A few months before, Alice Walker had appeared on the cover of *Essence*, her locks flowing with all the majesty of a Southern American Cleopatra. I was inspired. It was my family's superstition that the hours between New Year's Eve and New Year's Day were the

time to cast spells. "However New Year's catches you is how you'll spend the year," my mother always reminded me.

I decided to use the hours that remained to transform myself   8
into the vision I'd seen on the magazine. Unsure of how to begin, I washed my hair, carefully and lovingly. I dried it with a towel, then opened a jar of hair grease. Using a comb to part the sections, I began to twist each section into baby dreads. My hair, at the time, couldn't have been longer than an inch. I twisted for two hours, and in the end was far from smitten with what I saw: My full cheeks dominated my face now that my hair lay in flat twists around my head. My already short hair seemed shorter. I did not look like the African goddess I had imagined. I emerged from the bathroom and ran into my aunt Diana, whose luxuriously long, straight black hair always reminded me of Diahann Carroll on *Dynasty*. "Well, Vickie," she said, shaking her head. "Well, well." I knew that night my life would begin to change. I started my dreadlocks and began the process of seeing beauty where no one had ever seen beauty before.

There are, of course, those who see my hair and still consider it   9
"bad." A family friend touched my hair recently, then said, "Don't you think it's a waste? All that lovely hair twisted in those things?" I have been asked by more than one potential suitor if I had any pictures of myself before "you did that to your hair." A failure at small talk and countless other social graces, I sometimes let my hair do the talking for me. At a cocktail party, I stroll through the room, silently, and watch my hair tell white lies. In literary circles, it brands me "interesting, adventurous." In black middle-class circles, I'm "rebellious" or, more charitably. "Afro-centric." In predominantly white circles, my hair doubles my level of exotica. My hair says, "Unlike the black woman who reads you the evening news, I'm not even trying to blend in."

For those ignorant enough to think that they can read hair fol-   10
licles like tea leaves, my hair says a lot of things it doesn't mean. Taken to the extreme, it says that I am a pot-smoking Rastafarian wannabe who in her off-hours strolls through her house in an African dashiki, lighting incense and listening to Bob Marley. I don't smoke pot. In my house, I wear Calvin Klein nightshirts, and light tuberose candles that I buy from Diptyque in Paris. I play tennis in my off-hours and, while I love Bob Marley, I mostly listen to jazz vocalists like Ella Fitzgerald and Diana Krall.

Once after a dinner party in Beverly Hills, a white colleague of   11
mine lit up a joint. Everyone at the table passed and when I passed too, the man cajoled me relentlessly. "Come on," he kept saying. "Of all people, I thought you'd indulge." I shrugged and said nothing. As

we left the party that night, he kissed me good-bye. "Boy, were you a disappointment," he said, as if I had been a bad lay. But I guess I had denied him a certain sort of pleasure. It must have been his dream to smoke a big, fat spliff with a real live Rastafarian.

12   As much as I hate to admit it, I've been trained to turn my head to any number of names that aren't mine. I will answer to "Whoopi." I will turn when Jamaican men call out "Hey, Rasta" on the street. I am often asked if I am a singer, and I can only hope that I might be confused with the gorgeous Cassandra Wilson, whose dreadlocks inspired me to color my hair a jazzy shade of red. Walking through the streets of Marrakesh, I got used to trails of children who would follow me, trying to guess which country I came from. "Jamaica!" they would shout. "Ghana! Nigeria!" I shook my head no to them all. They did not believe me when I said I was from America: instead, they called me "Mama Africa" all day long. It's one of my favorite memories of the trip.

13   Once, after the end of a great love affair, I watched a man cut all of his dreadlocks off and then burn them in the backyard. This, I suspect, is the reason that might tempt me to change my hair. After all, a broken heart is what started me down this path of twisting hair. Because I do not cut my hair, I carry eight years of history on my head. One day, I may tire of this history and start anew. But one thing is for sure, whatever style I wear my hair in, I will live happily—and nappily—ever after.

QUESTIONS ON SUBJECT AND PURPOSE

1. What are *dreadlocks?* Do you know where the term came from?
2. When does Chambers first wear "dreads"?
3. How does wearing "dreads" change the way in which others perceive her? Does it also change the way in which she perceives herself?

QUESTIONS ON STRATEGY AND AUDIENCE

1. In what ways is this a cause and effect analysis?
2. In addition to cause and effect, what other organizational strategy can you find in the essay?.
3. What expectations might Chambers have of her audience? For example, what do the allusions or names mentioned in the essay suggest about Chambers's sense of her readers?

QUESTIONS ON VOCABULARY AND STYLE

1. Are the last two sentences in paragraph 1 really sentences? If not, what are they?
2. In paragraph 6, Chambers writes: "Hairdressers despaired like cowardly lion tamers at the thought of training my kinky hair." What figure of speech is she using?
3. Be prepared to define the following words: *Nubian* (2), *aka* (3), *cajoled* (11).

WRITING SUGGESTIONS

1. **For Your Journal.** Think about yourself, a sibling, or a friend. To what extent do you or that person adopt or affect an appearance? What has influenced how you or that person looks and acts? To what extent is the appearance intended to suggest or evoke something else? Think about the choices that can be made in physical appearances (such as hairstyles, clothing styles, piercings or tattoos, body jewelry) or in behavior (such as mannerisms, language habits, actions). In your journal try to list some possible causes and effects of such decisions.
2. **For a Paragraph.** Using your journal entry as a prewriting activity, expand your cause and effect analysis into a paragraph. Select one element in that appearance and try to explain what brought it about and what results that element has produced.
3. **For an Essay.** Expand your paragraph writing into an essay. Instead of concentrating on a single element in that appearance, expand your analysis to include all of the aspects of both appearance and behavior.
4. **For Research.** Not so long ago, one found tattoos mostly on former soldiers and sailors and on motorcyclists. Today, many young people sport tattoos. Why? What explanation can be given for the popularity of tattoos among young adults? In a research essay, explore the phenomenon and analyze why tattoos are so popular. Another possibility might be body piercings or extreme hairstyles or colors.

WEBSITE LINK

Additional information about Chambers and her books can be found on the Web as well as information about dreadlocks, Bob Marley, and Rastafarianism.

WRITING LINK: TOPIC SENTENCES

What is a topic sentence and what function does it have in a paragraph? Look carefully at Chambers's essay. Does she use topic sentences? If so, what role do they play in organizing the essay? What role do they play in helping you read the essay? What does this suggest about your own writing?

WHY THEY EXCEL

Fox Butterfield

Born in 1939 in Lancaster, Pennsylvania, Fox Butterfield earned a B.A. and an M.A. at Harvard University. He made his mark on American journalism as a member of The New York Times *reporting team that edited* The Pentagon Papers *(1971). That book, which earned the team a 1972 Pulitzer Prize for meritorious public service, revealed the scope of U.S. involvement in the Vietnam War. His most recent book is* All God's Children: The Bosket Family and the American Tradition of Violence *(1995). "Why They Excel" originally appeared in* Parade, *a Sunday newspaper magazine supplement.*

On Writing: *Of the job of a reporter Butterfield has said: "I was trained to think you've got to write what you find, warts and all, if you believe it to be accurate." An inveterate researcher, he describes his office as full of "lots of file cabinets and the floor littered with piles of paper that I could never put away."*

BEFORE READING

Connecting: What expectations do your parents have for you? How do those expectations influence you?

Anticipating: According to Butterfield, what are the main reasons that Asian and Asian-American students excel? Would or do these reasons motivate you?

Kim-Chi Trinh was just 9 in Vietnam when her father used his savings to buy a passage for her on a fishing boat. It was a costly and risky sacrifice for the family, placing Kim-Chi on the small boat, among strangers, in hopes she would eventually reach the United States, where she would get a good education and enjoy a better life. Before the boat reached safety in Malaysia, the supply of food and water ran out.

Still alone, Kim-Chi made it to the United States, coping with a succession of three foster families. But when she graduated from San Diego's Patrick Henry High School in 1988, she had a straight-A average and scholarship offers from Stanford and Cornell universities.

3   "I have to do well—it's not even a question," said the diminu-
tive 19-year-old, now a sophomore at Cornell. "I owe it to my parents in Vietnam."

4   Kim-Chi is part of a tidal wave of bright, highly motivated
Asian-Americans who are suddenly surging into our best colleges. Although Asian-Americans make up only 2.4 percent of the nation's
population, they constitute 17.1 percent of the undergraduates at
Harvard, 18 percent at the Massachusetts Institute of Technology and
27.3 percent at the University of California at Berkeley.

5   With Asians being the fastest-growing ethnic group in the
country—two out of five immigrants are now Asian—these figures
will increase. At the University of California at Irvine, a staggering
35.1 percent of the undergraduates are Asian-American, but the proportion in the freshman class is even higher: 41 percent.

6   Why are the Asian-Americans doing so well? Are they grinds,
as some stereotypes suggest? Do they have higher IQs? Or are they
actually teaching the rest of us a lesson about values we have long
treasured but may have misplaced—like hard work, the family and
education?

7   Not all Asians are doing equally well. Poorly educated Cambo-
dian and Hmong refugee youngsters need special help. And Asian-
Americans resent being labeled a "model minority," feeling that is just
another form of prejudice by white Americans, an ironic reversal of
the discriminatory laws that excluded most Asian immigration to
America until 1965.

8   But the academic success of many Asian-Americans has
prompted growing concern among educators, parents and other students. Some universities have what look like unofficial quotas, much
as Ivy League colleges did against Jews in the 1920s and '30s. Berkeley Chancellor Ira Heyman apologized last spring for an admissions
policy that, he said, had "a disproportionately negative impact on
Asian-Americans."

9   I have wondered about the reason for the Asians' success since
I was a fledgling journalist on Taiwan in 1969. That year, a team of
boys from a poor, isolated mountain village on Taiwan won the annual Little League World Series at Williamsport, Pa. Their victory
was totally unexpected. At the time, baseball was a largely unknown
sport on Taiwan, and the boys had learned to play with bamboo sticks
for bats and rocks for balls. But since then, teams from Taiwan, Japan
or South Korea have won the Little League championship in 16 out
of the 21 years. How could, these Asian boys beat us at our own game?

10   Fortunately, the young Asians' achievements have led to a series
of intriguing studies. "There is something going on here that we as

Americans need to understand," said Sanford M. Dornbusch, a professor of sociology at Stanford. Dornbusch, in surveys of 7000 students in six San Francisco-area high schools, found that Asian-Americans consistently get better grades than any other group of students, regardless of their parents' level of education or their families' social and economic status, the usual predictors of success. In fact, those in homes where English is spoken often, or whose families have lived longer in the United States, do slightly less well.

"We used to talk about the American melting pot as an advantage," Dornbusch said. "But the sad fact is that it has become a melting pot with low standards." 11

Other studies have shown similar results. Perhaps the most disturbing have come in a series of studies by a University of Michigan psychologist, Harold W. Stevenson, who has compared more than 7000 students in kindergarten, first grade, third grade and fifth grade in Chicago and Minneapolis with counterparts in Beijing; Sendai, Japan; and Taipei, Taiwan. On a battery of math tests, the Americans did worst at all grade levels. 12

Stevenson found no differences in IQ. But if the differences in performance are showing up in kindergarten, it suggests something is happening in the family, even before the children get to school. 13

It is here that the various studies converge: Asian parents are able to instill more motivation in their children. "My bottom line is, Asian kids work hard," said Professor Dornbusch. 14

In his survey of San Francisco-area high schools, for example, he reported that Asian-Americans do an average of 7.03 hours of homework a week. Non-Hispanic whites average 6.12 hours, blacks 4.23 hours and Hispanics 3.98 hours. Asians also score highest on a series of other measures of effort, such as fewer class cuts and paying more attention to the teacher. 15

Don Lee, 20, is a junior at Berkeley. His parents immigrated to Torrance, Calif., from South Korea when he was 5, so he could get a better education. Lee said his father would warn him about the danger of wasting time at high school dances or football games. "Instead," he added, "for fun on weekends, my friends and I would go to the town library to study." 16

The real question, then, is how do Asian parents imbue their offspring with this kind of motivation? Stevenson's study suggests a critical answer. When the Asian parents were asked why they think their children do well, they most often said "hard work." By contrast, American parents said "talent." 17

"From what I can see," said Stevenson, "we've lost our belief in the Horatio Alger myth that anyone can get ahead in life through 18 pluck and hard work. Instead, Americans now believe that some kids have it and some don't, so we begin dividing up classes into fast learners and slow learners, where the Chinese and Japanese believe all children can learn from the same curriculum."

19   The Asians' belief in hard work also springs from their common heritage of Confucianism, the philosophy of the 5th-century B.C. Chinese sage who taught that man can be perfected through practice. "Confucius is not just some character out of the past—he is an everyday reality to these people," said William Liu, a sociologist who directs the Pacific Asian-American Mental Health Research Center at the University of Illinois in Chicago.

20   Confucianism provides another important ingredient in the Asians' success. "In the Confucian ethic," Liu continued, "there is a centripetal family, an orientation that makes people work for the honor of the family, not just for themselves." Liu came to the United States from China in 1948. "You can never repay your parents, and there is a strong sense of guilt," he said. "It is a strong force, like the Protestant Ethic in the West."

21   Liu has found this in his own family. When his son and two daughters were young, he told them to become doctors or lawyers—jobs with the best guaranteed income, he felt. Sure enough, his daughters have gone into law, and his son is a medical student at UCLA, though he really wanted to be an investment banker. Liu asked his son why he picked medicine. The reply: "Ever since I was a little kid, I always heard you tell your friends their kids were a success if they got into med school. So I felt guilty. I didn't have a choice."

22   Underlying this bond between Asian parents and their children is yet another factor I noticed during 15 years of living in China, Japan, Taiwan and Vietnam. It is simply that Asian parents establish a closer physical tie to their infants than do most parents in the United States. When I let my baby son and daughter crawl on the floor, for example, my Chinese friends were horrified and rushed to pick them up. We think this constant attention is overindulgence and old-fashioned, but for Asians, who still live through the lives of their children, it is highly effective.

23   Yuen Huo, 22, a senior at Berkeley, recalled growing up in an apartment above the Chinese restaurant her immigrant parents owned and operated in Millbrae, Calif. "They used to tell us how they came from Taiwan to the United States for us, how they sacrificed for us, so I had a strong sense of indebtedness," Huo said. When she did not get all A's her first semester at Berkeley, she recalled, "I felt guilty and worked harder."

Here too is a vital clue about the Asians' success: Asian parents   24
expect a high level of academic performance. In the Stanford study
comparing white and Asian students in San Francisco high schools,
82 percent of the Asian parents said they would accept only an A or a
B from their children, while just 59 percent of white parents set such
a standard. By comparison, only 17 percent of Asian parents were
willing to accept a C, against 40 percent of white parents. On the average, parents of black and Hispanic students also had lower expectations for their children's grades than Asian parents.

Can we learn anything from the Asians? "I'm not naïve enough   25
to think everything in Asia can be transplanted," said Harold Stevenson, the University of Michigan psychologist. But he offered three
recommendations.

"To start with," he said, "we need to set higher standards for our   26
kids. We wouldn't expect them to become professional athletes without practicing hard."

Second, American parents need to become more committed to   27
their children's education, he declared. "Being understanding when a
child doesn't do well isn't enough." Stevenson found that Asian parents spend many more hours really helping their children with homework or writing to their teachers. At Berkeley, the mothers of some
Korean-American students move into their sons' apartments for
months before graduate school entrance tests to help by cooking and
cleaning for them, giving the students more time to study.

And, third, schools could be reorganized to become more   28
effective—without added costs, said Stevenson. One of his most surprising findings is that Asian students, contrary to popular myth, are
not just rote learners subjected to intense pressure. Instead, nearly 90
percent of Chinese youngsters said they actually enjoy school, and 60
percent can't wait for school vacations to end. These are vastly higher
figures for such attitudes than are found in the United States. One
reason may be that students in China and Japan typically have a re-
cess after each class; helping them to relax and to increase their attention spans. Moreover, where American teachers spend almost
their entire day in front of classes, their Chinese and Japanese counterparts may teach as little as three hours a day, giving them more
time to relax and prepare imaginative lessons.

Another study, prepared for the U.S. Department of Education,   29
compared the math and science achievements of 24,000 13-year-olds
in the United States and five other countries (four provinces of Canada,
plus South Korea, Ireland, Great Britain and Spain). One of the findings was that the more time students spent watching television, the

poorer their performance. The American students watched the most television. They also got the worst scores in math. Only the Irish students and some of the Canadians scored lower in science.

30   "I don't think Asians are any smarter," said Don Lee, the Korean-American at Berkeley. "There are brilliant Americans in my chemistry class. But the Asian students work harder. I see a lot of wasted potential among the Americans."

QUESTIONS ON SUBJECT AND PURPOSE

1. According to Butterfield, what are the "causes" of the success of Asian-American students?
2. Why do American students not excel to the same extent as Asian and Asian-American students?
3. In addition to providing an explanation for the high achievement of Asian students, what other purpose does Butterfield seem to have? What might his American readers take from his essay?

QUESTIONS ON STRATEGY AND AUDIENCE

1. Why might Butterfield have begun with the example of Kim-Chi Trinh? Why not begin, for example, with a thesis paragraph?
2. Why might Butterfield choose to end the essay the way he does?
3. What assumptions does Butterfield seem to make about his readers? How do you know?

QUESTIONS ON VOCABULARY AND STYLE

1. What aspects of the essay suggest that Butterfield is writing for a popular rather than a scholarly audience?
2. What types of sources does Butterfield use in his essay?
3. Be prepared to define the following words: *imbue* (paragraph 17), *pluck* (18), *centripetal* (20), *rote learners* (28).

WRITING SUGGESTIONS

1. **For Your Journal.** Are you "driven to excel"? In academics? In sports? In an artistic pursuit? In your career? Explore your motivations. Make a list of the ways you have sought to excel

and the reasons why. Conversely, if the phrase frightens you or seems contrary to your thinking, explore the reasons you react that way.

2. **For a Paragraph.** Butterfield basically attributes the motivation of Asian and Asian-American students to their desire to please their parents. In a paragraph, explore the typical motivations of students from another cultural group— your own or one to which friends of yours belong. (If you are Asian or Asian-American, or have many Asian-American friends, you might prefer to critique Butterfield's analysis.)

3. **For an Essay.** Expand your paragraph into an essay. Using a cause and effect analysis, either explain what motivates a particular group of students or compare what motivates Asian or Asian-American students to what motivates students from another cultural group. Try to define a specific audience—for example, readers of your college's newspaper.

4. **For Research.** In paragraph 28, Butterfield describes some differences between Asian schools and American schools. Research the nature and methods of high school education in China, Japan, or another Pacific Rim country. Then explain in an essay how that educational system prepares and motivates students. Be sure to acknowledge your sources wherever appropriate.

 WEBSITE LINK

A pair of Websites offer an extensive assortment of links devoted to Asian-American resources and students.

 WRITING LINK: WRITING CONCLUSIONS

Butterfield ends his essay with a quotation. He does not try to write a summarizing paragraph. Try writing a more conventional conclusion for his essay—the type that you think an English teacher would love. How effective is this new ending? What does this suggest about writing conclusions?

THE TROUBLE WITH FRIES

Malcolm Gladwell

Malcolm Gladwell (1963–   ) was born in England and grew up in Canada. A graduate of the University of Toronto with a degree in history, he was a reporter for The Washington Post *before becoming a staff writer for* The New Yorker *magazine. His most recent book is* The Tipping Point: How Little Things Can Make a Big Difference *(2000). "The Trouble with Fries" originally appeared in* The New Yorker.

On Writing: *Gladwell comments: "The most common question I get from readers is: 'Where do you get your ideas?' And the answer I always give is 'I don't know.' . . . It's just that the question seems to presuppose that there is a place where I find ideas—a system—and there isn't. . . . The process of generating ideas, for me, is entirely unpredictable and serendipitous. . . . The other important piece to the puzzle is that having an idea for a story is actually overrated. The idea is actually the easy part. The execution is the hard part."*

BEFORE READING

Connecting: How often do you eat at fast-food restaurants each week? Do you ever worry about the fat or the calories in that food?

Anticipating: Gladwell suggests that we already have the technology to make fast food more healthy for us. If so, why have changes not been made?

1   In 1954, a man named Ray Kroc, who made his living selling the five-spindle Multimixer milkshake machine, began hearing about a hamburger stand in San Bernardino, California. This particular restaurant, he was told, had no fewer than eight of his machines in operation, meaning that it could make forty shakes simultaneously. Kroc was astounded. He flew from Chicago to Los Angeles, and drove to San Bernardino, sixty miles away, where he found a small octagonal building on a corner lot. He sat in his car and watched as the workers showed up for the morning shift. They were in starched white shirts and paper hats, and moved with a purposeful discipline. As lunchtime approached, customers began streaming into the parking lot, lining up for bags of hamburgers. Kroc approached a strawberry blonde in a yellow convertible.

"How often do you come here?" he asked.   2

"Anytime I am in the neighborhood," she replied, and, Kroc   3
would say later, "it was not her sex appeal but the obvious relish with
which she devoured the hamburger that made my pulse begin to
hammer with excitement." He came back the next morning, and this
time set up inside the kitchen, watching the griddle man, the food
preparers, and, above all, the French-fry operation, because it was the
French fries that truly captured his imagination. They were made
from top-quality oblong Idaho russets, eight ounces apiece, deep-
fried to a golden brown, and salted with a shaker that, as he put it,
kept going like a Salvation Army girl's tambourine. They were crispy
on the outside and buttery soft on the inside, and that day Kroc had
a vision of a chain of restaurants, just like the one in San Bernardino,
selling golden fries from one end of the country to the other. He
asked the two brothers who owned the hamburger stand if he could
buy their franchise rights. They said yes. Their names were Mac and
Dick McDonald.

Ray Kroc was the great visionary of American fast food, the one   4
who brought the lessons of the manufacturing world to the restaurant
business. Before the fifties, it was impossible, in most American
towns, to buy fries of consistent quality. Ray Kroc was the man who
changed that. "The french fry," he once wrote, "would become almost sacrosanct for me, its preparation a ritual to be followed reli-
giously." A potato that has too great a percentage of water—and
potatoes, even the standard Idaho russet burbank, vary widely in their
water content—will come out soggy at the end of the frying process.
It was Kroc, back in the fifties, who sent out field men, armed with
hydrometers, to make sure that all his suppliers were producing potatoes in the optimal solids range of twenty to twenty-three per cent.
Freshly harvested potatoes, furthermore, are rich in sugars, and if you
slice them up and deep-fry them the sugars will caramelize and brown
the outside of the fry long before the inside is cooked. To make a crisp
French fry, a potato has to be stored at a warm temperature for several weeks in order to convert those sugars to starch. Here Kroc led
the way as well, mastering the art of "curing" potatoes by storing
them under a giant fan in the basement of his first restaurant, outside
Chicago.

Perhaps his most enduring achievement, though, was the so-   5
called potato computer—developed for McDonald's by a former elec-
trical engineer for Motorola named Louis Martino—which precisely
calibrated the optimal cooking time for a batch of fries. (The key:
when a batch of cold raw potatoes is dumped into a vat of cooking oil,
the temperature of the fat will drop and then slowly rise. Once the oil

has risen three degrees, the fries are ready.) Previously, making high-quality French fries had been an art. The potato computer, the hydrometer, and the curing bins made it a science. By the time Kroc was finished, he had figured out how to turn potatoes into an inexpensive snack that would always be hot, salty, flavorful, and crisp, no matter where or when you bought it.

This was the first fast-food revolution—the mass production of food that had reliable mass appeal. But today, as the McDonald's franchise approaches its fiftieth anniversary, it is clear that fast food needs a second revolution. As many Americans now die every year from obesity-related illnesses—heart disease and complications of diabetes—as from smoking, and the fast-food toll grows heavier every year. In the fine new book *Fast Food Nation*, the journalist Eric Schlosser writes of McDonald's and Burger King in the tone usually reserved for chemical companies, sweatshops, and arms dealers, and, as shocking as that seems at first, it is perfectly appropriate. Ray Kroc's French fries are killing us. Can fast food be fixed?

***

7   Fast-food French fries are made from a baking potato like an Idaho russet, or any other variety that is mealy, or starchy, rather than waxy. The potatoes are harvested, cured, washed, peeled, sliced, and then blanched—cooked enough so that the insides have a fluffy texture but not so much that the fry gets soft and breaks. Blanching is followed by drying, and drying by a thirty-second deep fry, to give the potatoes a crisp shell. Then the fries are frozen until the moment of service, when they are deep-fried again, this time for somewhere around three minutes. Depending on the fast-food chain involved, there are other steps interspersed in this process. McDonald's fries, for example, are briefly dipped in a sugar solution, which gives them their golden-brown color; Burger King fries are dipped in a starch batter, which is what gives those fries their distinctive hard shell and audible crunch. But the result is similar. The potato that is first harvested in the field is roughly eighty per cent water. The process of creating a French fry consists, essentially, of removing as much of that water as possible—through blanching, drying, and deep-frying—and replacing it with fat.

8   Elisabeth Rozin, in her book *The Primal Cheeseburger*, points out that the idea of enriching carbohydrates with fat is nothing new. It's a standard part of the cuisine of almost every culture. Bread is buttered; macaroni comes with cheese; dumplings are fried; potatoes are scalloped, baked with milk and cheese, cooked in the drippings of roasting meat, mixed with mayonnaise in a salad, or pan-fried in butterfat as latkes. But, as Rozin argues, deep-frying is in many ways the ideal method of adding fat to carbohydrates. If you put butter on a

mashed potato, for instance, the result is texturally unexciting: it simply creates a mush. Pan-frying results in uneven browning and crispness. But when a potato is deep-fried the heat of the oil turns the water inside the potato into steam, which causes the hard granules of starch inside the potato to swell and soften: that's why the inside of the fry is fluffy and light. At the same time, the outward migration of the steam limits the amount of oil that seeps into the interior, preventing the fry from getting greasy and concentrating the oil on the surface, where it turns the outer layer of the potato brown and crisp. "What we have with the french fry," Rozin writes, "is a near perfect enactment of the enriching of a starch food with oil or fat."

This is the trouble with the French fry. The fact that it is cooked   9 in fat makes it unhealthy. But the contrast that deep-frying creates between its interior and its exterior—between the golden shell and the pillowy whiteness beneath—is what makes it so irresistible. The average American now eats a staggering thirty pounds of French fries a year, up from four pounds when Ray Kroc was first figuring out how to mass-produce a crisp fry. Meanwhile, fries themselves have become less healthful. Ray Kroc, in the early days of McDonald's, was a fan of a hot-dog stand on the North Side of Chicago called Sam's, which used what was then called the Chicago method of cooking fries. Sam's cooked its fries in animal fat, and Kroc followed suit, prescribing for his franchises a specially formulated beef tallow called Formula 47 (in reference to the forty-seven-cent McDonald's "All-American meal" of the era: fifteen-cent hamburger, twelve-cent fries, twenty-cent shake). Among aficionados, there is general agreement that those early McDonald's fries were the finest mass-market fries ever made: the beef tallow gave them an unsurpassed rich, buttery taste. But in 1990, in the face of public concern about the health risks of cholesterol in animal-based cooking oil, McDonald's and the other major fast-food houses switched to vegetable oil. That wasn't an improvement, however. In the course of making vegetable oil suitable for deep-frying, it is subjected to a chemical process called hydrogenation, which creates a new substance called a trans unsaturated fat. In the hierarchy of fats, polyunsaturated fats—the kind found in regular vegetable oils—are the good kind; they lower your cholesterol. Saturated fats are the bad kind. But trans fats are worse: they wreak havoc with the body's ability to regulate cholesterol. According to a recent study involving some eighty thousand women, for every five-per-cent increase in the amount of saturated fats that a woman consumes, her risk of heart disease increases by seventeen per cent. But only a two-per-cent increase in trans fats will increase her heart-disease risk by ninety-three per cent. Walter Willett, an epidemiologist at Harvard—who helped design the study—estimates that the consumption of trans fats in the United States probably causes about thirty thousand premature deaths a year.

10   McDonald's and the other fast-food houses aren't the only purveyors of trans fats, of course; trans fats are in crackers and potato chips and cookies and any number of other processed foods. Still, a lot of us get a great deal of our trans fats from French fries, and to read the medical evidence on trans fats is to wonder at the odd selectivity of the outrage that consumers and the legal profession direct at corporate behavior. McDonald's and Burger King and Wendy's have switched to a product, without disclosing its risks, that may cost human lives. What is the difference between this and the kind of thing over which consumers sue companies every day?

11   The French-fry problem ought to have a simple solution: cook fries in oil that isn't so dangerous. Oils that are rich in monounsaturated fats, like canola oil, aren't nearly as bad for you as saturated fats, and are generally stable enough for deep-frying. It's also possible to "fix" animal fats so that they aren't so problematic. For example, K. C. Hayes, a nutritionist at Brandeis University, has helped develop an oil called Appetize. It's largely beef tallow, which gives it a big taste advantage over vegetable shortening, and makes it stable enough for deep-frying. But it has been processed to remove the cholesterol, and has been blended with pure corn oil, in a combination that Hayes says removes much of the heart-disease risk.

12   Perhaps the most elegant solution would be for McDonald's and the other chains to cook their fries in something like Olestra, a fat substitute developed by Procter & Gamble. Ordinary fats are built out of a molecular structure known as a triglyceride: it's a microscopic tree, with a trunk made of glycerol and three branches made of fatty acids. Our bodies can't absorb triglycerides, so in the digestive process each of the branches is broken off by enzymes and absorbed separately. In the production of Olestra, the glycerol trunk of a fat is replaced with a sugar, which has room for not three but eight fatty acids. And our enzymes are unable to break down a fat tree with eight branches—so the Olestra molecule can't be absorbed by the body at all. "Olestra" is as much a process as a compound: you can create an "Olestra" version of any given fat. Potato chips, for instance, tend to be fried in cottonseed oil, because of its distinctively clean taste. Frito-Lay's no-fat Wow! chips are made with an Olestra version of cottonseed oil, which behaves just like regular cottonseed oil except that it's never digested. A regular serving of potato chips has a hundred and fifty calories, ninety of which are fat calories from the cooking oil. A serving of Wow! chips has seventy-five calories and no fat.

If Procter & Gamble were to seek F.D.A. approval for the use of Olestra in commercial deep-frying (which it has not yet done), it could make an Olestra version of the old McDonald's Formula 47, which would deliver every nuance of the old buttery, meaty tallow at a fraction of the calories.

Olestra, it must be said, does have some drawbacks—in particular, a reputation for what is delicately called "gastrointestinal distress." The F.D.A. has required all Olestra products to carry a somewhat daunting label saying that they may cause "cramping and loose stools." Not surprisingly, sales have been disappointing, and Olestra has never won the full acceptance of the nutrition community. Most of this concern, however, appears to be overstated. Procter & Gamble has done randomized, double-blind studies—one of which involved more than three thousand people over six weeks—and found that people eating typical amounts of Olestra-based chips don't have significantly more gastrointestinal problems than people eating normal chips. Diarrhea is such a common problem in America— nearly a third of adults have at least one episode each month—that even F.D.A. regulators now appear to be convinced that in many of the complaints they received Olestra was unfairly blamed for a problem that was probably caused by something else. The agency has promised Procter & Gamble that the warning label will be reviewed.   13

Perhaps the best way to put the Olestra controversy into perspective is to compare it to fibre. Fibre is vegetable matter that goes right through you: it's not absorbed by the gastrointestinal tract. Nutritionists tell us to eat it because it helps us lose weight and it lowers cholesterol—even though if you eat too many baked beans or too many bowls of oat bran you will suffer the consequences. Do we put warning labels on boxes of oat bran? No, because the benefits of fibre clearly outweigh its drawbacks. Research has suggested that Olestra, like fibre, helps people lose weight and lowers cholesterol; too much Olestra, like too much fibre, may cause problems. (Actually, too much Olestra may not be as troublesome as too much bran. According to Procter & Gamble, eating a large amount of Olestra— forty grams—causes no more problems than eating a small bowl— twenty grams—of wheat bran.) If we had Olestra fries, then, they shouldn't be eaten for breakfast, lunch, and dinner. In fact, fast-food houses probably shouldn't use hundred-per-cent Olestra; they should cook their fries in a blend, using the Olestra to displace the most dangerous trans and saturated fats. But these are minor details. The point is that it is entirely possible, right now, to make a delicious French fry that does not carry with it a death sentence. A French fry can be much more than a delivery vehicle for fat.   14

15   Is it really that simple, though? Consider the cautionary tale of the efforts of a group of food scientists at Auburn University, in Alabama, more than a decade ago to come up with a better hamburger. The Auburn team wanted to create a leaner beef that tasted as good as regular ground beef. They couldn't just remove the fat, because that would leave the meat dry and mealy. They wanted to replace the fat. "If you look at ground beef, it contains moisture, fat, and protein," says Dale Huffman, one of the scientists who spearheaded the Auburn project. "Protein is relatively constant in all beef, at about twenty per cent. The traditional McDonald's ground beef is around twenty per cent fat. The remainder is water. So you have an inverse ratio of water and fat. If you reduce fat, you need to increase water." The goal of the Auburn scientists was to cut about two-thirds of the fat from normal ground beef, which meant that they needed to find something to add to the beef that would hold an equivalent amount of water—and continue to retain that water even as the beef was being grilled. Their choice? Seaweed, or, more precisely, carrageenan. "It's been in use for centuries," Huffman explains. "It's the stuff that keeps the suspension in chocolate milk—otherwise the chocolate would settle at the bottom. It has tremendous water-holding ability. There's a loose bond between the carrageenan and the moisture." They also selected some basic flavor enhancers, designed to make up for the lost fat "taste." The result was a beef patty that was roughly three-quarters water, twenty per cent protein, five per cent or so fat, and a quarter of a per cent seaweed. They called it AU Lean.

16   It didn't take the Auburn scientists long to realize that they had created something special. They installed a test kitchen in their laboratory, got hold of a McDonald's grill, and began doing blind taste comparisons of AU Lean burgers and traditional twenty-per-cent-fat burgers. Time after time, the AU Lean burgers won. Next, they took their invention into the field. They recruited a hundred families and supplied them with three kinds of ground beef for home cooking over consecutive three-week intervals—regular "market" ground beef with twenty per cent fat, ground beef with five per cent fat, and AU Lean. The families were asked to rate the different kinds of beef, without knowing which was which. Again, the AU Lean won hands down—trumping the other two on "likability," "tenderness," "flavorfulness," and "juiciness."

17   What the Auburn team showed was that, even though people love the taste and feel of fat—and naturally gravitate toward high-fat food—they can be fooled into thinking that there is a lot of fat in something when there isn't. Adam Drewnowski, a nutritionist at the University of Washington, has found a similar effect with cookies. He

did blind taste tests of normal and reduced-calorie brownies, biscotti, and chocolate-chip, oatmeal, and peanut-butter cookies. If you cut the sugar content of any of those cookies by twenty-five per cent, he found; people like the cookies much less. But if you cut the fat by twenty-five per cent they barely notice. "People are very finely attuned to how much sugar there is in a liquid or a solid," Drewnowski says. "For fat, there's no sensory break point. Fat comes in so many guises and so many textures it is very difficult to perceive how much is there." This doesn't mean we are oblivious of fat levels, of course. Huffman says that when his group tried to lower the fat in AU Lean below five per cent, people didn't like it anymore. But, within the relatively broad range of between five and twenty-five per cent, you can add water and some flavoring and most people can't tell the difference.

What's more, people appear to be more sensitive to the volume   18
of food they consume than to its calorie content. Barbara Rolls, a nutritionist at Penn State, has demonstrated this principle with satiety studies. She feeds one group of people a high-volume snack and another group a low-volume snack. Even though the two snacks have the same calorie count, she finds that people who eat the high-volume snack feel more satisfied. "People tend to eat a constant weight or volume of food in a given day, not a constant portion of calories," she says. Eating AU Lean, in short, isn't going to leave you with a craving for more calories; you'll feel just as full.

For anyone looking to improve the quality of fast food, all this   19
is heartening news. It means that you should be able to put low-fat cheese and low-fat mayonnaise in a Big Mac without anyone's complaining. It also means that there's no particular reason to use twenty-per-cent-fat ground beef in a fast-food burger. In 1990, using just this argument, the Auburn team suggested to McDonald's that it make a Big Mac out of AU Lean. Shortly thereafter, McDonald's came out with the McLean Deluxe. Other fast-food houses scrambled to follow suit. Nutritionists were delighted. And fast food appeared on the verge of a revolution.

Only, it wasn't. The McLean was a flop, and four years later it   20
was off the market. What happened? Part of the problem appears to have been that McDonald's rushed the burger to market before many of the production kinks had been worked out. More important, though, was the psychological handicap the burger faced. People liked AU Lean in blind taste tests because they didn't know it was AU Lean; they were fooled into thinking it was regular ground beef. But nobody was fooled when it came to the McLean Deluxe. It was sold as the healthy choice—and who goes to McDonald's for health food?

21   Leann Birch, a developmental psychologist at Penn State, has looked at the impact of these sorts of expectations on children. In one experiment, she took a large group of kids and fed them a big lunch. Then she turned them loose in a room with lots of junk food. "What we see is that some kids eat almost nothing," she says. "But other kids really chow down, and one of the things that predicts how much they eat is the extent to which parents have restricted their access to high-fat, high-sugar food in the past: the more the kids have been re-stricted, the more they eat." Birch explains the results two ways. First, restricting food makes kids think not in terms of their own hunger but in terms of the presence and absence of food. As she puts it, "The kid is essentially saying, 'If the food's here I better get it while I can, whether or not I'm hungry.' We see these five-year-old kids eating as much as four hundred calories." Birch's second finding, though, is more important. Because the children on restricted diets had been told that junk food was bad for them, they clearly thought that it had to taste good. When it comes to junk food, we seem to follow an im-plicit script that powerfully biases the way we feel about food. We like fries not in spite of the fact that they're unhealthy but because of it.

22   That is sobering news for those interested in improving the American diet. For years, the nutrition movement in this country has made transparency one of its principal goals: it has assumed that the best way to help people improve their diets is to tell them precisely what's in their food, to label certain foods good and certain foods bad. But transparency can back-fire, because sometimes nothing is more deadly for our taste buds than the knowledge that what we are eating is good for us. McDonald's should never have called its new offering the McLean Deluxe, in other words. They should have called it the Burger Supreme or the Monster Burger, and then buried the news about reduced calories and fat in the tiniest type on the remotest cor-ner of their Web site. And if we were to cook fries in some high-tech, healthful cooking oil—whether Olestrized beef tallow or something else with a minimum of trans and saturated fats—the worst thing we could do would be to market them as healthy fries. They will not taste nearly as good if we do. They have to be marketed as better fries, as Classic Fries, as fries that bring back the rich tallowy taste of the orig-inal McDonald's.

23   What, after all, was Ray Kroc's biggest triumph? A case could be made for the field men with their hydrometers, or the potato-curing techniques, or the potato computer, which turned the making of French fries from an art into a science. But we should not forget Ronald McDonald, the clown who made the McDonald's name irre-sistible to legions of small children. Kroc understood that taste com-

prises not merely the food on our plate but also the associations and assumptions and prejudices we bring to the table—that half the battle in making kids happy with their meal was calling what they were eating a Happy Meal. The marketing of healthful fast food will require the same degree of subtlety and sophistication. The nutrition movement keeps looking for a crusader—someone who will bring about better public education and tougher government regulations. But we need much more than that. We need another Ray Kroc.

QUESTIONS ON SUBJECT AND PURPOSE

1. What is the "trouble" with French fries? Is the essay just about fries?
2. Why is the problem difficult to solve?
3. What purpose might Gladwell have in the essay?

QUESTIONS ON STRATEGY AND AUDIENCE

1. Why might Gladwell begin his essay with the familiar story of Ray Kroc, the founder of McDonald's?
2. In paragraphs 15 through 22, Gladwell traces the rise and fall of the "lean" hamburger, marketed by McDonald's as the "McLean Deluxe." What does this story have to do with the "trouble with fries"?
3. What assumptions could Gladwell make about his audience?

QUESTIONS ON VOCABULARY AND STYLE

1. What is a rhetorical question? (You can check the Glossary.) How many rhetorical questions can you find in Gladwell's essay? Why might he use them?
2. Why does Gladwell return to Ray Kroc in his final paragraph?
3. Be prepared to define the following words: *sacrosanct* (paragraph 4), *calibrated* (5), *latkes* (8), *aficionados* (9), *purveyors* (10), *nuance* (12), *daunting* (13), *satiety* (18).

WRITING SUGGESTIONS

1. **For Your Journal.** Gladwell suggests that eating fast food is a health risk, likening it to cigarette smoking. The truth is that many people engage in dangerous behaviors, even though they supposedly know the risks. Why? In your journal make a

list of the risky behaviors that you, a sibling, or a friend has engaged in. Next to each behavior, suggest a reason why you or others knowingly have taken the risk.

2. **For a Paragraph.** Expand on your journal by writing a paragraph in which you examine either the causes or the effects of a specific risky act. In the paragraph, choose either to write about causes or about effects. Doing both would probably be attempting too much for a single paragraph.

3. **For an Essay.** Choose a single risky behavior that is commonly engaged in by your peers—things such as cigarette smoking, binge drinking, purging, unprotected sex, recreational drug use, criminal acts. In an essay, explore through a cause and effect analysis why such behavior has an appeal. Knowing that such things are risky or dangerous or even life threatening, why do people in your peer group engage in them? Remember that interviewing peers might prove to be an excellent source of information.

4. **For Research.** Expand the essay topic into a research paper using on-line and printed sources as well as interviews. What explanations have been offered by others to explain such decisions and behaviors? Is there any hope for changing or modifying such behaviors?

 WEBSITE LINK

Gladwell has his own Website where you can read some of his recent essays. In addition, the Web contains a number of interviews with him, particularly dealing with his most recent book.

 WRITING LINK: DASHES

Gladwell uses quite a few dashes in his essay. What is a dash? Why and when is it used? Make a list of each use of the dash in the essay. What other marks of punctuation might have been used instead? Are there any instances in which you could not substitute another punctuation mark? Do you ever have to rewrite the sentence in order to remove the dash?

PREWRITING SUGGESTIONS FOR CAUSE AND EFFECT

1. Spend several days thinking about possible topics. Try to take notes. Make a list of what seem like possible causes or effects. Test each possibility to make sure that it can be clearly related. During these first stages, just concentrate on getting ideas and testing those ideas.

2. Decide which direction your essay will go. Will you concentrate on causes? Or on effects? Remember that it is probably better to concentrate on one or the other rather than trying to go in both directions at the same time.

3. Remember that no one ever asked you to list every cause or every effect. You want to concentrate on the ones that seem the most significant. Decide which causes and which effects are the most important and then concentrate on developing them.

4. Plan out a middle for your essay. How will you arrange your causes or effects? Will you begin with the most important and move to the least or will you move in the other direction? Consider different arrangements of your essay's body paragraphs. Does changing their order seem to change the essay for the better?

5. Construct a rough outline for your essay. It is just a blueprint, a tentative plan. Do this at least a day before a complete draft of your essay is due. Take some time to look objectively at what you are planning.

REWRITING SUGGESTIONS FOR CAUSE AND EFFECT

1. Look again at your paragraphing. Probably the most typical arrangement would be to place each cause or each effect in a separate paragraph. Have you done that? Have you then adequately developed the idea so that each paragraph contains more than a single sentence?

2. Have you provided adequate transitions from one paragraph or section to another? Have you used transitional expressions or time and place markers to indicate that you are moving to another cause or another effect?

3. Check your draft by looking back at your thesis. Do you have a clear thesis? Does it adequately cover everything in your essay?

4. Reread your introduction and conclusion. Did you try to catch your reader's attention? Did you write a thesis

introduction? What type of conclusion does your paper have? Does it just stop? Does it just repeat the words in your introduction? Ask a friend or classmate to comment on just the opening and closing of your paper.

5. Make a list of the potential problems that you see in your essay—these may be grammatical or mechanical things, or they may be structural. Take your list and a copy of your paper to your school's Writing Center and ask a tutor for help; or take your list to your instructor—perhaps during office hours—and ask for advice.

DEFINITION

def • i • ni • tion (def′ ə nish′ə n) *n.* [ME *diffinicioun* < OR
definition & ML *diffinitio*, both < L *difinitio*] **1** a defining
or being defined **2** a statement of what a thing is **3** a
statement of the meaning of a word, phrase, etc.

On the midterm examination in your introductory economics class,
only the essay question remains to be answered: "What is capitalism?" You are tempted to write the one-sentence definition you
memorized from the glossary of your textbook and dash from the
room. But it is unlikely that your professor will react positively or
even charitably to such a skimpy (rote) response. Instead, you realize
that what is needed is an extended definition, one that explains what
factors were necessary before capitalism could emerge, what elements
are most characteristic of a capitalistic economy, how capitalism differs from other economic systems, how a capitalistic economy works,
how capitalism is linked to technology and politics. What you need is
a narrative, a division, a comparison and contrast, a process, and a
cause and effect analysis all working together to provide a full definition of what is finally a very complex term.

When you are asked to define a word, you generally do two
things: first, you provide a dictionary-like definition, normally a single sentence; and second, if the occasion demands, you provide a
longer, extended definition, analyzing the subject and giving examples or details. If you use technical or specialized words that may be
unfamiliar to your reader, you include a parenthetical definition:

"Macroeconomics, the portion of economics concerned with large-scale movements such as inflation and deflation, is particularly interested in changes in the GDP, or gross domestic product."

Definitions can be denotative, connotative, or a mixture of the two. Dictionary definitions are denotative; that is, they offer a literal and explicit definition of a word. A dictionary, for example, defines the word *prejudice* as "a judgment or opinion formed before the facts are known; preconceived idea." In most cases, however, a single sentence is not enough to give a reader a clear understanding of the word or concept.

Many words have more than just literal meanings; they also carry connotations, either positive or negative, and these connotations may make up part of an extended definition. For example, in 1944, when the United States was at war on two fronts, E. B. White was asked to write about the "meaning of democracy" for the Writers' War Board. White's one-paragraph response goes beyond a literal definition to explore the connotations and associations that surround the word *democracy:*

> Surely the Board knows what democracy is. It is the line that forms on the right. It is the don't in Don't Shove. It is the hole in the stuffed shirt through which the sawdust trickles; it is the dent in the high hat. Democracy is the recurrent suspicion that more than half of the people are right more than half of the time. It is the feeling of privacy in the voting booths, the feeling of communion in the libraries, the feeling of vitality everywhere. Democracy is the score at the beginning of the ninth. It is an idea which hasn't been disproved yet, a song the words of which have not gone bad. It's the mustard on the hot dog and the cream in the rationed coffee. Democracy is a request from a War Board, in the middle of a morning in the middle of a war, wanting to know what democracy is.

Democracy was, to White, not simply a form of government, but a whole way of life.

Most writing situations, especially those you encounter in college, require extended definitions. The selections in this chapter define a variety of subjects, and they suggest how differently extended definitions can be handled. Bob Greene's definition of the phrase "adults only" is drawn from a description of the content and the language found in products—films, music, television shows—so labeled. Judging from the products, Greene ironically concludes that adult behavior is violent and deviant and that adult language consists mostly of four-letter words. Judy Brady defines the word *wife* through the many associations that people have with that word. Robin D. G.

Kelley explains how a seemingly simple question, "What are you?", can be very difficult to answer. Amy Tan explores a definition of *mother tongue* based on her own mother's Chinese-inflected English. John Hollander describes the *mess* in his office, offering both a history of the word's meaning and examples of how artists have represented "messes." Finally Margaret Atwood uses multiple examples to define that "capacious" topic, the *female body*.

How Much Do You Include in a Definition?

Every word, whether it refers to a specific physical object or to the most theoretical concept, has a dictionary definition. Whether that one-sentence definition is sufficient depends on why you are defining the word. Complex words and words with many nuances and connotations generally require a fuller definition than a single sentence can provide. Moreover, one-sentence definitions often contain other words and phrases that also need to be defined.

For example, if you were asked, "What is a wife?" you could reply, "A woman married to a man." Although that definition is accurate, it does not convey any sense of what such a relationship might involve. Judy Brady's "I Want a Wife" defines the word by showing what men (or some men) expect in a wife. Brady divides and lists a wife's many responsibilities—things expected of her by an actual or potential husband. Brady's essay, comically overstated as it is, offers a far more meaningful definition of the term *wife* than any one-sentence dictionary entry. Her intention surely was to reveal inequality in marriage, and she makes her point by listing a stereotypical set of male expectations.

Writing a definition is a fairly common activity in college work. In your literature course, you are asked to define the romantic movement; in art history, the baroque period; in psychology, abnormal behavior. Since a single-sentence definition can never do justice to such complicated terms, an extended definition is necessary. In each case, the breadth and depth of your knowledge is being tested; your professor expects you to formulate a definition that accounts for the major subdivisions and characteristics of the subject. Your purpose is to convince your professor that you have read and mastered the assigned materials and can select among them and organize them, often adding some special insight of your own, into a logical and coherent response.

Politicians are not the only people who know how to manipulate meaning by changing the definitions of the words.
www.CartoonStock.com

HOW DO YOU STRUCTURE A DEFINITION?

Sentence definitions are relatively easy to write. You first place the word in a general class ("A wife is a *woman*") and then add any distinguishing features that set it apart from other members of the class ("married to a man"). But the types of definitions you are asked to write for college are generally more detailed than dictionary entries. How, then, do you get from a single sentence to a paragraph or an essay?

Extended definitions do not have a structure peculiar to themselves. That is, when you write a definition, you do not have a predetermined structural pattern as you do with comparison and contrast, division and classification, process, or cause and effect. Instead, definitions are constructed using all of the various strategies in this book. Bob Greene is not interested in how a dictionary might define the term "adults only," nor does he acknowledge the legal "signal" that lies behind the phrase. Instead, he focuses on the nature of the content and the language typically found in anything labeled "adults only." Judy Brady's definition of a wife uses division to organize the many types of responsibilities demanded of a wife. Robin D. G. Kelley and Amy Tan use narration as a vital part of their definitions. John Hollander uses description and comparison and contrast. Margaret

Atwood gathers a wide range of examples to suggest the complexity involved in the phrase "the female body," ending with an imaginative contrast between the brain of a man and that of a woman.

Once you have chosen a subject for definition, think first about its essential characteristics, steps, or parts. What examples would best define it? Then plan your organization by seeing how those details can be presented most effectively to your reader. If your definition involves breaking a subject into its parts, use division or possibly even process. If you are defining by comparing your subject to another, use a comparison and contrast structure. If your subject is defined as the result of some causal connection, use a cause and effect structure. Definitions can also involve narration, description, and even persuasion. The longer the extended definition, the greater the likelihood that your paper will involve a series of structures.

SAMPLE STUDENT ESSAY

Sherry Heck's essay started from a simple set of directions: "Write an extended definition of a word of your choice." Sherry's approach to the assignment, however, was very different from everyone else's in the class. In her purpose statement, Sherry wrote, "I wanted to inform a general audience in an amusing way of the connotations and associations that accrue to the word *fall*. I got the idea while thumbing through a dictionary looking for words!" Her first draft reads as follows.

EARLIER DRAFT

FALLING

When you were four years old, covered in scrapes and bruises, the word <u>fall</u> was probably too familiar. Perhaps you went exploring, discovering the creek in the woods, and following it to its falls. Summers would end too quickly and fall would arrive, and Mom would send you off to school.

You mastered the art of walking, yet it remained all too easy to fall over yourself in front of your peers. The popular kids would laugh, sending you to fall into the wrong crowd. As you sprayed graffiti triumphantly, you fell into agreement with your friends that this was the best way to slander the principal.

Then one day, you are sitting in school and you feel someone's glance fall on you. You fall silent and stare back. Soon you find yourself falling for that special someone, and you fall in love. Eventually, you have a huge falling out with that person. Your friends have long abandoned you, leaving you no one to fall back on. Your spirits fall, and you feel like the fall guy around your old peers.

Eventually, out of school, you fall into a good job, and you are able to fall out of your trance. Determined not to fall short of your career goals, you fall into line with society. Events seem to fall into place. The pace of the job speeds up, and several people fall out of the rat race. Their jobs fall to you, tripling your workload. It is difficult not to avoid falling from power, and your life's plans begin to fall through.

Alone, rejected, and jobless, you begin to blame your misfortunes on the root of all evil, the fall of Adam and Eve. Life continues, and you ponder this thought until your friends begin to fall off. Your face falls at the thought of your own fall. Your bones are weak, and falling means more than a scraped knee. Your blood pressure falls more easily. These physical worries all disappear when one day, after feeling a free-fall sensation, you fall asleep, peacefully, forever.

Sherry met with her instructor, Nathan Andrews, to go over her preliminary draft. He encouraged her to watch that she not repeat phrases—for example, in the fourth paragraph, Sherry had repeated *fall out* twice. After they had brainstormed some additional *fall* phrases, he encouraged her to search for more in the dictionaries in her school's library. He also suggested that she italicize each *fall* phrase so that the reader could more easily see the word play. In her revised essay, Sherry was able to add a number of new examples.

INFALLIBLE

When you were four years old, covered in scrapes and bruises, the word <u>fall</u> was probably too familiar. Perhaps you went exploring, discovering the creek in the woods, and following it to its <u>falls</u>. Summers would end too quickly and <u>fall</u> would arrive, and Mom would send you off to school.

You mastered the art of walking, yet it remained all too easy to <u>fall all over yourself</u> in front of your peers. The popular kids would laugh, sending you to <u>fall in with</u> the wrong crowd. As you sprayed the graffiti triumphantly, you <u>fell in agreement</u> with your friends that this was the best way to slander the principal. Your behavior was leading you to <u>fall afoul</u> of the law.

Then one day, you are sitting in school and you feel someone's glance <u>fall on</u> you. You <u>fall silent</u> and stare back. Soon you find yourself <u>falling for</u> that special someone, and you <u>fall in love</u>. Eventually, you have a huge <u>falling out</u> with that person. The relationship <u>falls apart</u>. Your friends have long abandoned you, leaving you no one to <u>fall back on</u>. Your cries for help <u>fall on deaf ears</u>. Your <u>spirits fall</u>, and you feel like the <u>fall guy</u> around your old peers.

Eventually, out of school, you <u>fall over backwards</u> to get a good job, and you are able to <u>fall out of your trance</u>. Your love life has <u>fallen by the wayside</u>. Determined not to <u>fall short</u> of your career goals, you <u>fall into line</u> with society. Events seem to <u>fall into place</u>. The pace of the job speeds up, and several people <u>fall on their faces</u>. Their jobs <u>fall to you</u>, tripling your workload. You <u>fall behind</u> in your work. It is difficult not to avoid <u>falling from power</u>, and your life's plans begin to <u>fall through</u>.

Alone, rejected and jobless, you begin to blame your misfortunes on the root of all evil, the <u>Fall</u> of Adam and Eve. Life continues, and you ponder this thought until your friends begin to <u>fall off</u>. Your <u>face falls</u> at the thought of your own <u>fall</u>. Your bones are weak, and <u>falling</u> means more than a scraped knee. Your <u>blood pressure falls</u> more easily. These physical worries all disappear when one day, after feeling a <u>free-fall</u> sensation, you <u>fall asleep</u>, peacefully, forever.

SOME THINGS TO REMEMBER

1. Choose a subject that can be reasonably and fully defined within the limits of your paper. That is, make sure it is neither too limited nor too large.
2. Determine a purpose for your definition.
3. Spend time analyzing your subject to see what its essential characteristics, steps, or parts are.
4. Write a dictionary-type definition for your subject. Do this even if you are writing an extended definition. The features that set your subject apart from others in its general class reveal what must be included in your definition.
5. Choose examples that are clear and appropriate.
6. Decide which of the organizational patterns will best convey the information you have gathered.
7. Be careful about beginning with a direct dictionary definition. There are usually more effective and interesting ways to announce your subject.

VISUALIZING DEFINITION

Central to our understanding of everything expressed in words—either spoken or written—is an understanding of what those words mean—we must know what the words refer to or how they are defined. The need to define is especially acute in college courses. As we move from one academic discipline to another, we constantly learn the meaning of new words and new concepts. Dictionaries and even textbooks, such as this one, provide us with lists or "glossaries" of new or unfamiliar terms, but often a subject is complex or unfamiliar enough that we need more than a one-sentence definition. Longer, extended definitions provide us with details, examples, explanations, even pictures and diagrams. Let's compare two definitions of the terms "hypocaust" and "hypocaust heating," used in archeology to refer to a type of under-the-floor hot-air heating found in ancient Roman buildings. A standard college dictionary offers this definition of the term "hypocaust": "A space below the floor in some ancient Roman buildings, into which hot air was piped to warm the rooms." In contrast, an illustrated book on archeology offers this extended example with two visuals to help us understand this heating concept more fully. Which of the two—the dictionary or the extended visual definition—is more helpful?

HYPOCAUST HEATING

This system of heating was based on under-floor hot-air circulation. A furnace situated outside the villa would have been fired with wood, heating the air that was fed into the flue pipes. The hot air would have circulated underneath the villa floor, which was supported on stone or ceramic pillars. It would then be fed through the walls in a series of pipes or flues made out of box tiles. The hot air and smoke would then escape through a series of chimneys or apertures. Only some rooms would have been heated, as the hypocaust would have required large quantities of wood and labor. This exposed hypocaust system was found at the Roman site of Chedworth in England.

Combed pattern to help fix the concrete

Air vent

Clay is used to make the box tile

COMPLETE BOX FLUE TILE

EXPOSED HYPOCAUST HEATING SYSTEM

The Atlas of Archaeology by M. Aston and T. Taylor (Dorling Kindersley © 1998). Photograph provided by the National Trust Photo Library/Ian Shaw.

DEFINITION AS A LITERARY STRATEGY

How and why might you define a "foot"? Alice Jones in her poem "The Foot" undertakes a definition that mixes anatomical terms with poetic images. As you read, notice how Jones organizes and develops her definition.

THE FOOT

Alice Jones

Our improbable support, erected
on the osseous architecture
of the calcaneus, talus, cuboid,
navicular, cuneiforms, metatarsals,
phalanges, a plethora of hinges,

all strung together by gliding
tendons, covered by the pearly
plantar fascia, then fat-padded
to form the sole, humble surface
of our contact with earth.

Here the body's broadest tendon
anchors the heel's fleshy base,
the finely wrinkled skin stretches
forward across the capillaried arch,
to the ball, a balance point.

A wide web of flexor tendons
and branched veins maps the dorsum,
fades into the stub-laden bone
splay, the stuffed sausage sacks
of toes, each with a tuft

of proximal hairs to introduce
the distal nail, whose useless
curve remembers an ancestor,
the vanished creature's wild
and necessary claw.

DISCUSSION QUESTIONS

1. Is the poem a denotative or a connotative definition? Or a mixture of both? Support your conclusion with specific evidence from the poem.
2. How is the definition (and the poem) organized? Is there a clear organizational plan?
3. Why might Jones have chosen to define the word *foot?* What does the poem do as a definition that a picture and a definition in an anatomy book might not do?
4. Do you sense any change in the poem—in its method of definition, in its diction—in stanzas 4 and 5?
5. What is the effect of the final three and a half lines of the poem?

WRITING SUGGESTIONS

Definitions can do many things. In part, they tell us what something is—we look up a word or a phrase in a dictionary or an encyclopedia so that we understand it. But definitions can also suggest or offer new perspectives on the familiar—they can allow us to see things in a fresh way. Write a definition for something in which you mix technical, precise language with a more creative and suggestive perception. Consider the following suggestions as possibilities:

a. A part of a face, a hand, teeth, hair
b. A common, useful object—a hairbrush, a comb, scissors, a pencil, a computer mouse
c. A term connected with school—dropping or adding a course, auditing, being a "work study" student, staying up all night to study or write a paper

Using Definition in Writing for Your Other Courses

In college writing, definition assignments are especially common on essay exams. You may also write extended definitions for certain kinds of research papers. Examples of assignments requiring definition include the following.

- **Marketing.** For a course in retail management, you might research and write a paper defining the concept of customer value management and its relation to a particular marketing plan using examples, process, and cause and effect.

- **Criminology.** For a course in juvenile justice, you might write an essay exam defining the characteristics of juvenile offenders using description, examples, and cause and effect.
- **Political Science.** For an American presidency course, you might research and write a paper examining changing conceptions of the presidency over the past two hundred years using examples, comparison, and cause and effect.
- **Communication.** For a course in persuasion, you might write an essay exam defining psychological resistance using example, narration, and cause and effect.
- **Environmental Studies.** For a course in environmental economics, you might research and write a paper defining public and private property rights in terms of pollution control using examples, description, and comparison and contrast.
- **Geography.** For a geography of the city course, you might research and write a paper about urban renewal using examples, description, comparison and contrast, and cause and effect.

VISIT THE PRENTICE HALL READER'S WEBSITE

When you have finished reading an essay, check out the additional material available at the *Reader*'s Website at www.prenhall.com/miller. For each reading, you will find a list of related readings connected with the topic or the author; additional background information; a group of relevant "hot-linked" Web resources (just click your computer's mouse and automatically visit the sites listed); and still more writing suggestions.

DEFINING

Are you frustrated when you see or hear words connected with computers that you don't understand? Answer your question on a Website devoted to definitions of computer-related terms and then try a paragraph-writing exercise in which you show off your new knowledge.

ADULTS ONLY

Bob Greene

Bob Greene's essay "Cut" is one of the readings in Chapter 1, and biographical information about Greene can be found in that headnote.

BEFORE READING

Connecting: When you see the label "adults only" (maybe with reference to a video, show, film, or CD), what do you expect? What associations do you have with that phrase?

Anticipating: What is it about the label "adults only" that Greene is objecting to?

It's one of the great untruths of our times, and it is so common that   1
it passes without notice.

You see it—or some variation of it—on television screens, in   2
movie advertisements, on the labels of recorded music. The wording
goes something like this:

"Adult content." Or: "Contains adult language."   3

Few people ever stop to think about what this means. What, ex-   4
actly, is adult content? What words constitute adult language?

In our contemporary culture, adult content usually means that   5
people are shown attacking each other with guns, hatchets and blow-
torches; that half-naked people are assaulting other people, ripping
their clothes off, treating humans like garbage; that people are deto-
nating other people's cars and houses, setting fire to property, bludgeoning and disemboweling and pumping holes in one another. That's
adult content; that's how adults behave.

Adult language? Adult language, by our current definition, con-   6
sists of the foulest synonyms for excrement, for sexual activity, for deviant conduct. Adult language usually consists of four letters; adult
language is the kind of language that civilized people are never supposed to use.

It makes you wonder what lesson we are sending—not only to   7
children, but to ourselves. If a TV show or a motion picture concerned
itself with responsible adults treating each other and the people
around them with kindness, with consideration, with thoughtfulness,

that TV show or movie would never be labeled as containing adult content. If a TV show or movie dealt quietly and responsibly with the many choices of conscience and generosity that adults face every day in the world, it would not warrant an "adult content" rating.

8   Similarly, if a movie featured adults talking with each other civilly, never resorting to gutter language or obscenities, choosing their words with care and precision, no one would ever think to describe the dialogue as "adult." A cable TV show or a music CD in which every word spoken or sung was selected to convey a thought or emotion without resorting to cheap and offensive vulgarities— that TV show or that CD would never be labeled as containing adult language.

9   We seem to be so sheepish about what our culture has become— so reluctant to concede the debasement of society—that we have decided to declare that darkness is light, that down is up, that wrong is right. We are sending a clear signal to young people: The things in our world that are violent, that are crude, that are dull and mean-spirited are the things that are considered "adult." The words that children are taught not to say because they are ugly and foul are "adult language." As if they are something to strive for, to grow into.

10   What is the solution? Truth in packaging might be a good idea, although it will never happen. No movie studio that has hired a top-money action star to headline in a film that consists of explosions, bloodshed and gore would ever agree to describe the movie truthfully. The lie of "adult content" is acceptable to Hollywood; the true label of "pathetic, moronic content, suitable for imbeciles" will never see the light of day.

11   Language? The movie studios, cable channels and record labels can live with the inaccurate euphemism of "adult language." To phrase it honestly—"infantile, ignorant, pitiful language"—would remove a certain sheen from a big-budget entertainment project.

12   Ours is becoming a society in which the best ideals of childhood— innocence, kindness, lack of spitefulness, rejection of violence—are qualities toward which adults ought to strive. A paradoxical society in which the things labeled "adult"—lack of restraint, conscienceless mayhem, vulgarity, raw and cynical carnality—are the things that children should be warned against growing up to embrace.

13   So perhaps we should learn to read the current "adult" warning labels in a different way. "Adult content" on a movie or television show should be read as a warning against becoming the kind of adult who welcomes such things into his or her life. The "adult language" label on a TV show or CD should be read as a genuine kind of warning, a warning to children against becoming the sort of adult who chooses to speak that way.

Then there is "For Mature Audiences Only," but that will have   14
to wait for another day. . . .

QUESTIONS ON SUBJECT AND PURPOSE

1. Why is the phrase "adults only" (or some variation) used to label potentially offensive or objectionable content or language?
2. What does Greene mean by his first sentence? What is "one of the great untruths of our times"? What is an "untruth"?
3. How does Greene feel about material that is labeled "adults only"?

QUESTIONS ON STRATEGY AND AUDIENCE

1. Why might Greene paragraph so frequently? What does the paragraphing suggest about where the essay was originally published?
2. Greene implies that a phrase like "adult content" (paragraph 13) could be defined in several ways. How many definitions could you give after reading Greene's essay?
3. How do you as a reader react to what Greene is saying? Does he win your agreement? Do you feel that he is being unfair?

QUESTIONS ON VOCABULARY AND STYLE

1. How does your dictionary define "adult"? What connotations does the word have for you?
2. Greene ends his essay with a series of spaced periods. What is this mark of punctuation called? Why does he use it here?
3. Be prepared to define the following words: *bludgeoning* (paragraph 5), *deviant* (6), *warrant* (7), *debasement* (9), *moronic* (10), *imbeciles* (10), *euphemism* (11), *sheen* (11), *mayhem* (12).

WRITING SUGGESTIONS

1. **For Your Journal.** What does the term "free speech" mean to you? In your journal, jot down your thoughts and reactions to that phrase. Are there, for example, any limits to "free" speech? Any restrictions?
2. **For a Paragraph.** Use your journal reactions as the basis for a paragraph definition of the term "free speech." Be sure to give

several examples of what you think might be covered or protected by this First Amendment guarantee.

3. **For an Essay.** Expand your paragraph writing into an essay-length extended definition of the term "free speech." Remember that the concept has been used to refer to not only sexually explicit material, but also material that advocates racial, ethnic, and religious hatred and material that promotes or describes dangerous or even terroristic activities (for example, how to build a bomb). Try to define the term as precisely as you can, making use of examples.

4. **For Research.** In an attempt to protect children from online pornography, Congress passed the Communications Decency Act in 1996. In 1997, the Supreme Court unanimously declared the law unconstitutional. Similarly, enforcement of the Child Online Protection Act of 1998 has been blocked by the courts. Part of the problem has been to define terms such as "indecent" or "patently offensive." In a research paper, write an extended definition of "indecent" as it might be defined in our culture.

 WEBSITE LINK

For additional information about the Communications Decency Act of 1996 and the Child Online Protective Act of 1998 and the debates that have raged over both, check out some of the sites listed at the *Reader*'s Website.

 WRITING LINK: VOCABULARY

Even though Greene's essay is easy to read, he does use a number of words that are relatively unfamiliar. Can you define all of the words in Greene's essay? Check each word that you are uncertain about in a dictionary. Can you find another, more common, word that means roughly the same thing? What would be gained or lost if Greene had used a more familiar word? What does that suggest about your own vocabulary in your papers?

I WANT A WIFE

Judy Brady

Judy Brady was born in 1937 in San Francisco, California, and received a B.F.A. in painting from the University of Iowa. As a freelance writer, Brady has written essays on topics such as union organizing, abortion, and the role of women in society. Currently an activist focusing on issues related to cancer and the environment, she has edited several books on the subject, including One in Three: Women with Cancer Confront an Epidemic *(1991).*

Brady's most frequently reprinted essay is "I Want a Wife," which originally appeared in Ms. magazine in 1971. After examining the stereotypical male demands in marriage, Brady concludes, "Who wouldn't want a wife?"

BEFORE READING

Connecting: In a relationship, what separates reasonable needs or desires from unreasonable or selfish ones?

Anticipating: What is the effect of the repetition of the phrase "I want a . . . " in the essay?

I belong to that classification of people known as wives. I am A Wife. And, not altogether incidentally, I am a mother. 1

Not too long ago a male friend of mine appeared on the scene 2 fresh from a recent divorce. He had one child, who is, of course, with his ex-wife. He is obviously looking for another wife. As I thought about him while I was ironing one evening, it suddenly occurred to me that I, too, would like to have a wife. Why do I want a wife?

I would like to go back to school so that I can become econom- 3 ically independent, support myself, and, if need be, support those dependent upon me. I want a wife who will work and send me to school. And while I am going to school I want a wife to take care of my children. I want a wife to keep track of the children's doctor and dentist appointments. And to keep track of mine, too. I want a wife to make sure my children eat properly and are kept clean. I want a wife who will wash the children's clothes and keep them mended. I want a wife who is a good nurturant attendant to my children, who arranges for their schooling, makes sure that they have an adequate social life with their peers, takes them to the park, the zoo, etc. I want a wife who takes care of the children when they are sick, a wife who arranges to be around when the children need special care, because, of course, I cannot miss classes at school. My wife must arrange to lose time at work, and not lose the job. It may mean a small cut in my wife's income from time to time, but I guess I can tolerate that. Needless to say, my wife will arrange and pay for the care of the children while my wife is working.

4   I want a wife who will take care of my physical needs. I want a wife who will keep my house clean. A wife who will pick up after me. I want a wife who will keep my clothes clean, ironed, mended, replaced when need be, and who will see to it that my personal things are kept in their proper place so that I can find what I need the minute I need it. I want a wife who cooks the meals, a wife who is a good cook. I want a wife who will plan the meals, do the necessary grocery shopping, prepare the meals, serve them pleasantly, and then do the cleaning up while I do my studying. I want a wife who will care for me when I am sick and sympathize with my pain and loss of time from school. I want a wife to go along when our family takes a vacation so that someone can continue to care for me and my children when I need a rest and change of scene.

5   I want a wife who will not bother me with rambling complaints about a wife's duties. But I want a wife who will listen to me when I feel the need to explain a rather difficult point I have come across in my course of studies. And I want a wife who will type my papers for me when I have written them.

6   I want a wife who will take care of the details of my social life. When my wife and I are invited out by my friends, I want a wife who will take care of the babysitting arrangements. When I meet people at school that I like and want to entertain, I want a wife who will have the house clean, will prepare a special meal, serve it to me and my friends, and not interrupt when I talk about the things that interest me and my friends. I want a wife who will have arranged that the children are fed and ready for bed before my guests arrive so that the children do not bother us. I want a wife who takes care of the needs of my guests so that they feel comfortable, who makes sure that they have an ashtray, that they are passed the hors d'oeuvres, that they are offered a second helping of the food, that their wine glasses are replenished when necessary, that their coffee is served to them as they like it. And I want a wife who knows that sometimes I need a night out by myself.

7   I want a wife who is sensitive to my sexual needs, a wife who makes love passionately and eagerly when I feel like it, a wife who

makes sure that I am satisfied. And, of course, I want a wife who will not demand sexual attention when I am not in the mood for it. I want a wife who assumes the complete responsibility for birth control, because I do not want more children. I want a wife who will remain sexually faithful to me so that I do not have to clutter up my intellectual life with jealousies. And I want a wife who understands that *my* sexual needs may entail more than strict adherence to monogamy. I must, after all, be able to relate to people as fully as possible.

If, by chance, I find another person more suitable as a wife than the wife I already have, I want the liberty to replace my present wife with another one. Naturally I will expect a fresh, new life; my wife will take the children and be solely responsible for them so that I am left free. 8

When I am through with school and have a job, I want my wife to quit working and remain at home so that my wife can more fully and completely take care of a wife's duties. 9

My God, who *wouldn't* want a wife? 10

QUESTIONS ON SUBJECT AND PURPOSE

1. In what way is this a definition of a wife? Why does Brady avoid a more conventional definition?
2. Is Brady being fair? Is there anything that she leaves out of her definition that you would have included?
3. What purpose might Brady have been trying to achieve?

QUESTIONS ON STRATEGY AND AUDIENCE

1. How does Brady structure her essay? What is the order of the development? Could the essay have been arranged in any other way?
2. Why does Brady identify herself by her roles—wife and mother—at the beginning of the essay? Is that information relevant in any way?
3. What assumptions does Brady have about her audience (readers of *Ms.* magazine in the early 1970s)? How do you know?

QUESTIONS ON VOCABULARY AND STYLE

1. How does Brady use repetition in the essay? Why? Does it work? What effect does it create?
2. How effective is Brady's final rhetorical question? Where else in the essay does she use a rhetorical question?
3. Be able to define the following words: *nurturant* (paragraph 3), *hors d'oeuvres* (6), *replenished* (6), *monogamy* (7).

WRITING SUGGESTIONS

1. **For Your Journal.** What do you look for in a possible spouse or "significant other"? Make a list of what you expect or want from a relationship with another person. Once you have brainstormed the list, rank each item in order of importance— which is most important, and which is least important? If you are in a relationship right now, try evaluating that relationship in light of your own priorities.
2. **For a Paragraph.** Using the material that you generated in your journal entry, write a paragraph definition of the kind of person you seek for a committed relationship. Be serious. Do not try to imitate Brady's style.
3. **For an Essay.** Define a word naming a central human relationship role, such as *husband, lover, friend, mother, father, child, sister, brother,* or *grandparent*. Define the term indirectly by showing what such a person does or should do.
4. **For Research.** What does it mean to be a wife in another culture? Choose at least two other cultures, and research those societies' expectations of a wife. Try to find cultures that show significant differences. Remember that interviews might be a good source of information—even e-mail interviews with wives in other cultures. Using your research, write an essay offering a comparative definition of *wife*. Assume that your audience is American. Be certain to document your sources, including any interviews or e-mail conversations.

WEBSITE LINK

Visit a group of Websites devoted to marriage and marital contracts—
the WWW offers a range of resources from the most conservative to
the most liberal. Some places to start can be found at www.prenhall.
com/miller.

WRITING LINK: REPETITION

The most distinctive stylistic feature of Brady's essay is the repetition
of the sentence opener "I want a wife who . . ." Normally, no one
would ever advise you to repeat the same sentence structure over and
over, let alone to repeat the same words again and again. How effective is the strategy in Brady's essay? Why might she have consciously
chosen to repeat this structure? How is this structure appropriate for
what the narrator is saying?

THE PEOPLE IN ME
Robin D. G. Kelley

Robin D. G. Kelley (1962–   ) was born in New York City and raised in Harlem, Seattle, and Pasadena, California. A graduate of California State University, Long Beach, Kelley earned his M.A. and Ph.D. at the University of California, Los Angeles. Currently a professor of history at New York University, Kelley has been called "the preeminent historian of black popular culture writing today." The author and editor of many books, Kelley's most recent collections of essays include Yo' Mama's DisFunktional!: Fighting the Culture Wars in Urban America *(1997) and* Freedom Dreams: The Black Radical Imagination *(2002).*

On Writing: *Complimented in an interview on the accessibility of his writing, Kelley replied, "That's the biggest compliment, because that's the one thing I try to achieve, only because I can't understand academic writing myself. I'm just not that smart."*

BEFORE READING

Connecting: Who are the people in you? What do you know about your ancestors?

Anticipating: Kelley prefers the word "polycultural" rather than "multicultural." Why? What is the difference?

1   "So, what are you?" I don't know how many times people have asked me that. "Are you Puerto Rican? Dominican? Indian or something? You must be mixed." My stock answer has rarely changed: "My mom is from Jamaica but grew up in New York, and my father was from North Carolina but grew up in Boston. Both black."

2   My family has lived with "the question" for as long as I can remember. We're "exotics," all cursed with "good hair" and strange accents—we don't sound like we from da Souf or the Norwth, and don't have that West Coast-by-way-of-Texas Calabama thang going on. The only one with the real West Indian singsong vibe is my grandmother, who looks even more East Indian than my sisters. Whatever Jamaican patois my mom possessed was pummeled out of her by cruel preteens who never had sensitivity seminars in diversity. The result for us was a nondescript way of talking, walking, and be-

ing that made us not black enough, not white enough—just a bunch of not-quite-nappy-headed enigmas.

My mother never fit the "black momma" media image. A beautiful, demure, light brown woman, she didn't drink, smoke, curse, or say things like "Lawd Jesus" or "hallelujah," nor did she cook chitlins or gumbo. A vegetarian, she played the harmonium (a foot-pumped miniature organ), spoke softly with textbook diction, meditated, followed the teachings of Paramahansa Yogananda, and had wild hair like Chaka Khan. She burned incense in our tiny Harlem apartment, sometimes walked the streets barefoot, and, when she could afford it, cooked foods from the East.

To this day, my big sister gets misidentified for Pakistani or Bengali or Ethiopian. (Of course, changing her name from Sheral Anne Kelley to Makani Themba has not helped.) Not long ago, an Oakland cab driver, apparently a Sikh who had immigrated from India, treated my sister like dirt until he discovered that she was not a "scoundrel from Sri Lanka," but a common black American. Talk about ironic. How often are black women spared indignities *because* they are African American?

"What are you?" dogged my little brother more than any of us. He came out looking just like his father, who was white. In the black communities of Los Angeles and Pasadena, my baby bro' had to fight his way into blackness, usually winning only when he invited his friends to the house. When he got tired of this, he became what people thought he was—a cool white boy. Today he lives in Tokyo, speaks fluent Japanese, and is happily married to a Japanese woman (who is actually Korean passing as Japanese!) He stands as the perfect example of our mulattoness: a black boy trapped in a white body who speaks English with a slight Japanese accent and has a son who will spend his life confronting "the question."

Although folk had trouble naming us, we were never blanks or aliens in a "black world." We were and are "polycultural," and I'm talking about all peoples in the Western world. It is not skin, hair, walk, or talk that renders black people so diverse. Rather, it is the fact that most of them are products of different "cultures"—living cultures, not dead ones. These cultures live in and through us every day, with almost no self-consciousness about hierarchy or meaning. "Polycultural" works better than "multicultural," which implies that cultures are fixed, discrete entities that exist side by side—a kind of zoological approach to culture. Such a view obscures power relations, but often reifies race and gender differences.

Black people were polycultural from the get-go. Most of our ancestors came to these shores not as Africans, but as Ibo, Yoruba,

Hausa, Kongo, Bambara, Mende, Mandingo, and so on. Some of our ancestors came as Spanish, Portuguese, French, Dutch, Irish, English, Italian. And more than a few of us, in North America as well as in the Caribbean and Latin America, have Asian and Native American roots.

8   Our lines of biological descent are about as pure as O. J.'s blood sample, and our cultural lines of descent are about as mixed up as a pot of gumbo. What we know as "black culture" has always been fluid and hybrid. In Harlem in the late 1960s and 1970s, Nehru suits were as popular—and as "black"—as dashikis, and martial arts films placed Bruce Lee among a pantheon of black heroes that included Walt Frazier of the New York Knicks and Richard Rountree, who played John Shaft in blaxploitation cinema. How do we understand the zoot suit—or the conk—without the pachuco culture of Mexican American youth, or low riders in black communities without Chicanos? How can we discuss black visual artists in the interwar years without reference to the Mexican muralists, or the radical graphics tradition dating back to the late 19th century, or the Latin American artists influenced by surrealism?

9   Vague notions of "Eastern" religion and philosophy, as well as a variety of Orientalist assumptions, were far more important to the formation of the Lost-Found Nation of Islam than anything coming out of Africa. And Rastafarians drew many of their ideas from South Asians, from vegetarianism to marijuana, which was introduced into Jamaica by Indians. Major black movements like Garveyism and the African Blood Brotherhood are also the products of global developments. We won't understand these movements until we see them as part of a dialogue with Irish nationalists from the Easter Rebellion, Russian and Jewish émigrés from the 1905 and 1917 revolutions, and Asian socialists like India's M. N. Roy and Japan's Sen Katayama.

10   Indeed, I'm not sure we can even limit ourselves to Earth. How do we make sense of musicians Sun Ra, George Clinton, and Lee "Scratch" Perry or, for that matter, the Nation of Islam, when we consider the fact that space travel and notions of intergalactic exchange constitute a key source of their ideas?

11   So-called "mixed race" children are not the only ones with a claim to multiple heritages. All of us are inheritors of European, African, Native American, and Asian pasts, even if we can't exactly trace our bloodlines to these continents.

12   To some people that's a dangerous concept. Too many Europeans don't want to acknowledge that Africans helped create so-called Western civilization, that they are both indebted to and descendants of those they enslaved. They don't want to see the world

as One—a tiny little globe where people and cultures are always on the move, where nothing stays still no matter how many times we name it. To acknowledge our polycultural heritage and cultural dynamism is not to give up our black identity. It does mean expanding our definition of blackness, taking our history more seriously, and looking at the rich diversity within us with new eyes.

So next time you see me, don't ask where I'm from or what I am,   13 unless you're ready to sit through a long-ass lecture. As singer/songwriter Abbey Lincoln once put it, "I've got some people in me."

QUESTIONS ON SUBJECT AND PURPOSE

1. Why is the question "What are you?" not a simple one?
2. The first section of the essay (through paragraph 5) deals with Kelley's family. What does their story have to do with the rest of the essay?
3. What might be Kelley's purpose in the essay?

QUESTIONS ON STRATEGY AND AUDIENCE

1. Does Kelley's opening paragraph catch your attention? Why or why not?
2. How would you characterize the first five paragraphs in Kelley's essay? What is he doing? What organizational strategy does he use?
3. In what way is the example of his brother's child (paragraph 5) a perfect example of the polyculturalism that Kelley is talking about?

QUESTIONS ON VOCABULARY AND STYLE

1. Can you find examples in the essay of informal, even colloquial word choices?
2. Can you find examples in the essay of formal word choices?
3. Be prepared to define the following words: *patois* (paragraph 2), *pummeled* (2), *nondescript* (2), *enigmas* (2), *demure* (3), *entities* (6), *reifies* (6).

WRITING SUGGESTIONS

1. **For Your Journal.** To what extent can you see in American culture, or perhaps in the things in which you are interested, evidence of polycultural heritage? Think about food, music, clothing or hairstyles, behavior, language habits, popular idols. Think about your friends—in high school, at college. In your journal make a list of things central to your life and your friends' lives that are clearly derived from cultures and heritages other than your own.

2. **For a Paragraph.** Select one example that you recorded in your journal (or a series of related examples) and in a paragraph explore the appeal that such a thing has for you and/or your friends.

3. **For an Essay.** Explore the question that Kelley begins with. If someone asked you, "What are you?", how would you reply? In an essay define yourself (and/or your family).

4. **For Research.** Select a word or phrase such as *race, nationality, ethnic origin, multicultural,* or *polycultural* and research what it means. Drawing upon your research, write an extended definition of that term. Be sure to document your sources fully.

 WEBSITE LINK

Interviews with Kelley and some of his essays can be found on the Web. Visit the *Reader*'s Website for places to start.

 WRITING LINK: QUOTATION MARKS

Kelley encloses quite a few words and phrases within quotation marks. When do we use quotation marks in this way? What is the difference between using quotation marks and using italics? After you have examined the essay, try writing some advice to student writers about when to put words and phrases in quotation marks.

MOTHER TONGUE

Amy Tan

Born in Oakland, California, in 1952 to Chinese immigrants, Amy Tan graduated from San Jose State University with a double major in English and linguistics and an M.A. in linguistics. Tan did not write fiction until 1985, when she began the stories that would become her first and very successful novel, The Joy Luck Club *(1989), also a popular film. Tan's children's book* The Chinese Siamese Cat *(1994) is the basis for the daily animated television series,* Sagwa, The Chinese Siamese Cat *(PBS). Her most recent novel is* The Bonesetter's Daughter *(2001).*

On Writing: *Asked about her writing, Tan responded: "I welcome criticism when I'm writing my books. I want to become better and better as a writer. I go to a writer's group every week. We read our work aloud." In another interview she commented, "I still think of myself, in many ways, as a beginning writer. I'm still learning my craft, learning what makes for a good story, what's an honest voice."*

BEFORE READING

Connecting: How sensitive are you to the language that you use or your family uses? Are you ever conscious of that language? Are you ever embarrassed by it? Are you proud of it?

Anticipating: In what ways does the language of Tan and her mother "define" them in the eyes of others?

I am not a scholar of English or literature. I cannot give you much   1
more than personal opinions on the English language and its variations in this country or others.

I am a writer. And by that definition, I am someone who has al-   2
ways loved language. I am fascinated by language in daily life. I spend a great deal of my time thinking about the power of language—the way it can evoke an emotion, a visual image, a complex idea, or a simple truth. Language is the tool of my trade. And I use them all—all the Englishes I grew up with.

Recently, I was made keenly aware of the different Englishes I   3
do use. I was giving a talk to a large group of people, the same talk I had already given to half a dozen other groups. The nature of the talk

was about my writing, my life, and my book, *The Joy Luck Club*. The talk was going along well enough, until I remembered one major difference that made the whole talk sound wrong. My mother was in the room. And it was perhaps the first time she had heard me give a lengthy speech, using the kind of English I have never used with her. I was saying things like, "The intersection of memory upon imagination" and "There is an aspect of my fiction that relates to thus-and-thus"—a speech filled with carefully wrought grammatical phrases, burdened, it suddenly seemed to me, with nominalized forms, past perfect tenses, conditional phrases, all the forms of standard English that I had learned in school and through books, the forms of English I did not use at home with my mother.

4 Just last week, I was walking down the street with my mother, and I again found myself conscious of the English I was using, the English I do use with her. We were talking about the price of new and used furniture and I heard myself saying this: "Not waste money that way." My husband was with us as well, and he didn't notice any switch in my English. And then I realized why. It's because over the twenty years we've been together I've often used that same kind of English with him, and sometimes he even uses it with me. It has become our language of intimacy, a different sort of English that relates to family talk, the language I grew up with.

5 So you'll have some idea of what this family talk I heard sounds like, I'll quote what my mother said during a recent conversation which I videotaped and then transcribed. During this conversation, my mother was talking about a political gangster in Shanghai who had the same last name as her family's, Du, and how the gangster in his early years wanted to be adopted by her family, which was rich by comparison. Later, the gangster became more powerful, far richer than my mother's family, and one day showed up at my mother's wedding to pay his respects. Here's what she said in part:

6 "Du Yusong having business like fruit stand. Like off the street kind. He is Du like Du Zong—but not Tsung-ming Island people. The local people call putong, the river east side, he belong to that side local people. That man want to ask Du Zong father take him in like become own family. Du Zong father wasn't look down on him, but didn't take seriously, until that man big like become a mafia. Now important person, very hard to inviting him. Chinese way, came only to show respect, don't stay for dinner. Respect for making big celebration, he shows up. Mean gives lots of respect. Chinese custom. Chinese social life that way. If too important won't have to stay too long. He come to my wedding. I didn't see, I heard it. I gone to boy's side, they have YMCA dinner. Chinese age I was nineteen."

You should know that my mother's expressive command of   7
English belies how much she actually understands. She reads the
Forbes report, listens to *Wall Street Week*, converses daily with her
stockbroker, reads all of Shirley MacLaine's books with ease—all
kinds of things I can't begin to understand. Yet some of my friends tell
me they understand 50 percent of what my mother says. Some say
they understand 80 to 90 percent. Some say they understand none of
it, as if she were speaking pure Chinese. But to me, my mother's English is perfectly clear, perfectly natural. It's my mother tongue. Her
language, as I hear it, is vivid, direct, full of observation and imagery.
That was the language that helped shape the way I saw things, expressed things, made sense of the world.

Lately, I've been giving more thought to the kind of English   8
my mother speaks. Like others, I have described it to people as
"broken" or "fractured" English. But I wince when I say that. It has
always bothered me that I can think of no way to describe it other
than "broken," as if it were damaged and needed to be fixed, as if it
lacked a certain wholeness and soundness. I've heard other terms
used, "limited English," for example. But they seem just as bad, as
if everything is limited, including people's perceptions of the limited English speaker.

I know this for a fact, because when I was growing up, my   9
mother's "limited" English limited *my* perception of her. I was
ashamed of her English. I believed that her English reflected the
quality of what she had to say. That is, because she expressed them
imperfectly her thoughts were imperfect. And I had plenty of empirical evidence to support me: the fact that people in department stores,
at banks, and at restaurants did not take her seriously, did not give her
good service, pretended not to understand her, or even acted as if they
did not hear her.

My mother has long realized the limitations of her English as   10
well. When I was fifteen, she used to have me call people on the
phone to pretend I was she. In this guise, I was forced to ask for information or even to complain and yell at people who had been rude
to her. One time it was a call to her stockbroker in New York. She had
cashed out her small portfolio and it just so happened we were going
to go to New York the next week, our very first trip outside California. I had to get on the phone and say in an adolescent voice that was
not very convincing, "This is Mrs. Tan."

And my mother was standing in the back whispering loudly,   11
"Why he don't send me check, already two weeks late. So mad he lie
to me, losing me money."

12   And then I said in perfect English, "Yes, I'm getting rather concerned. You had agreed to send the check two weeks ago, but it hasn't arrived."

13   Then she began to talk more loudly. "What he want, I come to New York tell him front of his boss, you cheating me?" And I was trying to calm her down, make her be quiet, while telling the stockbroker, "I can't tolerate any more excuses. If I don't receive the check immediately, I am going to have to speak to your manager when I'm in New York next week." And sure enough, the following week there we were in front of this astonished stockbroker, and I was sitting there red-faced and quiet, and my mother, the real Mrs. Tan, was shouting at his boss in her impeccable broken English.

14   We used a similar routine just five days ago, for a situation that was far less humorous. My mother had gone to the hospital for an appointment, to find out about a benign brain tumor a CAT scan had revealed a month ago. She said she had spoken very good English, her best English, no mistakes. Still, she said, the hospital did not apologize when they said they had lost the CAT scan and she had come for nothing. She said they did not seem to have any sympathy when she told them she was anxious to know the exact diagnosis, since her husband and son had both died of brain tumors. She said they would not give her any more information until the next time and she would have to make another appointment for that. So she said she would not leave until the doctor called her daughter. She wouldn't budge. And when the doctor finally called her daughter, me, who spoke in perfect English—lo and behind—we had assurances the CAT scan would be found, promises that a conference call on Monday would be held, and apologies for any suffering my mother had gone through for a most regrettable mistake.

15   I think my mother's English almost had an effect on limiting my possibilities in life as well. Sociologists and linguists probably will tell you that a person's developing language skills are more influenced by peers. But I do think that the language spoken in the family, especially in immigrant families which are more insular, plays a large role in shaping the language of the child. And I believe that it affected my results on achievement tests, IQ tests, and the SAT. While my English skills were never judged as poor, compared to math, English could not be considered my strong suit. In grade school I did moderately well, getting perhaps B's, sometimes B-pluses, in English and scoring perhaps in the sixtieth or seventieth percentile on achievement tests. But those scores were not good enough to override the opinion that my true abilities lay in math and science, because in those areas I achieved A's and scored in the ninetieth percentile or higher.

This was understandable. Math is precise; there is only one cor-   16
rect answer. Whereas, for me at least, the answers on English tests
were always a judgment call, a matter of opinion and personal experience. Those tests were constructed around items like fill-in-the-
blank sentence completion, such as, "Even though Tom was
_____ , Mary thought he was _____ ." And the correct answer always seemed to be the most bland combinations of thoughts,
for example, "Even though Tom was shy, Mary thought he was
charming," with the grammatical structure "even though" limiting
the correct answer to some sort of semantic opposites, so you wouldn't
get answers like, "Even though Tom was foolish, Mary thought he
was ridiculous." Well, according to my mother, there were very few
limitations as to what Tom could have been and what Mary might
have thought of him. So I never did well on tests like that.

The same was true with word analogies, pairs of words in which   17
you were supposed to find some sort of logical, semantic relationship—
for example, "*Sunset* is to *nightfall* as _____ is to _____ ."
And here you would be presented with a list of four possible pairs, one
of which showed the same kind of relationship: *red* is to *stoplight*, *bus*
is to *arrival*, *chills* is to *fever*, *yawn* is to *boring*. Well, I could never think
that way. I knew what the tests were asking, but I could not block out
of my mind the images already created by the first pair, "*sunset* is to
nightfall"—and I would see a burst of colors against a darkening sky,
the moon rising, the lowering of a curtain of stars. And all the other
pairs of words—*red, bus, stoplight, boring*—just threw up a mass of confusing images, making it impossible for me to sort out something as
logical as saying: "A sunset precedes nightfall" is the same as "a chill
precedes a fever." The only way I would have gotten that answer right
would have been to imagine an associative situation, for example, my
being disobedient and staying out past sunset, catching a chill at
night, which turns into feverish pneumonia as punishment, which indeed did happen to me.

I have been thinking about all this lately, about my mother's   18
English, about achievement tests. Because lately I've been asked, as a
writer, why there are not more Asian-Americans represented in
American literature. Why are there few Asian Americans enrolled in
creative writing programs? Why do so many Chinese students go into
engineering? Well, these are broad sociological questions I can't begin to answer. But I have noticed in surveys—in fact, just last week—
that Asian students, as a whole, always do significantly better on math
achievement tests than in English. And this makes me think that there
are other Asian-American students whose English spoken in the

home might also be described as "broken" or "limited." And perhaps they also have teachers who are steering them away from writing and into math and science, which is what happened to me.

19   Fortunately, I happen to be rebellious in nature and enjoy the challenge of disproving assumptions made about me. I became an English major my first year in college, after being enrolled as premed. I started writing nonfiction as a freelancer the week after I was told by my former boss that writing was my worst skill and I should hone my talents toward account management.

20   But it wasn't until 1985 that I finally began to write fiction. And at first I wrote using what I thought to be wittily crafted sentences, sentences that would finally prove I had mastery over the English language. Here's an example from the first draft of a story that later made its way into *The Joy Luck Club*, but without this line: "That was my mental quandary in its nascent state." A terrible line, which I can barely pronounce.

21   Fortunately, for reasons I won't get into today, I later decided I should envision a reader for the stories I would write. And the reader I decided upon was my mother, because these were stories about mothers. So with this reader in mind—and in fact she did read my early drafts—I began to write stories using all the Englishes I grew up with: the English I spoke to my mother, which for lack of a better term might be described as "simple"; the English she used with me, which for lack of a better term might be described as "broken"; my translation of her Chinese, which could certainly be described as "watered down"; and what I imagined to be her translation of her Chinese if she could speak in perfect English, her internal language, and for that I sought to preserve the essence, but neither an English nor a Chinese structure. I wanted to capture what language ability tests can never reveal: her intent, her passion, her imagery, the rhythms of her speech and the nature of her thoughts.

22   Apart from what any critic had to say about my writing, I knew I had succeeded where it counted when my mother finished reading my book and gave me her verdict: "So easy to read."

QUESTIONS ON SUBJECT AND PURPOSE

1. What does the title "Mother Tongue" suggest?
2. How many subjects does Tan explore in the essay?

3. How does Tan feel about her mother's "tongue"?

QUESTIONS ON STRATEGY AND AUDIENCE

1. In paragraph 6, Tan quotes part of one of her mother's conversations. Why?
2. After paragraphs 7 and 17, Tan uses additional space to indicate divisions in her essay. Why does she divide the essay into three parts?
3. Tan notes in paragraph 21 that she thinks of her mother as her audience when she writes stories. Why?

QUESTIONS ON VOCABULARY AND STYLE

1. How would you characterize Tan's tone (see the Glossary for a definition) in the essay?
2. In paragraph 20, Tan quotes a "terrible line" she once wrote: "That was my mental quandary in its nascent state." What is so terrible about that line?
3. Be prepared to define the following words: *belies* (7), *empirical* (9), *benign* (14), *insular* (15), *semantic* (16), *hone* (19), *quandary* (20), *nascent* (20).

WRITING SUGGESTIONS

1. **For Your Journal.** What makes up your "mother tongue"? To what extent is your language (such things as word choice, pronunciation, dialect, and second-language skills) influenced by your parents, your education, the part of the country in which you grew up, and your peers? Make a series of notes exploring those influences.
2. **For a Paragraph.** Using the information that you gathered for your journal entry, write a paragraph in which you define your "mother tongue." Try to define the influences that have shaped both how and what you say.
3. **For an Essay.** Tan suggests that a certain type or dialect of English is a language of power, that if you speak and write that English, people in authority will listen to you and respect you. How might that public, powerful English (sometimes referred to as "edited American English") be defined?

4. **For Research.** Linguists have defined a wide range of dialects
in the United States. Choose one of the dialects that interests
you—a reference librarian or your instructor can help you
find a list. You might choose one based on the geographical
area in which you live or one defined by your heritage. Using
the resources of your library, write a definition of that dialect.
What are its distinctive features? Where did those features
come from? Where is this dialect spoken in the United States?
What are some particularly colorful examples? Be sure to
document your sources wherever appropriate.

 WEBSITE LINK

Read on-line interviews with Tan, watch video clips of her talking
about her books, listen to audio excerpts from her works. Hot-linked
sites on Tan can be found at the *Reader*'s Website.

 WRITING LINK: SENTENCE STRUCTURE

Tan occasionally writes an extremely long sentence. For example,
look at the final sentences in paragraphs 3, 8, 13, 14, and 17 and the
next to last sentence in paragraph 21. How can Tan write such a long
sentence and still achieve clarity? Choose one or more of those sentences and analyze how it is constructed. What is essential in a very
long sentence?

MESS

John Hollander

Born in 1929, John Hollander is a distinguished and widely published poet, editor, and critic. He is Sterling Professor of English at Yale University and the author of many books of poetry. His most recent books are The Work of Poetry *(1997), a collection of essays, and* Figurehead: And Other Poems *(1999). "Mess" was originally published in the* Yale Review *in 1995.*

On Writing: *Commenting on this essay, Hollander observed: "This brief essay was generated more from within, like a poem, than most other prose of mine—nobody asked me to write it, but I felt impelled to observe something about one aspect of life that tends to get swept under the rug, as it were."*

BEFORE READING

Connecting: Are you "messy"? How do you feel about the messes that you make or about the messes of others?

Anticipating: In the final paragraph, Hollander refers to his essay as a "meditation on mess." What does the word *meditation* suggest to you? In what ways is the essay a meditation?

M ess is a state of mind. Or rather, messiness is a particular relation   1
between the state of arrangement of a collection of things and a state of mind that contemplates it in its containing space. For example, X's mess may be Y's delight—sheer profusion, uncompromised by any apparent structure even in the representation of it. Or there may be some inner order or logic to A's mess that B cannot possibly perceive. Consider: someone—Alpha—rearranges all the books on Beta's library shelf, which have been piled or stacked, sometimes properly, sometimes not, but all in relevant sequence (by author and, within that, by date of publication), and rearranges them neatly, by size and color. Beta surveys the result, and can only feel, if not blurt out, "WHAT A MESS!" This situation often occurs with respect to messes of the workplace generally.

For there are many kinds of mess, both within walls and outside   2
them: neglected gardens and the aftermath of tropical storms, and the indoor kinds of disorder peculiar to specific areas of our life with, and in and among, *things*. There are messes of one's own making, messes

not even of one's own person, places, or things. There are personal states of mind about common areas of messiness—those of the kitchen, the bedroom, the bathroom, the salon (of whatever sort, from half of a bed-sitter to some grand public parlor), or those of personal appearance (clothes, hair, etc.). Then, for all those who are in any way self-employed or whose avocations are practiced in some private space—a workshop, a darkroom, a study or a studio—there is the mess of the workplace. It's not the most common kind of mess, but it's exemplary: the eye surveying it is sickened by the roller-coaster of scanning the scene. And, alas, it's the one I'm most afflicted with.

3   I know that things are really in a mess when—as about ninety seconds ago—I reach for the mouse on my Macintosh and find instead a thick layer of old envelopes, manuscript notes consulted three weeks ago, favorite pens and inoperative ones, folders used hastily and not replaced, and so forth. In order to start working, I brush these accumulated impedimenta aside, thus creating a new mess. But this is, worse yet, absorbed by the general condition of my study: piles of thin books and thick books, green volumes of the Loeb Classical Library and slimy paperbacks of ephemeral spy-thrillers, mostly used notepads, bills paid and unpaid, immortal letters from beloved friends, unopened and untrashed folders stuffed with things that should be in various other folders, book-mailing envelopes, unanswered mail whose cries for help and attention are muffled by three months' worth of bank statements enshrouding them in the gloom of continued neglect. Even this fairly orderly inventory seems to simplify the confusion: in actuality, searching for a letter or a page of manuscript in this state of things involves crouching down with my head on one side and searching vertically along the outside of a teetering pile for what may be a thin, hidden layer of it.

4   Displacement, and lack of design, are obscured in the origins of our very word *mess*. The famous biblical "mess of red pottage" (lentil mush or dal) for which Esau sold his birthright wasn't "messy" in our sense (unless, of course, in the not very interesting case of Esau having dribbled it on his clothing). The word meant a serving of food, or a course in a meal: something *placed* in front of you (from the Latin *missus*, put or placed), hence "messmates" (dining companions) and ultimately "officers' mess" and the like. It also came to mean a dish of prepared mixed food—like an *olla podrida* or a minestrone—then by extension (but only from the early nineteenth century on) any hodgepodge: inedible, and outside the neat confines of a bowl or pot, and thus unpleasant, confusing, and agitating or depressing to contemplate. But for us, the association with food perhaps remains only in how much the state of mind of being messy is like that of being fat: for

example, X says, "God I'm getting gross! I'll have to diet!" Y, *really* fat, cringes on hearing this, and feels that for the slender X to talk that way is an obscenity. Similarly, X: "God, this place is a pigsty!" Y: (ditto). For a person prone to messiness, Cyril Connolly's celebrated observation about fat people is projected onto the world itself: inside every neat arrangement is a mess struggling to break out, like some kind of statue of chaos lying implicit in the marble of apparent organization. In Paradise, there was no such thing as messiness. This was 5 partly because unfallen, ideal life needed no supplemental *things*— objects of use and artifice, elements of any sort of technology. Thus there was nothing to leave lying around, messily or even neatly, by Adam and Eve—according to Milton—"at their savory dinner set / Of herbs and other country messes." But it was also because order, hence orderliness, was itself so natural that whatever bit of nature Adam and Eve might have been occupied with, or even using in a momentary tool-like way, flew or leapt or crept into place in some sort of reasonable arrangement, even as in our unparadised state things *fall* under the joyless tug of gravity. But messiness may seem to be an inevitable state of the condition of having so many *things*, precious or disposable, in one's life.

As I observed before, even to describe a mess is to impose order 6 on it. The ancient Greek vision of primal chaos, even, was not *messy* in that it was pre-messy: there weren't any categories by which to define order, so that there could be no disorder—no nextness or betweenness, no above, below, here, there, and so forth. *"Let there be light"* meant "Let there be perception of something," and it was then that order became possible, and mess possibly implied. Now, a list or inventory is in itself an orderly literary form, and even incoherent assemblages of items fall too easily into some other kind of order: in *Through the Looking-Glass*, the Walrus's "Of shoes, and ships, and sealing-wax, / Of cabbages, and kings," is given a harmonious structure by the pairs of alliterating words, and even by the half-punning association of "ships, [sailing] sealing-wax." The wonderful catalogue in *Tom Sawyer* of the elements of what must have been, pocketed or piled on the ground, a mess of splendid proportions, is a poem of its own. The objects of barter for a stint of fence whitewashing (Tom, it will be remembered, turns *having* to do a chore into *getting* to do it by sheer con-man's insouciance) comprise

> twelve marbles, part of a jewsharp, a piece of blue bottle-glass to
> look through, a spool cannon, a key that wouldn't unlock anything,
> a fragment of chalk, a glass stopper of a decanter, a tin soldier, a
> couple of tadpoles, six fire-crackers, a kitten with only one eye, a

brass door-knob, a dog collar—but no dog—the handle of a knife, four pieces of orange peel, and a dilapidated old window sash.

7   Thus such representations of disorder as lists, paintings, photos, etc., all compromise the purity of true messiness by the verbal or visual order they impose on the confusion. To get at the mess in my study, for example, a movie might serve best, alternately mixing midshot and zoom on a particular portion of the disaster, which would, in an almost fractal way, seem to be a mini-disaster of its own. There are even neatly conventionalized emblems of messiness that are, after all, all too neat; thus, whenever a movie wants to show an apartment or office that has been ransacked by Baddies (cop Baddies or baddy Baddies or whatever) in search of the Thing They Want, the designer is always careful to show at least one picture on the wall hanging carefully askew. All this could possibly tell us about a degree of messiness is that the searchers were so messy (at another level of application of the term) in their technique that they violated their search agenda to run over to the wall and tilt the picture (very messy procedure indeed), or that, hastily leaving the scene to avoid detection, they nonetheless took a final revenge against the Occupant for not having the Thing on his or her premises, and tilted the picture in a fit of pique. And yet a tilted picture gives good cueing mileage: it can present a good bit of disorder at the expense of a minimum of misalignment, after all.

8   A meditation on mess could be endless. As I struggle to conclude this one, one of my cats regards me from her nest in and among one of the disaster areas that all surfaces in my study soon become. Cats disdain messes in several ways. First, they are proverbially neat about their shit and about the condition of their fur. Second, they pick their way so elegantly among my piles of books, papers, and ancillary objects (dishes of paper clips, scissors, functional and dried-out pens, crumpled envelopes, outmoded postage stamps, boxes of slides and disks, staplers, glue bottles, tape dispensers—*you* know) that they cannot even be said to acknowledge the mess's existence. The gray familiar creature currently making her own order out of a region of mess on my desk—carefully disposing herself around and over and among piles and bunches and stacks and crazily oblique layers and thereby reinterpreting it as natural landscape—makes me further despair until I realize that what she does with her body, I must do with my perception of this inevitable disorder—shaping its forms to the disorder and thereby shaping the disorder to its forms. She has taught me resignation.

QUESTIONS ON SUBJECT AND PURPOSE

1. In what sense is a mess "a state of mind"?
2. What role do "things" play in creating a mess?
3. Having contemplated the "mess" in which he works, Hollander reaches what conclusion?

QUESTIONS ON STRATEGY AND AUDIENCE

1. In what way does describing a mess "impose order on it" (paragraph 6)?
2. Toward the end of the essay, Hollander notes that he "struggles" to conclude. Why is it a struggle?
3. Hollander makes reference throughout the essay to other writers and works of literature. What do these allusions suggest about Hollander and his sense of his audience?

QUESTIONS ON VOCABULARY AND STYLE

1. Hollander is a poet. Does he ever sound like a poet in the essay? Can you find examples of phrasing or language that sounds like something you would imagine a poet would write?
2. Find the two shortest sentences in the essay (not counting the exchange between X and Y in paragraph 4).
3. Make a list of words in the essay whose meanings are uncertain to you. Bring your list to class.

WRITING SUGGESTIONS

1. **For Your Journal.** In your journal, brainstorm a list of words that you might define. Try for a list of words that are somehow related to or associated with you. They might be words that describe your behavior (for example, *orderly, outgoing, shy, ambitious*), your physical self (*short, tall, athletic*), or your attitudes toward life or events (*optimistic, cynical*). Try for a substantial list.
2. **For a Paragraph.** In a paragraph, define one of the words. Do not write a dictionary definition; write an extended definition that includes examples, details, connotations.
3. **For an Essay.** Select one of the words from your journal, and write an essay definition of the word. Remember to get your instructor's approval of the word.

4. **For Research.** To judge from the number of books, videos, and products that are marketed to American consumers, messiness is clearly something that people would like to avoid. Whether it is how to clean up the clutter on your desk or in your closets at home or how to organize your every moment through elaborate daily planners and software programs, we seem to want desperately to be "neat." In a researched essay, define the word *neat*. You can draw examples from advertisements as well as from books, articles, and the electronic media. You will also want to research the history of the word (using, for example, some of the historical dictionaries in your school's library). Be sure to document all of your sources.

 WEBSITE LINK

A number of Hollander's poems can be found on the Web, as well as an audio file in which you can hear him read.

 WRITING LINK: COLON

Hollander has a fondness for linking sentences together with a colon. Make a list of each instance in which Hollander uses this construction, study those sentences, and then write a rule for the use of the colon as a mark to link sentences together. Do you ever use such a construction in your own writing?

THE FEMALE BODY

Margaret Atwood

Margaret Atwood was born in Ottawa, Canada, in 1939. She received a B.A. from the University of Toronto in 1961 and earned an M.A. at Radcliffe College in 1962. A poet, essayist, short story writer, and novelist, Atwood has enjoyed critical and popular acclaim throughout her writing career, winning numerous awards and honorary degrees. Her work has explored broad themes of feminism, dystopia, and the opposition of art and nature, but always through the eyes of an individual. Her best known novel is The Handmaid's Tale *(1986), in which a totalitarian state assigns roles to women according to their reproductive abilities.*

On Writing: *At a meeting of the Toronto Council of Teachers of English, Atwood was asked about the importance of punctuation in good writing. She commented on her own use of punctuation: "I've recently taken up a new device, which is the set of dashes. Some people overuse this quite a lot—everything is a set of dashes—but in prose I'm tending to prefer it to parentheses. In prose fiction a lot is associative, one idea suggests another which can lead to an interposition in the middle of a sentence. The question is, how do you set that off? Sometimes you can do it with parenthesis, but sets of dashes are often quite useful."*

BEFORE READING

Connecting: What image is suggested to you by the phrase "the female body"?

Anticipating: Does Atwood's essay fulfill your expectations of an essay on the "female body"? Why or why not?

> . . . entirely devoted to the subject of "The Female Body." Knowing how well you have written on this topic . . . this capacious topic . . .
>
> Letter from *Michigan Quarterly Review*

1

I agree, it's a hot topic. But only one? Look around, there's a wide range. Take my own, for instance.

I get up in the morning. My topic feels like hell. I sprinkle it with water, brush parts of it, rub it with towels, powder it, add lubricant. I dump in the fuel and away goes my topic, my topical topic, my controversial topic, my capacious topic, my limping topic, my nearsighted topic, my topic with back problems, my badly behaved topic, my vulgar topic, my outrageous topic, my aging topic, my topic that is out of the question and anyway still can't spell, in its oversized coat and worn winter boots, scuttling along the sidewalk as if it were flesh and blood, hunting for what's out there, an avocado, an alderman, an adjective, hungry as ever.

2

3   The basic Female Body comes with the following accessories: garter belt, panti-girdle, crinoline, camisole, bustle, brassiere, stomacher, chemise, virgin zone, spike heels, nose ring, veil, kid gloves, fishnet stockings, fichu, bandeau, Merry Widow, weepers, chokers, barrettes, bangles, beads, lorgnette, feather boa, basic black, compact, Lycra stretch one-piece with modesty panel, designer peignoir, flannel nightie, lace teddy, bed, head.

3

4   The Female Body is made of transparent plastic and lights up when you plug it in. You press a button to illuminate the different systems. The circulatory system is red, for the heart and arteries, purple for the veins; the respiratory system is blue; the lymphatic system is yellow; the digestive system is green, with liver and kidneys in aqua. The nerves are done in orange and the brain is pink. The skeleton, as you might expect, is white.

5   The reproductive system is optional, and can be removed. It comes with or without a miniature embryo. Parental judgment can thereby be exercised. We do not wish to frighten or offend.

4

6   He said, I won't have one of those things in the house. It gives a young girl a false notion of beauty, not to mention anatomy. If a real woman was built like that she'd fall on her face.

7   She said, If we don't let her have one like all the other girls she'll feel singled out. It'll become an issue. She'll long for one and she'll long to turn into one. Repression breeds sublimation. You know that.

8   He said, It's not just the pointy plastic tits, it's the wardrobes. The wardrobes and that stupid male doll, what's his name, the one with the underwear glued on.

9   She said, Better to get it over with when she's young. He said, All right, but don't let me see it.

10   She came whizzing down the stairs, thrown like a dart. She was stark naked. Her hair had been chopped off, her head was turned back to front, she was missing some toes and she'd been tattooed all over

her body with purple ink in a scrollwork design. She hit the potted azalea, trembled there for a moment like a botched angel, and fell.

He said, I guess we're safe.   11

5

The Female Body has many uses. It's been used as a door   12
knocker, a bottle opener, as a clock with a ticking belly, as something to hold up lampshades, as a nutcracker, just squeeze the brass legs together and out comes your nut. It bears torches, lifts victorious wreaths, grows copper wings and raises aloft a ring of neon stars; whole buildings rest on its marble heads.

It sells cars, beer, shaving lotion, cigarettes, hard liquor; it sells   13
diet plans and diamonds, and desire in tiny crystal bottles. Is this the face that launched a thousand products? You bet it is, but don't get any funny big ideas, honey, that smile is a dime a dozen.

It does not merely sell, it is sold. Money flows into this country   14
or that country, flies in, practically crawls in, suitful after suitful, lured by all those hairless pre-teen legs. Listen, you want to reduce the national debt, don't you? Aren't you patriotic? That's the spirit. That's my girl.

She's a natural resource, a renewable one luckily, because those   15
things wear out so quickly. They don't make 'em like they used to. Shoddy goods.

6

One and one equals another one. Pleasure in the female is not   16
a requirement. Pair-bonding is stronger in geese. We're not talking about love, we're talking about biology. That's how we all got here, daughter.

Snails do it differently. They're hermaphrodites, and work in   17
threes.

7

Each Female Body contains a female brain. Handy. Makes   18
things work. Stick pins in it and you get amazing results. Old popular songs. Short circuits. Bad dreams.

Anyway: each of these brains has two halves. They're joined to-   19
gether by a thick cord; neural pathways flow from one to the other, sparkles of electric information washing to and fro. Like light on waves. Like a conversation. How does a woman know? She listens. She listens in.

The male brain, now, that's a different matter. Only a thin con-   20
nection. Space over here, time over there, music and arithmetic in their own sealed compartments. The right brain doesn't know what

the left brain is doing. Good for aiming through, for hitting the target when you pull the trigger. What's the target? Who's the target? Who cares? What matters is hitting it. That's the male brain for you. Objective.

21   This is why men are so sad, why they feel so cut off, why they think of themselves as orphans cast adrift, footloose and stringless in the deep void. What void? she asks. What are you talking about? The void of the universe, he says, and she says Oh and looks out the window and tries to get a handle on it, but it's no use, there's too much going on, too many rustlings in the leaves, too many voices, so she says, Would you like a cheese sandwich, a piece of cake, a cup of tea? And he grinds his teeth because she doesn't understand, and wanders off, not just alone but Alone, lost in the dark, lost in the skull, searching for the other half, the twin who could complete him.

22   Then it comes to him: he's lost the Female Body! Look, it shines in the gloom, far ahead, a vision of wholeness, ripeness, like a giant melon, like an apple, like a metaphor for "breast" in a bad sex novel; it shines like a balloon, like a foggy noon, a watery moon, shimmering in its egg of light.

23   Catch it. Put it in a pumpkin, in a high tower, in a compound, in a chamber, in a house, in a room. Quick, stick a leash on it, a lock, a chain, some pain, settle it down, so it can never get away from you again.

QUESTIONS ON SUBJECT AND PURPOSE

1. What appears to be the occasion for Atwood's essay?
2. In what ways might this be considered a definition of the "female body"?
3. Is it true, as Atwood notes in section 7, that the structure of the brain varies with gender?

QUESTIONS ON STRATEGY AND AUDIENCE

1. Why might Atwood have chosen to divide the essay as she does?
2. Why doesn't Atwood write transitions to bridge from one section of the essay to another instead of dividing it into sections?
3. The letter from the magazine refers to the topic as "capacious." What does that word mean? In what way does that word suggest the shape and nature of Atwood's response?

QUESTIONS ON VOCABULARY AND STYLE

1. How would you characterize Atwood's tone in the essay? (See the Glossary for a definition of *tone*.)
2. In what context might you expect to find section 3 of the essay? What does it sound like?
3. Be prepared to define the words *alderman* (paragraph 2) and *sublimation* (7).

WRITING SUGGESTIONS

1. **For Your Journal.** Suppose you had been invited to write something (an essay, a poem, a story) about either the male or the female body. What would you say? In your journal, jot down some possible ideas for your response.
2. **For a Paragraph.** Select one of the ideas that you came up with in your journal writing, and expand that into a developed paragraph. Remember to use example—either a variety of different ones or a single, extended one—to develop your definition.
3. **For an Essay.** In section 5, Atwood makes numerous references to the ways in which the female body has been used to sell products. Similarily, advertisers today also use male bodies. Judging just from the images of women or of men presented in advertisements, write an essay about how the female or male body is defined in our culture.
4. **For Research.** How have society's definitions of *masculinity* and *femininity* changed over time? Choose one of the two terms, and research its shifting definitions over the past two hundred years. What did society expect of a man or a women in 1800? In 1900? In the early 2000s? What is considered masculine or feminine? Remember that no single reference source will provide you with the answers you need. You may need to infer the definitions from the roles that society forced on men and women and the images that represented those roles. Be sure to acknowledge your sources wherever appropriate.

WEBSITE LINK

Atwood maintains an extensive personal home page on the Web. Dozens of Websites contain a wide range of information about Atwood and her work, including the texts of a number of her short stories. Start at the *Reader's* Website.

WRITING LINK: SENTENCE FRAGMENTS

The first three paragraphs in Atwood's essay contain quite a few sentence fragments. How many can you find? What makes each a fragment? Try adding words to each fragment to make it into a sentence. What is gained or lost in the process? Can a sentence fragment be effective? Under what circumstances?

PREWRITING SUGGESTIONS FOR DEFINITION

1. Brainstorm some possible topics for your essay. Just jot down ideas in your notebook. Return to your list over the next day. Add to it. Scratch out topics that seem less promising. Remember that thinking about your topic is an important part of prewriting.

2. Once you have narrowed your topic, write out a dictionary definition for the term, idea, or subject. Regardless of how extended your definition is, start with a one-sentence statement.

3. Write a purpose statement for your essay: "My purpose in this essay is to. . . . " Use it to test what you are writing.

4. Since your essay will be an extended definition, think about the types of information or details that you will need to fill out your definition. Does your subject lend itself to observation? To research? To interviews with others? Plan a strategy to help you gather the details and examples that you will need.

Once you have a strategy, gather your information. Do this
before you start to write.

5. Look back over the details that you plan to include in your
   extended definition. What organizational strategy seems
   appropriate? Are you dividing your topic into parts? Are you
   defining through comparison and contrast? Does your
   definition involve narration or description? Process or cause
   and effect? Sketch out a possible framework that organizes the
   examples and details you plan to include.

REWRITING SUGGESTIONS FOR DEFINITION

1. Check each individual paragraph. Is there a unified idea that
   controls each one? Make a copy of your essay, and highlight
   the topic sentence or key idea of each paragraph with a color
   marker. Does each paragraph have a topic sentence?
2. Have you provided enough examples to support your
   generalizations? Go through a copy of your essay, underlining
   generalizations in one color and examples in another. Is there
   a good balance between the two?
3. Outline your draft. Do you see a clear, logical organization?
   Are there adequate transitions from section to section? Make a
   list of any problems you discover in the organization, and then
   devote some time to trying to solve just those problems.
4. Characterize the tone of what you have written. For example,
   are you serious or satirical? Is it formal or informal? Does
   your tone match your purpose?
5. Look again at your introduction and conclusion. Have you
   avoided beginning with a direct dictionary-like definition?
   Could you open with a catchy detail or example? Did you
   conclude or just stop? You want to end forcefully; you do not
   just want to repeat the same words used in your introduction.
   Ask someone to read just the beginning and the ending of the
   essay and offer some honest advice.

ARGUMENT AND PERSUASION

We live in a world of persuasive messages—billboards, advertisements in newspapers and magazines, commercials on television and radio, electronic advertisements on the Internet and the World Wide Web, signs on storefronts, bumper stickers, T-shirts and caps with messages, and manufacturers' logos prominently displayed on clothing. Advertisements demonstrate a wide range of persuasive strategies. Sometimes they appeal to logic and reason—they ask you to compare the features and price of one car stereo system with those of any competitor and judge for yourself. More often, though, they appeal to your emotions and feelings—you will not be stylish unless you wear this particular style and brand of athletic shoe; you are not a "real man" unless you smoke this brand of cigarette; you have not signaled your success in the world unless you drive this particular German automobile.

In the following paragraph, William Junius Wilson appeals to logic when he argues that the "school-to-work transition" confronts many young Americans by citing specific factual evidence to establish the magnitude of the problem:

> The problem of school-to-work transition confronts young people of all ethnic and racial backgrounds, but it is especially serious for black youths. According to a recent report by the U.S. Bureau of Labor Statistics, only 42 percent of black youths who had not enrolled in college had jobs in October after graduating from high school a few months earlier in June, compared with 69 percent of their white counterparts. The figures for black youngsters in inner-city ghetto neighborhoods are obviously even lower. The inadequate system of

Although we sometimes use "argument" and "persuasion" interchangeably, we generally think of the terms as implying a difference. Lawyers argue in court, we might say, and their arguments hopefully depend on reason and facts.

school-to-work transition has also contributed significantly to the growing wage gap between those with high school diplomas and those with college training. In the 1950s and 1960s, when school-to-work transition was compatible with the mass production system, the average earnings of college graduates was only about 20 percent higher than those of high school graduates. By 1979, it had increased to 49 percent, and then rapidly grew to 83 percent by 1992.

Thus, the school-to-work transition is a major problem in the United States, and it has reached crisis proportions in the inner-city ghetto.

In the face of such evidence, few readers would dispute the need to attack this problem. Later in this chapter you will find the editorial writer for *The New Yorker* in "Help for Sex Offenders" using a similar logical appeal to convince an audience of the truth of argument's claim.

As an example of an argument appealing to readers' emotions, notice how the writer of this editorial from the magazine *The Disability Rag* persuasively argues against the substitution of the phrase "physically challenged" for "physically disabled":

"Physically challenged" attempts to conceal a crucial fact: that the reason we can't do lots of things is not because we're lazy or because we won't accept a "challenge," but because many things are simply beyond our control—like barriers. Like discrimination. People who favor "physically challenged" are making a statement: Barriers, discrimination, are not *problems* for us, but *challenges.* We want those barriers, we almost seem to be saying—because by overcoming them we'll become better persons! Stronger. More courageous. After all, isn't that what challenges are for.

   Until you've made it your responsibility to get downtown, and discovered that there are no buses with lifts running on that route, you may not fully comprehend that it isn't a personal "challenge" you're up against, but a system resistant to change.

Similarly, later in this chapter Martin Luther King Jr., in his famous "I Have a Dream" speech, will appeal to his listeners' (and readers') emotions. Despite the differences in strategy, though, the objective in both argument and persuasion is the same: to convince readers to believe or act in a certain way.

   Whether you realize it or not, you have already had extensive experience in constructing arguments and in persuading an audience. Every time you try to convince someone to do or to believe something, you have to argue. Consider a hypothetical example. You are concerned about your father's health. He smokes cigarettes, avoids exercise, is overweight, and works long hours in a stressful job. Even though you are worried, he is completely unconcerned and has always resisted your family's efforts to change his ways. Your task is to persuade him to change or modify his lifestyle, and doing so involves

If we associate argument with reason and factual evidence, we tend to associate persuasion with emotional appeals. Salespeople are persuaders, as are those who use the "soapbox" approach.

making its dangers clear, offering convincing reasons for change, and urging specific action. Establishing the dangers is the first step, and you have a wide range of medical evidence from which to draw. That evidence involves statistics, testimony or advice from doctors, and case histories of men who have suffered the consequences of years of abusing or ignoring their health. From that body of material, you select the items that are most likely to get through to your obstinate father. He might not be moved by cold statistics citing life-expectancy tables for smokers and nonexercisers, but he might be touched by the story of a friend his age who suffered a heart attack or stroke. The evidence you gather and use becomes a part of the convincing reasons for change that you offer in your argument. If your father persists in ignoring his health, he is likely to suffer some consequences. You might at this point include emotional appeals in your strategy. If he is not concerned about what will happen to him, what about his family? What will they do if he dies?

Having gotten your father to realize and acknowledge the dangers inherent in his lifestyle and to understand the reasons why he should make changes, what remains is to urge specific action. In framing a plan for that action, you again need to consider your audience. If you urge your father to stop smoking immediately, join a daily exercise class at the local YMCA or health club, go on a thousand-calorie-a-day diet, and find a new job, chances are that he will think your proposal too drastic even to try. Instead, you might urge a more moderate plan, phasing in changes over a period of time or offering compromises (for example, that he work fewer hours).

How Do You Analyze Your Audience?

Argument or persuasion, unlike the other types of writing included in this text, has a special purpose—to persuade its audience. Because you want your reader to agree with your position or act as you urge, you need to analyze your audience carefully before you start to write. Try to answer each of the following questions:

- Who are my readers?
- What do they already know about this subject?
- How interested are they likely to be?
- How impartial or prejudiced are they going to be?
- What values do my readers share?

- Is my argument going to challenge any of my readers' beliefs or values?
- What types of evidence are most likely to be effective?
- Is my plan for requested action reasonable?

Your argumentative strategy should always reflect an awareness of your audience. Even in the hypothetical case of the unhealthy father, it is obvious that some types of evidence would be more effective than others and that some solutions or plans for action would be more reasonable and therefore more acceptable than others.

The second important consideration in any argument is to anticipate your audience's objections and be ready to answer them. Debaters study both sides of an argument so that they can effectively counter any opposition. In arguing the abortion issue, the right-to-life speaker has to be prepared to deal with subjects such as abnormal fetuses or pregnancy resulting from rape or incest. The pro-choice speaker must face questions about when life begins and when the rights of the unborn might take precedence over the mother's rights.

WHAT DOES IT TAKE TO PERSUADE YOUR READER?

In some cases, nothing will persuade your reader. For example, if you are arguing for legalized abortion, you will never convince a reader who believes that an embryo is a human being from the moment of conception. Abortion to that reader will always be murder. It is extremely difficult to argue any position that is counter to your audience's moral or ethical values. It is also difficult to argue a position that is counter to your audience's normal patterns of behavior. For example, you could reasonably argue that your readers ought to stop at all stop signs and to obey the speed limit. However, the likelihood of persuading your audience to always do these two things—even though not doing so breaks the law—is slim.

These cautions are not meant to imply that you should argue only "safe" subjects or that winning is everything. Choose a subject about which you feel strongly; present a fair, logical argument; express honest emotion; but avoid distorted evidence or inflammatory language. Even if no one is finally persuaded, at least you have offered a clear, intelligent explanation of your position.

In most arguments, you have two possible types of support: you can supply factual evidence, and you can appeal to your reader's values. Suppose you are arguing that professional boxing should be prohibited because it is dangerous. The reader may or may not accept your premise but at the very least would expect some support for your assertion. Your first task would be to gather evidence. The strongest evidence is factual—statistics dealing with the number of fighters each year who are fatally injured or mentally impaired. You might quote appropriate authorities—physicians, scientists, former boxers—on the risks connected with professional boxing. You might relate several instances of boxing injuries or even a single example of a particular fighter who was killed or permanently injured while boxing. You might describe in detail how blows affect the body or head; you might trace the process by which a series of punches can cause brain damage. You might catalog the effects that years of physical punishment can produce in the human body. In your argument you might use some or all of this factual evidence. Your job as a writer is to gather the best—the most accurate and the most effective—evidence and present it in a clear and orderly way for your reader.

You can also appeal to your reader's values. You could argue that a sport in which a participant can be killed or permanently injured is not a sport at all. You could argue that the objective of a boxing match—to render one's opponent unconscious or too impaired to continue—is different in kind from any other sport and not one that we, as human beings, should condone, let alone encourage. Appeals to values can be extremely effective.

Effective argumentation generally involves appealing to both reason and emotion. It is often easier to catch your reader's attention by using an emotional appeal. Demonstrators against vivisection, the dissecting of animals for laboratory research, display photographs of the torments suffered by these animals. Organizations that fight famine throughout the world use photographs of starving children. Advertisers use a wide range of persuasive tactics to touch our fears, our anxieties, our desires. But the types of argumentative writing that you are asked to do in college or in your job rarely allow for only emotional evidence.

One final thing is crucially important in persuading your reader. You must sound (and be) fair, reasonable, and credible in order to win the respect and possibly the approval of your reader. Readers distrust arguments that use unfair or inflammatory language, faulty logic, and biased or distorted evidence.

How Do You Make Sure That
Your Argument Is Logical?

Because logic or reason is so crucial to effective argumentation, you will want to avoid logical fallacies or errors. When you construct your argument, make sure that you have avoided the following common mistakes:

- **Ad hominem argument** (literally to argue "to the person"): criticizing a person's position by criticizing his or her personal character. If an underworld figure asserts that boxing is the manly art of self-defense, you do not counter his argument by claiming that he makes money by betting on the fights.

- **Ad populum argument** (literally to argue "to the people"): appealing to the prejudices of your audience instead of offering facts or reasons. You do not defend boxing by asserting that it is part of the American way of life and that anyone who criticizes it is a communist who seeks to undermine our society.

- **Appeal to an unqualified authority:** using testimony from someone who is unqualified to give it. In arguing against boxing, your relevant authorities would be physicians or scientists or former boxers—people who have had some direct experience. You do not quote a professional football player or your dermatologist.

- **Begging the question:** assuming the truth of whatever you are trying to prove. "Boxing is dangerous, and because it is dangerous, it ought to be outlawed." The first statement ("boxing is dangerous") is the premise you set out to prove, but the second statement uses that unproved premise as a basis for drawing a conclusion.

- **Either-or:** stating or implying that there are only two possibilities. Do not assert that the two choices are either to ban boxing or to allow this brutality to continue. Perhaps other changes might make the sport safer and hence less objectionable.

- **Faulty analogy:** using an inappropriate or superficially similar analogy as evidence. "Allowing a fighter to kill another man with his fists is like giving him a gun and permission to shoot to kill." The analogy might be vivid, but the two acts are much more different than they are similar.

- **Hasty generalization:** basing a conclusion on evidence that is atypical or unrepresentative. Do not assert that every boxer has suffered brain damage just because you can cite a few well-known cases.

- **Non sequitur** (literally "it does not follow"): arriving at a conclusion not justified by the premises or evidence. "My father has watched many fights on television; therefore, he is an authority on the physical hazards that boxers face."
- **Oversimplification:** suggesting a simple solution to a complex problem. "If professional boxers were made aware of the risks they take, they would stop boxing."

HOW DO YOU STRUCTURE AN ARGUMENT?

If you are constructing an argument based on a formal, logical progression, you can use either *inductive* or *deductive* reasoning. An *inductive* argument begins with specific evidence and then moves to a generalized conclusion that accounts for the evidence. The writer assumes the role of detective, piecing together the evidence in an investigation and only then arriving at a conclusion. An inductive structure is often effective because it can arouse the reader's interest or even anger by focusing on examples. If your thesis is likely to be rejected immediately by some readers, an inductive strategy can also be effective since it hides the thesis until the readers are involved in reading. Jonathan Rauch in "The Marrying Kind" begins with statistics about the increase in the number of cohabiting, unmarried couples and the corresponding decrease in the number of marriages. Rauch knows that many people would lament the change. He even "accepts" part of the blame as one engaged in a cohabiting relationship. And why are he and his partner unmarried? Because they are gay. Rauch subtly builds his argument, revealing his thesis only late in the essay. Want to encourage marriage in our society, want to make cohabiting seem less attractive? Then allow gays to marry, too.

A *deductive* argument moves in the opposite direction: It starts with a general truth or assumption and moves to provide evidence or support. Here the detective announces who the murderer is and then proceeds to show us how she arrived at that conclusion. Linda Lee in "The Case Against College" signals her thesis even in her title. Two paragraphs into the essay, she makes her argumentative, and provocative, assertion: "Not everyone needs a higher education." In the rest of her essay, Lee provides the support that leads to her conclusion, drawing from statistics and from her own experience with her son.

Since a deductive pattern immediately announces its thesis, it can run the risk of instantly alienating a reader, especially if it is arguing for something about which many of its readers might disagree. David Gelernter in "What Do Murderers Deserve?" is careful not to announce his point—murderers ought to be executed—until he has invited his readers to think about why we hesitate to exercise this "moral responsibility."

The simplest form of a deductive argument is the *syllogism*, a three-step argument involving a major premise, a minor premise, and a conclusion. Few essays—either those you write or those you read—can be reduced to a syllogism. Our thought patterns are rarely so logical; our reasoning is rarely so precise. Although few essays state a syllogism explicitly, syllogisms do play a role in shaping an argument. For example, a number of essays in this reader begin with the same syllogism, even though it is not directly stated:

Major premise: All people should have equal opportunities.
Minor premise: Minorities are people.
Conclusion: Minorities should have equal opportunities.

Despite the fact that a syllogism is a precise structural form, you should not assume that a written argument will imitate it—that the first paragraph or group of paragraphs will contain a major premise; the next, a minor premise; and the final, a conclusion. Syllogisms can be basic to an argument without being the framework on which it is constructed.

No matter how you structure your argument, one final consideration is important. Since the purpose of argumentation is to get a reader to agree with your position or to act in a particular way, it is always essential to end your paper decisively. Effective endings or conclusions to arguments can take a variety of forms. You might end with a call to action. For example, Martin Luther King's speech rises to an eloquent, rhythmical exhortation to his audience to continue to fight until they are "free at last." Jonathan Rauch uses his conclusion to reinforce his thesis: "Those who worry about the examples gays would set by marrying should be much more worried about the example gays are already setting by not marrying."

You might end with a thought-provoking question or image. *The New Yorker* editorial writer in "Help for Sex Offenders" challenges readers' attitudes toward sex offenders: "If castration helps, why not let them have what they want?" Richard Rodriguez, aware of the poor and the silent who are generally bypassed by opportunity despite affirmative action programs, chooses to end his essay with an arresting image: "They are distant, faraway figures like the boys I have seen peering down from freeway overpasses in some other part of town."

If you have used personal experience as evidence in your argument or injected yourself into the argument in some way, you might end as Linda Lee does in "The Case Against College." Throughout the essay, Lee has used her son as an example of a child not ready for college. After two years in school and two years of working, her son has found a job that he loves. Now, four years later, he has had, she notes, "his own graduation day . . . and he did it, for the most part, in spite of college." Or you might end by reaffirming the point that your argument has been making. David Gelernter in "What Do Murderers Deserve?" concludes: "In executing murderers, we declare that deliberate murder is absolutely evil and absolutely intolerable." Finally, Peter Singer, who in "The Singer Solution to World Poverty" has made us increasingly uncomfortable by pointing out our moral obligation to sacrifice to help the needy children of the world, reminds us one final time we are in the same situation as the fictional Bob who could save a child's life by sacrificing his savings.

SAMPLE STUDENT ESSAY

Beth Jaffe decided to tackle a subject on the minds of many career-minded, dollar-conscious college students: why do you have to take so many courses outside of your major? Beth's argument is sure to arouse the attention of every advocate of a liberal arts education, and you might consider exploring the subject in an argument of your own.

EARLIER DRAFT

REDUCING COLLEGE REQUIREMENTS

With the high costs of college still on the rise, it is not fair to make college students pay for courses labeled "requirements" which are not part of their major. Although many students want a well-rounded college education, many cannot afford to pay for one. By eliminating all of the requirements that do not pertain to a student's major, college costs could be cut tremendously. At the University of Delaware, for example, a student in the College of Arts and Science is required to take twelve credits of arts and humanities, twelve of culture and institutions of time, twelve of human beings and their environment, and thirteen of natural phenomena or science which include at least one lab. Although some of their major courses may fit into these categories, many others do not. Frequently students do not like and are not interested in the courses which fit into the four categories and feel they are wasting their money by paying for courses they do not enjoy, do not put much work into, and usually do not get much out of. It should be an option to the student to take these extra courses. Why should a humanities or social studies major have to take biology or chemistry? Many of these students thought their struggle with science was over after high school only to come to college and find yet more "requirements" in the sciences. Students are getting degrees in one area of concentration. They should be able to take only courses in their field of study and not have to waste their money on courses they have no desire to take.

Beth's essay, with her permission, was duplicated and discussed in class. Not surprisingly, it provoked a lively reaction. One student asked Beth whether she was serious and exactly what it was that she was proposing. Beth admitted that she did not advocate turning a college education into career training but that she had a number of friends who were deeply in debt because of their four-year education. "Why not just cut some requirements?" Beth asked. Several other students then suggested that since she did not really advocate an extreme position, maybe she could find a compromise proposal. Her instructor added that she might find a way of rewording her remarks about science classes. Few people, after all, are sympathetic to a position that seems to say, "I don't want to do that. It's too hard. It's too boring."

When Beth revised her paper, she tried to follow the advice the class had offered. In addition, she made the problem vivid by using her roommate as an example and by pointing out what specifically might be saved by her proposal.

LOWERING THE COST OF A COLLEGE EDUCATION

When my roommate graduates in June, she will be $20,000 in debt. The debt did not come from spring breaks in Fort Lauderdale or a new car. It came from four years of college expenses, expenses that were not covered by the money she earned as a part-time waitress or by the small scholarship she was awarded annually. So now in June at age 21, with her first full-time job (assuming she gets one), Alison can start repaying her student loans.

Alison's case is certainly not unusual. In fact, because she attends a state-assisted university, her debt is less than it might be. We cannot expect education to get cheaper. We cannot expect government scholarship programs to get larger. We cannot ask that students go deeper and deeper into debt. We need a new way of combating this cost problem. We need the Jaffe proposal.

If colleges would eliminate some of the general education course requirements, college costs could be substantially lowered. At the University of Delaware, for example, a student at the College of Arts and Science is required to take twelve credits of arts and humanities, twelve of culture and the institutions of time, twelve of human beings and their environment, and thirteen of natural phenomena or science, including at least one laboratory course. Approximately half of these requirements are fulfilled by courses which are required for particular majors. The others are not, and these are likely to be courses that students are not interested in and so get little out of.

If some of these requirements were eliminated, a student would need approximately twenty-five fewer credits for a bachelor's degree. A student who took a heavier load or went to summer school could graduate either one or two semesters earlier. The result would cut college costs by anywhere from one-eighth to one-fourth.

The Jaffe proposal does decrease the likelihood that a college graduate will receive a well-rounded education. On the other hand, it allows students to concentrate their efforts in courses which

they feel are relevant. Perhaps most important, it helps reduce the
burden that escalating college costs have placed on all of us.

SOME THINGS TO REMEMBER

1. Choose a subject that allows for the possibility of persuading
   your reader. Avoid emotionally charged subjects that resist
   logical examination.
2. Analyze your audience. Who are your readers? What do they
   already know about your subject? How are they likely to feel
   about it? How impartial or prejudiced are they going to be?
3. Make a list of the evidence or reasons you will use in your
   argument. Analyze each piece of evidence to see how effective
   it might be in achieving your end.
4. Honest emotion is fair, but avoid anything that is distorted,
   inaccurate, or inflammatory. Argue with solid, reasonable, fair,
   and relevant evidence.
5. Avoid the common logical fallacies listed in this introduction.
6. Make a list of all the possible counterarguments or objections
   your audience might have. Think of ways in which you can
   respond to those objections.
7. Decide how to structure your essay. You can begin with a
   position and then provide evidence, or you can begin with the
   evidence and end with a conclusion. Which structure seems to
   fit your subject and evidence better?
8. End forcefully. Conclusions are what listeners and readers are
   most likely to remember. Repeat or restate your position.
   Drive home the importance of your argument.

VISUALIZING ARGUMENT AND PERSUASION

We are surrounded each day by hundreds of examples of visual argumentation and persuasion—advertisements. Sometimes advertisements appeal to reason, citing specific facts, figures, and statistics to
buttress their claims. "Look at how our mutual fund has performed
over the past year, over the past five years. Check our line charts and
tables." Other times, we are assaulted by subtle persuasive appeals—
if we wore this cologne or perfume, we would be irresistible; if we
drove this automobile, we would be a hardy adventurer or an impor-

tant professional. Probably we like to think that we "see through" the claims of advertisers, that we are not susceptible to their appeals. The truth, however, is that we do respond to these visual appeals—otherwise, companies would stop advertising their goods and services. So powerful are advertisements that they can even sell products that don't exist! Graphic artist Fiona Jack designed a billboard campaign in New Zealand to sell "Nothing™." The poster appeared on 27 billboards around the Auckland area, and what happened? People telephoned the billboard company to find out where they could buy "Nothing™." Jack commented, "You can market anything if there's enough money behind it."

Copyright © 1998 by Fiona Jack.

ARGUMENT AND PERSUASION AS A LITERARY STRATEGY

British poet Wilfred Owen served as a British soldier during World War I. The human death toll in World War I was over 8.5 million soldiers; on a single day, the British lost more than 57,000 soldiers. The third leading cause of death was poison gas, used by both sides during the war. Owen's title is taken from the Latin quotation from Horace, cited at the end of the poem, which translates "It is sweet and fitting to die for one's country." As you read the poem, think about whether or not Owen agreed with Horace. See page 486.

DULCE ET DECORUM EST

Wilfred Owen

Bent double, like old beggars under sacks,
Knock-kneed, coughing like hags, we cursed through sludge,
Till on the haunting flares we turned our backs,
And towards our distant rest began to trudge.

Men marched asleep. Many had lost their boots,
But limped on, blood-shod. All went lame, all blind;
Drunk with fatigue; deaf even to the hoots
Of gas-shells dropping slowly behind.

Gas! GAS! Quick, boys! An ecstasy of fumbling,
Fitting the clumsy helmets just in time,
But someone still was yelling out and stumbling
And flound'ring like a man in fire or lime.—
Dim through the misty panes and thick green light,
As under a green sea, I saw him drowning.

If in some smothering dreams, you too could pace
Behind the wagon that we flung him in,
And watch the white eyes writhing in his face,
His hanging face, like a devil's sick of sin,
If you could hear, at every jolt, the blood
Come gargling from the froth-corrupted lungs
Bitter as the cud
Obscene as cancer,
Of vile, incurable sores on innocent tongues,—
My friend, you would not tell with such zest
To children ardent for some desperate glory,
The old lie: *Dulce et decorum est*
        Pro patria mori.

DISCUSSION QUESTIONS

1. How does Owen feel about war? How does he reveal his
   feelings in the poem?
2. Does the poem depend more on logical argument or on
   emotional persuasion? How is that strategy effective here?

3. Is describing the death of a single soldier an effective strategy? Why might Owen choose to focus on just one example and not on many? Would more examples make the poem more effective?
4. Do you think that Owen was being unpatriotic in writing this poem? Why or why not?
5. What purpose might Owen have had in writing the poem? Who might he have been trying to persuade? What might he have wanted his reader to see, feel, or understand?

WRITING SUGGESTIONS

Living as we do in a world full of advertisements, we are surrounded by persuasion—buy this, do this. Choose a social or moral issue about which you have strong feelings, and then using a single extended example persuade your audience to agree with you and/or to do something. Some possibilities might be:

a. The plight of the homeless in the United States
b. The dangers of addiction or at-risk behavior
c. Cloning or genetic engineering

Using Argument and Persuasion in Writing for Your Other Courses

A good deal of the writing you do for college courses is implicitly persuasive: you want to persuade an instructor that your mastery of a subject or area of inquiry is such that you deserve a good grade. You do this by presenting information accurately and in sufficient detail without oversimplification, by avoiding unnecessary repetition and padding, by achieving clarity through your organization and use of a thesis statement and topic sentences, by observing conventions of the particular discipline in terms of documenting sources and other matters, by the following standard English grammar and usage rules, and by adhering to the terms of the specific assignment. This is the case even when you are not arguing for a particular position.

Sometimes, however, your purpose in writing may be more explicitly argumentative—that is, to present your own position on a subject about which there is some controversy or disagreement or to try to convince your reader that an accepted conclusion or interpretation should be modified in some way. Keep in mind that academic argument should rely exclusively on logical rather than on emotional appeals. The following is a sampling of assignments involving argumentation.

- **Literature.** In writing about a particular literary work, you might argue against a prevailing interpretation of the work, presenting evidence from the text itself and perhaps the circumstances of its creation to support your own interpretation.

- **Environmental Studies.** For a research paper on global warming, you might weigh the differing scientific evidence on the extent of the phenomenon and its causes and then argue your own position based on your interpretation of that evidence.

- **Communication.** For a paper focusing on media analysis, you might closely analyze a broadcast news report to argue that it was put together in such a way as to promote a particular political or social viewpoint.

- **Philosophy.** For an ethics course, you might write a paper analyzing the competing values surrounding a particular ethical issue, such as assisted suicide or animal testing, and in so doing argue for your own position on the issue.

- **Marketing or Business Management.** For a marketing strategies course or technical writing requirement, you might be asked to draft a proposal for increasing the profits of a local small business with the ultimate purpose of convincing the owner of the effectiveness and ease of implementing your suggestions.

VISIT THE PRENTICE HALL READER'S WEBSITE

When you have finished reading an essay, check out the additional material available at the *Reader*'s Website at www.prenhall.com/ miller. For each reading, you will find a list of related readings connected with the topic or the author; additional background information; a group of relevant hot-linked Web resources (just click your computer's mouse and automatically visit the sites listed); and still more writing suggestions.

PERSUADING AND ARGUING

High school and college students have generally had extensive experiences with minimum wage jobs. But what if you faced a future of minimum wage jobs? Arguments for and against minimum wage hikes occur annually in Congress. The WWW can provide extensive information supporting both sides of the debate. Visit a site supporting such hikes and another in opposition to them and do a paragraph writing assignment at the *Reader*'s Website.

I HAVE A DREAM

Martin Luther King Jr.

Martin Luther King Jr. (1929–1968) was born in Atlanta, the son of a Baptist minister. Ordained in his father's church in 1947, King received a doctorate in theology from Boston University in 1955. That same year he achieved national prominence by leading a boycott protesting the segregation of the Montgomery, Alabama, city bus system, based on ideas of nonviolent civil resistance derived from Thoreau and Gandhi. A central figure in the civil rights movement, King was awarded the Nobel Peace Prize in 1964. He was assassinated in Memphis in 1968. His birthday, January 15, is celebrated as a national holiday.

King's "I Have a Dream" speech was delivered at the Lincoln Memorial to an audience of 250,000 people who assembled in Washington, D.C., on August 28, 1963. That march, commemorating in part the hundredth anniversary of Lincoln's Emancipation Proclamation, was intended as an act of "creative lobbying" to win the support of Congress and the president for pending civil rights legislation. King's speech is one of the most memorable and moving examples of American oratory.

BEFORE READING

Connecting: Probably every American has heard at least a small portion of King's speech. Before you begin to read, jot down what you know about the speech or the phrases that you remember from recordings and television clips.

Anticipating: King's speech is marked by the extensive use of images. As you read, make a note of the most powerful and recurrent images that he uses.

1   Five score years ago, a great American, in whose symbolic shadow we stand, signed the Emancipation Proclamation. This momentous decree came as a great beacon light of hope to millions of Negro slaves who had been seared in the flames of withering injustice. It came as a joyous daybreak to end the long night of captivity.

2   But one hundred years later, we must face the tragic fact that the Negro is still not free. One hundred years later, the life of the Negro is still sadly crippled by the manacles of segregation and the chains of

discrimination. One hundred years later, the Negro lives on a lonely island of poverty in the midst of a vast ocean of material prosperity. One hundred years later, the Negro is still languishing in the corners of American society and finds himself an exile in his own land. So we have come here today to dramatize an appalling condition.

In a sense we have come to our nation's capital to cash a check. 3 When the architects of our republic wrote the magnificent words of the Constitution and the Declaration of Independence, they were signing a promissory note to which every American was to fall heir. This note was a promise that all men would be guaranteed the unalienable rights of life, liberty, and the pursuit of happiness.

It is obvious today that America has defaulted on this promissory note insofar as her citizens of color are concerned. Instead of honoring this sacred obligation, America has given the Negro people a bad check; a check which has come back marked "insufficient funds." But we refuse to believe that the bank of justice is bankrupt. We refuse to believe that there are insufficient funds in the great vaults of opportunity of this nation. So we have come to cash this check—a check that will give us upon demand the riches of freedom and the security of justice. We have also come to this hallowed spot to remind America of the fierce urgency of *now*. This is no time to engage in the luxury of cooling off or to take the tranquilizing drugs of gradualism. *Now* is the time to make real the promises of Democracy. *Now* is the time to rise from the dark and desolate valley of segregation to the sunlit path of racial justice. *Now* is the time to open the doors of opportunity to all of God's children. *Now* is the time to lift our nation from the quicksands of racial injustice to the solid rock of brotherhood.

It would be fatal for the nation to overlook the urgency of the 5 moment and to underestimate the determination of the Negro. This sweltering summer of the Negro's legitimate discontent will not pass until there is an invigorating autumn of freedom and equality. 1963 is not an end, but a beginning. Those who hope that the Negro needed to blow off steam and will now be content will have a rude awakening if the nation returns to business as usual. There will be neither rest nor tranquility in America until the Negro is granted his citizenship rights. The whirlwinds of revolt will continue to shake the foundations of our nation until the bright day of justice emerges.

But there is something that I must say to my people who stand 6 on the warm threshold which leads into the palace of justice. In the process of gaining our rightful place we must not be guilty of wrongful deeds. Let us not seek to satisfy our thirst for freedom by drinking from the cup of bitterness and hatred. We must forever conduct our struggle on the high plane of dignity and discipline. We must not allow our creative protest to degenerate into physical violence. Again and again we must rise to the majestic heights of meeting physical force with soul force. The marvelous new militancy which has engulfed the Negro community must not lead us to a distrust of all white people, for many of our white brothers, as evidenced by their presence here today, have come to realize that their destiny is tied up with our destiny and their freedom is inextricably bound to our freedom. We cannot walk alone.

7   And as we walk, we must make the pledge that we shall march ahead. We cannot turn back. There are those who are asking the devotees of civil rights, "When will you be satisfied?" We can never be satisfied as long as the Negro is the victim of the unspeakable horrors of police brutality. We can never be satisfied as long as our bodies, heavy with the fatigue of travel, cannot gain lodging in the motels of the highways and the hotels of the cities. We cannot be satisfied as long as the Negro's basic mobility is from a smaller ghetto to a larger one. We can never be satisfied as long as a Negro in Mississippi cannot vote and a Negro in New York believes he has nothing for which to vote. No, no, we are not satisfied, and we will not be satisfied until justice rolls down like waters and righteousness like a mighty stream.

8   I am not unmindful that some of you have come here out of great trials and tribulations. Some of you have come fresh from narrow jail cells. Some of you have come from areas where your quest for freedom left you battered by the storms of persecution and staggered by the winds of police brutality. You have been the veterans of creative suffering. Continue to work with the faith that unearned suffering is redemptive.

9   Go back to Mississippi, go back to Alabama, go back to South Carolina, go back to Georgia, go back to Louisiana, go back to the slums and ghettos of our northern cities, knowing that somehow this situation can and will be changed. Let us not wallow in the valley of despair.

10   I say to you today, my friends, that in spite of the difficulties and frustrations of the moment I still have a dream. It is a dream deeply rooted in the American dream.

11   I have a dream that one day this nation will rise up and live out the true meaning of its creed: "We hold these truths to be self-evident: that all men are created equal."

12   I have a dream that one day on the red hills of Georgia the sons of former slaves and the sons of former slave owners will be able to sit down together at the table of brotherhood.

I have a dream that one day even the state of Mississippi, a   13
desert state sweltering with the heat of injustice and oppression, will
be transformed into an oasis of freedom and justice.

I have a dream that my four little children will one day live in a   14
nation where they will not be judged by the color of their skin but by
the content of their character.

I have a dream today.   15

I have a dream that one day the state of Alabama, whose gover-   16
nor's lips are presently dripping with the words of interposition and
nullification, will be transformed into a situation where little black
boys and black girls will be able to join hands with little white boys
and white girls and walk together as sisters and brothers.

I have a dream today.   17

I have a dream that one day every valley shall be exalted, every   18
hill and mountain shall be made low, the rough places will be made
plain, and the crooked places will be made straight, and the glory of
the Lord shall be revealed, and all flesh shall see it together.

This is our hope. This is the faith with which I return to the   19
South. With this faith we will be able to hew out of the mountain of
despair a stone of hope. With this faith we will be able to transform
the jangling discords of our nation into a beautiful symphony of
brotherhood. With this faith we will be able to work together, to pray
together, to struggle together, to go to jail together, to stand up for
freedom together, knowing that we will be free one day.

This will be the day when all of God's children will be able to   20
sing with new meaning

> *My country, 'tis of thee,*
> *Sweet land of liberty,*
> *Of thee I sing:*
> *Land where my fathers died,*
> *Land of the pilgrims' pride,*
> *From every mountain-side*
> *Let freedom ring.*

And if America is to be a great nation this must become true. So   21
let freedom ring from the prodigious hilltops of New Hampshire. Let
freedom ring from the mighty mountains of New York. Let freedom
ring from the heightening Alleghenies of Pennsylvania!

Let freedom ring from the snowcapped Rockies of Colorado!   22

Let freedom ring from the curvaceous peaks of California!   23

But not only that; let freedom ring from Stone Mountain of   24
Georgia!

Let freedom ring from Lookout Mountain of Tennessee!   25

26   Let freedom ring from every hill and molehill of Mississippi. From every mountainside, let freedom ring.

27   When we let freedom ring, when we let it ring from every village and every hamlet, from every state and every city, we will be able to speed up that day when all of God's children, black men and white men, Jews and Gentiles, Protestants and Catholics, will be able to join hands and sing in the words of the old Negro spiritual, "Free at last! free at last! thank God almighty, we are free at last!"

QUESTIONS ON SUBJECT AND PURPOSE

1. What is King's dream?
2. King's essay was a speech delivered before thousands of marchers and millions of television viewers. How are its oral origins revealed in the written version?
3. In what way is King's speech an attempt at persuasion? Whom was he trying to persuade to do what?

QUESTIONS ON STRATEGY AND AUDIENCE

1. Why does King begin with the words "Five score years ago"? Why does he say at the end of paragraph 6, "We cannot walk alone"? What do such words have to do with the context of King's speech?
2. How does King structure his speech? Is there an inevitable order or movement? How effective is his conclusion?
3. What expectations does King have of his audience? How do you know that?

QUESTIONS ON VOCABULARY AND STYLE

1. How many examples of figurative speech (images, metaphors, similes) can you find in the speech? What effect does such figurative language have?
2. The speech is full of parallel structures. See how many you can find. Why does King use so many?
3. Be able to define the following words: *seared* (paragraph 1), *manacles* (2), *languishing* (2), *promissory note* (3), *unalienable* (3), *invigorating* (5), *inextricably* (6), *tribulations* (8), *nullification* (16), *prodigious* (21).

WRITING SUGGESTIONS

1. **For Your Journal.** It is impossible for most people to read or hear King's speech without being moved. What is it about the speech that makes it so emotionally powerful? In your journal, speculate on the reasons the speech has such an impact. What does it suggest about the power of language?

2. **For a Paragraph.** In a paragraph, argue for equality for a minority group of serious concern on your campus (the disabled; a sexual, racial, or religious minority; returning adults, commuters).

3. **For an Essay.** Expand the argument you explored in Suggestion 2 to essay length.

4. **For Research.** According to the U.S. Census Bureau, 43 million Americans have some type of physical or mental disability. Like members of other minorities, the disabled regularly confront discrimination ranging from prejudice to physical barriers that deny them equal access to facilities. The federal government, with the passage of Title V of the Rehabilitation Act in 1973 and the Americans with Disabilities Act of 1990, has attempted to address these problems. Research the problem on your college's campus. What has been done to eliminate discrimination against the disabled? What remains to be done? Argue for the importance of such changes. Alternatively, you might argue that the regulations are burdensome and should be abandoned. Be sure to document your sources wherever appropriate.

   WEBSITE LINK

Extensive on-line resources are available for King including texts of speeches, video and audio clips, texts of sermons, and photographs. Some key sites, all with extensive additional Internet links, are available.

WRITING LINK: PARAGRAPHS

What is a paragraph? Once you have a definition, look at the 27 paragraphs in the essay. What rhetorical and grammatical principles does King seem to use in deciding when to begin a new paragraph? Do his principles change as the essay progresses? When and why? What does the essay suggest about structure and nature of paragraphs?

THE MARRYING KIND

Jonathan Rauch

Jonathan Rauch (1960–   ) graduated from Yale University in 1982 and begin his writing career as a newspaper reporter in North Carolina. In 1984, he moved to Washington, D.C., where he worked for the National Journal, *a nonpartisan magazine devoted to government and public policy. A columnist and the author of many essays and several books, he is currently a writer-in-residence at the Brookings Institute. His most recent book is* Government's End: Why Washington Stopped *(1999). "The Marrying Kind" originally appeared in the* Atlantic Monthly *magazine.*

On Writing: *Asked about his enthusiasm for a new topic, Rauch answered, "I think one of the exciting things about writing about this is that the sky's really the limit here. Many new social science ideas are applicable in one or maybe two fields. This is a kind of thinking that is applicable in almost any field that studies any aspect of human society. It's just a question of imagination, figuring out how many ways you can apply it."*

BEFORE READING

Connecting: What does the word *cohabiting* mean? Can you imagine yourself cohabiting with a partner without marriage?

Anticipating: According to Rauch, why should conservatives support same-sex marriage?

Last year the Census Bureau reported a statistic that deserved wider   1
notice than it received: during the 1990s the number of unmarried-partner households in the United States increased by 72 percent. Cohabitation has actually been on the rise for decades, but it started from a small base. Now the numbers (more than five million cohabiting couples) are beginning to look impressive.

Marriage, meanwhile, is headed in the other direction. The an-   2
nual number of weddings per 1,000 eligible women fell by more than a third from 1970 to 1996. A lot of factors are at work here—for example, people are marrying later—but it seems clear that one of them is the rise in cohabitation. Couples are simply more willing to live together without tying the knot.

3   Whether this is a bad thing is a contentious question, but it is almost certainly not a good thing. Cohabitation tends to be both less stable and less happy than marriage, and this appears to be true even after accounting for the possibility that the cohabiting type of person may often be different from the marrying type. Research suggests that marriage itself brings something beneficial to the table. Add the fact that a growing share of cohabiting households—now more than a third of them—contain children, and it is hard to be enthusiastic about the trend.

4   Whom to blame? In part, homosexual couples like me and my partner. Cohabitation used to be stigmatized. "Living in sin" it has been called in recent memory, even among the educated classes. Today cohabitation is often viewed as a different-but-equal alternative to wedlock. Although the drift toward cohabitation would no doubt have happened anyway, the growing visibility and acceptance of same-sex couples probably speeded the change. As one gay activist told the *Los Angeles Times* last year, "Just the term 'unmarried partner' gave it a dignity and social category."

5   So (conservatives say) it's true! Homosexuals undermine marriage! To the contrary. The culprit is not the presence of same-sex couples; it is the absence of same-sex marriage.

6   The emergence into the open of same-sex relationships is an irreversible fact in this country. Traditionalists may not like it, but they cannot change it, so they will have to decide how to deal with it. The far right's plan—try to push homosexuals back into the closet—is not going to work; the majority of Americans are too openhearted for that. Indeed, the currents of public opinion are running the other way. An annual survey of college freshmen found that last year 58 percent—a record high, and up from 51 percent in 1997—thought that same-sex couples should be able to marry.

7   Seeing those numbers and others like them, conservatives are desperate to stave off same-sex marriage. For that matter, many moderates remain queasy about legalizing gay marriage; they are sympathetic to homosexuals, but not *that* sympathetic. Liberation-minded leftists, who spent the 1970s telling us that our parents' marriages were outdated and stuffy, were never crazy about matrimony to begin with. As for gays, the vast majority want the right to marry, but most agree that domestic-partner benefits and other "marriage-lite" arrangements are a lot better than nothing.

8   The result is the ABM Pact: Anything But Marriage. Enroll same-sex partners in the company health plan, give them some of the legal prerogatives of spousehood, attend their commitment ceremonies, let them register at city hall as partners—just DON'T CALL

IT MARRIAGE. In America, and in Europe, too, ABM is rapidly establishing itself as the compromise of choice. Gay partnerships get some social and legal recognition, marriage remains the union of man and woman, and everybody moves on. A shrewd social bargain, no?

No. The last thing supporters of marriage should be doing is   9
setting up an assortment of alternatives, but that is exactly what the ABM Pact does, and not only for gays. Every year more companies and governments (at the state and local level) grant marriagelike benefits to cohabiting partners: "concessions fought for and won mostly by gay groups," as the *Los Angeles Times* notes, "but enjoyed as well by the much larger population of heterosexual unmarried couples." To which might be added what I think of as the *Will & Grace* effect: homosexuals are here, we're queer, and nowadays we're kind of cool. ABM, perversely, turns one of the country's more culturally visible minorities into an advertisement for just how cool and successful life outside of wedlock can be.

I doubt that most homosexuals would take their marital vows   10
less seriously than heterosexuals do, as some conservatives insist. Even if I'm wrong, however, surely the exemplary power of failed or unfaithful gay marriages would pale next to the example currently being set by a whole group—an increasingly fashionable group—among whom love and romance and sex and commitment flourish entirely outside of marriage. And can you imagine social conservatives telling any other group to cohabit rather than marry? Can you imagine them saying, "The young men of America's inner cities won't take marriage as seriously as they should, so let's encourage them to shack up with their girlfriends"?

Those who worry about the example gays would set by marry-   11
ing should be much more worried about the example gays are already setting by *not* marrying. In getting this backward the advocates of ABM make a mistake that is both ironic and sad. At a time when marriage needs all the support and participation it can get, homosexuals are pleading to move beyond cohabitation. We want the licenses, the vows, the rings, the honeymoons, the anniversaries, the benefits, and, yes, the responsibilities and the routines. And who is telling us to just shack up instead? Self-styled friends of matrimony. Someday conservatives will look back and wonder why they undermined marriage in an effort to keep homosexuals out.

QUESTIONS ON SUBJECT AND PURPOSE

1. What is *cohabitation*?
2. In what sense does Rauch feel that same-sex partnerships have undermined marriage?
3. What purpose might Rauch have in the essay? Does he expect to change his critics' minds about the issue?

QUESTIONS ON STRATEGY AND AUDIENCE

1. How far into the essay do you have to read until you are aware of what Rauch is writing about?
2. Why might Rauch wait so long to announce his real subject?
3. What expectations might Rauch have of his audience?

QUESTIONS ON VOCABULARY AND STYLE

1. Twice toward the end of the essay, Rauch argues that society is encouraging couples to "shack up." What would you call such an expression? Why might he use it?
2. What is a rhetorical question? How often does Rauch use that device?
3. Be prepared to define the following words: *contentious* (paragraph 3), *stigmatized* (4), *prerogatives* (8), *pale* (10).

WRITING SUGGESTIONS

1. **For Your Journal.** How do you react to the concept of cohabitation? Do you have any friends, siblings, or other relatives who are in an unmarried-partner relationship (remember this includes opposite-sex relationships). Jot down your reactions to the concept. Do you think that living together before marriage is appropriate? Immoral? Be honest.
2. **For a Paragraph.** Suppose that a friend or a sibling approached you for advice about such a relationship. In a paragraph, write a response to that person. Try to explain how you feel about such an idea and what you think he or she should do.
3. **For an Essay.** You have been asked by your school's campus newspaper to write an article aimed at your fellow students on the issue of cohabitation versus marriage. In an essay, state your position and your reasons for it.

4. **For Research.** In paragraph 3, Rauch notes, "research suggests that marriage itself brings something beneficial to the table." What evidence is there to support that statement? Do researchers agree that marriage is beneficial? That married couples are more "stable" and "happy" than cohabiting partners? Study the research and in an essay using that evidence, take a stand on marriage.

 WEBSITE LINK

Want to examine both sides of the argument? The Website can take you to an extensive on-line debate between Rauch and Stanley Kurtz, a contributing editor for the *National Review Online.*

 WRITING LINK: TOPIC SENTENCES

Does Rauch use topic sentences in his paragraphs? Underline all the examples that you can find. Are there any paragraphs without topic sentences? Why does a writer use topic sentences? What help are they to a reader?

THE CASE AGAINST COLLEGE
Linda Lee

Linda Lee (1947–   ), a graduate of Columbia University, is a writer and editor for The New York Times, *where she frequently contributes to the Style, Arts & Leisure, and Business sections. She is a widely published author, and her most recent book is* Success Without College: College May Not Be Right for Your Child, or Right Just Now *(2001). This essay originally appeared in* Family Circle *magazine.*

   On Writing: *A professional writer and editor, Lee remarked: "I have worked on both sides of the desk, as a writer and as an editor. The one gives you time but no money, the other gives you money but no time."*

BEFORE READING

Connecting: How did your parents feel about you going to college? Did they expect you to go? Did you expect to go? Did you ever consider not going?

Anticipating: How important to the essay is the experience that Lee had with her own son? To what extent does that influence her attitudes?

1   Do you, like me, have a child who is smart but never paid attention in class? Now it's high school graduation time. Other parents are talking Stanford this and State U. that. Your own child has gotten into a pretty good college. The question is: Is he ready? Should he go at all?

2   In this country two-thirds of high school graduates go on to college. In some middle-class suburbs, that number reaches 90 percent. So why do so many feel the need to go?

3   America is obsessed with college. It has the second-highest number of graduates worldwide, after (not Great Britain, not Japan, not Germany) Australia. Even so, only 27 percent of Americans have a bachelor's degree or higher. That leaves an awful lot who succeed without college, or at least without a degree. Many read books, think seriously about life and have well-paying jobs. Some want to start businesses. Others want to be electricians or wilderness guides or makeup artists. Not everyone needs a higher education.

4   What about the statistics showing that college graduates make more money? First, until the computer industry came along, all the

highest-paying jobs *required* a college degree: doctor, lawyer, engineer. Second, on average, the brightest and hardest-working kids in school go to college. So is it a surprise that they go on to make more money? And those studies almost always pit kids with degrees against those with just high school. An awful lot have additional training, but they are not included. Ponder for a moment: Who makes more, a plumber or a philosophy major?

These are tough words. I certainly wouldn't have listened to them five years ago when my son was graduating from high school. He had been smart enough to get into the Bronx High School of Science in New York and did well on his SATs. But I know now that he did not belong in college, at least not straight out of high school.

But he went, because all his friends were going, because it sounded like fun, because he could drink beer and hang out. He did not go to study philosophy. Nor did he feel it incumbent to go to class or complete courses. Meanwhile I was paying $1,000 a week for this pleasure cruise.

Eventually I asked myself, "Is he getting $1,000 a week's worth of education?" Heck no. That's when I began wondering why everyone needs to go to college. (My hair colorist makes $300,000 a year without a degree.) What about the famous people who don't have one, like Bill Gates (dropped out of Harvard) and Walter Cronkite (who left the University of Texas to begin a career in journalism)?

So I told my son (in a kind way) that his college career was over for now, but he could reapply to the Bank of Mom in two years if he wanted to go back. Meanwhile, I said, get a job.

If college is so wonderful, how come so many kids "stop out"? (That's the new terminology.) One study showed only 26 percent of those who began four-year colleges had earned a degree in six years. And what about the kids who finish, then can't find work? Of course, education is worth a great deal more than just employment. But most kids today view college as a way to get a good job.

I know, I know. What else is there to do? Won't he miss the "college experience?" First off, there are thousands of things for kids to do. And yes, he will miss the college experience, which may include binge drinking, reckless driving and sleeping in on class days. He can have the same experience in the Marine Corps, minus the sleeping in, and be paid good money for it and learn a trade and discipline.

If my son had gone straight through college, he would be a graduate by now. A number of his friends are, and those who were savvy enough to go into computers at an Ivy League school walked into $50,000-a-year jobs. But that's not everyone. An awful lot became teachers making half that. And some still don't know what they want to do.

12   They may, like my son, end up taking whatever jobs they can get. Over the last two years, he's done roofing, delivered UPS packages and fixed broken toilets. His phone was turned off a few times, and he began to pay attention to details, like the price of a gallon of gasoline.

13   But a year ago he began working at a telecommunications company. He loves his work, and over the last year, he's gotten a raise and a year-end bonus. He tells me now he plans to stay there and become a manager.

14   So, just about on schedule, my son has had his own graduation day. And although I won't be able to take a picture of him in cap and gown, I couldn't be any more proud. He grew up, as most kids do. And he did it, for the most part, in spite of college.

QUESTIONS ON SUBJECT AND PURPOSE

1. How does Lee feel about a college education? What reservations does she have? Under what circumstances does she have reservations?
2. The essay appeared in a June issue of *Family Circle* magazine, probably on sale by late May. How is that timing reflected in the essay?
3. What purpose might Lee have had in the essay?

QUESTIONS ON STRATEGY AND AUDIENCE

1. Judging just from the first sentence of the essay, to whom do you think Lee is writing?
2. Can you find a thesis statement in the essay? Where is it?
3. The essay originally appeared in *Family Circle* magazine. Have you ever seen *Family Circle*? Who is the audience for the magazine?

QUESTIONS ON VOCABULARY AND STYLE

1. What is the effect of opening the essay with a question and of addressing the reader as "you"?
2. How would you define the "tone" of Lee's essay? Is it formal or informal? Conversational?
3. Be prepared to define the following words: *incumbent* (paragraph 6) and *savvy* (11).

WRITING SUGGESTIONS

1. **For Your Journal.** Why did you come to college? Was it just expected of you? Did you just expect to do so? Did you consider other, noncollege options? Why or why not? In your journal jot down your thoughts, memories, and experiences connected with the decision to go to college.

2. **For a Paragraph.** Do you agree or disagree with Lee's argument? In a paragraph, respond to that argument. Focus on your own experience; probably just one aspect of that experience will be enough.

3. **For an Essay.** Whether you agree with Lee or not, write a rebuttal to her essay—title it something like "The Case for College." Think of your essay as something that might be published in *Family Circle* as the other side of the argument.

4. **For Research.** Lee cites a study that found that only "26 percent of those who began four-year colleges had earned a degree in six years." Is that statistic widely accepted? Locate other studies on the same subject; check with your school's admissions or alumni office. Why is the "stop out" rate so high? What explanations does the research offer for this phenomenon? Using your research, write an essay aimed at the incoming freshman class at your school in which you try to persuade them to make good use of their college experiences.

 WEBSITE LINK

Want to check out the statistics on college "stop out" rates? Try the suggestions on the *Reader*'s Website for places to begin your research.

 WRITING LINK: INTRODUCTIONS

How effective is Lee's introduction? Remember the audience for which it was written. What are they likely to find appealing in it? Why might Lee choose to begin with questions rather than with a thesis statement? What is gained by delaying the thesis statement? What does this suggest to you about introductions for your essays?

WHAT DO MURDERERS DESERVE?

David Gelernter

David Gelernter earned his B.A. at Yale and his Ph.D. at the State University of New York at Stony Brook. He joined the Yale faculty in 1982 *where he is a professor of computer science and chief scientist at Mirror Worlds Technologies in New Haven.* Gelernter's many books include a *semi-novel,* 1939: The Lost World of the Fair *(1995) and his recent* Machine Beauty: Elegance and the Heart of Technology *(1998).* Gelernter was a victim of Theodore Kaczynski, the so-called Unabomber, who mailed out anonymous packages containing explosives to a number of people involved in technological research. The injuries he suffered required ten operations.

On Writing: *Of his book about the Unabomber attack,* Drawing Life: Surviving the Unabomber *(1998), Gelernter has said: "An author writes because he has to, and it's a kind of compulsion, it's a personality type. . . . One of my first conscious thoughts coming to in the hospital is how soon I could get to a word processor and start writing. . . . The project changed in scope a little. When I actually sat down to tell the story, I found that I was struggling with questions that I really didn't have any particular desire to examine or to ask, but they were so urgent I couldn't avoid them."*

BEFORE READING

Connecting: How do you feel about the death penalty? If you had to vote in a referendum on legalizing or outlawing the death penalty in your state, how would you vote?

Anticipating: What does Gelernter mean by suggesting that society needs to assume "moral responsibility"?

1   A Texas woman, Karla Faye Tucker, murdered two people with a pickax, was said to have repented in prison, and was put to death. A Montana man, Theodore Kaczynski, murdered three people with mail bombs, did not repent, and struck a bargain with the Justice Department: He pleaded guilty and will not be executed. (He also attempted to murder others and succeeded in wounding some, myself included.) Why did we execute the penitent and spare the impenitent? However we answer this question, we surely have a duty to ask it.

And we ask it—I do, anyway—with a sinking feeling, because in   2
modern America, moral upside-downness is a specialty of the house.
To eliminate race prejudice we discriminate by race. We promote the
cultural assimilation of immigrant children by denying them schooling in English. We throw honest citizens in jail for child abuse, relying on testimony so phony any child could see through it. We make
a point of admiring manly women and womanly men. None of which
has anything to do with capital punishment directly, but it all obliges
us to approach any question about morality in modern America in the
larger context of this country's desperate confusion about elementary
distinctions.

Why execute murderers? To deter? To avenge? Supporters of   3
the death penalty often give the first answer, opponents the second.
But neither can be the whole truth. If our main goal were deterring
crime, we would insist on public executions—which are not on the
political agenda, and not an item that many Americans are interested
in promoting. If our main goal were vengeance, we would allow the
grieving parties to decide the murderer's fate; if the victim had no
family or friends to feel vengeful on his behalf, we would call the
whole thing off.

In fact, we execute murderers in order to make a communal   4
proclamation: that murder is intolerable. A deliberate murderer embodies evil so terrible that it defiles the community. Thus the late social philosopher Robert Nisbet wrote: "Until a catharsis has been
effected through trial, through the finding of guilt and then punishment, the community is anxious, fearful, apprehensive, and, above all,
contaminated."

When a murder takes place, the community is obliged to clear   5
its throat and step up to the microphone. Every murder demands a
communal response. Among possible responses, the death penalty is
uniquely powerful because it is permanent. An execution forces the
community to assume forever the burden of moral certainty; it is a
form of absolute speech that allows no waffling or equivocation.

Of course, we could make the same point less emphatically, by   6
locking up murderers for life. The question then becomes: Is the
death penalty overdoing it?

The answer might be yes if we were a community in which mur-   7
der was a shocking anomaly. But we are not. "One can guesstimate,"
writes the criminologist and political scientist John J. DiIulio Jr., "that
we are nearing or may already have passed the day when 500,000 murderers, convicted and undetected, are living in American society."

DiIulio's statistics show an approach to murder so casual as to   8
be depraved. Our natural bent in the face of murder is not to avenge

the crime but to shrug it off, except in those rare cases when our own near and dear are involved.

9   This is an old story. Cain murders Abel, and is brought in for questioning: "Where is Abel, your brother?" The suspect's response: "What am I, my brother's keeper?" It is one of the first human statements in the Bible; voiced here by a deeply interested party, it nonetheless expresses a powerful and universal inclination. Why mess in other people's problems?

10   Murder in primitive societies called for a private settling of scores. The community as a whole stayed out of it. For murder to count, as it does in the Bible, as a crime not merely against one man but against the whole community and against God is a moral triumph still basic to our integrity, and it should never be taken for granted. By executing murderers, the community reaffirms this moral understanding and restates the truth that absolute evil exists and must be punished.

11   On the whole, we are doing a disgracefully bad job of administering the death penalty. We are divided and confused: The community at large strongly favors capital punishment; the cultural elite is strongly against it. Consequently, our attempts to speak with assurance as a community sound like a man fighting off a chokehold as he talks. But a community as cavalier about murder as we are has no right to back down. The fact that we are botching things does not entitle us to give up.

12   Opponents of capital punishment describe it as a surrender to emotions—to grief, rage, fear, blood lust. For most supporters of the death penalty, this is false. Even when we resolve in principle to go ahead, we have to steel ourselves. Many of us would find it hard to kill a dog, much less a man. Endorsing capital punishment means not that we yield to our emotions but that we overcome them. If we favor executing murderers, it is not because we want to but because, however much we do not want to, we consider ourselves obliged to.

13   Many Americans no longer feel that obligation; we have urged one another to switch off our moral faculties: "Don't be judgmental!" Many of us are no longer sure evil even exists. The cultural elite oppose executions not (I think) because they abhor killing more than others do, but because the death penalty represents moral certainty, and doubt is the black-lung disease of the intelligentsia—an occupational hazard now inflicted on the whole culture.

14   Returning then to the penitent woman and the impenitent man: The Karla Faye Tucker case is the harder of the two. We are told that she repented. If that is true, we would still have had no business for-

giving her, or forgiving any murderer. As theologian Dennis Prager has written apropos this case, only the victim is entitled to forgive, and the victim is silent. But showing mercy to penitents is part of our religious tradition, and I cannot imagine renouncing it categorically. I would consider myself morally obligated to think long and 15 hard before executing a penitent. But a true penitent would have to have renounced (as Karla Faye Tucker did) all legal attempts to overturn the original conviction. If every legal avenue has been tried and has failed, the penitence window is closed.

As for Kaczynski, the prosecutors say they got the best outcome 16 they could, under the circumstances, and I believe them. But I also regard this failure to execute a cold-blooded, impenitent terrorist and murderer as a tragic abdication of moral responsibility. The community was called on to speak unambiguously. It flubbed its lines, shrugged its shoulders, and walked away.

In executing murderers, we declare that deliberate murder is 17 absolutely evil and absolutely intolerable. This is a painfully difficult proclamation for a self-doubting community to make. But we dare not stop trying. Communities in which capital punishment is no longer the necessary response to deliberate murder may exist. America today is not one of them.

QUESTIONS ON SUBJECT AND PURPOSE

1. How does Gelernter feel about the death penalty? Would there ever be circumstances that might affect his attitude?
2. In the first paragraph Gelernter mentions that he was one of the many victims of Theodore Kaczynski (the Unabomber). Does knowing that have any impact on your reading of the essay?
3. What might Gelernter's purpose be in writing?

QUESTIONS ON STRATEGY AND AUDIENCE

1. In paragraph 2, Gelernter cites a number of examples of what he regards as the "moral upside-downness" of American society. Does this strategy strengthen or weaken his argument for you?
2. What expectations does Gelernter's title create in your mind? Can you anticipate his position from his title?
3. Gelernter criticizes the "cultural elite" in this country in part because they lack "moral certainty." Who do you think those

"cultural elite" might be? Could you define the characteristics of such a group?

QUESTIONS ON VOCABULARY AND STYLE

1. What does it mean to be "penitent"? "Impenitent"?
2. How would you characterize the tone of Gelernter's essay? (See the Glossary for a definition of *tone*.)
3. Be prepared to define the following words: *assimilation* (paragraph 2), *catharsis* (4), *equivocation* (5), *anomaly* (7), *cavalier* (11), *abhor* (13), *apropos* (14), *abdication* (16).

WRITING SUGGESTIONS

1. **For Your Journal.** How do you feel about the death penalty? In your journal, brainstorm about your feelings.
2. **For a Paragraph.** Extend your journal writing into a paragraph. Given the space restrictions, focus on what you regard as your strongest argument about the issue.
3. **For an Essay.** Extend the paragraph writing into an essay. Your essay could be argumentative or persuasive or contain elements of both. That means that you might want to use specific examples, facts, and statistics to buttress your position. If you are going to take a qualified position (under certain circumstances), make sure that you make those circumstances clear.
4. **For Research.** Does your state (either the state in which you live or the state in which you go to school) enforce the death penalty? To what extent should states be allowed to decide independently whether or not murder should be punished by execution? Why should such a decision rest with the states? In an essay, argue either for or against uniform penalties for murder in all fifty states. Be sure to document all of your sources including information you gathered from the World Wide Web.

WEBSITE LINK

The Death Penalty Information Center is the place to begin your research. The WWW also has an on-line interview with Gelernter who was a victim of the Unabomber.

WRITING LINK: COLONS

Gelernter makes use of the colon at a number of points in his essay. Make a list of those times and then write a set of rules for using colons in writing. Compare those rules with those in a grammar handbook. Do you ever use colons in your own writing?

HELP FOR SEX OFFENDERS
The New Yorker

The New Yorker, *a weekly magazine famous for its high-caliber writing and witty cartoons, was founded by Harold Ross and first published in February 1925. Originally focused on life and amusements in New York City, the magazine gradually broadened its scope to appeal to a wide audience of sophisticated and well-educated readers. "Help for Sex Offenders" appeared in a section labeled "Comment," which is reserved for editorial opinions. Until recently, the "comments" were never signed. These essays were sometimes written by members of the magazine's staff and sometimes by outside contributors.*

BEFORE READING

Connecting: How should our legal system handle persons who have committed sex crimes?

Anticipating: Why as a society should we be concerned about how our legal system handles sex offenders?

1   Recently, a debate has arisen in this country over requests by sex criminals that they be permitted to undergo the surgical operation known as orchiectomy—more plainly, castration. The argument began in 1992, when Steve Allen Butler, a previously convicted child rapist, asked Judge Michael McSpadden, of the 209th Criminal District Court, in Houston, to let him be castrated rather than go to prison. McSpadden acceded to this request, setting off a hubbub that raged through the talk shows. Local black leaders contended that the bargain was racist, because the offender in the case was black. The director of the Rape Crisis Program at the Houston Area Women's Center opposed castration on principle, even when it was voluntary. She asserted that rape is a crime of violence, not of sex, and therefore the operation would not affect Butler's tendency to offend. The general counsel of the American Civil Liberties Union in Houston was already on record as opposing castration, having raised the spectre of Nazi sterilization programs. In the face of the controversy, doctors who had volunteered to perform the operation backed out, leaving the judge with no option but to send Butler to prison.

2   Since then, however, other sex offenders have come forward with similar requests. They draw attention to the failure of our pres-

ent approaches to dealing with sex criminals. A comprehensive study of the effectiveness of various therapies which appeared in the *Psychological Bulletin* in 1989 concluded that "the recidivism rate for treated offenders is not lower than that for untreated offenders; if anything, it tends to be higher." Other studies have reported equally dismal findings. Sex criminals reoffend at high rates no matter what the treatment.

The State of Florida, once a pioneer in the humane treatment   3 of sex offenders, has thrown up its hands and retreated to long prison sentences. Washington State recently enacted a "sexual predator" law, which provides indefinite terms of confinement for habitual offenders. Governor Pete Wilson, of California, now running for re-election, has proposed life sentences for some *first-time* sex offenders. Other states have continued to explore therapeutic approaches ranging from role-playing to olfactory aversion therapy. According to Dr. William Pithers, the psychologist who directs Vermont's program, "the most successful candidates for treatment are men who have no other criminal record, have an established network of family and friends, and are not so preoccupied by their fantasies that they think of them hours a day." Few offenders meet such standards.

One out of six prisoners in the federal and state systems is a sex   4 offender. The offenses include everything from exhibitionism to pedophilia and rape. Given the compulsive nature of the behavior of sex criminals, their share of the prison population is bound to rise with the passage of the "three strikes and you're out" proposals now sweeping through Congress and the legislatures. Although there are differences between men who fondle and men who rape, most sex criminals actually commit a variety of offenses as well as an appalling number of them. An eight-year study by Emory University researchers of five hundred and sixty-one male offenders who had voluntarily sought treatment reported a total of 291,737 specific acts committed against 195,407 victims. The average offender had been arrested in about one out of thirty crimes he committed; some had never been arrested at all.

Can a sex offender be cured of his need to offend? Of course he   5 can, given the will to change, given the opportunity, given the proper care and treatment. Unfortunately, these elements rarely meet in the case of the chronic offender, and, even when they do, the struggle toward reform is likely to be lengthy and marked by failure. Anyone who has gone through the torment of giving up smoking or drinking or of following a prolonged diet can testify to the difficulty of changing a compulsive behavior. And yet, when the urge to eat or smoke becomes overwhelming, the consequences are merely personal. When sex offenders fail, other lives are destroyed.

6   Why, then, resist the demands of men who are willing to risk sacrificing sexual activity in order to be free of their damaging impulses? Most of the arguments against voluntary castration are based on misconceptions, such as the common belief that it is a barbaric practice that has been used only in Third World countries. The fact is that it has been effectively and humanely used as treatment in Denmark, Czechoslovakia, Holland, Switzerland, Norway, Iceland, Sweden, and Finland. A 1973 Swiss study of a hundred twenty-one castrated offenders found that the rate of reoffending dropped to 4.1 per cent, compared with 76.9 per cent before the operation. A Danish study in the sixties which followed as many as nine hundred castrated sex offenders, found that recidivism rates dropped to 2.2 per cent.

7   Many European countries have turned to so-called chemical castration, which involves injections of female hormones, and this treatment is also common in the United States and Canada. But, while chemical castration effectively blunts the male sex drive, it may place the subject at risk for certain medical problems, including gallstones and diabetes. Moreover, such programs, both here and abroad, are plagued by dropouts; and as soon as the injections cease the sexual drive returns to its previous level.

8   That surgical castration is permanent and irreversible is a source of alarm to its opponents and of security to its advocates. An orchiectomy is not a Bobbitt-like mutilation. It involves removing the testicles from the scrotum and replacing them with silicone prostheses that make the procedure virtually undetectable. The operation is far less invasive than a hysterectomy, for instance, or many forms of cosmetic surgery. Nor is it necessarily a "sexual death sentence," as some opponents have called it. A 1991 Czech study of eighty-four castrated sexual delinquents found that eighteen per cent were capable of occasional intercourse and that twenty-one per cent lived in a stable heterosexual partnership. Only three men committed another sexual offense after castration, and those offenses were not of an aggressive character. Similarly, in the Danish study none of the rapists were found to rape again.

9   Some opponents of the castration option, while conceding its effectiveness, attack it on moral grounds. Here an odd double standard comes into play. A woman who suffers from excessive premenstrual tension may choose to have her uterus removed. A woman who is carrying a baby she doesn't want (and many such women are rape victims) may elect to have an abortion. But a man who molests chil-

dren or brutalizes women can't ask to have his testicles removed, because that would be barbarous.

Our society is so squeamish when it comes to discussing sexual deviance that we tend to demonize sex offenders, forgetting that in many cases they themselves are victims, not only of sexual abuse in their own childhood but also of their overwhelming sexual impulses. Most of them, every time they exercise their sexual preference, break the law. It amounts to fraud when we offer these men treatment that doesn't work. If castration helps, why not let them have what they want? 10

QUESTIONS ON SUBJECT AND PURPOSE

1. Specifically, what does the essay argue for?
2. Why types of sexual activities are included under the rubric "sexual crimes"?
3. Why should the public be concerned about the treatment that sexual offenders receive?

QUESTIONS ON STRATEGY AND AUDIENCE

1. What strategy does the author use in beginning the essay?
2. What objections do people have to voluntary castration?
3. What might the author be able to assume about his or her audience?

QUESTIONS ON VOCABULARY AND STYLE

1. What does *recidivism* mean?
2. What does the title, "Help for Sex Offenders," suggest?
3. Be prepared to define the following words: *acceded* (paragraph 1), *spectre* (1), *habitual* (3), *therapeutic* (3), *chronic* (5), *prostheses* (8), *squeamish* (10).

WRITING SUGGESTIONS

1. **For Your Journal.** The Internet and the World Wide Web contain material that many people find offensive—sexually explicit material, calls to hatred and violence, directions for building bombs, pages promoting the use of drugs. Should such information be policed or censored? By the government?

By parents? By the companies that provide Websites? In your journal, freewrite about the need for censoring or the importance of not censoring the dissemination of information through electronic means.

2. **For a Paragraph.** In a paragraph, focus on one aspect of the argument that you began in your journal. If your instructor approves, you could concentrate on either logical argument or emotional appeal.

3. **For an Essay.** Extend your paragraph into an essay. Again you can argue either for or against such censorship. Remember that in part you will need to define the nature of such offensive documents and images.

4. **For Research.** What should be done about sex offenders once they have been released back into their communities? Should they be required to register with the police? Should neighbors be informed of their presence in neighborhoods? Should their houses or apartments or even their persons be labeled in some way? Do any of these actions seem unreasonable? Unconstitutional? Research the problems and suggested solutions for dealing with sex offenders who are returning to society. Argue for or against specific measures. Don't rely on just your own opinions. Research what is happening, how effective such measures are, and what objections have been raised. Be sure to document your sources.

   WEBSITE LINK

As more states are considering chemical castration as a punishment for sexual offenders, the debate over such practices has been growing. Some good places to start gathering information are hot-linked at the *Reader*'s Website.

   WRITING LINK: PARAGRAPHS

Look at the paragraphing in the essay, concentrating on paragraphs 3, 5, 8, and 9. How are the paragraphs structured and organized? What do such examples suggest about how you can and should structure your own paragraphs?

THE SINGER SOLUTION
TO WORLD POVERTY

Peter Singer

Peter Singer (1946–   ), born in Australia, is Ira W. DeCamp Professor of Bioethics at the University Center for Human Values at Princeton. A prolific author on a wide range of ethical issues, Singer has been referred to as "maybe the most controversial [ethicist] alive . . . [and] certainly among the most influential." His most recent book is One World: The Ethics of Globalization *(2002). This essay originally appeared in* The New York Times Magazine.

On Writing: *In an interview, Singer had this to say about the effects of argument: "I think we are (mostly) rational beings and rational argument does move people to action particularly when it gets them to see that what they are doing is inconsistent with other beliefs that they have and other values that they have that are important to them. But it is also true that we are self-interested beings to some extent. That's part of our nature and you can't get away from that. . . . If we put a rational argument in front of people, some are moved by it a lot of the way, it moves others a little bit of the way, and some people just shrug it off because it is too much against what they want to do."*

BEFORE READING

Connecting: How much money do you contribute annually to organizations seeking to care for children in need throughout the world?

Anticipating: As you read, think about whether or not Singer's essay has persuaded you to change your own behavior. Why or why not?

IN THE BRAZILIAN FILM *Central Station*, Dora is a retired school-   1
teacher who makes ends meet by sitting at the station writing letters for illiterate people. Suddenly she has an opportunity to pocket a thousand dollars. All she has to do is persuade a homeless nine-year-old boy to follow her to an address she has been given. (She is told he will be adopted by wealthy foreigners.) She delivers the boy, gets the money, spends some of it on a television set, and settles down to enjoy her new acquisition. Her neighbor spoils the fun, however, by telling her that the boy was too old to be adopted—he will be killed and his organs sold for transplantation. Perhaps Dora knew this all

along, but after her neighbor's plain speaking, she spends a troubled night. In the morning Dora resolves to take the boy back.

2   Suppose Dora had told her neighbor that it is a tough world, other people have nice new TVs too, and if selling the kid is the only way she can get one, well, he was only a street kid. She would then have become, in the eyes of the audience, a monster. She redeems herself only by being prepared to bear considerable risks to save the boy.

3   At the end of the movie, in cinemas in the affluent nations of the world, people who would have been quick to condemn Dora if she had not rescued the boy go home to places far more comfortable than her apartment. In fact, the average family in the United States spends almost one third of its income on things that are no more necessary to them than Dora's new TV was to her. Going out to nice restaurants, buying new clothes because the old ones are no longer stylish, vacationing at beach resorts—so much of our income is spent on things not essential to the preservation of our lives and health. Donated to one of a number of charitable agencies, that money could mean the difference between life and death for children in need.

4   All of which raises a question: in the end, what is the ethical distinction between a Brazilian who sells a homeless child to organ peddlers and an American who already has a TV and upgrades to a better one, knowing that the money could be donated to an organization that would use it to save the lives of kids in need?

5   Of course, there are several differences between the two situations that could support different moral judgments about them. For one thing, to be able to consign a child to death when he is standing right in front of you takes a chilling kind of heartlessness; it is much easier to ignore an appeal for money to help children you will never meet. Yet for a utilitarian philosopher like myself—that is, one who judges whether acts are right or wrong by their consequences—if the upshot of the American's failure to donate the money is that one more kid dies on the streets of a Brazilian city, then it is in some sense just as bad as selling the kid to the organ peddlers. But one doesn't need to embrace my utilitarian ethic to see that at the very least, there is a troubling incongruity in being so quick to condemn Dora for taking the child to the organ peddlers while at the same time not regarding the American consumer's behavior as raising a serious moral issue.

6   In his 1996 book, *Living High and Letting Die*, the New York University philosopher Peter Unger presented an ingenious series of imaginary examples designed to probe our intuitions about whether it is wrong to live well without giving substantial amounts of money to help

people who are hungry, malnourished, or dying from easily treatable illnesses like diarrhea. Here's my paraphrase of one of these examples: Bob is close to retirement. He has invested most of his savings 7 in a very rare and valuable old car, a Bugatti, which he has not been able to insure. The Bugatti is his pride and joy. In addition to the pleasure he gets from driving and caring for his car, Bob knows that its rising market value means that he will always be able to sell it and live comfortably after retirement. One day when Bob is out for a drive, he parks the Bugatti near the end of a railway siding and goes for a walk up the track. As he does so, he sees that a runaway train, with no one aboard, is running down the railway track. Looking farther down the track, he sees the small figure of a child very likely to be killed by the runaway train. He can't stop the train and the child is too far away to warn of the danger, but he can throw a switch that will divert the train down the siding where his Bugatti is parked. Then nobody will be killed—but the train will destroy his Bugatti. Thinking of his joy in owning the car and the financial security it represents, Bob decides not to throw the switch. The child is killed. For many years to come, Bob enjoys owning his Bugatti and the financial security it represents.

Bob's conduct, most of us will immediately respond, was gravely 8 wrong. Unger agrees. But then he reminds us that we too have opportunities to save the lives of children. We can give to organizations like UNICEF or Oxfam America. How much would we have to give one of these organizations to have a high probability of saving the life of a child threatened by easily preventable diseases? (I do not believe that children are more worth saving than adults, but since no one can argue that children have brought their poverty on themselves, focusing on them simplifies the issues.) Unger called up some experts and used the information they provided to offer some plausible estimates that include the cost of raising money, administrative expenses, and the cost of delivering aid where it is most needed. By his calculation, $200 in donations would help a sickly two-year-old transform into a healthy six-year-old—offering safe passage through childhood's most dangerous years. To show how practical philosophical argument can be, Unger even tells his readers that they can easily donate funds by using their credit card and calling one of these toll-free numbers: (800) 367-5437 for UNICEF; (800) 693-2687 for Oxfam America.

Now you too have the information you need to save a child's life. 9 How should you judge yourself if you don't do it? Think again about Bob and his Bugatti. Unlike Dora, Bob did not have to look into the eyes of the child he was sacrificing for his own material comfort. The child was a complete stranger to him and too far away to relate to in an intimate, personal way. Unlike Dora too, he did not mislead the child or initiate the chain of events imperiling him. In all these respects, Bob's situation resembles that of people able but unwilling to donate to overseas aid and differs from Dora's situation.

10   If you still think that it was very wrong of Bob not to throw the switch that would have diverted the train and saved the child's life, then it is hard to see how you could deny that it is also very wrong not to send money to one of the organizations listed above. Unless, that is, there is some morally important difference between the two situations that I have overlooked.

11   Is it the practical uncertainties about whether aid will really reach the people who need it? Nobody who knows the world of overseas aid can doubt that such uncertainties exist. But Unger's figure of $200 to save a child's life was reached after he had made conservative assumptions about the proportion of the money donated that will actually reach its target.

12   One genuine difference between Bob and those who can afford to donate to overseas aid organizations but don't is that only Bob can save the child on the tracks, whereas there are hundreds of millions of people who can give $200 to overseas aid organizations. The problem is that most of them aren't doing it. Does this mean that it is all right for you not to do it?

13   Suppose that there were more owners of priceless vintage cars—Carol, Dave, Emma, Fred, and so on, down to Ziggy—all in exactly the same situation as Bob, with their own siding and their own switch, all sacrificing the child in order to preserve their own cherished car. Would that make it all right for Bob to do the same? To answer this question affirmatively is to endorse follow-the-crowd ethics—the kind of ethics that led many Germans to look away when the Nazi atrocities were being committed. We do not excuse them because others were behaving no better.

14   We seem to lack a sound basis for drawing a clear moral line between Bob's situation and that of any reader of this article with $200 to spare who does not donate it to an overseas aid agency. These readers seem to be acting at least as badly as Bob was acting when he chose to let the runaway train hurtle toward the unsuspecting child. In the light of this conclusion, I trust that many readers will reach for the phone and donate that $200. Perhaps you should do it before reading further.

*

15   Now that you have distinguished yourself morally from people who put their vintage cars ahead of a child's life, how about treating yourself and your partner to dinner at your favorite restaurant? But wait.

The money you will spend at the restaurant could also help save the lives of children overseas! True, you weren't planning to blow $200 tonight, but if you were to give up dining out just for one month, you would easily save that amount. And what is one month's dining out compared to a child's life? There's the rub. Since there are a lot of desperately needy children in the world, there will always be another child whose life you could save for another $200. Are you therefore obliged to keep giving until you have nothing left? At what point can you stop?

Hypothetical examples can easily become farcical. Consider   16 Bob. How far past losing the Bugatti should he go? Imagine that Bob had got his foot stuck in the track of the siding, and if he diverted the train, then before it rammed the car it would also amputate his big toe. Should he still throw the switch? What if it would amputate his foot? His entire leg?

As absurd as the Bugatti scenario gets when pushed to extremes,   17 the point it raises is a serious one: only when the sacrifices become very significant indeed would most people be prepared to say that Bob does nothing wrong when he decides not to throw the switch. Of course, most people could be wrong; we can't decide moral issues by taking opinion polls. But consider for yourself the level of sacrifice that you would demand of Bob, and then think about how much money you would have to give away in order to make a sacrifice that is roughly equal to that. It's almost certainly much, much more than $200. For most middle-class Americans, it could easily be more like $200,000.

Isn't it counterproductive to ask people to do so much? Don't we run   18 the risk that many will shrug their shoulders and say that morality, so conceived, is fine for saints but not for them? I accept that we are unlikely to see, in the near or even medium-term future, a world in which it is normal for wealthy Americans to give the bulk of their wealth to strangers. When it comes to praising or blaming people for what they do, we tend to use a standard that is relative to some conception of normal behavior. Comfortably off Americans who give, say, 10 percent of their income to overseas aid organizations are so far ahead of most of their equally comfortable fellow citizens that I wouldn't go out of my way to chastise them for not doing more. Nevertheless, they should be doing much more, and they are in no position to criticize Bob for failing to make the much greater sacrifice of his Bugatti.

At this point various objections may crop up. Someone may say,   19 "If every citizen living in the affluent nations contributed his or her share, I wouldn't have to make such a drastic sacrifice, because long before such levels were reached the resources would have been there to save the lives of all those children dying from lack of food or medical care. So why should I give more than my fair share?" Another, related objection is that the government ought to increase its overseas aid allocations, since that would spread the burden more equitably across all taxpayers.

20   Yet the question of how much we ought to give is a matter to be decided in the real world—and that, sadly, is a world in which we know that most people do not, and in the immediate future will not, give substantial amounts to overseas aid agencies. We know too that at least in the next year, the United States government is not going to meet even the very modest United Nations–recommended target of 0.7 percent of gross national product; at the moment it lags far below that, at 0.09 percent, not even half of Japan's 0.22 percent or a tenth of Denmark's 0.97 percent. Thus, we know that the money we can give beyond that theoretical "fair share" is still going to save lives that would otherwise be lost. While the idea that no one need do more than his or her fair share is a powerful one, should it prevail if we know that others are not doing their fair share and that children will die preventable deaths unless we do more than our fair share? That would be taking fairness too far.

21   Thus, this ground for limiting how much we ought to give also fails. In the world as it is now, I can see no escape from the conclusion that each one of us with wealth surplus to his or her essential needs should be giving most of it to help people suffering from poverty so dire as to be life-threatening. That's right: I'm saying that you shouldn't buy that new car, take that cruise, redecorate the house, or get that pricy new suit. After all, a thousand-dollar suit could save five children's lives.

22   So how does my philosophy break down in dollars and cents? An American household with an income of $50,000 spends around $30,000 annually on necessities, according to the Conference Board, a nonprofit economic research organization. Therefore, for a household bringing in $50,000 a year, donations to help the world's poor should be as close as possible to $20,000. The $30,000 required for necessities holds for higher incomes as well. So a household making $100,000 could cut a yearly check for $70,000. Again, the formula is simple: whatever money you're spending on luxuries, not necessities, should be given away.

23   Now, evolutionary psychologists tell us that human nature just isn't sufficiently altruistic to make it plausible that many people will sacrifice so much for strangers. On the facts of human nature, they might be right, but they would be wrong to draw a moral conclusion from those facts. If it is the case that we ought to do things that, pre-

dictably, most of us won't do, then let's face that fact head-on. Then, if we value the life of a child more than going to fancy restaurants, the next time we dine out we will know that we could have done something better with our money. If that makes living a morally decent life extremely arduous, well, then that is the way things are. If we don't do it, then we should at least know that we are failing to live a morally decent life—not because it is good to wallow in guilt but because knowing where we should be going is the first step toward heading in that direction.

When Bob first grasped the dilemma that faced him as he stood   24
by that railway switch, he must have thought how extraordinarily unlucky he was to be placed in a situation in which he must choose between the life of an innocent child and the sacrifice of most of his savings. But he was not unlucky at all. We are all in that situation.

QUESTIONS ON SUBJECT AND PURPOSE

1. Singer labels himself a "utilitarian" philosopher. How does he explain what that means?
2. Is there any limit for Singer to how much money one ought to give away for overseas aid?
3. What type of response do you think that Singer hopes from his audience? Expects from his audience?

QUESTIONS ON STRATEGY AND AUDIENCE

1. Why might Singer choose to begin with the example of Dora in the Brazilian film *Central Station*?
2. The text of the essay is separated after paragraph 14 by a centered asterisk (*). What division does this indicate in the essay itself?
3. What assumptions could Singer make about his audience?

QUESTIONS ON VOCABULARY AND STYLE

1. What is an analogy? Does Singer use analogy in his argument?
2. Why is the effect of including the telephone numbers for UNICEF and Oxfam America in the essay?
3. Be prepared to define the following words: *affluent* (paragraph 3), *incongruity* (5), *ingenious* (6), *altruistic* (23), *arduous* (23).

WRITING SUGGESTIONS

1. **For Your Journal.** Over the course of a week, jot down in your journal a detailed list of how you spent your money. Try to record everything. For each expenditure of over 50 cents, write an explanation for where and why the money was spent. At the end of the week, make some notes about your spending habits.

2. **For a Paragraph.** What did your journal reveal? In a paragraph, explore your values and either defend or criticize your behavior.

3. **For an Essay.** Singer notes (citing the research of someone else) that a $200 donation would "help a sickly two-year-old transform into a healthy six-year-old." That works out to about 55 cents per day yearly. Could you and your friends, even as college students, find a way to trim 55 cents a day (or less than $4 a week) out of what you already spend? In an essay aimed at undergraduates at your school, argue for a schoolwide campaign to get everyone to contribute to such a cause.

4. **For Research.** Why is it that the richest nation in the world is one of the world's poorest contributors to overseas aid? In an essay research this situation. How much does the United States contribute? What factors have accounted for our current position? Are there good reasons why we as a nation should not contribute more? In an essay arguing either side, take a stand on the United States' overseas aid policy.

 WEBSITE LINK

The Web offers a number of sites where you can read more of Singer's work, explore the objections that some critics have to some of his ethical stands, and make a contribution to UNICEF, Oxfam America, or to the relief agency of your choice.

 WRITING LINK: PARAGRAPH STRUCTURE

Choose one or more of Singer's longer paragraphs and look closely at how it is organized. You might want to outline it. Does the paragraph achieve unity and coherence? How? Does the paragraph have a topic sentence? Does it use transitional devices to link sentences together? What observations could you make about effective body paragraphs based on the example(s) you examined?

NONE OF THIS IS FAIR

Richard Rodriguez

Born in 1944 in San Francisco to Spanish-speaking Mexican-American parents, Richard Rodriguez first learned English in grade school. Educated in English literature at Stanford, Columbia, and the University of California at Berkeley, Rodriguez is best known for his conservative opinions on bilingual education and affirmative action, and in "None of This Is Fair" he uses his personal experience to argue that affirmative action programs are ineffective in reaching the seriously disadvantaged. Yet he also suggests in his two autobiographical works, Hunger of Memory: The Education of Richard Rodriguez *(1982) and* Days of Obligation: An Argument with My Mexican Father *(1992), that he harbors deep regret at losing his own Hispanic heritage when he became assimilated into the English-speaking world. His most recent book is* Brown: The Last Discovery of America *(2002).*

Basically, the phrase "affirmative action" refers to policies and programs that try to redress past discrimination by increasing opportunities for underrepresented or minority groups. In the United States, the major classifications affected by affirmative action are defined by age, race, religion, national origin, and sex. The phrase was coined in 1965 in an executive order issued by President Lyndon Johnson that required any contractor dealing with the federal government to "take affirmative action to ensure that applicants are employed . . . without regard to their race, creed, color, or national origin." In the decades following, affirmative action, in the form of weighted admissions policies, became a potent tool for colleges and universities seeking increased enrollments of previously underrepresented students. Controversy has always surrounded such policies, and in recent years a number of states have enacted legislation banning race-based admissions selection.

*   **On Writing:** In an interview, Rodriguez noted: "It takes me a very long time to write. What I try to do when I write is break down the line separating the prosaic world from the poetic world. I try to write about everyday concerns—an educational issue, say, or the problems of the unemployed—but to write about them as powerfully, as richly, as well as I can."*

BEFORE READING

Connecting: To what extent has your education—in elementary and secondary schools—provided you with opportunities that others have not had?

Anticipating: Why did it trouble Rodriguez to be labeled as a "minority student"?

1   My plan to become a professor of English—my ambition during long years in college at Stanford, then in graduate school at Columbia and Berkeley—was complicated by feelings of embarrassment and guilt. So many times I would see other Mexican-Americans and know we were alike only in race. And yet, simply because our race was the same, I was, during the last years of my schooling, the beneficiary of their situation. Affirmative Action programs had made it all possible. The disadvantages of others permitted my promotion; the absence of many Mexican-Americans from academic life allowed my designation as a "minority student."

2   For me opportunities had been extravagant. There were fellowships, summer research grants, and teaching assistantships. After only two years in graduate school, I was offered teaching jobs by several colleges. Invitations to Washington conferences arrived and I had the chance to travel abroad as a "Mexican-American representative." The benefits were often, however, too gaudy to please. In three published essays, in conversations with teachers, in letters to politicians and at conferences, I worried the issue of Affirmative Action. Often I proposed contradictory opinions. Though consistent was the admission that—because of an early, excellent education—I was no longer a principal victim of racism or any other social oppression. I said that but still I continued to indicate on applications for financial aid that I was a Hispanic-American. It didn't really occur to me to say anything else, or to leave the question unanswered.

3   Thus I complied with and encouraged the odd bureaucratic logic of Affirmative Action. I let government officials treat the disadvantaged condition of many Mexican-Americans with my advancement. Each fall my presence was noted by Health, Education, and Welfare department statisticians. As I pursued advanced literary studies and learned the skill of reading Spenser and Wordsworth and Empson, I would hear myself numbered among the culturally disadvantaged. Still, silent, I didn't object.

4   But the irony cut deep. And guilt would not be evaded by averting my glance when I confronted a face like my own in a crowd. By late 1975, nearing the completion of my graduate studies at Berkeley, I was so wary of the benefits of Affirmative Action that I feared my inevitable success as an applicant for a teaching position. The months of fall—traditionally that time of academic job-searching—passed without my applying to a single school. When one of my professors

chanced to learn this in late November, he was astonished, then furious. He yelled at me: Did I think that because I was a minority student jobs would just come looking for me? What was I thinking? Did I realize that he and several other faculty members had already written letters on my behalf? Was I going to start acting like some other minority students he had known? They struggled for success and then when it was almost within reach, grew strangely afraid and let it pass. Was that it? Was I determined to fail?

I did not respond to his questions. I didn't want to admit to him, 5 and thus to myself, the reason I delayed.

I merely agreed to write to several schools. (In my letter I wrote: 6 "I cannot claim to represent disadvantaged Mexican-Americans. The very fact that I am in a position to apply for this job should make that clear.") After two or three days, there were telegrams and phone calls, invitations to interviews, then airplane trips. A blur of faces and the murmur of their soft questions. And, over someone's shoulder, the sight of campus buildings shadowing pictures I had seen years before when I leafed through Ivy League catalogues with great expectations. At the end of each visit, interviewers would smile and wonder if I had any questions. A few times I quietly wondered what advantage my race had given me over other applicants. But that was an impossible question for them to answer without embarrassing me. Quickly, several persons insisted that my ethnic identity had given me no more than a "foot inside the door"; at most, I had a "slight edge" over other applicants. "We just looked at your dossier with extra care and we liked what we saw. There was never any question of having to alter our standards. You can be certain of that."

In the early part of January, offers arrived on stiffly elegant sta- 7 tionery. Most schools promised terms appropriate for any new assistant professor. A few made matters worse—and almost more tempting—by offering more: the use of university housing; an unusually large starting salary; a reduced teaching schedule. As the stack of letters mounted, my hesitation increased. I started calling department chairmen to ask for another week, then 10 more days—"more time to reach a decision"—to avoid the decision I would need to make.

At school, meantime, some students hadn't received a single job 8 offer. One man, probably the best student in the department, did not even get a request for his dossier. He and I met outside a classroom one day and he asked about my opportunities. He seemed happy for me. Faculty members beamed. They said they had expected it. "After all, not many schools are going to pass up getting a Chicano with a Ph.D. in Renaissance literature," somebody said, laughing. Friends wanted to know which of the offers I was going to accept. But I couldn't make up my mind. February came and I was running out of time and excuses. (One chairman guessed my delay was a bargaining ploy and increased his offer with each of my calls.) I had to promise a decision by the 10th; the 12th at the very latest.

9   On the 18th of February, late in the afternoon, I was in the office I shared with several other teaching assistants. Another graduate student was sitting across the room at his desk. When I got up to leave, he looked over to say in an uneventful voice that he had some big news. He had finally decided to accept a position at a faraway university. It was not a job he especially wanted, he admitted. But he had to take it because there hadn't been any other offers. He felt trapped, and depressed, since his job would separate him from his young daughter.

10   I tried to encourage him by remarking that he was lucky at least to have found a job. So many others hadn't been able to get anything. But before I finished speaking I realized that I had said the wrong thing. And I anticipated his next question.

11   "What are your plans?" he wanted to know. "Is it true you've gotten an offer from Yale?"

12   I said that it was. "Only, I still haven't made up my mind."

13   He stared at me as I put on my jacket. And smiling, then unsmiling, he asked if I knew that he too had written to Yale. In his case, however, no one had bothered to acknowledge his letter with even a postcard. What did I think of that?

14   He gave me no time to answer.

15   "Damn!" he said sharply and his chair rasped the floor as he pushed himself back. Suddenly, it was to *me* that he was complaining. "It's just not right, Richard. None of this is fair. You've done some good work, but so have I. I'll bet our records are just about equal. But when we look for jobs this year, it's a different story. You get all of the breaks."

16   To evade his criticism, I wanted to side with him. I was about to admit the injustice of Affirmative Action. But he went on, his voice hard with accusation. "It's all very simple this year. You're a Chicano. And I am a Jew. That's the only real difference between us."

17   His words stung me: there was nothing he was telling me that I didn't know. I had admitted everything already. But to hear someone else say these things, and in such an accusing tone, was suddenly hard to take. In a deceptively calm voice, I responded that he had simplified the whole issue. The phrases came like bubbles to the tip of my tongue: "new blood"; "the importance of cultural diversity"; "the goal of racial integration." These were all the arguments I had proposed several years ago—and had long since abandoned. Of course the offers were unjustifiable. I knew that. All I was saying amounted to a

frantic self-defense. I tried to find an end to a sentence. My voice faltered to a stop.

"Yeah, sure," he said. "I've heard all that before. Nothing you say 18 really changes the fact that Affirmative Action is unfair. You see that, don't you? There isn't any way for me to compete with you. Once there were quotas to keep my parents out of certain schools; now there are quotas to get you in and the effect on me is the same as it was for them."

I listened to every word he spoke. But my mind was really on 19 something else. I knew at that moment that I would reject all of the offers. I stood there silently surprised by what an easy conclusion it was. Having prepared for so many years to teach, having trained myself to do nothing else, I had hesitated out of practical fear. But now that it was made, the decision came with relief. I immediately knew I had made the right choice.

My colleague continued talking and I realized that he was sim- 20 ply right. Affirmative Action programs *are* unfair to white students. But as I listened to him assert his rights, I thought of the seriously disadvantaged. How different they were from white, middle-class students who come armed with the testimony of their grades and aptitude scores and self-confidence to complain about the unequal treatment they now receive. I listen to them. I do not want to be careless about what they say. Their rights are important to protect. But inevitably when I hear them or their lawyers, I think about the most seriously disadvantaged, not simply Mexican-Americans, but of all those who do not ever imagine themselves going to college or becoming doctors: white, black, brown. Always poor. Silent. They are not plaintiffs before the court or against the misdirection of Affirmative Action. They lack the confidence (my confidence!) to assume their right to a good education. They lack the confidence and skills a good primary and secondary education provides and which are prerequisites for informed public life. They remain silent.

The debate drones on and surrounds them in stillness. They are 21 distant, faraway figures like the boys I have seen peering down from freeway overpasses in some other part of town.

QUESTIONS ON SUBJECT AND PURPOSE

1. In paragraph 4, Rodriguez makes reference to the "irony" of the situation. In what ways was it ironic?

2. Why does Rodriguez decide to reject all of the offers?

3. Is Rodriguez criticizing affirmative action policies? How could such policies reach or change the lives of those who are really seriously disadvantaged?

QUESTIONS ON STRATEGY AND AUDIENCE

1. To what extent does Rodriguez present a formal argument based on an appeal to reason? To what extent does he attempt to persuade through an appeal to emotion? Which element is stronger in the piece?
2. What is the difference between objectively stating an opinion and narrating a personal experience? Do we as readers react any differently to Rodriguez's story as a result?
3. What expectations does Rodriguez have of his audience? How do you know that?

QUESTIONS ON VOCABULARY AND STYLE

1. In paragraphs 11–18, Rodriguez dramatizes a scene with a fellow student. He could have just summarized what was said without using dialogue. What advantage is gained by developing the scene?
2. Be prepared to discuss the significance of the following sentences:
   a. "For me opportunities had been extravagant" (paragraph 2).
   b. "The benefits were often, however, too gaudy to please" (2).
   c. "The phrases came like bubbles to the tip of my tongue" (17).
   d. "Always poor. Silent" (20).
3. What is the effect of the simile ("like the boys I have seen . . . ") Rodriguez uses in the final line?

WRITING SUGGESTIONS

1. **For Your Journal.** What made you pursue your education? What are the important motivating factors? Explore the questions in your journal.
2. **For a Paragraph.** Describe a time when you encountered an obstacle because of your age, gender, race, religion, physical ability, physical appearance, or socioeconomic status. Describe the experience briefly, and then argue against the unfairness of such discrimination.
3. **For an Essay.** Are minorities and women fairly represented on the faculty of your college or university? Check the proportion of white males to minority and women faculty

members, looking not only at raw numbers but also at rank, tenure, and so forth. Then, in an essay, argue for or against the need to achieve a better balance.

4. **For Research.** Rodriguez feels that as a result of "an early, excellent education" (paragraph 2), he was no longer "a principal victim of racism or any other social oppression." If the key to helping the "seriously disadvantaged" lies in improving the quality of elementary and secondary education, how successful have American schools been? Has the quality of education for the disadvantaged improved in the past twenty years? Research the problem, and then write an essay in which you evaluate some existing programs and make recommendations about continuing, expanding, modifying, or dropping them. Be sure to document your sources wherever appropriate.

 WEBSITE LINK

In 1997 Rodriguez won the George Foster Peabody Award for his essays on the PBS *NewsHour.* Many of these essays are available on-line.

 WRITING LINK: WRITING DIALOGUE

Rewrite paragraphs 11 to 18, changing the dialogue into indirect discourse (a model would be paragraphs 4 to 6). What is the difference between the two strategies? What are the advantages and disadvantages of each? What happens to the essay when this change is made? What does Rodriguez gain by dramatizing the situation with the other teaching assistant? What does this activity suggest about using dialogue at appropriate times in your own essays?

PREWRITING SUGGESTIONS FOR ARGUMENT AND PERSUASION

1. Brainstorm both sides of the issue that you are considering writing about. Remember that the quality of your argument is always improved when you understand the issue from various points of view.

2. Remember that you will need specific, accurate information to write convincingly about a subject. Most arguments need more than unsubstantiated personal opinion.

3. Write a specific statement of the action or reaction that you want to elicit from your audience. As you write, use that statement as a way of checking your developing argument.

4. Arrange your points in an order, deciding which should come first and which last. Make these decisions carefully. For example, do you want to begin or end with your strongest point? Experiment with different orders.

5. Try out your argument on someone who disagrees with you. You can debate the issue orally. Which pieces of evidence seem particularly powerful and persuasive? Use the experience to reshape your draft.

REWRITING SUGGESTIONS FOR ARGUMENT AND PERSUASION

1. Make a copy of your essay, and highlight in colored marker all the emotionally charged words and phrases. Look carefully at these highlighted sections. How will your audience react to them? Have you avoided distorted or inflammatory language?

2. Look carefully at how you have structured your essay. Did you begin with a position and then provide evidence (deductive) or did you begin with specific examples and then draw your conclusion (inductive)? Is the structure you chose the more effective one for the essay?

3. Highlight all of the specific evidence in your essay. Remember that details are generally vital to making an argument effective. Have you included enough? Each body paragraph needs specifics, not just generalizations.

4. Remember that conclusions are especially important in argument and persuasion. Plan a specific, forceful concluding strategy. Are you asking people to do something? Make it clear what they are to do.

5. Find a classmate or a peer to read your essay. Ask that reader to evaluate honestly your position. Does the reader agree with you? Why or why not? Listen carefully to your reader's reactions.

REVISING

Not even the best professional writers produce only perfect sentences and paragraphs. Good writing almost always results from rewriting or revising. Although the terms *rewriting* and *revising* are interchangeable, *revising* suggests some important aspects of this vital stage of your writing process: a "re-vision" is a reseeing of what you have written. In its broadest sense, this reseeing can be a complete rethinking of a paper from idea through execution. As such, revising a paper is quite different from proofreading it for mechanical and grammatical errors. When you proofread, you are mostly looking for small things—misspellings or typographical errors, incorrect punctuation, awkwardly constructed sentences. When you *revise*, however, you look for larger concerns as well—such things as a clear thesis, an effective structure, or adequate and relevant details.

Revising does not occur only after you have written a complete draft of a paper. In fact, many writers revise as they draft. They may write a sentence, then stop to change its structure, even erase it and start over; they may shift the positions of sentences and paragraphs or delete them altogether. In this search for the right words, the graceful sentence, the clear structure, writers revise constantly.

But rewriting does not end with the first draft. For one thing, revision while writing usually focuses on the sentence or paragraph being composed. When you are struggling to find the right word or the right sentence structure, you're probably not thinking much about the larger whole.

Consequently, allowing some time to elapse between drafts of your paper is important. You need to put the draft aside for a while if you are to get a perspective on what you have written and read your paper objectively. For this reason, it is important to finish a complete draft at least one day before you have to hand in the paper. If circumstances prevent you from finishing a paper until an hour or two before class, you will not have a chance to revise. You will have time only to proofread.

ANALYZING YOUR OWN WRITING

The key to improving your writing is self-awareness. You have to look carefully and critically at what you have written, focus on areas that caused you the most problems, and then work to correct them. Most writers are, in fact, able to identify the key problems they faced in a particular paper or in writing in general, even though they might not know how to solve those problems. Knowing what causes you problems is the essential first step toward solving them.

When you analyze the first draft of a paper, begin by asking a series of specific questions, starting with the larger issues and working toward the smaller ones. Ideally, you should write out your answers—doing so will force you to have a specific response. Here are some questions you might consider:

1. What were you asked to do in this paper? Look again at the assignment. Circle the key action words, verbs such as *analyze, argue, classify, compare, criticize, define, describe, evaluate, narrate, recommend,* and *summarize.* Have you done what you were asked to do?

2. What is the thesis of your paper? Can you find a single sentence in your essay that sums up that thesis? If so, underline it. If not, write a one-sentence thesis statement.

3. How have you organized your paper? That organization ought to be conveyed in the way the paper has been paragraphed. Make an outline that contains only as many subdivisions as you have paragraphs.

4. Is each paragraph focused around a single idea? Is there an explicit statement of that idea? If so, underline it. If not, jot down in the margin the key word or words. Should that idea be specifically stated in the paragraph? Is that idea developed

adequately? Are there enough supporting details and examples?

5. What strategies did you use to begin and end your essay? Does your introduction seem likely to catch the reader's attention? Do you have a concluding paragraph, or do you just stop?

Only after you have asked and answered these kinds of questions about the larger elements of your paper should you move to questions directed toward style, grammar, and mechanics:

6. Is everything you punctuated as a sentence in fact a complete sentence? Check each sentence to make sure.
7. Look carefully at every mark of punctuation. Is it the right choice for this place in the sentence?
8. Check your choice of words. Are you certain of what each word means? Are there any words that might be too informal or too colloquial (words that are appropriate in a conversation with friends but not in academic writing)? Is every word spelled correctly? (If you have *any* doubt about *any* word, look it up in a dictionary.)

KEEPING A REVISION LOG

Keeping a log of writing problems you most often encounter is an excellent way of promoting self-awareness. Your log should include subdivisions for a wide range of writing problems, not just grammatical and mechanical errors. The log will help you keep track of the areas that you know you have trouble with and those your instructor, peer readers, or writing tutors point out as needing improvement. Do you have a tendency to overparagraph? To stop rather than conclude? To have trouble with parallelism? Each time you discover a problem or one is pointed out to you, list it in your log. Then, as you revise your papers, look back through your revision log to remind yourself of these frequent problems and look closely for them in your current draft.

If a revision log seems a lot of trouble, remember that only you can improve your own writing. Improvement, in turn, comes with recognizing your weaknesses and working to correct them.

Using Peer Readers

Most of the writing you'll do in school is aimed toward only one reader—a teacher. Writing just for a teacher has both advantages and disadvantages. A teacher is a critical reader who evaluates your paper by a set of standards. But a teacher can also be a sympathetic reader, one who understands the difficulties of writing and is patient with the problems that writers have. Classmates, colleagues, or supervisors can be just as critical as teachers but less sympathetic.

Only in school, however, do you have someone who will read everything that you write and offer constructive comments. After you graduate, your letters and reports will be read by many different readers, but you will no longer have a teacher to offer advice or a tutor to conference with you. Instead, you will have to rely on your own analysis of your writing and on the advice of your fellow workers. For this reason, learning to use a peer reader as a resource in your revising process is extremely important. At first, you might feel a little uncomfortable asking someone other than your instructor to read your papers, but after some experience, you will feel better about sharing. Remember that every reader is potentially a valuable resource for suggestions.

Peer Editing

Many college writing courses use peer editing as a regular classroom activity. On a peer editing day, students swap papers with their classmates and then critique one another's work, typically using a list of peer editing guidelines. But you don't have to do peer editing in class to reap the benefits of such an arrangement. If your instructor approves, you can arrange to swap papers with a classmate outside of class, or you can ask a roommate or a friend to do a peer reading for you.

From the start, though, several ground rules are important. First, when you ask a peer to edit your paper, you are asking for criticism. You want advice; you want reaction. You cannot expect that your reader will love everything that you have written.

Second, peer editing is not proofreading. You should not ask your reader to look for misspelled words and missing commas. Rather, you want your reader to react to the whole paper. Is the thesis clear? Does the structure seem appropriate? Are there enough examples or details? Does the introduction catch the reader's attention and make him or her want to keep reading? You need to keep your reader's attention focused on these larger, significant issues. One good way to do so is to give your reader a checklist or a set of questions that reflect the criteria appropriate for evaluating this kind of paper.

Third, you want a peer reader to offer specific and constructive criticism. To get that type of response, you must ask questions that invite—or even require—a reader to comment in more than "yes" and "no" answers. For example, do not ask your reader, "Is the thesis clear?"; instead ask, "What is the thesis of this paper?" If your reader has trouble answering that question or if the answer differs from your own, you know that this aspect of your paper needs more work.

Group Editing

Sharing your writing in a small group is another good way to get reader reaction to your papers. Such an editing activity can take place either inside or outside of the classroom. In either case, you can prepare for a group editing session in the same way. Plan to form a group of four or five students, and make a copy of your paper for each group member. If possible, distribute those copies prior to the group editing session so that each member will have a chance to read and prepare some comments for the discussion. Then follow these guidelines:

Before the group editing session

1. Read each paper carefully, marking or underlining the writer's main idea and key supporting points. Make any other notes about the paper that seem appropriate.
2. On a separate sheet, comment specifically on one or two aspects of the paper that most need improvement.

At the group editing session

1. When it is your turn, read your own paper aloud to the group. Since you might hear problems as you read, keep a pen or pencil handy to jot down notes.
2. When you are finished, tell the group members what you would like them to comment on.
3. Listen to their remarks, and make notes. Feel free to ask group members to explain or expand on their observations. Remember, you want as much advice as you can get.
4. Collect the copies of your paper and the sheets on which the group members have commented on specific areas that need improvement.

After the group editing session

1. Carefully consider both the oral and written comments of your group. You may not agree with everything that was said, but you need to weigh each comment.
2. Revise your paper. Remember that you are responsible for your own work. No one else—not your instructor, your peer editors, or your group readers—can or should tell you *everything* that you need to change.

Using Your School's Writing Center or a Writing Tutor

Most colleges operate writing centers, writing labs, or writing tutor programs. Their purpose is to provide individual assistance to any student who has a question about writing. They are staffed by trained tutors who want to help you. In part, such services are intended to supplement the instruction that you receive in a writing class, since most writing teachers have too many students to be able to offer extensive help outside of class to everyone. These services also exist to provide advice to students writing papers for courses in other disciplines where writing might be required but not discussed.

If you are having trouble with grammar or mechanics, if you consistently have problems with beginnings or middles or ends of papers, if you are baffled by a particular assignment, do not be afraid to ask for help. After all, every writer can benefit from constructive advice or additional explanations, and writing centers and tutors exist to provide that help. Remember, though, that a writing tutor is a teacher whose job is to explain and to instruct. You do not drop off your paper at the writing center like you drop off your automobile at the service station. Your tutor will suggest ways that *you* can improve your paper or follow a particular convention. A tutor will not do the work for you.

Come to your appointment with a specific set of questions or problems. Why are you there? What do you want to discuss? What don't you understand? After all, when you have a medical problem, you make an appointment with a doctor to discuss a specific set of symptoms. A conference with a writing tutor should work in a similar way.

Finally, make sure that you keep some form of written record of your conference. Jot down the tutor's advice and explanations. Those notes will serve as a valuable reminder of what to do when you are revising your paper.

Using an OWL

For students who have access to the Internet and the World Wide Web—either from home or from school—another source of help in revising is an on-line writing lab, or OWL. Most OWLs are operated by traditional writing centers at colleges and universities. Although most provide help predominantly to students enrolled at those schools, many have services also available to students from anywhere who access the site through the Internet.

The services that OWLs provide range widely. Some offer e-mail tutoring; some provide access to MOOs ("multiple user dimensions, object-oriented"), where you can hold conversations with other writers. Most provide access to writing reference materials and extensive links to other related sites. One of the oldest OWLs is Purdue University's. Purdue's site offers information about writing based on reference materials and also maintains a listing of other OWLs and their e-mail addresses. A good place to start in a search for on-line revising help is the National Writing Centers Association List of Online Writing Labs and Centers. Visit the *Reader's* Website (www.prenhall.com/miller) for a list of hot-linked resources for revision.

Conferencing with Your Instructor

Your instructor in a writing class is always willing to talk with you about your writing. You can, of course, visit your instructor during scheduled office hours. In addition, many instructors, if their teaching schedule permits it, will schedule a set of regular conference times spaced throughout the semester. Whatever the arrangement, such a conference is an opportunity for you to ask questions about your writing in general or about a particular paper.

Whether you have asked for the conference or the instructor has scheduled it as a part of the class requirements, several ground rules apply. As with a tutoring session, you should always come to an instructor conference with a definite agenda in mind and a specific set of questions to ask. Writing these questions out is an excellent way to prepare for a conference. Generally, a conference is intended to be a dialogue, and so your active participation is expected. Do not be surprised, for example, if your instructor begins by asking you what you want to talk about. Since time is always limited (remember that your instructor might have to see dozens of students), you will not be able to ask about everything. Try to concentrate on the issues that trouble you the most.

Instructors like to use conferences as opportunities to discuss the larger issues of a paper: Is the thesis well defined? Is the structure as clear as it might be? Are there adequate transitions? Although your instructor will be happy to explain a troublesome grammatical or mechanical problem, do not expect your instructor to find and fix every mistake in your paper. A conference is not a proofreading session.

A conference is also not an oral grading of your paper. Grading a paper is a complicated task and one that frequently involves seeing your essay in the context of the other papers from the class. As a result, your instructor cannot make a quick judgment. Do not ask what grade the paper might receive.

As the conference proceeds, make notes for yourself about what is said. Do not rely on your memory. Those notes will constitute a plan for revising your paper.

PROOFREADING YOUR PAPER

At one point or another, virtually everyone has had the injunction "proofread!" written on a paper. (*Proofreading* comes from printing terminology: a printer reads and corrects "proofs"—trial impressions made of the pages of set type—before printing a job.) You probably stared in dismay at those obvious slips that somehow managed to escape your eye. Why, you may have asked yourself, was I penalized for what were obviously just careless mistakes? In response, you could ask another question: why do businesses and industries spend so much money making sure that their final written products are as free from errors as possible?

Basically, the answer is related to an audience's perception of the writer (or the business). If a paper, letter, report, or advertisement contains even minor mistakes, they act as a form of "static" that interferes with the communication process. The reader's attention is shifted away from the message to some fundamental questions about the writer. A reader might wonder why you did not have enough pride in your work to check it before handing it in. Even worse, a reader might question your basic competence as a writer and researcher. As the number of errors in proportion to the total number of words rises, the reader's distraction grows. In college such static can have serious consequences. Studies conducted in New York City colleges, for example, revealed that readers would tolerate on the average only five to six basic errors in a three-hundred-word passage before assigning a student to a remedial English course. The point is that careless mistakes are rhetorically damaging to you as a writer; they undermine your voice and authority.

Once you have revised your paper thoroughly—considering the effectiveness of the thesis, the clarity of the organization, the strength of the opening and the conclusion, and any other problems in previous papers that you have listed in your revision log—you are ready to proofread. The secret of proofreading is to make sure that you read each word as you have written it. If you read too quickly, your mind often "corrects" or skips over problems. Force yourself to read each word exactly by moving a ruler or a piece of paper slowly down the page, reading aloud as you go. When you combine looking at the page with listening to the words, you increase your chances of catching mistakes that are visual (such as misspellings) and those that are aural (such as awkward phrasings).

Misspellings are so common that they need special attention. Everyone misspells some words; even the most experienced writer, teacher, or editor, has to check a dictionary for correct spellings of certain words. English is a particularly tricky language, for words are not always spelled the way in which they are pronounced. English has silent *e*'s as in *live*; *ph*'s and *gh*'s that sound like *f*'s as in *phone* and *tough*; silent *ough*'s and *gh*'s as in *through* and *bright*. It is easy to get confused about when to double consonants before adding *–ed* to the end of a word or when to drop the final *e* before adding *–able*. All of these difficulties are perfectly natural and common. No one expects you to remember how to spell every word in your speaking vocabulary, but people do expect that you will check your writing for misspelled words.

Most misspellings can be eliminated if you do two things. First, recognize the kinds of words you are likely to misspell; learn when not to trust your instinct, particularly with words that sound alike, such as *there* and *their* and *its* and *it's*. Second, once you have finished your paper, go back and check your spelling. If you have written your paper on a word processor that has a spell check function, be sure to run it. However, do not rely on that type of checking alone; for example, spell checkers won't show you that you've used *there* when you mean *their*. Always have a dictionary at hand. Go through your essay and look up every word that might be a problem. Doing these two things will go a long way toward eliminating misspellings in your papers.

VISUALIZING REVISION

Robert Mankoff's cartoon does not really "visualize" revision, but it does remind us, as writers, that even when we have what we regard as a "final" draft, our writing task is not always over. Even though we have labored over every sentence, word, and mark of punctuation, now it is time to recruit friends, colleagues, and significant others for additional editing and proofreading tasks. "Does this make sense?" we ask. "Is my point clear? What do you think about my opening? Does my title work?" And, then, after we have cleared these hurdles, we still have one more: Published writing—books, essays, articles, advertisements—has all had the careful scrutiny of professional editors who, in turn, suggest changes, deletions, and additions to our "final" product. The process of revision is demanding (and yes, every writer gets tired and frustrated), but every writer knows that the final product is that much better for all the attention that it has received.

"I like it—it's wonderfully editable."

REVISERS AT WORK

To help you think about what is involved in revising and to help you see how it actually takes place, earlier chapters of this text include draft and final revised versions of student papers. In this chapter you can see a professional writer at work. You can follow the evolution of Gordon Grice's essay on the black widow spider from its earliest journal entries through its published form in *Harper's* magazine. This case study includes sample journal entries and an interview with Grice in which he discusses how he revises his work and why he made some of the changes that he did in the course of revising. See page 544.

VISIT THE PRENTICE HALL READER'S WEBSITE

When you have finished reading an essay, check out the additional material available at the *Reader's* Website at www.prenhall. com/miller. For each reading, you will find a list of related readings connected with the topic or the author; additional background information; a group of relevant hot-linked Web resources; and still more writing suggestions.

REVISING

Does your school have a Writing Lab or a Writing Center where you can get help with your papers? Does it have a Website? Can you get on-line help? Can you submit a draft by e-mail? The Web has extensive resources available for writers trying to revise. You can find advice, visit a "virtual" Writing Center, and discover what an OWL is. Check out the links on the *Reader's* Website.

Revision Case Study
Caught in the Widow's Web

Gordon Grice

Gordon Grice earned his B.A. at Oklahoma State University and his M.F.A. at the University of Arkansas. Grice has published essays and poems in a wide range of literary magazines. His first collection of essays was The Red Hourglass: Lives of the Predators *(1998). The following essay, originally titled "The Black Widow," first appeared in the* High Plains Literary Review. *Grice reworked it for its appearance in* Harper's *magazine and then again for* The Red Hourglass. *The version reproduced here appeared in* Harper's.

On Writing: *Widely praised for his precise and detailed attention to the "micro-world," Grice has said, "Personal observation and experience are part of my approach to writing as a whole. I like to delve into the details and give my readers the feeling of being there and having their own hands in it."*

BEFORE READING

Connecting: How do you feel about spiders? To what do you attribute your reaction?

Anticipating: In the Glossary at the back of this book, look up the word *symbol.* As you read, think about the extent to which the black widow is a symbol for Grice.

1   I hunt black widows. When I find one, I capture it. I have found them in discarded wheels and tires and under railroad ties. I have found them in house foundations and cellars, in automotive shops and toolsheds, in water meters and rock gardens, against fences and in cinder-block walls.

2   Black widows have the ugliest webs of any spider, messy-looking tangles in the corners and bends of things and under logs and debris. Often the widow's web is littered with leaves. Beneath it lie the husks of consumed insects, their antennae stiff as gargoyle horns; on them and the surrounding ground are splashes of the spider's white urine, which looks like bird guano and smells of ammonia even at a distance of several feet.

This fetid material draws scavengers—ants, sow bugs, crickets, roaches, and so on—which become tangled in vertical strands of silk reaching from the ground up into the web. The widow climbs down and throws gummy silk onto this new prey. When the insect is seriously tangled but still struggling, the widow cautiously descends and bites it, usually on a leg joint. This is a killing bite; it pumps poison into the victim. As the creature dies, the widow delivers still more bites, injecting substances that liquefy the organs. Finally it settles down to suck the liquefied innards out of the prey, changing position two or three times to get it all.

Widows reportedly eat mice, toads, tarantulas—anything that 4 wanders into that remarkable web. I have never witnessed a widow performing a gustatory act of that magnitude, but I have seen them eat scarab beetles heavy as pecans, carabid beetles strong enough to prey on wolf spiders, cockroaches more than an inch long, and hundreds of other arthropods of various sizes.

Many widows will eat as much as opportunity allows. One ag- 5 gressive female I raised had an abdomen a little bigger than a pea. She snared a huge cockroach and spent several hours subduing it, then three days consuming it. Her abdomen swelled to the size of a largish marble, its glossy black stretching to a tight red-brown. With a different widow, I decided to see whether that appetite really was insatiable. I collected dozens of large crickets and grasshoppers and began to drop them into her web at a rate of one every three or four hours. After catching and devouring her tenth victim, this bloated widow fell from her web, landing on her back. She remained in this position for hours, making only feeble attempts to move. Then she died.

The first thing people ask when they hear about my fascination with 6 the widow is why I am not afraid. The truth is that my fascination is rooted in fear.

I have childhood memories that partly account for this. When 7 I was six my mother took my sister and me into the cellar of our farmhouse and told us to watch as she killed a widow. With great ceremony she produced a long stick (I am tempted to say a ten-foot pole) and, narrating her technique in exactly the hushed voice she used for discussing religion or sex, went to work. Her flashlight beam found a point halfway up the cement wall where two marbles hung together— one a crisp white, the other a shiny black. My mother ran her stick through the dirty silver web around them. As it tore it sounded like the crackling of paper in fire. The black marble rose on thin legs to fight off the intruder. My mother smashed the widow onto the stick and carried it up into the light. It was still kicking its remaining legs. Mom scraped it against the floor, grinding it into a paste. Then she returned for the white marble—the widow's egg sac. This, too, came to an abrasive end.

8   My mother's stated purpose was to teach us how to recognize and deal with a dangerous creature that we would probably encounter on the farm. But, of course, we also took away the understanding that widows were actively malevolent, that they waited in dark places to ambush us, that they were worthy of ritual disposition, like an enemy whose death is not sufficient but must be followed by the murder of his children and the salting of his land and whose unclean remains must not touch our hands.

9   The odd thing is that so *many* people, some of whom presumably did not first encounter the widow in such an atmosphere of mystic reverence, hold the widow in awe. Various friends have told me that the widow's bite is always fatal to humans—in fact, it almost never is. I have heard told for truth that goods imported from the Orient are likely to be infested with widows and that women with bouffant hairdos have died of widow infestation. Any contradiction of such tales is received as if it were a proclamation of atheism.

10   We project our archetypal terrors onto the widow. It is black; it avoids the light; it is a voracious carnivore. Its red markings suggest blood. The female's habit of eating her lovers invites a strangely sexual discomfort; the widow becomes an emblem for a man's fear of extending himself into the blood and darkness of a woman, something like the legendary Eskimo vampire that takes the form of a fanged vagina.

11   The widow's venom is, of course, a sound reason for fear. The venom contains a neurotoxin that can produce sweats, vomiting, swelling, convulsions, and dozens of other symptoms. The variation in symptoms from one person to the next is remarkable. The constant is pain. A useful question for a doctor trying to diagnose an uncertain case: "Is this the worst pain you've ever felt?" A "yes" suggests a diagnosis of a black widow bite. Occasionally people die from widow bites. The very young and the very old are especially vulnerable. Some people seem to die not from the venom but from the infection that may follow: because of its habitat, the widow carries dangerous microbes.

12   Researchers once hypothesized that the virulence of the venom was necessary for killing beetles of the scarabaeidae family. This family contains thousands of species, including the June beetle and the famous dung beetle that the Egyptians thought immortal. All the scarabs have thick, strong bodies and unusually tough exoskeletons, and many of them are common prey for the widow. The tough hide was supposed to require a particularly nasty venom. As it turns out,

the venom is thousands of times more virulent than necessary for this purpose.

No one has ever offered a sufficient explanation for the dangerous venom. It provides no evolutionary advantages: all of the widow's prey would find lesser toxins fatal, and there is no particular benefit in killing or harming larger animals. A widow that bites a human being or other large animal is likely to be killed.

Natural selection favors the inheritance of useful characteristics that arise from random mutation and tends to extinguish disadvantageous traits. All other characteristics, the ones that neither help nor hinder survival, are preserved or extinguished at random as mutation links them with useful or harmful traits. Many people—even many scientists—assume that every animal is elegantly engineered for its ecological niche, that every bit of an animal's anatomy and behavior has a functional explanation. This assumption is false. Evolution sometimes produces flowers of natural evil—traits that are neither functional nor vestigial but utterly pointless.

We want the world to be an ordered room, but in a corner of that room there hangs an untidy web. Here the analytical mind finds an irreducible mystery, a motiveless evil in nature; here the scientist's vision of evil comes to match the vision of a God-fearing country woman with a ten-foot pole. No idea of the cosmos as elegant design accounts for the widow. No idea of a benevolent God is comfortable in a world with the widow. She hangs in her web, that marvel of design, and defies reason.

QUESTIONS ON SUBJECT AND PURPOSE

1. Why is Grice so fascinated by black widow spiders? To what does he trace his fascination?
2. What particular aspects of the black widow spider does Grice focus on?
3. What does the spider symbolize to Grice?

QUESTIONS ON STRATEGY AND AUDIENCE

1. Why does Grice begin with the simple sentence "I hunt black widows." What is the effect of that sentence?
2. Grice divides his essay into three sections through the use of additional white space (after paragraphs 5 and 10). How does that division reflect the structure of the essay?

3. What assumptions could Grice make about his audience and their attitudes toward spiders?

QUESTIONS ON VOCABULARY AND STYLE

1. In describing how his mother killed the spider, Grice writes, "With great ceremony she produced a long stick (I am tempted to say a ten-foot pole)" (paragraph 7). Why does he add the material in the parentheses?

2. What is the effect of labeling the spider a "voracious carnivore"? To what extent is that an accurate phrase?

3. Be prepared to define the following words: *fetid* (paragraph 3), *gustatory* (4), *malevolent* (8), *bouffant* (9), *voracious* (10), *carnivore* (10), *virulence* (12), *niche* (14), *vestigial* (14).

WRITING SUGGESTIONS

1. For Your Journal. We tend to ignore the natural details that surround us. Try looking closely, even minutely, at the things around you. For example, take a magnifying glass and carefully examine an insect or a plant leaf. Take a walk and sit down with your journal. Study the landscape around you. Make journal entries about what you are suddenly able to see.

2. For a Paragraph. Select one of your journal entries and expand the entry into a descriptive paragraph. Try to make your reader see with you.

3. For an Essay. Nature can be seen and interpreted in many ways. Look back over your journal entries, look around you, select some natural thing—a living creature, a plant or leaf, an event, or even a landscape. In an essay, describe it to your reader in such a way as to reveal a significance. You are not writing an encyclopedia article or a guide book for tourists; you are seeing a meaning.

4. For Research. Grice does not attempt to tell the "full" story of the black widow. Research the black widow (or any other poisonous insect or reptile) using traditional library resources. You could also explore resources on the World Wide Web and various other on-line electronic information sources. Your object is not to present an informational report—"here is everything about the subject." Rather, try to formulate a thesis about your subject. For example, you might explore the myths and symbols that have attached themselves to your subject or the role of the creature in our environment or the "lethalness" of its venom.

WEBSITE LINK

How did Grice get interested in black widow spiders? In an on-line interview at one of the electronic bookstores he explains his interest in spiders, snakes, and other predatory creatures.

WRITING LINK: CREATING VIVID DESCRIPTIONS

Look closely at the first five paragraphs in Grice's essay. How does he create vivid images? To what extent does he use precise nouns, vivid verbs, and arresting details? What can writers learn from Grice's descriptive techniques?

JOURNAL ENTRIES:
THE BLACK WIDOW

Gordon Grice

Grice began his essay in January 1993 in a journal. He wrote a series of consecutive entries through February, essentially drafting the essay from beginning to end. Then he put the essay aside for a year. "One day, when I was substitute-teaching a shop class in high school and the kids were all busy," Grice commented, "I took it out and rewrote the opening. The next journal I sent it to accepted it for publication." This published version, originally titled "The Black Widow," appeared in the High Plains Literary Review. *The essay was then rewritten and reprinted in* Harper's *magazine as "Caught in the Widow's Web." He continued to work on the piece for inclusion in his collection of essays,* The Red Hourglass: Inner Lives of the Predators *(1998).*

Reproduced here are some of the original journal entries for the essay. Grice printed his entries in ink in a spiral-bound notebook. His revisions of those entries are preserved here. Crossed-out words are indicated by a line running through the word. Additions added above or to the side of the crossouts are reproduced here in brackets.

ENTRY 1

1/16/93

1 Idea for essay: What people have nightmares about. Paul dreamed of people vomiting up human flesh, knew he was in hell.

1/16/93

2 The black widow has the ugliest web of any spider. The orb weavers ~~have~~ make those seemingly delicate nets that poets have ~~turned~~ traditionally used as symbols of imagination (~~Dickinson~~), order (~~Shakespeare~~), [and] perfection. The sheet-web weavers make spiders weave crisp linens for the lawn [on the lawn] — ~~some of these have impressive-looking underlayers and tunnels~~. But the widow makes messy-looking tangles in the corners and bends of things and under logs and debris. Often the web ~~has~~ is littered with leaves. Beneath ~~the web~~ it lie the ~~corpses~~ husks of insect prey, [their antenna stiff as gargoyle horns], cut loose and dropped; on them and the surrounding ground are splashes of the spider's white ~~dung~~ [urine], which looks like bird ~~urine~~ [guano] and smells of ammonia even at a distance of several feet.

~~If these spiders this ground is biolog~~ This fetid material draws scavengers—ants, sow bugs, crickets, roaches, and so on—which ~~walk into~~ become tangled in vertical strands of ~~web~~ [silk] reaching from the ground up into the web. The widow comes down and, with a bicycling ~~motion~~ of the hind [pair of] legs, throws [gummy] ~~liquid~~ silk onto this new prey.

Point of Comparison: Compare this entry with paragraphs 2 and 3 in "Caught in the Widow's Web."

ENTRY 2

1/20/93
When the prey is seriously tangled but still struggling, the widow   3
cautiously descends and bites the creature, usually on a leg joint. This is ~~the~~ a killing bite. ~~She will~~; it pumps neurotoxin into the victim. She will deliver a series of bites as the creature dies; these later bites inject substances that liquify the organs. And finally she will settle down to suck the liquified innards out of the prey, changing her ~~position~~ [place] two or three times to get [it] all.

Point of Comparison: Compare this entry with paragraph 3 in "Caught in the Widow's Web."

ENTRY 3

The [architectural] complexity[ities] of the widow-web ~~are beyond~~   4
~~us. As a home~~ do not particularly impress the widow. ~~She~~ They move around in these webs ~~essentially~~ [almost] blind, yet they never snare themselves, misstep, or ~~lose their wa~~ get lost. In fact, a widow forcibly removed from her web and put back at a different point does not seem confused; she will quickly return to her habitual resting place. ~~All this~~

Point of comparison: This material does not appear in "Caught in the Widow's Web."

ENTRY 4

2/3/93
The first thing people ask when they [hear] about my fascination with   5
the widow is why ~~I'm~~ [am] not afraid. The truth is that my fascination is rooted in fear.

I know a man who as a child was frightened by ~~the~~ his preacher's   6
~~claim that~~ invitation to eat the flesh of Jesus. The man's [worst] night-

mares are about ~~cannibals. His hobby~~ vomiting up human meat. The thing he likes best to watch [horror] ~~movies~~ [films] about cannibals.

Point of comparison: Compare this entry with paragraph 6 in "Caught in the Widow's Web."

ENTRY 5

2/4/93

7   There is, of course, one pragmatic reason for fearing the widow.

8   These markings include a pair of triangles on the ventral side of the abdomen—the infamous "hourglass"

9   The widow's venom is, of course, a soundly pragmatic reason for fear. The venom contains a neurotoxin that produces chills, [sweats], vomiting, ~~and~~ fiery pain, ~~sometimes~~ [and] convulsions and death. ~~Death It is [And]~~ Occasionally ~~a person~~ [people] dies from ~~the~~ widow bites ~~but less than the~~ Some researchers ~~have theorized~~ [hypothesized] that the virulence of the venom was necessary for killing ~~scarab~~ beetles of the scarab family. This family contains thousands of ~~beetles~~ [species], including the june bug and the famous ~~Egyptian~~ dung beetle the Egyptians thought immortal. All the scarabs have thick, strong bodies and [unusually] tough exoskeletons, and ~~these~~ many of them are common prey for the widow.

Point of Comparison: Compare this entry with paragraphs 11 and 12 in "Caught in the Widow's Web."

ENTRY 6

2/9/93

10   The widow, it was proposed, needs a strong venom to kill such thick-hided creatures. But this idea is yet another that owes more to ~~the widow's~~ dark romance ~~than~~ with the widow than to hard evidence. The venom is thousands of times too virulent ~~for this than~~ [for] this purpose. ~~We see~~ An emblem of immortality ~~trapped~~, killed by a creature ~~thing~~ whose most distinctive [blood-colored] markings people invariably describe as an hourglass: scientists, being human, want to see a deep causality.

11   But no one has ever offered a sufficient explanation for the widow's [dangerous] venom. It ~~has no~~ provides no evolutionary advantages: all of ~~its~~ [the widow's] prey items ~~are~~ would find lesser toxins fatal, and there is no particular ~~advantage to~~ benefit in harming or killing larger animals. A widow biting a human or other large animal is almost certain to be killed. Evolution does occasionally produce such flowers of [natural] evil—traits that are not functional, but ves-

tiges of lost functions, but ~~pure~~ utterly pointless. ~~This~~ Such ~~things~~ [traits] come about because natural selection merely ~~works against~~ [favors] the inheritance of useful ~~traits~~ [characteristics] that arise from random mutation and extinguishes disadvantageous characteristics. All other characteristics, the ones that neither help nor hinder survival, are preserved [or not] (almost) randomly; when mutation links a useless but harmless trait to a useful one, both are preserved. Many people—even many scientists—assume that every animal is elegantly engineered for its ecological niche, that every bit of an animal's anatomy and behavior ~~can be~~ has a functional explanation. This assumption is false. Nothing in evolutionary theory sanctions it; fact refutes it. ~~It is in fact a lapse into magical thinking. But we want to order and explain things. But We all want order and order in the world and in the room of order In the ordered rooms~~

We want the world to be an ordered room, but in a corner of   12
that room there hangs an untidy web ~~that says~~. Here the analytic mind finds an irreducible mystery, a motiveless evil in nature; [and] the scientist's vision of evil comes to match the vision of a religious woman with a ten-foot pole. No picture of the cosmos as elegant design accounts for the widow. No picture of a benevolent God explains the widow. She hangs in her haphazard web (that marvel of design) defying teleology.

Point of Comparison: Compare the entry with paragraphs 12–15 of "Caught in the Widow's Web."

QUESTIONS FOR DISCUSSION

1. What thought or idea appears to trigger Grice's essay? Does he ever return to that idea in the sections of the journal reproduced here?

2. How does the black widow's web differ from those of most spiders?

3. What is puzzling about the widow's venom?

4. What associations do we have with the hourglass (paragraph 10)?

5. In what sense does the widow's web "defy teleology" (paragraph 12)? What is teleology?

6. What are the most common types of revisions that Grice makes in these journal entries?

7. Be prepared to define the following words: *gargoyle* (paragraph 2), *scavengers* (2), *neurotoxin* (3), *innards* (3), *habitual* (4), *pragmatic* (9), *exoskeletons* (9), *causality* (10), *vestiges* (11), *benevolent* (12).

WRITING SUGGESTIONS ON THE REVISIONS

1. **For Your Journal.** First, make a list of each revision that Grice made as he wrote in his journal. See if you can group these changes in any categories. Then make a list of the differences between one of the original entries in the journal and the corresponding paragraphs in the published version of the essay.

2. **For a Paragraph.** Formulate a thesis that explains one of the categories or types of revision that Grice made as he wrote in his journal. Use examples to support that thesis. Then formulate a thesis that explains the nature of the revision that Grice made from one of the journal entries to the corresponding paragraphs in the published version of the essay.

3. **For an Essay.** Using the evidence that you gathered for your journal entry, write an essay in which you analyze the revisions that Grice made as he wrote the first version of the essay in his journal. Alternatively, using the evidence that you gathered for your journal entry, write an essay in which you analyze the revisions that Grice made from the entries in the journal to the published version of the essay.

A CONVERSATION
WITH GORDON GRICE

Q: "The Black Widow" began as a series of dated entries in a notebook. Is that your usual way of working?

A: No, I rarely use that technique. I don't use it when I have a good idea of where I'm going. Keeping a journal helps me when I don't really have a good subject in mind. I kept this one while I was taking a nonfiction workshop, because I had to turn in pieces on deadline and didn't really know how to start.

Q: An entry in your notebook mentioned a friend's nightmare about cannibalism and hell. This idea comes up again in the notebook draft of "The Black Widow," but you dropped it in the published versions.

A: That idea somehow launched me into the essay about the widow. It set me thinking on the subject of things that are simultaneously attractive and terrifying—for me, the widow is such a thing. I mentioned my friend in the essay to make this point about the widow. As soon as I brought the piece into the workshop, however, someone pointed out that the dream didn't fit in. I hated to drop it because I thought it was really interesting, but I realized it was distracting.

Q: In the notebook, you started with a section about the web. In the first printed version, that section comes later, after a new part about your personal experiences with black widows. Why did you add the new beginning?

A: I had tried to get the essay published, but I wasn't having any luck. I theorized that the opening wasn't catchy enough. I also thought the piece didn't quite fit any magazine I could think of— it was too arty for a science magazine, and most of the essays I saw in literary journals had more personal material than I had used. My idea was to let editors see right away that it was a personal essay and at the same time to jazz up the opening.

I wrote about getting young widows all over my arms because I thought the danger made it interesting. I carried the piece around with me until I got the chance to work on it. I was substitute-teaching a middle school shop class when I scribbled down the new opening. That was almost two years after I started the essay.

Q: Most of that new introduction was dropped when the essay was reprinted in *Harper's*. Why?

A: An editor at *Harper's* made that cut. I simple agreed to it. She was trimming for space and considered that part expendable.

Q: The *Harper's* version also changed the final word of the essay, from *teleology* to *reason*.

A: The editor at *Harper's* asked me to change *teleology* because she thought the word was too obscure. She thought a lot of readers wouldn't be familiar with it. Unfortunately, neither of us could come up with a good synonym. Our compromise was *reason*, which I didn't like. I reinstated *teleology* when I rewrote the piece for *The Red Hourglass*.

Q: What other changes have you made in the book version?

A: It's five or six times longer, so I covered a lot of new material. For example, I developed the section about the widow's venom with some case studies. I added details and changed the overall shape of the essay. I changed word choices and sentence structures as well.

Q: In general, how do you approach the job of revising?

A: It's different every time. Basically, I have a bag of tricks, and I try them until something works.

When I started revising the black widow piece, I went to a junkyard with an empty mayonnaise jar and caught a widow. I kept her on my desk as I wrote. I kept observing interesting things I had never thought of putting in the piece before. If I'm writing about something I can't catch in a jar, I find some other way to research it. I hit the library or interview people. This helps me find interesting details that will fire up a boring draft.

I try to figure out what's working in a draft and what's not. I put it away for a while so I can get some distance on it. I get other people to criticize it. I don't trust anybody who likes everything I write or anybody who hates everything I write.

I analyze a draft like this: I want something interesting in the first sentence. Usually my first draft begins badly, so my job on revision is to decapitate the essay. I cut until I hit something interesting. Or I may find an interesting part somewhere else in the draft and move it to the beginning. I move things around a lot. If I get frustrated trying to keep it all straight on the computer, I print it out and sit on the floor with scissors rearranging things.

I look for long sections of exposition or summary and try to break these up with vivid examples or details. If some part is boring, I try to think of ways to make it into a story.

I fiddle with the sentences as I go. I try to cut all the passive voice verbs and all the *be* verbs. I strike filler words like *very*. If it doesn't sound right without the filler, I take that as a clue that something's wrong with the ideas themselves. I aim for the prose to sound simple, even if the ideas are complex.

FINDING, USING, AND DOCUMENTING SOURCES

FINDING SOURCES

All effective writing involves some form of research. To write a laboratory report in chemistry, you use the information gathered from performing the experiment. To write an article for the student newspaper on your college's latest tuition increase, you include information gathered in interviews with those involved in making that decision. To answer a midterm examination, you marshal evidence from lecture notes and from required reading.

As these examples demonstrate, you may use a wide variety of sources when you research any particular topic.

- *Firsthand knowledge.* Your own observations and experiences play a major role in much of your writing. Such knowledge can be simple and acquired easily (before writing a review of a restaurant, you would sample the cuisine and service) or complex and gathered laboriously (scientists will study a virus for years, gathering information and testing out hypotheses by performing experiments).

- *Printed knowledge.* The bulk of your knowledge for the papers you will typically write in college comes from printed sources, including reference works such as dictionaries and encyclopedias, books, articles in magazines and journals, articles in newspapers, and government publications.

- *Electronic documents.* The Internet and the World Wide Web contain important sources of information. Many magazines, newspapers, and academic journals can be found in electronic form. Some journals, in fact, are available only electronically. Organizations and even individuals maintain home pages with valuable information. Our research in the future increasingly will be done through computers.

- *Interviewing.* On many topics, you can gather information by talking with the people involved. A newspaper reporter writing about the latest tuition increase, for example, would have to rely on information provided by administrators and budget analysts. Thanks to the increasing use of electronic mail (e-mail), interviewing no longer requires face-to-face contact or a telephone call.

Although all writing uses sources, not all writing meets the special considerations that we associate with a research paper. Not only does a research paper document its sources, but it also exhibits a particular approach to its subject. A research paper is not just a collection of information about a subject. Instead, a research paper poses a particular question or thesis about its subject and then sets out to answer that question or test the validity of that thesis.

In important ways, you should approach the research that you do for a college paper in the same way that a scientist sets about exploring a problem. The idea behind research—all research—is to isolate a particular aspect of a subject, to become an expert in that defined area, and to present an original or new conclusion about that material. Because research papers have a thesis, they differ significantly from the informational overviews that we find in encyclopedia articles. Many writers confuse the two forms of writing. The confusion probably dates back to grade school when a teacher assigned a report on, say, Jupiter. What most of us did was go to the encyclopedia, look up "Jupiter," and copy down the entry. That might have been an appropriate response for a grade school assignment, but such a strategy will never work for a college research paper.

USING REFERENCE BOOKS AS A STARTING POINT: ENCYCLOPEDIAS AND DICTIONARIES

If you do not already have a fairly detailed knowledge about your subject, encyclopedias and dictionaries can be good places to begin your research. Before using such reference works, however, you should remember three important points. First, encyclopedias and dictionaries are only good as *starting points*, providing just a basic overview of a subject. You will never be able to rely solely on such sources for college-level research. Second, encyclopedias and dictionaries range from general works that cover a wide range of subjects (such as the *Encyclopaedia Britannica*, *Encyclopedia Americana*, and *Collier's Encyclopedia*) to highly specialized works focused around a single area or subject. Third, although some encyclopedias are available in electronic formats (for example, the *Encyclopaedia Britannica* has a version known as *Britannica Online*), many of the most detailed specialized encyclopedias and dictionaries are currently available only in print form.

Because general encyclopedias provide information about a variety of subjects, they can never contain as much information about a single subject as you can find in an encyclopedia that specializes in that subject. For this reason, you might begin any search with a specialized encyclopedia. The word *specialized* in this sense refers primarily to the more focused subject coverage that these works offer; most of the articles are still written in nontechnical language. The word *dictionary*, as it is used in the titles of these works, means essentially the same thing as *encyclopedia*—a collection of articles of varying lengths arranged alphabetically.

Your school is likely to have a wide range of specialized encyclopedias and dictionaries. To locate these reference tools, try the following steps:

1. Consult a guide to reference works. The following guides to reference books are widely available in college and university libraries. Use one or more of them to establish a list of possible works to consult.

   - Annie M. Brewer, *Dictionaries, Encyclopedias, and Other Word-Related Books* (3 vols), 4th ed. (1988). Volume 1 is devoted to English-language sources.

   - Kenneth F. Kister, *Kister's Best Encyclopedias: A Comparative Guide to General and Specialized Encyclopedias*, 2nd ed. (1994). This provides detailed descriptions of over five hundred works.

   - Robert Balay, *Guide to Reference Books*, 11th ed. (1996).

2. Check in the library's catalog under the headings "Encyclopedias and Dictionaries—Bibliography," "[Your subject]—Dictionaries," and "[Your subject]—Dictionaries and Encyclopedias."

3. Ask a reference librarian for advice on the specialized sources likely to be relevant to your topic.

4. If your school's library maintains an electronic database, check to see if any dictionaries or encyclopedias are networked into it.

FINDING BOOKS: YOUR LIBRARY'S CATALOG

Every library maintains an index or catalog that lists the material kept in its collections. The record for each item often provides a wide range of information, but it always includes the author's name, the title of the item, and a few of the most important subject headings. Most college and university libraries are now computerized. With all the information about each item contained in one large database, users can access holdings through a computer terminal, searching by keyword(s), by author, by title, by subject, and often by date or place of publication. Most on-line catalogs not only display call numbers but also tell you whether the item you want has been checked out or is on the shelves. Often you no longer need to visit the library to search its catalog; it is accessible at home or in your dorm room via modem or network cabling.

When you start a search for books in your library's catalog, remember these key points:

- Always read the "help" menu the first time you use an on-line catalog. Do not assume that you know how the search functions work. Knowing *how* to search often makes the difference between disappointment and success.
- All catalogs—whether filed in drawers or stored on-line—list only material owned by that particular library or other libraries in the area or state. No library owns a copy of every book.
- Library catalogs list books (by author, title, and a few subject headings) and journals (*only* by title). Library catalogs never include the authors or titles of individual articles contained in journals or magazines.
- Much information on any subject—and generally the most current information—is found in journal articles, not in books. Remember as well that certain subjects may not be treated in books. For example, if a subject is very current or too specialized, no book may have been written about it. Therefore, a search for sources should *never* be limited to the references found in a library catalog.
- In initial searches for information, you are typically looking for subjects—that is, you do not yet have a specific title or author to look up. Searching for subjects in a library

catalog can be considerably more complicated than it might initially seem since the subject headings used in library catalogs are often not what you might expect. Unless you use the subject heading or keyword that the catalog uses, you will not find what you are looking for. The next section offers some advice about subject headings.

CHOOSING THE RIGHT SUBJECT HEADING

The success of any research paper depends in part on finding reliable and appropriate sources of information. For most college papers, your information will come from *secondary* sources, typically books and articles that report the research done by others. Depending on your subject, you might also be able to use *primary* sources—original documents (historical records, letters, works of literature) or the results of original research (laboratory experiments, interviews, questionnaires).

Finding sources is not hard, no matter what your subject, but it does require knowing *how* and *where* to look. A quick tour of your college or university library, with its rows of shelves, or an hour on the World Wide Web will vividly demonstrate that you need a *search strategy*. The first step in that strategy is to find subject headings and keywords that can be used to retrieve information.

The subject headings used in library catalogs and periodical indexes are part of a fixed, interlocking system that is both logically organized and highly structured. The idea is not to list every possible subject heading under which a particular subject might be found but to establish general headings under which related subjects can be grouped. Most libraries use the subject headings suggested by the Library of Congress and published in the *Library of Congress Subject Headings* (LCSH), a five-volume set of books typically found near your library's catalog or in the reference area. In addition, most periodical indexes also use either the same system or one so similar that the LCSH headings will still serve your purpose. As a result, the most efficient way to begin a subject search is to check the LCSH for appropriate subject headings under which books and articles on your subject will be listed.

For example, suppose you were surprised to read that even today, women earn less than 80 percent of what men earn doing the same job. You want to research why that disparity exists and what is being done to remedy that inequity. Exactly what keywords or subject headings would you look under in a catalog, a database, or a periodical index to find appropriate sources: *Women? Work? Job discrimination? Salaries?* Unless you know where to begin, you might waste a considerable amount of time guessing randomly or con-clude (quite wrongly) that your library had no information on the topic.

If you consulted the *Library of Congress Subject Headings*, you would find cross-references that would lead you to the following:

Equal pay for work of comparable value
    USE Pay equity
Equal pay for equal work *(May Subd Geog)*
    Here are entered works on equal pay for jobs that require
    identical skills, responsibilities, and effort. Works on comparable
    pay for jobs that require comparable skills, responsibilities, effort,
    and working conditions are entered under Pay equity.
    BT   Discrimination in employment Wages
    RT   Women—Employment
    —Law and registration *(May Subd Geog)*
        BT Labor laws and legislation
Equal pay for work of comparable value
    USE Pay equity

The LCSH use abbreviations to indicate the relationships among subjects. By following the cross-references, you can conduct a more thorough search. The relationships that are signaled include these:

Equivalence:	USE
Hierarchy:	BT (broader term)
	NT (narrower term)
Association:	RT (related term)

Having checked the key to using the headings, you know from these entries not to search under "Equal pay for comparable work" since the heading is not in bold type; instead, you are told to use "Pay eq-uity." The best heading under which to search for books and articles related to your topic is **"Equal pay for equal work."** The abbrevia-tion *May Subd Geog* indicates that the heading might be subdivided geographically, for example, "Equal pay for equal work—Delaware." The LCSH also suggests other possibilities: for a broader term, use "Discrimination in employment" or "Wages"; for a related term, use "Woman—Employment." You will find relevant information under all of these possible headings. In general, no one subject heading will lead you to all of the books your library has on a particular topic.

Here are a few cautions to keep in mind when using subject headings:

1. Always check the *Library of Congress Subject Headings* first to find the best headings to use for your subject. The quickest way to short-circuit your search strategy is to begin with a heading that you think will work, find nothing, and conclude that your library has no information on that topic.
2. Remember that the headings used might not be as specific as you want. You might need to browse through a group of related materials to find the more precise information you are seeking.

Subject headings use a *controlled vocabulary;* that is, all information about a particular subject is grouped under a single heading with appropriate cross-references from other related headings. For example, if your subject was "capital punishment," you would not also need to look under the headings "death penalty," "execution," or "death row." Controlled vocabularies do, however, place some restrictions on your search strategy. As we've mentioned, subject headings aren't always as precise as you would like them to be. Furthermore, timely or very recent subjects might not appear within the classification scheme for several years.

An on-line alternative to subject heading searches is *keyword* searching. A keyword is a significant word, almost always a noun, that is used in the titles (or someplace else in the computerized record) of books, reports, or articles. By combining keywords, you can conduct very precise searches. You will learn how to combine keywords and what "operators" to use (words such as *and, near,* and *or* that indicate the relationships between those keywords) only if you take the time to study the help menu. Keyword searches that do not specify the relationship between the words tend to produce unwieldy strings of "hits"—records that contain those words. The computer just lists every record that contains those words anywhere in it, even if the records themselves are completely unrelated to your topic or to each other. Keyword searches are especially valuable when you cannot find the appropriate subject heading (for example, "glass ceiling," referring to the limited promotion possibilities for someone within a company or organization) or when you want to combine several concepts (for example, "children and violence and television").

FINDING SOURCES ON THE WORLD WIDE WEB

The Web is expanding at a prodigious rate—in 1997, it contained an estimated 320 million pages; in 1999, it had grown to 800 million pages; by the time you read this, it will probably be several billion pages. Given that growth, it is not surprising that no single search engine (the term applied to software programs that index information on the Web) can retrieve it all. What this means is that for the best results on a research project, you should use at least two different search engines. Unfortunately, every list of relevant sites retrieved is likely to contain some dead links—that is, the information is no longer available at the listed site. It's frustrating to encounter such links, but it's also common.

Retrieving relevant sites of information is only one problem. Anyone can post anything on the Web. Just because it is there, just because the Web pages look professional, there is no guarantee that you can trust every document you retrieve. Evaluating Web sources is covered a little later in this appendix. Don't forget to look at the advice there (and on the *Reader*'s Website at www.prenhall.com/miller) before you start using Web sources to write your research paper.

Choosing a Search Engine

In searching the Web, like searching most libraries' computerized catalogs, you have two initial choices: you can search by subject or by keyword. A number of sites offer indexes or catalogs of Web documents arranged by subject. A good place to start is Netscape's Search page, which contains an up-to-date index linked to the major commercial directories. One popular and effective subject organized site is Yahoo!, where human editors have selected the best information available on the Web and presented it in a large, comprehensive, and well-organized directory.

You can also search the Web by keywords or key phrases. Search engines such as AltaVista and Google.com are both highly rated keyword engines. The problem with most keyword searches—like keyword searches in an on-line library catalog—is that they deliver a huge number of "hits" or references that are listed together only because each one contains—somewhere—the word or phrase you typed in. An initial search for a single word might turn up thousands of documents, the majority of which are irrelevant to the topic you want. Just as in the case of a keyword search in an on-line library catalog, you need to narrow your search by using precise terms and "operators." If your search turns up 100,000 seemingly relevant sites, don't just walk away from the computer in frustration. You need to learn how to tailor your requests to control the information you get back. For some starting tips, see the box "Web Searching Tips."

Web Searching Tips

A good place to start is to visit the *Reader*'s Website at www.prenhall.com/miller. There you will find:

- A hot-linked list of the major research engines with comments on their strengths and weaknesses.
- Detailed suggestions for defining your Web queries more precisely.
- Advice on how to evaluate the accuracy of Web information, with some helpful hotlinks.
- Some tips on how searching on-line databases can help you better define your searches on the Web.
- How to find photographs or images on the Web using a search engine.

Some essentials:

1. As you research, develop a list of synonyms or related subjects. Vital resources might be irretrievable, if you don't enter the right key word or the exact subject heading. A good search generally involves searching multiple terms rather than searching a single word or phrase.

2. Use at least two search engines in every Web search. Remember different engines will retrieve different documents.

3. Read the help screens on each search engine to get the most precise advice on tailoring your search and organizing its results.

4. Learn to use *operators*—words or symbols that signal the relationship between words in a search entry. A large list of common ones can be found at the *Reader*'s Website. Here are a few examples from that list that are particularly effective in Web searches:

" "   Place a phrase in quotation marks to find occurrences of that particular phrase in exactly that order rather than occurrences of each individual word in a phrase.

Disadvantage: In finding names, such a query would not retrieve names where a middle name or initial intervened or where the first and last name were inverted.

+ or and	Attach the plus as a prefix to a word or the "and" between words to indicate that the word(s) must appear on a page.
− or and not	Attach the minus as a prefix to a word or the "and not" between words to indicate the second word cannot also appear on the page.

Example:

+ Frankenstein + Dracula (both must appear on the same page, although not necessarily side by side)

+ Frankenstein − Dracula (only references to Frankenstein without references to Dracula

* or ?	Most search engines have a symbol for truncation, sometimes called a wild card. Truncation symbols are essential when a word might have alternate spellings (theater or theatre) or alternate endings (theater, theaters, theatrical).

Using Your Search for Subject Headings and Keywords to Revise Your Topic

Your search for subject headings and keywords is also a valuable tool in helping you sharpen and define your topic. Typically, despite the most diligent efforts to find a specific topic within a larger subject, you will begin your research strategy with a topic that is really still a subject, too large to research effectively or write about within the limits of a freshman English research paper. If the subject headings you use yield a mountain of published research, obviously you need to focus your topic more precisely.

Finding Magazines, Journals, and Newspapers

The greater amount of information on almost any topic will be found not in books but in magazines and journals. (College and university libraries generally do not use the term *magazine;* they refer to *periodicals* or *serials.* These two terms indicate that the publication appears periodically or that it is an installment of a larger series.) You'll find that most of the thousands of magazines sold at your local newsstand—whether issued weekly, biweekly, or monthly—cannot be found in your college or university library. Correspondingly, most of the journals found in your college's periodical room cannot be purchased on a newsstand. They are too specialized; they appeal to too limited an audience. Most, if not all, of your research for college papers should be done in the journals that your library holds.

Increasingly, the way in which libraries provide access to journals is changing. More and more libraries are discontinuing their subscriptions to printed copies of journals that do not have widespread use. Instead, they are providing electronic access to journals. The switch has some significant advantages. Many electronic databases include not just a bare bibliographical citation, or a short abstract, but also the full text of the essay. Some journals are exclusively available as electronic documents. In general, computer technologies have significantly increased our access to periodical literature, although that access is often through an electronic copy.

Increased access doesn't necessarily mean, however, that it is always easier to find the information that you need. For example, there is no single index to all periodical literature. (Similarly, many newspapers are not indexed at all). Instead, you have to consult a variety of indexes, depending on the particular subject that you are researching. Indexes to periodicals are found in two forms. Some come as printed volumes, with regular supplements, that are typically kept in the reference section of your library. Others are available in electronic formats and you search for information using a computer.

Printed indexes require that you search your subject through a series of separate volumes devoted to particular years. Once you have the citations you need, you then have to find the appropriate bound volume of the journals in your library. Admittedly, it can be a slow process. Electronic databases, on the other hand, allow you instantly to conduct a search of many sources published over a multiyear period. If the database includes full-text formats, you can retrieve on the computer screen the text of the article (sometimes even with illustrations). Electronic databases make the task of retrieving the articles simpler. Not surprisingly, printed indexes are gradually being replaced by electronic ones.

When you start your research, first visit your school's library and explore what types of indexes are available. Where are they located? How can you access them? Visit the reference section of the library. Are there printed indexes available? Check your library's computer network or Web page. Are the electronic databases listed there? How are they organized? What is available varies from school to school; there are no absolute certainties about what you will find.

For example, at my university, the library maintains a listing of 190 different databases that are available for searching. This listing includes some that are still only available in print and some that are only available in electronic form. The listing—which can be found on the library's Website—also indicates the date at which the databases started indexing and the subjects and periodicals included in it. The indexes are grouped so that you are first directed to general databases that are good places to start in any search. From here, the indexes are arranged in a series of subject areas: arts and humanities, business and economics, engineering, government, law, and politics, health sciences, life science, physical sciences, and social sciences.

The list of indexes that follows is representative. Your library might have all or only some of these. Different publishers market different databases, so the names might change as well, depending upon the service to which your library subscribes.

- *General Indexes: Good Places to Start.* These four sets of indexes are held by many libraries. Check to see if any or all are available at your school's library.

    Expanded Academic ASAP (Covers 1980–   ). Provides coverage of nearly every discipline. Also indexes national news magazines and newspapers. The largest version includes approximately 1,900 periodicals, 900 of which are offered in a full-text format.

    LexisNexis Academic (Coverage varies depending on the section). Composed of five sections—news, business, legal research, medical, and reference. Also has a detailed "Help" on how to use the different sections.

    The Readers' Guide to Periodical Literature (Covers 1900–   ). Indexes about 240 popular periodicals, most of which can be purchased at newsstands. Available in both printed and electronic forms. Likely to be available in almost every library.

    The New York Times Index (Covers 1851–   ). Indexes news and articles in the newspaper. Since many libraries subscribe to *The Times* and since it is a national newspaper, it can be a useful source of information. The *Index* and a group of other specialized indexes to *The Times* are available in both print and electronic formats.

- *Specialized Periodical Indexes: The Next Step.* About 200 different indexes to the periodical literature in specialized subject areas are available. Any library is likely to have a number of these; most will not have them all. Visit your library and ask what is available. In some cases, similar coverages are provided by indexes that have different names. The listing below includes those most widely held and used:

Art Abstracts/Art Index (Covers 1929–) for indexing; 1994– for abstracts). Indexes periodicals, yearbooks, and museum bulletins in art areas such as archaeology, architecture, art history, city planning, crafts, films, graphic arts, photography.

Biography and Genealogy Master Index. The place to begin for biographical information about people living or dead. Indexes biographical dictionaries, encyclopedias, and other reference sources. Contains references to 12.7 million people. Widely available in print and also in an electronic format.

Biological and Agricultural Index (Covers 1983–). Indexes articles on biology, agriculture, and related sciences in some 240 scholarly and popular periodicals.

Computer Database (Covers 1996–). Indexes journals devoted to computer science, electronic, telecommunications, and microcomputer applications. Full-text format is available for about 100 journals.

ERIC [U.S. Department of Education Resources Information Center] (Covers 1966–). Indexes, with abstracts, articles in professional journals in educations and other educational documents. Most libraries will also have print guides to ERIC materials as well.

General BusinessFile ASAP (Covers 1980–). Indexes and abstracts more than 900 periodicals on a broad range of business, management, trade, technology, marketing, and advertising issues. Full-text format is provided for 400 of the periodicals.

Health Reference Center (Covers 1995–). Indexes medical journals and consumer health magazines as well as health-related articles in more than 1,500 general interest magazines. Many essays are available as full-text.

MLA International Bibliography (Covers 1922–) in print format; 1963–) in electronic format). Indexes articles and books on modern languages, literature, linguistics, and folklore.

PsycINFO (Covers 1887–). Indexes and abstracts over 1,300 journals in areas such as psychiatry, nursing, sociology, education, pharmacology, and physiology.

Sociological Abstracts (Covers 1963–   ). Indexes and abstracts over 2,500 journals in sociology and related areas such as anthropology, economics, demography, political science, and social psychology.

FINDING GOVERNMENT DOCUMENTS

The United States government is the world's largest publisher of statistical information. On many research topics, government documents represent an excellent source of information. Most college libraries house collections of such documents, often located in a special area. Government documents are arranged by a Superintendent of Documents call number system that indicates the agency that released the document. Check with your reference or government documents librarian for help in locating relevant documents for your research. Depending on what indexes your library owns, the following are good starting points for research.

- *Marcive Web DOCS* (Covers 1976–   ). Indexes U.S. government publications cataloged by the Government Printing Office.
- *LexisNexis Statistical* (Covers 1973–   ). Indexes and abstracts statistical publications produced by the federal and state governments, by international and intergovernmental organizations, and by private publishers. Includes a searchable version of the information contained within the *Statistical Abstract of the United States*.
- *Monthly Catalog of U.S. Government Publications* (Covers 1895–   ). Printed catalog held by most libraries.

INTERVIEWING

Depending on your topic, you may find that people—and not just books and articles—will be an important source of information. If you decide to interview someone in the course of your research, you must first choose a person who has special credentials or knowledge about the subject. For example, while working on an essay about campus drinking, you might realize that it would be valuable and interesting to include specific information about the incidence of drinking at your school. To get such data, you could talk to the dean of students or the director of health services. You might also talk to students who acknowledge that they have had problems with alcohol.

Once you have drawn up a list of possible people to interview, you need to plan your interviewing strategy. When you first contact someone to request an interview, always explain who you are, what you want to know, and how you will use the information. Whether you are doing the interview in person, on the telephone, or via e-mail, establish first any crucial guidelines for the interview—students who have problems with binge drinking, for instance, would probably not want to have their real names used in an essay. Once you have agreed on a time for an in-person or telephone interview, be on time. If you are using e-mail for the interview, make sure that your source knows when you will need a reply.

No matter what the circumstances of the interview, always be prepared—do some fairly thorough research about the topic ahead of time. Do not impose on your source by stating, "I've just started to research this problem, and I would like you to tell me everything you know about it." Prepare a list of questions in advance, the more specific the better. However, do not be afraid to ask your source to elaborate on a response. Take notes, but expand those notes as soon as you leave the interview, while the conversation is still fresh in your mind. If you plan to use any direct quotations, make sure that your source is willing to be quoted and that your wording of the quotation is accurate. If possible, check the quotations with your source one final time.

Quotations from interviews should be integrated into your text in the same way as quotations from printed texts—make sure they are essential to your paper, keep them short, use ellipses to indicate omissions, and try to position them at the ends of your sentences. When you are quoting someone who is an expert or an authority, it is best to include a reference to his or her position within your text, setting off that description or job title with commas:

> "We've inherited this notion that if it pops up on a screen and looks good, we think of it as fairly credible," said Paul Gilster, author at *Digital Literacy* (Wiley Computer Publishing, 1997).

USING SOURCES

Most researched writing—and virtually every college research paper—needs to be based on a variety of sources, not just one or two. A single source always represents only one point of view and necessarily contains a limited amount of information. In fact, a wide range of sources are available for any subject—encyclopedias and other reference tools;

books; articles in specialized journals, popular magazines, and newspapers; pamphlets; government documents; interviews; research experiments or studies; electronic mail postings or documents from World Wide Web home pages. Your instructor might specify both the number and the nature of the sources that you are to use, but even if the choice is up to you, make sure that you have a varied set of sources.

EVALUATING SOURCES

Primarily, you want your sources to be accurate, specific, up-to-date, and unbiased. Not every source will meet those criteria. Just because something is in print or posted on a Website doesn't mean that it is true or accurate—just think of the tabloids displayed at any supermarket checkout. In your search for information, you need to evaluate the reliability and accuracy of each source, because you don't want to base your paper on inaccurate, distorted, or biased information.

Obviously, evaluating sources is less difficult if you are already an expert on the subject you are researching. But how can you evaluate sources when you first start to gather information? The problem is not as formidable as it at first seems, for you regularly evaluate written sources when you try to answer day-to-day questions.

For example, if you are interested in information about the best way to lose weight, which of the following sources would you be most likely to trust?

- An article in the *National Enquirer* ("Lose 10 Pounds This Weekend on the Amazing Prune Diet!")
- An article in a popular magazine ("How to Lose a Pound a Week")
- A Web document urging the value of a particular weight reduction program (for example, electrotherapy treatments, a liquid diet plan, or wraps)
- A newspaper article offering advice on weight loss
- A magazine article published in 1930 dealing with diets
- A book written by medical doctors, dietitians, and fitness experts published in 2002
- The Website maintained by the American College of Sports Medicine

You would probably reject the *National Enquirer* article (not necessarily objective, accurate, or reliable), the Web document urging a particular program (potentially biased and likely to exaggerate the value of that particular treatment), and the article published in 1930 (out-of-date). The articles in the popular magazine and the newspaper might have some value but, given the limitations of space and the interests of their audiences, would probably be too general and too sketchy to be of much use. Presumably, the best source of information would be the new book written by obvious experts or the electronic information provided by a recognizable medical authority.

Evaluating printed sources for a research paper is pretty much a comparable activity. A good source must meet the following tests:

1. **Is the source objective?** You can assess objectivity in several ways. For example, does the language used in the work, and even in its title, seem sensational or biased? Is the work published by an organization that might have a special and hence possibly distorted interest in the subject? Does it contain documented facts? Are there bibliographical references, footnotes, and lists of works consulted? How reliable are the "authorities" quoted? Are their titles or credentials cited? The more scholarly and impartial the source seems, the greater the likelihood that the information it contains can be trusted.

2. **Is the source accurate?** Reputable newspapers and magazines make serious efforts to ensure that what they publish is accurate. Similarly, books published by university presses or by large, well-known publishing houses are probably reliable, and journals published by scholarly or professional organizations and the Websites they maintain very likely contain accurate information. For books, you could check reviews to see critical readers' evaluations. The *Book Review Index* and *Book Review Digest* can be found in your library's reference room.

3. **Is the source current?** In general, the more current the source, the greater the likelihood that new discoveries will be considered. Current information might not be crucial in discussing literary works, but it makes a great deal of difference in many other fields.

4. **Is the source authoritative?** What can you find out about the author's or sponsor's credentials? Are they cited anywhere? What does the nature of the source tell you about the author's expertise?

Knowing How Much Quotation to Use

Even though much of the information in a research paper—facts, opinions, statistics, and so forth—will be taken from outside sources, a research paper should never be just a cut-and-paste collection of quotations with a few bridge sentences written by you. The major part of your research paper should be in *your* own words. You can achieve this balance by remembering several points:

- Ask yourself if the quotation is really necessary. If something is common knowledge, you do not need to quote an authority for that information; any information that is widely known or that can be found in general reference works may be included in your own words.
- Keep your quotations as short as possible. Use large chunks of indented direct quotations sparingly, if at all.
- Avoid strings of quotations. You should never pile up quotations in a row. Rather, you should interpret and control the material that you are using and provide transitions for the reader that tie the quotations into your text.
- Learn to paraphrase and summarize instead of giving direct quotations. What is generally important is the idea or the facts that you find in your sources, not the exact words. Paraphrasing means putting the source material into your own words; summarizing goes even further in that you try to condense the quotation into the fewest possible words.
- Use ellipses to shorten quotations. An ellipsis consists of three spaced periods. It is used to indicate that a word, part of a sentence, a whole sentence, or a group of sentences has been omitted from the quotation.

Working Quotations into Your Text

Unless the quotation is only a few words long, try to place it at the end of your sentence. Avoid "sandwich" sentences in which a quotation comes between two parts of your own sentence. If you introduce a several-line quotation into the middle of a sentence, by the end of the sentence the reader will probably have forgotten how your sentence began.

When you place a quotation at the end of a sentence, use a colon or a comma to introduce it. The colon signals that the quotation supports, clarifies, or illustrates the point being made.

One advice book, *Common Sense for Maid, Wife, and Mother,* stated:
"Heated discussion and quarrels, fretfulness and sullen taciturnity
while eating, are as unwholesome as they are unchristian."

Joan Jacobs Brumberg, "The Origins of Anorexia Nervosa" (Chapter 7)

If the introductory statement is not a dependent clause, always use a
comma before the quotation. For example, in the following sentence,
the introductory clause ("As Brian Johnson . . . says") is not a complete sentence.

As Brian Johnson, co-owner of the Dogwater Cafe, a fast-growing
restaurant chain in Florida, says, "When I'm interviewing, I'm
looking for someone with a lot of energy who wants this job more
than anything else."

Charlie Drozdyk, "Into the Loop" (Chapter 6)

If a complete sentence follows a colon, the first word after the colon
may or may not be capitalized. The choice is yours, as long as you are
consistent. However, if the colon introduces a quotation, the first
word following that colon is capitalized.

DOCUMENTING YOUR SOURCES

Research papers require documentation—that is, you need to document or acknowledge all information that you have taken from your
sources. The documentation serves two purposes. First, it acknowledges your use of someone else's work. Whenever you take something
from a published source—statistics, ideas, or opinions, whether quoted
or in your own words—you must indicate where it comes from
(thereby acknowledging that it is not your original work). Otherwise,
you will be guilty of academic dishonesty. Students who borrow material from sources without acknowledgment—that is, who plagiarize—
are subject to some form of academic penalty. Writers and people in
the business world who do so can be sued. Documentation is necessary
for researchers to maintain their integrity. Documentation also serves
a second purpose, however: it gives you greater credibility because your
readers know they can consult and evaluate the sources that you used.

Different disciplines use different citation systems. In most introductory writing classes, you will be asked to use either the MLA
or the APA form of documentation. MLA stands for the Modern
Language Association, an organization of teachers of modern

foreign languages and of English. A full guide to that system can be
found in the *MLA Handbook for Writers of Research Papers* (6th edition, 2003). The APA is the American Psychological Association,
and its style guide, *Publication Manual of the American Psychological
Association* (5th edition, 2001) is widely used in the social sciences.

Documentation systems are standardized; that is, the systems have
a fixed format in which the bibliographical information about the source
is given. Even the marks of punctuation are specified. No one, however,
expects you to memorize a particular citation system. The style guides are
intended to serve as models. You should look at each of your sources, noting its particular features (What type of source was it? How many authors
did it have? In what type of book or journal did it appear?). You then look
for a similar example in the style guide for the citation system that you are
using, and use that sample as a model for your own citation. Citation formats for the types of sources most commonly used in a freshman English
research paper are given on the next few pages. But because the range of
possible sources on any topic is very large, you might have a source that
does not match any of these common examples. For a complete guide,
consult the *MLA Handbook* or the APA *Publication Manual.* Both can be
found in the reference area of your school's library.

ACKNOWLEDGING SOURCES IN YOUR TEXT

Both the MLA and APA systems acknowledge sources with brief parenthetical citations in the text. The reader can then check the "List of
Works Cited" (the MLA title) or "References" (the APA title) at the end
of the paper for the full bibliographical reference. In the MLA system,
the author's last name is given along with the number of the page on
which the information appears. In the APA system, the author's last name
is given along with the year the source was published and, for direct quotations, the page number. Notice in the following examples that the
punctuation within the parentheses varies between the two systems.

Here is how a quotation from an article, "Immuno-Logistics,"
written by Gary Stix, that appeared in the June 1994 issue of *Scientific
American* would be cited in the two systems:

MLA: The major vaccines—those for diphtheria, pertussis,
tetanus, polio, measles, and tuberculosis—cost less to make
than they do to distribute: "The United Nations Children's
Fund, for example, spends a total of $1.50 on the vaccines. .
. . A tenth of what a government then has to disburse for
labor, transportation, training and refrigeration to get these
vaccines to infants and young children" (Stix 102).

APA: The major vaccines—those for diphtheria, pertussis, tetanus, polio, measles, and tuberculosis—cost less to make than they do to distribute: "The United Nations Children's Fund, for example, spends a total of $1.50 on the vaccines. . . . A tenth of what a government then has to disburse for labor, transportation, training and refrigeration to get these vaccines to infants and young children" (Stix, 1994, p. 102).

Note that in both cases, the parenthetical citation comes before any final punctuation.

If you include the author's name in your sentence, you omit that part of the reference within the parentheses.

MLA: According to Gary Stix, the major vaccines—those for diphtheria, pertussis, tetanus, polio, measles, and tuberculosis—cost less to make than they do to distribute: "The United Nations Children's Fund, for example, spends a total of $1.50 on the vaccines. . . . A tenth of what a government then has to disburse for labor, transportation, training and refrigeration to get these vaccines to infants and young children" (102).

APA: According to Gary Stix (1994), the major vaccines—those for diphtheria, pertussis, tetanus, polio, measles, and tuberculosis—cost less to make than they do to distribute: "The United Nations Children's Fund, for example, spends a total of $1.50 on the vaccines. . . . A tenth of what a government then has to disburse for labor, transportation, training and refrigeration to get these vaccines to infants and young children" (p. 102).

Note that in the APA system the date in such cases goes in parentheses after the author's name in the text.

A quotation of more than four lines (MLA) or more than forty words (APA) should be indented or set off from your text. In such cases, the parenthetical citation comes after the indented quotation. Here is how a quotation from "A Weight That Women Carry" by Sallie Tisdale, which appeared in the March 1993 issue of *Harper's* magazine, would be cited in the two systems:

MLA: Sallie Tisdale points out the links between weight "reduction" and the "smallness" that society presses upon women:

> Small is what feminism strives against, the
> smallness that women confront everywhere. All of

> women's spaces are smaller than those of men,
> often inadequate, without privacy. Furniture
> designers distinguish between a man's and a
> woman's chair, because women don't spread out
> like men. (A sprawling woman means only one
> thing.) Even our voices are kept down. (53)

APA: Sallie Tisdale (1993) points out the links between weight
"reduction" and the "smallness" that society presses upon
women:

> Small is what feminism strives against, the
> smallness that women confront everywhere. All of
> women's spaces are smaller than those of men,
> often inadequate, without privacy. Furniture
> designers distinguish between a man's and a
> woman's chair, because women don't spread out
> like men. (A sprawling woman means only one
> thing.) Even our voices are kept down. (p. 53)

Note in both cases that the parenthetical citation comes after the final period.

If you are quoting material that has been quoted by someone else, cite the secondary source from which you took the material. Do not cite the original if you did not consult it directly. Here is how a quotation from an original source—a nuclear strategist writing in 1967—quoted on page 357 in a 1985 book written by Paul Boyer and titled *By the Bomb's Early Light: American Thought and Culture at the Dawn of the Atomic Age* would be cited.

MLA: Explaining how Americans' views of the atom bomb shifted
during the 1950's, Albert Wohlstetter, a nuclear strategist,
commented in 1967: "Bright hopes for civilian nuclear
energy" proved to be "an emotional counterweight to . . .
nuclear destruction" (qtd. in Boyer 357).

APA: Explaining how Americans' views of the atom bomb shifted
during the 1950's, Albert Wohlstetter, a nuclear strategist,
commented in 1967: "Bright hopes for civilian nuclear
energy" proved to be "an emotional counterweight to . . .
nuclear destruction" (cited in Boyer, 1985, p. 357).

In certain situations, you may need to include additional or slightly different information in your parenthetical citation. For example, when two or more sources on your list of references are by the same author, your citation will need to make clear to which of these you are referring; in the MLA system you do this by including a brief version of the title along with the author and page number: (Tisdale, "Weight," 53). (Note that this is generally not a problem in the APA system because works by the same author will already be distinguished by date.) For works that do not indicate an author, mention the title fully in your text or include a brief version in the parenthetical citation.

THE "LIST OF WORKS CITED" OR "REFERENCES"

At the end of your essay, on a separate sheet of paper, you should list all of those works that you cited in your paper. In the MLA system, this page is titled "List of Works Cited" (with no quotation marks); in the APA system, it is titled "References" (also no quotation marks). The list should be alphabetized by the authors' last names so that readers can easily find full information about particular sources. Both systems provide essentially the same information, although arranged in a slightly different order.

- *For books:* the author's or authors' names, the title, the place of publication, the publisher's name, and the year of publication
- *For articles:* the author's or authors' names, the title, the name of the journal, the volume number and/or the date of that issue, and the pages on which the article appeared
- *For electronic sources:* the author's or authors' names, the title, data of publication, the URL (Uniform Resource Locator, the electronic address) or other information on how the sources can be accessed, and the date on which you accessed the material (Dates are important in citing electronic sources because the source may change its URL or even disappear after a short period of time.)

Note in the following sample entries that in MLA style, the first line of each entry is flush with the left margin and subsequent lines are indented five spaces. Ask your instructor which of the APA's two recommended formats you should use: the first line flush left and subsequent lines indented five spaces (as shown here) or the first line indended five spaces and subsequent lines flush left.

Books

A book by a single author
MLA:
Boyer, Paul. By the Bomb's Early Light: American Thought and Culture at the Dawn of the Atomic Age. New York: Random House, 1985.
APA:
Boyer, P. (1985). *By the bomb's early light: American thought and culture at the dawn of the atomic age.* New York: Random House.

An anthology
MLA:
Ibieta, Gabriella, ed. Latin American Writers: Thirty Stories. New York: St. Martin's, 1993.
APA:
Ibieta, G. (Ed.). (1993). *Latin American writers: Thirty stories.* New York: St. Martin's Press.

A book by more than one author
MLA:
Burns, Ailsa, and Cath Scott. Mother-Headed Families and Why They Have Increased. Hillsdale, NJ: Erlbaum, 1994.
APA:
Burns, A., & Scott, C. (1994). *Mother-headed families and why they have increased.* Hillsdale, NJ: Erlbaum.

A book with no author's name
MLA:
Native American Directory. San Carlos, AZ: National Native American Co-operative, 1982.
APA:
Native American Directory. (1982). San Carlos, AZ: National Native American Co-operative.

An article or story in an edited anthology
MLA:
Quartermaine, Peter. "Margaret Atwood's Surfacing: Strange Familiarity." Margaret Atwood: Writing and Subjectivity. Ed. Colin Nicholson. New York: St. Martin's, 1994. 119–32.
APA:
Quartermaine, P. (1994). Margaret Atwood's Surfacing: Strange familiarity. In C. Nicholson (Ed.), *Margaret Atwood: Writing and subjectivity* (pp. 119–132). New York: St. Martin's Press.

An article in a reference work
MLA:
"Film Noir." Oxford Companion to Film. Ed. Liz-Anne Bawden.
New York: Oxford UP, 1976. 249.
APA:
Film Noir. (1976). In L.-A. Bawden (Ed.), *Oxford companion to film*
(p. 249). New York: Oxford University Press.

Articles

*An article in a journal that is continuously paginated (that is, issues
after the first in a year do not start at page 1)*
MLA: Lenz, Nygel. "'Luxuries' in Prison: The Relationship Between
Amenity Funding and Public Support." Crime &
Delinquency 48 (2002): 499–525.
APA:
Lenz, N. (2002). "Luxuries" in prison: The relationship between
amenity funding and public support. *Crime & Delinquency,
48*, 499–525.
Note: When each issue of a journal does begin with page 1, also
indicate the issue number after the volume number. For
MLA style, separate the two with a period: 9.2. For APA
style, use parentheses: *9*(2).

An article in a monthly magazine
MLA:
Milgrom, Mordehai. "Does Dark Matter Really Exist?" Scientific
American Aug. 2002: 42–52.
APA:
Milgrom, M. (2002, August). Does dark matter really exist?
Scientific American, 42–52.

An article in a weekly or biweekly magazine
MLA:
Weaver, Mary Anne. "The Real bin Laden." New Yorker 24 Jan.
2000: 32–38.
APA:
Weaver, M. (2000, Jan. 24). The real bin Laden. *New Yorker,* 32–38.

An article in a daily newspaper
MLA:
Lacey, Marc. "Engineering Food for Africans." New York Times 8
Sep. 2002, Sunday National Edition, sec. 1:8.

APA:

Lacey, M. (2002, September 8). Engineering food for Africans. *New York Times,* Sunday National Edition, sec. 1, p. 8.

An editorial in a newspaper

MLA:

"Spinning on Iraq." Editorial. Washington Post 26 Sep. 2002, sec. A: 32.

APA:

Spinning on Iraq. (2002, September 26). [Editorial]. *Washington Post,* sec. A, p. 32.

A review

MLA:

Hitchens, Christopher. "The Misfortune of Poetry." Rev. of Byron: Life and Legend, by Fiond MacCarthy. Atlantic Monthly Oct. 2002: 149–56.

APA:

Hitchens, C. (2002, October). The misfortune of poetry. [Review of *Byron: Life and legend,* by Fiond MacCarthy]. *Atlantic Monthly,* 149–56.

Other Sources

An interview

MLA:

Quintana, Alvina. Personal interview. 13 June 2002.

Worthington, Joanne. Telephone interview. 12 Dec. 2002.

Note: APA style does not include personal interviews on the Reference list, but rather cites pertinent information parenthetically in the text.

A film

MLA:

Silkwood. Writ. Nora Ephron and Alice Arden. Dir. Mike Nichols. With Meryl Streep. ABC, 1983.

APA:

Ephron, N. (Writer), & Nichols, M. (Director). (1983). *Silkwood* [Motion picture]. Hollywood: ABC.

More than one work by the same author

MLA:

Didion, Joan. Miami. New York: Simon & Schuster, 1987.

———. "Why I Write." New York Times Book Review 9 Dec. 1976: 22.

APA:

Didion, J. (1976, December 9). Why I write. *New York Times Book Review*, p. 22.

Didion, J. (1987). *Miami*. New York: Simon & Schuster.

Note: MLA style lists multiple works by the same author alphabetically by title. APA style lists such works chronologically beginning with the earliest.

ELECTRONIC SOURCES

Increasingly the sources that we use for writing research papers are electronic—full-text articles taken from electronic databases available through libraries, journals that exist only in electronic form, documents taken from Websites, e-mail from people whom we have interviewed. Even books today are available—and sometimes only available—in an electronic format. The most recent edition of the *MLA Handbook for Writers of Research Papers* (6th edition, 2003) includes a section on citing electronic publications, as does the *Publication of the American Psychological Association* (5th edition, 2001). What follows here is a guide to citing three of the most common types of electronic sources used in Freshman English research papers. For a fuller guide consult the *MLA Handbook*. For additional help, ask your instructor or the reference department in your library for assistance in locating a published style guide in your area of study.

An e-mail message

MLA:

Miller, George. "On revising." E-mail to Eric Gray. 7 March 2002.

APA:

Miller, G. (2002, March 7). On revising.

The crucial pieces of information in citing an e-mail include the name of the writer, the title of the message (taken from the subject line), the recipient, and the date on which the message was sent.

A full-text article from a periodical available through a library database

MLA:

Seligman, Dan. "The Grade-Inflation Swindle." <u>Forbes</u> 18 Mar. 2002: 94. Online. Expanded Academic ASAP. 27 Sept. 2002.

APA:

Seligman, D. (2002, March 18). The grade-inflation swindle. *Forbes*
p. 94. Retrieved September 30, 2002, from Expanded
Academic ASAP.

Information from a Website

MLA:

Barndt, Richard. <u>Fiscal Policy Effects on Grade Inflation</u>. 27 Sept.
2002 < http://www.newfoundations.com/Policy/Barndt.html>.

APA:

Barndt, R. (2002, September 27). Fiscal policy effects on grade
inflation. Retrieved October 3, 2002, from
http://www.newfoundations.com/Policy/Barndt.html.

ANNOTATED SAMPLE STUDENT RESEARCH PAPER: MLA DOCUMENTATION STYLE

The following paper was written to fulfill the research component of
a freshman composition course and is documented according to
guidelines of the Modern Language Association, as required by the
instructor. Be sure to consult with your instructor to determine which
documentation style you should follow.

This paper has been annotated to point out important conventions
of research writing and documentation. Note that it does not begin with
a title page. If, however, your instructor requires an introductory outline, your first page should be a title page (ask about the preferred format), and the next page should be headed with only the title of the essay.

Amy Rubens

ENGL 110

Instructor Dan Lane

① Page numbers in upper right corner, with author's last name.

③ Title centered.

Ecotourism: Friend or Foe?

② Double-spacing throughout.

Humans from all parts of the globe share a common feature: curiosity. While there are many ways to fulfill the urge to seek out the unknown, tourism is a way many people choose to satisfy this inquisitiveness. Every year, the number of plane tickets sold, hotel rooms booked, and tour packages put on the market increases, and many of these items are geared towards one of the fastest growing types of tourism: ecotravel. Ecotravel, also called ecotourism, is multifaceted. As Hector

④ Definition of "ecotourism"

Ceballos-Lascurain notes, ecotourism involves "traveling to relatively undisturbed or uncontaminated natural areas with the specific objective of studying, admiring, and enjoying the scenery and its wild plants and animals"

⑤ Quotation moved to the end of the writer's sentence.

(qtd. in Boo XIV). Besides providing the traveler

⑥ Citing an indirect source

with breath-taking sights, ecotravel is a way to link tourism's economic benefits with environmental conservation because it can justify the "retention, enhancement, and enlargement of these areas in the face of competition" from forces that would otherwise halt or slow the conservation process (Carter

⑦ Citing a book— author's last name and page number

169). Researchers have proven that ecotourism is an effective means to preserve unique natural areas.

Despite the benefits of ecotourism, it does present some problems. Now more than ever before travelers are descending upon many protected areas of the world—especially marine environments. In particular, ecotourism is increasing drastically in the Caribbean areas

⑧ Author's last name is in the sentence so parenthetica l reference contains only page number.

because of their reputation, as Carter puts it, as "3-S" areas—places of sun, sand, and sea (160). The escalation of ecotourism has a direct correlation with an ecosystem's preservation and protection, but many of these environments and the animals that inhabit

⑨ Thesis statement

them are threatened. Thus, although ecotourism is mostly beneficial in that it boosts conservation and protection, there is a potential for environmental damage, especially in marine areas. To lessen the negative impacts of ecotourism, governments should devise plans and enact legislation to counteract the degradation of these environmental treasures.

Marine environments throughout the world are popular tourist destinations. Countries in Latin and South America, like Costa Rica and Ecuador, are discovering different ways to market their coastlines' recreational capabilities and aesthetic values.

Rubens 3

One way to increase a nation's marketability to tourists is to exploit its most abundant resource. In the Caribbean area, for example, the ocean is more dominant than the land—tiny island nations seem to be swallowed up by the sea—and naturally these countries would try to take advantage of their largest resource. The main idea of this strategy is that most people come to tropical locations for "traditional" reasons, but some of these tourists may take an extra day or two out of their itinerary to explore natural areas. Therefore, tourists are not only spending money in resorts, but in other areas like national parks and preserves as well.

Many of these marine environments, ranging from beaches to wetlands to tidal pools to coral reefs, remain untouched by man and are thus prime destinations for developers who wish to capitalize on the booming ecotourism industry. Developers are planning and building beach resorts in Mexico and other countries. Along Costa Rica's Bahia Culebra, for example, an "ecodevelopment" venture called the Papagayo Project has plans for 1144 homes, 6270 condo-hotel units, and 6584 hotel rooms as well as a shopping center and a golf course (McLaren 105). In addition to the eco-developments, more eco-resorts, eco-lodges, and eco-marine parks are sprouting up in

⑩ Citation indicates that the statistics came from the source cited, but that the sentence is not a direct quotation.

Rubens 4

marine environments. This construction results

from the countries' desire to entice more

ecotourists to discover what their nations have

to offer.

Most authorities of coastal communities

believe that projects geared towards

recreational and tourist-based interests are

important to the financial health of a

community (Heiman 13). The infrastructure

ecotourism brings, for instance, creates jobs for

local citizens. At the same time, the area is

protected because the new jobs help slow the

natives' destruction of the environment. A

native who would probably employ the "slash

and burn" technique to clear the land for crops

would now have a new job and no longer a

need to destroy the forest.

Development of natural areas to augment

profits and increase infrastructure does come

with some potentially disastrous effects. In

Ecotourism: A Sustainable Option, Carter notes

that among numerous other negative impacts,

an influx of people brings pollution and can

even change the behavior of wildlife (173). For

ecotourism to truly attain its goal, the

ecotourist must at least leave the area in the

same condition as he or she found it (McLaren

98). Yet, this rarely happens. To illustrate, all

types of transportation require potentially

⑪Since the sentence has no quotation marks, the citation indicates that the ideas—and not the sentence itself—came from the source.

Rubens 5

damaging fossil fuels; planes and cars that

transport tourists, food, and other supplies

such as building materials are dependent upon

these kinds of fuels. Consequently, tourists

often damage the natural environment.

Moreover, tourists create a "transient but

permanent population increase in destination

sites . . . [that] creates monumental waste and

pollution" (McLaren 98). Heiman, another

expert on recreation's impact on marine

environments, agrees with McLaren. Small

⑫ Ellipses (the 3 spaced periods) are used to shorten the quotation.

marine towns must expand in order to

accommodate the multitudes of tourists who

flock to these communities each year and often

damage delicate environments like dune

systems (Heiman 33). Even when the number

of incoming ecotourists is restricted, as it is in

the Galapagos Islands of Ecuador, within a few

years these limits are regularly surpassed. For

example, in 1982, the Galapagos Islands

allowed a maximum of 25,000 visitors, but in

1994 the number had crept to 60,000 who

brought with them more cars, tourist boats,

and pollution (McLaren 106).

Ecotourists also need support facilities in

addition to the hotels, motels, and resorts

where they stay during their trip. Waste

disposal, parking, and roads are necessary to

fully accommodate large groups of people

Rubens 6

touring the natural areas of a particular region,
and all of these have negative impacts on the
environment. Soil erosion caused by building
activities, for example, leads to coral reef
destruction by increasing the dirt particles in
the water surrounding the reef and decreasing
the amount of available light. Without an
adequate supply of solar energy, the coral
cannot obtain sufficient food from the water.
Just as the dirt harms the coral, so does
sewage from ecotourist facilities. In bays
where tidal movement is limited, sewage will
cause a thick growth of algae to spread over
the coral reef. Since coral is a filter-feeding
animal because it extracts nutrients from the
ocean, the algae blanket prevents the coral
from getting an adequate food supply. In
addition, coral reefs act as breakwaters that
help dissipate the intense energy of waves
that pound the shore. Without coral reefs to
lessen the continual blows of waves along
the surf, one storm could wash the beach
away. While no ecotourist or ecotourist
facility has a direct intention of destroying
coral reefs, it happens nonetheless. Coral reef
destruction both deprives the visitor of
seeing such a unique formation in a pristine
state, and also exposes beaches to
destructive erosion.

Rubens 7

Another environmental consequences of sewage pollution from tourist areas is the excess growth of algae that results. This filamentous algae, also known as "blanket weed" because of its appearance, is a thick mass of slime that rests on the ocean's surface. It produces less than desirable swimming conditions and often ruins fishing lines and nets. The sewage can also cause an event called "water bloom," caused by the microorganisms microcystis and anabaena that thrive in raw sewage and similar environments. These two nasty bacteria can afflict beach goers with rashes and stomach problems, and are poisonous to several species of fish (Edington 173). Edible refuse in the ocean is just as bad as non-edible refuse. Garbage thrown from ships into the ocean or left behind by beach goers who are staying in area hotels usually contain food scraps that can attract sharks, scavenging gulls, and rats to the beach.

Not every ecotourist facility turns away from its responsibility to preserve the environment. Located on the coast of Mexico's Yucatan Peninsula, the Hotel Eco Paraiso Xixim claims to be the paradigm of an earth-friendly tourist facility. Here, there is "no grass in the garden . . . and the beach is littered with sea shells, seaweed, and starfish" (Malkin). Not

⑬ Citation to an article from an electronic database. Such sources do not have page numbers.

Rubens 8

only are the creators of this ecotourist facility
intent on preserving the natural marine setting
of the region, they are also focused on reducing
the impact of human by-products that
inevitably result from these settlements: the
hotel treats its waste water and sewage. Their
conscientious efforts to improve the
environment (combined with the investors'
decision to leave a large portion of the
surrounding land in its wild state) are
expensive, though. Accordingly, many investors
choose to perpetuate Mexico's current school of
thought—megatourism—by choosing to
construct large and more economical
accommodations that are almost sure routes to
financial success (Malkin). It is no surprise that
environmentally supportive places like the
Hotel Eco Paraiso Xixim are rare.

Since many ecotourism programs are
designed to complement more traditional types
of tourism, ecotourists often engage in
activities other than viewing the local flora and
fauna. One of the most popular types of tourist
recreation is boating because it allows visitors
access to marine areas other than the beach
(Heiman 15). Guided boat tours are extremely
popular, and this popularity does not come
without problems. Large tour boats, for
instance, allow gas and oil to enter the ocean,

Rubens 9

causing damage along the coastline and in sea
caves. Similarly, exhaust produced from
burning these fuels can disrupt sediments if the
boat is in shallow water (Heiman 9) and, as has
been previously pointed out, swirling sediment
in the ocean is detrimental to coral reefs. Also,
large boats frequently dump sewage into the
water, threatening human health and
destroying shellfish.

Cruise ships are also culprits in damaging
the ocean. When guests disembark at ports of
call, they engage in recreational activities that
highlight the natural beauty of the region. By
definition, these tourists are actually
ecotravelers. Snorkeling near coral reefs, for
example, often proves to be too much of a
temptation, and snorkelers seldom refrain
from stealing a small piece of the reef as a
souvenir. Snorkelers also threaten the local
fishing economy because some of these
underwater adventure seekers may spearfish.
McLaren likens cruise ships to "mobile
[resorts] that simply [float] away without any
sense of obligation" to the preservation of the
community's natural areas of wildlife (92-93).
Popular ports of call for cruise lines often
become the "dumping grounds" of
inconsiderate tourists, and the local
community is left to deal with the

consequences of the environmental

destruction.

Land development due to the booming

ecotourism industry also negatively influences

the aquatic animals that inhabit the marine

environments. Road construction and the

consequent influx of traffic to areas

unaccustomed to human activity have

profoundly affected the behavior of several

species of marine turtles. The types of turtles

affected are those who lay their eggs in nests

located just above the high tide line on the

beach. After two months of gestation, the

turtles hatch and make their way to the sea.

The turtles instinctively know where the ocean

is, and they also rely on the moon's light over

the ocean's horizon that acts as a signal for the

direction in which to swim. Biologists have

discovered that turtles associate a brighter

horizon with the sea. Headlights of cars near

the beach, however, can greatly "disorient [the]

hatchlings and cause them to crawl inland

rather than towards the sea" (Edington 170).

Consequently, turtles that cannot find the

ocean—their natural home—have a decreased

chance of survival. Lights from streets, hotels,

and floodlights can disorient turtles, too. Some

coastal communities have recognized the plight

of these marine turtles, and are using shrubs

Rubens 11

and trees to help screen the beach from artificial lights. Another threat to marine turtles are steep road embankments. Turtles that attempt to climb these embankments often find the task too challenging. The embankments are usually quite steep, and turtles can roll over easily. If the turtles remain upside-down, they will die.

Despite its detrimental effects, ecotourism is helping some animals to survive better. Environmentalists successfully convinced fishermen of Baja California to reduce their takes of certain kinds of fish. The fishermen responded by "[rolling] up their nets and [rolling] out the red carpet" to provide services for rich tourists who frequent the area (Padgett). The result: fish populations flourished, producing an increase in the number of gray and right whales off the coast of this part of Mexico. In 1996, Mexico expected 20,000 tourists to visit Baja California to participate in whale-watching activities (Padgett). Whale-watching is growing in popularity in other areas of the world, too. In the waters surrounding Spain's Canary Islands there are so many whale-watching expeditions that whales are often frightened by all the activity. To escape the commotion, whales retreat to the depths of the ocean for extremely

Rubens 12

long periods and could potentially run out of
breathable air. While whales are hassled by
ecotourists intent on glimpsing these
magnificent creatures, the whales are still
alive, and as they continue to make profits for
natives, their fates do not include "blubber
factories and jewelry shops" (Padgett).

It is unfortunate that ecotourism's main
goal of preserving irreplaceable natural
biospheres cannot be realized. Ecotourism was
first conceived to help protect the environment,
but its popularity has threatened these
conservation goals. Ecotourism has also
brought to certain areas of the world,
particularly to marine and coastal regions,
pollution, destruction, and harm to animals.
Halting ecotourism, however, is not an
adequate solution to this problem since
ecotourism can be greatly beneficial to the
environment. The governments of those
countries where ecotourism is a main source of
revenue should understand the need for
reforms in ecotravel policies. In <u>Coastal
Recreation in California</u>, Heiman argues that
coastal communities should implement plans,
as well as legislation, to limit things that are
pleasing or that would harm or alter the
environment (44). Already, developers planning
new hotels in Costa Rica are spacing them

Rubens 13

farther apart. Officials should also consider the possibility of educating ecotourists (and tourists) about how their visit will impact the precious environment they will be visiting. The Canary Islands, for example, have already responded to this idea. A marine naturalist is on board each whale-watching vessel to help curtail any harassment of the creatures. The Cayman Islands' new plan is an illustration of one of the most impressive attempts of ecotourism reform. Their new plan calls for an improvement of the visitor's awareness of the environment, a quota for visitors at specific marine sites, a reef management program that would regulate scuba diving activities, and new standards for all types of water recreation ("Cayman Islands").

Ecotourism is effective in preserving the environment: it slows down the indigenous peoples' destruction of natural areas by providing jobs, and it has been successful in helping to preserve animal populations. However, ecotourism is becoming increasingly destructive. Ecotravel is quite popular in marine areas, but an increase of tourists has produced more damage to these special ecosystems. Rather than eliminating ecotourism (or allowing it to continue at its present state), countries should realize the

Rubens 14

need for reform. An important recommendation of the Final Report of the 2002 World Ecotourism Summit, for example, was that governmental tourism and environmental agencies work more closely together to ensure that ecotourism destinations are more thoughtfully planned and regulated. If countries and localities do not sufficiently protect the environment and the animals that inhabit it, tourists and ecotourists alike will not have the opportunity to visit or admire these unique treasures.

WORKS CITED

Boo, Elizabeth. Ecotourism: The Potentials and Pitfalls. 2 vols. Washington, D. C.: World Wildlife Fund, 1990.

Carter, Erlet and Gwen Lowman, eds. Ecotourism: A Sustainable Option? New York: John Wiley and Sons, 1994.

"Cayman Islands Offers Five-Year Tourism Plan." Travel Agent Caribbean and Bahamas Supplement 15 July 1996: 5. LexisNexis Academic. U. of Delaware Library. 3 Nov. 2002 < http://web.lexis-nexis.com/universe>.

Edington, John M. and M. Ann Edington. Ecology, Recreation, and Tourism. Cambridge, England: Cambridge U P, 1986.

⑭ Citation to an article accessed through a library's database includes publication information and how and when it was accessed.

Rubens 15

Heiman, Michael. Coastal Recreation in

California. Berkeley: Institute of

Governmental Studies, 1986.

Malkin, Elisabeth. "Betting on the Eco-Tourism

Craze . . . And on Adventure and Travel,

Too." Business Week 1 Mar. 1999: 4.

Lexis-Nexis Academic Universe. U. of

Delaware Library. 3 Nov. 2002 <

http://web.lexis-nexis.com/universe>.

McLaren, Deborah. Rethinking Tourism and

Ecotravel: The Paving of Paradise and

What You Can Do to Stop It. West

Hartford, CT: Kumarian Press, Inc., 1998.

Padgett, Tim, Sharon Begley, and Joshua

Hammer. "Beware of the Humans."

Newsweek 5 Feb. 1996: 52. Lexis-Nexis

Academic Universe. U. of Delaware

Library. 3 Nov. 2002 < http://web.lexis-

nexis.com/universe>.

World Ecotourism Summit. Final Report. 2002 <

http://www.ecotourism2002.org/anglais/i

ndex_a.html>.

⑮ Work by three authors lists all names.

GLOSSARY

Abstract words refer to ideas or generalities—words such as *truth, beauty,* and *justice.* The opposite of an abstract word is a *concrete* one. Margaret Atwood in "The Female Body" (p. 465) explores the abstract phrase "female body," offering a series of more concrete examples or perspectives on the topic.

Allusion is a reference to an actual or fictional person, object, or event. The assumption is that the reference will be understood or recognized by the reader. For that reason, allusions work best when they draw on a shared experience or heritage. Allusions to famous literary works or to historically prominent people or events are likely to have meaning for many readers for an extended period of time. Martin Luther King Jr. in "I Have a Dream" (p. 490) alludes to biblical verses, spirituals, and patriotic songs. If an allusion is no longer recognized by an audience, it loses its effectiveness in conjuring up a series of significant associations.

Analogy is an extended comparison in which an unfamiliar or complex object or event is likened to a familiar or simple one in order to make the former more vivid and more easily understood. Inappropriate or superficially similar analogies should not be used, especially as evidence in an argument. See *Faulty analogy* in the list of logical fallacies on pp. 478–479.

Argumentation or *persuasion* seeks to move a reader, to gain support, to advocate a particular type of action. Traditionally, argumentation appeals to logic and reason, while persuasion appeals to emotion and sometimes prejudice. See the introduction to Chapter 9.

Cause and effect analyses explain why something happened or what the consequences are or will be from a particular occurrence. See the introduction to Chapter 7.

Classification is a form of division, but instead of starting with a single subject as a *division* does, classification starts with many items, and groups or sorts them into categories. See the introduction to Chapter 4.

Cliché is an overused common expression. The term is derived from a French word for a stereotype printing block. Just as many identical copies can be made from such a block, so clichés are typically words and phrases used so frequently that they become stale and ineffective. Everyone uses clichés in speech: "in less than no time" they "spring to mind," but "in the last analysis," a writer ought to "avoid them like the plague," even though they always seem "to hit the nail on the head."

Coherence is achieved when all parts of a piece of writing work together as a harmonious whole. If a paper has a well-defined thesis that controls its structure, coherence will follow. In addition, relationships between sentences, paragraphs, and ideas can be made clearer for the reader by using pronoun references, parallel structures (see *Parallelism*), and transitional words and phrases (see *Transitions*).

Colloquial expressions are informal words and phrases used in conversation but inappropriate for more formal writing situations. Occasionally, professional writers use colloquial expressions to create intentional informality. David Bodanis in "What's in Your Toothpaste?" (p. 204) mixes colloquial words (*gob, stuff, goodies, glop*) with formal words (*abrading, gustatory, intrudant*).

Comparison involves finding similarities between two or more things, people, or ideas. See the introduction to Chapter 5.

Conclusions should always leave the reader feeling that a paper has come to a logical and inevitable end, that the communication is now complete. As a result, an essay that simply stops, weakly trails off, moves into a previously unexplored area, or raises new or distracting problems lacks that necessary sense of closure. Endings often cause problems because they are written last and hence are often rushed. With proper planning, you can always write an effective and appropriate ending. Keep the following points and strategies in mind:

1. An effective conclusion grows out of a paper—it must be logically related to what has been said. It might restate the thesis, summarize the exposition or argument, apply or reflect on the subject under discussion, tell a related story, call for a course of action, or state the significance of the subject.

2. The extent to which a conclusion can repeat or summarize is determined in large part by the length of the paper. A short paper should not have a conclusion that repeats the introduction in slightly varied words. A long essay, however, often needs a conclusion that conveniently summarizes the significant facts or points discussed in the paper.

3. The appropriateness of a particular type of ending is related to a paper's purpose. An argumentative or persuasive essay—one that asks the reader to do or believe something—can always conclude with a statement of the desired action—vote for, do this, do not support. A narrative essay can end at the climactic moment in the action. An expository essay in which points are arranged according to significance can end with the major point.

4. The introduction and conclusion can be used as a related pair to frame the body of an essay. Often in a conclusion you can return to or allude to an idea, an expression, or an illustration used at the beginning of the paper and so enclose the body.

Concrete words describe things that exist and can be experienced through the senses. Abstractions are rendered understandable and specific through concrete examples. See *Abstract*.

Connotation and **denotation** refer to two different types of definition of words. A dictionary definition is denotative—it offers a literal and explicit definition of a word. But words often have more than just literal meanings, for they can carry positive or negative associations or connotations. The denotative definition of *wife* is "a woman married to a man," but as Judy Brady shows in "I Want a Wife" (p. 441), the word *wife* carries a series of connotative associations as well.

Contrast involves finding differences between two or more things, people, or ideas. See the introduction to Chapter 5.

Deduction is the form of argument that starts with a general truth and then moves to a specific application of that truth. See the introduction to Chapter 9.

Definition involves placing a word first in a general class and then adding distinguishing features that set it apart from other members of that class: "A dalmatian is a breed of dog (general class) with a white, short-haired coat and dark spots (distinguishing feature)." Most college writing assignments in definition require extended definitions in which a subject is analyzed with appropriate examples and details. See the introduction to Chapter 8.

Denotation. See *Connotation.*

Description is the re-creation of sense impressions in words. See the introduction to Chapter 3.

Dialect. See *Diction.*

Diction is the choice of words used in speaking or writing. It is frequently divided into four levels: formal, informal, colloquial, and slang. Formal diction is found in traditional academic writing, such as books and scholarly articles; informal diction, generally characterized by words common in conversation contexts, by contractions, and by the use of the first person *(I)*, is found in articles in popular magazines. Bernard R. Berelson's essay "The Value of Children" (p. 231) uses formal diction; Judy Brady's "I Want a Wife" (p. 441) is informal. See *Colloquial expressions* and *Slang.*

Two other commonly used labels are also applied to diction:

- **Nonstandard** words or expressions are not normally used by educated speakers. An example would be *ain't.*

- **Dialect** reflects regional or social differences with respect to word choice, grammatical usage, and pronunciation. Dialects are primarily spoken rather than written but are often reproduced or imitated in narratives. William Least Heat Moon in "Nameless, Tennessee" (p. 164) captures the dialect of his speakers.

Division breaks a subject into parts. It starts with a single subject and then subdivides that whole into smaller units. See the introduction to Chapter 4.

Essay literally means "attempt," and in writing courses the word is used to refer to brief papers, generally five hundred to one thousand words long, on tightly delimited subjects. Essays can be formal and academic, like Bernard Berelson's "The Value of Children" (p. 231), or informal and humorous, like Judy Brady's "I Want a Wife" (p. 441).

Example is a specific instance used to illustrate a general idea or statement. Effective writing requires examples to make generalizations clear and vivid to a reader. See the introduction to Chapter 1.

Exposition comes from a Latin word meaning "to expound or explain." It is one of the four modes into which writing is subdivided, the other three being *narration, description,* and *argumentation.* Expository writing is information-conveying; its purpose is to inform its reader. This purpose is achieved through a variety of organizational patterns including *division and classification, comparison and contrast, process analysis, cause and effect,* and *definition.*

Figures of speech are deliberate departures from the ordinary and literal meanings of words in order to provide fresh, insightful perspectives or emphasis. Figures of speech are most commonly used in descriptive passages and include the following:

- **Simile** is a comparison of two dissimilar things, introduced by the word *as* or *like.* Lynne Sharon Schwartz in "The Page Turner" (p. 358) describes the skin of the young woman turning pages as "an off-white like heavy cream or the best butter."

- **Metaphor** is an analogy that directly identifies one thing with another. After Scott Russell Sanders in "The Inheritance of Tools" (p. 180) accidentally strikes his thumb with a hammer, he describes the resulting scar using a metaphor: "A white scar in the shape of a crescent moon began to show above the cuticle, and month by month it rose across the pink sky of my thumbnail."

- **Personification** is an attribution of human qualities to an animal, idea, abstraction, or inanimate object. Gordon Grice in "The Black Widow" (p. 550) refers to male and female spiders as "lovers."

- **Hyperbole** is a deliberate exaggeration, often done to provide emphasis or humor. Margaret Atwood in comparing the female brain with the male brain (p. 465) resorts to hyperbole: "[Female brains are] joined together by a thick cord; neural pathways flow from one to the other, sparkles of electronic information washing to and fro. The male brain, now, that's a different matter. Only a thin connection. Space over here, time over here, music and arithmetic in their sealed compartments. The right brain doesn't know what the left brain is doing."

- **Understatement** is the opposite of hyperbole; it is a deliberate minimizing done to provide emphasis or humor. In William Least Heat Moon's "Nameless, Tennessee" (p. 164), Miss Ginny Watts explains how she asked her husband to call the doctor unless he wanted to be "shut of" (rid of) her. Her husband, Thurmond, humorously uses understatement in his reply: "I studied on it."

- **Rhetorical questions** are questions not meant to be answered but instead to provoke thought. Barbara Ehrenreich in "In

Defense of Talk Shows" (p. 209) poses a series of rhetorical questions toward the end of her essay: "This is class exploitation, pure and simple. What next—'homeless people so hungry they eat their own scabs'? Or would the next step be to pay people outright to submit to public humiliation? For $50 would you confess to adultery in your wife's presence? For $500 would you reveal your thirteen-year-old's girlish secrets on *Ricki Lake*?"

- **Paradox** is a seeming contradiction used to catch a reader's attention. An element of truth or rightness often lurks beneath the contradiction. John Hollander in "Mess" observes that "to describe a mess is to impose order on it" (p. 459), making it paradoxically not a mess.

Generalizations are assertions or conclusions based on some specific instances. The value of a generalization is determined by the quality and quantity of examples on which it is based. Bob Greene in "Cut" (p. 57) formulates a generalization—being cut from an athletic team makes men superachievers later in life—on the basis of five examples. For such a generalization to have validity, however, a proper statistical sample would be essential.

Hyperbole. See *Figures of speech.*

Illustration is providing specific examples for general words or ideas. A writer illustrates by using *examples.*

Induction is the form of argument that begins with specific evidence and then moves to a generalized conclusion that accounts for the evidence. See the introduction to Chapter 9.

Introductions need to do two essential things: first, catch or arouse a reader's interest, and second, state the thesis of the paper. In achieving both objectives, an introduction can occupy a single paragraph or several. The length of an introduction should always be proportional to the length of the essay—short papers should not have long introductions. Because an introduction lays out what is to follow, it is always easier to write after a draft of the body of the paper has been completed. When writing an introduction, keep the following strategies in mind:

1. Look for an interesting aspect of the subject that might arouse the reader's curiosity. It could be a quotation, an unusual statistic, a narrative, or a provocative question or statement. It

should be something that will make the reader want to continue reading, and it should be appropriate to the subject at hand.

2. Provide a clear statement of purpose and thesis, explaining what you are writing about and why.

3. Remember that an introduction establishes a tone or point of view for what follows, so be consistent—an informal personal essay can have a casual, anecdotal beginning, but a serious academic essay needs a serious, formal introduction.

4. Suggest to the reader the structure of the essay that follows. Knowing what to expect makes it easier for the audience to read actively.

Irony occurs when a writer says one thing but means another. E. M. Forster ends "My Wood" (p. 381) ironically by imagining a time when he will "wall in and fence out until I really taste the sweets of property"—which is actually the opposite of the point he is making.

Metaphor. See *Figures of speech.*

Narration involves telling a story, and all stories—whether they are personal-experience essays, imaginative fiction, or historical narratives—have the same essential ingredients: a series of events arranged in an order and told by a narrator for some particular purpose. See the introduction to Chapter 2.

Nonstandard diction. See *Diction.*

Objective writing takes an impersonal, factual approach to a particular subject. Bernard Berelson's "The Value of Children" (p. 231) is primarily objective in its approach. Writing frequently blends the objective and subjective together. See *Subjective.*

Paradox. See *Figures of speech.*

Parallelism places words, phrases, clauses, sentences, or even paragraphs equal in importance in equivalent grammatical form. The similar forms make it easier for the reader to see the relationships that exist among the parts; they add force to the expression. Martin Luther King Jr.'s "I Have a Dream" speech (p. 490) exhibits each level of parallelism: words ("When all God's children, black and white men, Jews and Gentiles, Protestants and Catholics"), phrases ("With this faith, we will be able to work together, to pray together, to struggle together, to go to jail together, to stand up for freedom together"), clauses ("Go back to Mississippi, go back to Alabama, go back to South Carolina, go back to Georgia, go back to Louisiana, go back to the slums and ghettos of our northern cities"), sentences (the "one hundred years later" pattern in paragraph 2), and paragraphs (the "I have a dream" pattern in paragraphs 11–18).

Person is a grammatical term used to refer to a speaker, the individual being addressed, or an individual being referred to. English has three persons: first (*I* or *we*), second (*you*), and third (*he, she, it,* or *they*).

Personification. See *Figures of speech*.

Persuasion. See *Argumentation*.

Point of view is the perspective the writer adopts toward a subject. In narratives, point of view is either first person (*I*) or third person (*he, she, it*). First-person narration implies a *subjective* approach to a subject; third-person narration promotes an *objective* approach. Point of view can be limited (revealing only what the narrator knows) or omniscient (revealing what anyone else in the narrative thinks or feels). Sometimes the phrase "point of view" is used simply to describe the writer's attitude toward the subject.

Premise in logic is a proposition—a statement of a truth—that is used to support or help support a conclusion. For an illustration, see p. 480.

Process analysis takes one of two forms: either a set of directions intended to allow a reader to duplicate a particular action or a description intended to tell a reader how something happens. See the introduction to Chapter 6.

Proofreading is the systematic checking of a piece of writing for grammatical and mechanical errors. Proofreading is quite different from revision; see *Revision*.

Purpose involves intent, the reason why a writer writes. Three purposes are fundamental: to entertain, to inform, or to persuade. These are not necessarily separate or discrete; they can be combined. An effective piece of writing has a well-defined purpose.

Revision means "to see again." Revision involves the careful, active scrutiny of every aspect of a paper—subject, audience, thesis, paragraph structures, sentence constructions, and word choice. Revising is more complicated and more wide-ranging than proofreading; see *Proofreading*.

Rhetorical questions. See *Figures of speech*.

Satire pokes fun at human behavior or institutions in an attempt to correct them. Judy Brady in "I Want a Wife" (p. 441) satirizes the stereotypical male demands of a wife, implying that marriage should be a more understanding partnership.

Simile. See *Figures of speech.*

Slang is common, casual, conversational language that is inappropriate in formal speaking or writing. Slang often serves to define social groups by virtue of being a private, shared language not understood by outsiders. Slang changes constantly and is therefore always dated. For that reason alone, it is wise to avoid using slang in serious writing.

Style is the arrangement of words that a writer uses to express meaning. The study of an author's style would include an examination of diction or word choice, figures of speech, sentence constructions, and paragraph divisions.

Subject is what a piece of writing is about. See also *Thesis.* Linda Lee's thesis in "The Case Against College" (p. 502) is "not everyone needs a higher education."

Subjective writing expresses an author's feelings or opinions about a particular subject. Editorials or columns in newspapers and personal essays tend to rely on subjective judgments. The editorial from *The New Yorker,* "Help for Sex Offenders" (p. 512), is an example of subjective journalism. Writing frequently blends the subjective and the objective; see *Objective.*

Syllogism is a three-step deductive argument involving a major premise, a minor premise, and a conclusion. For an illustration, see p. 480.

Thesis is a particular idea or assertion about a subject. Effective writing will always have an explicit or implicit statement of thesis; it is the central and controlling idea, the thread that holds the essay together. Frequently a thesis is stated in a thesis or *topic sentence.* See *Subject.*

Tone refers to a writer's or speaker's attitude toward both subject and audience. Tone reflects human emotions and so can be characterized or described in a wide variety of ways, including serious, sincere, concerned, humorous, sympathetic, ironic, indignant, and sarcastic.

Topic sentence is a single sentence in a paragraph that contains a statement of *subject* or *thesis.* The topic sentence is to the paragraph what the thesis statement is to an essay—the thread that holds the whole together, a device to provide clarity and unity. Because paragraphs have various purposes, not every paragraph will have a topic sentence. The topic sentence is often the first or last sentence in the paragraph.

Transitions are links or connections made between sentences, paragraphs, or groups of paragraphs. By using transitions, a writer achieves *coherence* and *unity*. Transitional devices include the following:

1. Repeated words, phrases, or clauses

2. Transitional sentences or paragraphs that act as bridges from one section or idea to the next

3. Transition-making words and phrases

Transitional words and phrases can express relationships of various types:

- Addition: *again, next, furthermore, last*
- Time: *soon, after, then, later, meanwhile*
- Comparison: *but, still, nonetheless, on the other hand*
- Example: *for instance, for example*
- Conclusion: *in conclusion, finally, as a result*
- Concession: *granted, of course*

Understatement. See *Figures of speech.*

Unity is a oneness in which all of the individual parts of a piece of writing work together to form a cohesive and complete whole. It is best achieved by having a clearly stated *purpose* and *thesis* against which every sentence and paragraph can be tested for relevance.

CREDITS

Definition" from *New American Webster's Handy College Dictionary* by Philip D. Morehead and Andrew T. Morehead, copyright 1951 (renewed), © 1955, 1956, 1957, 1961 by Albert H. Morehead, 1972, 1981, 1985, 1995 by Philip D. Morehead and Andrew T. Morehead. Used by permission of Dutton Signet, a division of Penguin Putnam Inc.

"Help for Sex Offenders" from *The New Yorker* (March 7, 1994). Reprinted by permission; © 1994. Originally published in *The New Yorker.* All rights reserved.

Dulce et Decorum Est" by Wilfred Owen, from *The Collected Poems of Wilfred Owen,* copyright © 1963 by Chatto &ampersand; Windus, Ltd. Reprinted by permission of New Directions Publishing Corp.

Barbie Doll" from *Circles of the Water* by Marge Piercy, copyright © 1982 by Marge Piercy. Used by permission of Alfred A. Knopf, a division of Random House, Inc.

Academic Selves", from *Reviving Ophelia* by Mary Pipher, Ph.D., copyright © 1994 by Mary Pipher, Ph.D. Used by permission of G.P. Putnam's Sons, a division of Penguin Putnam Inc.

Anna Quindlen, "The Name is Mine" originally published as "Life in the 30's" from THE NEW YORK TIMES, March 4, 1987 by the New York Times Co. reprinted by permission.

Jonathan Rauch, "The Marrying Kind," © 2002 by Jonathan Rauch. First published in *The Atlantic Monthly,* May 2002. Reprinted by permission of the author.

Reprinted courtesy of *Sports Illustrated:* "The Biggest Play of His Life" by Rick Reilly, May 8, 2000. Copyright © 2000, Time Inc. All rights reserved.

Richard Rodriguez, "None of This Is Fair" from *Politicks & Other Human Interests.* Copyright © 1977 by Richard Rodriguez. Reprinted with the permission of Georges Borchardt, Inc. for the author.

Scott Russell Sanders, "The Inheritance of Tools" from *The Paradise of Bombs.* First published in the *North American Review* (1986). Copyright © 1986 by Scott Russell Sanders. Reprinted with the permission of the author and the Virginia Kidd Agency, Inc.

Esmerelda Santiago, "Guavas" from *WHEN I WAS PUERTO RICAN.* Copyright © 1993 by Esmerelda Santiago. Reprinted by permission of Perseus Books Publishers, a member of Perseus Books, L.L.C.

Lynne Sharon Schwartz, "The Page Turner" from *Face to Face: A Reader in the World* (Boston: Beacon Press, 2000). Copyright © 2000 by Lynne Sharon Schwartz. Reprinted with the permission of Sterling Lord Literistic, Inc.

Danzy Senna, "The Color of Love" from *O, The Oprah Magazine.* Reprinted by permission of International Creative Management, Inc. Copyright © 2000 by Danzy Senna.

Peter Singer, "The Singer Solution to Poverty," *New York Times Magazine*, September 5, 1999. Copyright © 1999 by the New York Times Co. Reprinted by permission.

Brent Staples, "Black Men and Public Space" from *Ms.* (September 1986) and *Harper's.* Copyright © 1986 by Brent Staples. Reprinted with the permission of the author.

Amy Tan, "Mother Tongue." Copyright © 1990 by Amy Tan. First appeared in *The Threepenny Review.* Reprinted by permission of the author and the Sandra Dijkstra Literary Agency.

Lewis Thomas, "On Cloning a Human Being," from *The Medusa and the Snail* by Lewis Thomas, copyright © 1974, 1975, 1976, 1977, 1978, 1979 by Lewis Thomas. Used by permission of Viking Penguin, a division of Penguin Putnam Inc.

The Village Watchman" from *An Unspoken Hunger* by Terry Tempest Williams, copyright © 1994 by Terry Tempest Williams. Used by permission of Pantheon Books, a division of Random House, Inc.

William Zinsser, "Simplicity" from *On Writing Well, Sixth Edition* (New York: HarperCollins Publishers, 1994). Copyright © 1976, 1980, 1985, 1988, 1990, 1994, 1998 by William Zinsser. Reprinted with the permission of the author and Carol Brissie.

INDEX OF TITLES

Academic Selves, 279
Adults Only, 437
Angelou, Maya
  Sister Monroe, 106
Atwood, Margaret
  Female Body, The, 465

Barbie Doll, 378
Being Brians, 71
Berelson, Bernard
  *Value of Children: A Taxonomical
    Essay, The*, 231
BigEagle, Duane
  Traveling to Town, 144
Biggest Play of His Life, The, 111
Black Men and Public Space, 393
Bodanis, David
  What's in Your Toothpaste?, 204
Brady, Judy
  I Want a Wife, 441
Brooks, David
  Culture of Martyrdom, The, 341
Browning, Elizabeth Barrett
  How Do I Love Thee?, 201
Brumberg, Joan Jacobs
  *Origins of Anorexia Nervosa,
    The*, 387

Burton, Tina
  Watermelon Wooer, The, 31
Butterfield, Fox
  Why They Excel, 405

Case Against College, The, 502
Caught in the Widow's Web, 544
Chambers, Veronica
  Dreadlocked, 399
Coca-Cola and Coco Frio, 267
Cofer, Judith Ortiz
  Marina, 116
  *Myth of the Latin Woman,
    The*, 223
Cole, Diana
  Don't Just Stand There, 333
Color of Love, The, 289
*Conversation with Gordon Grice,
    A*, 555
Culture of Martyrdom, The, 341
Cut, 57

Danticat, Edwidge
  Westbury Court, 65
Daum, Meghan
  Virtual Love, 296
Don't Just Stand There, 333

Doyle, Brian
Being Brians, 71
Dreadlocked, 399
Drozdyk, Charlie
Into the Loop: How to Get the Job You Want after Graduation, 348
Dulce et Decorum Est, 486

Ecotourism: Friend or Foe?, 584
Ehrenreich, Barbara
In Defense of Talk Shows, 209
Eighner, Lars
My Daily Dives in the Dumpster, 320
English 99: Literacy among the Ruins, 214
Ephron, Nora
Revision and Life: Take It from the Top–Again, 327
Espada, Martin
Coca-Cola and Coco Frio, 267

Female, Body, The , 465
Ferguson, Cathy
TV Aggression and Children, 373
Foot, The, 434
Forster, E. M.
My Wood, 381
Fun Ethic vs. Work Ethic?, 284

Gannon, Frank
English 99: Literacy among the Ruins, 214
Gelernter, David
What Do Murderers Deserve?, 506
Gladwell, Malcolm
Trouble with Fries, The, 412
Gray, Alicia
Subject vs. Keyword Searches, 261
Greene, Bob
Adults Only, 437
Cut, 57
Grice, Gordon
Caught in the Widow's Web, 544

Conversation with Gordon Grice, A, 555
Journal Entries: The Black Widow, 550
Guavas, 271

Halbfish, Julie Anne
How to Play Dreidel, 312
Heck, Sherry
Infallible, 429
Help for Sex Offenders, 512
Heywood, Leslie
One of the Girls, 78
Hollander, John
Mess, 459
Hopkins, Evans D.
Lockdown, 125
How Do I Love Thee?, 201
How to Play Dreidel, 312
Hughes, Langston
Salvation, 101

I Have a Dream , 490
I Want a Wife, 441
In Defense of Talk Shows, 209
Infallible, 429
Inheritance of Tools, The, 180
Into the Loop: How to Get the Job You Want after Graduation, 348
Iyer, Pico
Why We Travel, 240

Jaffe, Beth
Lowering the Cost of a College Education, 481
James, Evan
Riding the Rails: The American Hobo, 197
Jones, Alice,
The Foot, 434
Journal Entries: The Black Widow, 550

Kelley, Robin D. G.
People in Me, The, 446

King, Jr., Martin Luther
  I Have a Dream, 490

Least Heat Moon, William
  Nameless, Tennessee, 164
Lee, Linda
  Case Against College, The , 502
Liu, Eric
  Po-Po, 150
Lockdown, 125
Looking for Love, 45
Lott, Bret
  Night, 48
*Lowering the Cost of a College
  Education*, 481

McNally, Peggy
  Waiting, 96
Marina, 116
Marrying Kind, The, 497
Mess, 459
Mirikitani, Janice
  Recipe, 317
Momaday, N. Scott
  Way to Rainy Mountain, The, 156
Mother Tongue, 451
My Daily Dives in the Dumpster, 320
My Wood, 381
Myth of the Latin Woman, The, 223

Name is Mine, The, 52
Nameless, Tennessee, 164
Natalie, 140
New Yorker, The
  Help for Sex Offenders, 512
Night, 48
None of This Is Fair, 525

On Cloning a Human Being, 7
One of the Girls, 78
Origins of Anorexia Nervosa, The,
  387
Owen, Wilfred
  Dulce et Decorum Est, 486

Page Turner, The, 358
People in Me, The, 446

Piercy, Marge
  Barbie Doll, 378
Pipher, Mary
  Academic Selves, 279
Po-Po, 150

Quindlen, Anna
  Name is Mine, The, 52

Rauch, Jonathan
  Marrying Kind, The, 497
Recipe, 317
Reilly, Rick
  Biggest Play of His Life, The, 111
Resnick, Nadine
  Natalie, 140
*Revision and Life: Take It from the
  Top–Again*, 327
*Riding the Rails: The American
  Hobo*, 197
Rodriguez, Richard
  None of This Is Fair, 525
Rubens, Amy
  Ecotourism: Friend or Foe?, 584
Ruby Slippers, The, 92

Salvation, 101
Samuelson, Robert J.
  Fun Ethic vs. Work Ethic?, 284
Sanders, Scott Russell
  Inheritance of Tools, The, 180
Santiago, Esmeralda
  Guavas, 271
Schwartz, Lynne Sharon
  Page Turner, The, 358
Senna, Danzy
  Color of Love, The, 289
Singer, Peter
  *Singer Solution to World Poverty,
  The*, 515
*Singer Solution to World Poverty,
  The*, 515
Sister Monroe, 106
Smite, Frank
  Looking for Love, 45
Staples, Frank
  Black Men and Public Space, 393

Subject vs. Keyword Searches, 261

Tan, Amy
  Mother Tongue, 451
Thomas, Lewis
  On Cloning a Human Being, 7
Transaction, The, 275
Traveling to Town, 144
Trouble with Fries, The, 412
TV Aggression and Children, 373

*Value of Children: A Taxonomical
  Essay, The*, 231
Village Watchman, The, 172
Virtual Love, 296

Waiting, 96
Watermelon Wooer, The, 31
Way to Rainy Mountain, The, 156
Westbury Court, 65
What Do Murderers Deserve?, 506
What's in Your Toothpaste?, 204
Why They Excel, 405
Why We Travel, 240
Williams, Terry Tempest
  Village Watchman, The, 172

Zinsser, William
  Transaction, The, 275
Zucker, Hope
  Ruby Slippers, The, 92